Criti
Readi ng

NINTH EDITION

Critical Thinking, Reading, and Writing

A Brief Guide to Argument

SYLVAN BARNET
Professor of English, Late of Tufts University

HUGO BEDAU
Professor of Philosophy, Late of Tufts University

JOHN O'HARA
*Associate Professor of Critical Thinking,
Reading, and Writing, Stockton University*

bedford/st.martin's
Macmillan Learning
Boston | New York

For Bedford/St. Martin's

Vice President, Editorial, Macmillan Learning Humanities: Edwin Hill
Editorial Director, English: Karen S. Henry
Senior Publisher for Composition, Business and Technical Writing, Developmental Writing: Leasa Burton
Executive Editor: John E. Sullivan III
Developmental Editor: Alicia Young
Senior Production Editor: Jessica Gould
Media Producers: Allison Hart and Rand Thomas
Production Supervisor: Victoria Anzalone
Marketing Manager: Joy Fisher Williams
Copy Editor: Alice Vigliani
Photo Editor: Martha Friedman
Photo Researcher: Jen Simmons
Permissions Editor: Elaine Kosta
Senior Art Director: Anna Palchik
Text Design: Laura Shaw Feit
Cover Design: John Callahan
Cover Photo: Martin Hardman/Getty Images
Composition: Jouve
Printing and Binding: LSC Communications

Manufactured in the United States of America.

1 0 9 8 7 6
f e d c b a

For information, write: Bedford/St. Martin's, 75 Arlington Street, Boston, MA 02116 (617-399-4000)

ISBN 978-1-319-03545-7

Acknowledgments

Text acknowledgments and copyrights appear at the back of the book on page 477, which constitutes an extension of the copyright page. Art acknowledgments and copyrights appear on the same page as the art selections they cover.

Preface

This book is a text — a book about reading other people's arguments and writing your own arguments — and it is also an anthology — a collection of dozens of selections, ranging from Plato to the present, with a strong emphasis on contemporary arguments and, in this edition, the first in full color, new modes of argument. Before we describe these selections further, we'd like to describe our chief assumptions about the aims of a course that might use *Critical Thinking, Reading, and Writing: A Brief Guide to Argument*.

Probably most students and instructors would agree that, as *critical readers*, students should be able to

- summarize accurately an argument they have read;

- locate the thesis (the claim) of an argument;

- locate the assumptions, stated and unstated, of an argument;

- analyze and evaluate the strength of the evidence and the soundness of the reasoning offered in support of the thesis; and

- analyze, evaluate, and account for discrepancies among various readings on a topic (for example, explain why certain facts are used, why probable consequences of a proposed action are examined or are ignored, or why two sources might interpret the same facts differently).

Probably, too, students and instructors would agree that, as *thoughtful writers*, students should be able to

- imagine an audience and write effectively for it (for instance, by using the appropriate tone and providing the appropriate amount of detail);

- present information in an orderly and coherent way;

- be aware of their own assumptions;

- locate sources and incorporate them into their own writing, not simply by quoting extensively or by paraphrasing but also by having digested material so that they can present it in their own words;

- properly document all borrowings — not merely quotations and paraphrases but also borrowed ideas; and

- do all these things in the course of developing a thoughtful argument of their own.

In the first edition of this book we quoted Edmund Burke and John Stuart Mill. Burke said,

> He that wrestles with us strengthens our nerves, and sharpens our skill.
> Our antagonist is our helper.

Mill said,

> He who knows only his own side of the cause knows little.

These two quotations continue to reflect the view of argument that underlies this text: In writing an essay one is engaging in a serious effort to know what one's own ideas are and, having found them, to contribute to a multisided conversation. One is not setting out to trounce an opponent, and that is partly why such expressions as "marshaling evidence," "attacking an opponent," and "defending a thesis" are misleading. True, on television talk shows we see right-wingers and left-wingers who have made up their minds and who are concerned only with pushing their own views and brushing aside all others. But in an academic community, and indeed in our daily lives, we learn by listening to others and also by listening to ourselves.

We draft a response to something we have read, and in the very act of drafting we may find — if we think critically about the words we are putting down on paper — we are changing (perhaps slightly, perhaps radically) our own position. In short, one reason that we write is so that we can improve our ideas. And even if we do not drastically change our views, we and our readers at least come to a better understanding of why we hold the views we do.

Features

THE TEXT

Part One: Critical Thinking and Reading (Chapters 1–4) and Part Two: Critical Writing (Chapters 5–7) together offer a short course in methods of thinking about and writing arguments. By "thinking," we mean serious analytic thought, including analysis of one's own assumptions (Chapter 1); by "writing" we mean the use of effective, respectable techniques, not gimmicks (such as the notorious note a politician scribbled in the margin of the text of his speech: "Argument weak; shout here"). For a delightfully wry account of the use of gimmicks, we recommend that you consult "The Art of Controversy" in *The Will to Live* by the nineteenth-century German philosopher Arthur Schopenhauer. Schopenhauer reminds readers that a Greek or Latin quotation (however irrelevant) can be impressive to the uninformed and that one can knock down almost any proposition by loftily saying, "That's all very well in theory, but it won't do in practice."

We offer lots of advice about how to set forth an argument, but we do not offer instruction in one-upmanship. Rather, we discuss responsible ways of arguing persuasively. We know, however, that before one can write a persuasive argument, one must clarify one's own ideas — a process that includes arguing with oneself — to find out what one really thinks about a problem. Therefore, we devote Chapter 1 to critical thinking; Chapters 2, 3, and 4 to critical reading (Chapter 4 is about reading images); and Chapters 5, 6, and 7 to critical writing.

Parts One and Two together contain thirty readings (seven are student papers) for analysis and discussion. Some of these essays originated as op-ed newspaper pieces, and we reprint some of the letters to the editor that they generated, so students can easily see several sides to a given issue. In this way students can, in their own responses, join the conversation, so to speak. (We have found, by the way, that using the format of a letter helps students to frame their ideas, and therefore in later chapters we occasionally suggest writing assignments in the form of a letter to the editor.)

All of the essays in the book are accompanied by a list of Topics for Critical Thinking and Writing.[1] This is not surprising, given the emphasis we place on asking questions in order to come up with ideas for writing. Among the chief questions that writers should ask, we suggest, are "What is X?" and "What is the value of X?" (pp. 226–27). By asking such questions — for instance (to look only at these two types of questions), "Is the fetus a person?" or "Is Arthur Miller a better playwright than Tennessee Williams?" — a writer probably will find ideas coming, at least after a few moments of head scratching. The device of developing an argument by identifying issues is, of course, nothing new. Indeed, it goes back to an ancient method of argument used by classical rhetoricians, who identified a stasis (an issue) and then asked questions about it: Did X do such and such? If so, was the action bad? If bad, how bad? (Finding an issue or stasis — a position where one stands — by asking questions is discussed in Chapter 6.)

In keeping with our emphasis on writing as well as reading, we raise issues not only of what can roughly be called the "content" of the essays but also of what can (equally roughly) be called the "style" — that is, the *ways* in which the arguments are set forth. Content and style, of course, cannot finally be kept apart. As Cardinal Newman said, "Thought and meaning are inseparable from each other. . . . *Style is thinking out into language.*" In our Topics for Critical Thinking and Writing, we sometimes ask the student

- to evaluate the effectiveness of an essay's opening paragraph,

- to explain a shift in tone from one paragraph to the next, or

- to characterize the persona of the author as revealed in the whole essay.

---

1   The paragraphs in the essays are, for ease of reference, numbered in increments of five (5, 10, 15, and so on).

In short, the book is not designed as an introduction to some powerful ideas (though in fact it is that, too); it is designed as an aid to *writing* thoughtful, effective arguments on important political, social, scientific, ethical, legal, and religious issues.

The essays reprinted in this book also illustrate different styles of argument that arise, at least in part, from the different disciplinary backgrounds of the various authors. Essays by journalists, lawyers, judges, social scientists, policy analysts, philosophers, critics, activists, and other writers — including first-year undergraduates — will be found in these pages. The authors develop and present their views in arguments that have distinctive features reflecting their special training and concerns. The differences in argumentative styles found in these essays foreshadow the differences students will encounter in the readings assigned in many of their other courses.

Parts One and Two, then, offer a preliminary (but we hope substantial) discussion of such topics as

- identifying assumptions;

- getting ideas by means of invention strategies;

- finding, evaluating, and citing printed and electronic sources;

- interpreting visual sources;

- evaluating kinds of evidence; and

- organizing material as well as an introduction to some ways of thinking.

Part Three: Further Views on Argument consists of Chapters 8 through 12.

- Chapter 8, A Philosopher's View: The Toulmin Model, is a summary of the philosopher Stephen Toulmin's method for analyzing arguments, covering claims, grounds, warrants, backing, modal qualifiers, and rebuttals. This summary will assist those who wish to apply Toulmin's methods to the readings in our book.

- Chapter 9, A Logician's View: Deduction, Induction, Fallacies, offers a more rigorous analysis of these topics than is usually found in composition courses and reexamines from a logician's point of view material already treated briefly in Chapter 3.

- Chapter 10, A Psychologist's View: Rogerian Argument, with an essay by psychotherapist Carl R. Rogers and an essay by a student, complements the discussion of audience, organization, and tone in Chapter 6.

- Chapter 11, A Literary Critic's View: Arguing about Literature, should help students to see the things literary critics argue about and *how* they argue. Students can apply what they learn not only to the literary readings that appear in the chapter (poems by Robert Frost and Andrew Marvell and a story by Kate Chopin) but also to the readings that appear in Part Four, A Casebook on the State and the Individual. Part Three concludes with

- Chapter 12, A Debater's View: Individual Oral Presentations and Debate, which introduces students to standard presentation strategies and debate format.

Finally, Part Four: A Casebook on the State and the Individual consists of Chapter 13, which asks the question, How Free Is the Will of the Individual within Society? Nine authors explore this enduring question through essays, letters, poems, and a play.

What's New in the Ninth Edition

This ninth edition brings highly significant changes. The authors of the previous eight editions established a firm foundation for the book: Hugo Bedau, professor of philosophy, brought analytical rigor to the instruction in argumentation. and Sylvan Barnet, professor of English, contributed expertise in writing instruction. They have now turned the project over to John O'Hara, professor of critical thinking, to contribute a third dimension, augmenting and enriching the material on critical thinking throughout, especially in the early chapters. Other changes have been made to ensure practical instruction and current topics.

Fresh and timely new readings. One-third are new, as are topics such as genetically engineered foods, protection of religious rights in prison, and marijuana regulation.

A revised casebook in Part Four. Chapter 13 offers selections from Plato, George Orwell, Walter T. Stace, Martin Luther King Jr., Peter Cave, Thomas Hardy, T. S. Eliot, Susan Glaspell, and Mitsuye Yamada that explore a question both timeless and current: How Free Is the Will of the Individual within Society?

A vibrant new design. A new full-color layout makes the book more engaging and easier for students to navigate, and an expanded trim size allows more space for students to annotate and take notes. Over fifty new visuals, including ads, cartoons, photographs, and Web pages, provide occasions for critical inquiry.

Expanded coverage of critical thinking in Part One. Part One has been heavily revised to help better show students how effective reading, analysis, and writing all begin with critical thinking. Enhancements include an expanded vocabulary for critical thinking, instruction on writing critical summaries, guidance on confronting unfamiliar issues in reading and writing, new strategies for generating essay topics, and extended critical reading approaches.

New "Thinking Critically" activities. Throughout the text, new interactive exercises test students' ability to apply critical thinking, reading, and writing concepts. Students can also complete these exercises online in LaunchPad.

Expanded discussion of developing thesis statements in Chapter 6. This updated section helps better illustrate for students what the difference is between taking a truly critical position versus resting on their laurels in argumentative essays.

Updated coverage of visual rhetoric in Chapter 4. The "Visual Rhetoric" chapter has been expanded to include discussion of how to analyze images rhetorically, including how to recognize and resist the meanings of images, how to identify visual emotional appeals, and what the difference is exactly between *seeing* passively and truly *looking* critically.

LaunchPad for *Critical Thinking, Reading, and Writing.* This edition of *Critical Thinking, Reading, and Writing* includes access to LaunchPad—an interactive platform that brings together the resources students need to prepare for class, working with the textbook. Features include interactive questions and exercises and quizzes on all of the readings and instructional content, allowing instructors to quickly get a sense of what students understand and what they need help with. You and your students can access LaunchPad at **macmillanhighered.com /barnetbedauohara**. Students receive access automatically with the purchase of a new book. Students can purchase standalone access at **macmillanhighered.com/barnetbedauohara**. To get instructor access, register as an instructor at this site.

Acknowledgments

Finally, the authors would like to thank those who have strengthened this book by their comments and advice on the ninth edition: Stacia Bensyl, Missouri Western State University; Christine Brooks, Community College of Vermont; Syble Davis, Houston Community College–Central; Africa Fine, Palm Beach State College; Erin Fujinami, Clovis Center Community College; Deanna Gabrielson, Morehead State University; Melinda Mejia, Houston Community College–Central; Veronica Reyes, California State University Los Angeles; Daniel Sabol, Mercy College; Rachel Savorelli, University of Pittsburgh; Kay Siebler, Missouri Western State University; Celeste Sonnier, Morton College; Jim Wilkins-Luton, Clark College; and our anonymous reviewers from Los Angeles Mission College, Mission College, and Palm Beach State College. We would also like to thank Kalina Ingham, Elaine Kosta, Martha Friedman, Angela Boehler, and Jen Simmons, who adeptly managed art research and text permissions.

We are also deeply indebted to the people at Bedford/St. Martin's, especially to our editor, Alicia Young, who is wise, patient, supportive, and unfailingly helpful. Steve Scipione, Maura Shea, John Sullivan, and Adam Whitehurst, our editors for all of the preceding editions, have left a lasting impression on us and on the book; without their work on the first eight editions, there probably would not be a ninth. Others at Bedford/St. Martin's to whom we are deeply indebted include Edwin Hill, Leasa Burton, Karen Henry, Joy Fisher Williams, Jennifer Prince, Elise Kaiser, and Jessica Gould, all of whom have offered countless valuable (and invaluable) suggestions. Intelligent, informed, firm yet courteous, persuasive—all of these folks know how to think and how to argue.

Get the Most Out of Your Course with *Critical Thinking, Reading, and Writing*

Bedford/St. Martin's offers resources and format choices that help you and your students get even more out of your book and course. To learn more about or to order any of the following products, contact your Macmillan sales representative, e-mail sales support (**sales_support@ bfwpub.com**), or visit the Web site at **macmillanhighered.com/criticalthinking9e/catalog**.

LAUNCHPAD FOR *CRITICAL THINKING, READING, AND WRITING*: WHERE STUDENTS LEARN

LaunchPad provides engaging content and new ways to get the most out of your book. Get an **interactive e-book** combined with **useful, highly relevant materials** in a fully customizable course space; then assign and mix our resources with yours.

- Auto-graded **reading quizzes, comprehension quizzes on argument topics**, and **interactive writing templates** help students to engage actively with the material you assign.

- **Pre-built units** — including readings, videos, quizzes, discussion groups, and more — are **easy to adapt and assign** by adding your own materials and mixing them with our high-quality multimedia content and ready-made assessment options, such as **LearningCurve** adaptive quizzing. LearningCurve now includes argument modules focusing on topic, purpose, and audience, arguable claims, reasoning and logical fallacies, and persuasive appeals (*logos, pathos,* and *ethos*).

- LaunchPad also provides access to a **Gradebook** that provides a clear window on the performance of your whole class, individual students, and even results of individual assignments.

- A **streamlined interface** helps students focus on what's due, and social commenting tools let them **engage**, make connections, and learn from each other. Use LaunchPad on its own or integrate it with your school's learning management system so that your class is always on the same page.

To get the most out of your book, order LaunchPad for *Critical Thinking, Reading, and Writing* packaged with the print book. (LaunchPad for *Critical Thinking, Reading, and Writing* can also be purchased on its own.) An activation code is required. To order LaunchPad for *Critical Thinking, Reading, and Writing* with the print book, use ISBN 978-1-319-10223-4.

CHOOSE FROM ALTERNATIVE FORMATS OF *CRITICAL THINKING, READING, AND WRITING*

Critical Thinking, Reading, and Writing is available in a variety of e-book formats. For details about our e-book partners, visit **macmillanlearning.com/ebooks**.

SELECT VALUE PACKAGES

Add value to your text by packaging one of the following resources with *Critical Thinking, Reading, and Writing*. To learn more about package options for any of the following products, contact your Bedford/St. Martin's sales representative or visit **macmillanhighered.com /criticalthinking9e/catalog**.

Writer's Help 2.0 is a powerful online writing resource that helps students find answers whether they are searching for writing advice on their own or as part of an assignment.

- **Smart search:** Built on research with more than 1,600 student writers, the smart search in Writer's Help 2.0 provides reliable results even when students use novice terms, such as *flow* and *unstuck*.

- **Trusted content from our best-selling handbooks:** Choose *Writer's Help 2.0, Hacker Version* or *Writer's Help 2.0, Lunsford Version* and ensure that students have clear advice and examples for all of their writing questions.

- **Adaptive exercises that engage students:** Writer's Help 2.0 includes *LearningCurve*, game-like online quizzing that adapts to what students already know and helps them focus on what they need to learn.

Student access is packaged with *Critical Thinking, Reading, and Writing* at a significant discount. Order ISBN 978-1-319-10221-0 for *Writer's Help 2.0, Hacker Version* or ISBN 978-1-319-10220-3 for *Writer's Help 2.0, Lunsford Version* to ensure your students have easy access to online writing support. Students who rent a book or buy a used book can purchase access to Writer's Help 2.0 at **macmillanhighered.com/writershelp2**.

Instructors may request free access by registering as an instructor at **macmillanhighered.com/writershelp2**.

For technical support, visit **macmillanhighered.com/getsupport**.

Portfolio Keeping, **Third Edition, by Nedra Reynolds and Elizabeth Davis**, provides all the information students need to use the portfolio method successfully in a writing course. *Portfolio Teaching*, a companion guide for instructors, provides the practical information instructors and writing program administrators need to use the portfolio method successfully in a writing course. To order *Portfolio Keeping* packaged with this text, contact your sale representative for a package ISBN.

INSTRUCTOR RESOURCES

macmillanhighered.com/criticalthinking9e/catalog

You have a lot to do in your course. Bedford/St. Martin's wants to make it easy for you to find the support you need — and to get it quickly.

Resources for Teaching Critical Thinking, Reading, and Writing is available as a PDF that can be downloaded from the Bedford/St. Martin's online catalog at the URL above. In addition to chapter overviews and teaching tips, the instructor's manual includes a sample syllabus and suggested classroom activities.

Join Our Community! The Macmillan English Community is now Bedford/St. Martin's home for professional resources, featuring Bedford *Bits*, our popular blog site offering new ideas for the composition classroom and composition teachers. Connect and converse with a growing team of Bedford authors and top scholars who blog on *Bits*: Andrea Lunsford, Nancy

Sommers, Steve Bernhardt, Traci Gardner, Barclay Barrios, Jack Solomon, Susan Bernstein, Elizabeth Wardle, Doug Downs, Liz Losh, Jonathan Alexander, and Donna Winchell.

In addition, you'll find an expanding collection of additional resources that support your teaching:

- Sign up for webinars.

- Download resources from our professional resource series that support your teaching.

- Start a discussion.

- Ask a question.

- Follow your favorite members.

- Review projects in the pipeline.

Visit **community.macmillan.com** to join the conversation with your fellow teachers.

Brief Contents

Contents

Critical Thinking,
Reading, and Writing

PART ONE

Critical Thinking and Reading

Critical Thinking

What is the hardest task in the world? To think.　　　　— RALPH WALDO EMERSON

In all affairs it's a healthy thing now and then to hang a question mark on the things you have long taken for granted.　　　　— BERTRAND RUSSELL

Although Emerson said the hardest task in the world is simply "to think," he was using the word *think* in the sense of *critical thinking*. By itself, *thinking* can mean almost any sort of cognitive activity, from idle daydreaming ("I'd like to go camping") to simple reasoning ("but if I go this week, I won't be able to study for my chemistry exam"). Thinking by itself may include forms of deliberation and decision-making that occur so automatically they hardly register in our consciousness ("What if I do go camping? I won't be likely to pass the exam. Then what? I better stay home and study").

When we add the adjective *critical* to the noun *thinking,* we begin to examine this thinking process consciously. When we do this, we see that even our simplest decisions involve a fairly elaborate series of calculations. Just in choosing to study and not to go camping, for instance, we weighed the relative importance of each activity (both are important in different ways); considered our goals, obligations, and commitments (to ourselves, our parents, peers, and professors); posed questions and predicted outcomes (using experience and observation as evidence); and resolved to take the most prudent course of action.

Many people associate being critical with fault-finding and nit-picking. The word *critic* might conjure an image of a sneering art or food critic eager to gripe about everything that's wrong with a particular work of art or menu item. People's low estimation of the stereotypical critic comes to light humorously in Samuel Beckett's play *Waiting for Godot*, when the two vagabond heroes, Vladimir and Estragon, engage in a name-calling contest to see who can hurl the worst insult at the other. Estragon wins hands-down when he fires the ultimate invective:

V: Moron!
E: Vermin!
V: Abortion!

E: Morpion!
V: Sewer-rat!
E: Curate!
V: Cretin!
E: (*with finality*) Crritic!
V: Oh! (*He wilts, vanquished, and turns away*)

However, being a good *critical* thinker isn't the same as being a "critic" in the derogatory sense. Quite the reverse: Because critical thinkers approach difficult questions and seek intelligent answers, they must be open-minded and self-aware, and they must interrogate *their own* thinking as rigorously as they interrogate others'. They must be alert to *their own* limitations and biases, the quality of evidence and forms of logic *they themselves* tentatively offer. In college, we may not aspire to become critics, but we all should aspire to become better critical thinkers.

Becoming more aware of our thought processes is a first step in practicing critical thinking. The word *critical* comes from the Greek word *krinein*, meaning "to separate, to choose"; above all, it implies *conscious* inquiry. It suggests that by breaking apart, or examining, our reasoning we can understand better the basis of our judgments and decisions — ultimately, so that we can make better ones.

Thinking through an Issue: Gay Marriage Licenses

By way of illustration, let's examine a case from Kentucky that was reported widely in the news in 2015. After the U.S. Supreme Court's landmark decision making gay marriage legal in all fifty states, a Rowan County clerk, Kim Davis, refused to begin issuing marriage licenses to same-sex couples. Citing religious freedom as her reason, Davis contended that the First Amendment of the Constitution protects her from being forced to act against her religious convictions and conscience. As a follower of Apostolic Christianity, she believes gay marriage is not marriage at all. To act against her belief, she said, "I would be asked to violate a central teaching of Scripture and of Jesus Himself regarding marriage. . . . It is not a light issue for me. It's a Heaven or Hell decision."

Let's think critically about this — and let's do it in a way that's fair to all parties and not just a snap judgment. Critical thinking means questioning not only the beliefs and assumptions of others, but also *one's own* beliefs and assumptions. We'll discuss this point at some length later, but for now we'll say only that when writing an argument you ought to be *thinking* — identifying important problems, exploring relevant issues, and evaluating available evidence — not merely collecting information to support a pre-established conclusion.

In 2015, Kim Davis was an elected county official. She couldn't be fired from her job for not performing her duties because she had been placed in that position by the vote of her constituency. And as her lawyers pointed out, "You don't lose your conscience rights, or your religious freedom rights, or your constitutional rights just because you accept public employment." However, once the Supreme Court established the legality of same-sex marriage,

Davis's right to exercise her religious freedom impinged upon others' abilities to exercise their equal right to marriage (now guaranteed to them by the federal government). And so there was a problem: Whose rights have precedence?

We may begin to identify important problems and explore relevant issues by using a process called *clustering*. (We illustrate clustering again on p. 13.) Clustering is a method of brainstorming, a way of getting ideas on paper to see what develops, what conflicts and issues exist, and what tentative conclusions you can draw as you begin developing an argument. To start clustering, take a sheet of paper, and in the center jot down the most basic issue you can think of related to the problem at hand. In our example, we wrote a sentence that we think gets at the heart of the matter. It's important to note that we conducted this demonstration in "real time" — just a few minutes — so if our thoughts seem incomplete or off-the-cuff, that's fine. The point of clustering is to get ideas on paper. Don't be afraid to write down whatever you think, because you can always go back, cross out, rethink. This process of working through an issue can be messy. In a sense, it involves conducting an argument with yourself.

At the top of our page we wrote, "The law overrides individual religious freedom." (Alternatively, we could have written from the perspective of Davis and her supporters, saying "Individual religious freedom supersedes the law," and seen where that might have taken us.) Once we have a central idea, we let our minds work and allow one thought to lead to another. We've added numbers to our thoughts so you can follow the progression of our thinking.

1. The law overrides individual religious freedom.

2. Not always. The law can't tell people what to believe or how to practice religion.

4. What are the limits of individual religious freedom? When *can* the law compel or prohibit behavior?

3. What about drugs or animal sacrifice? What is *not* allowed under religious exemption? Murder? Jail? Polygamy? **Not really the issue. Real issue is Kim Davis.**

5. The law can limit some things, but it cannot force a person to act against his or her religion (how to speak, think, dress, etc.).

6. But Davis is not just any citizen. She is a government representative sworn to act according to law, not her religion.

7. Maybe she should resign or be fired?

10. Impeachment? Complicated, not a long-term solution.

8. Why should she resign? Should one's religion prevent one from public employment?

9. She can't be fired. She was elected to the county office by vote.

11. Davis as crusader, civil disobedience, the American individualist tradition?

12. Davis isn't signing religious licenses to marry. She is signing civil licenses. The legal terms of marriage are secular.

13. Any workarounds? Someone else in the office could sign the licenses? Or maybe same-sex couples could simply go to a different county clerk? But how far should they have to go and why? And what if the next county had another clerk like Kim Davis?

14. Why is the county clerkship an elected position, after all? If it were an appointed position, it would be clear. Davis could be removed from office for not upholding her oath to execute the law.

Notice that from our first idea about the law being more important than individual religious freedom, we immediately challenged our initial thinking. The law, in fact, protects religious freedom (2), and in some cases allows individuals to "break the law" if their religious rituals require it. We learned this when we wrote down a number of illegal activities sometimes associated with religion, and quickly looked up whether or not there was a legal precedent protecting these activities. We found the Supreme Court has allowed for the use of illegal drugs in some ceremonies (*Gonzalez v. O Centro Espirita*), and for the ritual sacrifice of animals in another (*Church of Lakumi Bablu Aye v. Hialeah*). Still, religions cannot do *anything they want* in the name of religious freedom. Religions cannot levy taxes, or incarcerate or kill people, for example. We then realized that what religions do as part of their ceremonies is not really the issue at all. The questions we are asking have to do with Kim Davis, her individual religious freedom, and what the law might force her to do (4).

Individuals cannot simply break the law and claim religious exemption. But the government cannot force people to act against their religious beliefs (5). Then (6) it occurred to us that Davis isn't just any citizen but a government employee whose job is to issue marriage licenses under the law. She may be free to believe what she wants and exercise her rights accordingly, but she cannot use her authority legally as a government official to deny people the rights they've been afforded by law.

We then posed several questions to ourselves in trying to determine the right way to think. We considered whether Davis should resign or be fired (7), which we then realized isn't possible (8, 9), and we wondered how else a person may be removed from office (10). We considered her as a figure of civil disobedience, defying the law in defense of religious liberties (11), trying to see the situation from her perspective. But we returned again to the idea that she isn't just a regular citizen but an agent of the law whose oath compels her to uphold the law (6). She shouldn't be able to use her authority to deprive others of exercising their rights. We also considered that the government doesn't take particular interest in the religious basis of marriage (12), so why should Davis be permitted to impose her religious beliefs on a lawful act of marriage?

By the time we got to (13), we thought, "Isn't there some workaround? Can't *deputy clerks* continue to sign the licenses as long as the state accepts them?" This way, Davis wouldn't have to violate the deeply held beliefs that she is free to hold, and yet those seeking to exercise their rights to marriage would still be satisfied. Later, on page 374, we discuss a facet of compromise solutions to difficult problems when we explore Rogerian argument (named for Carl Rogers, a psychologist), a way of arguing that promotes finding common ground and solutions in which both sides win by conceding some elements to the opposition. We also thought in (13) that maybe same-sex couples could just get their licenses from a different place, one where Davis doesn't work.

At this point, it may be useful to mention another facet of critical thinking and argument that we'll also explore in more detail later: considering the implications of the decisions to which our thinking leads. What happens when our judgments on matters are settled and we draw a reasonable conclusion? If we were to settle on a compromise in the Davis case, it might work for the moment, but what would happen if other clerks in the state held the same beliefs as Davis (13)? In (13), we also considered the implications if same-sex couples were simply asked to go to a different office. How far should a same-sex couple have to go to find someone willing to issue the license if all clerks can decide based on their religious convictions what kinds of marriage they will authorize? Additionally, and maybe even more important, why should same-sex couples be hindered in any way in acquiring their license or be treated as a different class of citizens?

Again, if you think with pencil and paper in hand and let your mind make associations by clustering, you'll find (perhaps to your surprise) that you have plenty of interesting ideas and that some can lead to satisfying conclusions. Doubtless you'll also have some ideas that represent gut reactions or poorly thought-out conclusions, but that's okay. When clustering, allow your thoughts to take shape without restriction; you can look them over again and organize them later. Originally, we wrote in our cluster (7) that Davis could be fired for not performing her job according to its requirements. We then realized that this wouldn't involve a simple process. Because she's an elected official, there would have to be a state legislative action to impeach her (9). This made us think, "The state of Kentucky could impeach Davis" (10). But then we also considered the consequences and decided this would not be a long-term solution. What if the next election cycle brought someone else who shares Davis's beliefs into the same position? In fact, what if citizens in Kentucky continued to elect county clerks in Rowan County — or any county — who refused to issue marriage licenses based on religious convictions? Would the state have to impeach clerks over and over again? We then thought, "Why is the county clerkship an elected position" (14)? Could it become an appointed position instead, such that governors could emplace county clerks, whose primary job is to administer legislative policy? Perhaps this is the argument we'll want to make. (Of course, it might open up new questions and issues that we would have to explore: What else does the clerk do? Is the autonomy of an elected position necessary? Do all states elect county clerks? And so on.)

> **A RULE FOR WRITERS**
> One good way to start writing an essay is to generate ideas by clustering — and at this point not to worry that some ideas may be off-the-cuff or even nonsense. Just get ideas down on paper. You can evaluate them later.

At the time of this writing, Kim Davis had continued to refuse signing marriage licenses for same-sex couples. When ordered by a judge to do so or face contempt of court, she held firm to her position and spent six days in jail as a result. Her supporters cheered her act of civil disobedience (defined as breaking a law based on moral or religious conscience) and even compared her to Rosa Parks, Martin Luther King Jr., and other civil rights leaders who fought against unjust laws on the basis of religious principles. Davis returned to her position as Rowan County clerk and authorized her deputy clerks to issue marriage licenses to same-sex couples, but without her signature. Time will tell how the case plays out.

Topics for Critical Thinking and Writing

1. As noted, some of Kim Davis's supporters have compared her to celebrated figures from American history like Rosa Parks who practiced civil disobedience by breaking laws they believed were immoral, unfair, or unjust. What are the similarities and differences in the case

of Rosa Parks, who violated the law in Montgomery, Alabama, in 1955 by refusing to move to the "black" section of a public bus, and that of Kim Davis, who has refused to abide by laws established by the U.S. Supreme Court regarding gay marriage? How do the similarities and differences justify or not justify Davis's actions?

2. On a Facebook page dedicated to Davis's case, one commenter wrote, "Davis is a hero for all of us Christians who feel this country is abandoning our God." Think critically about this statement by writing about the assumptions it reveals.

3. In denying Davis's appeal to a federal court to not be forced to authorize same-sex marriage licenses, Judge David Bunning wrote that individuals "cannot choose what orders they follow" and that religious conscience "is not a viable defense" for not adhering to the law. At the same time, the free exercise clause of the First Amendment of the U.S. Constitution says that Congress shall make no law prohibiting the free exercise of religion. What do you think about Kim Davis's exercise of religion? Is it fair that in order to keep her job after the Court's decision about the legality of gay marriage, she has to regularly violate one of her religion's central beliefs about marriage? Explain your response.

On Flying Spaghetti Monsters: Analyzing and Evaluating from Multiple Perspectives

Let's think critically about another issue related to religious freedom, equality, and the law — one that we hope brings some humor to the activity but also inspires careful thinking and debate.

In 2005, in response to pressure from some religious groups, the Kansas Board of Education gave preliminary approval for teaching alternatives to evolution in public school science classes. New policies would require science teachers to present "intelligent design" — the idea that the universe was created by an intentional, conscious force such as God — as an equally plausible explanation for natural selection and human development.

In a quixotic challenge to the legislation, twenty-four-year-old physics graduate Bobby Henderson wrote an open letter that quickly became popular on the Internet and then was published in the *New York Times*. Henderson appealed for recognition of another theory that he said was equally valid: that an all-powerful deity called the Flying Spaghetti Monster created the world. While clearly writing satirically on behalf of science, Henderson nevertheless kept a straight face and argued that if creationism were to be taught as a theory in science classes, then "Pastafarianism" must also be taught as another legitimate possibility. "I think we can all look forward to the time," he wrote, "when these three theories are given equal time in our science classes. . . . One third time for Intelligent Design; one third time for Flying Spaghetti Monsterism (Pastafarianism); and one third time for logical conjecture based on overwhelming observable evidence."

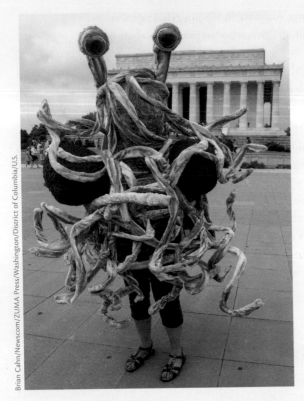

Brian Cahn/Newscom/ZUMA Press/Washington/District of Columbia/U.S.

Since that time, the Church of the Flying Spaghetti Monster has become a creative venue where secularists and atheists construct elaborate mythologies, religious texts, and rituals, most of which involve cartoonish pirates and various noodle-and-sauce images. ("R'amen," they say at the end of their prayers.) However, although tongue-in-cheek, many followers have also used the organization seriously as a means to champion the First Amendment's establishment clause, which prohibits government institutions from *establishing*, or preferring, any one religion over another. Pastafarians have challenged policies and laws in various states that appear to discriminate among religions or to provide exceptions or exemptions based on religion. In Tennessee, Virginia, and Wisconsin, church members have successfully petitioned for permission to display statues or signs of the Flying Spaghetti Monster in places where other religious icons are permitted, such as on state government properties. One petition in Oklahoma argued that because the state allows a marble and granite Ten Commandments monument on the state courthouse lawn, then a statue of the Flying Spaghetti Monster must also be permitted; this effort ultimately forced the state to remove the Ten Commandments monument in 2015. In the past three years, individuals in California, Georgia, Florida, Texas, California, and Utah have asserted their right to wear religious head coverings in their driver's license photos — a religious exemption afforded to Muslims in those states — and have had their pictures taken with colanders on their heads.

Let's stop for a moment. Take stock of your initial reactions to the Church of the Flying Spaghetti Monster. Some responses might be quite uncritical, quite unthinking: "That's outrageous!" or "What a funny idea!" Others might be the type of snap judgment we discussed earlier: "These people are making fun of real religions!" or "They're just causing trouble." Think about it: If your hometown approved placing a Christmas tree on the town square during the holiday season, and the Church of the Flying Spaghetti Monster argued that it too should be allowed to set up its holiday symbol as a matter of religious equality — perhaps a statue like the one pictured above — should it be afforded equal space? Why, or why not?

Be careful here, and exercise critical thinking. Can one simply say, "No, that belief is ridiculous," in response to a religious claim? What if members of a different religious group were asking for equal space? Should a menorah (a Jewish holiday symbol) be allowed? A mural celebrating Kwanzaa? A Native American symbol? Can some religious expressions be included in public spaces and not others? If so, why? If not, why not?

In thinking critically about a topic, we must try to see it from all sides before reaching a conclusion. We conduct an argument with ourselves, advancing and then questioning different opinions:

- What can be said *for* the proposition?
- What can be said *against* it?

Critical thinking requires us to support our position and also see the other side. The heart of critical thinking is a *willingness to face objections to one's own beliefs,* to adopt a skeptical attitude not only toward views opposed to our own but also toward our own common sense — that is, toward views that seem to us as obviously right. If we assume we have a monopoly on the truth and dismiss those who disagree with us as misguided fools, or if we say that our opponents are acting out of self-interest (or a desire to harass the community) and we don't analyze their views, we're being critical but we aren't engaging in critical thinking.

When thinking critically, it's important to ask key questions about any position, decision, or action we take and any regulation, policy, or law we support. We must ask:

- Is it fair?
- What is its purpose?
- Is it likely to accomplish its purpose?
- What will its effects be? Might it unintentionally cause some harm?
- If it might cause harm, to whom? What kind of harm? Can we weigh the potential harm against the potential good?
- Who gains something and who loses something as a result?
- Are there any compromises that might satisfy different parties?

What do you think? If you were on your hometown's city council, how would you answer the above questions in relation to a petition from the Church of the Flying Spaghetti Monster to permit a Spaghetti Monster display alongside the traditional Christmas tree on the town square? How would you vote, and why? What other questions and issues might arise from your engagement with this issue? (*Hint:* Try clustering. Place the central question in the middle of a sheet of a paper, and brainstorm the issues that flower from it.)

CALL-OUT: OBSTACLES TO CRITICAL THINKING   Because critical thinking requires engaging seriously with potentially difficult topics, topics about which you may already have strong opinions, and topics that elicit powerful emotional responses, it's important to recognize the ways in which your thinking may be compromised or clouded. Write down or discuss how each of the following attitudes might impede or otherwise negatively affect your critical thinking in real life. How might each one be detrimental in making conclusions?

1. The topic is too controversial and will never be resolved.
2. The topic hits "too close to home" (i.e., "I've had direct experience with this").

3. The topic disgusts me.

4. The topic angers me.

5. Everyone I know thinks roughly the same thing I do about this topic.

6. Others may judge me if I verbalize what I think.

7. My opinion on this topic is *X* because it benefits me, my family, or my kind the most.

8. My parents raised me to think *X* about this topic.

9. One of my favorite celebrities believes *X* about this topic, so I do too.

10. I know what I think, but my solutions are probably unrealistic. It's impossible to change the system.

Think of some more obstacles to critical thinking, and provide examples of how they might lead to unsound conclusions or poor solutions.

> **A RULE FOR WRITERS**
> Early in the process of jotting down your ideas on a topic, stop to ask yourself, "What might someone reasonably offer as an *objection* to my view?"

In short, as we will say several times (because the point is key), *argument is an instrument of learning* as well as of persuasion. In order to formulate a reasoned position and make a vote, you'll have to gather some information, find out what experts say, and examine the points on which they agree and disagree. You'll likely want to gather opinions from religious leaders, community members, and legal experts (after all, you wouldn't want the town to be sued for discrimination). You'll want to think beyond a knee-jerk value judgment like, "No, a Spaghetti Monster statue would be ugly."

Seeing the issue from multiple perspectives will require familiarizing yourself with current debates — perhaps about religious equality, free speech, or the separation of church and state — and considering the responsibility of public institutions to accommodate different viewpoints and various constituencies. Remember, the Church of the Flying Spaghetti Monster didn't gain so much traction by being easy to dismiss. Thus, you must do the following:

Survey, considering as many perspectives as possible.

Analyze, identifying and then separating out the parts of the problem, trying to see how its pieces fit together.

Evaluate, judging the merit of various ideas and claims and the weight of the evidence in their favor or against them.

If you survey, analyze, and evaluate comprehensively, you'll have better and more informed ideas; you'll generate a wide variety of ideas, each triggered by your own responses and the ideas your research brings to light. As you form an opinion and prepare to vote, you'll be constructing an argument to yourself at first, but also one you may have to present to the community, so you should be as thorough as possible and sensitive to the ideas and rights of many different people.

CRITICAL THINKING AT WORK: FROM JOTTINGS TO A SHORT ESSAY

We have already seen an example of clustering on page 6, which illustrates the prewriting process of thinking through an issue and generating ideas by imagining responses — counterthoughts — to our initial thoughts. Here's another example, this time showing an actual student's thoughts about an issue related to the Church of the Flying Spaghetti Monster. The student, Alexa Cabrera, was assigned to write approximately 500 words about a specific legal challenge made by a member of the Church of the Flying Spaghetti Monster. She selected the case of Stephen Cavanaugh, a prisoner who made a complaint against the Nebraska State Penitentiary after being denied the right to practice Pastafarianism while incarcerated there. Because the Department of Corrections denied him those privileges, Cavanaugh filed suit citing civil rights violations and asked for his rights to be accommodated. Notice that in the essay — the product of several revised drafts — the student introduced points she had *not* thought of while clustering. The cluster, in short, was a *first* step, not a road map of the final essay.

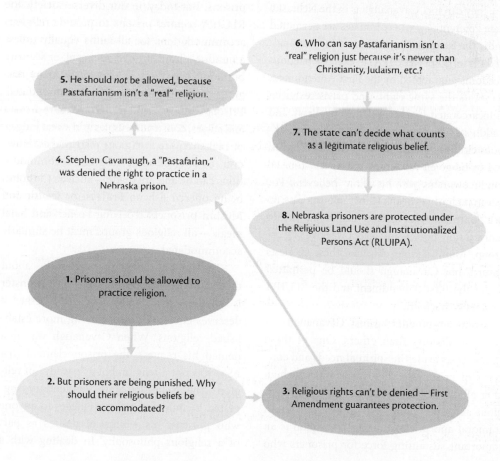

5. He should *not* be allowed, because Pastafarianism isn't a "real" religion.

6. Who can say Pastafarianism isn't a "real" religion just because it's newer than Christianity, Judaism, etc.?

7. The state can't decide what counts as a legitimate religious belief.

4. Stephen Cavanaugh, a "Pastafarian," was denied the right to practice in a Nebraska prison.

8. Nebraska prisoners are protected under the Religious Land Use and Institutionalized Persons Act (RLUIPA).

1. Prisoners should be allowed to practice religion.

2. But prisoners are being punished. Why should their religious beliefs be accommodated?

3. Religious rights can't be denied — First Amendment guarantees protection.

Stirred and Strained: Pastafarians Should Be Allowed to Practice in Prison

Stephen Cavanaugh is a member of the Church of the Flying Spaghetti Monster, a mostly Web-based religious group that has earned notoriety for its members' demands that they be treated under the First Amendment like any other religion. The group strives to show that if Christians can place Nativity scenes on public grounds, or if Muslims can wear head coverings in state driver's license photographs, then by god (or pasta, as the case may be), they can too. Cavanaugh is in the Nebraska State Penitentiary, where inmates are permitted under the Religious Land Use and Institutionalized Persons Act (RLUIPA) to exercise religious freedoms guaranteed by the First Amendment. He wants the same rights and privileges given to incarcerated Christians, Muslims, Jews, and Buddhists — namely, to be able to wear religious clothing, to eat specially prepared meals, and to be given resources, space, and time to conduct worship with his fellow "believers." For Cavanaugh, this means being able to dress up as a pirate, eat pasta on selected holidays, order satirical holy books, and lead a weekly "prayer" group. Many people consider these requests absurd, but Cavanaugh should be permitted under the First Amendment and the RLUIPA to practice his faith.

Some arguments against Cavanaugh are easier to dismiss than others. One of these simply casts aside the spiritual needs and concerns of prisoners: They are being punished, after all, so why should they receive any religious accommodations? This position is both immoral and unconstitutional. Religion is an important sustaining force for prisoners who might otherwise struggle to find meaning and purpose in life, and it is protected by the First Amendment *because* it helps prisoners find purpose and become rehabilitated — the fundamental goal of correctional facilities (even for those serving life without parole). Another argument sees religion as important as long as it conforms to Judeo-Christian belief structures, which has for a long time been the only spiritual path available in American prisons. But today, in our diverse society, the RLUIPA *requires* prisons to provide religious accommodations for all faiths equally unless an undue administrative, financial, or security burden can be proven. Obviously, many religious observances cannot be accommodated. Prisons cannot permit inmates to carry crosses and staves, construct temples and sweat lodges, or make required religious pilgrimages. However, as long as some religious accommodations can be and are made — such as Catholics being offered fish on Fridays, or Jewish and Muslim prisoners receiving kosher and halal meals — all religious groups must be similarly accommodated.

The more challenging question about the Church of the Flying Spaghetti Monster is whether it is a religion at all, whether it deserves equal treatment among more established religions. When Cavanaugh was first denied his request, the prison claimed that FSM was not a religion but a "parody" of religion. The Nebraska State Penitentiary suggested it could not grant privileges to anyone who presents his whimsical desires as part of a religious philosophy. In dealing with a humorous and politically motivated "religion" without a strong tradition and whose founder may write a new gospel at any time, should the prison have to keep up with the possibility of constantly changing prisoner demands? Can anyone just make up a religion and then expect to be accommodated?

For better or worse, the answer is yes—as long as the accommodations represent valid forms of observance, are reasonable, and do not pose a substantial burden to the institution. Many religions have councils that at times alter the tenets of their faith. The state does not have the authority to determine what is or is not a "real" religion or religious practice. It does have an obligation under the RLUIPA to accommodate not just some but all forms of faith for incarcerated persons. As long as individuals sincerely hold certain beliefs, and as long as the accommodations requested meet the standards of reasonability and equity, state prisons, like all other government agencies and institutions, cannot discriminate. Some might argue that Cavanaugh's faith is not sincere—that he does not *really* believe that the Earth was literally created by a ball of pasta with meatball-shaped eyes. But this is not the point. The government cannot apply a religious test to measure the degree of one's sincerity or faith. Like others in the Flying Spaghetti Monster movement—secularists, atheists, and professed believers—Cavanaugh should not be treated as an exploiter of religious freedom. In fact, in a pluralistic society with laws to ensure religious freedom and equality, his challenge helps protect all faiths.

THE ESSAY ANALYZED

The title, in its words *stirred* and *strained,* engages readers' attention by playing with words related to pasta, prison, and the frustration likely to be encountered by an individual who is denied religious freedom. The subtitle states the thesis. This introductory material—a paper begins with its title, not with its first paragraph—makes readers curious and lets them know where the essay will take them.

Paragraph 1 sets the stage. The first sentence clarifies what the Church is and uses a nifty turn of phrase, "by god (or by pasta)," to encourage engagement and make the author's voice, like the FSM, playful but dead serious. The second, third, and fourth sentences provide the basis for Cavanaugh's claims. The last sentence presents a clear thesis.

Paragraph 2 draws on the student's preliminary map. It sets forth objections to making religious accommodations for prisoners and disputes them, providing a citation of the law that guarantees religious freedom in prison, a definition of its limits, and a few examples of these limits. The last sentence sustains the thesis by arguing that accommodations must be equal among religions. However, it also anticipates that readers are likely to agree on this point but still not consider the FSM as a religion.

Paragraph 3 addresses the potential counterargument set up by paragraph 2 and highlights the most common criticism of the FSM: that it isn't *really* a religion at all. The writer raises the problematic question that if prisons must accommodate Cavanaugh, then where would the protest end? What new accommodations might he ask for in the future? Paragraph 3 in effect suggests the *implications* of granting Cavanaugh his request, inviting the reader to imagine a potentially slippery argumentative slope.

Paragraph 4 halts readers' imaginings, reminding them that the writer is still in the realm of talking about *reasonable* and *fair* treatment among inmates, not an "anything goes" proposition. It reminds readers that the state cannot determine a "real" or "unreal" religion, just as it cannot judge the depth, rigor, or literalness of an inmate's belief (Christian, Pastafarian, or otherwise). The fact is that our society has laws to ensure religious freedom and equality for all citizens. In this way, the writer makes a shrewd rhetorical move, presenting Cavanaugh's complaint not just as antagonistic but also as something essential to protecting prisoners of all faiths. Such an appeal to democratic insistence on fairness is normally effective, although in this instance a reader may wonder if the writer has demonstrated convincingly that fairness requires prisons to accommodate Pastafarians. Are you convinced that it would be *unfair* to deny Cavanaugh and other Pastafarian inmates their demands? Why, or why not?

Generating Ideas: Writing as a Way of Thinking

We have already seen, in the clusters that students have generated, concise examples of how the act of writing helps thinkers to think better. "To learn to write," Robert Frost said, "is to learn to have ideas." But how does one "learn to have ideas"? Often we discover ideas while talking with others. A friend says X about some issue, and we — who have never really thought much about the matter — say,

- "Well, yes, I see what you're saying, but come to think of it, I'm not of your opinion. I see it differently — *not as* X *but as* Y."

Or maybe we say,

- "*Yes, X, sure, and also a bit of* Y, *too.*"

Mere chance — a friend's comment — has led us to an idea that we didn't know we had. This sort of discovery may seem like the one we make when reaching under the couch to retrieve the dog's ball and finding a ten-dollar bill instead: "How it got there, I'll never know, but I'm sure glad I found it."

In fact, learning to have ideas is not largely a matter of chance. Or if chance *is* involved, well, as Louis Pasteur put it, "Chance favors the prepared mind." This means that lurking in the mind are bits of information or hints or hunches that in the unexpected circumstance — when talking, when listening to a lecture or a classroom discussion, or especially when reading — are triggered and lead to useful thoughts. This is a sort of seat-of-the-pants knowledge that, when brought to the surface in the right circumstances, produces good results.

Consider the famous example of Archimedes, the ancient Greek mathematician who discovered a method to determine the volume of an irregularly shaped object. The problem: A king gave a goldsmith a specific weight of gold with which to make a crown in the shape of laurel leaves. When the job was finished, the king weighed the crown and found that it matched the weight of the gold he had provided, but he nevertheless suspected that the goldsmith might have substituted some silver for some of the gold. How could the king find out (without melting or otherwise damaging the crown) if the crown was pure gold? For Archimedes, meditating on this problem produced no ideas, but when he entered a bathtub he noticed that the water level rose as he immersed his body. He suddenly realized that he could thus determine the volume of the crown — by measuring the amount of displaced water. Since silver is less dense than gold, it takes a greater volume of silver to equal a given weight of gold. That is, a given weight of gold will displace less water than the same weight of silver. Archimedes then immersed the given weight of gold, measured the water it displaced, and found that indeed the crown displaced more water than the gold did. In his excitement at confirming his idea, Archimedes is said to have leaped out of the tub and run naked through the street, shouting "Eureka!" (Greek for "I have found [it]!").

Why do we tell this story? Partly because we like it, but chiefly because the word *eureka* comes from the same Greek word that has given our language the word **heuristic** (pronounced hyoo-RIS-tik), which refers to a method or process of discovering ideas — in short, of thinking. In this method, one thought triggers another. (*Note:* In computer science, *heuristic* has a more specialized meaning.) Of course, one of the best ways of generating ideas is to hear what's going on around you — and that is talk, both in and out of the classroom, as well as in the world of books. You'll find, as we said early in this discussion, that your response may be, "Well, yes, I see what you're saying, but come to think of it, I don't see it quite that way. I see it differently — not as X but as Y." As we've said, argument is an instrument of learning as well as of persuasion. For instance:

> *Yes,* solar power is a way of conserving energy, *but* do we need to despoil the Mojave Desert and endanger desert life with — literally — fifty thousand solar mirrors so that folks in Los Angeles can heat their pools? Doesn't it make sense to reduce our use of energy, rather than develop sources of renewable energy that violate the environment? Some sites should be off-limits.

Maybe your response to the proposal (now at least fifteen years old) that wind turbines be placed in the waters off Cape Cod, Massachusetts, would go like this:

> *Given our need* for wind power, *how can a reasonable person object* to the proposal that we put 130 wind turbines in the waters off Cape Cod, Massachusetts? *Yes,* the view will be changed, *but* in fact the turbines are quite attractive. No one thinks that windmills in Holland spoil the landscape. So the view will be changed, but not spoiled; *and furthermore,* the verdict is still out on whether or not wind turbines pose a significant risk to birds or aquatic life.

When you're asked to write about something you've read in this book, if your first response is that you have no ideas, remember the responses that we have mentioned — "No, I don't see it that way" or "Yes, but" or "Yes, and moreover" — and see if one of them helps you respond to the work — helps you, in short, to develop ideas.

CONFRONTING UNFAMILIAR ISSUES

Generating ideas can be a challenge when you, as a student, are asked to read about and respond to an unfamiliar issue. Sometimes, students wonder why they have to engage in particular topics and generate ideas about them. "I want to be a speech pathologist," you might say, "so why do I need to read essays and formulate ideas about capital punishment?"

One answer is that a college curriculum should spur students to think about pressing issues facing our society, so learning about capital punishment is important to all students. But this isn't the only answer. One could never study "all" the important social problems we face (anyway, many of them change very rapidly). Instead, colleges seek to equip students with tools, methods, and habits of mind that enable them to confront arguments about *any* potential issue or problem (including those within the field of speech pathology!). The primary goal of a college education (and of this book) is to help students develop an *intellectual apparatus* — a toolkit that can be applied to any subject matter, any issue.

The techniques presented in this book offer a practical framework for approaching issues, thinking about them carefully, asking good questions, identifying problems, and offering reasonable solutions — not necessarily because we want you to form opinions about the issues we have selected (though we hope you do), but because we want you to practice critical thinking, reading, and writing in ways that transfer to other aspects of your education as well as to your personal, professional, and civic life.

The playwright Edward Albee once said, "Good writers define reality; bad ones merely restate it." Rather than thinking that you must "agree or disagree" with the authors whose works you'll read in this book, imagine that you'll be practicing how to discover your unique point of view by finding pathways into debates, negotiating different positions, and generating new ideas. So when you confront an unfamiliar issue in this book (or elsewhere), consider the strategies discussed below as practical methods for generating new ideas. That is what critical thinking (and writing) is all about.

TOPICS

One way of generating ideas, practiced by the ancient Greeks and Romans and still regarded as among the best ways, is to consider what the ancients called **topics** — from the Greek *topos*, meaning "place," as in our word *topography* (a description or representation of a place). For the ancients, certain topics, when formulated as questions, were places where they went to find ideas. Among the classical topics were *definition, comparison, relationship,* and *testimony*. By prompting oneself with questions about these topics, one moves toward answers.

If you're at a loss for ideas when confronted with an issue (and an assignment to write about it), you might discover ideas by turning to the relevant classical topics and jotting down your responses. (In classical terminology, this means engaging in the process of invention, from the Latin *invenire*, "to come upon, to find.") Seeing your ideas on paper — even in the briefest form — will help bring other ideas to mind and will also help you evaluate them. For instance, after jotting down ideas as they come and your responses to them, you might do the following:

1. First, organize them into two lists, pro and con.
2. Next, delete ideas that, upon consideration, seem wrong or irrelevant.
3. Finally, develop the ideas that strike you as pretty good.

You probably won't know where you stand until you've gone through such a process. It would be nice to be able to make a quick decision, immediately justify it with three excellent reasons, and then give three further reasons showing why the opposing view is inadequate. In fact, however, people almost never can reach a reasoned decision without a good deal of preliminary thinking.

Consider the following brief essay about the Food and Drug Administration's approval, in 2015, of a genetically engineered salmon. Although GMO (genetically modified organisms) foods and medicines are common in the United States, this salmon will soon be the first genetically modified animal approved for food consumption in the United States. After you read the essay, refer to Thinking Critically: Generating Topics, which asks you to begin jotting down ideas on a sheet of paper along the lines of the classical topics. As an example of how to respond to the questions, we've included columns related to the Kim Davis and Stephen Cavanaugh cases. As you attempt to formulate ideas related to the essay about genetically engineered salmon, answer the questions related to the classical topics. There's no need to limit yourself to one answer per item as we did.

NINA FEDOROFF

Nina Fedoroff (b. 1942) is the Evan Pugh professor emerita at Penn State University. She served as science and technology adviser to the U.S. secretary of state from 2007 to 2010. The following essay originally appeared in the New York Times *in December 2015.*

The Genetically Engineered Salmon Is a Boon for Consumers and Sustainability

This is great news for consumers and the environment. Wild salmon populations have long been in deep trouble because of overfishing, and open-water cage farming of salmon pollutes coastal waters, propagates fish diseases, and sacrifices a lot of wild-caught fish to be consumed as salmon feed.

The fish is virtually identical to wild salmon, but it is a more sustainable food source, growing faster to maturity.

But just imagine, you'll soon be able to eat salmon guilt-free. AquaBounty has spent more than 20 years developing and testing this faster-growing salmon that will require less feed to bring it to a marketable size. It can be farmed economically in closed, on-land facilities that recirculate water and don't dump waste into the sea. Since the fish live in clean, managed water, they don't get diseases that are spread among caged fish in the sea. And the growing facilities could be closer to markets, cutting shipping costs.

All of these elements take pressure off wild salmon and make salmon farming more sustainable.

Much of the concern about AquaBounty's 5 salmon centers around several bits of added DNA, taken from another fish, that let the salmon grow continuously, not just seasonally. That does not make them "unnatural" or dangerous, it just makes them grow to market size on less feed.

We've been tinkering with our plants and animals to serve our food needs for somewhere between 10 and 20 thousand years. We created corn, for example. The seed-bearing structure of the original "wild" version, called teosinte, looked very different from the modern-day ear, packed with hundreds of soft, starch-and-protein-filled kernels. And it's people who developed the tomatoes we eat today. Mother Nature's are tiny: A pioneering breeder described them in an 1893 grower's guide as "small, hollow, tough, watery" fruits.

But there's money (and fame) in being anti-G.M.O. The organic food marketers want to sell their food, which is over-priced because organic farming is inefficient — not because the food's better — so they tell scare stories about the dangers of G.M.O.s.

There is also no reason to fear that these genetically engineered salmon will escape and destroy wild populations. Only sterile females will be grown for food. And since the fish will be grown in contained facilities on land, escapees can't survive either.

AquaBounty's salmon is salmon, plain and simple. I, for one, can't wait to taste it.

THINKING CRITICALLY *Generating Topics*

Provide the relevant information for the topic of genetically engineered salmon.

TOPICS	QUESTIONS	DAVIS	CAVANAUGH	GENETICALLY ENGINEERED SALMON
Definition *Categories Descriptions Definitions Explanations*	*What is it?*	"The Kim Davis case involves one woman's dissent against the Supreme Court decision of 2015 legalizing gay marriage. The law says *X*, but Davis draws upon *Y*."	"The RLUIPA requires state prisons to provide religious accommodations under the First Amendment, which says *X*. Cavanaugh asserted his 'right' to . . ."	

Comparison	What is it like or unlike?	"Other cases in which individuals defied the law because of conscience include X, Y, and Z. The Davis case is similar/different because . . ."	"This case is like other challenges made by the FSM Church; however, since he is a prisoner asking for XYZ, Cavanaugh's case is different because . . ."	
Similarities *Differences* *Analogies* *Applications*				
Relationship	What caused it, and what will it cause?	"The issue of gay marriage had been a state's rights issue but was unevenly applied across states. When the Court legalized it at the federal level, it required all public officials including judges and clerks to abide by the law, yet the result is . . ."	"Prisoners deserve to exercise their religious freedom, but for most of U.S. history Christianity was the only available option, which violated the establishment clause . . ."	
Antecedents *Precedents* *Consequences* *Outcomes*				
Testimony	What is known or said about it, especially by experts?	"Supreme Court Justice Kennedy asserted in his opinion that the Constitution guarantees X, though Justice Scalia in his dissent said . . ."	"In American prisons, there are *over X* number of recognized religious groups, including Satanists and Wiccans. If they can have their rights, then . . ."	
Statistics *Maxims* *Laws* *Quotations*				

LaunchPad To complete this activity online, go to **macmillanhighered.com/barnetbedauohara**

Here's an inner dialogue that you might engage in as you think critically about the question of genetically engineered salmon:

> The purpose of genetically engineered salmon is to protect against the ecological effects of overfishing — that seems to be a good thing.
>
> Another purpose is to protect consumers by ensuring that the price of salmon, one of the most commonly eaten fish, will not become so high that few people could afford it.
>
> But other issues are apparent. Should we turn to altering the genes of animals to protect the environment or consumer prices? Are there other solutions, like eating less salmon or regulating overfishing?
>
> Who gains and who loses, and what do they stand to gain or lose, by this FDA approval of genetically modified salmon?
>
> The author says no one should worry about "several bits of DNA added"; but come to think of it, is this modification unethical or dangerous in any way? Is it okay to create a new type of animal by altering genes?
>
> The author attacks anti-GMO activists, saying they're just after money (and fame — why fame?). Isn't money (and fame?) also the goal of AquaBounty and other GMO food producers?

Notice how part of the job is *analytic*, recognizing the elements or complexities of the whole, and part is *evaluative*, judging the adequacy of all the ideas, one by one. Both tasks require critical thinking in the form of analyzing and evaluating, and those processes themselves require a disciplined *imagination*.

So far we have jotted down a few thoughts and then immediately given some second thoughts contrary to the first. Be aware that your own counterthoughts might not come to mind right away. For instance, they might not occur until you reread your notes or try to explain the issue to a friend, or until you begin drafting an essay aimed at supporting or undermining the new FDA rules. Most likely, in fact, some good ideas won't occur until a second or third or fourth draft.

Here are some further thoughts on the genetically modified salmon. We list them more or less as they occurred to us and as we typed them into a computer — not sorted neatly into two groups, pro and con, or evaluated as you should do in further critical thinking of your own. Of course, a later step would be to organize the material into a useful pattern. As you read, try writing your responses in the margin.

> According to one article, the FDA is not requiring companies to label the salmon as genetically engineered. Should this information at least be made available to consumers? Maybe their religious, ethical, or personal preferences would be not to eat modified fish species. If the fish were properly labeled and people knew of any risks associated with eating it, they could avoid it if they wished.
>
> Are there any animal rights issues at stake here? Is it okay to breed "only sterile females"? Critics say that scientists shouldn't create new kinds of animals. Is this even what AquaBounty is doing?

The author says we shouldn't worry about these fish breeding with other salmon, but is she understating the risks? I hadn't thought of the possibility, but clearly someone has. Is there an actual risk of threatening the natural species? If there was really zero risk, why are they bothering to breed only *sterile* females?

Maybe the FDA shouldn't have approved genetically modified salmon for food. If we start with the salmon, where will it end? What other foods are being reviewed for similar kinds of farming? Is this really the same as the development of corn and other vegetables, as the author suggests — or is animal life something different?

Doubtless there is much that we haven't asked or thought about, but we hope you'll agree that the issue deserves careful thought, given that the availability of genetically modified food animals has serious implications for the environment and the future of food production.

If you worked for the FDA and were part of this decision, you would *have* to think about these questions and issues. As a thought experiment, imagine you had to contribute to the decision about approving these fish. Try to put your tentative views into writing.

Note that you would want to get answers to questions such as the following:

- What sort of evidence exists about the safety of genetically engineered salmon? Who has studied it?

- What do biologists and bioethicists say about the genetically engineered salmon?

- What kind of people and organizations oppose the approval of this genetically engineered salmon, and what are their primary critiques?

Some of these questions require you to do **research** on the topic. Some raise issues of fact, and relevant evidence probably is available. In order to reach a conclusion in which you have confidence, you'll have to do some research to find out what the facts — the objective data — are. Merely explaining your position without giving the evidence will not be convincing.

Even without doing any research, however, you might want to look over the pros and cons, perhaps adding some new thoughts or modifying or even rejecting (for reasons that you can specify) some of those already given. If you do

> ## A CHECKLIST FOR CRITICAL THINKING
>
> Attitudes:
>
> - ☐ Does my thinking show imaginative open-mindedness and intellectual curiosity?
>
> - ☐ Am I willing to examine my assumptions?
>
> - ☐ Am I willing to entertain new ideas — both those that I encounter while reading and those that come to mind while writing?
>
> - ☐ Am I willing to exert myself — for instance, to do research — to acquire information and to evaluate evidence?
>
> Skills:
>
> - ☐ Can I summarize an argument accurately?
>
> - ☐ Can I evaluate assumptions, evidence, and inferences?
>
> - ☐ Can I present my ideas effectively — for instance, by organizing and by writing in a manner appropriate to my imagined audience?

think further about this issue (and we hope that you will), notice an interesting point about *your own* thinking: It probably isn't *linear* (moving in a straight line from *A* to *B* to *C*) but *recursive*, moving from *A* to *C* and back to *B* or starting over at *C* and then back to *A* and *B*. By zigging and zagging almost despite yourself, you'll reach a conclusion that may finally seem correct. In retrospect, it might seem obvious; *now* you can chart a nice line from *A* to *B* to *C* — but that probably wasn't at all evident at the start.

A Short Essay Calling for Critical Thinking

When reading an essay, we expect the writer to have thought carefully about the topic. We don't want to read every false start, every fuzzy thought, every ill-organized paragraph that the writer knocked off. Yes, writers make false starts, put down fuzzy thoughts, write ill-organized paragraphs; but then they revise and revise yet again, ultimately producing a readable essay that seems effortlessly written. Still — and this is our main point — writers of argumentative essays need to show readers that they have made some effort; they need to show *how* they got to their final (for the moment) views. It isn't enough for the writer to say, "I believe *X*"; rather, he or she must in effect say, "I believe *X* — and I hope you'll believe it also — because *Y* and *Z*, though attractive, just don't stand up to inquiry as well as *X* does. *Y* is superficially plausible, but . . . , and *Z*, which is an attractive alternative to *Y*, nevertheless fails because. . . ."

Notice in the following short essay — on employers using biometric devices to monitor employees' performance — that the author, Lynn Stuart Parramore, positions herself against these workplace technologies in a compelling way. As you read, think critically about how she presents her position, how she encourages readers to sympathize with her views. Ask questions about what she includes and excludes, whether she presents other perspectives amply or fairly, and what additional positions might be valid on these recent developments in the rapidly growing field of biometrics in business.

LYNN STUART PARRAMORE

Lynn Stuart Parramore is a contributing editor of AlterNet, *a frequent contributor to* Al-Jazeera America, Reuters, *and the* Huffington Post, *and a member of the editorial board of* Lapham's Quarterly. *Reprinted here is an essay published by* Al-Jazeera America *on September 18, 2015.*

Fitbits for Bosses

Imagine you've just arrived at your job with the Anywhere Bank call center. You switch on your computer and adjust the height of your chair. Then, you slide on the headset, positioning the mic in front of your lips. All that's left to do is to activate your behavior-monitoring device — the gadget hanging from your neck that tracks your tone of voice, your heart rate, and your physical movements throughout the day, sending real-time reports to your supervisor.

A scene from a dystopian movie? Nope. It's already happening in America. Welcome to the brave new world of workplace biosurveillance.

It's obvious that wearable tracking technology has gone mainstream: Just look at the explosion of smart watches and activity monitors that allow people to count steps and check their calorie intake. But this technology has simultaneously been creeping into workplaces: The military uses sensors that scan for injuries, monitor heart rate, and check hydration. More and more, professional athletes are strapping on devices that track every conceivable dimension of performance. Smart ice skates that measure a skater's jump. Clothes that measure an athlete's breathing and collect muscle data. At this year's tryouts in Indianapolis, some NFL hopefuls wore the "Adidas miCoach," a device that sends data on speed and acceleration straight to trainers' iPads. Over the objection of many athletes, coaches and team owners are keen to track off-the-field activity, too, such as sleep patterns and diet. With million-dollar players at stake, big money seems poised to trump privacy.

Now employers from industries that don't even require much physical labor are getting in on the game.

Finance is adopting sophisticated analytics to ensure business performance from high-dollar employees. Cambridge neuroscientist and former Goldman Sachs trader John Coates works with companies to figure out how monitoring biological signals can lead to trading success; his research focuses on measuring hormones that increase confidence and other desirable states as well as those that produce negative, stressful states. In a report for Bloomberg, Coates explained that he is working with "three or four hedge funds" to apply an "early-warning system" that would alert supervisors when traders are getting into the hormonal danger zone. He calls this process "human optimization."

People who do the most basic, underpaid work in our society are increasingly subject to physical monitoring, too — and it extends far beyond the ubiquitous urine test. Bank of America has started using smart badges that monitor the voice and behavior patterns of call-center workers, partnering with the creepily named Humanyze, a company specializing in "people analytics." Humanyze is the brainchild of the MIT Media Lab, the fancy research institute at the Massachusetts Institute of Technology dedicated to the "betterment of humanity," which, incidentally, receives a quarter of its funding from taxpayers. Humanyze concocted a computer dashboard complete with graphs and pie charts that can display the location of employees (Were you hanging out in the lounge today?) and their "social context" (Do you spend a lot of time alone?).

Humanyze founder Ben Waber points out that companies already spend enormous resources collecting analytics on their customers. Why not their employees?

A growing number of workers are being monitored by GPS, often installed on their smartphones. In the U.S. the Supreme Court ruled that law enforcement officials need a warrant to use GPS devices to track a suspect. But employers don't worry over such formalities in keeping tabs on employees, especially those who are mobile, such as truck drivers. A *Washington Post* report on GPS surveillance noted a 2012 study by the research firm Aberdeen Group, which showed that 62 percent of "field employees" — those who regularly perform duties away from the office — are tracked this way. In May, a California woman filed a lawsuit against her former employer, Intermex Wire Transfer, for forcing her to install a tracking app on her phone, which she was required to keep on 24/7. She described feeling like a prisoner wearing an ankle bracelet. After removing the app, the woman was fired.

Sensitive to Big Brother accusations, the biosurveillance industry is trying to keep testing and tool evaluations under the radar. Proponents of the technology point to its potential to improve health conditions in the workplace and enhance public safety. Wouldn't it be better, they argue, if nuclear power plant operators, airline pilots, and oil rig operatives had their physical state closely monitored on the job?

Young Americans nurtured in a digital world where their behavior is relentlessly collected and monitored by advertisers may shrug at an employer's demands for a biosurveillance badge. In a world of insecure employment, what choice do they have, anyway? Despite the revelations of alarming National Security Agency spying and increased government and corporate surveillance since 9/11, the young haven't had much experience yet with what's at stake for them personally. What could possibly go wrong?

A lot: Surveillance has a way of dehumanizing workers. It prevents us from experimenting and exercising our creativity on the job because it tends to uphold the status quo and hold back change. Surveillance makes everyone seem suspicious, creating perceptions and expectations of dishonesty. It makes us feel manipulated. Some researchers have found that increased monitoring actually decreases productivity.

Philosopher and social theorist Michel Foucault observed that the relationship between the watcher and the watched is mostly about power. The power of the observer is enhanced, while the person observed feels more powerless. When an employer or manager interprets our personal data, she gets to make categorical judgments about us and determine how to predict our behavior.

What if she uses the information to discriminate? Coerce? Selectively apply the rules?

The data she uses to make her judgments may not even be telling the truth: Researchers have warned that big data can produce big errors. People looking at numbers tend to use them to confirm their own biases, cherry-picking the information that supports their beliefs and ditching the rest. And since algorithms are constructed by human beings, they are not immune to human biases, either. A consumer might be labeled "unlikely to pay a credit card bill" because of an ethnic name, thus promulgating a harmful stereotype.

As Americans, we like to tell ourselves that we value freedom and undue interference from authority. But when we are subjected to surveillance, we feel disempowered and disrespected. We may be more inclined to accept the government getting involved because of fears about terrorism — but when it comes to surveillance on the job, our tendency to object may be chilled by weakened worker protections and increased employment insecurity.

Instead of producing an efficient and productive workplace, biosurveillance may instead deliver troops of distracted, apathetic employees who feel loss of control and decreased job satisfaction. Instead of feeling like part of a team, surveilled workers may develop an us-versus-them mentality and look for opportunities to thwart the monitoring schemes of Big Boss.

Perhaps what we really need is biosurveillance from the bottom up — members of Congress and CEOs could don devices that could, say, detect when they are lying or how their hormones are behaving. Colorful PowerPoints could display the results of data collection on public billboards for the masses to pore over. In the name of safety and efficiency, maybe we ought to ensure that those whose behavior can do society the most harm do not escape the panopticon.

OVERALL VIEW OF THE ESSAY

Before we comment in detail on Parramore's essay, we need to say that in terms of the length of some of its paragraphs, it isn't necessarily a model for you to imitate. Material in print or online news sources is typically presented in very short paragraphs (notice Parramore's one-sentence-long paragraph 4). This is partly because people read it while eating breakfast or commuting to work, and in the case of print newspapers partly because the columns are narrow (a paragraph of only two or three sentences may still be an inch or two deep).

The title, "Fitbits for Bosses," is provocative, captures readers' attention, and leaves them with a sense of where Parramore's argument is heading.

Paragraph 1 compels readers by asking them to imagine an ordinary day at work, presenting the routine activities of getting work under way — turning on the computer, adjusting the chair — before throwing in the "behavior-monitoring device" almost as an afterthought, as if to shock us with the possibility that such devices could become routine.

Paragraph 2 presses the idea of invasion of privacy, almost aggressively, by using words like *dystopian* and a reference to a science fiction novel ("brave new world") whose title has become a shorthand for technological intrusions into individuals' lives.

Paragraph 3 presents as "obvious" the fact that self-monitoring technology has gone mainstream. (One of the authors of this book just purchased a new mobile device that came pre-installed with an application that records the number of steps and miles the user walks in a day. Going deeper into the menu, it includes functions for recording everything from nutrient intake to sexual activity.) The writer is clearly drawing on readers' familiarity with these technologies. Then she presents the portent of these devices "creeping" into the workplace, first by showing how such technologies have already been used in military applications and in businesses like professional sports. "So what?" we might think, but Parramore is about tell us.

Paragraph 4 is a single-sentence paragraph, turning the essay's focus from two specialized fields to the everyday jobs that millions of people hold. Notice how the language ("getting in on the game") reveals Parramore's position that this trend signals something new and troubling.

Paragraph 5 turns to the finance industry to show how some industries are beginning to monitor not just employee health but hormonal flows that have been correlated to emotional and psychological states. The dystopian theme is extended here as these technologies are presented as reaching into new realms where independent action and decision-making occur. Phrases like "human optimization" and references to an "early warning system" that would "alert supervisors" hint at potential limitations on human independence and deeper control of employees by managers.

Paragraph 6 focuses on Bank of America's partnership with Humanyze and shows more ways in which biosurveillance technologies could be used to monitor employees. Parramore is enhancing her argument through careful language use. In fact, her position is arguably coming most strongly through tone. What language cues indicate her position on these technologies? What specific words and phrases does she use ironically or sardonically?

Paragraph 7 quotes Humanyze's founder, Ben Waber, who rationally states that companies spend enormous amounts of money tracking consumers, so why not track employees too?

But Parramore presents this statement as anything but appealing; instead, it comes across as a kind of dangerous rationality.

Paragraph 8 starts out by noting that the government doesn't permit law enforcement to do what employers regularly do in various industries. It cites a study showing how widespread the use of these devices is, and a case in which a woman lost her job by refusing to be monitored.

Paragraph 9 provides the defense offered by the industries that create these technologies, pointing out that some highly sensitive jobs such as power plant operator and airline pilot require the closest scrutiny of individuals' physical conditions.

Paragraph 10 mentions "Young Americans," raised in a digital world, who may just "shrug" at the latest developments in surveillance technology without realizing the implications to them personally. "What could go wrong?" Parramore asks.

Paragraph 11 answers that question, first with the word *dehumanizing*, then by claiming that surveillance dampens creativity and change, encourages suspicion, presumes dishonesty, and hurts productivity.

Paragraph 12 brings into the mix a philosopher, Michel Foucault — one of the twentieth century's most recognized theorists of power. Foucault leads Parramore to wonder about what kinds of power may be exercised by using the information gained from surveillance technology.

Paragraph 13 considers hypothetical scenarios in which a manager might be able to discriminate or coerce an employee by using collected data. Parramore seems to be asking how employees are protected from such strict oversight.

Paragraph 14 reminds readers that measurements are just measurements, prone to error and to biases that could lead to unfair or discriminatory uses of data.

Paragraph 15 presents a summary of the potentially harmful outcomes of widespread implementation of biometric surveillance of employees, pointing especially to decreased job satisfaction and an "us-versus-them" mentality among employees and employers.

Paragraph 16 drives home the author's point by offering a reversal of the expected order of surveillance arrangements. What if, Parramore suggests, the public demanded surveillance of those in power, especially since those in important managerial positions are presumably the ones whose behaviors and actions might impact the most people? The essay finishes with a suggestion that it is those in power who most need to be watched "in the name of safety and efficiency" — ostensibly the terms used to justify the practice as applied to workers.

Topics for Critical Thinking and Writing

1. Do you think biometric measurement by employers is ever justified, or do the privacy and security of one's own body always trump the concerns of employers? Why, or why not?

2. If your teachers or parents could monitor the time you spent, and how you felt, while doing homework and studying, what benefits and drawbacks might result? What types of personal

monitoring are already in place (or possible) in schools and homes, and are these different from biometric surveillance?

3. Do you think Lynn Parramore fairly portrays the founder of Humanyze and others who see potential in the possibilities for biometric monitoring? Why, or why not? In what other ways might biometric measurements help employees and employers?

4. List some examples of Parramore's use of language, word choice, and phrasing that would influence readers to be suspicious of biometric monitoring. How does this language make the essay more or less effective or convincing?

5. In what way does Parramore's recommendation in the final paragraph support or contradict her argument about individuals' basic rights to privacy?

Examining Assumptions

In Chapter 3, we will discuss **assumptions** in some detail, but here we introduce the topic by emphasizing the importance of *identifying* and *examining* assumptions — those you'll encounter in the writings of others and those you'll rely on in your own essays.

With this in mind, let's again consider some of the assumptions suggested in this chapter's earlier readings. The student who wrote about Stephen Cavanaugh's case pointed out that Nebraska prison officials simply did not see the Church of the Flying Spaghetti Monster as a real religion. Their assumption was that some religions can be more or less "real" than others or can make more sense than others. Assumptions may be *explicit* or *implicit*, stated or unstated. In this case, the prison officials were forthright about their assumptions in their stated claim about the Church, perhaps believing their point was obvious to anyone who thought seriously about the idea of a Flying Spaghetti Monster. It didn't occur to them to consider that even major and mainstream religions honor stories, claims, and rituals that seem absurd to others.

An implicit assumption is one that is not stated but, rather, is taken for granted. It works like an underlying belief that structures an argument. In Lynn Stuart Parramore's essay on workplace biometric devices, the unstated assumption is that these sorts of technology in the workplace represent a kind of evil "big brother" intent on subduing and exploiting employees with newer and newer forms of invasion of privacy. Parramore's assumption, while not stated directly, is evident in her choice of language, as we've pointed out above. Another way to discern her assumption is by looking at the scenarios and selections of examples she chooses. For example, in imagining a company that would seek to know how much time an employee spends in the lounge area or alone, Parramore sees only obsessive monitoring of employees for the purposes of regulating their time. But what if these technologies could enable a company to discover that productivity or worker satisfaction increases in proportion to the amount of time employees spend collaborating in the lounge? Maybe workplace conditions would improve instead of deteriorating (a bigger lounge, more comfortable chairs), and maybe more efforts would be made for team-building and improving interpersonal employee relations.

Consider now two of the assumptions involved in the Kim Davis case. Thanks to the clustering exercise (p. 6), these and other assumptions are already on display. Perhaps the most important and fundamental assumption Davis and her supporters made is this:

> Where private religious beliefs conflict with duly enacted laws, the former should prevail.

This assumption is widely held in our society; it is by no means unique to Davis and her supporters. Opponents, however, probably assumed a very different but equally fundamental proposition:

> Private religious practices and beliefs must yield to the demands of laws guaranteeing citizens equal rights.

Obviously, these two assumptions are opposed to each other, and neither side can prevail so long as the key assumption of the other side is ignored.

Assumptions can be powerful sources of ideas and opinions, and understanding our own and others' assumptions is a major part of critical thinking. Assumptions about race, class, disability, sex, and gender are among the most powerful sources of social inequality. The following essay arguing that women should be permitted to serve in combat roles in the military was published in 2012, well before the Department of Defense lifted the ban on women in combat roles in the armed forces in 2013. More recently, Defense Secretary Ashton Carter further lifted exclusions pertaining to women by granting them access to serve in all capacities in combat, including in elite special forces units. Following that development, General Lori J. Robinson made history as the first female combatant commander when she was appointed leader of the North American Aerospace Defense Command and U.S. Northern Command in Colorado in May 2016. Still, we reprint McGregor's essay because it compels readers to consider some of their assumptions about women (and men). Topics for discussion appear after the essay.

JENA McGREGOR

Jena McGregor, a graduate of the University of Georgia, is a freelance writer and a daily columnist for the Washington Post. *This article was published on May 25, 2012.*

Military Women in Combat: Why Making It Official Matters

It's been a big couple of weeks for women in the military.

Last week, female soldiers began formally moving into jobs in previously all-male battalions, a program that will later go Army-wide. The move is a result of rule changes following a February report that opened some 14,000 new positions to women in critical jobs much closer to the front lines. However, some 250,000 combat jobs still remain officially closed to them.

The same week, Rep. Loretta Sanchez (D, Calif.) and Sen. Kirsten Gillibrand (D, N.Y.) introduced legislation in both houses of Congress that would encourage the "repeal of the Ground Combat Exclusion policy" for women in the armed forces. Then this Wednesday, two female U.S. Army reservists filed a lawsuit that seeks to overturn the remaining restrictions on women in combat, saying they limit "their current and future earnings, their potential for promotion and advancement, and their future retirement benefits." (A Pentagon spokesperson told Bloomberg News that Defense Secretary Leon Panetta "is strongly committed to examining the expansion of roles for women in the U.S. military, as evidenced by the recent step of opening up thousands of more assignments to women.")

One of the arguments behind both the lawsuit and the new legislation is that the remaining restrictions hurt women's opportunities for advancement. Advocates for women in the military say that even if women like Gen. Ann Dunwoody have reached four-star general status, she and women like her without official frontline combat experience apparently haven't been considered for the military's very highest posts. "If women remain restricted to combat service and combat service support specialties, we will not see a woman as Commandant of the Marine Corps, or CENTCOM commander, or Chairman of the Joint Chiefs of Staff," writes Greg Jacob, policy director for the Service Women's Action Network. "Thus women in the military are being held back simply because they are women. Such an idea is not only completely at odds with military ethics, but is distinctly un-American."

Women have been temporarily "attached" to battalions for the last decade; still, allowing women to formally serve in combat operations could help to break down the so-called brass ceiling.

Another way to break down the ceiling would be to consider talented women for top military leadership positions, whether or not they've officially held certain combat posts. Presidents have chosen less-senior officers for Joint Chiefs roles, which are technically staff jobs, wrote Laura Conley and Lawrence Korb, a former assistant defense secretary in the Reagan administration and a senior fellow at the Center for American Progress, in the *Armed Forces Journal* last year. They argue that putting a woman on the Joint Chiefs would help the military grapple with rising sexual harassment issues, bring nontraditional expertise (which women have developed because of some of their role exclusions) at a time when that's increasingly critical, and send the signal that the military is not only open to women, but puts no barriers in their way.

Yes, putting women in combat roles beyond those that have been recently formalized would require many adjustments, both logistical and psychological, for the military and for its male troops. There are plenty of women who may not be interested in these jobs, or who do not meet the physical demands required of them. And gradual change may be prudent. The recent openings are a start; Army Chief of Staff Ray Odierno's acknowledgment last week that if women are allowed into infantry, they will at some point probably go through Ranger School, is encouraging.

But at a time when experience like the infantry is reportedly crucial for getting top posts, it's easy to see how official and sizable policy changes are needed in order to create a system that lets talented women advance to the military's highest echelons. In any field where there are real or perceived limitations for women's advancement, it's that much harder to attract the best and brightest. Indeed, the Military Leadership Diversity Commission recommended last March that the services end combat exclusion policies for women, along with other "barriers and inconsistencies, to create a level playing field for all qualified service members." As the commission chairman, Retired Air Force Gen. Lester L. Lyles, told the American Forces Press Service at the time, "we know that [the exclusion] hinders women from promotion."

For the military to achieve the diverse workforce it seeks, interested and capable women should either not face exclusions, or the culture of the armed forces needs to change so that women without that particular experience can still reach the very top. Both changes may be difficult, but the latter is extraordinarily so. Ending the restrictions is the shortest route to giving the military the best pool of talent possible and the most diverse viewpoints for leading it.

Topics for Critical Thinking and Writing

1. How would you characterize Jena McGregor's tone (her manner)? Is it thoughtful? Pushy? Identify passages that support your view.

2. Explain the term *brass ceiling* (para. 5).

3. One argument *against* sending women onto an actual battlefield, as infantry or as members of a tank crew, is that if they're captured they might be gang-raped. In your view, how significant is this argument? Explain your response.

4. Here is a second argument against sending women into direct combat: Speaking generally, women do not have the upper-body strength that men have, and a female soldier (again, speaking generally, not about a particular individual) would thus be less able to pull a wounded companion out of a burning tank or off a battlefield. To put the matter differently: Male soldiers might feel that they couldn't count on their female comrades in a time of need. What is your reply?

5. In her final paragraph, McGregor suggests that if the armed forces were to change their policy and not require battlefield experience for the very highest jobs, the military would

achieve diversity at the top and women would have an opportunity for top pay. What are your thoughts? For instance, is the idea that the top officers should have experienced hand-to-hand combat out of date, romantic, hopelessly macho, or irrelevant to modern warfare? Explain.

6. What do you make of the following question? Since women are now permitted to serve in all military combat positions, should all women, like all men, have to register for Selective Service and be subject to the military draft, if one were needed? Construct an argument to defend your position on this question.

Four Exercises in Critical Thinking

As you draft essays for one or more of the assignments, consider typing your notes in a Google document or in Microsoft OneNote, or using another collaborative application or service (perhaps offered free by your school), so that you can easily share your thoughts and writing on the topic. As always, submit and complete assignments in the way that your instructor directs. However, remember that services such as Google and OneNote can be good places to maintain copies of your notes and essays for later consultation.

1. Think further about the issues of privacy and surveillance raised by Lynn Parramore's essay. Consider several different kinds of work, types of employers, and the various types of employee monitoring that do or may occur. Jot down pros and cons, and then write a balanced dialogue between two imagined speakers who hold opposing views on the issue. You'll doubtless have to revise your dialogue several times, and in revising your drafts you'll likely come up with further ideas. Present *both* sides as strongly as possible. (You may want to give the two speakers distinct characters; for instance, one may be an employer seeking to introduce a new technology, and the other may be an employee intent on protecting his privacy and freedom. Alternatively, one could be an employee looking forward to a new "healthy workplace" initiative using biometrics, and the other could be a colleague suspicious of the new program.)

2. Choose one of the following topics, and write down all the pro and con arguments you can think of in, say, ten minutes. Then, at least an hour or two later, return to your notes and see whether you can add to them. Finally, as in Exercise 1, write a balanced dialogue, presenting each idea as strongly as possible. (If none of these topics interests you, ask your instructor about the possibility of choosing a topic of your own.) Suggested topics:

    a. Colleges with large athletic programs should pay student athletes a salary or stipend.
    b. Bicyclists and motorcyclists should be required by law to wear helmets.
    c. High school teachers should have the right to carry concealed firearms in schools.
    d. Smoking should be prohibited on all college campuses, including in all buildings *and* outdoors.
    e. College students should have the right to request alternative assignments from their professors if class material is offensive or traumatic.

f. Students should have the right to drop out of school at any age.

g. Sororities and fraternities should be coeducational (allowing both males and females).

h. The government should tax sugary foods and drinks in order to reduce obesity.

3. In April 2012, Williams College in Williamstown, Massachusetts, hosted a lecture and film screening of work by Jiz Lee, described in campus advertisements as a "genderqueer porn star." After inviting the adult entertainer to campus, the college came under fire by some students and members of the public (especially after the story was reported by national media). Opponents questioned the appropriateness and academic value of the event, which was brought to campus by the Mike Dively Committee, an endowment established to help "develop understanding of human sexuality and sexual orientation and their impact on culture." Proponents argued that (1) pornography is a subject that deserves critical analysis and commentary; (2) the Dively series is intended to create conversations about sexuality and sexual orientation in society and culture; and (3) treating any potential subject in an academic setting under the circumstances of the program is appropriate. What are your views? Should adult film stars ever be invited to college campuses? Should pornography constitute a subject of analysis on campus? Why, or why not?

Imagine you're a student member of the campus programming board, and the Gender and Sexuality Program comes to your committee seeking funds to invite a female former adult film star to campus to lecture on "The Reality of Pornography." Faculty and student sponsors have assured your committee that the visit by the actress in question is part of an effort to educate students and the public about the adult film industry and its impact on popular culture. Images and short film clips may be shown. Pose as many questions as you can about the potential benefits and risks of approving this invitation. How would you vote, and why? (If you can find a peer who has an opposing view, construct a debate on the issue.)

4. In 1985, the U.S. Congress passed the National Minimum Drinking Age Act, mandating that all states implement and enforce raising the minimum drinking age from eighteen to twenty-one years. Through this legislation, the United States became one of a handful of developed countries to have such a high drinking age. In 2009, John McCardell, president of Middlebury College in Vermont, wrote a declaration signed by 135 college presidents supporting returning the drinking age to eighteen. McCardell's organization, Choose Responsibly, says that people age eighteen to twenty should be treated as the adults they are — for example, in terms of voting, serving on juries and in the military, or buying legal weapons. The organization encourages educational programs and awareness efforts that would introduce alcohol-related issues to young college students and demystify and discourage problem drinking. Such a move is opposed by Mothers Against Drunk Drivers (MADD), whose members argue that raising the drinking age to twenty-one has curbed traffic accidents and fatalities caused by drunk driving. Opponents to lowering the drinking age also claim that it would introduce alcohol to even younger people, as many eighteen-year-olds would inevitably interact in social situations with underage peers.

2

Critical Reading: Getting Started

Some books are to be tasted, others to be swallowed, and some few to be chewed and digested.
— FRANCIS BACON

Active Reading

In the passage that we quote above, Bacon makes two good points. One is that books are of varying worth; the second is that a taste of some books may be enough.

But even a book (or an essay) that you will chew and digest is one that you first may want to taste. How can you get a taste — that is, how can you get some sense of a piece of writing — *before* you sit down to read it carefully?

PREVIEWING

Even before reading a work, you may have some ideas about it, perhaps because you already know something about the **author**. You know, for example, that a work by Martin Luther King Jr. will probably deal with civil rights. You know, too, that it will be serious and eloquent. In contrast, if you pick up an essay by Stephen King, you'll probably expect it to be about fear, the craft of writing, or his experiences as a horror novelist. It may be about something else, but it's probable the essay will follow your expectations. For one thing, you know that King writes for a broad audience, so his essay won't be terribly difficult to understand.

In short, a reader who has knowledge of the author probably has some idea of what the subject will be and what the writing will be like, so the reader approaches it in a certain light. But even if you don't know the author, you can often discern important information about him or her by looking at biographical information provided in the text or by doing a quick Internet search. You can use this information to predict not only the essay's subject and style but also the author's approach to the topic, which helps when trying to diagnose assumptions and biases, among other things.

The **place of publication** may also reveal something about the essay in terms of its subject, style, and approach. For instance, the *National Review* is a conservative journal. If you notice that an essay on affirmative action was published in the *National Review,* you're probably safe in tentatively assuming that the essay will not endorse affirmative action. In contrast, *Ms.* magazine is a liberal publication, and an essay on affirmative action published there will probably be an endorsement. You often can learn a good deal about a journal or magazine simply by flipping through it and noticing the kinds of articles and advertisements in it.

The **title** of an essay, too, may give an idea of what to expect. Of course, a title may announce only the subject and not the author's thesis or point of view ("On Gun Control"; "Should Drugs Be Legal?"), but fairly often it will indicate the thesis too (as in "Give Children the Vote" or "We Need Campaign Finance Reform Now"). By knowing more or less what to expect, you can probably take in some of the major points even on a quick reading.

When engaging with an essay, you can also consider the role of **context** — the situational conditions in which it was written. Context can refer to the time period, geographical location, cultural climate, political environment, or any other setting for a piece of writing. Recognizing the context of any piece of writing can reveal a lot about how an author treats a subject. For example, an essay written before September 11, 2001, about how to contain global terrorism might have a less urgent approach and advocate more lenient measures than one written today. An article about transgender identity or police brutality might convey different assumptions about those topics depending on whether it was written before or after Bruce Jenner publicly became Caitlyn Jenner, for instance, or before or after the events of Ferguson, Missouri, brought the issue of race and police violence into the public's consciousness in new ways.

Anything you read exists in at least two broad contexts: the context of its *production* (where and when it was written or published) and the context of its *consumption* (where and when it is encountered and read). One thing all good critical thinkers do when considering the validity of claims and arguments is to take *both* types of context into account. This means asking questions not only about the approach, assumptions, and beliefs that were in place when an essay was written, but also about how current events and understandings generate new issues and challenges within the subject of the essay. The state of affairs in the time and place in which that argument is made *and received* shapes the questions you might ask, the evidence you might consider, and the responses you might produce.

Notice that you can apply these previewing techniques before reading a single word of the essay. And once you have a good sense of the what, who, where, and when of an essay, you should keep them in mind while reading.

Your first reading might involve another previewing technique, **skimming**. Sometimes, you can find the **thesis** (the main point or major claim) of an essay by looking at the first paragraph. Other times, especially if the paragraphs are short, you can locate the thesis within the first several paragraphs. Depending on what you discover while skimming, you can speed up or slow down your reading as needed while you locate the thesis and get a sense of how the argument for it is structured. If the essay has sections, pay attention to *headings* and *subheadings*. Look for key expressions that indicate an author's conclusive statements, such as "Finally, then, it is time that we . . ." or "Given this evidence, it is clear that. . . ." These kinds of sentences frequently appear at the beginnings or endings of paragraphs and sections. Final paragraphs are particularly important because they often summarize the argument and restate the thesis.

By previewing and skimming effectively, you can quickly ascertain quite a bit of information about an article or essay. You can detect the author's claims and methods, see the evidence he or she uses (experience, statistics, quotations, etc.), ascertain the tone and difficulty level, and determine whether the piece of writing offers useful ideas for you. This strategy works well if you're researching a topic and need to review many essays — you can read efficiently to find those that are most important or relevant to you, or those that offer different perspectives. Of course, if you do find an essay to be compelling during previewing, you can begin "chewing and digesting," as Francis Bacon put it — reading more closely and carefully (or else putting it aside for later when you can give it more time).

CALL OUT: CRITICAL READING TIP   Instead of imagining previewing and close reading as two separate stages to be completed consecutively, think of previewing as an activity that might at any time develop into close reading.

A SHORT ESSAY FOR PREVIEWING PRACTICE

Before skimming the following essay, apply the previewing techniques discussed above, and complete the Thinking Critically: Previewing activity on page 41.

SANJAY GUPTA

Dr. Sanjay Gupta (b. 1969) is a neurosurgeon and multiple Emmy award–winning television personality. As a leading public health expert, he has appeared widely on television, including the Oprah Winfrey Show, *the* Late Show *with David Letterman,* the *Jon Stewart* Show, *and* 60 Minutes. *He is most well known as CNN's chief medical correspondent. In 2011,* Forbes *magazine named him one of the ten most influential celebrities in America. The essay reprinted below originally appeared on CNN.com in August 2013.*

Why I Changed My Mind on Weed

Over the last year, I have been working on a new documentary called "Weed." The title "Weed" may sound cavalier, but the content is not.

I traveled around the world to interview medical leaders, experts, growers and patients. I spoke candidly to them, asking tough questions. What I found was stunning.

Long before I began this project, I had steadily reviewed the scientific literature on medical marijuana from the United States and thought it was fairly unimpressive. Reading these papers five years ago, it was hard to make a case for medicinal marijuana. I even wrote about this in a *Time* magazine article, back in 2009, titled "Why I Would Vote No on Pot."

Well, I am here to apologize.

I apologize because I didn't look hard 5 enough, until now. I didn't look far enough. I didn't review papers from smaller labs in other countries doing some remarkable research, and I was too dismissive of the loud chorus of legitimate patients whose symptoms improved on cannabis.

Instead, I lumped them with the high-visibility malingerers, just looking to get high. I mistakenly believed the Drug Enforcement Agency listed marijuana as a Schedule 1 substance because of sound scientific proof. Surely, they must have quality reasoning as to why marijuana is in the category of the most dangerous drugs that have "no accepted medicinal use and a high potential for abuse."

They didn't have the science to support that claim, and I now know that when it comes to marijuana neither of those things are true. It doesn't have a high potential for abuse, and there are very legitimate medical applications. In fact, sometimes marijuana is the only thing that works. Take the case of Charlotte Figi, whom I met in Colorado. She started having seizures soon after birth. By age 3, she was having 300 a week, despite being on 7 different medications. Medical marijuana has calmed her brain, limiting her seizures to 2 or 3 per month.

I have seen more patients like Charlotte first hand, spent time with them and come to the realization that it is irresponsible not to provide the best care we can as a medical community, care that could involve marijuana.

We have been terribly and systematically misled for nearly 70 years in the United States, and I apologize for my own role in that.

I hope this article and upcoming docu- 10 mentary will help set the record straight.

On August 14, 1970, the Assistant Secretary of Health, Dr. Roger O. Egeberg, wrote a letter recommending the plant, marijuana, be classified as a Schedule 1 substance, and it has remained that way for nearly 45 years. My research started with a careful reading of that decades-old letter. What I found was unsettling. Egeberg had carefully chosen his words:

"Since there is still a considerable void in our knowledge of the plant and effects of the active drug contained in it, our recommendation is that marijuana be retained within Schedule 1 at least until the completion of certain studies now under way to resolve the issue."

Not because of sound science, but because of its absence, marijuana was classified as a Schedule 1 substance. Again, the year was 1970. Egeberg mentions studies that are under way, but many were never completed. As my investigation continued, however, I realized Egeberg did in fact have important research already available to him, some of it from more than 25 years earlier.

HIGH RISK OF ABUSE

In 1944, New York mayor Fiorello LaGuardia commissioned research to be performed by the New York Academy of Science. Among their conclusions: they found marijuana did not lead to significant addiction in the medical sense of the word. They also did not find any evidence marijuana led to morphine, heroin or cocaine addiction.

We now know that while estimates vary, 15 marijuana leads to dependence in around 9 to 10% of its adult users. By comparison, cocaine, a Schedule 2 substance "with less abuse potential than Schedule 1 drugs," hooks 20% of those who use it. Around 25% of heroin users become addicted.

The worst is tobacco, where the number is closer to 30% of smokers, many of whom go on to die because of their addiction.

There is clear evidence that in some people marijuana use can lead to withdrawal symptoms, including insomnia, anxiety and nausea. Even considering this, it is hard to make a case that it has a high potential for abuse. The physical symptoms of marijuana addiction are nothing like those of the other drugs I've mentioned. I have seen the withdrawal from alcohol, and it can be life threatening.

I do want to mention a concern that I think about as a father. Young, developing brains are likely more susceptible to harm from marijuana than adult brains. Some recent studies suggest that regular use in teenage years leads to a permanent decrease in IQ. Other research hints at a possible heightened risk of developing psychosis.

Much in the same way I wouldn't let my own children drink alcohol, I wouldn't permit marijuana until they are adults. If they are adamant about trying marijuana, I will urge them to wait until they're in their mid 20s, when their brains are fully developed.

MEDICAL BENEFIT

While investigating, I realized something [20] else quite important. Medical marijuana is not new, and the medical community has been writing about it for a long time. There were in fact hundreds of journal articles, mostly documenting the benefits. Most of those papers, however, were written between the years 1840 and 1930. The papers described the use of medical marijuana to treat "neuralgia, convulsive disorders, emaciation," among other things.

A search through the U.S. National Library of Medicine this past year pulled up nearly 20,000 more recent papers. But the majority were research into the harm of marijuana, such as "Bad trip due to anticholinergic effect of cannabis," or "Cannabis induced pancreatitis" and "Marijuana use and risk of lung cancer."

In my quick running of the numbers, I calculated about 6% of the current U.S. marijuana studies investigate the benefits of medical marijuana. The rest are designed to investigate harm. That imbalance paints a highly distorted picture.

THE CHALLENGES OF MARIJUANA RESEARCH

To do studies on marijuana in the United States today, you need two important things.

First of all, you need marijuana. And marijuana is illegal. You see the problem. Scientists can get research marijuana from a special farm in Mississippi, which is astonishingly located in the middle of the Ole Miss campus, but it is challenging. When I visited this year, there was no marijuana being grown.

The second thing you need is approval, and [20] the scientists I interviewed kept reminding me how tedious that can be. While a cancer study may first be evaluated by the National Cancer Institute, or a pain study may go through the National Institute for Neurological Disorders, there is one more approval required for marijuana: NIDA, the National Institute on Drug Abuse. It is an organization that has a core mission of studying drug abuse, as opposed to benefit.

Stuck in the middle are the legitimate patients who depend on marijuana as a medicine, oftentimes as their only good option.

Keep in mind that up until 1943, marijuana was part of the United States drug pharmacopeia. One of the conditions for which it was prescribed was neuropathic pain. It is a miserable pain that's tough to treat. My own patients have described it as "lancinating, burning and a barrage of pins and needles."

While marijuana has long been documented to be effective for this awful pain, the most common medications prescribed today come from the poppy plant, including morphine, oxycodone and dilaudid.

Here is the problem. Most of these medications don't work very well for this kind of pain, and tolerance is a real problem.

Most frightening to me is that someone dies in the United States every 19 minutes from a prescription drug overdose, mostly accidental. Every 19 minutes. It is a horrifying statistic. As much as I searched, I could not find a documented case of death from marijuana overdose.

It is perhaps no surprise then that 76% of physicians recently surveyed said they would approve the use of marijuana to help ease a woman's pain from breast cancer.

When marijuana became a Schedule 1 substance, there was a request to fill a "void in our knowledge." In the United States, that has been challenging because of the infrastructure surrounding the study of an illegal substance, with a drug abuse organization at the heart of the approval process. And yet, despite the hurdles, we have made considerable progress that continues today.

Looking forward, I am especially intrigued by studies like those in Spain and Israel looking at the anti-cancer effects of marijuana and its components. I'm intrigued by the neuro-protective study by Lev Meschoulam in Israel, and research in Israel and the United States on whether the drug might help alleviate symptoms of PTSD. I promise to do my part to help, genuinely and honestly, fill the remaining void in our knowledge.

Citizens in 20 states and the District of Columbia have now voted to approve marijuana for medical applications, and more states will be making that choice soon. As for Dr. Roger Egeberg, who wrote that letter in 1970, he passed away 16 years ago.

I wonder what he would think if he were alive today.

THE "FIRST AND LAST" RULE   As noted above, authors often place main points of emphasis at the beginnings and endings of *essays*. They also place important material at the beginnings and endings of *paragraphs* and *sentences*.

When writing, you can emphasize main points by using the first and last rule. Don't bury your most important material in the middle of sentences, paragraphs, or entire papers. Make it stand out.

Consider the following observations. Select two that you find to be most important.

1. Gupta is one of the most respected voices in public health.

2. Gupta argues for the legalization of medical marijuana.

3. Gupta's article was written for CNN News in 2011.

4. Gupta rejects his previous position on medical marijuana and apologizes for his oversight.

5. The article was important because it represented a shift in approach by a leading doctor.

THINKING CRITICALLY Previewing

Provide the missing information for Sanjay Gupta and his essay "Why I Changed My Mind on Weed."

PREVIEWING STRATEGIES	TYPES OF QUESTIONS	ANSWERS
Author	Who is he? What expertise does he have? What credibility does he have? How difficult is the writing likely to be?	
Title	What does the title reveal about the essay's content? Does it give any clues about how the argument will take shape?	
Place of Publication	How does the place of publication help you understand the argument? What type of audiences will it be likely to target?	
Context	By placing the article in the context of its time — given trends in the conversations about or popular understandings of the subject — what can you expect about the author's position?	
Skimming	As you skim over the first several paragraphs, where do you first realize the purpose of the essay? What is Gupta's argument? What major forms of evidence does he offer?	

LaunchPad   To complete this activity online, go to **macmillanhighered.com/barnetbedauohara**

Now arrange these statements in a short paragraph, using the first and last rule to emphasize the two that you selected as most important. Compare your paragraph to your classmates' paragraphs. How do they compare?

READING WITH A CARFUL EYE: UNDERLINING, HIGHLIGHTING, ANNOTATING

Once you have a general idea of the work — not only an idea of its topic and thesis but also a sense of the way in which the thesis is argued — you can go back and start reading it carefully.

As you read, **underline** or **highlight** key passages, and make **annotations** in the margins. Because you're reading actively, or interacting with the text, you won't simply let your eye rove across the page.

- Highlight what seem to be the chief points, so that later when reviewing the essay you can easily locate the main passages.

- But don't overdo a good thing. If you find yourself highlighting most of a page, you're probably not thinking carefully enough about what the key points are.

- Similarly, your marginal annotations should be brief and selective. They will probably consist of hints or clues, comments like "doesn't follow," "good," "compare with Jones," "check this," and "really?"

- In short, in a paragraph you might highlight a key definition, and in the margin you might write "good," or "in contrast," or "?" if you think the definition is unclear or incorrect.

- With many electronic formats, you can use tools to highlight or annotate. Also consider copying and pasting passages that you would normally highlight in a Google document. Include a link to the piece, and create an RSS feed to the journal's Web site. Having your notes in an electronic format makes it easy to access and use them later.

In all these ways, you interact with the text and lay the groundwork for eventually writing your own essay on what you have read.

What you annotate will depend largely on your **purpose**. If you're reading an essay in order to see how the writer organizes an argument, you'll annotate one sort of thing. If you're reading in order to challenge the thesis, you'll annotate other things. Here is a passage from an essay entitled "On Racist Speech," with a student's rather skeptical, even aggressive, annotations. But notice that the student apparently made at least one of the annotations — "Definition of 'fighting words'" — chiefly in order to remind herself to locate where the definition of an important term appears in the essay. The essay, printed in full on page 71, is by Charles R. Lawrence III, a professor of law at Georgetown University. It originally appeared in the *Chronicle of Higher Education* (October 25, 1989), a publication read chiefly by college and university faculty members and administrators.

Example of such a policy?

University officials who have formulated <u>policies</u> to respond to incidents of racial harassment have been characterized in the press as "thought police," but such policies generally do nothing more than impose ⟨sanctions⟩ against intentional face-to-face insults. When <u>racist speech</u> takes the form of <u>face-to-face insults</u>, catcalls, or other assaultive speech aimed at an individual or small group of persons, it falls directly within the "fighting words" exception to First Amendment protection. The Supreme Court has held that <u>words "which 'by their very utterance inflict</u> injury or tend to incite an immediate breach of the peace'"</u> are not protected by the First Amendment.

?
Example?
What about sexist speech?

Definition of "fighting words"

If the purpose of the First Amendment is to foster the greatest amount of speech, racial insults disserve that purpose. Assaultive racist speech functions as a preemptive strike. The <u>invective</u> is experienced as a blow, not as a <u>proffered idea,</u> and once the blow is struck, it is unlikely that a dialogue will follow. Racial insults are particularly undeserving of First Amendment protection because the perpetrator's <u>intention is not to discover truth</u> or initiate dialogue but to injure the victim. <u>In most situations,</u> members of minority groups realize that they are likely to lose if they respond to epithets by fighting and are forced to remain silent and submissive.

Really? Probably depends
on the Individual.

Why must speech always
seek "to discover truth"?
How does he know?

"THIS; THEREFORE, THAT"

To arrive at a coherent thought or series of thoughts that will lead to a reasonable conclusion, a writer has to go through a good deal of preliminary effort. When we discussed heuristics in Chapter 1 (p. 17), we talked about patterns of thought that stimulate initial ideas. The path to sound conclusions involves similar thought patterns that carry forward the arguments presented in the essay:

- While these arguments are convincing, they fail to consider . . .
- While these arguments are convincing, they must also consider . . .
- These arguments, rather than being convincing, instead prove . . .
- While these authors agree, in my opinion . . .
- Although it is often true that . . .
- Consider also . . .
- What sort of audience would agree with such an argument?
- What sort of audience would be opposed?
- What are the differences in values between these two kinds of audiences?

All of these patterns can serve as heuristics or prompts — that is, they can stimulate the creation of ideas.

Moreover, for the writer to convince the reader that the conclusion is sound, the reasoning behind the conclusion must be set forth in detail, with a good deal of "This; therefore, that"; "If this, then that"; and "Others might object at this point that. . . ." The arguments in this book require more comment than President Calvin Coolidge supposedly provided when his wife, who hadn't been able to attend church one Sunday, asked him what the preacher talked about in his sermon. "Sin," Coolidge said. His wife persisted: "What did the preacher say about it?" Coolidge's response: "He was against it."

But, again, when we say that most of the arguments in this book are presented at length and require careful reading, we don't mean that they are obscure; we mean, rather, that you have to approach the sentences thoughtfully, one by one. In this vein, recall an episode from Lewis Carroll's *Through the Looking-Glass:*

> "Can you do Addition?" the White Queen asked. "What's one and one and one and one and one and one and one and one and one and one?"
>
> "I don't know," said Alice. "I lost count."
>
> "She can't do Addition," the Red Queen said.

Alice with the Red Queen and the White Queen

It's easy enough to add one and one and one and so on, and of course Alice can do addition — but not at the pace that the White Queen sets. Fortunately, you can set your own pace in reading the cumulative thinking set forth in the essays we reprint in this book. Skimming won't work, but slow reading — and thinking about what you're reading — will.

When you first pick up an essay, you may indeed want to skim it, for some of the reasons mentioned on page 36, but sooner or later you have to settle down to read it and think about it. The effort will be worthwhile. Consider what John Locke, a seventeenth-century English philosopher, said:

> *Reading* furnishes the mind with materials of knowledge; it is *thinking* [that] makes what we read ours. We are of the ruminating kind, and it is not enough to cram ourselves with a great load of collections; unless we chew them over again they will not give us strength and nourishment.

Often students read an essay just once, supposing that to reread would be repetitious. But much can be gleaned from a second reading, as new details will likely emerge and new ideas will be generated. Roland Barthes, a twentieth-century philosopher, warned against accepting a first reading as final. Far from being repetitive, "[r]e-reading," he wrote, "*saves* the text from repetition, multiplies it in its variety and plurality." What may actually be repetitious is reading something only once and, thinking you have it pinned down, repeating it (in your writing) and thereby sticking to your first and only impression.

DEFINING TERMS AND CONCEPTS

Suppose you're reading an argument about whether a certain set of images is pornography or art. For the present purpose, let's use a famous example from 1992, when American photographer Sally Mann published *Immediate Family*, a controversial book featuring numerous images of her three children (then ages 12, 10, and 7) in various states of nakedness during their childhood on a rural Kentucky farm. Mann is considered a great photographer and artist ("America's Best Photographer," according to *Time* magazine in 2001), and *Immediate Family* is very well regarded in the art community ("one of the great photograph books of our time," according to the *New Republic*). But some critics couldn't separate the images of Mann's own naked children from the label "child pornography."

When reading, attend carefully to how terms and concepts are used for the purposes of advancing an argument. In this case, you might begin by asking, "What is *pornography*? What is *art*?" If writers and readers cannot agree on basic definitions of the terms and concepts that structure the debate, then argument is futile. And if an author doesn't share *your* definition of a term or concept, then you might challenge the premise of his or her argument. If someone were to define pornography to include *any* images of nude children, that definition would include photographs taken for any reason — medical, sociological, anthropological, scientific — and would include even the innocent photographs taken by proud parents of their children swimming, bathing, and so on. It would also apply to some of the world's great art. Most people do not seriously think the mere image of the naked body, adult or child, is pornography.

Pornography is often defined according to its intended effect on the viewer ("genital commotion," Father Harold Gardiner, S.J., called it in *Catholic Viewpoint on Censorship*). In this definition, if images are eroticized (i.e., made erotic through style or symbolism), if they invite a sexual gaze, they are pornographic. This seems to be the definition that novelist Mary Gordon applied in a 1996 critique of Sally Mann:

> Unless we believe it is ethically permissible for adults to have sex with children, we must question the ethics of an art which allows the adult who has the most power over these children — a parent, in this case a mother — to place them in a situation where they become the imagined sexual partner of adults. . . . It is inevitable that Sally Mann's photographs arouse the sexual imaginations of strangers.

But is it enough to say something is pornographic if it "arouses the sexual imagination"? No, you might contend, because there is no way to predict what will arouse people's sexual imaginations. Many kinds of images might arouse the sexual imaginations of different people. You might say in rebutting Gordon, "These are just pictures of children. Sure, they're naked in some of them, but children have been symbols of purity and innocence in art since the dawn of civilization. If some people see these images as sexual, that's their problem, not Mann's."

Writers often attempt to provide a provisional definition of important terms and concepts in their arguments. They may write, for example, "For the purposes of this argument, let's define terrorism as *X*" (a broad definition) or "According to federal law, the term 'international terrorism' means *A*, *B*, and *C*" (a technical definition). If you do this and a reader wants to challenge your ideas, he must argue on your terms or else offer a different definition.

So that we are consistent with our own recommendations, allow us to define the difference between a "term" and a "concept." A rule of thumb is that a *term* is more concrete and fixed than a *concept*. You may be able to find an authoritative source (like a federal law or an official policy) to help define a *term*. A *concept* is more open-ended and

A RULE FOR WRITERS
Be alert to how terms and concepts are defined both in your source material and in your own writing. Are your terms broadly, narrowly, or technically construed?

THINKING CRITICALLY *Defining Terms and Concepts*

Examine each claim, and note the terms and concepts used. Provide a terminological (strict, codified by an authoritative source) or a conceptual (loose, self-generated) definition for each. What sources did you use? Compare your answers to those of your peers to see if they are similar or different.

STATEMENT	DEFINITION	TYPE OF DEFINITION
Video games are **addictive.**		
Poor people will suffer most from the new law.		
The **epidemic of obesity** needs to be solved.		
We must send troops to protect **the national interest.**		
The Internet has ushered in a new age of **progress.**		

LaunchPad To complete this activity online, go to **macmillanhighered.com/barnetbedauohara**

may have a generally agreed-upon definition, but rarely a strict or unchanging one. Concepts can be abstract but can also function powerfully in argumentation; love, justice, morality, psyche, health, freedom, bravery, obscenity, masculinity — these are all concepts. You may look up such words in the dictionary for general definitions, but the source won't say much about how to apply the concepts.

Since you cannot assume that everyone has a shared understanding of concepts you may be using, it's prudent for the purposes of effective writing to define them. You may find a useful definition of a concept given by an authoritative person, such as an expert in a field, as in "Stephen Hawking defines time as. . . ." You might cite a respected authority, as in "Mahatma Gandhi defines love as. . . ." Alternatively, you can combine several views and insert your own provisional definition. See "Thinking Critically: Defining Terms and Concepts" for an exercise.

Summarizing and Paraphrasing

After a first reading, perhaps the best approach to a fairly difficult essay is to reread it and simultaneously take notes on a sheet of paper, summarizing each paragraph in a sentence or two. Writing a summary will help you to:

- understand the contents and
- see the strengths and weaknesses of the piece.

Don't confuse a summary with a paraphrase. A paraphrase is a word-by-word or phrase-by-phrase rewording of a text, a sort of translation of the author's language into your own. A paraphrase is therefore as long as the original or even longer; a summary is much shorter. An entire essay, even a whole book, may be summarized in a page, in a paragraph, even in a sentence. Obviously, the summary will leave out most details, but it will accurately state the essential thesis or claim of the original.

Why would anyone summarize, and why would anyone paraphrase? Because, as we've already said, these two activities — in different ways — offer a way to introduce other authors' ideas into your arguments in a way that readers can follow. You may do this for a number of reasons. Summaries and paraphrases can accomplish the following:

- **validate** the basis of your argument by providing an instance in which someone else wrote about the same topic
- **clarify** in short order the complex ideas contained in another author's work
- **support** your argument by showing readers where someone else "got it right" (corroborating your ideas) or "got it wrong" (countering your ideas, but giving you a chance to refute that position in favor of your own)
- **lend authority** to your voice by showing readers that you have considered the topic carefully by consulting other sources
- **help you build new ideas** from existing ideas on the topic, enabling you to insert your voice into an ongoing debate made evident by the summary or paraphrase

When you summarize, you're standing back, saying briefly what the whole adds up to; you're seeing the forest, as the saying goes, not the individual trees. **When you paraphrase**, you're inching through the forest, scrutinizing each tree — finding a synonym for almost every word in the original in an effort to ensure you know exactly what the original is saying. (*Caution:* Do not incorporate a summary or a paraphrase into your own essay without acknowledging the source and stating that you are summarizing or paraphrasing.)

Let's examine the distinction between summary and paraphrase in connection with the first two paragraphs of Paul Goodman's essay "A Proposal to Abolish Grading," excerpted from Goodman's book *Compulsory Miseducation and the Community of Scholars* (1966).

> Let half a dozen of the prestigious universities — Chicago, Stanford, the Ivy League — abolish grading, and use testing only and entirely for pedagogic purposes as teachers see fit.

> Anyone who knows the frantic temper of the present schools will understand the transvaluation of values that would be effected by this modest innovation. For most of the students, the competitive grade has come to be the essence. The naive teacher points to the beauty of the subject and the ingenuity of the research; the shrewd student asks if he is responsible for that on the final exam.

A **summary** of these two paragraphs might read like this:

> If some top universities used tests only to help students to learn and not for grades, students would stop worrying about whether they got an A, B or C and might begin to share the teacher's interest in the beauty of the subject.

Notice that the summary doesn't convey Goodman's style or voice (e.g., the wry tone in his pointed contrast between "the naive teacher" and "the shrewd student"). That is not the purpose of summary.

Now for a **paraphrase**. Suppose you're not sure what Goodman is getting at, maybe because you're uncertain about the meanings of some words (e.g., *pedagogic* and *transvaluation*), or else you just want to make sure you understand the point. In such a case, you may want to move slowly through the sentences, restating them in your own words. You might turn Goodman's "pedagogic purposes" into "goals in teaching," "attempts to help students to learn," or something else. Here is a paraphrase — not a summary, but a rewording — of Goodman's paragraphs:

> Suppose some of the top universities — such as Chicago, Stanford, Harvard, Yale, and others in the Ivy League — stopped using grades and instead used tests only in order to help students to learn.

> Everyone who is aware of the rat race in schools today will understand the enormous shift in values about learning that would come about by this small change. At present, idealistic instructors talk about how beautiful their subjects are, but smart students know that grades are what count. They only want to know if it will be on the exam.

In short, you may decide to paraphrase an important text if you want the reader to see the passage itself but you know that the full passage will be puzzling. In this situation, you offer help, *paraphrasing* before making your own point about the author's claim.

A second good reason to offer a paraphrase is if there is substantial disagreement about what the text says. The Second Amendment to the U.S. Constitution is a good example of this sort of text:

> A well regulated Militia being necessary to the security of a free State, the right of the people to keep and bear Arms shall not be infringed.

Exactly what, one might ask, is a "Militia"? What does it mean for a militia to be "well regulated"? And does "the people" mean each individual or the citizenry as a unified group? After all, elsewhere in the document, where the Constitution speaks of individuals, it speaks of a "man" or a "person," not "the people." To speak of "the people" is to use a term (some argue) that sounds like a reference to a unified group — perhaps the citizens of each of the thirteen states — rather than a reference to individuals. However, if Congress did mean a unified group rather than individuals, why didn't it say, "Congress shall not prohibit the states from organizing militias"?

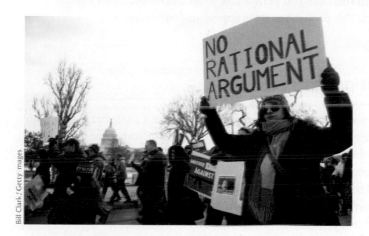

Gun control supporters marching in 2013 at the Washington Monument in Washington, D.C.

Bill Clark / Getty images

In fact, thousands of pages have been written about this sentence, and if you're going to talk about it, you certainly have to let readers know exactly how you interpret each word. In short, you almost surely will paraphrase the sentence, going word by word, giving readers your own sense of what each word or phrase means. Here is one possible paraphrase:

> Because an independent society needs the protection of an armed force if it is to remain free, the government may not limit the right of the individuals (who may someday form the militia needed to keep the society free) to possess weapons.

In this interpretation, the Constitution grants individuals the right to possess weapons, and that is that.

Other students of the Constitution, however, offer very different paraphrases, usually along these lines:

> Because each state that is now part of the United States may need to protect its freedom (from the new national government), the national government may not infringe on the right of each state to form its own disciplined militia.

This paraphrase says that the federal government may not prevent each state from having a militia; it says nothing about every individual person having a right to possess weapons.

The first paraphrase might be offered by the National Rifle Association or any other group that interprets the Constitution as guaranteeing individuals the right to own guns. The second paraphrase might be offered by groups that seek to limit the ownership of guns.

Why paraphrase? Here are two reasons why you might paraphrase a passage:

- To help yourself to understand it. In this case, the paraphrase does not appear in your essay.

- To help your reader to understand a passage that is especially important but that is not immediately clear. In this case, you paraphrase to let the reader know exactly what the passage means. This paraphrase does appear in your essay.

Paraphrase, Patchwriting, and Plagiarism

We have indicated that only rarely will you have reason to introduce a paraphrase into your essays. But in your preliminary work, when taking notes, you might sometimes do one or more of the following: copy word for word, paraphrase (usually to establish an author's idea clearly in your mind), summarize, and / or produce a medley of borrowed words and original words. The latter strategy is known as *patchwriting*, and it can be dangerous: If you submit such a medley in your final essay, you risk the charge of **plagiarism** *even if you have rearranged the phrases and clauses, and even if you have cited your source.*

Here's an example. First, we give the source: a paragraph from Jena McGregor's essay on whether women serving in the armed forces should be allowed to participate directly in combat. (The entire essay is printed on pp. 31–32.)

> Last week, female soldiers began formally moving into jobs in previously all-male battalions, a program that will later go Army-wide. The move is a result of rule changes following a February report that opened some 14,000 new positions to women in critical jobs much closer to the front lines. However, some 250,000 combat jobs still remain officially closed to them.

Here is a student's patchwriting version:

> Women in the army recently began to formally move into jobs in battalions that previously were all-male. This program later will go throughout the Army. According to author Jena McGregor,

the move comes from changes in the rules following a February report that opened about 14,000 new jobs to women in critical jobs that are much closer to the front lines. About 250,000 jobs, however — as McGregor points out — continue to be officially closed to women.

As you can see, the student writer has followed the source almost phrase by phrase — certainly, sentence by sentence — making small verbal changes, such as substituting *Women in the army recently* for McGregor's *Last week, female soldiers* and substituting *the move comes from changes in the rules* for McGregor's *The move is a result of rule changes. . . .*

What the student should have done is either (1) *quote the passage exactly,* setting it off to indicate that it's a quotation and indicating the source, or (2) *summarize it briefly* and credit the source — maybe in a sentence such as this:

Jena McGregor points out that although a recent change in army rules has resulted in new jobs being opened for women in the military, some 250,000 jobs "continue to be officially closed."

As opposed to the above example of a sentence that frankly summarizes a source, patchwriting is *not* the student's writing but, rather, the source material thinly disguised. In a given paragraph of patchwriting, usually some of the words are copied from the source, and all or most of the rest consists of synonyms substituted for the source's words, with minor rearrangement of phrases and clauses. That is, the sequence of ideas and their arrangement, as well as most of the language, are entirely or almost entirely derived from the source, even if some of the words are different.

The fact that you may cite a source is not enough to protect you from the charge of plagiarism. Citing a source tells the reader that some fact or idea — or some groups of words enclosed within quotation marks or set off by indentation — comes from the named source; it does *not* tell the reader that almost everything in the paragraph is, in effect, someone else's writing with a few words changed, a few words added, and a few phrases moved.

The best way to avoid introducing patchwriting into your final essay is to make certain that when taking notes you indicate, *in the notes themselves,* what sorts of notes they are. For example:

- When quoting word for word, put the passage within quotation marks, and cite the page number(s) of the source.

- When paraphrasing — perhaps to ensure that you understand the writer's idea, or because your readers won't understand the source's highly technical language unless you put it into simpler language — use some sign, perhaps *(par)*, to remind yourself later that this passage is a paraphrase and thus is not really *your* writing.

- When summarizing, use a different key, such as *(sum)*, and cite the page(s) of the source.

Make certain that your notes indicate the degree of indebtedness to your source, and again, do *not* think that if you name a source in a paraphrase you're not plagiarizing. The reader assumes that the name indicates the source of a fact or an idea — not that the paragraph is a rewriting of the original with an occasional phrase of your own inserted here and there.

If you have taken notes properly, with indications of the sort we've mentioned, when writing your paper you can say things like the following:

X's first reason is simple. He says, ". . ." (here you quote X's words, putting them within quotation marks).

X's point can be summarized thus . . . (here you cite the page).

X, writing for lawyers, uses some technical language, but we can paraphrase her conclusion in this way: . . . (here you give the citation).

In short:

- Avoid patchwriting; it is *not* acceptable.
- Enclose direct quotations within quotation marks, or, if the quotations are long, set them off as a block quotation. (Consult your specific style guide for instructions on how to set off block quotations.)
- If you offer a paraphrase, tell readers that you are paraphrasing and explain *why* you are doing so rather than quoting directly or summarizing.

For additional information about plagiarism, see pages 275–278.

A CHECKLIST FOR A PARAPHRASE

❑ Do I have a good reason for offering a paraphrase rather than a summary?

❑ Is the paraphrase entirely in my own words — a word-by-word "translation" — rather than a patchwork of the source's words and my own, with some of my own rearrangement of phrases and clauses?

❑ Do I not only cite the source but also explicitly say that the entire passage is a paraphrase?

STRATEGIES FOR SUMMARIZING

As with paraphrases, summaries can be useful for helping you to establish your understanding of an essay or article. Summarizing each paragraph or each group of closely related paragraphs will enable you to follow the threads of the argument and will ultimately provide a useful map of the essay. Then, when rereading the essay, you may want to underline passages that you now realize are the author's key ideas — for instance, definitions, generalizations, summaries. You may also want to jot notes in the margins, questioning the logic, expressing your uncertainty, or calling attention to other writers who see the matter differently.

Summaries are also useful for your readers, for the reasons noted on page 47. How long should your summaries be? They can be as short as a single sentence or as long as an entire paragraph. Here's a one-sentence summary of Martin Luther King Jr.'s famous essay "Letter from Birmingham Jail." King wrote this essay after his arrest for marching against racial segregation and injustice in Birmingham, Alabama.

In his letter, King argues that the time is ripe for nonviolent protest throughout the segregated South, dismissing claims by local clergymen who opposed him, and arguing that unjust laws need to be challenged by black people who have been patient and silent for too long.

A RULE FOR WRITERS
Your essay is *likely to include brief summaries* of points of view with which you agree or disagree, but it will *rarely include a paraphrase* unless the original is obscure and you feel compelled to present a passage at length in words that are clearer than those of the original. If you do paraphrase, explicitly identify the material as a paraphrase. Never submit patchwriting.

King's essay, however, is quite long. Obviously, our one-sentence summary cannot convey substantial portions of King's eloquent arguments, sacrificing almost all the nuance of his rationale, but it serves as an efficient summation and allows the writer to move on to his own analysis promptly.

A longer summary might try to capture more nuance, especially if, for the purposes of your essay, you need to capture more. How much you summarize depends largely on the *purpose* of your summary (see again our list of reasons to summarize on p. 47). Here is a longer summary of King's letter:

In his letter, King argues that the time is ripe for nonviolent protest in the segregated South despite the criticism he and his fellow civil rights activists received from various authorities, especially the eight local clergymen who wrote a public statement against him. King addresses their criticism point by point, first claiming his essential right to be in Birmingham with his famous statement, "injustice anywhere is a threat to justice everywhere," and then saying that those who see the timing of his group's nonviolent direct action as inconvenient must recognize at least two things: one, that his "legitimate and unavoidable impatience" resulted from undelivered promises by authorities in the past; and two, that African Americans had long been told over and over again to wait for change with no change forthcoming. "This 'wait' has almost always meant 'never,'" King writes. For those who criticized his leadership, which encouraged people to break laws prohibiting their march, King says that breaking *unjust* laws may actually be construed as a *just* act. For those who called him an extremist, he revels in the definition ("was not Jesus an extremist in love?" he asks) and reminds them of the more extremist groups who call for violence in the face of blatant discrimination and brutality (and who will surely rise, King suggests, if no redress is forthcoming for the peaceful southern protestors he leads). Finally, King rails against "silence," saying that to hold one's tongue in the face of segregation is tantamount to supporting it—a blow to "white moderates" who believe in change but do nothing to help bring it about.

This summary, obviously much longer than the first, raises numerous points from King's argument and preserves through quotation some of King's original tone and substance. It sacrifices much, of course, but seeks to provide a thorough account of a long and complex document containing many primary and secondary claims.

If your instructor asks for a summary of an essay, most often he or she won't want you to include your own thoughts about the content. Of course, you'll be using your own words, but try to "put yourself in the original author's shoes" and provide a summary that reflects the approach taken by the source. It should *not* contain ideas that the original piece doesn't express. If you use exact words and phrases drawn from the source, enclose them in quotation marks.

Summaries may be written for exercises in reading comprehension, but the point of summarizing when writing an essay is to assist your own argument. A faithful summary — one without your own ideas interjected — can be effective when using a source as an example or showing another writer's concordance with your argument. Consider the following paragraph written by a student who was arguing that if a person today purchases goods manufactured in sweatshops or under other inadequate labor conditions, then he or she is just as responsible for the abuses of labor as the companies who operate them. Notice how the student provides a summary (underlined) along the way and how it assists her argument.

Americans today are so disconnected from the source and origins of the products they buy that it is entirely possible for them one day to march against global warming and the next to collect a dividend in their 401k from companies that are the worst offenders. It is possible to weep over a news report on child labor in China and then post an emotional plea for justice on Facebook using a mobile device made by Chinese child laborers. In 1849, Henry David Thoreau wrote in "Resistance to Civil Government" how ironic it was to see his fellow citizens in Boston opposed to slavery in the South, yet who read the daily news and commodity prices and "fall asleep over them both," not recognizing their own investments in, or patronage of, the very thing that offends their consciences. To Thoreau, such "gross inconsistency" makes even well-intentioned people "agents of injustice." Similarly, today we do not see the connections between our consumer habits and the various kinds of oppression that underlie our purchases — forms of oppression we would never support directly and outright.

The embedded short summary addresses only one point of Thoreau's original essay, but it shows how summaries may serve in an integrative way — as analogy, example, or illustration — to support an argument even without adding the writer's own commentary or analysis.

CRITICAL SUMMARY

When writing a longer summary that you intend to integrate into your argument, you may interject your own ideas; the appropriate term for this is **critical summary**. It signifies that you're offering more than a thorough and accurate account of an original source, because you're adding your evaluation of it as well. Think of this as weaving together your neutral summary with your own argument so that the summary meshes seamlessly with your overall writing goal. Along the way, during the summary, you may appraise the original author's ideas, commenting on them as you go — even while being faithful to the original.

How can you faithfully account for an author's argument while commenting on its merits or shortcomings? One way is to offer examples from the original. In addition, you might assess the quality of those examples or present others that the author didn't consider. Remember, being critical doesn't necessarily mean refuting the author. Your summary can refute, support, or be more balanced, simply recognizing where the original author succeeds and fails.

A STRATEGY FOR WRITING A CRITICAL SUMMARY   Follow these five steps when writing a critical summary:

1. **Introduce** the summary. You don't have to provide all these elements, but consider offering the *author's name* and *expertise*, the *title* of the source, the *place* of publication, the *year* of publication, or any other relevant information. You may also start to explain the author's main point that you are summarizing:

> Pioneering feminist Betty Friedan, in her landmark book *The Feminine Mystique* (1963), argued that . . .

> In an essay on the state of higher education today, University of Illinois English professor Cary Nelson complains about . . .

2. **Explain** the major point the source makes. Here you have a chance to tell your readers what the original author is saying, so be faithful to the original but also highlight the point you're summarizing:

> Pioneering feminist Betty Friedan, in her landmark book *The Feminine Mystique* (1963), argued that women of the early 1960s were falling victim to a media-created image of ideal femininity that pressured them to prioritize homemaking, beauty, and maternity above almost all other concerns.

Here you can control the readers' understanding through simple adjectives such as *pioneering* and *landmark*. (Compare how "*stalwart* feminist Betty Friedan, in her *provocative* book" might dispose the reader to interpret your material differently.)

> In a *blunt critique* of the state of higher education today, University of Illinois professor Cary Nelson complains that universities are underpaying and overworking part-time, adjunct teachers.

3. **Exemplify** by offering one or more representative examples or evidence on which the original author draws. Feel free to quote if needed, though it is not required in a summary.

> Friedan examines post–World War II trends that included the lowering of the marriage age, the rise of the mass media, and what she calls "the problem that has no name" — that of feminine un-fulfillment, or what we might today call "depression."

4. **Problematize** by placing your assessment, analysis, or question into the summary.

> While the word *depression* never comes up in Friedan's work, one could assume that terms like *malaise, suffering,* and *housewives' fatigue* signal an emerging

understanding of the relationship between stereotypical media representations of social identity and mental health.

If you're working toward a balanced critique or rebuttal, here is a good place to insert your ideas or those of someone with a slightly different view.

> Nelson is right to say that schools should model themselves on the ideals being taught in classrooms, but having a flexible workforce is perfectly logical for a large organization (something probably also taught in many business classes).

5. **Extend** by tying the summary to your argument, helping transition out of the critical summary and back into your own analysis.

> Friedan's work should raise questions about how women are portrayed in the media today, and about what mental health consequences are attributable to the ubiquitous and consistent messages given to women about their bodies, occupations, and social roles.

> The biggest problem with using too many contingent faculty is with preserving the quality of undergraduate education and the basic principles of academic freedom. Paying contingent faculty more money while increasing the number of tenure-track positions is not just a question of principles but a hallmark of the investment a university makes in its students.

It is possible to use this method — **Introduce**, **Explain**, **Exemplify**, **Problematize**, and **Extend** — in many ways, but essentially it is a way of providing a critical summary, any element of which can be enhanced or built upon as needed.

<table>
<tr>
<td>

A RULE FOR WRITERS
Remember that when writing a summary you are putting yourself into the author's shoes.

</td>
<td>

Having insisted earlier that you should read the essays in this book slowly because the writers build one reason on another, we will now seem to contradict ourselves by presenting an essay that you can almost skim. Susan Jacoby's piece originally appeared in the *New York Times*, a thoroughly respectable newspaper but not one that requires readers to linger over every sentence. Still, compared with most news accounts, Jacoby's essay requires close reading. Notice that it zigs and zags, not because Jacoby is careless but because in building a strong

</td>
</tr>
</table>

case to support her point of view, she must consider some widely held views that she does *not* accept; she must set these forth and then give her reasons for rejecting them.

SUSAN JACOBY

Susan Jacoby (b. 1946), a journalist since the age of seventeen, is well known for her feminist writings. "A First Amendment Junkie" (our title) appeared in the Hers *column in the* New York Times *in 1978.*

A First Amendment Junkie

It is no news that many women are defecting from the ranks of civil libertarians on the issue of obscenity. The conviction of Larry Flynt, publisher of *Hustler* magazine — before his metamorphosis into a born-again Christian — was greeted with unabashed feminist approval. Harry Reems, the unknown actor who was convicted by a Memphis jury for conspiring to distribute the movie *Deep Throat*, has carried on his legal battles with almost no support from women who ordinarily regard themselves as supporters of the First Amendment. Feminist writers and scholars have even discussed the possibility of making common cause against pornography with adversaries of the women's movement — including opponents of the Equal Rights Amendment and "right-to-life" forces.

All of this is deeply disturbing to a woman writer who believes, as I always have and still do, in an absolute interpretation of the First Amendment. Nothing in Larry Flynt's garbage convinces me that the late Justice Hugo L. Black was wrong in his opinion that "the Federal Government is without any power whatsoever under the Constitution to put any type of burden on free speech and expression of ideas of any kind (as distinguished from conduct)." Many women I like and respect tell me I am wrong; I cannot remember having become involved in so many heated discussions of a public issue since the end of the Vietnam War. A feminist writer described my views as those of a "First Amendment junkie."

Many feminist arguments for controls on pornography carry the implicit conviction that porn books, magazines, and movies pose a greater threat to women than similarly repulsive exercises of free speech pose to other offended groups. This conviction has, of course, been shared by everyone — regardless of race, creed, or sex — who has ever argued in favor of abridging the First Amendment. It is the argument used by some Jews who have withdrawn their support from the American Civil Liberties Union because it has defended the right of American Nazis to march through a community inhabited by survivors of Hitler's concentration camps.

If feminists want to argue that the protection of the Constitution should not be extended to *any* particularly odious or threatening form of speech, they have a reasonable argument (although I don't agree with it). But it is ridiculous to suggest that the porn shops on 42nd Street are more disgusting to women than a march of neo-Nazis is to survivors of the extermination camps.

The arguments over pornography also blur 5 the vital distinction between expression of ideas and conduct. When I say I believe unreservedly in the First Amendment, someone always comes back at me with the issue of "kiddie porn." But kiddie porn is not a First Amendment issue. It is an issue of the abuse of power — the power adults have over children — and not of obscenity. Parents and promoters have no more right to use their children to make porn movies than they do to send them to work in coal mines. The responsible adults should be prosecuted, just as adults who use children for back-breaking farm labor should be prosecuted.

Susan Brownmiller, in *Against Our Will: Men, Women, and Rape,* has described pornography as "the undiluted essence of antifemale propaganda." I think this is a fair description of some types of pornography, especially of the brutish subspecies that equates sex with death and portrays women primarily as objects of violence.

The equation of sex and violence, personified by some glossy rock record album covers as well as by *Hustler,* has fed the illusion that censorship of pornography can be conducted on a more rational basis than other types of censorship. Are all pictures of naked women obscene? Clearly not, says a friend. A Renoir nude is art, she says, and *Hustler* is trash. "Any reasonable person" knows that.

But what about something between art and trash — something, say, along the lines of *Playboy* or *Penthouse* magazines? I asked five women for their reactions to one picture in *Penthouse* and got responses that ranged from "lovely" and "sensuous" to "revolting" and "demeaning." Feminists, like everyone else, seldom have rational reasons for their preferences in erotica. Like members of juries, they tend to disagree when confronted with something that falls short of 100 percent vulgarity.

In any case, feminists will not be the arbiters of good taste if it becomes easier to harass, prosecute, and convict people on obscenity charges. Most of the people who want to censor girlie magazines are equally opposed to open discussion of issues that are of vital concern to women: rape, abortion, menstruation, contraception, lesbianism — in fact, the entire range of sexual experience from a woman's viewpoint.

Feminist writers and editors and filmmakers have limited financial resources: Confronted by a determined prosecutor, Hugh Hefner[1] will fare better than Susan Brownmiller. Would the Memphis jurors who convicted Harry Reems for his role in *Deep Throat* be inclined to take a more positive view of paintings of the female genitalia done by sensitive feminist artists? *Ms.* magazine has printed color reproductions of some of those art works; *Ms.* is already

banned from a number of high school libraries because someone considers it threatening and / or obscene.

Feminists who want to censor what they regard as harmful pornography have essentially the same motivation as other would-be censors: They want to use the power of the state to accomplish what they have been unable to achieve in the marketplace of ideas and images. The impulse to censor places no faith in the possibilities of democratic persuasion.

It isn't easy to persuade certain men that they have better uses for $1.95 each month than to spend it on a copy of *Hustler.* Well, then, give the men no choice in the matter.

I believe there is also a connection between the impulse toward censorship on the part of people who used to consider themselves civil libertarians and a more general desire to shift responsibility from individuals to institutions. When I saw the movie *Looking for Mr. Goodbar,* I was stunned by its series of visual images equating sex and violence, coupled with what seems to me the mindless message (a distortion of the fine Judith Rossner novel) that casual sex equals death. When I came out of the movie, I was even more shocked to see parents standing in line with children between the ages of ten and fourteen.

I simply don't know why a parent would take a child to see such a movie, any more than I understand why people feel they can't turn off a television set their child is watching. Whenever I say that, my friends tell me I don't know how it is because I don't have children. True, but I do have parents. When I was a child, they did turn off the TV. They didn't expect the Federal Communications Commission to do their job for them.

I am a First Amendment junkie. You can't OD on the First Amendment, because free speech is its own best antidote.

10

15

---

[1]**Hugh Hefner** Founder and longtime publisher of *Playboy* magazine.

SUMMARIZING JACOBY

Suppose we want to make a *rough summary*, more or less paragraph by paragraph, of Jacoby's essay. Our summary might look like this:

Paragraph 1. Although feminists usually support the First Amendment, when it comes to pornography many feminists take pretty much the position of those who oppose the Equal Rights Amendment and abortion and other causes of the women's movement.

Paragraph 2. Larry Flynt produces garbage, but I think his conviction represents an unconstitutional limitation of freedom of speech.

Paragraphs 3, 4. Feminists who want to control (censor) pornography argue that it poses a greater threat to women than similar repulsive speech poses to other groups. If feminists want to say that all offensive speech should be restricted, they can make a case, but it is absurd to say that pornography is a "greater threat" to women "than a march of neo-Nazis is to survivors of the extermination camps."

Paragraph 5. Trust in the First Amendment is not refuted by kiddie porn; kiddie porn is not a First Amendment issue but an issue of child abuse.

Paragraphs 6, 7, 8. Some feminists think censorship of pornography can be more "rational" than other kinds of censorship, but a picture of a nude woman strikes some women as base and others as "lovely." There is no unanimity.

Paragraphs 9, 10. If feminists censor girlie magazines, they will find that they are unwittingly helping opponents of the women's movement to censor discussions of rape, abortion, and so on. Some of the art in the feminist magazine *Ms.* would doubt-less be censored.

Paragraphs 11, 12. Like other would-be censors, feminists want to use the power of the state to achieve what they have not achieved in "the marketplace of ideas." They display a lack of faith in "democratic persuasion."

Paragraphs 13, 14. This attempt at censorship reveals a "desire to shift responsibility from individuals to institutions." The responsibility — for instance, to keep young people from equating sex with violence — is properly the parents'.

Paragraph 15. We can't have too much of the First Amendment.

Jacoby's **thesis** (i.e., major claim or chief proposition) — that any form of censorship of pornography is wrong — is clear enough, even as early as the end of paragraph 1, but it gains force from the **reasons** she offers throughout the essay. If we want to reduce our summary further, we might say that she supports her thesis by arguing several subsidiary points. Here we'll merely assert them briefly, but Jacoby **argues** them — that is, she gives reasons:

- Pornography can scarcely be thought of as more offensive than Nazism.
- Women disagree about which pictures are pornographic.
- Feminists who want to censor pornography will find that they help antifeminists to censor discussions of issues advocated by the women's movement.

- Feminists who favor censorship are in effect turning to the government to achieve what they haven't achieved in the free marketplace.

- One sees this abdication of responsibility in the fact that parents allow their children to watch unsuitable movies and television programs.

If we want to present a *brief summary* in the form of one coherent paragraph — perhaps as part of an essay arguing for or against — we might write something like the one shown in the paragraph below. (Of course, we would **introduce** it with a lead-in along these lines: "Susan Jacoby, writing in the *New York Times,* offers a forceful argument against censorship of pornography. Jacoby's view, briefly, is. . . .")

> When it comes to censorship of pornography, some feminists take a position shared by opponents of the feminist movement. They argue that pornography poses a greater threat to women than other forms of offensive speech offer to other groups, but this interpretation is simply a mistake. Pointing to kiddie porn is also a mistake, for kiddie porn is an issue involving not the First Amendment but child abuse. Feminists who support censorship of pornography will inadvertently aid those who wish to censor discussions of abortion and rape or censor art that is published in magazines such as *Ms.* The solution is not for individuals to turn to institutions (i.e., for the government to limit the First Amendment) but for individuals to accept the responsibility for teaching young people not to equate sex with violence.

In contrast, a *critical summary* of Jacoby — an evaluative summary in which we introduce our own ideas and examples — might look like this:

> Susan Jacoby, writing for the *New York Times* in 1978, offers a forceful argument against censorship of pornography, but one that does not have foresight of the Internet age and the new availability of extreme and exploitative forms of pornography. While she dismisses claims by feminists that pornography should be censored because it constitutes violence against women, what would Jacoby think of such things as "revenge porn" and "voyeuristic porn" today, or the array of elaborate sadistic fantasies readily available to anyone with access to a search engine? Jacoby says that censoring pornography is a step toward censoring art, and she proudly wears the tag "First Amendment junkie," ostensibly to protect what she finds artistic (such as images of female genitalia in *Ms.* Magazine). However, her argument does not help us account for these new forms of exploitation and violence disguised as art or "free speech." Perhaps she would see revenge porn and voyeur porn in the same the way she sees kiddie porn — not so much as an issue of free speech but as an issue of other crimes. Perhaps she would hold her position that we can avoid pornography by just "turning off the TV," but the new Internet pornography is intrusive, entering our lives and the lives of our children whether we like it or not. Education is part of the solution, Jacoby would agree, but we could also consider. . . .

The example above not only summarizes and applies the other techniques presented in this chapter (e.g., accounting for context and questioning definitions of terms and concepts) but also weaves them together with a central argument that offers a new response and a practicable solution.

Topics for Critical Thinking and Writing

1. What does Susan Jacoby mean by saying she is a "First Amendment junkie" (para. 15)?

2. The essay is primarily an argument against the desire of some feminists to censor the sort of pornography that appealed to some heterosexual adult males in 1978. How does the context of the article's publication reflect events and perspectives of that period? How are conditions different now, and how do these new contexts offer ways to support or challenge Jacoby's argument?

3. Evaluate the final paragraph as a conclusion. (Effective final paragraphs are not all of one sort. Some round off the essay by echoing one or more points from the opening; others suggest that the reader, having now seen the problem, should think further about it or act on it. No matter what form it takes, a good final paragraph should make the reader feel that the essay has come to a satisfactory conclusion, not a sudden breaking-off of the argument.)

4. This essay originally appeared in the *New York Times.* If you're unfamiliar with this newspaper, consult an issue or two in your school library. Next, in a paragraph, try to characterize the paper's readers — that is, Jacoby's audience.

5. Jacoby claims in paragraph 2 that she "believes . . . in an absolute interpretation of the First Amendment." What does such an interpretation involve? Would it permit shouting "Fire!" in a crowded theater even when there is no fire? Posting racist insults on the Internet? Spreading untruths about someone's past? (*Does* the First Amendment, as actually interpreted by the Supreme Court today, permit any or all of these claims? Consult your reference librarian for help in answering this question.)

6. Jacoby implies that permitting prosecution of persons on obscenity charges will lead eventually to censorship of "open discussion" of important issues such as "rape, abortion, menstruation, contraception, lesbianism" (para. 9). Do you find her fears convincing? Does she give evidence to support her claim? Explain your responses.

A CHECKLIST FOR GETTING STARTED

☐ Have I adequately previewed the work?

☐ Can I state the thesis?

☐ If I have written a summary, is it accurate?

☐ Does my summary mention all the chief points?

☐ If there are inconsistencies, are they in the summary or the original selection?

☐ Will my summary be clear and helpful?

☐ Have I considered the audience for whom the author is writing?

ZACHARY SHEMTOB AND DAVID LAT

Zachary Shemtob teaches criminal justice at Central Connecticut State University; David Lat is a former federal prosecutor. Their essay originally appeared in the New York Times *in 2011.*

Executions Should Be Televised

Earlier this month, Georgia conducted its third execution this year. This would have passed relatively unnoticed if not for a controversy surrounding its videotaping. Lawyers for the condemned inmate, Andrew Grant DeYoung, had persuaded a judge to allow the recording of his last moments as part of an effort to obtain evidence on whether lethal injection caused unnecessary suffering.

Though he argued for videotaping, one of Mr. DeYoung's defense lawyers, Brian Kammer, spoke out against releasing the footage to the public. "It's a horrible thing that Andrew DeYoung had to go through," Mr. Kammer said, "and it's not for the public to see that."

We respectfully disagree. Executions in the United States ought to be made public.

Right now, executions are generally open only to the press and a few select witnesses. For the rest of us, the vague contours are provided in the morning paper. Yet a functioning democracy demands maximum accountability and transparency. As long as executions remain behind closed doors, those are impossible. The people should have the right to see what is being done in their name and with their tax dollars.

This is particularly relevant given the current debate on whether specific methods of lethal injection constitute cruel and unusual punishment and therefore violate the Constitution.

There is a dramatic difference between reading or hearing of such an event and observing it through image and sound. (This is obvious to those who saw the footage of Saddam Hussein's hanging in 2006 or the death of Neda Agha-Soltan during the protests in Iran in 2009.) We are not calling for opening executions completely to the public — conducting them before a live crowd — but rather for broadcasting them live or recording them for future release, on the Web or TV.

When another Georgia inmate, Roy Blankenship, was executed in June, the prisoner jerked his head, grimaced, gasped, and lurched, according to a medical expert's affidavit. The *Atlanta Journal-Constitution* reported that Mr. DeYoung, executed in the same manner, "showed no violent signs in death." Voters should not have to rely on media accounts to understand what takes place when a man is put to death.

Cameras record legislative sessions and presidential debates, and courtrooms are allowing greater television access. When he was an Illinois state senator, President Obama successfully pressed for the videotaping of homicide interrogations and confessions. The most serious penalty of all surely demands equal if not greater scrutiny.

Opponents of our proposal offer many objections. State lawyers argued that making Mr. DeYoung's execution public raised safety concerns. While rioting and pickpocketing occasionally marred executions in the public square in the eighteenth and nineteenth centuries, modern security and technology obviate this concern. Little would change in the death chamber; the faces of witnesses and executioners could be edited out, for privacy reasons, before a video was released.

Of greater concern is the possibility that broadcasting executions could have a numbing effect. Douglas A. Berman, a law professor, fears that people might come to equate human executions with putting pets to sleep. Yet this seems overstated. While public indifference might result over time, the initial broadcasts would undoubtedly get attention and stir debate.

Still others say that broadcasting an execution would offer an unbalanced picture—making the condemned seem helpless and sympathetic, while keeping the victims of the crime out of the picture. But this is beside the point: the defendant is being executed precisely because a jury found that his crimes were so heinous that he deserved to die.

Ultimately the main opposition to our idea seems to flow from an unthinking disgust—a sense that public executions are archaic, noxious, even barbarous. Albert Camus related in his essay "Reflections on the Guillotine" that viewing executions turned him against capital punishment. The legal scholar John D. Bessler suggests that public executions might have the same effect on the public today; Sister Helen Prejean, the death penalty abolitionist, has urged just such a strategy.

That is not our view. We leave open the possibility that making executions public could strengthen support for them; undecided viewers might find them less disturbing than anticipated.

Like many of our fellow citizens, we are deeply conflicted about the death penalty and how it has been administered. Our focus is on accountability and openness. As Justice John Paul Stevens wrote in *Baze v. Rees*, a 2008 case involving a challenge to lethal injection, capital punishment is too often "the product of habit and inattention rather than an acceptable deliberative process that weighs the costs and risks of administering that penalty against its identifiable benefits."

A democracy demands a citizenry as informed as possible about the costs and benefits of society's ultimate punishment.

Topics for Critical Thinking and Writing

1. In paragraphs 9–13, the authors discuss objections to their position. Are you satisfied with their responses to the objections, or do you think they do not satisfactorily dispose of one or more of the objections? Explain.

2. In paragraph 4, the authors say that "[t]he people should have the right to see what is being done in their name and with their tax dollars." But in terms of *rights*, should the person being executed have a right to die in privacy? Articulate a position that weighs the public's right to see what is being done with its tax dollars against death row prisoners' rights to privacy.

3. In the concluding paragraph, the authors imply that their proposal, if enacted, will help to inform citizens "about the costs and benefits of society's ultimate punishment." Do you agree? Why, or why not? What reasons do the authors offer to support their proposal?

4. In your view, what is the strongest argument the authors give on behalf of their proposal? What is the weakest? Explain why you made these choices.

GWEN WILDE

This essay was written for a composition course at Tufts University.

Why the Pledge of Allegiance Should Be Revised (Student Essay)

All Americans are familiar with the Pledge of Allegiance, even if they cannot always recite it perfectly, but probably relatively few know that the *original* Pledge did *not* include the words "under God." The original Pledge of Allegiance, published in the September 8, 1892, issue of the *Youth's Companion,* ran thus:

> I pledge allegiance to my flag, and to the Republic for which it stands: one Nation indivisible, with Liberty and justice for all (Djupe 329).

In 1923, at the first National Flag Conference in Washington, D.C., it was argued that immigrants might be confused by the words "my Flag," and it was proposed that the words be changed to "the Flag of the United States." The following year it was changed again, to "the Flag of the United States of America," and this wording became the official — or, rather, unofficial — wording, unofficial because no wording had ever been nationally adopted (Djupe 329).

In 1942, the United States Congress included the Pledge in the United States Flag Code (4 USC 4, 2006), thus for the first time officially sanctioning the Pledge. In 1954, President Dwight D. Eisenhower approved adding the words "under God." Thus, since 1954 the Pledge reads:

> I pledge allegiance to the flag of the United States of America, and to the Republic for which it stands: one nation under God, indivisible, with Liberty and Justice for all. (Djupe 329)

In my view, the addition of the words "under God" is inappropriate, and they are needlessly divisive — an odd addition indeed to a nation that is said to be "indivisible."

Very simply put, the Pledge in its latest 5 form requires all Americans to say something that some Americans do not believe. I say "requires" because although the courts have ruled that students may not be compelled to recite the Pledge, in effect peer pressure does compel all but the bravest to join in the recitation. When President Eisenhower authorized the change, he said, "In this way we are reaffirming the transcendence of religious faith in America's heritage and future; in this way we shall constantly strengthen those spiritual weapons which forever will be our country's most powerful resource in peace and war" (Sterner).

Exactly what did Eisenhower mean when he spoke of "the transcendence of religious faith in America's heritage" and when he spoke of "spiritual weapons"? I am not sure what "the transcendence of religious faith in America's heritage" means. Of course, many Americans have been and are deeply religious — no one doubts it — but the phrase certainly goes far beyond saying that many Americans have been devout. In any case, many Americans have *not* been devout, and many Americans have *not* believed in "spiritual weapons," but they have nevertheless been patriotic Americans. Some of them have fought and died to keep America free.

In short, the words "under God" cannot be uttered in good faith by many Americans. True, something like 70 or even 80% of Americans say they are affiliated with some form of Christianity, and approximately another 3% say they are Jewish. I don't have the figures for persons of other faiths, but in any case we can surely all agree that although a majority of Americans say they have a religious affiliation, nevertheless several million Americans do *not* believe in God.

If one remains silent while others are reciting the Pledge, or even if one remains silent only while others are speaking the words "under God," one is open to the charge that one is unpatriotic, is "unwilling to recite the Pledge of Allegiance." In the Pledge, patriotism is connected with religious belief, and it is this connection that makes it divisive and (to be blunt) un-American. Admittedly, the belief is not very specific: one is not required to say that one believes in the divinity of Jesus, or in the power of Jehovah, but the fact remains, one is required to express belief in a divine power, and if one doesn't express this belief one is — according to the Pledge — somehow not fully an American, maybe even un-American.

Please notice that I am not arguing that the Pledge is unconstitutional. I understand that the First Amendment to the Constitution says that "Congress shall make no law respecting an establishment of religion, or prohibiting the free exercise thereof." I am not arguing that the words "under God" in the Pledge add up to the "establishment of religion," but they certainly do assert a religious doctrine. Like the words "In God we trust," found on all American money, the words "under God" express an idea that many Americans do not hold, and there is no reason why these Americans — loyal people who may be called upon to defend the country with their lives — should be required to say that America is a nation "under God."

It has been argued, even by members of the Supreme Court, that the words "under God" are not to be taken terribly seriously, not to be taken to say what they seem to say. For instance, Chief Justice Rehnquist wrote:

> To give the parent of such a child a sort of "heckler's veto" over a patriotic ceremony willingly participated in by other students, simply because the Pledge of Allegiance contains the descriptive phrase "under God," is an unwarranted extension of the establishment clause, an extension which would have the unfortunate effect of prohibiting a commendable patriotic observance. (qtd. in Stephens et al. 104)

Chief Justice Rehnquist here calls "under God" a "descriptive phrase," but descriptive of *what*? If a phrase is a "descriptive phrase," it describes something, real or imagined. For many Americans, this phrase does *not* describe a reality. These Americans may perhaps be mistaken — if so, they may learn of their error at Judgment Day — but the fact is, millions of intelligent Americans do not believe in God.

Notice, too, that Chief Justice Rehnquist goes on to say that reciting the Pledge is "a commendable patriotic observance." Exactly. That is my point. It is a *patriotic* observance, and it should not be connected with religion. When we announce that we respect the flag — that we are loyal Americans — we should not also have to announce that we hold a particular religious belief, in this case a belief in monotheism, a belief that there is a God and that God rules.

One other argument defending the words "under God" is often heard: The words "In God We Trust" appear on our money. It is claimed that these words on American money are analogous to the words "under God" in the Pledge. But the situation really is very different. When we hand some coins over, or some paper money, we are concentrating on the business transaction, and we are not making any affirmation about God or our country. But when we recite the Pledge — even if we remain silent at the point when we are supposed to say "under God" — we are very conscious that we are supposed to make this affirmation, an affirmation that many Americans cannot in good faith make, even though they certainly can unthinkingly hand over (or accept) money with the words "In God We Trust."

Because I believe that *reciting* the Pledge is to be taken seriously, with a full awareness of the words that is quite different from when we hand over some money, I cannot understand the recent comment of Supreme Court Justice Souter, who in a case said that the phrase "under God" is "so tepid, so diluted, so far from compulsory prayer, that it should, in effect, be beneath the constitutional radar" (qtd. in "Guide"). I don't follow his reasoning that the phrase should be "beneath the constitutional radar," but in any case I am willing to put aside the issue of constitutionality. I am willing to grant that this phrase does not in any significant sense signify the "establishment of religion" (prohibited by the First Amendment) in the United States. I insist, nevertheless, that the phrase is neither "tepid" nor "diluted." It means what it says — it *must* and *should* mean what it says, to everyone who utters it — and, since millions of loyal Americans cannot say it, it should not be included in a statement in which Americans affirm their loyalty to our great country.

15 In short, the Pledge, which ought to unite all of us, is divisive; it includes a phrase that many patriotic Americans cannot bring themselves to utter. Yes, they can remain silent when others recite these two words, but, again, why should they have to remain silent? The Pledge of Allegiance should be something that *everyone* can say, say out loud, and say with pride. We hear much talk of returning to the ideas of the Founding Fathers. The Founding Fathers did not create the Pledge of Allegiance, but we do know that they never mentioned God in the Constitution. Indeed, the only reference to religion, in the so-called establishment clause of the First Amendment, says, again, that "Congress shall make no law respecting an establishment of religion, or prohibiting the free exercise thereof." Those who wish to exercise religion are indeed free to do so, but the place to do so is not in a pledge that is required of all schoolchildren and of all new citizens.

WORKS CITED

Djupe, Paul A. "Pledge of Allegiance." *Encyclopedia of American Religion and Politics*. Edited by Paul A. Djupe and Laura R. Olson, Facts on File, 2003.

"Guide to Covering 'Under God' Pledge Decision." *ReligionLink*, 17 Sept. 2005, religionlink.com/database/guide-to-covering-under-god/.

Stephens, Otis H., et al., editors. *American Constitutional Law*. 6th ed., vol. 1, Cengage Learning, 2014.

Sterner, Doug. "The Pledge of Allegiance." *Home of Heroes*, homeofheroes.com/hallofheroes/1st_floor/flag/1bfc_pledge_print.html. Accessed 13 Apr. 2016.

Topics for Critical Thinking and Writing

1. Summarize the essay in a paragraph.

2. What terms and concepts are defined in this essay? Explain how one term or concept is defined.

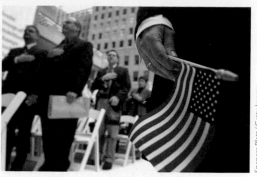

Spencer Platt / Getty Images

3. Does the writer, Gwen Wilde, give enough weight to the fact that no one is compelled to recite the Pledge? Explain your answer.

4. What arguments does Wilde offer in support of her position?

5. Does Wilde show an adequate awareness of counterarguments? Identify one place where she raises and refutes a counterargument.

6. What is Wilde's strongest argument? Are any of her arguments notably weak? If so, how could they be strengthened?

7. What assumptions — tacit or explicit — does Wilde make? Do you agree or disagree with them? Explain your response.

8. What do you take the words "under God" to mean? Do they mean "under God's special protection"? Or "acting in accordance with God's rules"? Or "accountable to God"? Or something else? Explain.

9. Chief Justice Rehnquist wrote that the words "under God" are a "descriptive phrase." What do you think he meant by this?

10. What is the purpose of the Pledge of Allegiance? Does the phrase "under God" promote or defeat that purpose? Explain your answer.

11. What do you think about substituting "with religious freedom" for "under God"? Set forth your response, supported by reasons, in about 250 words.

12. Wilde makes a distinction between the reference to God on U.S. money and the reference to God in the Pledge. Do you agree with her that the two cases are not analogous? Explain.

13. What readers might *not* agree with Wilde's arguments? What values do they hold? How might you try to persuade an audience who disagrees with Wilde to consider her proposal?

14. Putting aside your own views on the issue, what grade would you give this essay as a work of argumentative writing? Support your evaluation with reasons.

A CASEBOOK FOR CRITICAL READING:
Should Some Kinds of Speech Be Censored?

Now we present a series of essays that are somewhat more difficult than Jacoby's, Shemtob and Lat's, and Wilde's but that address in more detail some of the free speech issues raised by the earlier essays. We suggest you read each one through to get its gist and then read it a second time, writing down after each paragraph a sentence or two summarizing the paragraph. Keep in mind the First Amendment to the Constitution, which reads, in its entirety, as follows:

> Congress shall make no law respecting an establishment of religion, or prohibiting the free exercise thereof; or abridging the freedom of speech, or of the press; or the right of the people peaceably to assemble, and to petition the government for a redress of grievances.

SUSAN BROWNMILLER

Susan Brownmiller (b. 1935), a graduate of Cornell University, is the founder of Women against Pornography and the author of several books, including Against Our Will: Men, Women, and Rape *(1975). The essay reprinted here is from* Take Back the Night *(1980), a collection of essays edited by Laura Lederer. The book has been called "the manifesto of antipornography feminism."*

Let's Put Pornography Back in the Closet

Free speech is one of the great foundations on which our democracy rests. I am old enough to remember the Hollywood Ten, the screenwriters who went to jail in the late 1940s because they refused to testify before a congressional committee about their political affiliations. They tried to use the First Amendment as a defense, but they went to jail because in those days there were few civil liberties lawyers around who cared to champion the First Amendment right to free speech, when the speech concerned the Communist Party.

The Hollywood Ten were correct in claiming the First Amendment. Its high purpose is the protection of unpopular ideas and political dissent. In the dark, cold days of the 1950s, few civil libertarians were willing to declare themselves First Amendment absolutists. But in the brighter, though frantic, days of the 1960s, the principle of protecting unpopular political speech was gradually strengthened.

It is fair to say now that the battle has largely been won. Even the American Nazi Party has found itself the beneficiary of the dedicated, tireless work of the American Civil Liberties Union. But — and please notice the quotation marks coming up — "To equate the free and robust exchange of ideas and political debate with commercial exploitation of obscene material demeans the grand conception of the First Amendment and its high purposes in the historic struggle for freedom. It is a misuse of the great guarantees of free speech and free press."

I didn't say that, although I wish I had, for I think the words are thrilling. Chief Justice Warren Burger said it in 1973, in the United States Supreme Court's majority opinion in *Miller v. California*. During the same decades that the right to political free speech was being strengthened in the courts, the nation's obscenity laws also were undergoing extensive revision.

It's amazing to recall that in 1934 the question of whether James Joyce's *Ulysses* should be banned as pornographic actually went before the Court. The battle to protect *Ulysses* as a work of literature with redeeming social value was won. In later decades, Henry Miller's *Tropic* books, *Lady Chatterley's Lover,* and the *Memoirs of Fanny Hill* also were adjudged not obscene. These decisions have been important to me. As the author of *Against Our Will,* a study of the history of rape that does contain explicit sexual material, I shudder to think how my book would have fared if James Joyce, D. H. Lawrence, and Henry Miller hadn't gone before me.

I am not a fan of *Chatterley* or the *Tropic* books, I should quickly mention. They are not to my literary taste, nor do I think they represent female sexuality with any degree of accuracy. But I would hardly suggest that we ban them. Such a suggestion wouldn't get very far anyway. The battle to protect these books is ancient history. Time does march on, quite methodically. What, then, is unlawfully obscene, and what does the First Amendment have to do with it?

In the *Miller* case of 1973 (not Henry Miller, by the way, but a porn distributor who sent unsolicited stuff through the mails), the Court came up with new guidelines that it hoped would strengthen obscenity laws by giving more power to the states. What it did in actuality was throw everything into confusion. It set up a three-part test by which materials can be adjudged obscene. The materials are obscene if they depict patently offensive, hard-core sexual conduct; lack serious scientific, literary, artistic, or political value; and appeal to the prurient interest of an average person — as measured by contemporary community standards.

"Patently offensive," "prurient interest," and "hard-core" are indeed words to conjure with. "Contemporary community standards" are what we're trying to redefine. The feminist objection to pornography is not based on prurience, which the dictionary defines as lustful,

itching desire. We are not opposed to sex and desire, with or without the itch, and we certainly believe that explicit sexual material has its place in literature, art, science, and education. Here we part company rather swiftly with old-line conservatives who don't want sex education in the high schools, for example.

No, the feminist objection to pornography is based on our belief that pornography represents hatred of women, that pornography's intent is to humiliate, degrade, and dehumanize the female body for the purpose of erotic stimulation and pleasure. We are unalterably opposed to the presentation of the female body being stripped, bound, raped, tortured, mutilated, and murdered in the name of commercial entertainment and free speech.

These images, which are standard pornographic fare, have nothing to do with the hallowed right of political dissent. They have everything to do with the creation of a cultural climate in which a rapist feels he is merely giving in to a normal urge and a woman is encouraged to believe that sexual masochism is healthy, liberated fun. Justice Potter Stewart once said about hard-core pornography, "You know it when you see it," and that certainly used to be true. In the good old days, pornography looked awful. It was cheap and sleazy, and there was no mistaking it for art.

Nowadays, since the porn industry has become a multimillion dollar business, visual technology has been employed in its service. Pornographic movies are skillfully filmed and edited, pornographic still shots using the newest tenets of good design artfully grace the covers of *Hustler, Penthouse,* and *Playboy,* and the public — and the courts — are sadly confused.

The Supreme Court neglected to define "hard-core" in the *Miller* decision. This was a mistake. If "hard-core" refers only to explicit sexual intercourse, then that isn't good enough.

When women or children or men — no matter how artfully — are shown tortured or terrorized in the service of sex, that's obscene. And "patently offensive," I would hope, to our "contemporary community standards."

Justice William O. Douglas wrote in his dissent to the *Miller* case that no one is "compelled to look." This is hardly true. To buy a paper at the corner newsstand is to subject oneself to a forcible immersion in pornography, to be demeaned by an array of dehumanized, chopped-up parts of the female anatomy, packaged like cuts of meat at the supermarket. I happen to like my body and I work hard at the gym to keep it in good shape, but I am embarrassed for my body and for the bodies of all women when I see the fragmented parts of us so frivolously, and so flagrantly, displayed.

Some constitutional theorists (Justice Douglas was one) have maintained that any obscenity law is a serious abridgement of free speech. Others (and Justice Earl Warren was one) have maintained that the First Amendment was never intended to protect obscenity. We live quite compatibly with a host of free-speech abridgements. There are restraints against false and misleading advertising or statements — shouting "fire" without cause in a crowded movie theater, etc. — that do not threaten, but strengthen, our societal values. Restrictions on the public display of pornography belong in this category.

The distinction between permission to 15 publish and permission to display publicly is an essential one and one which I think consonant with First Amendment principles. Justice Burger's words which I quoted above support this without question. We are not saying "Smash the presses" or "Ban the bad ones," but simply "Get the stuff out of our sight." Let the legislatures decide — using realistic and humane contemporary community standards — what can be displayed and what cannot. The courts, after all, will be the final arbiters.

Topics for Critical Thinking and Writing

1. Objecting to Justice Douglas's remark that no one is "'compelled to look'" (para. 13), Brownmiller says, "This is hardly true. To buy a paper at the corner newsstand is to subject oneself to a forcible immersion in pornography, to be demeaned by an array of dehumanized, chopped-up parts of the female anatomy, packaged like cuts of meat at the supermarket." How does the ubiquity (high visibility) of pornography in the Internet age trouble Douglas's argument and assist Brownmiller's? How does the advent of the Internet hurt Brownmiller's call for restrictions on what can be shown?

2. Who is Brownmiller's intended audience? Do you think she holds their attention? Why, or why not?

3. When Brownmiller attempts to restate the "three-part test" for obscenity established by the Supreme Court in *Miller v. California*, she writes (para. 7): "The materials are obscene if they depict . . ." and so on. She should have written: "The materials are obscene if and only if they depict . . ." and so on. Explain what is wrong here with her "if," and why "if and only if" is needed.

4. When Brownmiller accuses "the public — and the courts" of being "sadly confused" (para. 11), what does she think is making them confused? The definition of *pornography* or

obscenity? The effects of such literature on men and women? Something else? Explain your response.

5. In paragraph 14, Brownmiller reminds us that we already live quite "compatibly" with some "free-speech abridgements." Her examples are that we may not make false statements such as shouting "fire" in a crowded theater and may not issue misleading advertisements. Do you think that these widely accepted restrictions are valid evidence in arguing on behalf of limiting the display of what Brownmiller considers pornography? Why, or why not?

6. Brownmiller insists that defenders of the First Amendment, who will surely oppose laws that interfere with the freedom to publish, need not condemn laws that regulate the freedom to publicly display pornographic publications. Do you agree? Why, or why not? Suppose a publisher insists that he cannot sell his product at a profit unless he is permitted to display it to advantage and that restriction on the latter amounts to interference with his freedom to publish. How might Brownmiller reply?

7. In her last paragraph, Brownmiller says that "contemporary community standards" should be decisive. Can it be argued that because standards vary from one community to another and from time to time even in the same place, her recommendation subjects the rights of a minority to the whims of a majority? Why, or why not? (The Bill of Rights, after all, was supposed to safeguard the constitutional rights of the minority from the possible tyranny of the majority.) How is "contemporary community standards" defined in the essay? How do you define the phrase?

CHARLES R. LAWRENCE III

Charles R. Lawrence III (b. 1943), author of numerous articles in law journals and coauthor of We Won't Go Back: Making the Case for Affirmative Action *(1997), teaches law at Georgetown University. This essay originally appeared in the* Chronicle of Higher Education *(October 25, 1989), a publication read chiefly by faculty and administrators at colleges and universities. An amplified version of the essay appeared in the* Duke Law Journal *(February 1990).*

On Racist Speech

I have spent the better part of my life as a dissenter. As a high school student, I was threatened with suspension for my refusal to participate in a civil defense drill, and I have been a conspicuous consumer of my First Amendment liberties ever since. There are very strong reasons for protecting even racist speech. Perhaps the most important of these is that such protection reinforces our society's commitment to tolerance as a value, and that by protecting bad speech from government regulation, we will be forced to combat it as a community.

But I also have a deeply felt apprehension about the resurgence of racial violence and the corresponding rise in the incidence of verbal and symbolic assault and harassment to which blacks and other traditionally subjugated and excluded groups are subjected. I am troubled by the way the debate has been framed in response to the recent surge of racist incidents on college and university campuses and in response to some universities' attempts to regulate harassing speech. The problem has been framed as one in which the liberty of free speech is in conflict with the elimination of racism. I believe this has placed the bigot on the moral high ground and fanned the rising flames of racism.

Above all, I am troubled that we have not listened to the real victims, that we have shown so little understanding of their injury, and that we have abandoned those whose race, gender, or sexual preference continues to make them second-class citizens. It seems to me a very sad irony that the first instinct of civil libertarians has been to challenge even the smallest, most narrowly framed efforts by universities to provide black and other minority students with the protection the Constitution guarantees them.

The landmark case of *Brown v. Board of Education* is not a case that we normally think of as a case about speech. But *Brown* can be broadly read as articulating the principle of equal citizenship. *Brown* held that segregated schools were inherently unequal because of the *message* that segregation conveyed — that black children were an untouchable caste, unfit to go to school with white children. If we understand the necessity of eliminating the system of signs and symbols that signal the inferiority of blacks, then we should hesitate before proclaiming that all racist speech that stops short of physical violence must be defended.

University officials who have formulated 5 policies to respond to incidents of racial harassment have been characterized in the press as "thought police," but such policies generally do nothing more than impose sanctions against intentional face-to-face insults. When racist speech takes the form of face-to-face insults, catcalls, or other assaultive speech aimed at an individual or small group of persons, it falls directly within the "fighting words" exception to First Amendment protection. The Supreme Court has held that words which "by their very utterance inflict injury or tend to incite an immediate breach of the peace" are not protected by the First Amendment.

If the purpose of the First Amendment is to foster the greatest amount of speech, racial insults disserve that purpose. Assaultive racist speech functions as a preemptive strike. The invective is experienced as a blow, not as a proffered idea, and once the blow is struck, it is unlikely that a dialogue will follow. Racial insults are particularly undeserving of First Amendment protection because the perpetrator's intention is not to discover truth or initiate dialogue but to injure the victim. In most situations, members of minority groups realize that they are likely to lose if they respond to epithets by fighting and are forced to remain silent and submissive.

Courts have held that offensive speech may not be regulated in public forums such as streets where the listener may avoid the speech by moving on, but the regulation of otherwise protected speech has been permitted when the speech invades the privacy of the unwilling listener's home or when the unwilling listener cannot avoid the speech. Racist posters, fliers, and graffiti in dormitories, bathrooms, and other common living spaces would seem to clearly fall within the reasoning of these cases. Minority students should not be required to remain in their rooms in order to avoid racial assault. Minimally, they should find a safe haven in their dorms and in all other common rooms that are a part of their daily routine.

I would also argue that the university's responsibility for ensuring that these students receive an equal educational opportunity provides a compelling justification for regulations that ensure them safe passage in all common areas. A minority student should not have to risk becoming the target of racially assaulting speech every time he or she chooses to walk across campus. Regulating vilifying speech that cannot be anticipated or avoided would not preclude announced speeches and rallies — situations that would give minority-group members and their allies the chance to organize counterdemonstrations or avoid the speech altogether.

The most commonly advanced argument against the regulation of racist speech proceeds something like this: We recognize that minority groups suffer pain and injury as the result of racist speech, but we must allow this hate mongering for the benefit of society as a whole. Freedom of speech is the lifeblood of our democratic system. It is especially important for minorities because often it is their only vehicle for rallying support for the redress of their grievances. It will be impossible to formulate a prohibition so precise that it will prevent the racist speech you want to suppress without catching in the same net all kinds of speech that it would be unconscionable for a democratic society to suppress.

Whenever we make such arguments, we 10 are striking a balance on the one hand between our concern for the continued free flow of ideas and the democratic process dependent on that flow, and, on the other, our desire to further the cause of equality. There can be no meaningful discussion of how we should reconcile our commitment to equality and our commitment to free speech until it is acknowledged that there is real harm inflicted by racist speech and that this harm is far from trivial.

To engage in a debate about the First Amendment and racist speech without a full understanding of the nature and extent of that harm is to risk making the First Amendment an instrument of domination rather than a vehicle of liberation. We have not all known the experience of victimization by racist, misogynist, and homophobic speech, nor do we equally share the burden of the societal harm it inflicts. We are often quick to say that we have heard the cry of the victims when we have not.

The *Brown* case is again instructive because it speaks directly to the psychic injury inflicted by racist speech by noting that the symbolic message of segregation affected "the hearts and minds" of Negro children "in a way unlikely ever to be undone." Racial epithets and harassment often cause deep emotional scarring and feelings of anxiety and fear that pervade every aspect of a victim's life.

Brown also recognized that black children did not have an equal opportunity to learn and participate in the school community if they bore the additional burden of being subjected to the humiliation and psychic assault contained in the message of segregation. University students bear an analogous burden when they are forced to live and work in an environment where at any moment they may be subjected to denigrating verbal harassment and assault. The same injury was addressed by the Supreme Court when it held that sexual harassment that creates a hostile or abusive work environment violates the ban on sex discrimination in employment of Title VII of the Civil Rights Act of 1964.

Carefully drafted university regulations would bar the use of words as assault weapons and leave unregulated even the most heinous of ideas when those ideas are presented at times and places and in manners that provide an opportunity for reasoned rebuttal or escape from immediate injury. The history of the development of the right to free speech has been one of carefully evaluating the importance of free expression and its effects on other important societal interests. We have drawn the line between protected and unprotected speech before without dire results. (Courts have, for example, exempted from the protection of the First Amendment obscene speech and speech that disseminates official secrets, that defames or libels another person, or that is used to form a conspiracy or monopoly.)

Blacks and other people of color are skepti-cal about the argument that even the most injurious speech must remain unregulated because, in an unregulated marketplace of ideas, the best ones will rise to the top and gain acceptance. Our experience tells us quite the opposite. We have seen too many good liberal politicians shy away from the issues that might brand them as being too closely allied with us.

Whenever we decide that racist speech must be tolerated because of the importance of maintaining societal tolerance for all unpopular speech, we are asking blacks and other subordinated groups to bear the burden for the good of all. We must be careful that the ease with which we strike the balance against the regulation of racist speech is in no way influenced by the fact that the cost will be borne by others. We must be certain that those who will pay that price are fairly represented in our deliberations and that they are heard.

At the core of the argument that we should resist all government regulation of speech is the ideal that the best cure for bad speech is good, that ideas that affirm equality and the worth of all individuals will ultimately prevail. This is an empty ideal unless those of us who would fight racism are vigilant and unequivocal in that fight. We must look for ways to offer assistance and support to students whose speech and political participation are chilled in a climate of racial harassment.

Civil rights lawyers might consider suing on behalf of blacks whose right to an equal education is denied by a university's failure to ensure a nondiscriminatory educational climate or conditions of employment. We must embark upon the development of a First Amendment jurisprudence grounded in the reality of our history and our contemporary experience. We must think hard about how best to launch legal attacks against the most indefensible forms of hate speech. Good lawyers can create exceptions and narrow interpretations that limit the harm of hate speech without opening the floodgates of censorship.

Everyone concerned with these issues must find ways to engage actively in actions that resist and counter the racist ideas that we would have the First Amendment protect. If we fail in this, the victims of hate speech must rightly assume that we are on the oppressors' side.

Topics for Critical Thinking and Writing

1. Summarize Charles Lawrence's essay in a paragraph. (You may find it useful first to summarize each paragraph in a sentence and then to revise these summary sentences into a paragraph.)

2. In one sentence, state Lawrence's thesis (his main point).

3. Why do you suppose Lawrence included his first paragraph? What does it contribute to his argument?

4. In paragraph 8, Lawrence speaks of "racially assaulting speech" and of "vilifying speech." It's easy to think of words that fit these descriptions, but what about other words? Is *Uncle Tom,* used by an African American about another African American who is eager to please whites, an example of "racially assaulting speech"? Or consider the word *gay.* Surely this word is acceptable because it's widely used by homosexuals, but what about *queer* (used by some homosexuals but usually derogatory when used by heterosexuals)? What might make these words seem "assaulting" or "vilifying"?

5. Think about the provisions in the Code of Conduct of Shippensburg University in Pennsylvania. The code says that each student has a "primary" right to be free from harassment, intimidation, physical harm, and emotional abuse and has a "secondary" right to express personal beliefs in a manner that does not "provoke, harass, demean, intimidate, or harm" another. The code prohibits conduct that "annoys, threatens, or alarms a person or group," such as sexual harassment, "innuendo," "comments, insults," "propositions," "humor / jokes about sex or gender-specific traits," and "suggestive or insulting sounds, leering, whistling, [and] obscene gestures." The university's president has said (according to the *New York Times,* April 24, 2003, p. A23) that the university encourages free speech as a means to examine ideas and that the university is "committed to the principle that this discussion be conducted appropriately. We do have expectations that our students will conduct themselves in a civil manner that allows them to express their opinions without interfering with the rights of others." Use this material to generate your own thoughts about speech on college campuses.

6. Find out if your college or university has a code — perhaps online — governing hate speech. If it does, evaluate it. If your college has no such code, make a case for why such a policy should be readily available to students and faculty. Compose a blog entry evaluating your current code, or draft your own code.

DEREK BOK

Derek Bok was born in 1930 in Bryn Mawr, Pennsylvania, and educated at Stanford University and Harvard University, where he received a law degree. From 1971 to 1991 he served as president of Harvard University. The following essay, first published in the Boston Globe *in 1991, was prompted by the display of Confederate flags hung from a window of a Harvard dormitory.*

Protecting Freedom of Expression on the Campus

For several years, universities have been struggling with the problem of trying to reconcile the rights of free speech with the desire to avoid racial tension. In recent weeks, such a controversy has sprung up at Harvard. Two students hung Confederate flags in public view, upsetting students who equate the Confederacy with slavery. A third student tried to protest the flags by displaying a swastika.

These incidents have provoked much discussion and disagreement. Some students have urged that Harvard require the removal

BOK | PROTECTING FREEDOM OF EXPRESSION ON THE CAMPUS   75

of symbols that offend many members of the community. Others reply that such symbols are a form of free speech and should be protected.

Different universities have resolved similar conflicts in different ways. Some have enacted codes to protect their communities from forms of speech that are deemed to be insensitive to the feelings of other groups. Some have refused to impose such restrictions.

It is important to distinguish between the appropriateness of such communications and their status under the First Amendment. The fact that speech is protected by the First Amendment does not necessarily mean that it is right, proper, or civil. I am sure that the vast majority of Harvard students believe that hanging a Confederate flag in public view — or displaying a swastika in response — is insensitive and unwise because any satisfaction it gives to the students who display these symbols is far outweighed by the discomfort it causes to many others.

I share this view and regret that the stu- 5 dents involved saw fit to behave in this fashion. Whether or not they merely wished to manifest their pride in the South — or to demonstrate the insensitivity of hanging Confederate flags, by mounting another offensive symbol in return — they must have known that they would upset many fellow students and ignore the decent regard for the feelings of others so essential to building and preserving a strong and harmonious community.

To disapprove of a particular form of communication, however, is not enough to justify prohibiting it. We are faced with a clear example of the conflict between our commitment to free speech and our desire to foster a community founded on mutual respect. Our society has wrestled with this problem for many years. Interpreting the First Amendment, the Supreme Court has clearly struck the balance in favor of free speech.

While communities do have the right to regulate speech in order to uphold aesthetic standards (avoiding defacement of buildings) or to protect the public from disturbing noise, rules of this kind must be applied across the board and cannot be enforced selectively to prohibit certain kinds of messages but not others.

Under the Supreme Court's rulings, as I read them, the display of swastikas or Confederate flags clearly falls within the protection of the free-speech clause of the First Amendment and cannot be forbidden simply because it offends the feelings of many members of the community. These rulings apply to all agencies of government, including public universities.

Although it is unclear to what extent the First Amendment is enforceable against private institutions, I have difficulty understanding why a university such as Harvard should have less free speech than the surrounding society — or than a public university.

One reason why the power of censorship 10 is so dangerous is that it is extremely difficult to decide when a particular communication is offensive enough to warrant prohibition or to weigh the degree of offensiveness against the potential value of the communication. If we begin to forbid flags, it is only a short step to prohibiting offensive speakers.

I suspect that no community will become humane and caring by restricting what its members can say. The worst offenders will simply find other ways to irritate and insult.

In addition, once we start to declare certain things "offensive," with all the excitement and attention that will follow, I fear that much ingenuity will be exerted trying to test the limits, much time will be expended trying to draw tenuous distinctions, and the resulting publicity will eventually attract more attention to the offensive material than would ever have occurred otherwise.

Rather than prohibit such communications, with all the resulting risks, it would be better to ignore them, since students would then have little reason to create such displays and would soon abandon them. If this response is not possible—and one can understand why—the wisest course is to speak with those who perform insensitive acts and try to help them understand the effects of their actions on others.

Appropriate officials and faculty members should take the lead, as the Harvard House Masters have already done in this case. In talking with students, they should seek to educate and persuade, rather than resort to ridicule or intimidation, recognizing that only persuasion is likely to produce a lasting, beneficial effect. Through such efforts, I believe that we act in the manner most consistent with our ideals as an educational institution and most calculated to help us create a truly understanding, supportive community.

Topics for Critical Thinking and Writing

1. Derek Bok sketches the following argument (paras. 8 and 9): The First Amendment protects free speech in public universities and colleges; Harvard is not a public university; therefore, Harvard does not enjoy the protection of the First Amendment. Bok finds this argument invalid. He clearly rejects the conclusion. "I have difficulty understanding why . . . Harvard should have less free speech . . . than a public university." What would need to be revised in the premises to make the argument valid? Do you think Bok would accept or reject such a revision? Why, or why not?

2. Bok objects to censorship that simply prevents students from being "offended." He would not object to the campus police preventing students from being harmed. In an essay of 100 words, explain the difference between conduct that is *harmful* and conduct that is *offensive*. (If you think that such a distinction cannot be made, explain why.)

3. Bok advises campus officials (and students) to "ignore" offensive words, flags, and so forth (para. 13). Do you agree with this advice? Or do you favor a different kind of response? Write a 250-word essay on the theme "How We Ought to Respond to the Offensive Misconduct of Others."

THINKING FURTHER: FREEDOM OF EXPRESSION AND SOCIAL MEDIA

On February 8, 2009, the *New York Times* reported that a high school senior, Katherine Evans, believed that her English teacher, Sarah Phelps, behaved offensively in two ways: Evans said that the teacher ignored her requests for help with assignments and, further, that Phelps brusquely reproached her when Evans missed a class because she had attended a blood drive. Evans, an honor student, logged into Facebook and wrote about her teacher:

> To those select students who have had the displeasure of having Ms. Sarah Phelps, or simply knowing her and her insane antics: Here is the place to express your feelings of hatred.

The posting drew several responses, including some that criticized the student and supported the teacher. Here is one, written by a former student of Ms. Phelps, quoted by the *Times*:

> Whatever your reasons for hating her are, they're probably very immature.

Ms. Evans removed the posting a few days later, but subsequently she was nevertheless reprimanded by the principal and received a three-day suspension for "cyberbullying." Ms. Evans sued the principal of the high school. She was not asking for money other than legal fees. Moreover, she wanted the suspension removed from her record. (She eventually settled the suit, and the suspension was wiped from her record.)

The issue to consider: Was the suspension an attack on Ms. Evans's right to free speech? Or did her comment and her invitation to "express feelings of hatred" constitute a verbal assault that crossed the line of freedom of expression? Howard Simon, executive director of the American Civil Liberties Union of Florida, takes the first position. The *Times* quotes him as saying, "Since when did criticism of a teacher morph into assault? If Katie Evans said what she said over burgers with her friends at the mall, there is no question it would be protected by free speech."

Three-Part Exercise in Definition

1. Construct a definition (three to five sentences) of *cyberbullying*. If you use sources, cite them.

2. Find a technical definition of cyberbullying as defined by a law, rule, or code, and compare it to your definition in #1 above. What limits and restrictions are included? (Be sure to cite your source.)

3. Given the admittedly scanty information that we have on the Evans case, do you think a suspension was reasonable, in light of the definitions of cyberbullying above? If you think it was reasonable, explain why. If you think it was unreasonable, explain why. Indicate also whether you think a different punishment might have been appropriate. Your essay should be about 250 to 300 words in length.

Exercise: Letter to the Editor

Your college newspaper has published a letter that links a hateful attribute to a group and that clearly displays hatred for the entire group. (For instance, the letter charges that interracial marriages should be made illegal because "African Americans carry a criminal gene" or that "Jews should not be elected to office because their loyalty is to Israel, not the United States" or that "Muslims should not be allowed to enter the country because they are intent on destroying America.") The letter generates many letters of response; some, supporting the editor's decision to publish the letter, make these points:

- The writer of the offending letter is a student in the college, and she has a right to express her views.

- The point of view expressed is probably held only by a few persons, but conceivably it expresses a view held by a significant number of students.

- Editors should not act as censors.

- The First Amendment guarantees freedom of speech.

- Freedom of expression is healthy — that is, society gains.

In contrast, among the letters opposing the editor's decision to publish, some make points along these lines:

- Not every view of every nutty student can be printed; editors must make responsible choices.

- The First Amendment, which prohibits the government from controlling the press, has nothing to do with a college newspaper.

- Letters of this sort do not foster healthy discussion; they merely heat things up.

Write a 250- to 500-word letter to the editor expressing your view of the decision to publish the first letter. (If you wish, you can assume that the letter addressed one of the topics we specify in the second sentence of this exercise. In any case, address the general issue of the editor's decision, not just the specific issue of the charge or charges made in the first letter.)

3

Critical Reading: Getting Deeper into Arguments

He that wrestles with us strengthens our nerves, and sharpens our skill.
Our antagonist is our helper.

— EDMUND BURKE

Persuasion, Argument, Dispute

When we think seriously about an argument, not only do we encounter ideas that may be unfamiliar but also we are forced to examine our own cherished opinions — and perhaps for the first time really see the strengths and weaknesses of what we believe. As John Stuart Mill put it, "He who knows only his own side of the case knows little."

It is useful to distinguish between **persuasion** and **argument**. Persuasion has the broader meaning. To **persuade** is to convince someone else to accept or adopt your position, which can be accomplished in a number of ways, including

- by giving reasons (i.e., by argument, by logic),
- by appealing to the emotions, or
- by using torture.

Argument, we mean to say, represents only one form of persuasion, one that relies on the cognitive or intellectual capacity for reason. Rhetoricians often use the Greek word *logos*, which means "word" or "reason," to denote this aspect of persuasive writing. An appeal to reason may by conducted by using such things as

- physical evidence,
- the testimony of experts,
- common sense, and
- probability.

We can put it this way: The goal of *argument* is to convince by demonstrating the truth (or probable truth) of an assertion, whereas the goal of *persuasion* is simply to convince by one means or another. *Logos*, the root word of *logic*, means appealing to the intellect to make rational claims and reasoned judgments.

The appeal to the emotions is known as **pathos**. Strictly speaking, *pathos* is Greek for "feeling." It covers all sorts of emotional appeals — for instance, appeals that elicit pity or sympathy (derived from the Greek for "feeling with"), or one's sense of duty or patriotism.

Notice that an argument doesn't require two speakers or writers with opposing positions. In practice, of course, they may, but it is not a requirement that arguments advance claims in opposition to another position. **Dispute** is a special kind of argument in which two or more people express views that are at odds. But the Declaration of Independence is also an argument, setting forth the colonists' reasons for declaring their independence. An essay showing indecisiveness to be Hamlet's tragic flaw would present an argument. Even when writing only for oneself, trying to clarify one's thinking by setting forth reasons and justifications for an idea, the result is an argument.

Most of this book is about argument in the sense of presenting reasonable support of claims, but reason is not the whole story. If an argument is to be effective, it must be presented persuasively. For instance, the writer's **tone** (presentation of self, topic, and audience) must be appropriate if the discourse is to persuade the reader. The careful presentation of the self is not something disreputable, nor is it something that publicity agents or advertising agencies invented. Aristotle (384–322 B.C.E.) emphasized the importance of impressing on the audience that the speaker is a person of good sense and high moral character. (He called this aspect of persuasion **ethos**, the Greek word for "character," a basis of persuasion different from *logos,* which involves persuasion by appealing to reason, and *pathos*, which persuades by appealing to emotion.)

Writers convey their *ethos*, their good character or trustworthiness, by doing the following:

- using language appropriate to the setting, avoiding vulgar language, slang, and colloquialism;
- showing an awareness of the issue's complexity (e.g., by offering other points of view in goodwill and by recognizing that contrary points of view may have some merit); and
- showing attention to detail (e.g., by citing relevant statistics).

In short, writers who are concerned with *ethos* — and all writers should be — employ devices that persuade readers that the writers are reliable, fair-minded, intelligent persons in whom their readers can have confidence.

We talk at length about tone, along with other matters such as the organization of an argument, in Chapter 5, Writing an Analysis of an Argument, but here we deal with some of the chief devices used in reasoning, and we glance at emotional appeals.

We should note at once, however, that an argument presupposes a fixed **topic**. Suppose we're arguing about Thomas Jefferson's assertion, in the Declaration of Independence, that "all men are created equal." Jones subscribes to this statement, but Smith says it's nonsense and argues that some people are obviously brighter than others, or healthier, or better coordinated, and so on. Jones and Smith, if they intend to argue the point, will do well to examine what Jefferson actually wrote:

> We hold these truths to be self-evident, that all men are created equal: that they are endowed by their Creator with certain unalienable rights; and that among these are life, liberty, and the pursuit of happiness.

There is room for debate over what Jefferson really meant and whether he is right, but clearly he was talking about *equality of rights*. If Smith and Jones wish to argue about Jefferson's view of equality — that is, if they wish to offer their reasons for accepting, rejecting, or modifying it — they must first agree on what Jefferson said or probably meant to say. Jones and Smith

THINKING CRITICALLY *Establishing Trustworthiness and Credibility*

For each method listed, provide your own example of a sentence that helps to establish trustworthiness and credibility. (Pick a topic that interests you. If you need ideas, look at the topics addressed by the authors presented in this chapter.) Be sure to use a tone and language that are appropriate and respectful of your audience.

METHOD	EXAMPLE	YOUR TURN
Acknowledge weaknesses, exceptions, and complexities.	"Although the unemployment rate continues to decline, further investigation into underemployment and the loss of jobless benefits is necessary in order to truly understand the unemployment crisis in the United States."	
Use personal experience when appropriate.	"As a student who works and attends school full-time, I can speak firsthand about the importance of increased availability of financial aid."	
Mention the qualifications of any sources as a way to boost your own credibility.	"According to Deborah Tannen, author and noted professor of linguistics at Georgetown University, . . ."	

LaunchPad   To complete this activity online, go to **macmillanhighered.com/barnetbedauohara**

may still hold different views; they may continue to disagree on whether Jefferson was right and proceed to offer arguments and counterarguments to settle the point. But only if they can agree on *what* they disagree about will their dispute get somewhere.

Reason versus Rationalization

Reason may not be the only way of finding the truth, but it is a way on which we often rely. "The subway ran yesterday at 6:00 A.M. and the day before at 6:00 A.M. and the day before that, so I infer from this evidence that it will also run today at 6:00 A.M." (a form of reasoning known as **induction**). "Bus drivers require would-be passengers to present the exact change; I don't have the exact change; therefore, I infer I cannot ride on the bus" (**deduction**). (The terms *deduction* and *induction* are discussed in more detail on pp. 91 and 95.)

We also know that if we set our minds to a problem, we can often find reasons (not always necessarily sound ones) for almost anything we want to justify. Here's an entertaining example from Benjamin Franklin's *Autobiography:*

> I believe I have omitted mentioning that in my first voyage from Boston, being becalmed off Block Island, our people set about catching cod and hauled up a great many. Hitherto I had stuck to my resolution of not eating animal food, and on this occasion, I considered with my master Tryon the taking of every fish as a kind of unprovoked murder, since none of them had or ever could do us any injury that might justify the slaughter. All this seemed very reasonable. But I had formerly been a great lover of fish, and when this came hot out of the frying pan, it smelt admirably well. I balanced some time between principle and inclination, till I recollected that when the fish were opened I saw smaller fish taken out of their stomachs. Then thought I, if you eat one another, I don't see why we mayn't eat you. So I dined upon cod very heartily and continued to eat with other people, returning only now and then occasionally to a vegetable diet. So convenient a thing it is to be a *reasonable creature,* since it enables one to find or make a reason for everything one has a mind to do.

Franklin is being playful; he is *not* engaging in critical thinking. He tells us that he loved fish and that this fish "smelt admirably well," so we're prepared for him to find a reason (here one as weak as "Fish eat fish, therefore people may eat fish") to abandon his vegetarianism. (But think: Fish also eat their own young. May we therefore eat ours?)

Still, Franklin touches on a truth: If necessary, we can find reasons to justify whatever we want. That is, instead of reasoning, we may *rationalize* (devise a self-serving but dishonest reason), like the fox in Aesop's fables who, finding the grapes he desired were out of reach, consoled himself with the thought that they were probably sour.

Perhaps we can never be certain that we aren't rationalizing, except when being playful like Franklin. But we can seek to think critically about our own beliefs, scrutinizing our assumptions, looking for counterevidence, and wondering if it's reasonably possible to draw different conclusions.

Some Procedures in Argument

DEFINITION

Definition, we mentioned in Chapter 1, is one of the classical topics, a "place" to which one goes with questions; in answering the questions, one finds ideas. When we define, we're answering the question "What is it?" In answering this question as precisely as we can, we will find, clarify, and develop ideas.

We have already glanced at an argument over the proposition that "all men are created equal," and we saw that the words needed clarification. *Equal* meant, in the context, not physically or mentally equal but something like "equal in rights," equal politically and legally. (And, of course, *men* meant "white men and women.") Words don't always mean exactly what they seem to mean: There's no lead in a lead pencil, and a standard 2-by-4 is currently 1⅝ inches in thickness and 3⅜ inches in width.

DEFINITION BY SYNONYM   Let's return for a moment to *pornography,* a word that is not easy to define. One way to define a word is to offer a **synonym**. Thus, pornography can be defined, at least roughly, as "obscenity" (something indecent). But definition by synonym is usually only a start because then we have to define the synonym; besides, very few words have exact synonyms. (In fact, *pornography* and *obscenity* are not exact synonyms.)

DEFINITION BY EXAMPLE   A second way to define a word is to point to an example (this is often called **ostensive definition**, from the Latin *ostendere,* "to show"). This method can be very helpful, ensuring that both writer and reader are talking about the same thing, but

Tom Cheney, The New Yorker Collection / The Cartoon Bank

"It all depends on how you define 'chop.'"

it also has limitations. A few decades ago, many people pointed to James Joyce's *Ulysses* and D. H. Lawrence's *Lady Chatterley's Lover* as examples of obscene novels, but today these books are regarded as literary masterpieces. It's possible that they can be obscene and also be literary masterpieces. (Joyce's wife is reported to have said of her husband, "He may have been a great writer, but . . . he had a very dirty mind.")

One of the difficulties of using an example, however, is that the example is richer and more complex than the term it's being used to define, and this richness and complexity get in the way of achieving a clear definition. Thus, if one cites *Lady Chatterley's Lover* as an example of pornography, a reader may erroneously think that pornography has something to do with British novels (because Lawrence was British) or with heterosexual relationships outside of marriage. Yet neither of these ideas relates to the concept of pornography.

We are not trying here to formulate a satisfactory definition of *pornography*. Our object is to make the following points clear:

- An argument will be most fruitful if the participants first agree on what they are talking about.
- One way to secure such agreement is to define the topic ostensively.
- Choosing the right example, one that has all the central or typical characteristics, can make a topic not only clear but also vivid.

DEFINITION BY STIPULATION   Arguments frequently involve matters of definition. In a discussion of gun control, for instance, you probably will hear one side speak of *assault weapons* and the other side speak instead of *so-called assault weapons*. In arguing, you can hope to get agreement — at least on what the topic of argument is — by offering a **stipulative definition** (from a Latin verb meaning "to bargain"). For instance, you and a representative of the other side can agree on a definition of *assault weapon* based on the meaning of the term in the ban approved by Congress in 1994, which expired in 2004, and which President Obama in 2013 asked Congress to renew. Although the renewal of the ban was unsuccessful, the definition was this: a semiautomatic firearm (the spent cartridge case is automatically extracted, and a new round is automatically reloaded into the chamber but isn't fired until the trigger is pulled again) with a detachable magazine *and at least two of the following five characteristics*:

- collapsible or folding stock
- pistol grip (thus allowing the weapon to be fired from the hip)
- bayonet mount
- grenade launcher
- flash suppressor (to keep the shooter from being blinded by muzzle flashes)

Again, this was the agreed-upon definition for the purposes of the legislation. Congress put *fully* automatic weapons into an entirely different category, and the legislatures of California and of New York each agreed on a stipulation different from that of Congress: In these two states, an assault weapon is defined as a semiautomatic firearm with a detachable magazine and with any *one* (not two) of the five bulleted items. The point is that for an argument to proceed rationally, and especially in the legal context, the key terms need to be precisely defined and agreed upon by all parties.

Let's now look at stipulative definitions in other contexts. Who is a *Native American*? In discussing this issue, you might stipulate that *Native American* means any person with any Native American blood; or you might say, "For the purpose of the present discussion, I mean that a *Native American* is any person who has at least one grandparent of pure Native American blood." A stipulative definition is appropriate in the following cases:

- when no fixed or standard definition is available, and
- when an arbitrary specification is necessary to fix the meaning of a key term in the argument.

Not everyone may accept your stipulative definition, and there will likely be defensible alternatives. In any case, when you stipulate a definition, your audience knows what *you* mean by the term.

It would *not* be reasonable to stipulate that by *Native American* you mean anyone with a deep interest in North American aborigines. That's too idiosyncratic to be useful. Similarly, an essay on Jews in America will have to rely on a definition of the key idea. Perhaps the writer will stipulate the definition used in Israel: A Jew is a person who has a Jewish mother or, if not born of a Jewish mother, a person who has formally adopted the Jewish faith. Perhaps the writer will stipulate another meaning: Jews are people who consider themselves to be Jews. Some sort of reasonable definition must be offered.

To stipulate, however, that *Jews* means "persons who believe that the area formerly called Palestine rightfully belongs to the Jews" would hopelessly confuse matters. Remember the old riddle: If you call a dog's tail a leg, how many legs does a dog have? The answer is four. Calling a tail a leg doesn't make it a leg.

Later in this chapter you will see, in an essay titled "When 'Identity Politics' Is Rational," that the author, Stanley Fish, begins by stipulating a definition. His first paragraph begins thus:

> If there's anything everyone is against in these election times, it's "identity politics," a phrase that covers a multitude of sins. Let me start with a definition. (It may not be yours, but it will at least allow the discussion to be framed.) You're practicing identity politics when you vote for or against someone because of his or her skin color, ethnicity, religion, gender, sexual orientation, or any other marker that leads you to say yes or no independently of a candidates' ideas or policies.

Fish will argue in later paragraphs that sometimes identity politics makes very good sense, that it is *not* irrational, is *not* logically indefensible; but here we simply want to make two points — one about how a definition helps the writer, and one about how it helps the reader:

- A definition is a good way to get started when drafting an essay, a useful stimulus (idea prompt, pattern, template, heuristic) that will help *you* to think about the issue, a device that will stimulate your further thinking.
- A definition lets readers be certain that they understand what the author means by a crucial word.

Readers may disagree with Fish, but at least they know what he means when he speaks of identity politics.

A stipulation may be helpful and legitimate. Here's the opening paragraph of a 1975 essay by Richard B. Brandt titled "The Morality and Rationality of Suicide." Notice that the author does two things:

- He first stipulates a definition.
- Then, aware that the definition may strike some readers as too broad and therefore unreasonable or odd, he offers a reason on behalf of his definition.

> "Suicide" is conveniently defined, for our purposes, as doing something which results in one's death, either from the intention of ending one's life or the intention to bring about some other state of affairs (such as relief from pain) which one thinks it certain or highly probable can be achieved only by means of death or will produce death. It may seem odd to classify an act of heroic self-sacrifice on the part of a soldier as suicide. It is simpler, however, not to try to define "suicide" so that an act of suicide is always irrational or immoral in some way; if we adopt a neutral definition like the above we can still proceed to ask when an act of suicide in that sense is rational, morally justifiable, and so on, so that all evaluations anyone might wish to make can still be made. (61)

Sometimes, a definition that at first seems extremely odd can be made acceptable by offering strong reasons in its support. Sometimes, in fact, an odd definition marks a great intellectual step forward. For instance, in 1990 the U.S. Supreme Court recognized that *speech* includes symbolic nonverbal expression such as protesting against a war by wearing armbands or by flying the American flag upside down. Such actions, because they express ideas or emotions, are now protected by the First Amendment. Few people today would disagree that *speech* should include symbolic gestures. (We include an example of controversy over this issue in Derek Bok's essay "Protecting Freedom of Expression on the Campus" in Chapter 2.)

A definition that seems notably eccentric to many readers and thus far has not gained much support is from Peter Singer's *Practical Ethics*, in which the author suggests that a non-human being can be a *person*. He admits that "it sounds odd to call an animal a person" but says that it seems so only because of our habit of sharply separating ourselves from other species. For Singer, *persons* are "rational and self-conscious beings, aware of themselves as distinct entities with a past and a future." Thus, although a newborn infant is a human being, it isn't a person; however, an adult chimpanzee isn't a human being but probably is a person. You don't have to agree with Singer to know exactly what he means and where he stands. Moreover, if you read his essay, you may even find that his reasons are plausible and that by means of his unusual definition he has broadened your thinking.

THE IMPORTANCE OF DEFINITIONS   Trying to decide on the best way to define a key idea or a central concept is often difficult as well as controversial. *Death*, for example, has been redefined in recent years. Traditionally, a person was considered dead when there was no longer any heartbeat. But with advancing medical technology, the medical profession has persuaded legislatures to redefine death as cessation of cerebral and cortical functions — so-called brain death.

Some scholars have hoped to bring clarity into the abortion debate by redefining *life*. Traditionally, human life has been seen as beginning at birth or perhaps at viability (the capacity of a fetus to live independently of the uterine environment). However, others have proposed a *brain birth* definition in the hope of resolving the abortion controversy. Some thinkers want abortion to be prohibited by law at the point where "integrated brain functioning begins to emerge," allegedly about seventy days after conception. Whatever the merits of such a redefinition may be, the debate is convincing evidence of just how important the definition of certain terms can be.

LAST WORDS ABOUT DEFINITION   Since Plato's time in the fourth century B.C.E, it has often been argued that the best way to give a definition is to state the *essence* of the thing being defined. Thus, the classic example defines *man* as "a rational animal." (Today, to avoid sexist implications, instead of *man* we would say *human being* or *person*.) That is, the property of *rational animality* is considered to be the essence of every human creature, so it must be mentioned in the definition of *man*. This statement guarantees that the definition is neither too broad nor too narrow. But philosophers have long criticized this alleged ideal type of definition on several grounds, one of which is that no one can propose such definitions without assuming that the thing being defined has an essence in the first place — an assumption that is not necessary. Thus, we may want to define *causality,* or *explanation,* or even *definition* itself, but it's doubtful whether it is sound to assume that any of these concepts has an essence.

A much better way to provide a definition is to offer a set of **sufficient and necessary conditions**. Suppose we want to define the word *circle* and are conscious of the need to keep circles distinct from other geometric figures such as rectangles and spheres. We might express our definition by citing sufficient and necessary conditions as follows: "Anything is a circle *if and only if* it is a closed plane figure and all points on the circumference are equidistant from the center." Using the connective "if and only if" (called the *biconditional*) between the definition and the term being defined helps to make the definition neither too exclusive (too narrow) nor too inclusive (too broad). Of course, for most ordinary purposes we don't require such a formally precise definition. Nevertheless, perhaps the best criterion to keep in mind when assessing a proposed definition is whether it can be stated in the "if and only if" form, and whether, if so stated, it is true; that is, if it truly specifies *all and only* the things covered by the word being defined. The Thinking Critically exercise that follows provides examples.

We aren't saying that the four sentences in the table below are incontestable. In fact, they are definitely arguable. We offer them merely to show ways of defining, and the act of defining is one way of helping to get your own thoughts going. Notice, too, that the fourth example, a "statement of necessary and sufficient conditions" (indicated by *if and only if*), is a bit stiff for ordinary writing. An informal prompt along this line might begin, "Essentially, something can be called *pornography* if it presents. . . ."

THINKING CRITICALLY *Giving Definitions*

In the spaces provided, define one of the "new terms" provided according to the definition type stipulated.

DEFINITION TYPE	EXAMPLE	NEW TERM	YOUR DEFINITION
Synonym	"*Pornography*, simply stated, is obscenity."	Police brutality Helicopter parenting Alternative music Organic foods	
Example	"*Pornography* can be seen, for example, in D. H. Lawrence's *Lady Chatterley's Lover*, in the scene where . . ."	Police brutality Helicopter parenting Alternative music Organic foods	
Stipulation	"For the purposes of this essay, *pornography* means any type of media that . . ."	Police brutality Helicopter parenting Alternative music Organic foods	
Statement of necessary and sufficient conditions	"Something can be called *pornography* if and only if it presents sexually stimulating material without offering anything of redeeming social value."	Police brutality Helicopter parenting Alternative music Organic foods	

LaunchPad   To complete this activity online, go to **macmillanhighered.com/barnetbedauohara**

ASSUMPTIONS

In Chapter 1, we discussed the **assumptions** made by the authors of two essays on religious freedoms. But we have more to say about assumptions. We've already said that in the form of discourse known as argument, certain statements are offered as reasons for other statements. But even the longest and most complex chain of reasoning or proof is fastened to assumptions — one or more *unexamined beliefs*. (Even if writer and reader share such a belief, it is no less an assumption.) Benjamin Franklin argued against paying salaries to the holders of executive offices in the federal government on the grounds that men are moved by ambition (love of power) and by avarice (love of money) and that powerful positions conferring wealth incite men to do their worst. These assumptions he stated, although he felt no need to argue them at length because he assumed that his readers shared them.

An assumption may be unstated. A writer, painstakingly arguing specific points, may choose to keep one or more of the argument's assumptions tacit. Or the writer may be completely unaware of an underlying assumption. For example, Franklin didn't even bother to state another assumption. He must have assumed that persons of wealth who accept an unpaying job (after all, only persons of wealth could afford to hold unpaid government jobs) will have at heart the interests of all classes of people, not only the interests of their own class. Probably Franklin didn't state this assumption because he thought it was perfectly obvious, but if you think critically about it, you may find reasons to doubt it. Surely one reason we pay our legislators is to ensure that the legislature does not consist only of people whose incomes may give them an inadequate view of the needs of others.

As another example, here are two assumptions in the argument for permitting abortion:

1. Ours is a pluralistic society, in which we believe that the religious beliefs of one group should not be imposed on others.

2. Personal privacy is a right, and a woman's body is hers, not to be violated by laws that forbid her from doing certain things to her body.

But these (and other) arguments *assume* that a fetus is not — or not yet — a person and therefore is not entitled to the same protection against assaults that we are. Virtually all of us assume that it is usually wrong to kill a human being. Granted, there may be instances in which we believe it's acceptable to take a human life, such as self-defense against a would-be murderer. But even here we find a shared assumption that persons are ordinarily entitled not to be killed.

The argument about abortion, then, usually depends on opposed assumptions. For one group, the fetus is a human being and a potential person — and this potentiality is decisive. For the other group, it is not. Persons arguing one side or the other of the abortion issue ought to be aware that opponents may not share their assumptions.

PREMISES AND SYLLOGISMS

Premises are stated assumptions that are used as reasons in an argument. (The word comes from a Latin word meaning "to send before" or "to set in front.") A premise thus is a statement set down — assumed — before the argument begins. The joining of two premises — two statements taken to be true — to produce a conclusion, a third statement, is a **syllogism** (from the Greek for "a reckoning together"). The classic example is this:

Major premise: All human beings are mortal.

Minor premise: Socrates is a human being.

Conclusion: Socrates is mortal.

DEDUCTION

The mental process of moving from one statement ("All human beings are mortal") through another ("Socrates is a human being") to yet a further statement ("Socrates is mortal") is **deduction**, from the Latin for "lead down from." In this sense, deductive reasoning doesn't give us any new knowledge, although it's easy to construct examples that have so many premises, or premises that are so complex, that the conclusion really does come as news to most who examine the argument. Thus, the great fictional detective Sherlock Holmes was credited by his admiring colleague, Dr. Watson, with having unusual powers of deduction. Watson meant in part that Holmes could see the logical consequences of apparently disconnected reasons, the number and complexity of which left others at a loss. What is common in all cases of deduction is that the reasons or premises offered are supposed to contain within themselves, so to speak, the conclusion extracted from them.

Often a syllogism is abbreviated. Martin Luther King Jr., defending a protest march, wrote in "Letter from Birmingham Jail":

> You assert that our actions, even though peaceful, must be condemned because they precipitate violence.

Fully expressed, the argument that King attributes to his critics would be stated thus:

> Society must condemn actions (even if peaceful) that precipitate violence.
>
> This action (though peaceful) will precipitate violence.
>
> Therefore, society must condemn this action.

An incomplete or abbreviated syllogism in which one of the premises is left unstated, of the sort found in King's original quotation, is an **enthymeme** (from the Greek for "in the mind").

Here is another, more whimsical example of an enthymeme, in which both a premise and the conclusion are left implicit. Henry David Thoreau remarked that "circumstantial evidence can be very strong, as when you find a trout in the milk." The joke, perhaps intelligible only to people born before 1930 or so, depends on the fact that milk used to be sold "in bulk" — that is, ladled out of a big can directly to the customer by the farmer or grocer. This practice was prohibited in the 1930s because for centuries the sellers, seeking to increase their profit, were diluting the milk with water. Thoreau's enthymeme can be fully expressed thus:

> Trout live only in water.
>
> This milk has a trout in it.
>
> Therefore, this milk has water in it.

These enthymemes have three important properties: Their premises are *true*, the form of their argument is *valid*, and they leave *implicit* either the conclusion or one of the premises.

Robert Mankoff, The New Yorker Collection/The Cartoon Bank

SOUND ARGUMENTS

The purpose of a syllogism is to present reasons that establish its conclusion. This is done by making sure that the argument satisfies both of two independent criteria:

- First, all of the premises must be *true*.
- Second, the syllogism must be *valid*.

Once these criteria are satisfied, the conclusion of the syllogism is guaranteed. Any such argument is said to establish or to prove its conclusion — to use another term, it is said to be **sound**. Here's an example of a sound argument, a syllogism that proves its conclusion:

> Extracting oil from the Arctic Wildlife Refuge would adversely affect the local ecology.
>
> Adversely affecting the local ecology is undesirable, unless there is no better alternative fuel source.
>
> Therefore, extracting oil from the Arctic Wildlife Refuge is undesirable, unless there is no better alternative fuel source.

Each premise is **true**, and the syllogism is **valid**, so it establishes its conclusion.

But how do we tell in any given case that an argument is sound? We perform two different tests, one for the truth of each of the premises and another for the validity of the argument.

The basic test for the **truth** of a premise is to determine whether what it asserts corresponds with reality; if it does, then it is true, and if it doesn't, then it is false. Everything earlier this morning. Whatever the explanation might be, we relied on a sample that wasn't large enough (a larger sample might have included some early morning breakdowns) or representative enough (a more representative sample would have included the later starts on Sundays and holidays).

A WORD ABOUT SAMPLES   When we reason inductively, much depends on the size and the quality of the sample (we say "sample" because a writer probably cannot examine every instance). If, for example, we're offering an argument concerning the politics of members of sororities and fraternities, we probably cannot interview *every* member. Rather, we select a sample. But is the sample a fair one? Is it representative of the larger group? We may interview five members of Alpha Tau Omega and find that all five are Republicans, yet we cannot legitimately conclude that all members of ATO are Republicans. The problem doesn't always involve failing to interview an adequately large sample group. For example, a poll of ten thousand college students tells us very little about "college students" if all ten thousand are white males at the University of Texas. Because such a sample leaves out women and minority males, it isn't sufficiently *representative* of "college students" as a group. Further, though not all students at the University of Texas are from Texas or even from the Southwest, it's quite likely that the student body is not fully representative (e.g., in race and in income) of American college students. If this conjecture is correct, even a truly representative sample of University of Texas students wouldn't enable us to draw firm conclusions about American college students.

In short: An argument that uses samples ought to tell the reader how the samples were chosen. If it doesn't provide this information, the reader should treat the argument with suspicion.

EVIDENCE: EXPERIMENTATION, EXAMPLES, AUTHORITATIVE TESTIMONY, STATISTICS

Different disciplines use different kinds of evidence:

- In literary studies, the texts are usually the chief evidence.
- In the social sciences, field research (interviews, surveys) usually provides evidence.
- In the sciences, reports of experiments are the usual evidence; if an assertion cannot be tested — if one cannot show it to be false — it is a *belief*, an *opinion*, not a scientific hypothesis.

EXPERIMENTATION   Induction is obviously useful in arguing. If, for example, one is arguing that handguns should be controlled, one will point to specific cases in which handguns caused accidents or were used to commit crimes. In arguing that abortion has a traumatic effect on women, one will point to women who testify to that effect. Each instance constitutes **evidence** for the relevant generalization.

depends on the premise's content — what it asserts — and the evidence for it. (In the preceding syllogism, it's possible to test the truth of the premises by checking the views of experts and interested parties, such as policymakers, environmental groups, and experts on energy.)

The test for **validity** is quite different. We define a valid argument as one in which the conclusion follows from the premises, so that if all the premises are true, then the conclusion *must* be true, too. The general test for validity, then, is this: If one grants the premises, one must also grant the conclusion. In other words, if one grants the premises but denies the conclusion, is one caught in a self-contradiction? If so, the argument is valid; if not, the argument is invalid.

The preceding syllogism passes this test. If you grant the information given in the premises but deny the conclusion, you contradict yourself. Even if the information were in error, the conclusion in this syllogism would still follow from the premises — the hallmark of a valid argument! The conclusion follows because the validity of an argument is a purely formal matter concerning the *relation* between premises and conclusion based on what they mean.

It's possible to see this relationship more clearly by examining an argument that is valid but that, because one or both of the premises are false, does *not* establish its conclusion. Here's an example of such a syllogism:

> The whale is a large fish.
>
> All large fish have scales.
>
> Therefore, whales have scales.

We know that the premises and the conclusion are false. Whales are mammals, not fish, and not all large fish have scales (sharks have no scales, for instance). But in determining the argument's validity, the truth of the premises and the conclusion is beside the point. Just a little reflection assures us that *if* both premises were true, then the conclusion would have to be true as well. That is, anyone who grants the premises of this syllogism yet denies the conclusion contradicts herself. So the validity of an argument does not in any way depend on the truth of the premises or the conclusion.

A sound argument, as we said, is one that passes both the test of true premises and the test of valid inference. To put it another way, a sound argument does the following:

- It passes the test of content (the premises are true, as a matter of fact).
- It passes the test of form (its premises and conclusion, by virtue of their very meanings, are so related that it is impossible for the premises to be true and the conclusion false).

Accordingly, an unsound argument, one that fails to prove its conclusion, suffers from one or both of two defects:

- Not all the premises are true.
- The argument is invalid.

Usually, we have in mind one or both defects when objecting to someone's argument as "illogical." In evaluating a deductive argument, therefore, you must always ask: Is it vulnerable to criticism on the grounds that one (or more) of its premises is false? Or is the inference itself vulnerable because even if all the premises are true, the conclusion still wouldn't follow?

A deductive argument proves its conclusion if and only if *two conditions* are satisfied: (1) All the premises are true, and (2) it would be inconsistent to assert the premises and deny the conclusions.

A WORD ABOUT FALSE PREMISES   Suppose that one or more of a syllogism's premises are false but the syllogism itself is valid. What does that indicate about the truth of the conclusion? Consider this example:

> All Americans prefer vanilla ice cream to other flavors.
>
> Jimmy Fallon is an American.
>
> Therefore, Jimmy Fallon prefers vanilla ice cream to other flavors.

The first (or major) premise in this syllogism is false. Yet the argument passes our formal test for validity; if one grants both premises, then one must accept the conclusion. So we can say that the conclusion *follows from* its premises, even though the premises *do not prove* the conclusion. This is not as paradoxical as it may sound. For all we know, the argument's conclusion may in fact be true; Jimmy Fallon may indeed prefer vanilla ice cream, and the odds are that he does because consumption statistics show that a majority of Americans prefer vanilla. Nevertheless, if the conclusion in this syllogism is true, it's not because this argument proved it.

A WORD ABOUT INVALID SYLLOGISMS   Usually, one can detect a false premise in an argument, especially when the suspect premise appears in someone else's argument. A trickier business is the invalid syllogism. Consider this argument:

> All terrorists seek publicity for their violent acts.
>
> John Doe seeks publicity for his violent acts.
>
> Therefore, John Doe is a terrorist.

In this syllogism, let's grant that the first (major) premise is true. Let's also grant that the conclusion may well be true. Finally, the person mentioned in the second (minor) premise could indeed be a terrorist. But it's also possible that the conclusion is false; terrorists aren't the only ones who seek publicity for their violent acts — consider, for example, the violence committed against doctors, clinic workers, and patients at clinics where abortions are performed. In short, the truth of the two premises is no guarantee that the conclusion is also true. It's possible to assert both premises and deny the conclusion without being self-contradictory.

How do we tell, in general and in particular cases, whether a syllogism is valid? Chemists use litmus paper to determine instantly whether the liquid in a test tube is an acid or a base. Unfortunately, logic has no litmus test to tell us instantly whether an argument is valid or invalid. Logicians beginning with Aristotle have developed techniques to test any given argument, no matter how complex or subtle, to determine its validity. But the results of their labors cannot be expressed in a paragraph or even a few pages; this is why entire semester-long

courses are devoted to teaching formal deductive logic. Apart from advising you to consult Chapter 9, A Logician's View: Deduction, Induction, Fallacies, all we can do here is repeat two basic points.

First, the validity of deductive arguments is a matter of their *form* or *structure*. Even syllogisms like the one on the Arctic Wildlife Refuge on page 92 come in a large variety of forms (256 forms, to be precise), and only some of these forms are valid. Second, all valid deductive arguments (and only such arguments) pass this test: If one accepts all the premises, then one must accept the conclusion as well. Hence, if it's possible to accept the premises but reject the conclusion (without self-contradiction, of course), then the argument is invalid.

Let's exit from further discussion of this important but difficult subject on a lighter note. Many illogical arguments masquerade as logical. Consider this example: If it takes a horse and carriage four hours to go from Pinsk to Chelm, does it follow that a carriage with two horses will get there in two hours?

Note: In Chapter 9, we discuss at some length other kinds of deductive arguments, as well as **fallacies**, which are kinds of invalid reasoning.

INDUCTION

Whereas deduction takes beliefs and assumptions and extracts their hidden consequences, **induction** uses information about observed cases to reach a conclusion about unobserved cases. (The word comes from the Latin *in ducere,* "to lead into" or "to lead up to.") If we observe that the bite of a certain snake is poisonous, we may conclude on the basis of this evidence that the bite of another snake of the same general type is also poisonous. Our inference might be even broader: If we observe that snake after snake of a certain type has a poisonous bite and that these snakes are all rattlesnakes, then we're tempted to **generalize** that all rattlesnakes are poisonous.

By far the most common way to test the adequacy of a generalization is to consider one or more **counterexamples**. If the counterexamples are genuine and reliable, then the generalization must be false. For example, Ronald Takaki's essay on the "myth" of Asian racial superiority (p. 124) is full of examples that contradict the alleged superiority of Asians; they are counterexamples to that thesis, and they help to expose it as a "myth." What is true of Takaki's reasoning is true generally in argumentative writing: We constantly test our generalizations by considering them against actual or possible counterexamples, or by doing research on the issue.

Unlike deduction, induction yields conclusions that go beyond the information contained in the premises used in their support. It's not surprising that the conclusions of inductive reasoning are not always true, even when all the premises are true. On page 83, we gave as an example our observation that on previous days a subway has run at 6:00 A.M. and that therefore we conclude that it runs at 6:00 A.M. every day. Suppose, following this reasoning, we arrive at the subway platform just before 6:00 A.M. on a given day and wait for an hour without seeing a single train. What inference should we draw to explain this? Possibly today is Sunday, and the subway doesn't run before 7:00 A.M. Or possibly there was a breakdown

In a courtroom, evidence bearing on the guilt of the accused is introduced by the prosecution, and evidence to the contrary is introduced by the defense. Not all evidence is admissible (e.g., hearsay is not, even if it's true), and the law of evidence is a highly developed subject in jurisprudence. In the forum of daily life, the sources of evidence are less disciplined. Daily experience, a particularly memorable observation, an unusual event — any or all of these may serve as evidence for (or against) some belief, theory, hypothesis, or explanation. Science involves the systematic study of what experience can yield, and one of the most distinctive features of the evidence that scientists can marshal on behalf of their claims is that it is the result of **experimentation**. Experiments are deliberately contrived situations, often complex in their technology, that are designed to yield particular observations. What the ordinary person does with unaided eye and ear, the scientist does, much more carefully and thoroughly, with the help of laboratory instruments.

The variety, extent, and reliability of the evidence obtained in daily life are quite different from those obtained in the laboratory. It's no surprise that society attaches much more weight to the "findings" of scientists than to the corroborative (much less the contrary) experiences of ordinary people. No one today would seriously argue that the sun really does go around the earth just because it looks that way; nor would we argue that because viruses are invisible to the naked eye they cannot cause symptoms such as swellings and fevers, which are plainly evident.

EXAMPLES   One form of evidence is the **example**. Suppose we argue that a candidate is untrustworthy and shouldn't be elected to public office. We point to episodes in his career — his misuse of funds in 2008 and the false charges he made against an opponent in 2016 — as examples of his untrustworthiness. Or if we're arguing that President Truman ordered the atom bomb dropped to save American (and, for that matter, Japanese) lives that otherwise would have been lost in a hard-fought invasion of Japan, we point to the stubbornness of the Japanese defenders in battles on the islands of Saipan, Iwo Jima, and Okinawa, where Japanese soldiers fought to the death rather than surrender.

These examples, we say, indicate that the Japanese defenders of the main islands would have fought to their deaths without surrendering, even though they knew defeat was certain. Or if we argue that the war was nearly won when Truman dropped the bomb, we can cite secret peace feelers as examples of the Japanese willingness to end the war.

An *example* is a *sample*. These two words come from the same Old French word, *essample,* from the Latin *exemplum,* which means "something taken out" — that is, a selection from the group. A Yiddish proverb shrewdly says, "'For example' is no proof," but the evidence of well-chosen examples can go a long way toward helping a writer to convince an audience.

In arguments, three sorts of examples are especially common:

- real events
- invented instances (artificial or hypothetical cases)
- analogies

We will treat each of these briefly.

Real Events In referring to Truman's decision to drop the atom bomb, we've already touched on examples drawn from real events — the battles at Saipan and elsewhere. And we've also seen Ben Franklin pointing to an allegedly real happening, a fish that had consumed a smaller fish. The advantage of an example drawn from real life, whether a great historical event or a local incident, is that its reality gives it weight. It cannot simply be brushed off.

Yet an example drawn from reality may not be as clear cut as we would like. Suppose, for instance, that someone cites the Japanese army's behavior on Saipan and on Iwo Jima as evidence that the Japanese later would have fought to the death in an American invasion of Japan and would therefore have inflicted terrible losses on themselves and on the Americans. This example is open to the response that in June and July 1945 certain Japanese diplomats sent out secret peace feelers, so that in August 1945, when Truman authorized dropping the bomb, the situation was very different.

Similarly, in support of the argument that nations will no longer resort to using atomic weapons, some people have offered as evidence the fact that since World War I the great powers have not used poison gas. But the argument needs more support than this fact provides. Poison gas wasn't decisive or even highly effective in World War I. Moreover, the invention of gas masks made its use obsolete.

In short, any *real* event is so entangled in historical circumstances that it might not be adequate or relevant evidence in the case being argued. In using a real event as an example (a perfectly valid strategy), the writer must demonstrate that the event can be taken out of its historical context for use in the new context of argument. Thus, in an argument against using atomic weapons in warfare, the many deaths and horrible injuries inflicted on the Japanese at Hiroshima and Nagasaki can be cited as effects of nuclear weapons that would invariably occur and did not depend on any special circumstances of their use in Japan in 1945.

Invented Instances **Artificial** or **hypothetical cases** — **invented instances** — have the great advantage of being protected from objections of the sort we have just given. Recall Thoreau's trout in the milk; that was a colorful hypothetical case that illustrated his point well. An invented instance ("Let's assume that a burglar promises not to shoot a householder if the householder swears not to identify him. Is the householder bound by the oath?") is something like a drawing of a flower in a botany textbook or a diagram of the folds of a mountain in a geology textbook. It is admittedly false, but by virtue of its simplifications it sets forth the relevant details very clearly. Thus, in a discussion of rights, the philosopher Charles Frankel says:

> Strictly speaking, when we assert a right for *X*, we assert that *Y* has a duty. Strictly speaking, that *Y* has such a duty presupposes that *Y* has the capacity to perform this duty. It would be nonsense to say, for example, that a nonswimmer has a moral duty to swim to the help of a drowning man.

This invented example is admirably clear, and it is immune to charges that might muddy the issue if Frankel, instead of referring to a wholly abstract person, *Y*, talked about some real person, Jones, who did not rescue a drowning man. For then Frankel would get bogged down over arguing about whether Jones *really* couldn't swim well enough to help, and so on.

Yet invented examples have drawbacks. First and foremost, they cannot serve as evidence. A purely hypothetical example can illustrate a point or provoke reconsideration of a generalization, but it cannot substitute for actual events as evidence supporting an inductive inference. Sometimes, such examples are so fanciful that they fail to convince the reader. Thus, the philosopher Judith Jarvis Thomson, in the course of an argument entitled "A Defense of Abortion," asks the reader to imagine waking up one day and finding that against her will a celebrated violinist whose body is not adequately functioning has been hooked up into her body for life support. Does she have the right to unplug the violinist? As you read the essays we present in this textbook, you'll have to decide for yourself whether the invented cases proposed by various authors are helpful or whether they are so remote that they hinder thought. Readers will have to decide, too, about when they can use invented cases to advance their own arguments.

But we add one point: Even a highly fanciful invented case can have the valuable effect of forcing us to see where we stand. A person may say that she is, in all circumstances, against vivisection — the practice of performing operations on live animals for the purpose of research. But what would she say if she thought that an experiment on one mouse would save the life of someone she loves? Conversely, if she approves of vivisection, would she also approve of sacrificing the last giant panda to save the life of a senile stranger, a person who in any case probably wouldn't live longer than another year? Artificial cases of this sort can help us to see that we didn't really mean to say such-and-such when we said so-and-so.

Analogies   The third sort of example, **analogy**, is a kind of comparison. An analogy asserts that things that are alike in some ways are alike in yet another way as well. Here's an example:

> Before the Roman Empire declined as a world power, it exhibited a decline in morals and in physical stamina; our society today shows a decline in both morals (consider the high divorce rate and the crime rate) and physical culture (consider obesity in children). America, like Rome, will decline as a world power.

Strictly speaking, an analogy is an extended comparison in which different things are shown to be similar in several ways. Thus, if one wants to argue that a head of state should have extraordinary power during wartime, one can argue that the state at such a time is like a ship in a storm: The crew is needed to lend its help, but the decisions are best left to the captain. (Notice that an analogy compares things that are relatively *un*like. Comparing the plight of one ship to another or of one government to another isn't an analogy; it's an inductive inference from one case of the same sort to another such case.)

Let's consider another analogy. We have already glanced at Judith Thomson's hypothetical case in which the reader wakes up to find

"*Do you mind if I use yet another sports analogy?*"

herself hooked up to a violinist in need of life support. Thomson uses this situation as an analogy in an argument about abortion. The reader stands for the mother; the violinist, for the unwanted fetus. You may want to think about whether this analogy is close enough to pregnancy to help illuminate your own thinking about abortion.

The problem with argument by analogy is this: Two admittedly different things are agreed to be similar in several ways, and the arguer goes on to assert or imply that they are also similar in another way — the point being argued. (That's why Thomson argues that if something is true of the reader-hooked-up-to-a-violinist, it is also true of the pregnant-mother-hooked-up-to-a-fetus.) But the two things that are said to be analogous and that are indeed similar in characteristics *A, B,* and *C* are also different — let's say in characteristics *D* and *E*. As Bishop Butler is said to have remarked in the early eighteenth century, "Everything is what it is, and not another thing."

Analogies can be convincing, especially because they can make complex issues seem simple. "Don't change horses in midstream" isn't a statement about riding horses across a river but, rather, about choosing new leaders in critical times. Still, in the end, analogies don't necessarily prove anything. What may be true about riding horses across a stream may not be true about choosing new leaders in troubled times. Riding horses across a stream and choosing new leaders are fundamentally different things, and however much they may be said to resemble each other, they remain different. What is true for one need not be true for the other.

Analogies can be helpful in developing our thoughts and in helping listeners or readers to understand a point we're trying to make. It is sometimes argued, for instance — on the analogy of the doctor–patient, the lawyer–client, or the priest–penitent relationship — that newspaper and television reporters should not be required to reveal their confidential sources. That is worth thinking about: Do the similarities run deep enough, or are there fundamental differences? Consider another example: Some writers who support abortion argue that the fetus is not a person any more than the acorn is an oak. That is also worth thinking about. But one should also think about this response: A fetus is not a person, just as an acorn is not an oak; but an acorn is a potential oak, and a fetus is a potential person, a potential adult human being. Children, even newborn infants, have rights, and one way to explain this claim is to call attention to their potentiality to become mature adults. Thus, some people argue that the fetus, by analogy, has the rights of an infant, for the fetus, like the infant, is a potential adult.

Three analogies for consideration: First, let's examine a brief comparison made by Jill Knight, a member of the British Parliament, speaking about abortion:

> Babies are not like bad teeth, to be jerked out because they cause suffering.

Her point is effectively put; it remains for the reader to decide whether fetuses are *babies* and if a fetus is not a baby, *why* it can or cannot be treated like a bad tooth.

Now a second bit of analogical reasoning, again about abortion: Thomas Sowell, an economist at the Hoover Institute, grants that women have a legal right to abortion, but he objects to a requirement that the government pay for abortions:

> Because the courts have ruled that women have a legal right to an abortion, some
> people have jumped to the conclusion that the government has to pay for it. You have

a constitutional right to privacy, but the government has no obligation to pay for your window shades. (*Pink and Brown People*, 1981, p. 57)

We leave it to you to decide whether the analogy is compelling — that is, if the points of resemblance are sufficiently significant to allow you to conclude that what's true of people wanting window shades should be true of people wanting abortions.

And one more: A common argument on behalf of legalizing gay marriage drew an analogy between gay marriage and interracial marriage, a practice that was banned in sixteen states until 1967, when the Supreme Court declared miscegenation statutes unconstitutional. The gist of the analogy was this: Racism and discrimination against gay and lesbian people are the same. If marriage is a fundamental right — as the Supreme Court held in its 1967 decision striking down bans on miscegenation — then it is a fundamental right for gay and lesbian people as well as heterosexual people.

AUTHORITATIVE TESTIMONY   Another form of evidence is **testimony**, the citation or quotation of authorities. In daily life, we rely heavily on authorities of all sorts: We get a doctor's opinion about our health, we read a book because an intelligent friend recommends it, we see a movie because a critic gave it a good review, and we pay at least a little attention to the weather forecaster.

In setting forth an argument, one often tries to show that one's view is supported by notable figures — perhaps Jefferson, Lincoln, Martin Luther King Jr., or scientists who won the Nobel Prize. You may recall that in Chapter 2, in talking about medical marijuana legalization, we presented an essay by Sanjay Gupta. To make certain that you were impressed by his ideas, we described him as CNN's chief medical correspondent and a leading public health expert. In our Chapter 2 discussion of Sally Mann, we qualified our description of her controversial photographs by noting that *Time* magazine called her "America's Best Photographer" and the *New Republic* called her book "one of the great photograph books of our time." But heed some words of caution:

- Be sure that the authority, however notable, is *an authority on the topic in question*. (A well-known biologist might be an authority on vitamins but not on the justice of war.)

- Be sure that the authority is *unbiased*. (A chemist employed by the tobacco industry isn't likely to admit that smoking may be harmful, and a producer of violent video games isn't likely to admit that playing those games stimulates violence.)

- Beware of *nameless* authorities: "a thousand doctors," "leading educators," "researchers at a major medical school." (If possible, offer at least one specific name.)

- Be careful when using authorities who indeed were great authorities in their day but *who now may be out of date*. (Examples would include Adam Smith on economics, Julius Caesar on the art of war, Louis Pasteur on medicine).

- Cite authorities *whose opinions your readers will value.* (William F. Buckley Jr.'s conservative/libertarian opinions mean a good deal to readers of the magazine that he founded, the *National Review*, but probably not to most liberal thinkers. Gloria Steinem's liberal/feminist opinions carry weight with readers of the magazines that she cofounded, *New York* and *Ms.* magazine, but probably not with most conservative thinkers.) When writing for the general reader — your usual audience — cite authorities whom the general reader is likely to accept.

One other point: *You* may be an authority. You probably aren't nationally known, but on some topics you might have the authority of personal experience. You may have been injured on a motorcycle while riding without wearing a helmet, or you may have escaped injury because you wore a helmet. You may have dropped out of school and then returned. You may have tutored a student whose native language isn't English, you may be such a student who has received tutoring, or you may have attended a school with a bilingual education program. In short, your personal testimony on topics relating to these issues may be invaluable, and a reader will probably consider it seriously.

STATISTICS   The last sort of evidence we discuss here is quantitative, or statistical. The maxim "More is better" captures a basic idea of quantitative evidence: Because we know that 90 percent is greater than 75 percent, we're usually ready to grant that any claim supported by experience in 90 percent of cases is more likely to be true than an alternative claim supported by experience in only 75 percent of cases. The greater the difference, the greater our confidence. Consider an example. Honors at graduation from college are often computed on the basis of a student's cumulative grade-point average (GPA). The undisputed assumption is that the nearer a student's GPA is to a perfect record (4.0), the better scholar he or she is and therefore the more deserving of highest honors. Consequently, a student with a GPA of 3.9 at the end of her senior year is a stronger candidate for graduating summa cum laude than another student with a GPA of 3.6. When faculty members on the honors committee argue over the relative academic merits of graduating seniors, we know that these quantitative, statistical differences in student GPAs will be the basic (if not the only) kind of evidence under discussion.

Graphs, Tables, Numbers   Statistical information can be presented in many forms, but it tends to fall into two main types: the graphic and the numerical. Graphs, tables, and pie charts are familiar ways of presenting quantitative data in an eye-catching manner. (See pp. 165–70.) To prepare the graphics, however, one first has to decide how best to organize and interpret the numbers, and for some purposes it may be more appropriate to directly present the numbers themselves.

But is it better to present the numbers in percentages or in fractions? Should a report say that the federal budget (1) underwent a twofold increase over the decade; (2) increased by 100 percent; (3) doubled; or (4) at the beginning of the decade was one-half what it was at the end? These are equivalent ways of saying the same thing. Making a choice among them, therefore, will likely rest on whether one's aim is to dramatize the increase (a 100 percent increase looks larger than a doubling) or to play down its size.

Thinking about Statistical Evidence   Statistics often get a bad name because it's so easy to misuse them (unintentionally or not) and so difficult to be sure that they were gathered correctly in the first place. (One old saying goes, "There are lies, damned lies, and statistics.") Every branch of social science and natural science needs statistical information, and countless decisions in public and private life are based on quantitative data in statistical form. It's important, therefore, to be sensitive to the sources and reliability of the statistics and to develop a healthy skepticism when you confront statistics whose parentage is not fully explained.

Consider statistics that pop up in conversations about wealth distribution in the United States. In 2014, the Census Bureau calculated that the **median** household income in the United States was $53,657, meaning that half of households earned less than this amount and half earned above it. However, the **average** — technically, the **mean** — household income in the same year was $72,641, about $19,000 (or 39 percent) higher. Which number more accurately represents the typical household income? Both are "correct," but both are calculated with different measures, median and mean. If a politician wanted to argue that the United States has a strong middle class, he might use the average (mean) income as evidence, a number calculated by dividing the total income of all households by the total number of households. If another politician wished to make a rebuttal, she could point out that the average income paints a rosy picture because the wealthiest households skew the average higher. The median income (representing the number above and below which two halves of all households fall) should be the measure we use, the rebutting politician could argue, because it helps reduce the effect of the limitless ceiling of higher incomes and the finite floor of lower incomes at zero.

Consider the following statistics: Suppose in a given city in 2014, 1 percent of the victims in fatal automobile accidents were bicyclists. In the same city in 2015, the percentage of bicyclists killed in automobile accidents was 2 percent. Was the increase 1 percent (not an alarming figure), or was it 100 percent (a staggering figure)? The answer is both, depending on whether we're comparing (1) bicycle deaths in automobile accidents *with all deaths in automobile accidents* (that's an increase of 1 percent), or (2) bicycle deaths in automobile accidents *only with other bicycle deaths in automobile accidents* (an increase of 100 percent). An honest statement would say that bicycle deaths due to automobile accidents doubled in 2015, increasing from 1 to 2 percent. But here's another point: Although every such death is lamentable, if there was one such death in 2014 and two in 2015, the increase from one death to two (an increase of 100 percent!) hardly suggests a growing problem that needs attention. No one would be surprised to learn that in the next year there were no deaths at all, or only one or two.

If it's sometimes difficult to interpret statistics, it's often at least equally difficult to establish accurate statistics. Consider this example:

> Advertisements are the most prevalent and toxic of the mental pollutants. From the moment your radio alarm sounds in the morning to the wee hours of late-night TV, microjolts of commercial pollution flood into your brain at the rate of about three thousand marketing messages per day. (Kalle Lasn, *Culture Jam* [1999], 18–19)

Lasn's book includes endnotes as documentation, so, being curious about the statistics, we turn to the appropriate page and find this information concerning the source of his data:

> "three thousand marketing messages per day." Mark Landler, Walecia Konrad, Zachary Schiller, and Lois Therrien, "What Happened to Advertising?" *BusinessWeek,* September 23, 1991, page 66. Leslie Savan in *The Sponsored Life* (Temple University Press, 1994), page 1, estimated that "16,000 ads flicker across an individual's consciousness daily." I did an informal survey in March 1995 and found the number to be closer to 1,500 (this included all marketing messages, corporate images, logos, ads, brand names, on TV, radio, billboards, buildings, signs, clothing, appliances, in cyberspace, etc., over a typical twenty-four hour period in my life). (219)

Well, this endnote is odd. In the earlier passage, the author asserted that about "three thousand marketing messages per day" flood into a person's brain. In the documentation, he cites a source for that statistic from *BusinessWeek* — though we haven't the faintest idea how the authors of the *BusinessWeek* article came up with that figure. Oddly, he goes on to offer a very different figure (16,000 ads) and then, to our confusion, offers yet a third figure, 1,500, based on his own "informal survey."

Probably the one thing we can safely say about all three figures is that none of them means very much. Even if the compilers of the statistics explained exactly how they counted — let's say that among countless other criteria they assumed that the average person reads one magazine per day and that the average magazine contains 124 advertisements — it would be hard to take them seriously. After all, in leafing through a magazine, some people may read many ads and some may read none. Some people may read some ads carefully — but perhaps just to enjoy their absurdity. Our point: Although the author in his text said, without implying any uncertainty, that "about three thousand marketing messages per day" reach an individual, it's evident (by checking the endnote) that even he is confused about the figure he gives.

Unreliable Statistics   We'd like to make a final point about the unreliability of some statistical information — data that looks impressive but that is, in fact, insubstantial. For instance, Marilyn Jager Adams studied the number of hours that families read to their children in the five or so years before the children start attending school. In her book *Beginning to Read: Thinking and Learning about Print* (1994), she pointed out that in all those preschool years, poor families read to their children only 25 hours, whereas in the same period middle-income families read 1,000 to 1,700 hours. The figures were much quoted in newspapers and by children's advocacy groups. Adams could not, of course, interview every family in these two groups; she had to rely on samples. What were her samples? For poor families, she selected 24 children in 20 families, all in Southern California. Ask yourself: Can families from only one geographic area provide an adequate sample for a topic such as this? Moreover, let's think about Adams's sample of middle-class families. How many families constituted that sample? Exactly one — her own. We leave it to you to judge the validity of her findings.

Quiz

What is wrong with the following statistical proof that children do not have time for school?

One-third of the time they are sleeping (about 122 days).

One-eighth of the time they are eating (three hours a day, totaling 45 days).

One-fourth of the time they are on summer and other vacations (91 days).

Two-sevenths of the year is weekends (104 days).

Total: 362 days — so how can a kid have time for school?

Nonrational Appeals

SATIRE, IRONY, SARCASM, HUMOR

In talking about definition, deduction, and evidence, we've been talking about means of rational persuasion. However, as mentioned earlier, there are also other means of persuasion. Force is an example. If *X* kicks *Y*, threatens to destroy *Y*'s means of livelihood, or threatens *Y*'s life, *X* may persuade *Y* to cooperate. But writers, of course, cannot use such kinds of force on their readers. Instead, one form of irrational but sometimes highly effective persuasion is **satire** — that is, witty ridicule. A cartoonist may persuade viewers that a politician's views are unsound by caricaturing (thus ridiculing) her appearance or by presenting a grotesquely distorted (funny, but unfair) picture of the issue she supports.

Satiric artists often use caricature; satiric writers, also seeking to persuade by means of ridicule, often use **verbal irony**. This sort of irony contrasts what is said and what is meant. For instance, words of praise may actually imply blame (when Shakespeare's Cassius says, "Brutus is an honorable man," he wants his hearers to think that Brutus is dishonorable), and words of modesty may actually imply superiority ("Of course, I'm too dumb to understand this problem"). Such language, when heavy-handed, is **sarcasm** ("You're a great guy," said to someone who won't lend the speaker ten dollars). If it's witty and clever, we call it irony rather than sarcasm.

Although ridicule isn't a form of argument (because it isn't a form of reasoning), passages of ridicule, especially verbal irony, sometimes appear in argument essays. These passages, like reasons or like appeals to the emotions, are efforts to persuade the reader to accept the writer's point of view. The key to using humor in an argument is, on the one hand, to avoid wisecracking like a smart aleck, and on the other hand, to avoid mere clownishness. Later in this chapter (p. 110), we print an essay by George F. Will that is (or seeks to be) humorous in places. You be the judge.

EMOTIONAL APPEALS

It is sometimes said that good argumentative writing appeals only to reason, never to emotion, and that any emotional appeal is illegitimate and irrelevant. "Tears are not arguments," the Brazilian writer Machado de Assis said. Logic textbooks may even stigmatize with Latin labels the various sorts of emotional appeal — for instance, *argumentum ad populam* (appeal to the prejudices of the mob, as in "Come on, we all know that schools don't teach anything anymore") and *argumentum ad misericordiam* (appeal to pity, as in "No one ought to blame this poor kid for stabbing a classmate because his mother was often institutionalized for alcoholism and his father beat him").

True, appeals to emotion may distract from the facts of the case; they may blind the audience by, in effect, throwing dust in its eyes or by provoking tears.

LEARNING FROM SHAKESPEARE   A classic example is in Shakespeare's *Julius Caesar,* when Marc Antony addresses the Roman populace after Brutus, Cassius, and others have assassinated Caesar. The real issue is whether Caesar was becoming tyrannical (as the assassins claim) and would have curtailed the freedom of the Roman people. Antony turns from the evidence and stirs the mob against the assassins by appealing to its emotions. In the ancient Roman biographical writing that Shakespeare drew on, Sir Thomas North's translation of Plutarch's *Lives of the Noble Grecians and Romans,* Plutarch says this about Antony:

> perceiving that his words moved the common people to compassion, . . . [he] framed
> his eloquence to make their hearts yearn [i.e., grieve] the more, and, taking Caesar's
> gown all bloody in his hand, he laid it open to the sight of them all, showing what a
> number of cuts and holes it had upon it. Therewithal the people fell presently into
> such a rage and mutiny that there was no more order kept.

Here are a few extracts from Antony's speeches in Shakespeare's play. Antony begins by asserting that he will speak only briefly:

> Friends, Romans, countrymen, lend me your ears;
> I come to bury Caesar, not to praise him.

After briefly offering insubstantial evidence that Caesar gave no signs of behaving tyrannically (e.g., "When that the poor have cried, Caesar hath wept"), Antony begins to play directly on his hearers' emotions. Descending from the platform so that he may be in closer contact with his audience (like a modern politician, he wants to work the crowd), he calls attention to Caesar's bloody toga:

> If you have tears, prepare to shed them now.
> You all do know this mantle; I remember
> The first time ever Caesar put it on:
> 'Twas on a summer's evening, in his tent,
> That day he overcame the Nervii.
> Look, in this place ran Cassius' dagger through;
> See what a rent the envious Casca made;
> Through this, the well-belovèd Brutus stabbed. . . .

In these few lines, Antony accomplishes the following:

- He prepares the audience by suggesting to them how they should respond ("If you have tears, prepare to shed them now").
- He flatters them by implying that they, like Antony, were intimates of Caesar (he credits them with being familiar with Caesar's garment).
- He then evokes a personal memory of a specific time ("a summer's evening") — not just any specific time, but a very important one, the day that Caesar won a battle against the Nervii (a particularly fierce tribe in what is now France).

In fact, Antony was not at the battle, and he did not join Caesar until three years later.

Antony doesn't mind being free with the facts; his point here is not to set the record straight but to stir the mob against the assassins. He goes on, daringly but successfully, to identify one particular slit in the garment with Cassius's dagger, another with Casca's, and a third with Brutus's. Antony cannot know which dagger made which slit, but his rhetorical trick works.

Notice, too, that Antony arranges the three assassins in climactic order, since Brutus (Antony claims) was especially beloved by Caesar:

> Judge, O you gods, how dearly Caesar loved him!
> This was the most unkindest cut of all;
> For when the noble Caesar saw him stab,
> Ingratitude, more strong than traitor's arms,
> Quite vanquished him. Then burst his mighty heart. . . .

Nice. According to Antony, the noble-minded Caesar—Antony's words have erased all thought of the tyrannical Caesar—died not from wounds inflicted by daggers but from the heartbreaking perception of Brutus's ingratitude. Doubtless there wasn't a dry eye in the house. Let's all hope that if we are ever put on trial, we'll have a lawyer as skilled in evoking sympathy as Antony.

ARE EMOTIONAL APPEALS FALLACIOUS?   Antony's oration was obviously successful in the play and apparently was successful in real life, but it is the sort of speech that prompts logicians to write disapprovingly of attempts to stir feeling in an audience. (As mentioned earlier, the evocation of emotion in an audience is **pathos,** from the Greek word for "emotion" or "suffering.") There is nothing inherently wrong in stimulating an audience's emotions when attempting to establish a claim, but when an emotional appeal confuses the issue being argued or shifts attention away from the facts, we can reasonably speak of the fallacy of emotional appeal.

No fallacy is involved, however, when an emotional appeal heightens the facts, bringing them home to the audience rather than masking them. In talking about legislation that would govern police actions, for example, it's legitimate to show a photograph of the battered, bloodied face of an alleged victim of police brutality. True, such a photograph cannot tell the whole truth; it cannot tell if the subject threatened the officer with a gun or repeatedly resisted an order to surrender. But it can demonstrate that the victim was severely beaten and (like a comparable description in words) evoke emotions that may properly affect the audience's decision about the permissible use of police evidence. Similarly, an animal rights activist who argues that calves are cruelly confined might reasonably talk about the inhumanely small size of their pens, in which they cannot turn around or even lie down. Others may argue that calves don't care about turning around or have no right to turn around, but the evocative verbal description of their pens, which makes an emotional appeal, cannot be called fallacious or irrelevant.

In appealing to emotions, then, important strategies are as follows:

- Do not falsify (especially by oversimplifying) the issue.
- Do not distract attention from the facts of the case.
- Do think ethically about how emotional appeals may affect the audience.

You should focus on the facts and offer reasons (essentially, statements linked with "because"), but you may also legitimately bring the facts home to your readers by seeking to provoke appropriate emotions. Your words will be fallacious only if you stimulate emotions that aren't connected with the facts of the case.

Does All Writing Contain Arguments?

Our answer to the question above is no—however, *most* writing probably *does* contain an argument of sorts. The writer wants to persuade the reader to see things the way the writer sees them—at least until the end of the essay. After all, even a recipe for a cherry pie in a food magazine — a piece of writing that's primarily expository (how to do it) rather than argumentative (how a reasonable person ought to think about this topic) — probably starts out with a hint of an argument, such as "*Because* [a sign that a *reason* will be offered] this pie can be made quickly and with ingredients (canned cherries) that are always available, give it a try. It will surely become one of your favorites." Clearly, such a statement cannot stand as a formal argument — a discussion that addresses counter-arguments, relies chiefly on logic and little if any emotional appeal, and draws a conclusion that seems irrefutable.

Still, the statement is an argument on behalf of making a pie with canned cherries. In this case, we can identify a claim (the pie will become a favorite) and two *reasons* in support of the claim:

- It can be made quickly.
- The chief ingredient — because it is canned — can always be at hand.

There are two underlying *assumptions*:

- Readers don't have a great deal of time to waste in the kitchen.
- Canned cherries are just as tasty as fresh cherries — and even if they aren't, no one who eats the pie will know the difference.

A CHECKLIST FOR ANALYZING AN ARGUMENT

What is the writer's claim or thesis? Ask yourself:

- ❏ What claim is asserted?
- ❏ What evidence is imagined?
- ❏ What assumptions are being made — and are they acceptable?
- ❏ Are important terms satisfactorily defined?

What support (evidence) is offered on behalf of the claim? Ask yourself:

- ❏ Are the examples relevant and convincing?
- ❏ Are the statistics (if any) relevant, accurate, and complete? Do they allow only the interpretation that is offered in the argument?
- ❏ If authorities are cited, are they indeed authorities on this topic, and can they be considered impartial?
- ❏ Is the logic   deductive and inductive — valid?
- ❏ If there is an appeal to emotion (e.g., if satire is used to ridicule the opposing view), is this appeal acceptable?

Does the writer seem to be fair? Ask yourself:

❑ Are counterarguments adequately considered?

❑ Is there any evidence of dishonesty or of a discreditable attempt to manipulate the reader?

❑ How does the writer establish the image of himself or herself that readers sense in the essay? What is the writer's tone, and is it appropriate?

When we read a lead-in to a recipe, then, we won't find a formal argument, but we'll probably see a few words that seek to persuade us to keep reading. And most writing does contain such material — sentences that engage our interest and give us a reason to keep reading. If the recipe is difficult and time consuming, the lead-in may say:

> Although this recipe for a cherry pie, using fresh cherries that you will have to pit, is a bit more time consuming than the usual recipes that call for canned cherries, once you have tasted it you will never go back to canned cherries.

Again, although the logic is scarcely compelling, the persuasive element is evident. The assumption is that readers have a discriminating palate; once they've tasted a pie made with fresh cherries, they'll never again enjoy the canned stuff. The writer isn't making a formal argument with abundant evidence and detailed refutation of counterarguments, but we know where he stands and how he wishes us to respond.

In short, almost all writers are trying to persuade readers to see things *their* way.

An Example: An Argument and a Look at the Writer's Strategies

This essay concerns President George W. Bush's proposal to allow drilling in part of the Arctic National Wildlife Refuge (ANWR, pronounced "An-war"). The ANWR section where drilling is proposed is called the 1002 area, as defined by Section 1002 of the Alaska National Interest Lands Conservation Act of 1980. In March 2003, the Senate rejected the Bush proposal, but the issue remains alive.

We follow George F. Will's essay with some comments about the ways in which he constructs his argument.

GEORGE F. WILL

George F. Will (b. 1941), a syndicated columnist whose writing appears in 460 newspapers, was born in Champaign, Illinois, and educated at Trinity College (in Hartford), Oxford University, and Princeton University. Will has served as the Washington, D.C., editor of the National

Review *and now writes a regular column for* Newsweek. *His essays have been collected in several books.*

This essay was originally published in 2002, so it is in some respects dated—for instance, in its reference to the price of gasoline—but it still serves as an excellent model of certain ways to argue.

Being Green at Ben and Jerry's
Some Environmental Policies Are Feel-Good Indulgences for an Era of Energy Abundance

If you have an average-size dinner table, four feet by six feet, put a dime on the edge of it. Think of the surface of the table as the Arctic National Wildlife Refuge in Alaska. The dime is larger than the piece of the coastal plain that would have been opened to drilling for oil and natural gas. The House of Representatives voted for drilling, but the Senate voted against access to what Sen. John Kerry, Massachusetts Democrat and presidential aspirant, calls "a few drops of oil." ANWR could produce, for twenty-five years, at least as much oil as America currently imports from Saudi Arabia.

Six weeks of desultory Senate debate about the energy bill reached an almost comic culmination in . . . yet another agriculture subsidy. The subsidy is a requirement that will triple the amount of ethanol, which is made from corn, that must be put in gasoline, ostensibly to clean America's air, actually to buy farmers' votes.

Over the last three decades, energy use has risen about 30 percent. But so has population, which means per capita energy use is unchanged. And per capita GDP has risen substantially, so we are using 40 percent less energy per dollar output. Which is one reason there is no energy crisis, at least none as most Americans understand such things—a shortage of, and therefore high prices of, gasoline for cars, heating oil for furnaces and electricity for air conditioners.

In the absence of a crisis to concentrate the attention of the inattentive American majority, an intense faction—full-time environmentalists—goes to work. Spencer Abraham, the secretary of Energy, says "the previous administration . . . simply drew up a list of fuels it *didn't* like—nuclear energy, coal, hydropower, and oil—which together account for 73 percent of America's energy supply." Well, there are always windmills.

Sometimes lofty environmentalism is a cover for crude politics. The United States has the world's largest proven reserves of coal. But Mike Oliver, a retired physicist and engineer, and John Hospers, professor emeritus of philosophy at USC, note that in 1996 President Clinton put 68 billion tons of America's cleanest-burning coal, located in Utah, off-limits for mining, ostensibly for environmental reasons. If every existing U.S. electric power plant burned coal, the 68 billion tons could fuel them for forty-five years at the current rate of consumption. Now power companies must import clean-burning coal, some from mines owned by Indonesia's Lippo Group, the heavy contributor to Clinton, whose decision about Utah's coal vastly increased the value of Lippo's coal.

The United States has just 2.14 percent of the world's proven reserves of oil, so some people say it is pointless to drill in places like ANWR because "energy independence" is a chimera.[1] Indeed it is. But domestic supplies can provide important insurance against uncertain foreign supplies. And domestic supplies can mean exporting hundreds of billions of dollars less to oil-producing nations, such as Iraq.

Besides, when considering proven reserves, note the adjective. In 1930 the United States had proven reserves of 13 billion barrels. We then fought the Second World War and fueled the most fabulous economic expansion in human history, including the electricity-driven "New Economy." (Manufacturing and running computers consume 15 percent of U.S. electricity. Internet use alone accounts for half of the growth in demand for electricity.) So by 1990 proven reserves were . . . 17 billion barrels, not counting any in Alaska or Hawaii.

In 1975 proven reserves in the Persian Gulf were 74 billion barrels. In 1993 they were 663 billion, a ninefold increase. At the current rate of consumption, today's proven reserves would last 150 years. New discoveries will be made, some by vastly improved techniques of deep-water drilling. But environmental policies will define opportunities. The government estimates that beneath the U.S. outer continental shelf, which the government owns, there are at least 46 billion barrels of oil. But only 2 percent of the shelf has been leased for energy development.

Opponents of increased energy production usually argue for decreased consumption. But they flinch from conservation measures. A new $1 gasoline tax would dampen demand for gasoline, but it would stimulate demands for the heads of the tax increasers. After all, Americans get irritable when impersonal market forces add 25 cents to the cost of a gallon. Tougher fuel-efficiency requirements for vehicles would save a lot of energy. But who would save the legislators who passed those requirements? Beware the wrath of Americans who like to drive, and autoworkers who like to make cars that are large, heavy, and safer than the gasoline-sippers that environmentalists prefer.

Some environmentalism is a feel-good [10] indulgence for an era of energy abundance, which means an era of avoided choices. Or ignored choices — ignored because if acknowledged, they would not make the choosers feel good. Karl Zinsmeister, editor in chief of the *American Enterprise* magazine, imagines an oh-so-green environmentalist enjoying the most politically correct product on the planet — Ben & Jerry's ice cream. Made in a factory that depends on electricity-guzzling refrigeration, a gallon of ice cream requires four gallons of milk. While making that much milk, a cow produces eight gallons of manure, and flatulence with another eight gallons of methane, a potent "greenhouse" gas. And the cow consumes lots of water plus three pounds of grain and hay, which is produced with tractor fuel, chemical fertilizers, herbicides and insecticides, and is transported with truck or train fuel:

"So every time he digs into his Cherry Garcia, the conscientious environmentalist should visualize (in addition to world peace) a pile of grain, water, farm chemicals, and energy inputs much bigger than his ice cream bowl on one side of the table, and, on the other side of the table, a mound of manure eight times the size of his bowl, plus a balloon of methane that would barely fit under the dining room table."

Cherry Garcia. It's a choice. *Bon appétit.*

---

[1] **chimera** Something that is hoped or wished for but is impossible to actually achieve. [Editors' note.]

GEORGE F. WILL'S STRATEGIES

Now let's look at Will's essay to see what techniques he uses to engage readers' interest and perhaps enable him to convince them — or at least make them think — that he is on to something. If you think some or all of his strategies are effective, consider adapting them for use in your own essays.

The title, "Being Green at Ben and Jerry's," does not at all prepare readers for an argument about drilling in the National Arctic Wildlife Refuge. But if you have read any of Will's other columns in *Newsweek*, you probably know that he is conservative and can guess that in this essay he'll poke some fun at the green folk — the environmentalists. Will can get away with using a title that isn't focused because he has a body of loyal readers who will read his pieces no matter what the topic is, but the rest of us have to give our readers some idea of our topic. In short, let your readers know early, perhaps in the title, where you'll be taking them.

The subtitle, "Some Environmental Policies Are Feel-Good Indulgences for an Era of Energy Abundance," perhaps added by the magazine's editor, suggests that the piece will concern energy. Moreover, the words "feel-good indulgences" signal to readers that Will believes the environmentalists are indulging themselves.

Paragraph 1 offers a striking comparison. Will wants his readers to believe that the area proposed for drilling is tiny, so he says that if they imagine the entire Arctic National Wildlife Refuge as a dinner table, the area proposed for drilling is the size of a dime. We think you'll agree that this opening seizes a reader's attention. Although some opponents to drilling in the ANWR have contested Will's analogy (saying the area would be much larger, perhaps comparable to the size of a dinner plate, or even a dinner plate broken in pieces, with roads and pipelines crossing between the fragments), the image is still highly effective. A dime is so small! And worth so little!

Another point about paragraph 1: Will's casual voice sounds like one you might hear in your own living room: "If you have an average-size dinner table," "The dime is larger," "at least as much oil." Your own essays need not adopt a highly formal style. Readers should think of you as serious but not solemn.

Will goes on to say that Senator John Kerry, an opponent of drilling and therefore on the side that Will opposes, dismisses the oil in the refuge as "a few drops." Will replies that it "could produce, for twenty-five years, at least as much oil as America currently imports from Saudi Arabia." Kerry's "a few drops" isn't literal, of course; he means that the oil is a drop in the bucket. But when one looks into the issue, one finds that estimates by responsible sources vary considerably — from 3.2 billion barrels to 11.5 billion barrels.

Paragraph 2 dismisses the Senate's debate ("almost comic . . . actually to buy farmers' votes").

Paragraph 3 offers statistics to make the point that "there is no energy crisis." Here, as in paragraph 1 (where he showed his awareness of Kerry's view), Will indicates that he's familiar with views other than his own. In arguing a case, it's important for a writer to let readers know that indeed there are other views — which the writer then shows are less substantial than the writer's own. Will is correct in saying that "per capita energy use is unchanged," but opponents might say, "Yes, per capita consumption hasn't increased; but given the population increase, the annual amount has vastly increased, which means that resources are being depleted and that pollution is increasing."

Paragraph 4 asserts again that there is no energy crisis, pokes fun at "full-time environmentalists" (perhaps even implying that such people ought to get respectable jobs), and ends with a bit of whimsy: These folks probably think we should go back to using windmills.

Paragraph 5, in support of the assertion that "Sometimes lofty environmentalism is a cover for crude politics," cites an authority (often an effective technique). Since readers aren't likely to recognize the name, Will also identifies him ("professor emeritus of philosophy at USC") and then offers further statistics. The paragraph begins by talking about "crude politics" and ends with this assertion: "Now power companies must import clean-burning coal, some from mines owned by Indonesia's Lippo Group, the heavy contributor to Clinton." In short, Will makes several strategic moves to suggest that at least some environmentalists' views are rooted in money and politics.

Paragraph 6 offers another statistic ("The United States has just 2.14 percent of the world's proven reserves of oil") and turns it against those who argue that therefore it's pointless to drill in Alaska. In effect, Will is replying to people like Senator Kerry who say that the Arctic refuge provides only "a few drops of oil." The point, Will suggests, is not that it's impossible for the nation to achieve independence; rather, the point is that "domestic supplies can provide important insurance against uncertain foreign supplies."

Paragraph 7 begins smoothly with a transition, "Besides," and then offers additional statistics concerning the large amount of oil that the United States has held in proven reserves. For instance, by the end of World War II these reserves were enough to fuel "the most fabulous economic expansion in human history."

Paragraph 8 offers additional statistics, first about "proven reserves in the Persian Gulf" and then about an estimate — but only an estimate — of oil "beneath the U.S. outer continental shelf." We are not certain of Will's point here, but in any case the statistics suggest that he has done some homework.

Paragraph 9 summarizes the chief position (as Will sees it) of those on the other side of this issue: They "usually argue for decreased consumption," but they're afraid to argue for the sort of gasoline tax that might indeed decrease consumption because they know that many Americans want to drive large, heavy cars. Further, the larger, heavier cars that the environmentalists object to are in fact "safer than the gasoline-sippers that environmentalists prefer."

Paragraph 10 uses the term "feel-good indulgence," which also appears in the essay's subtitle; and now in the paragraph's third sentence we hear again of Ben and Jerry, whose names we haven't seen since reading the essay's title, "Being Green at Ben and Jerry's." Perhaps we've been wondering all this time why the title mentions Ben and Jerry. Surely most readers know that Ben and Jerry are associated with ice cream and therefore with cows and meadows, and probably many readers know that Ben and Jerry support environmentalism and other liberal causes. Drawing on an article by Karl Zinsmeister, editor of the *American Enterprise*, Will writes an extremely amusing paragraph in which he points out that the process of making ice cream "depends on electricity-guzzling refrigeration" and that the cows are essentially supported by fuel that transports fertilizers, herbicides, and insecticides. Further, in the course of producing the four gallons of milk required for one gallon of ice cream, the cows themselves — those darlings of the environmentalists — contribute "eight gallons of manure, and flatulence with another eight gallons of methane, a potent 'greenhouse' gas." As we'll soon see in Will's next paragraph, the present paragraph is largely a lead-in for the quotation he gives in the next paragraph. He knows it isn't enough to give a quotation; a writer has to make use of it — by leading in to it, by commenting on it after inserting it, or both.

Paragraph 11 is entirely devoted to quoting Zinsmeister, who imagines an environmentalist digging into a dish of one of Ben and Jerry's most popular flavors, Cherry Garcia. We're invited to see the bowl of ice cream on one side of the table — here Will effectively evokes the table of paragraph 1 — and a pile of manure on the other side, "plus a balloon of methane that would barely fit under the dining room table." This statement is vulgar, no doubt, but it's funny too. Will knows that humor as well as logic (and statistics and other evidence) can be among the key tools a writer uses in getting an audience to consider or accept an argument.

Paragraph 12 consists of three short sentences, adding up to less than a single line of type: "Cherry Garcia. It's a choice. *Bon appétit.*" None of the sentences mentions oil or the Arctic Refuge or statistics; therefore, this ending might seem irrelevant to the topic, but Will is very effectively saying, "Sure, you have a choice about drilling in the Arctic Refuge; any sensible person will choose the ice cream (drilling) rather than the manure and the gas (not drilling)."

Topics for Critical Thinking and Writing

1. What, if anything, makes George Will's essay interesting to you? What, if anything, makes it highly persuasive? How might it be made more persuasive?

2. In paragraph 10, Will clowns about the gas that cows emit, but apparently this gas, which contributes to global warming, is no laughing matter. The government of New Zealand, in an effort to reduce livestock emissions of methane and nitrous oxide, proposed a tax that would subsidize future research on the emissions. The tax would cost the average farmer $300 a year. Imagine that you're a New Zealand farmer. Write a letter to your representative, arguing for or against the tax.

3. Senator Barbara Boxer, campaigning against the proposal to drill in ANWR, spoke of the refuge as "God's gift to us" (*New York Times*, March 20, 2002). How strong an argument is this? Some opponents of the proposal have said that drilling in ANWR is as unthinkable as drilling in Yosemite or the Grand Canyon. Again, how strong is this argument? Can you imagine circumstances in which you would support drilling in these places? Why, or why not? Do we have a moral duty to preserve certain unspoiled areas? Explain your response.

4. The Inupiat (Eskimo) who live in and near ANWR by a large majority favor drilling, seeing it as a source of jobs and a source of funding for schools, hospitals, and police. But the Ketchikan Indians, who speak of themselves as the "Caribou People," see drilling as a threat to the herds on which they depend for food and hides. How is it possible to balance the conflicting needs of these two groups?

5. Opponents of drilling in ANWR argue that over its lifetime of fifty years, the area would produce less than 1 percent of the fuel we need during the period and that therefore we

shouldn't risk disturbing the area. Further, they argue that drilling in ANWR is an attempt at a quick fix to U.S. energy needs, whereas what the nation really needs are sustainable solutions, such as the development of renewable energy sources (e.g., wind and sun) and fuel-efficient automobiles. How convincing do you find these arguments? Explain your response.

6. Proponents of drilling include a large majority — something like 75 percent — of the people of Alaska, including its governor and its two senators. How much attention do their voices deserve?

7. Analyze the essay in terms of its use of *ethos*, *pathos*, and *logos*.

8. What sort of audience do you think Will is addressing? What values do his readers probably share? What makes you think so?

Arguments for Analysis

STANLEY FISH

Stanley Fish (b. 1938) established his reputation as a scholar of English literature — he has taught literature at the University of California–Berkeley, Johns Hopkins University, and Duke University — but he has also published on legal issues. He now teaches at Florida International University's College of Law. This essay was published in 2008, when Hillary Clinton and Barack Obama were candidates for the Democratic Party's nomination for president. Inevitably, there was much talk about the candidacy of a woman and an African American.

When "Identity Politics" Is Rational

If there's anything everyone is against in these election times, it's "identity politics," a phrase that covers a multitude of sins. Let me start with a definition. (It may not be yours, but it will at least allow the discussion to be framed.) You're practicing identity politics when you vote for or against someone because of his or her skin color, ethnicity, religion, gender, sexual orientation, or any other marker that leads you to say yes or no independently of a candidate's ideas or policies. In essence identity politics is an affirmation of the tribe against the claims of ideology, and by ideology I do not mean something bad (a mistake frequently made), but any agenda informed by a vision of what the world should be like.

An identity politics voter says, in effect, I don't care what views he holds, or even what bad things he may have done, or what lack of ability he may display; he's my brother, or he's my kinsman, or he's my landsman, or he comes from the neighborhood, or he's a Southerner, or (and here the tribe is really big) my country right or wrong. "My country right or wrong" is particularly useful in making clear how identity politics differs from politics as many Americans would prefer to see it practiced. Rather than saying she's right on immigration or he's wrong on the war, the identity-politics voter says he looks like me or she and I belong to the same church.

Identity politics is illiberal. That is, it is particularist whereas liberalism is universalist. The history of liberalism is a history of extending the franchise to those who were once excluded from it by their race, gender, or national origin. Although these marks of identification were retained (by the census and other forms of governmental classification) and could still be celebrated in private associations like the church and the social club, they were not supposed to be the basis of decisions one might make "as a citizen," decisions about who might best lead the country or what laws should be enacted or voted down. Deciding as a citizen means deciding not as a man or a woman or a Jew or an African American or a Caucasian or a heterosexual, but as a human being.

Stanley Crouch believes that the project of liberal universalizing is now pretty much complete and that "elements of distinction" — his phrase for the thinking that was fashionable in "the era of 'identity politics'" — "have become secondary to the power of human qualities with which anyone can identify or reject" (*Daily News*, Feb. 11). But his judgment is belied by almost everything that is going on in this campaign. As I write this I am watching the returns from the "Potomac Primary" and the news is being presented entirely in racial, ethnic, and gender terms. Every newspaper or magazine article I read does the same thing. The Obama and Clinton campaigns accuse each other of playing the race card or the gender card. An Hispanic superdelegate warns that by replacing her Latino campaign manager with a black one, Senator Clinton risks losing his vote and the vote of other Hispanic delegates he is in the process of contacting.

Christopher Hitchens looks at the scene 5 and is disgusted by behavior that, in his view, "keeps us anchored in the past" (*Wall Street Journal*, Jan. 18). He will not, he tells us, vote for Clinton just so that we can have the "'first woman president'" (I don't remember that one from the past); and he won't vote for Obama who, he says, "wants us to transcend something at the same time he implicitly asks us to give that same something as a reason to vote for him." It would seem that we are far from realizing Ken Connor's dream that we might judge "all of the presidential hopefuls on the basis of the content of their character and their qualifications to serve" (Townhall.com, Jan. 20).

But is it as bad as all that? Is it so irrational and retrograde to base one's vote on the gender or race or religion or ethnicity of a candidate? Not necessarily. If the vote is given (or withheld) only because the candidate looks like you or has the same religion, it does seem a shallow and meretricious act, for it is an act unsupported by reasons. "Because she is a woman as I am" is of course a reason, but it is not a reason of the relevant kind, a reason that cites goals and programs, and argues for them. But suppose what was said was something like this: "As a woman I find government sponsored research skewed in the direction of diseases that afflict men and inattentive to the medical problems faced by women, and it is my belief that a woman president will devote resources to the solution of those problems." That's an identity politics argument which is thick, not thin; the she's-like-me point is not invoked as sufficient unto itself, but as it relates to a matter of policy. The calculation may or may not pan out (successful candidates both disappoint and surprise), but it is a calculation of the right kind.

One objection to identity politics (Crouch makes it in the same column) is that groups and populations are not monolithic, but display a diversity of attitudes and positions. Yes they do, but members of a group who might disagree with each other on any number of things could nevertheless come together on a matter of shared concern. American Jews, for example, have widely varying views on many important issues — tax cuts, tort reform, gay marriage, the Iraq war. Still, the vast majority believes that it is important to defend the security of Israel. This is a belief shared even by those American Jews who are strongly critical of Israel's treatment of the Palestinians. They may deplore Israel's actions and agree with Jimmy Carter when he likens them to apartheid, but if the choice is between a politician who pledges to support Israel and a politician who would withdraw support and leave the Jewish state to fend for itself, most of them would vote for the first candidate every time.

African Americans are no less heterogeneous in their views than Jewish Americans. Yet every African American — conservative or liberal, rich or poor, barely educated or highly educated — meets with obstacles to his or her success and mobility that are all the more frustrating because they are structural (built into the culture's ways of perceiving) rather than official. To the non–African American these obstacles will be more or less invisible, especially in a country where access to opportunity is guaranteed by law. It makes sense, therefore, that an African American voter could come to the conclusion that an African American candidate would be likely to fight for changes that could remove barriers a white candidate might not even see. A vote given for that reason would be a vote based on identity, but it would be more than a mere affirmation of fellowship (he's one of mine and I have to support him); it would be a considered political judgment as to which candidate will move the country in a preferred direction. Identity might be the trigger of the vote, but it would not be the whole of its content.

We should distinguish, I think, between two forms of identity politics. The first I have already named "tribal"; it is the politics based on who a candidate is rather than on what he or she believes or argues for. And that, I agree, is usually a bad idea. (I say "usually" because it is possible to argue that the election of a black or female president, no matter what his or

her positions happen to be, will be more than a symbolic correction of the errors that have marred the country's history, and an important international statement as well.) The second form of identity politics is what I call "interest" identity politics. It is based on the assumption (itself resting on history and observation) that because of his or her race or ethnicity or gender a candidate might pursue an agenda that would advance the interests a voter is committed to. Not only is there nothing wrong with such a calculation — it is both rational and considered — I don't see that there is an alternative to voting on the basis of interest.

The alternative usually put forward is Crouch's: Vote "for human qualities" rather than sectarian qualities. That is, vote on the basis of reasons everyone, no matter what his or her identity, will acknowledge as worthy. But there are no such reasons and no such human qualities. To be sure, there are words often attached to this chimera — integrity, dedication, honesty, intellect, to name a few. But these qualities, even when they are found, will always be in the service of some set of policies you either favor or reject. It is those policies, not the probity[1] of their proposer, that you will be voting for. (If your candidate is also a good person, that's a nice bonus, but it isn't the essential thing.) You will be voting, in short, for interests, and those who do not have an investment in those interests will be voting for someone else.

What this means is that the ritual deprecation of "special interests" makes no sense. All interests are special interests — they proceed from some contestable point of view — and none is "generally human." And that is why identity interests, as long as they are ideological and not merely tribal, constitute a perfectly respectable reason for awarding your vote.

[1] **probity** Integrity or morality; goodness. [Editors' note.]

Topics for Critical Thinking and Writing

1. Stanley Fish begins his essay with a formal and explicit definition of "identity politics." What do you think of that definition? Is it too broad? Too narrow? Too vague? Can you think of any ways to improve it? Explain your responses.

2. What is the origin of the epigram "My country right or wrong"? Does Fish endorse it? Do you? Why, or why not? Why does Fish offer it as an example of identity politics? Explain your views.

3. Suppose someone says that it's naïve to advocate deciding issues of public concern by appealing to one's status as "a human being" (para. 3). How would you reply? Do so in an essay of 300 words.

4. Fish speaks of two different practices under the rubric of "identity politics." What are they? Which one, if either, does Fish prefer, and why? Is either of these practices related to what Fish's essay title refers to as "rational" politics? Explain.

5. Is the appeal of Fish's essay entirely to *logos* and *ethos,* or do you also find some humor and some *pathos*? If so, cite passages.

GLORIA JIMÉNEZ

Gloria Jiménez married immediately after she graduated from high school, worked briefly, had two children, and then, after her younger child started school, continued her own formal education. This essay, written for a composition course at Tufts University in 2003, was her first publication.

Against the Odds, and against the Common Good (Student Essay)

State-run lotteries are now so common — thirty-nine states and Washington, D.C., operate lotteries — that the states probably will never get out of the lottery business. Still, when all is said and done about lotteries bringing a bit of excitement into the lives of many people and bringing a vast amount of money into the lives of a few, the states should not be in the business of urging people to gamble.

And they *do* urge people. Consider a slogan used in Maryland, "Play Today. Cash Tomorrow." If the statement were, "Get a job today and you will have cash tomorrow," it would be true; it would make sense, however small the earnings might be. But "Play Today. Cash Tomorrow" falsely suggests that the way to have money tomorrow is to buy a ticket today. In fact, buying a ticket is an almost sure-fire way of getting nothing for something.

Maryland is not the only state that uses a clever slogan to get its citizens to part with hard-earned money. New York's ads say, "You Can't Win If You Don't Play," and Oregon's ads say, "There Is No Such Thing as a Losing

Ticket." This last slogan — which at first glance seems to say that every ticket will benefit the purchaser — is built on the idea that the state's share of the money goes to a worthy cause, usually education or some social service. But no matter how you look at it, this slogan, like the others, urges people to buy a product — a jackpot — that they have almost no chance of receiving.

The chief arguments *in favor* of state-run lotteries seem to be these: (1) people freely choose to participate; (2) funds are used for education or for other important services; (3) if this source of funding disappears, the states will have to compensate by imposing taxes of one sort or another; (4) operation by the government ensures that the lotteries are run honestly; and (5) lotteries create jobs. We can respond briefly to the last two points, and then concentrate on the first three.

It probably is true that the lotteries are run honestly (though I seem to recall reading in the newspaper about one state in which corruption was found in administering the lottery), but that is not the point. If it is wrong to encourage people to gamble, it is hardly relevant to say that the game is run honestly. The other point that can be dismissed briefly is that lotteries create jobs. This argument is usually advanced in connection with the creation of casinos, which surely do create jobs, not only in the casinos but also in nearby restaurants, parking lots, movie theaters, and so forth. But lottery tickets are sold in places where the clerks are already employed. Presumably the only new jobs created by the lottery are the relatively few jobs of the people who dream up the slogans or who are in charge of collecting and processing the receipts.

The three other claims require more attention. The first, that people freely choose to participate, probably is largely true. Although some buyers are compulsive gamblers, people who are addicted and therefore cannot really be said to choose freely, I grant that most people do have a free choice — although, as I have already said, I think that some of the slogans that states use are deceptive, and if this is the case, purchasers who are misled by the ads are not entirely free. Consider a slogan that Illinois used on billboards, especially in poor neighborhoods: "This Could Be Your Ticket Out." Yes, a person might hit the jackpot and get out of poverty, but the chances are one in several million, and to imply that the lottery is a reasonable option to get out of present poverty is to be deceptive. Further, the message is essentially unwholesome. It implies that the way out is luck, rather than education and hard work. Of course, luck plays a part in life, but 99.99 percent of the people who rely on the ticket as the "ticket out" of poverty are going to be terribly disappointed. But again, we can grant that except for gambling addicts, people who buy lottery tickets are freely doing so.

Probably the strongest claim is that the funds are used for important purposes, usually education. This claim apparently is true: the legislators are smart enough to package the lottery bills this way. And the revenue gained seems enormous — $20 billion in 2002, according to the *New York Times* (May 18, 2003, sec. 4, p. 1). On the other hand, this amount is only about 4 percent of the total revenue of the states. That is, this amount *could* be raised by other means, specifically by taxation, but legislators understandably do not want to be associated with increasing taxes. And so, again, advocates of state lotteries emphasize the voluntary nature of the lottery: by buying lottery tickets, they say, people are in effect volunteering to give money to the states, in exchange for the chance (however remote) of getting a ticket out. Buying a ticket, in this view, is paying an optional tax; if you don't want to pay the tax, don't buy the ticket.

I now get to the point in my argument where I may sound condescending, where I may offend decent people. The point is this: studies show that most of the tickets are bought by people who don't have much money, people who are near the bottom of the economic scale. According to one study, adults whose income was under $10,000 spent nearly three times as much buying lottery tickets as did adults who earned $50,000 or more.[1] I say that this argument is delicate because anyone who advances it is liable to be accused of being snobbish and paternalistic, of saying, in effect, "Poor people don't know how to manage their money, so we ought to remove temptation from their eyes." But such a reply does not get to the central issues: the central issues are (1) that the state should not tempt people, rich or poor, with dreams of an easy buck and (2) that education and social services are immensely important to the whole of society, so they should not be disproportionately financed by the poor and the addicted.

Let me end a bit indirectly. Surely everyone will grant that tobacco is a harmful product.

---
[1] Verna V. Gehring, "The American State Lottery: Sale or Swindle?" *Report from the Institute for Philosophy and Public Policy* 20 (Winter/Spring 2000): 15.

Yes, it is legal, but everyone knows it is harmful. The state puts very heavy taxes on it, presumably not to raise revenue but to discourage the use of tobacco. We agree, surely, that it would be almost criminal if, in an effort to increase its revenues, the state *enticed* people to smoke — for example, by posting billboards showing attractive people smoking or cartoon characters that appealed to children. Would we say, "Oh, well, we need the revenue (from the taxes) to provide services, so let's make smoking as attractive as we can to get people to buy cigarettes"? No, we would say, "People should not smoke, but if they will, well, let's use the revenue from the taxes for two chief purposes: *to dissuade* people from smoking and *to treat* people who have become ill from smoking."

State legislators who genuinely have the 10 interests of their constituents at heart will not pass bills that put the state into the lottery business and that cause the state to engage in an activity that is close to pickpocketing. Rather, they will recognize that, however unpopular taxes are, taxes may have to be raised to support education and social services that the people rightly expect the state to provide. It's against the odds to expect politicians to act this way, but let's hope that some politicians will do the right thing and will vote for the common good.

Topics for Critical Thinking and Writing

1. Gloria Jiménez omits at least one important argument that advocates of state-run lotteries sometimes offer: If our state doesn't run a lottery, residents will simply go to nearby states to buy tickets, so we will just be losing revenue that other states pick up; poor people will still be spending money that they can't afford, and our state will in no way benefit. What do you suppose Jiménez might say in reply? And what is your own view of this argument?

2. A bit of humor appears at the end of paragraph 2. Is it appropriate? Or is the essay too solemn, too preachy? If you think it's too preachy, cite some sentences, and then revise them to make them more acceptable.

3. What are the strengths and weaknesses of this essay? What grade would you give it, and why? If you were the instructor in a first-year composition course, what comment (three or four sentences) would you write at the end of the essay?

4. Jiménez wrote the essay in a composition course. If you were the editor of your college's newspaper, might you run it as an op-ed piece? Why, or why not?

ANNA LISA RAYA

Daughter of a second-generation Mexican American father and a Puerto Rican mother, Anna Lisa Raya grew up in Los Angeles. In 1994, while she was an undergraduate at Columbia University in New York, she wrote and published this essay on identity.

It's Hard Enough Being Me (Student Essay)

When I entered college, I *discovered* I was Latina. Until then, I had never questioned who I was or where I was from: My father is a second-generation Mexican American, born and raised in Los Angeles, and my mother was born in Puerto Rico and raised in Compton, California. My home is El Sereno, a predominantly Mexican neighborhood in L.A. Every close friend I have back home is Mexican. So I was always just Mexican. Though sometimes I was just Puerto Rican — like when we would visit Mamo (my grandma) or hang out with my Aunt Titi.

Upon arriving in New York as a first-year student, 3,000 miles from home, I not only experienced extreme culture shock, but for the first time I had to define myself according to the broad term "Latina." Although culture shock and identity crisis are common for the newly minted collegian who goes away to school, my experience as a newly minted Latina was, and still is, even more complicating. In El Sereno, I felt like I was part of a majority, whereas at the College I am a minority.

I've discovered that many Latinos like myself have undergone similar experiences. We face discrimination for being a minority in this country while also facing criticism for being "whitewashed" or "sellouts" in the countries of our heritage. But as an ethnic group in college, we are forced to define ourselves according to some vague, generalized Latino experience. This requires us to know our history, our language, our music, and our religion. I can't even be a content "Puerto Mexican" because I have to be a politically-and-socially-aware-Latina-with-a-chip-on-my-shoulder-because-of-how-repressed-I-am-in-this-country.

I am none of the above. I am the quintessential imperfect Latina. I can't dance salsa to save my life, I learned about Montezuma and the Aztecs in sixth grade, and I haven't prayed to the *Virgen de Guadalupe* in years.

Apparently I don't even look Latina. I 5 can't count how many times people have just assumed that I'm white or asked me if I'm Asian. True, my friends back home call me *güera* ("whitey") because I have green eyes and pale skin, but that was as bad as it got. I never thought I would wish my skin were a darker shade or my hair a curlier texture, but since I've been in college, I have — many times.

Another thing: My Spanish is terrible. Every time I call home, I berate my mama for not teaching me Spanish when I was a child. In fact, not knowing how to speak the language of my home countries is the biggest problem that I have encountered, as have many Latinos. In Mexico there is a term, *pocha*, which is used by native Mexicans to ridicule Mexican Americans. It expresses a deep-rooted antagonism and dislike for those of us who were raised on the other side of the border. Our failed attempts to speak pure, Mexican Spanish are largely responsible for the dislike. Other Latin American natives have this same attitude. No matter how well a Latino speaks Spanish, it can never be good enough.

Yet Latinos can't even speak Spanish in the U.S. without running the risk of being called "spic" or "wetback." That is precisely why my mother refused to teach me Spanish when I was a child. The fact that she spoke Spanish was constantly used against her: It prevented her from getting good jobs, and it would have placed me in bilingual education — a construct of the Los Angeles public school system that has proved to be more of a hindrance to intellectual development than a help.

To be fully Latina in college, however, I *must* know Spanish. I must satisfy the equation: Latina [equals] Spanish-speaking.

So I'm stuck in this black hole of an identity crisis, and college isn't making my life any easier, as I thought it would. In high school, I was being prepared for an adulthood in which I would be an individual, in which I wouldn't have to wear a Catholic school uniform anymore. But though I led an anonymous adolescence, I knew who I was. I knew I was different from white, black, or Asian people. I knew there was a language other than English that I could call my own if I only knew how to speak it better. I knew there were historical reasons why I was in this country, distinct reasons that make my existence here easier or more difficult than other people's existence. Ultimately, I was content.

Now I feel pushed into a corner, always 10 defining, defending, and proving myself to classmates, professors, or employers. Trying to understand who and why I am, while understanding Plato or Homer, is a lot to ask of myself.

A month ago, I heard three Nuyorican (Puerto Ricans born and raised in New York) writers discuss how New York City has influenced their writing. One problem I have faced as a young writer is finding a voice that is true to my community. I was surprised and reassured to discover that as Latinos, these writers had faced similar pressures and conflicts as myself; some weren't even taught Spanish in childhood. I will never forget the advice that one of them gave me that evening: She said that I need to be true to myself. "Because people will always complain about what you are doing — you're a 'gringa' or a 'spic' no matter what," she explained. "So you might as well do things for yourself and not for them."

I don't know why it has taken 20 years to hear this advice, but I'm going to give it a try. *Soy yo* and no one else. *Punto.*[1]

---

[1] **Soy yo . . . Punto.** I'm me . . . Period (Spanish). [Editors' note.]

Topics for Critical Thinking and Writing

1. When Anna Lisa Raya says she "*discovered*" she was Latina (para. 1), to what kind of event is she referring? Was she coerced or persuaded to declare herself as Latina, or did it come about in some other way? Explain.

2. Is Raya glad or sorry that she didn't learn Spanish as a child? What evidence in her essay indicates one way or the other?

3. What is an "identity crisis" (para. 9)? Does everyone go through such a crisis upon entering college? Did you? Or is this an experience that only racial minorities in predominantly white American colleges undergo? Explain your responses.

RONALD TAKAKI

Ronald Takaki (1939–2009), the grandson of agricultural laborers who immigrated from Japan, was a professor of ethnic studies at the University of California–Berkeley. He edited From Different Shores: Perspectives on Race and Ethnicity in America *(1987) and wrote (among other works)* Strangers from a Different Shore: A History of Asian-Americans *(1989). The essay reprinted here appeared originally in the* New York Times *on June 16, 1990.*

The Harmful Myth of Asian Superiority

Asian Americans have increasingly come to be viewed as a "model minority." But are they as successful as claimed? And for whom are they supposed to be a model?

Asian Americans have been described in the media as "excessively, even provocatively" successful in gaining admission to universities. Asian American shopkeepers have been congratulated, as well as criticized, for their ubiquity and entrepreneurial effectiveness.

If Asian Americans can make it, many politicians and pundits ask, why can't African Americans? Such comparisons pit minorities against each other and generate African American resentment toward Asian Americans. The victims are blamed for their plight, rather than racism and an economy that has made many young African American workers superfluous.

The celebration of Asian Americans has obscured reality. For example, figures on the high earnings of Asian Americans relative to Caucasians are misleading. Most Asian Americans live in California, Hawaii, and New York—states with higher incomes and higher costs of living than the national average.

Even Japanese Americans, often touted for 5 their upward mobility, have not reached equality. While Japanese American men in California earned an average income comparable to Caucasian men in 1980, they did so only by acquiring more education and working more hours.

Comparing family incomes is even more deceptive. Some Asian American groups do have higher family incomes than Caucasians. But they have more workers per family.

The "model minority" image homogenizes Asian Americans and hides their differences. For example, while thousands of Vietnamese American young people attend universities, others are on the streets. They live in motels and hang out in pool halls in places like East Los Angeles; some join gangs.

Twenty-five percent of the people in New York City's Chinatown lived below the poverty level in 1980, compared with

17 percent of the city's population. Some 60 percent of the workers in the Chinatowns of Los Angeles and San Francisco are crowded into low-paying jobs in garment factories and restaurants.

"Most immigrants coming into Chinatown with a language barrier cannot go outside this confined area into the mainstream of American industry," a Chinese immigrant said. "Before, I was a painter in Hong Kong, but I can't do it here. I got no license, no education. I want a living; so it's dishwasher, janitor, or cook."

Hmong and Mien refugees from Laos 10 have unemployment rates that reach as high as 80 percent. A 1987 California study showed that three out of ten Southeast Asian refugee families had been on welfare for four to ten years.

Although college-educated Asian Americans are entering the professions and earning good salaries, many hit the "glass ceiling" — the barrier through which high management positions can be seen but not reached. In 1988, only 8 percent of Asian Americans were "officials" and "managers," compared with 12 percent for all groups.

Finally, the triumph of Korean immigrants has been exaggerated. In 1988, Koreans in the New York metropolitan area earned only 68 percent of the median income of non-Asians. More than three-quarters of Korean greengrocers, those so-called paragons of bootstrap entrepreneurialism, came to America with a college education. Engineers, teachers, or administrators while in Korea, they became shopkeepers after their arrival. For many of them, the greengrocery represents dashed dreams, a step downward in status.

For all their hard work and long hours, most Korean shopkeepers do not actually earn very much: $17,000 to $35,000 a year, usually representing the income from the labor of an entire family.

But most Korean immigrants do not become shopkeepers. Instead, many find themselves trapped as clerks in grocery stores, service workers in restaurants, seamstresses in garment factories, and janitors in hotels.

Most Asian Americans know their "suc- 15 cess" is largely a myth. They also see how the celebration of Asian Americans as a "model minority" perpetuates their inequality and exacerbates relations between them and African Americans.

Topics for Critical Thinking and Writing

1. What is the thesis of Ronald Takaki's essay? What evidence does he offer for its truth? Do you find his argument convincing? Explain your answers to these questions in an essay of 500 words. Alternatively, write a 500-word blog post that responds to the essay.

2. Takaki several times uses statistics to make a point. What effect do the statistics have on the reader? Do some of the statistics seem more convincing than others? Explain your responses.

3. Consider the title of Takaki's essay. To what group(s) is the myth of Asian superiority harmful?

4. Suppose you believed that Asian Americans are economically more successful in America today, relative to white Americans, than African Americans are. Does Takaki agree

or disagree with you? Why, or why not? What evidence, if any, does he cite to support or reject the belief?

5. Takaki attacks the "myth" of Asian American success and thus rejects the idea that Asian Americans are a "model minority" (recall the opening and closing paragraphs). What do you think a genuine model minority would be like? Can you think of any racial or ethnic minority in the United States that can serve as a model? Explain why or why not in an essay of 500 words.

JAMES Q. WILSON

James Q. Wilson (1931–2012) was Collins Professor of Management and Public Policy at the University of California–Los Angeles. Among his books are Thinking about Crime *(1975),* Bureaucracy *(1989),* The Moral Sense *(1993), and* Moral Judgment *(1997). The essay reprinted here appeared originally in the* New York Times Magazine *on March 20, 1994.*

Just Take Away Their Guns

The president wants still tougher gun control legislation and thinks it will work. The public supports more gun control laws but suspects they won't work. The public is right.

Legal restraints on the lawful purchase of guns will have little effect on the illegal use of guns. There are some 200 million guns in private ownership, about one-third of them handguns. Only about 2 percent of the latter are employed to commit crimes. It would take a Draconian,[1] and politically impossible, confiscation of legally purchased guns to make much of a difference in the number used by criminals. Moreover, only about one-sixth of the handguns used by serious criminals are purchased from a gun shop or pawnshop. Most of these handguns are stolen, borrowed, or obtained through private purchases that wouldn't be affected by gun laws.

What is worse, any successful effort to shrink the stock of legally purchased guns (or of ammunition) would reduce the capacity

of law-abiding people to defend themselves. Gun control advocates scoff at the importance of self-defense, but they are wrong to do so. Based on a household survey, Gary Kleck, a criminologist at Florida State University, has estimated that every year, guns are used — that is, displayed or fired — for defensive purposes more than a million times, not counting their use by the police. If his estimate is correct, this means that the number of people who defend themselves with a gun exceeds the number of arrests for violent crimes and burglaries.

Our goal should not be the disarming of law-abiding citizens. It should be to reduce the number of people who carry guns unlawfully, especially in places — on streets, in taverns — where the mere presence of a gun can increase the hazards we all face. The most effective way to reduce illegal gun-carrying is to encourage the police to take guns away from people who carry them without a permit. This means encouraging the police to make street frisks.

The Fourth Amendment to the Constitution bans "unreasonable searches and 5

---

[1] **Draconian** Harsh or severe, often excessively so. [Editors' note.]

seizures." In 1968 the Supreme Court decided (*Terry v. Ohio*) that a frisk — patting down a person's outer clothing — is proper if the officer has a "reasonable suspicion" that the person is armed and dangerous. If a pat-down reveals an object that might be a gun, the officer can enter the suspect's pocket to remove it. If the gun is being carried illegally, the suspect can be arrested.

The reasonable-suspicion test is much less stringent than the probable-cause standard the police must meet in order to make an arrest. A reasonable suspicion, however, is more than just a hunch; it must be supported by specific facts. The courts have held, not always consistently, that these facts include someone acting in a way that leads an experienced officer to conclude criminal activity may be afoot; someone fleeing at the approach of an officer; a person who fits a drug courier profile; a motorist stopped for a traffic violation who has a suspicious bulge in his pocket; a suspect identified by a reliable informant as carrying a gun. The Supreme Court has also upheld frisking people on probation or parole.

Some police departments frisk a lot of people, but usually the police frisk rather few, at least for the purpose of detecting illegal guns. In 1992 the police arrested about 240,000 people for illegally possessing or carrying a weapon. This is only about one-fourth as many as were arrested for public drunkenness. The average police officer will make *no* weapons arrests and confiscate *no* guns during any given year. Mark Moore, a professor of public policy at Harvard University, found that most weapons arrests were made because a citizen complained, not because the police were out looking for guns.

It is easy to see why. Many cities suffer from a shortage of officers, and even those with ample law-enforcement personnel worry about having their cases thrown out for constitutional reasons or being accused of police harassment. But the risk of violating the Constitution or engaging in actual, as opposed to perceived, harassment can be substantially reduced.

Each patrol officer can be given a list of people on probation or parole who live on that officer's beat and be rewarded for making frequent stops to insure that they are not carrying guns. Officers can be trained to recognize the kinds of actions that the Court will accept as providing the "reasonable suspicion" necessary for a stop and frisk. Membership in a gang known for assaults and drug dealing could be made the basis, by statute or Court precedent, for gun frisks.

The available evidence supports the claim [10] that self-defense is a legitimate form of deterrence. People who report to the National Crime Survey that they defended themselves with a weapon were less likely to lose property in a robbery or be injured in an assault than those who did not defend themselves. Statistics have shown that would-be burglars are threatened by gun-wielding victims about as many times a year as they are arrested (and much more often than they are sent to prison) and that the chances of a burglar being shot are about the same as his chances of going to jail. Criminals know these facts even if gun control advocates do not and so are less likely to burgle occupied homes in America than occupied ones in Europe, where the residents rarely have guns.

Some gun control advocates may concede these points but rejoin that the cost of self-defense is self-injury: Handgun owners are more likely to shoot themselves or their loved ones than a criminal. Not quite. Most gun accidents involve rifles and shotguns, not handguns. Moreover, the rate of fatal gun accidents has been declining while the level of gun ownership has been rising. There are fatal gun accidents just as there are fatal car accidents, but in fewer than 2 percent of the gun fatalities was the victim someone mistaken for an intruder.

Those who urge us to forbid or severely restrict the sale of guns ignore these facts. Worse, they adopt a position that is politically absurd. In effect, they say, "Your government, having failed to protect your person and your property from criminal assault, now intends to deprive you of the opportunity to protect yourself."

Opponents of gun control make a different mistake. The National Rifle Association and its allies tell us that "guns don't kill, people kill" and urge the Government to punish more severely people who use guns to commit crimes. Locking up criminals does protect society from future crimes, and the prospect of being locked up may deter criminals. But our experience with meting out tougher sentences is mixed. The tougher the prospective sentence the less likely it is to be imposed, or at least to be imposed swiftly. If the Legislature adds on time for crimes committed with a gun, prosecutors often bargain away the add-ons; even when they do not, the judges in many states are reluctant to impose add-ons.

Worse, the presence of a gun can contribute to the magnitude of the crime even on the part of those who worry about serving a long prison sentence. Many criminals carry guns not to rob stores but to protect themselves from other armed criminals. Gang violence has become more threatening to bystanders as gang members have begun to arm themselves. People may commit crimes, but guns make some crimes worse. Guns often convert spontaneous outbursts of anger into fatal encounters. When some people carry them on the streets, others will want to carry them to protect themselves, and an urban arms race will be under way.

And modern science can be enlisted to help. Metal detectors at airports have reduced the number of airplane bombings and skyjackings to nearly zero. But these detectors only work at very close range. What is needed is a device that will enable the police to detect the presence of a large lump of metal in someone's pocket from a distance of ten or fifteen feet. Receiving such a signal could supply the officer with reasonable grounds for a pat-down. Underemployed nuclear physicists and electronics engineers in the post-cold-war era surely have the talents for designing a better gun detector.

Even if we do all these things, there will still be complaints. Innocent people will be stopped. Young black and Hispanic men will probably be stopped more often than older white Anglo males or women of any race. But if we are serious about reducing drive-by shootings, fatal gang wars and lethal quarrels in public places, we must get illegal guns off the street. We cannot do this by multiplying the forms one fills out at gun shops or by pretending that guns are not a problem until a criminal uses one.

Topics for Critical Thinking and Writing

1. If you had to single out one sentence in James Wilson's essay that best states his thesis, what sentence would that be? Why do you think it states, better than any other sentence, the essay's thesis?

2. In paragraph 3, Wilson reviews research by a criminologist purporting to show that guns are important for self-defense in American households. Does the research as reported show that displaying or firing guns in self-defense actually prevented crimes? Or wounded

aggressors? Suppose you were also told that in households where guns may be used defensively, thousands of innocent people are injured and hundreds are killed — for instance, children who find a loaded gun and play with it. Would you regard these injuries and deaths as a fair trade-off? Explain. What does the research presented by Wilson really show?

3. In an essay of no more than 100 words, explain the difference between the "reasonable-suspicion" test (para. 5) and the "probable-cause standard" (para. 6) that the courts use in deciding whether a street frisk is lawful. (You may want to organize your essay into two paragraphs, one on each topic, or perhaps into three if you include a brief introductory paragraph.)

4. Wilson reports in paragraph 7 that the police arrest four times as many drunks on the streets as they do people carrying unlicensed firearms. Does this strike you as absurd, reasonable, or mysterious? Does Wilson explain it to your satisfaction? Why, or why not?

5. In paragraph 12, Wilson says that people who want to severely restrict the ownership of guns are in effect saying, "'Your government, having failed to protect your person and your property from criminal assault, now intends to deprive you of the opportunity to protect yourself.'" What reply might an advocate of severe restrictions make? (Even if you strongly believe Wilson's summary is accurate, put yourself in the shoes of an advocate of gun control, and come up with the best reply that you can.)

6. In his final paragraph, Wilson grants that his proposal entails a difficulty: "Innocent people will be stopped. Young black and Hispanic men will probably be stopped more often than older white Anglo males or women of any race." Assuming that his predictions are accurate, is his proposal therefore fatally flawed and worth no further thought, or (taking the other extreme view) will innocent people who fall into certain classifications just have to put up with frisking for the public good? Explain your response.

7. Wilson criticizes both gun control advocates and the National Rifle Association for their ill-advised views. In an essay of 500 words, state his criticisms of each side, and explain whether and to what extent you agree.

KAYLA WEBLEY

Kayla Webley, education correspondent for Time *magazine, did her undergraduate work at the University of Washington, concentrating on journalism and political science, and her graduate work at Northwestern University, specializing in new media. The essay reprinted here originally appeared in* Time *magazine on April 20, 2012.*

Is Forgiving Student Loan Debt a Good Idea?

Every few weeks now a petition pops up in my Facebook newsfeed urging the government to forgive all student debt. The comment from the person posting the petition usually goes something like this, "Guessing this will never happen, but can't hurt to sign on!"

The petition now has nearly 670,000 signatures. Scrolling through the stories posted on the petition (and similar stories told on the related Occupy Student Debt site) can be a heart-wrenching experience. Former students tell stories of unemployment, worthless majors, low-paying jobs and resulting six-figure debt, insurmountable interest, forbearance, and default. From a human standpoint, it's easy to see why forgiving student debt holds some appeal. But many have questioned not only the enormous and economically unfeasible cost, but the purported benefits and fairness of a one-time student loan bailout.

Feeling shackled by an estimated $88,000 in student loan debt, Robert Applebaum started the petition in 2009 and has seen its popularity skyrocket since last fall as some members of the Occupy Wall Street movement adopted the battle cry. His proposal is simple: Provide a one-time bailout of student loan debt — currently valued at $1 trillion — as a way to stimulate the still-limping economy. After all, college graduates are the type of people society needs to do things like start businesses, buy homes and cars, invent things, and make babies — and people burdened with debt are less likely to make those kinds of decisions. Unburden them and the housing market might improve, along with the overall economy. "With the stroke of the President's pen, millions of Americans would suddenly have hundreds, or in some cases, thousands of extra dollars in their pockets each and every month with which to spend on ailing sectors of the economy," Applebaum writes in the petition.

That sounds like a very expensive proposition, of course. But so were the bank and auto bailouts — and, the thinking goes, if "fat cat" bankers and auto makers got a bailout, why not college graduates?

Well, as Justin Wolfers writes on the Freak- 5 onomics blog, one reason why not is that such a scheme wouldn't be a particularly efficient fiscal stimulus. Someone who has $50,000 in debt forgiven isn't likely to pump all those dollars back into the economy in a short amount of time. A much more effective stimulus, Wolfers says, would be to give fifty poor people $1,000 each because that money would almost immediately be spent.

Another problem with such a plan is that most borrowers actually can afford to pay off their student loan debt. There are some borrowers who desperately need relief, but there are many others who would just rather not have to fork over a certain percentage of their income each month to pay for the education they received years ago. But if forgiveness was offered, who wouldn't take the handout?

As it turns out, the six-figure debts that we keep hearing about in the media are actually pretty unusual. By most estimates, only a tiny minority of student loan borrowers — as little as 1 percent — graduate with more than $100,000 in debt. Mark Kantrowitz of FinAid.org and FastWeb.com says that only a few thousand students out of the several million who finish college each year graduate with that much debt. The average debt total at graduation is a much more reasonable — yet still significant — $27,500.

What's more, even borrowers who can't afford the standard repayment plan have existing alternatives if the loan is from the government. There are already programs in place that offer forgiveness, not to mention the government's effective and underutilized Income Based Repayment program. What might be a more politically viable approach to student debt — although it would provide less fiscal stimulus — would be for the government and loan providers to have a better way of distinguishing between those borrowers who really need help and those who don't. But of course that's no easy task.

Many of the concerns surrounding Applebaum's plan involve the idea of fairness. Why should current debt holders be forgiven when for years people have paid their debts? Why should taxpayers — especially those who never attended college in the first place — foot the bill for the borrowers' education? What about future generations? Will they just take out loads of money in college and cross their fingers for a bailout? There are no easy answers to these questions other than to say, life isn't fair.

But perhaps the biggest roadblock to Applebaum's plan is that a one-time bailout is a temporary fix to an ongoing problem. What's really needed is a long look at how higher education in the United States is financed. Many would argue the current model is fundamentally broken.

Virtually everyone who applies is approved for almost unlimited student loans, regardless of how likely they are to be able to pay them back. But lenders aren't really concerned about that because student loans cannot be discharged in bankruptcy. They know they'll get their money back one way or another.

As a result, lenders have no incentive to work with students toward a reasonable repayment plan. And further, colleges have no incentive to keep tuition low — tuition is increasing at a rate double that of inflation — because whether they can afford it or not, students will find a way to pay the bill.

Applebaum's proposal offers a radical and wildly unfeasible solution, both politically and economically, but it's an idea nonetheless. "I'm not saying my solution to the student debt crisis is the very best," he says. "If you disagree with me, what's your solution?"

Topics for Critical Thinking and Writing

1. Why do you suppose Kayla Webley prefaces her argument by telling readers in paragraph 2 that some of the stories on the Occupy Student Debt site are "heart-wrenching"?

2. What do you think of Webley's final paragraph as a way of concluding her essay? Is it effective? Why, or why not?

3. Do you have any ideas about forgiving student debt that Webley's essay doesn't address? If so, what are they? How would you work them into the essay?

Ron Bailey / Getty Images

ALFRED EDMOND JR.

Alfred Edmond Jr. (b. 1960) is senior vice president/multimedia editor-at-large of Black Enterprise, a media organization that publishes Black Enterprise *magazine. He appears often on television and on nationally syndicated radio programs. The following essay was originally published in* Black Enterprise *in 2012.*

Why Asking for a Job Applicant's Facebook Password Is Fair Game

"Should business owners be allowed to ask job applicants for their Facebook passwords?" Many people who watched me on MSNBC's *Your Business* on Sunday were surprised to hear that my answer is "Yes," including the show's host, J. J. Ramberg. This question became a hot news topic last week, especially in business and social media circles, when Congress failed to pass legislation that would have banned the practice of employers asking employees to reveal their Facebook passwords.

Now, if I was asked the same question as a guest on a show called *Your Career*, I would have been hard-pressed to think of a situation where I would share my Facebook password with a potential employer. For me to consider it, I would have to want the job pretty badly, with the amount and type of compensation (including benefits, perks, and even an equity stake in the company) being major considerations. But before doing so, I would see if there were other ways I could address the potential employer's concerns without revealing my password, such as changing my privacy settings to give them the ability to view all of my Facebook content. If they persisted with their request for my password, I would try to negotiate terms to strictly limit both their use of the password and the length of time the potential employer would have access to it before I could change it. I might even consider getting an employment attorney to negotiate an agreement, including terms of confidentiality, to be signed by both me and the potential employer before sharing my password.

Of course, for the vast majority of positions, neither I nor a company looking to hire would deem it worth the time and expense to jump through all of these hoops. Most companies would not care to have password access to an applicant's social media accounts. (For what it's worth, Facebook's terms of rights and responsibilities forbids users from sharing their passwords.) In probably 99 percent of such cases, if a potential employer made such a request, my answer would be, "No, I will not share my password. Are there alternatives you are willing to consider to satisfy your concerns?" I'd accept that I'd risk not being hired as a result. On the other hand, if that was all it took for me not to be hired, I'd question how badly they really wanted me in the first place, as well as whether that was the kind of place I would have been happy working for. But for certain companies and positions, especially if I wanted the job badly enough, I'd consider a request for my Facebook password at least up for negotiation.

That said, my response on *Your Business* was from the perspective of the business owner. And if I'm the owner of certain types of businesses, or trying to fill certain types of positions, I believe I should be able to ask job applicants for access to their Facebook accounts. The applicant may choose not to answer, but I should be able to ask. Depending on the position, knowing everything I possibly can about an applicant is critical to not only making the best hire, but to protecting the interests of my current employees, customers, and partners as well as the financial interests of the company.

On *Your Business*, I pointed to an example 5 where I believe a request for a Facebook password as part of the hiring process is entirely reasonable: the child care industry. If I am running a school or a day care center, the time to find out that a teacher or other worker has a record of inappropriate social media communication with minors, or worse, a history of or predilection for sexual relationships with students, is during the hiring process—as New York City is finding out the hard way, with an epidemic of public school employees being revealed to have had such relationships with students. To me, such a request falls into the same category of checking the backgrounds of potential employees as the common (also still debated) practice of asking job applicants to agree to a credit check, especially for jobs that will require them to handle money, keep the books, or carry out other fiscal duties on behalf of a company. In these and other cases, safety and security issues, and the legal liability that they create for business owners if they are not adequately addressed during the hiring process, outweigh the job applicant's expectation of privacy when it comes to their social media activities.

Speaking of which, I can still hear people screaming (actually tweeting and retweeting) that an employer asking for your Facebook password is a horrible invasion of privacy. Well, for those of you who still believe in Santa Claus, I strongly recommend that you read *The Filter Bubble: What the Internet Is Hiding from You* by Eli Pariser (Penguin Press). Or you can just take my advice and let go of the illusion of privacy on social media. The courts are conflicted, at best, on whether we as social media users have a right to an expectation of privacy, with many cases being decided against such expectations. The last place you want to share anything that is truly private is on your Facebook page or any other social media platform. Better to think of social media as the ultimate

"Front Street." No matter what Facebook's privacy policies are (which they can change at will without your permission) and what privacy tools and settings they offer (which they also change whenever it suits their business models), always assume that posting on Facebook is just the ticking time bomb version of you shouting your private business from the middle of Times Square—on steroids.

To paraphrase a quote shared in *The Filter Bubble*, if you're getting something for free, you're not the customer, you're the product. Social media is designed for the information shared on it to be searched and shared—and mined for profit. The business model is the very antithesis of the expectation of privacy. To ignore that reality is to have blind faith in Facebook, Google, Twitter, etc., operating in your best interests above all else, at all times. (I don't.)

Whether you agree with me or not about whether a potential employer asking you for your Facebook password is fair game, I hope you'll take my advice: When considering what to share via social media, don't think business vs. personal. Think public vs. private. And if something is truly private, do not share it on social media out of a misplaced faith in the expectation of privacy.

This debate is far from over, and efforts to update existing, but woefully outdated, privacy laws—not to mention the hiring practices of companies—to catch up with the realities of social media will definitely continue. I'd like to know where you stand, both as entrepreneurs and business owners, as well as potential job applicants. And I'd especially like to hear from human resources and recruiting experts. How far is too far when it comes to a potential employer investigating the social media activity of a job applicant?

Topics for Critical Thinking and Writing

1. Employers *do* (at least at the time we're writing this textbook) have the right to require drug tests and personality tests. Do you think they should also legally be allowed to ask for a password to Facebook, or should Congress pass legislation outlawing the practice? If employers are legally allowed to ask, would you provide your password? Why, or why not?

2. Would Alfred Edmond Jr.'s case be strengthened if he gave one or two additional examples — beyond the "child care industry" that he mentions in paragraph 5 — of jobs that, a reader might agree, require a thorough background check? What examples can you suggest? Would you say that applicants for these jobs should be willing to reveal their Facebook password to a potential employer? Why, or why not?

3. In paragraph 7, Edmond paraphrases: "if you're getting something for free, you're not the customer, you're the product." Paraphrase this passage yourself (on paraphrase, see p. 48) so that it would be clear to a reader who finds it puzzling.

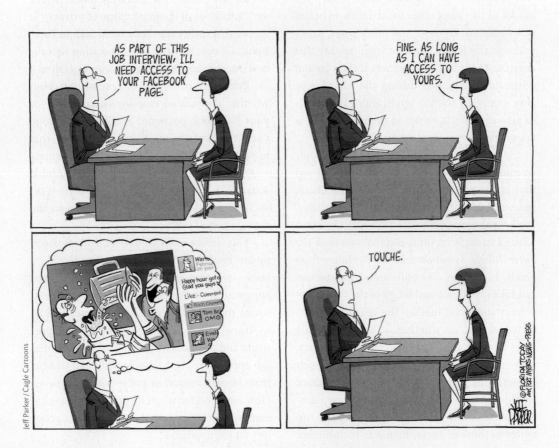

Jeff Parker / Cagle Cartoons

SHERRY TURKLE

Sherry Turkle, born in Brooklyn, New York, in 1948, is Professor of the Social Studies of Science and Technology at the Massachusetts Institute of Technology. The author of numerous books, including Alone Together *(2011), Turkle often appears on television as a commentator on media. Here we reprint an essay that originally appeared in the* New York Times *on April 22, 2012.*

The Flight from Conversation

We live in a technological universe in which we are always communicating. And yet we have sacrificed conversation for mere connection.

At home, families sit together, texting and reading e-mail. At work, executives text during board meetings. We text (and shop and go on Facebook) during classes and when we're on dates. My students tell me about an important new skill. It involves maintaining eye contact with someone while you text someone else; it's hard, but it can be done.

Over the past fifteen years, I've studied technologies of mobile connection and talked to hundreds of people of all ages and circumstances about their plugged-in lives. I've learned that the little devices most of us carry around are so powerful that they change not only what we do, but also who we are.

We've become accustomed to a new way of being "alone together." Technology-enabled, we are able to be with one another, and also elsewhere, connected to wherever we want to be. We want to customize our lives. We want to move in and out of where we are because the thing we value most is control over where we focus our attention. We have gotten used to the idea of being in a tribe of one, loyal to our own party.

Our colleagues want to go to that board meeting but pay attention only to what interests them. To some this seems like a good idea, but we can end up hiding from one another, even as we are constantly connected to one another.

A businessman laments that he no longer has colleagues at work. He doesn't stop by to talk; he doesn't call. He says that he doesn't want to interrupt them. He says they're "too busy on their e-mail." But then he pauses and corrects himself. "I'm not telling the truth. I'm the one who doesn't want to be interrupted. I think I should. But I'd rather just do things on my BlackBerry."

A sixteen-year-old boy who relies on texting for almost everything says almost wistfully, "Someday, someday, but certainly not now, I'd like to learn how to have a conversation."

In today's workplace, young people who have grown up fearing conversation show up on the job wearing earphones. Walking through a college library or the campus of a high-tech start-up, one sees the same thing: We are together, but each of us is in our own bubble, furiously connected to keyboards and tiny touch screens. A senior partner at a Boston law firm describes a scene in his office. Young associates lay out their suite of technologies: laptops, iPods, and multiple phones. And then they put their earphones on. "Big ones. Like pilots. They turn their desks into cockpits." With the young lawyers in their cockpits, the office is quiet, a quiet that does not ask to be broken.

In the silence of connection, people are comforted by being in touch with a lot of people — carefully kept at bay. We can't get enough of one another if we can use technology to keep one another at distances we can control: not too close, not too far, just right. I think of it as a Goldilocks effect.

Texting and e-mail and posting let us 10 present the self we want to be. This means we can edit. And if we wish to, we can delete. Or retouch: the voice, the flesh, the face, the body. Not too much, not too little — just right.

Human relationships are rich; they're messy and demanding. We have learned the habit of cleaning them up with technology. And the move from conversation to connection is part of this. But it's a process in which we shortchange ourselves. Worse, it seems that over time we stop caring, we forget that there is a difference.

We are tempted to think that our little "sips" of online connection add up to a big gulp of real conversation. But they don't. E-mail, Twitter, Facebook, all of these have their places — in politics, commerce, romance, and friendship. But no matter how valuable, they do not substitute for conversation.

Connecting in sips may work for gathering discrete bits of information or for saying, "I am thinking about you." Or even for saying, "I love you." But connecting in sips doesn't work as well when it comes to understanding and knowing one another. In conversation we tend to one another. (The word itself is kinetic; it's derived from words that mean to move, together.) We can attend to tone and nuance. In conversation, we are called upon to see things from another's point of view.

Face-to-face conversation unfolds slowly. It teaches patience. When we communicate on our digital devices, we learn different habits. As we ramp up the volume and velocity of online connections, we start to expect faster answers. To get these, we ask one another simpler questions; we dumb down our communications, even on the most important matters. It is as though we have all put ourselves on cable news. Shakespeare might have said, "We are consum'd with that which we were nourish'd by."

And we use conversation with others to 15 learn to converse with ourselves. So our flight from conversation can mean diminished chances to learn skills of self-reflection. These days, social media continually asks us what's "on our mind," but we have little motivation to say something truly self-reflective. Self-reflection in conversation requires trust. It's hard to do anything with 3,000 Facebook friends except connect.

As we get used to being shortchanged on conversation and to getting by with less, we seem almost willing to dispense with people altogether. Serious people muse about the future of computer programs as psychiatrists. A high school sophomore confides to me that he wishes he could talk to an artificial intelligence program instead of his dad about dating; he says the A.I. would have so much more in its database. Indeed, many people tell me they hope that as Siri, the digital assistant on Apple's iPhone, becomes more advanced, "she" will be more and more like a best friend — one who will listen when others won't.

During the years I have spent researching people and their relationships with technology, I have often heard the sentiment "No one is listening to me." I believe this feeling helps explain why it is so appealing to have a Facebook page or a Twitter feed — each provides so many automatic listeners. And it helps explain why — against all reason — so many of us are willing to talk to machines that seem to care about us. Researchers around the world are busy inventing sociable robots, designed to be companions to the elderly, to children, to all of us.

One of the most haunting experiences during my research came when I brought one of these robots, designed in the shape of a baby seal, to an elder-care facility, and an older woman began to talk to it about the loss of her child. The robot seemed to be looking into her eyes. It seemed to be following the conversation. The woman was comforted.

And so many people found this amazing. Like the sophomore who wants advice about dating from artificial intelligence and those who look forward to computer psychiatry, this enthusiasm speaks to how much we have confused conversation with connection and collectively seem to have embraced a new kind of delusion that accepts the simulation of compassion as sufficient unto the day. And why would we want to talk about love and loss with a machine that has no experience of the arc of human life? Have we so lost confidence that we will be there for one another?

We expect more from technology and less 20 from one another and seem increasingly drawn to technologies that provide the illusion of companionship without the demands of relationship. Always-on/always-on-you devices provide three powerful fantasies: that we will always be heard; that we can put our attention wherever we want it to be; and that we never have to be alone. Indeed our new devices have turned being alone into a problem that can be solved.

When people are alone, even for a few moments, they fidget and reach for a device. Here connection works like a symptom, not a cure, and our constant, reflexive impulse to connect shapes a new way of being.

Think of it as "I share, therefore I am." We use technology to define ourselves by sharing our thoughts and feelings as we're having them. We used to think, "I have a feeling; I want to make a call." Now our impulse is, "I want to have a feeling; I need to send a text."

So, in order to feel more, and to feel more like ourselves, we connect. But in our rush to connect, we flee from solitude, our ability to be separate and gather ourselves. Lacking the capacity for solitude, we turn to other people but don't experience them as they are. It is as though we use them, need them as spare parts to support our increasingly fragile selves.

We think constant connection will make us feel less lonely. The opposite is true. If we are unable to be alone, we are far more likely to be lonely. If we don't teach our children to be alone, they will know only how to be lonely.

I am a partisan for conversation. To make 25 room for it, I see some first, deliberate steps. At home, we can create sacred spaces: the kitchen, the dining room. We can make our cars "device-free zones." We can demonstrate the value of conversation to our children. And we can do the same thing at work. There we are so busy communicating that we often don't have time to talk to one another about what really matters. Employees asked for casual Fridays; perhaps managers should introduce conversational Thursdays. Most of all, we need to remember — in between texts and e-mails and Facebook posts — to listen to one another, even to the boring bits, because it is often in unedited moments, moments in which we hesitate and stutter and go silent, that we reveal ourselves to one another.

I spend the summers at a cottage on Cape Cod, and for decades I walked the same dunes that Thoreau once walked. Not too long ago, people walked with their heads up, looking at the water, the sky, the sand, and at one another, talking. Now they often walk with their heads down, typing. Even when they are with friends, partners, children, everyone is on their own devices.

So I say, look up, look at one another, and let's start the conversation.

Topics for Critical Thinking and Writing

1. Imagine a period when the book — or even the handwritten manuscript — was not yet invented. Now look at Sherry Turkle's first paragraph. Think of someone saying what Turkle says, but saying it about the invention of writing, and of the manuscript or book. Write a brief (250–500 words) expression of concern about the perils of the "new" inventions of writing and books.

2. In paragraph 3, Turkle says that the little devices that we carry "change not only what we do, but also who we are." We might reply that yes, of course, almost everything that touches us changes what we are. The invention of the movie theater changed us: Instead of conversing with family or friends and generating our own entertainment, we sat isolated in the dark for several hours. The possession of an automobile changes us, the move to a new address brings us into contact with new people who may change us (we may even marry one of them), and certainly the engendering of children changes us (or it ought to). But do you agree with Turkle that today's electronic devices produce changes of an unexpected sort? Why, or why not?

3. In paragraph 14, Turkle suggests that when we communicate electronically, as opposed to when communicating face-to-face or with pen and paper, "we dumb down our communications, even on the most important matters." Is she describing your behavior? Explain.

4. In paragraph 23, Turkle says, "we flee from solitude, our ability to be separate and gather ourselves." Is this passage true for you? Explain. Might a case be made that far from being lonely, people who use Facebook and comparable sites are often stimulated to participate in civic and political activities? Does your own experience offer evidence one way or the other? Explain.

5. Do you think Turkle's final two paragraphs make an effective ending? Why, or why not?

4

Visual Rhetoric: Thinking about Images as Arguments

A picture is worth a thousand words.   — PROVERB

"What is the use of a book," thought Alice, "without pictures or conversations?"
                                                                        — LEWIS CARROLL

Uses of Visual Images

Most visual materials that accompany written arguments serve one of several functions. One of the most common is to appeal to the reader's emotions (e.g., a photograph of a sad-eyed calf in a narrow pen can assist an argument against eating meat by inspiring sympathy for the animal). Pictures can also serve as visual evidence, offering proof that something occurred or appeared in a certain way at a certain moment. Pictures can help clarify numerical data (e.g., a graph showing five decades of law school enrollment by males and females). They can also add humor or satire to an essay. In this chapter, we concentrate on thinking critically about visual images. This means reading images in the same way we read print (or electronic) texts: by looking closely at them and discerning not only *what* they show but also *how* and *why* they convey a particular message, or argument.

When we discussed the **appeal to emotion** in Chapter 3 (p. 106), we quoted from Marc Antony's speech to the Roman populace in Shakespeare's play *Julius Caesar*. You'll recall that Antony stirred the mob by displaying Caesar's blood-stained mantle. He wasn't holding up a picture, but in a similar way he supplemented his words with visual material:

> Look, in this place ran Cassius' dagger through;
> See what a rent the envious Casca made;
> Through this, the well-belovèd Brutus stabbed. . . .

In courtrooms today, trial lawyers and prosecutors accomplish the same thing when doing the following:

- exhibiting photos of a bloody corpse, or
- holding up a murder weapon for jurors to see, or
- introducing victims as witnesses who sob while describing their ordeal.

Lawyers know that such visuals help make good arguments. Whether presented sincerely or gratuitously, visuals can have a significantly persuasive effect. Such appeals to emotion work on feelings, not logic. Think about the suit and tie that lawyers advise their male clients to wear: The attire helps make an argument to the jury about the defendant's character or credibility, even if he is actually lacking these qualities. Images, too, may be rationally connected to an argument (e.g., a gruesome image of a diseased lung in an anti-smoking ad makes a reasonable claim), but their immediate impact is more on the viewer's heart than the mind.

Like any kind of evidence, images make statements and support arguments. When Congress debated over whether to allow drilling in the Arctic National Wildlife Refuge (ANWR), both opponents and supporters made use of images:

- *Opponents* of drilling showed beautiful pictures of polar bears frolicking, wildflowers in bloom, and caribou on the move.
- *Proponents* of drilling showed bleak pictures of what they called "barren land" and "a frozen wasteland."

Both sides knew very well that images are powerfully persuasive, and they didn't hesitate to use them as supplements to words.

We invite you to think about the appropriateness of using such images in arguments. Was either side manipulating the "reality" of the ANWR? Or do images such as those described provide reasonable support for the ideas under consideration? Should argument be entirely a matter of reason, of logic (*logos*), without appeals to the emotions (*pathos*)? A statement that "the Arctic National Wildlife Refuge is a home for abundant wildlife, notably polar bears, caribou, and wildflowers" may not mean much until it is reinforced with breathtakingly beautiful images. Similarly, a statement that "most of the ANWR land is barren" may not mean much until it is corroborated by images of the vast bleakness. Each side selected a particular kind of image for a specific purpose — to support its position on drilling in the ANWR. Neither side was being dishonest, but both were appealing to emotions.

TYPES OF EMOTIONAL APPEALS

We began the preceding chapter by distinguishing between *argument,* which relies on reason (*logos*), and *persuasion,* which is a broad term that can include appeals to the emotions (*pathos*) — for example, an **appeal to pity**, such as an image of a sad-eyed calf. You might say, "Well, eating meat implies confining and killing animals," and regard the image as both reasonable and emotionally powerful. Or you might say, "Although it's emotionally powerful, this appeal to pity doesn't describe the condition of every meat animal. Some are treated humanely, slaughtered humanely, and eaten ethically." You might write a counterargument and include an image of free-range cattle on a farm (although in doing this, you too would be appealing to emotions).

The point is that images can be persuasive even if they don't make good arguments, in the same way threats of violence can be persuasive but do not make good arguments. The gangster Al Capone famously said, "You can get a lot more done with a kind word and a gun than with a kind word alone." Threats of violence appeal exclusively to the emotions — specifically, fear.

Advertisers commonly use the **appeal to fear** as a persuasive technique. While it is not a threat of violence, the appeal to fear is a threat of sorts. Showing a burglary, a car crash, embarrassing age spots, or a cockroach infestation can successfully convince consumers to buy a product — a home security system, a new car insurance policy, an age-defying skin cream, or a pesticide. Such images generate fear and anxiety at the same time that they offer the solution for it.

Appeal to self-interest is another persuasive tactic that writers can use. Consider these remarks, which use the word *interest* in the sense of "self-interest":

Would you persuade, speak of Interest, not Reason. — BENJAMIN FRANKLIN

There are two levers for moving men — interest and fear. — NAPOLEON BONAPARTE

Appeals to self-interest may be quite persuasive because they speak directly to what benefits you the most, not necessarily what benefits others in the community, society, or world. Such appeals are also common in advertising. "You can save bundles by shopping at Maxi-Mart," a commercial might claim, without making reference to sweatshop labor conditions, the negative impact of global commerce, or other troublesome aspects of what you see only as a great savings for yourself. You may be familiar with other types of emotional appeals in advertising that speak to the senses more than to the rational mind. Again, these kinds of appeals don't necessarily make good arguments for the products in question, but each can be highly persuasive — sometimes affecting us subconsciously. (The same applies to appeals in written arguments. This is why thinking critically about both words and images is so important.)

Here is a list of some additional kinds of appeals to emotion:

Sexual appeals (Example: showing a bikini-clad model standing near a product)

Bandwagon appeals (Example: showing crowds of people rushing to a sale)

Humor appeals (Example: showing a cartoon animal drinking X brand of beverage)

Celebrity appeals (Example: showing a famous person driving X brand of car)

Testimonial appeals (Example: showing a doctor giving X brand of vitamins to her kids)

Identity appeals (Example: showing a "good family" going to X restaurant)

Prejudice appeals (Example: showing a "loser" drinking X brand of beer)

Lifestyle appeals (Example: showing a jar of X brand of mustard on a silver platter)

Stereotype appeals (Example: showing a Latino person enjoying X brand of salsa)

Patriotic appeals (Example: showing X brand of mattress alongside an American flag)

Exercise

Watch the commercials that air during a television show, or examine the print advertisements in a popular magazine. Identify as many examples as possible of the types of appeals mentioned on the preceding pages. Is there a rational basis for any of the appeals you see? Are any appeals irrational even if they are effective? Why, or why not?

Images played an important role in the antislavery movement in the nineteenth century. On the top left is a diagram showing how human cargo was packed into a slave ship; it was distributed with Thomas Clarkson's *Essay on the Slavery and Commerce of the Human Species* (1804). On the top right is Frederick W. Mercer's photograph (April 2, 1863) of Gordon, a "badly lacerated" runaway slave. Images such as the slave ship and the runaway slave worked against slave owners' claims that slavery was a humane institution — claims that also were supported by illustrations, such as the woodcut at the bottom, titled *Attention Paid to a Poor Sick Negro*, from *Josiah Priest's In Defense of Slavery* (1843).

Top left: "Description of a Slave Ship, 1789 (print)/English School, (18th century)/WILBERFORCE HOUSE MUSEUM/© Wilberforce House, Hull City Museums and Art Galleries, UK/Bridgeman Images. *Top right:* Bettmann/Getty Images. *Bottom:* Josiah Priest's In Defense of Slavery, Rare Books and Manuscripts Department, Boston Public Library.

Seeing versus Looking: Reading Advertisements

Advertising is one of the most common forms of visual persuasion we encounter in everyday life. The influence of advertising in our culture is pervasive and subtle. Part of its power comes from our habit of internalizing the intended messages of words and images without thinking deeply about them. Once we begin decoding the ways in which advertisements are constructed — once we view them critically — we can understand how (or if) they work as arguments. We may then make better decisions about whether to buy particular products and what factors convinced us or failed to convince us.

To read an advertisement — or any image — critically, it helps to consider some basic rules from the field of **semiotics**, the study of signs and symbols. Fundamental to semiotic analysis is the idea that visual signs have shared meanings in a culture. If you approach a sink and see a red faucet and a blue faucet, you can be pretty sure which one will produce hot water and which one will produce cold. In a similar way, we almost subconsciously recognize the meanings of images in advertisements. Thus, one of the first strategies we can use in reading advertisements critically is **deconstructing** them, taking them apart to see what makes them work. It's helpful to remember that advertisements are enormously expensive to produce and disseminate, so nothing is left to chance. Teams of people typically scrutinize every part of an advertisement to ensure it communicates the intended message — although this doesn't imply that viewers must accept those messages. In fact, taking advertisements apart is the first step in being critical about them.

Taking apart an advertisement means examining each visual element. Consider this advertisement for Nike shoes featuring basketball star LeBron James. Already, you should see the celebrity appeal — an implicit claim that Nike shoes help make James a star player. The ad creates an association between the shoes and the sports champion. James's uniform number, 23, assists

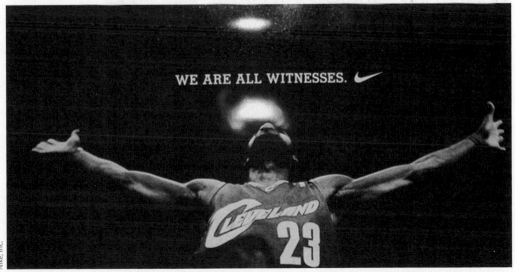

Nike, Inc.

in this association by referencing another basketball legend (and Nike spokesperson), Michael Jordan. James is, in a way, presented as the progeny of Michael Jordan, as a new incarnation of a sports "god." WE ARE ALL WITNESSES, the text reads, drawing on language commonly used in religious settings to describe the second coming of Christ. James's arms are outstretched, Christ-like, and seem to be illuminated by divine light from above. The uniform also references James's famous return to the Cleveland Cavaliers, his hometown team, after leaving the team abruptly to play four seasons with the Miami Heat. His "return" to Cleveland — his own second coming — the son of a sports god — and with the resonance of forgiveness, redemption, and salvation for Cleveland sports fans: All these associations work together to elevate James, Jordan, and Nike to exalted status. Of course, our description here is tongue-in-cheek. We're not gullible enough to believe this literally, and the ad's producers don't expect us to be; but they do hope that such an impression will be powerful enough to make us think of Nike the next time we shop for athletic shoes. If sports gods wear Nike, why shouldn't we?

This kind of analysis is possible when we recognize a difference between *seeing* and *looking*. **Seeing** is a physiological process involving light, the eye, and the brain. **Looking**, however, is a social process involving the mind. It suggests apprehending an image in terms of symbolic, metaphorical, and other social and cultural meanings. To do this, we must think beyond the *literal* meaning of an image or image element and consider its *figurative* meanings. If you look up *apple* in the dictionary, you'll find its literal, **denotative** meaning — a round fruit with thin red or green skin and a crisp flesh. But an apple also communicates figurative, **connotative** meanings. Connotative meanings are the cultural or emotional associations that an image suggests.

The long-running ABC television series *Desperate Housewives*, which dramatized the furtive sex lives and exploits of suburban women, featured apples prominently in its advertisements.

How does the DKNY advertisement use the symbolic, connotative meanings of the apple? In what ways does the advertisement for Bulova watches attempt to make an argument about the product?

The connotative meaning of an apple in Western culture dates back to the biblical story of the Garden of Eden, where Eve, tempted by a serpent, eats the fruit from the forbidden tree of knowledge and brings about the end of paradise on earth. Throughout Western culture, apples have come to represent knowledge and the pursuit of knowledge. Think of the ubiquitous Apple logo gracing so many mobile phones, tablets, and laptops: With its prominent bite, it symbolizes the way technology opens up new worlds of knowing. Sometimes, apples represent forbidden knowledge, temptation, or seduction—and biting into one suggests giving in to desires for new understandings and experiences. The story of Snow White offers just one example of an apple used as a symbol of temptation.

Let's look at two additional advertisements (pictured on p. 146), each of which relies almost entirely on images rather than words. The first, an ad for a TV comedy that made its debut in 2009, boldly displays the show's title and highlights the network name by setting it apart, but the most interesting words are in much smaller print:

Funny. On so many levels.

These words flatter the ad's readers, thus making them susceptible to the implicit message: "Look at this program." Why do we say the words are flattering? For three reasons:

- The small type size implies that the reader isn't someone whose attention can be caught only by headlines.

- The pun on "levels" (physical levels, and levels of humor) is a witty way of saying that the show offers not only the low comedy of physical actions but also the high comedy of witty talk — talk that, for instance, may involve puns.

- The two terse, incomplete sentences assume that the sophisticated reader doesn't need to have things explained at length.

The picture itself is attractive, showing what seems to be a wide variety of people (though not any faces or body types that in real life might cause viewers any uneasiness) posed in the style of a family portrait. Indeed, these wholesome figures, standing in affectionate poses, are all dressed in white (no real-life ketchup stains here) and are neatly framed — except for the patriarch, at the extreme right — by a pair of seated youngsters whose legs dangle down from the levels. The modern family, we're told, is large and varied (this one includes a gay son and his partner, and their adopted Vietnamese baby), smart and warm. Best of all, it is "Funny. On so many levels."

The second ad features just a single line of text: "No In-App Purchases." These words are set below the image of a shopping cart with a plus sign, which has come to be an almost universally recognized symbol for an electronic shopping cart. Both the text and the icon are textured and look a little rough at the edges, suggesting that they are made out of the very item they are advertising. After all, Play-Doh has been around since the 1930s; though the way children play has changed dramatically since then (most kids born now will grow up knowing what an "in-app purchase" is), by fashioning the electronic icon and text out of a nearly century-old product, the ad implies that just because a toy—or anything else—is new and high-tech, that does not make it inherently better than old-fashioned things. After all, the product being advertised has been around for nearly a century; how long will an app on a smartphone or tablet last until it is replaced with a newer version?

A CHECKLIST FOR ANALYZING IMAGES (ESPECIALLY ADVERTISEMENTS)

- ☐ What is the overall effect of the design? Colorful and busy (suggesting activity)? Quiet and understated (e.g., chiefly white and grays, with lots of empty space)? Old-fashioned or cutting edge?

- ☐ What single aspect of the image immediately captures your attention? Its size? Its position on the page? The beauty of the image? The grotesqueness of the image? Its humor?

- ☐ Who is the audience for the image? Affluent young men? Housewives? Retired persons?

- ☐ What is the argument?

- ☐ Does the text make a rational appeal (*logos*)? ("Tests at a leading university prove that . . ."; "If you believe X, you should vote 'No' on this referendum" appeal to our sense of reason.)

- ☐ Does the image appeal to the emotions or to dearly held values (*pathos*)? (Images of starving children or maltreated animals appeal to our sense of pity; images of military valor may appeal to our patriotism; images of luxury may appeal to our envy; images of sexually attractive people may appeal to our desire to be like them; images of violence or of extraordinary ugliness — as in ads showing a human fetus being destroyed — may seek to shock us.)

- ☐ Does the image make an ethical appeal — that is, does it appeal to our character as a good human being (*ethos*)? (Ads by charitable organizations often appeal to our sense of decency, fairness, and pity; but ads that appeal to our sense of prudence — such as ads for insurance companies or investment houses — also make an ethical appeal).

- ☐ What is the relation of print to image? Does the image do most of the work, or does it serve to attract us and lead us on to read the text?

Topics for Critical Thinking and Writing

1. Imagine that you work for a business — for instance, a vacation resort, a clothing manufacturer, or an automaker — that advertises in a publication such as *Time* or *Newsweek*. Design an advertisement for the business: Describe the picture and write the text, and then, in an essay of 500 words, identify your target audience (college students? young couples about to

buy their first home? retired persons?) and explain your purpose in choosing certain types of appeals (e.g., to reason, to the emotions, to the audience's sense of humor).

2. It is often said that colleges, like businesses, are selling a product. Examine a brochure or catalog that is sent to prospective college applicants, or locate your own college's view book, and analyze the kinds of appeals that some of the images make.

Other Aspects of Visual Appeals

As we saw with the uses of images relating to the Arctic National Wildlife Refuge, photographs can serve as evidence but have a peculiar relationship to the truth. We must never forget that images are constructed, selected, and used for specific purposes. When advertisers use images, they're trying to convince consumers to purchase a product or service. But when images serve as documentary evidence, we often assume they're showing the "truth" of the matter at hand. Our skepticism may be lower when we see an image in the newspaper or a magazine, assuming it captures a particular event or moment in time *as it really happened*. But historical images, images of events, news photographs, and other forms of visual evidence are not free from the potential for conscious or unconscious bias. Consider how liberal and conservative media sources portray the nation's president in images: One source may show him proud and smiling in bright light with the American flag behind him, while another might show him scowling in a darkened image suggestive of evil intent. Both are "real" images, but the framing, tinting, setting, and background can inspire significantly different responses in viewers.

As we saw with the image of LeBron James, certain postures, facial expressions, and settings can contribute to a photograph's interpretation. Martin Luther King Jr.'s great speech of

Bettmann/Getty Images

Martin Luther King Jr. delivering his "I Have a Dream" speech on August 28, 1963, from the steps of the Lincoln Memorial.

August 28, 1963, "I Have a Dream," still reads very well on the page, but part of its immense appeal derives from its setting: King spoke to some 200,000 people in Washington, D.C., as he stood on the steps of the Lincoln Memorial. That setting, rich with associations of slavery and freedom, strongly assists King's argument. In fact, images of King delivering his speech are nearly inseparable from the very argument he was making. The visual aspects — the setting (the Lincoln Memorial with the Washington Monument and the Capitol in the distance) and King's gestures — are part of the speech's persuasive rhetoric.

Derrick Alridge, a historian, examined dozens of accounts of Martin Luther King Jr. in history books, and he found that images of King present him overwhelmingly as a messianic figure — standing before crowds, leading them, addressing them in postures reminiscent of a prophet. While King is an admirable figure, Alridge asserts, history books err by presenting him as more than human. Doing so ignores his personal struggles and failures and makes a myth out of the real man. This myth suggests he was the epicenter of the civil rights movement, an effort that was actually conducted in different ways via different

Martin Luther King Jr. on "Chicken Bone Beach" in Atlantic City.

strategies on the part of many other figures whom King eclipsed. We may even get the idea that the entire civil rights movement began and ended with King alone. When he's presented as a holy prophet, it becomes easier to focus on his abstract messages about love, equality, and justice, and not on the specific policies and politics he advocated — his avowed socialist stances, for instance. While photographs of King seek to help us remember, they may actually portray him in a way that causes us to forget other things — for example, the fact that his approval rating among whites at the time of his death was lower than 30 percent, and among blacks lower than 50 percent.

LEVELS OF IMAGES

One helpful way of discerning the meanings of images by *looking* at them (see p. 143) is to utilize *seeing* first as a way to define what is plainly or literally present in them. You can begin by *seeing* — identifying the elements that are indisputably "there" in an image (the denotative level). Then you move on to *looking* — interpreting the meanings suggested by the elements that are present (the connotative level).

Semioticians distinguish between images' surface levels and deeper levels. The surface level is the **syntagmatic level**, and the deeper level is the **paradigmatic level**. The words *syntagmatic* and *paradigmatic* are related to the words *syntax* and *paradigm*.

Arguably, when we *see*, we pay attention only to the syntagmatic level. We notice the various elements included in an image. We *see* denotatively — that is, we observe just the explicit elements of the image. We aren't concerned with the meaning of the image's elements, but just with the fact that they're present.

When we *look*, we move to the paradigmatic level. That is, we speculate on the elements' deeper meanings — what they suggest figuratively, symbolically, or metaphorically in our cultural system. We may also consider the relationship of different elements to one another. When we do this, we look connotatively.

Syntagmatic analysis	Paradigmatic analysis
Seeing	Looking
Denotation	Connotation
Literal	Figurative
What is present	What it means
Understanding / Textual	Interpreting / Subtextual / Contextual

Exercise

Examine the images on this page and the next. As you examine each one, do the following:

1. *See* the image. Perform a syntagmatic analysis thoroughly describing the image elements you observe. Write down as many elements as possible that you see.

2. *Look* at the image. Perform a paradigmatic analysis in which you take the elements you have observed and relate what they suggest by considering their figurative meanings, their meanings in relation to one another, and their meanings in the context of the images' production and consumption.

Margaret Bourke-White/Time & Life Pictures/Getty Images

Residents of Louisville, Kentucky, waiting in a bread line in 1937. A massive flood from January to February that year left nearly four hundred people dead and roughly one million people homeless across five states.

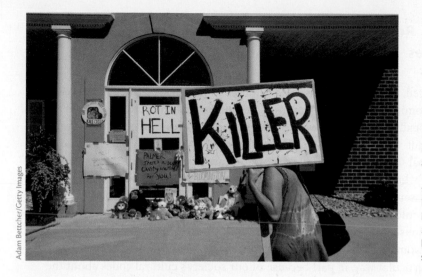

Protestors rallying outside the office of Dr. Walter Palmer, a dentist from Bloomington, Minnesota. In July 2015, Palmer was accused of poaching a 13-year-old lion named Cecil that was living at Hwange National Park in Zimbabwe. Palmer reportedly paid $50,000 for the hunt and lured Cecil out of the sanctuary to shoot him.

The point here is that photographs promise a clear window into a past reality but are not unassailable guarantors of truth. In the digital age, it's remarkably easy to alter photographs, and we have become more suspicious of photographs as direct evidence of reality. Yet we still tend to trust certain sources more than others. To counteract this tendency, we can be more critical about images by asking three overarching questions about the contexts in which they are created, disseminated, and received. Within each question, other questions arise.

1. *Who produced the image?*   Who was the photographer? Under what circumstances was the picture taken? How is the subject of the image framed? What other visual information is included in the frame? What is emphasized and de-emphasized? What do you think is the image's intended effect?

2. *Who distributed the image?*   How widely has the image been distributed? Where has it been published (magazine, newspaper, blog, social media page)? What is the intended audience of the publication where the image appears? What purpose does the image serve? How does the image support the accompanying text? What alternative images exist?

3. *Who consumed the image?*   What type of audience is the likeliest viewer of the image? Are they likely to see it as negative or positive? Does the image inspire an emotional response? If so, what kind? What elements in the photograph are likely to generate certain kinds of responses?

> **A RULE FOR WRITERS**
> If you think that pictures will help you to make the point you are arguing, include them with captions explaining their sources and relevance.

Accommodating, Resisting, and Negotiating the Meaning of Images

Most images are produced, selected, and published in order to have a specific effect on readers and viewers. This dominant meaning of an image supposes that the audience will react in a predictable way, usually based on the widespread **cultural codes** that operate within a society. Images of elegant women in designer dresses, rugged men driving pickup trucks, stodgy teachers, cutthroat CEOs, hipster computer programmers, and so on speak to generally accepted notions of what certain types of people are like. An image of a suburban couple in an automobile advertisement washing their new car subconsciously confirms and perpetuates a certain ideal of middle-class suburban life (a heterosexual couple, a well-trimmed lawn, a neatly painted house and picket fence—and a brand-new midsize sedan). An image of a teary-eyed young woman accepting a diamond ring from a handsome man will likely touch the viewer in a particular way, in part because of our society's cultural codes about the rituals of romantic love and marriage, gender roles, and the diamond ring as a sign of love and commitment.

These examples demonstrate that images can be constructed according to dominant connotations of gender, class, and racial, sexual, and political identity. When analyzing an image, ask yourself what cultural codes it endorses, what ideals it establishes as natural, what social norms or modes of everyday life it idealizes or assumes.

As image consumers, we often *accommodate* (i.e., passively accept) the cultural codes promoted in the media. For example, in the hypothetical advertisement featuring a wedding proposal, you might accept the producer's communicated ideals that men should propose to women, that women are emotional beings, and that diamond rings are the appropriate objects to represent love and commitment. When you **accommodate** cultural codes without understanding them critically, you allow the media that perpetuate these codes to interpret the world for you. That is, you accept their interpretations without questioning the social and cultural values implicit in their assumptions, many of which may actually run counter to your own or others' social and cultural values.

If you *resist* the cultural codes of an image, you actively criticize its message and meaning. Suppose you (1) question how the ad presents gender roles and marriage, (2) claim that it idealizes heterosexual marriage, and (3) point out that it confirms and extends traditional gender roles in which men are active and bold and women are passive and emotional. Moreover, you (4) argue that the diamond ring represents a misguided commodification of love because diamonds are kept deliberately scarce by large companies and, as such, are overvalued and overpriced; meanwhile, the ad prompts young couples to spend precious money at a time when their joint assets might be better saved, and because many diamonds come from third-world countries under essentially slave labor conditions, the diamond is more a symbol of oppression than of love. If your analysis follows such paths, you **resist** the dominant message of the image in question. Sometimes, this is called an *oppositional reading*.

Negotiation, or a *negotiated reading*, the most useful mode of reading and viewing, involves a middle path—a process of revision that seeks to recognize and change the conditions that give rise to certain negative aspects of cultural codes. Negotiation implies a practical intervention into common viewing processes that help construct and maintain social conditions and relations. This intervention can be important when inequalities or stereotypes are perpetuated by cultural codes. A negotiated reading enables you to emphasize the ways in which individuals, social groups, and others relate to images and their dominant meanings, and how different personal and cultural perspectives can challenge those meanings. Without intervention there can be no revision, no positive social or cultural change. You **negotiate** cultural codes when:

Image courtesy of The Advertising Archives

- you understand the underlying messages of images and accept the general cultural implications of these codes, *but*
- you acknowledge that in some circumstances the general codes do not apply.

Using this scheme will help you analyze diverse kinds of images as well as develop more nuanced arguments about the messages those images convey.

Exercise

Examine the image above, which is an advertisement for Lego building blocks. Provide brief examples of how a viewer could accommodate, resist, or negotiate the images in the ad.

Are Some Images Not Fit to Be Shown?

Images of suffering—either human or animal—can be immensely persuasive. In the nineteenth century, for instance, the antislavery movement made extremely effective use of images in its campaign. We reproduce two antislavery images earlier in this chapter, as well as a counterimage that sought to assure viewers that slavery is a beneficent system (p. 142). But are there some images not fit to print?

Until recently, many newspapers did not print pictures of lynched African Americans, hanged and burned and maimed. The reasons for not printing such images probably differed between South and North: Southern papers may have considered the images to be discreditable to whites, while northern papers may have deemed the images too revolting. Even today, when it's commonplace for newspapers and television news to show pictures of dead victims of war, famine, or traffic accidents, one rarely sees bodies that are horribly maimed. (For traffic accidents, the body is usually covered, and we see only the smashed car.) The U.S. government has refused to release photographs showing the bodies of American soldiers killed in the war in Iraq, and it has been most reluctant to show pictures of dead Iraqi soldiers and civilians. Only after many Iraqis refused to believe that former Iraqi president Saddam Hussein's two sons had been killed did the U.S. government reluctantly release pictures showing the two men's blood-spattered faces — and some American newspapers and television programs refused to use the images.

There have been notable exceptions to this practice, such as Huynh Cong (Nick) Ut's 1972 photograph of children fleeing a napalm attack in Vietnam (below), which was widely reproduced in the United States and won the photographer a Pulitzer Prize in 1973. It's impossible to measure the influence of this particular photograph, but many people believe that it played a substantial role in increasing public pressure to end the Vietnam War. Another widely reproduced picture of horrifying violence is Eddie Adams's 1968 picture (p. 155) of a South Vietnamese chief of police firing a pistol into the head of a Viet Cong prisoner.

AP Photo/Nick Ut

Huynh Cong (Nick) Ut, *The Terror of War: Children on Route 1 near Trang Bang, 1972*

Eddie Adams, *Execution of Viet Cong Prisoner, Saigon,* 1968

The issue remains: Are some images unacceptable? For instance, although capital punishment — by methods including lethal injection, hanging, shooting, and electrocution — is legal in parts of the United States, every state in the Union prohibits the publication of pictures showing a criminal being executed.[1]

The most famous recent example of an image widely thought to be unprintable showed the murder of Daniel Pearl, a reporter for the *Wall Street Journal.* Pearl was captured and murdered in June 2002 by Islamic terrorists in Pakistan. His killers videotaped Pearl reading a statement denouncing American policy and then being decapitated. The video also shows a man's arm holding Pearl's head. The video ends with the killers making demands (such as the release of Muslim prisoners being held by the United States in Guantánamo Bay, Cuba) and asserting, "if our demands are not met, this scene will be repeated again and again."

The chief arguments against newspapers reproducing material from this video were as follows:

- The video and still images from it are unbearably gruesome.

- Showing the video would traumatize the Pearl family.

- The video is enemy propaganda.

---

[1]For more on this topic, see Wendy Lesser, *Pictures at an Execution* (1993).

Alexander Gardner, *Home of a Rebel Sharpshooter*, 1863. This photo illustrates the devastation wrought by the Battle of Gettysburg through focusing on a single dead soldier splayed out in a "sharpshooter's den."

Those who favored broadcasting the video on television and printing still images from it in newspapers offered these arguments:

- The photos would show the world what sort of enemy the United States is fighting.
- Newspapers have published pictures of other terrifying sights (notably, people leaping out of windows of the World Trade Center's Twin Towers on 9/11 and the space shuttle *Challenger* exploding in 1986).
- No one was worried about protecting the families of 9/11 or *Challenger* victims from seeing those traumatic images.

But is the comparison of the Daniel Pearl video to the photos of the Twin Towers and the *Challenger* valid? You may respond that individuals in the Twin Towers pictures aren't specifically identifiable and that the *Challenger* images, although horrifying, aren't as visually revolting as the picture of a severed head held up for view.

The *Boston Phoenix*, a weekly newspaper, published some images from the Pearl video and also put a link to the video (with a warning that the footage is "extremely graphic") on its Web site. The weekly's editor justified publication on the three grounds we list above. Pearl's wife, Mariane Pearl, was quoted in various newspapers as condemning the "heartless decision to air this despicable video." And a spokeswoman for the Pearl family, when asked for comment, referred reporters to a statement issued earlier, which said that broadcasters who show the video

fall without shame into the terrorists' plan. . . . Danny believed that journalism was a tool to report the truth and foster understanding — not perpetuate propaganda and sensationalize tragedy. We had hoped that no part of this tape would ever see the

light of day. . . . We urge all networks and news outlets to exercise responsibility and
not aid the terrorists in spreading their message of hate and murder.[2]

Although some journalists expressed regret that Pearl's family was distressed, they insisted
that journalists have a right to reproduce such material and that the images can serve the
valuable purpose of shocking viewers into awareness.

POLITICS AND PICTURES

Consider, too, the controversy that erupted in 1991, during the Persian Gulf War, when
the U.S. government decided that news media would not be allowed to photograph coffins
returning with the bodies of military personnel killed during the war. In later years the policy
was sometimes ignored, but in 2003 the George W. Bush administration decreed that there
would be "no arrival ceremony for, or media coverage of, deceased military personnel returning [from Iraq or Afghanistan] . . . to the Dover (Delaware) base." The government enforced
the policy strictly.

Members of the news media strongly protested, as did many others, chiefly on the basis
of these arguments:

- The administration was trying to sanitize the war; that is, the government was
  depriving the public of important information — images — that showed the war's
  real cost.

- Grief for the deaths of military personnel is not a matter only for the families of
  the deceased. The sacrifices were made on behalf of the nation, and the nation
  should be allowed to grieve. Canada and Britain have no such ban; when military
  coffins are transported there, the public lines the streets to honor the fallen
  warriors. In fact, in Canada a portion of the highway near the Canadian base has
  been renamed "Highway of Heroes."

- The coffins at Dover Air Force base are not identified by name, so there is no issue
  about intruding on the privacy of grieving families.

The chief arguments in defense of the ban were as follows:

- Photographs violate the families' privacy.

- If the arrival of the coffins at Dover is publicized, some grieving families will think
  they should travel to Dover to be present when the bodies arrive. This may cause a
  financial hardship on the families.

- If the families give their consent, the press is *not* barred from individual graveside
  ceremonies at hometown burials. The ban extends only to the coffins' arrival at
  Dover Air Force Base.

---

[2]Quoted in the *Hartford Courant*, June 5, 2002, and reproduced on the Internet by the Freedom of Information Center, under the
heading "Boston Paper Creates Controversy."

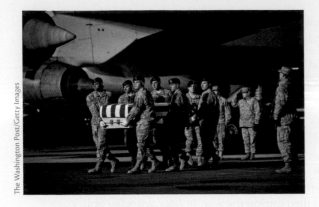

The Washington Post/Getty Images

In February 2009, President Obama changed the policy and permitted coverage of the transfer of bodily remains. In his Address to the Joint Session of Congress on February 24, 2009, he said, "For seven years we have been a nation at war. No longer will we hide its price." On February 27, Defense Secretary Robert M. Gates announced that the government ban was lifted and that families will decide whether to allow photographs and videos of the "dignified transfer process at Dover."

Exercise

In an argumentative essay of about 250 words — perhaps two or three paragraphs — give your view of the issue of permitting photos of military coffins. In an opening paragraph, you may want to both explain the issue and summarize the arguments that you reject. The second paragraph of a two-paragraph essay may present your reasons for rejecting those arguments. Additionally, you might devote a third paragraph to a more general reflection.

Topics for Critical Thinking and Writing

1. Marvin Kalb, a distinguished journalist, was quoted as saying that the public has a right to see the tape of Daniel Pearl's murder but that "common sense, decency, [and] humanity would encourage editors . . . to say 'no, it is not necessary to put this out.' There is no urgent demand on the part of the American people to see Daniel Pearl's death." What is your view?

2. In June 2006, two American soldiers were captured in Iraq. Later their bodies were found, dismembered and beheaded. Should newspapers have shown photographs of the mutilated bodies? Why, or why not? (In July 2006, insurgents in Iraq posted images on the Internet showing a soldier's severed head beside his body.)

Another issue concerning the appropriateness of showing certain images arose early in 2006. In September 2005, a Danish newspaper, accused of being afraid to show political cartoons that were hostile to Muslim terrorists, responded by publishing twelve cartoons. One cartoon showed the prophet Muhammad wearing a turban that looked like a bomb. The images at first didn't arouse much attention, but when they were reprinted in Norway in January 2006, they attracted worldwide attention and outraged Muslims, most of whom regard any depiction of Muhammad as blasphemous. Some Muslims in various Islamic nations burned Danish embassies and engaged in other acts of violence. Most non-Muslims agreed that the images were in bad taste; and apparently in deference to Islamic sensibilities (but possibly also out of fear of reprisals), very few Western newspapers reprinted the cartoons when they covered the news events. Most newspapers (including the *New York Times*) merely described the images. The editors of these papers believed that readers should be told the news, but that because the drawings were so offensive to some persons, they should be described rather than reprinted. A controversy then arose: Do readers of a newspaper deserve to *see* the evidence for themselves, or can a newspaper adequately fulfill its mission by offering only a verbal description? These questions arose again after the 2007 bombing of the French satirical newspaper *Charlie Hebdo*, and then after another mass shooting at the same newspaper in 2015 that claimed the lives of twelve editors and staff members.

Persons who argued that the images should be reproduced in the media generally made these points:

- Newspapers should yield neither to the delicate sensibilities of some readers nor to threats of violence.

- Jews for the most part do not believe that God should be depicted (the prohibition against "graven images" appears in Exodus 20.3), but they raise no objections to such Christian images as Michelangelo's painting of God awakening Adam, depicted on the ceiling of the Sistine Chapel. Further, when Andres Serrano (a Christian) in 1989 exhibited a photograph of a small plastic crucifix submerged in urine, it outraged a wider public (several U.S. senators condemned it because the artist had received federal funds), but virtually all newspapers showed the image, and many even printed its title, *Piss Christ*. The subject was judged to be newsworthy, and the fact that some viewers would regard the image as blasphemous was not considered highly relevant.

- Our society values freedom of speech, and newspapers should not be intimidated. When certain pictures are a matter of news, readers should be able to see them.

In contrast, opposing voices made these points:

- Newspapers must recognize deep-seated religious beliefs. They should indeed report the news, but there is no reason to *show* images that some people regard as blasphemous. The images can be adequately *described* in words.

- The Jewish response to Christian images of God, and even the tolerant Christians' response to Serrano's image of the crucifix immersed in urine, are irrelevant to the issue of whether a Western newspaper should represent images of the prophet Muhammad. Virtually all Muslims regard depictions of Muhammad as blasphemous, and that's what counts.

- Despite all the Western talk about freedom of the press, the press does *not* reproduce all images that become matters of news. For instance, news items about the sale of child pornography do not include images of the pornographic photos.

Exercises: Thinking about Images

1. Does the display of the Muhammad cartoons constitute an argument? If so, what is the conclusion, and what are the premises? If not, then what sort of statement, if any, does publishing these cartoons constitute?

2. Hugh Hewitt, an Evangelical Christian, offered a comparison to the cartoon of Muhammad wearing a bomblike turban. Suppose, he asked, an abortion clinic were bombed by someone claiming to be an Evangelical Christian. Would newspapers publish "a cartoon of Christ's crown of thorns transformed into sticks of TNT"? Do you think they would? If you were the editor of a newspaper, would you? Why, or why not?

3. One American newspaper, the *Boston Phoenix*, didn't publish any of the cartoons "out of fear of retaliation from the international brotherhood of radical and bloodthirsty Islamists who seek to impose their will on those who do not believe as they do. . . . We could not in good conscience place the men and women who work at the *Phoenix* and its related companies in physical jeopardy." Evaluate this position.

4. A week after the 2015 attack on *Charlie Hebdo*, and in response to media hesitancy to re-publish the offending images of Muhammad, the Index on Censorship and several other journalistic organizations called for all newspapers to publish them simultaneously and globally on January 8, 2015. "This unspeakable act of violence has challenged and assailed the entire press," said Lucie Morillon of Reporters Without Borders. "Journalism as a whole is in mourning. In the name of all those who have fallen in the defence of these fundamental values, we must continue *Charlie Hebdo*'s fight for the right to freedom of information." Evaluate this position.

Writing about a Political Cartoon

Most editorial pages print political cartoons as well as editorials. Like the writers of editorials, cartoonists seek to persuade, but they rarely use words to *argue* a point. True, they may use a few words in speech balloons or in captions, but generally the drawing does most of the work. Because their aim usually is to convince the viewer that some person's action or proposal is ridiculous, cartoonists almost always **caricature** their subjects:

- They exaggerate the subject's distinctive features to the point at which . . .
- . . . the subject becomes grotesque and ridiculous — absurd, laughable, contemptible.

We agree that it's unfair to suggest that because, say, the politician who proposes such-and-such is short, fat, and bald, his proposal is ridiculous; but that's the way cartoonists work. Further, cartoonists are concerned with producing a striking image, not with exploring an issue, so they almost always oversimplify, implying that there really is no other sane view.

In the course of saying that (1) the figures in a cartoon are ridiculous and *therefore* their ideas are contemptible, and (2) there is only one side to the issue, cartoonists often use **symbolism**. Here's a list of common symbols:

- symbolic figures (e.g., the U.S. government as Uncle Sam)
- animals (e.g., the Democratic Party as donkey and the Republican Party as elephant)
- buildings (e.g., the White House as representing the nation's president)
- things (e.g., a bag with a dollar sign on it as representing a bribe)

For anyone brought up in U.S. culture, these symbols (like the human figures they represent) are obvious, and cartoonists assume that viewers will instantly recognize the symbols and figures, will get the joke, and will see the absurdity of whatever issue the cartoonist is seeking to demolish.

In writing about the argument presented in a cartoon, normally you will discuss the ways in which the cartoon makes its point. Caricature usually implies, "This is ridiculous, as you can plainly see by the absurdity of the figures depicted" or "What *X*'s proposal adds up to, despite its apparent complexity, is nothing more than. . . ." As we have said, this sort of persuasion, chiefly by ridicule, probably is unfair: An unattractive person certainly can offer a thoughtful political proposal, and almost always the issue is more complicated than the cartoonist indicates. But cartoons work largely by ridicule and the omission of counterarguments, and we shouldn't reject the possibility that the cartoonist has indeed highlighted the absurdity of the issue.

Your essay will likely include an *evaluation* of the cartoon. Indeed, the *thesis* underlying your analytic/argumentative essay may be that the cartoon is effective (persuasive) for such-and-such reasons but unfair for such-and-such other reasons.

In analyzing the cartoon — in determining the cartoonist's attitude — consider the following elements:

- the relative size of the figures in the image
- the quality of the lines (e.g., thin and spidery, or thick and seemingly aggressive)
- the amount of empty space in comparison with the amount of heavily inked space (a drawing with lots of inky areas conveys a more oppressive tone than a drawing that's largely open)
- the degree to which text is important, as well as its content and tone (is it witty, heavy-handed, or something else?)

Caution: If your instructor lets you choose a cartoon, be sure to select one with sufficient complexity to make the exercise worthwhile. (See also Thinking Critically: Analysis of a Political Cartoon.)

Let's look at an example. Jackson Smith wrote this essay in a composition course at Tufts University.

THINKING CRITICALLY *Analysis of a Political Cartoon*

Look at the cartoon on page 161. For each Type of Analysis section in the chart below, provide your own answer based on the cartoon. (Sample answers appear in the third column.)

TYPE OF ANALYSIS	QUESTIONS TO ASK	SAMPLE ANSWER	YOUR ANSWER
Context	*Who is the artist? Where and when was the cartoon published?*	"This cartoon by Walt Handelsman was originally published in *Newsday* on September 12, 2009. Handelsman, a Pulitzer Prize–winning cartoonist, drew this cartoon in response to recent breaches of political decorum."	
Description	*What does the cartoon look like?*	"It depicts a group of Washington, D.C., tourists being driven past what the guide calls 'The Museum of Modern American Political Discourse,' a building in the shape of a giant toilet."	
Analysis	*How does the cartoon make its point? Is it effective?*	"The toilet as a symbol of the level of political discussion dominates the cartoon, effectively driving home the point that Americans are watching our leaders sink to new lows as they debate the future of our nation. By drawing the toilet on a scale similar to that of familiar monuments in Washington, Handelsman may be pointing out that today's politicians, rather than being remembered for great achievements like those of George Washington or Abraham Lincoln, will instead be remembered for their rudeness and aggression."	

LaunchPad / To complete this activity online, go to **macmillanhighered.com/barnetbedauohara**

JACKSON SMITH

Pledging Nothing? (Student Essay)

Gary Markstein's cartoon about the Pledge of Allegiance is one of dozens that can be retrieved by a search engine. It happens that every one of the cartoons that I retrieved mocked the courts for ruling that schools cannot require students to recite the Pledge of Allegiance in its present form, which includes the words "under God." I personally object to these words, so the cartoons certainly do not speak for me, but I'll try as impartially as possible to analyze the strength of Markstein's cartoon.

Markstein shows us, in the cartoon, four schoolchildren reciting the Pledge. Coming out of all four mouths is a speech balloon with the words, "One nation under nothing in particular." The children are facing a furled American flag, and to the right of the flag is a middle-aged female teacher, whose speech balloon is in the form of a cloud, indicating that she is *thinking* rather than saying the words, "God help us."

Certainly the image grabs us: little kids lined up reciting the Pledge of Allegiance, an

American flag, a maternal-looking teacher, and, in fact, if one examines the cartoon closely, one sees an apple on the teacher's desk. It's almost a Norman Rockwell scene, except, of course, it is a cartoon, so the figures are all a bit grotesque — but, still, they are nice folks. What is *not* nice, Markstein says, is what these kids must recite, "One nation under nothing in particular." In fact, the cartoon is far from telling the truth. Children who recite the Pledge without the words "under God" will still be saying that they are pledging allegiance to something quite specific — the United States:

> I pledge allegiance to the flag of the United States of America, and to the Republic for which it stands: one nation indivisible, with Liberty and Justice for all.

That's really quite a lot, very far from Markstein's "under nothing in particular." But no one, I suppose, expects fairness in a political cartoon — and of course this cartoon *is* political, because the issue of the Pledge has become a political football, with liberals on the whole wanting the words "under God" removed and conservatives on the whole wanting the words retained.

Let's now look at some of the subtleties of the cartoon. First, although, as I have said, cartoons present grotesque caricatures, the figures here are all affectionately presented. None of these figures is menacing. The teacher, with her spectacles and her rather dumpy figure, is clearly a benevolent figure, someone who in the eyes of the cartoonist rightly is disturbed about the fate of these little kids who are not allowed to say the words "under God." (Nothing, of course, prevents the children from speaking about God when they are not in the classroom. Those who believe in God can say grace at mealtime, can go to Sunday School, can go to church regularly, can pray before they go to bed, etc.) Markstein suggests that the absence of these words makes the entire Pledge meaningless ("under nothing in particular"), and in a master stroke he has conveyed this idea of impoverishment by showing a tightly furled flag, a flag that is presented as minimally as possible. After all, the flag could have been shown more fully, perhaps hanging from a pole that extended from a wall into the classroom, or the flag could have been displayed extended against a wall. Instead we get the narrowest of flags, something that is not much more than a furled umbrella, identifiable as the American flag by its stripes and a few stars in the upper third. Markstein thus cleverly suggests that with the loss of the words "under God," the flag itself is reduced to almost nothing.

Fair? No. Effective? Yes, and that's the job 5 of a cartoonist. Readers probably give cartoons no more than three or four seconds, and Markstein has made the most of those few seconds. The reader gets his point, and if the reader already holds this view, he or she probably says, "Hey, here's a great cartoon." I don't hold that view, but I am willing to grant that it is a pretty good cartoon, effectively making a point that I think is wrong-headed.

Visuals as Aids to Clarity: Maps, Graphs, and Pie Charts

Maps were part of the argument in the debate over drilling in the Arctic National Wildlife Refuge.

- Advocates of drilling argued that it would take place only in a tiny area. Their map showed Alaska, with an indication (in gray) of the much smaller part of Alaska that was the Refuge, and a further indication (cross-hatched) of what the advocates emphasized was a minuscule part of the Refuge.
- Opponents showed maps indicating the path of migrating caribou and the roads that would have to be constructed across the Refuge to get to the area where the drilling would take place.

Graphs, tables, and pie charts usually present quantitative data in visual form, helping writers to clarify dry statistical assertions. For instance, a line graph may illustrate how many immigrants came to the United States in each decade of the last century.

A bar graph (with bars running either horizontally or vertically) offers similar information. In the Coming to America graph, we can see at a glance that, say, the second bar on the lower left is almost double the length of the first, indicating that the number of immigrants almost doubled between 1850 and 1860.

A pie chart is a circle divided into wedges so that we can see, literally, how a whole comprises its parts. We can see, for instance, on page 166, that of an entire pie representing the regions of foreign-born U.S. immigrants, 36 percent were born in Central America and Mexico, 26 percent in Asia, 14 percent in Europe, and so on.

COMING TO AMERICA . . .

Both the percentage and number of foreign-born people in the United States dropped during much of the twentieth century, but after 1970, the tide was turning again.

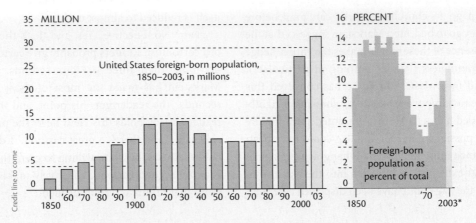

. . . FROM NEAR AND FAR

Central America, Mexico, and Asia contribute most to the foreign-born population.

Foreign-born population by region of birth, 2002

*Most recent estimate
Data from: United States Census Bureau

Because maps, charts, and graphs offer empirical data to support arguments, they communicate a high degree of reliability and tend to be convincing. "Numbers don't lie," it is sometimes said, and to some extent this is true. It's difficult to spin a fact like 1 + 1 = 2. However, as Charles Seife (whose essay on video games we reprint in Chapter 22) notes in his book,

Proofiness, numbers are cold facts, but the measurements that numbers actually chart aren't always so clear or free from bias and manipulation. Consider two examples of advertising claims that Seife cites — one for a L'Oréal mascara offering "twelve times more impact," and another for a new and improved Vaseline product that "delivers 70% more moisture in every drop." Such measurements *sound* good but remain relatively meaningless. (How was eyelash "impact" measured? What is a percentage value of moisture?)

Another way in which data can be relatively meaningless is by addressing only part of the question at stake. In 2013, a Mayo Clinic study found that drinking coffee regularly lowered participants' risk of the liver disease known as primary sclerosing cholangitis (PSC). But PSC is already listed as a "rare disease" by the Centers for Disease Control and Prevention, affecting fewer than 1 in 2,000 people. So even if drinking coffee lowered the risk of PSC by 25 percent, a person's chances would improve only slightly from .0005 percent chance to .0004 percent chance — hardly a change at all, and hardly a rationale for drinking more coffee. Yet, statistical information showing a 25 percent reduction in PSC sounds significant, even more so when provided under a headline proclaiming "Drinking coffee helps prevent liver disease."

Consider other uses of numbers that Seife shows in his book to constitute "proofiness" (his title and word to describe the misuse of numbers as evidence):

- In 2006, George W. Bush declared No Child Left Behind a success in his State of the Union Address: "[B]ecause we acted," he said, "students are performing better in reading and math." (True, fourth to eighth graders showed improved scores, but other grade levels declined. In addition, fourth- to eighth-grade reading and math scores had been improving at an unchanged rate both before and after the NCLB legislation.)

- In 2000, the *New York Times* reported "Researchers Link Bad Debt to Bad Health" (the "dark side of the economic boom"). The researchers claimed that debt causes more illness, but in doing so they committed the correlation-causation fallacy: Just because two phenomena are correlated does not mean they are causally related. (Example: More people wear shorts in the summer and more people eat ice cream in the summer than during other seasons, but wearing shorts does not *cause* higher ice cream consumption.)

Finally, consider the following graph showing that eating Quaker Oats decreases cholesterol levels after just four weeks of daily servings. The bar graph suggests that cholesterol levels will plummet. But a careful look at the graph reveals that the vertical axis doesn't begin

---

A CHECKLIST FOR CHARTS AND GRAPHS

- ☐ Is the source authoritative?
- ☐ Is the source cited?
- ☐ Will the chart or graph be intelligible to the intended audience?
- ☐ Is the caption, if any, clear and helpful?

at zero. In this case, a relatively small change has been (mis)represented as much bigger than it actually is.

Representative Cholesterol Point Drop

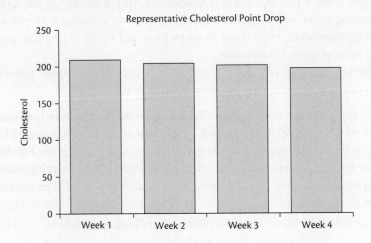

Representative Cholesterol Point Drop

A more accurate representation of cholesterol levels after four weeks of eating Quaker Oats, using a graph that starts at zero, would look more like the second graph—showing essentially unchanged levels.

Here is another example showing unemployment rates during the Obama presidency. Note that here, too, the vertical axis doesn't start at zero, making the "rise" appear more dramatic than it actually was in reality.

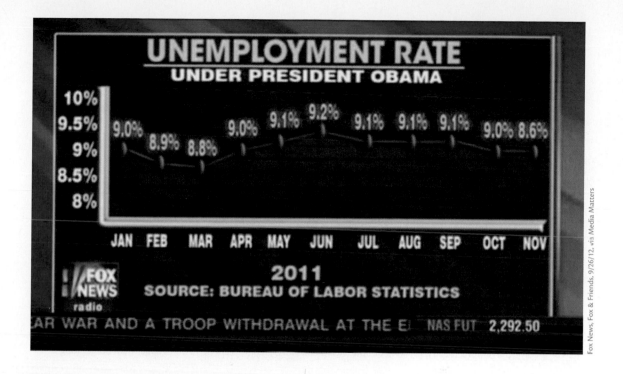

Fox News, Fox & Friends, 9/26/12, via Media Matters

Using Visuals in Your Own Paper

Every paper uses some degree of visual persuasion, merely in its appearance. Consider these elements of a paper's "look": title page; margins (ample, but not so wide that they indicate the writer's inability to produce a paper of the assigned length); double-spacing for the reader's convenience; headings and subheadings that indicate the progression of the argument; paragraphing; and so on. But you may also want to use visuals such as pictures, graphs, or pie charts. Keep a few guidelines in mind as you work with visuals, "writing" them into your own argument with as much care as you would read them in others' arguments:

- Consider your audience's needs and attitudes, and select the type of visuals — graphs, drawings, photographs — likely to be most persuasive to that audience.

- Consider the effect of color, composition, and placement within your document. Because images are most effective when they appear near the text that they supplement, do not group all images at the end of the paper.

Remember especially that images are almost never self-supporting or self-explanatory. They may be evidence for your argument (e.g., Ut's photograph of napalm victims is *very* compelling evidence of suffering), but they aren't arguments themselves.

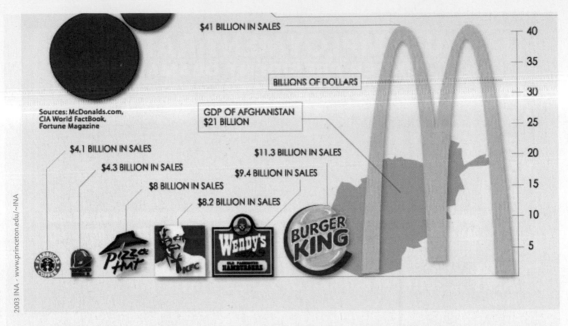

$41 BILLION IN SALES

BILLIONS OF DOLLARS

Sources: McDonalds.com,
CIA World FactBook,
Fortune Magazine

GDP OF AFGHANISTAN
$21 BILLION

$4.1 BILLION IN SALES

$4.3 BILLION IN SALES

$8 BILLION IN SALES

$8.2 BILLION IN SALES

$11.3 BILLION IN SALES

$9.4 BILLION IN SALES

In this graph, McDonald's $41 billion in sales are shown to be about 3.5 times higher than the revenues of its next closest competitor, Burger King (at $11.3 billion), but the McDonald's logo graphic is about 13 times larger than Burger King's.

- Be sure to explain each visual that you use, integrating it into the verbal text that provides the logic and principal support behind your thesis.
- Be sure to cite the source of any visual that you paste into your argument.

Be alert to common ways in which graphs can be misleading:

- Vertical axis doesn't start at zero or skips numbers.
- Scale is given in very small units to make changes look big.
- Pie charts don't accurately divide on scale with percentages shown.
- Oversized graphics don't match the numbers they represent.

Additional Images for Analysis

In 1936, photographer Dorothea Lange (1895–1965) took a series of pictures, including the two below, of a migrant mother and her children. Widely reprinted in the nation's newspapers, these photographs helped to dramatize for the American public the poverty of displaced workers during the Great Depression.

Art Resource, NY

Digital Image © The Museum of Modern Art/Licensed by SCALA/Art Resource, NY

Topics for Critical Thinking and Writing

1. Dorothea Lange drew increasingly near to her subject as she took a series of pictures. Make a list of details gained and lost by framing the mother and children more closely. The final shot in the series (above) became the most famous and most widely reprinted. Do you find it more effective than the other? Why, or why not?

2. Note the expression on the mother's face, the position of her body, and the way she interacts with her children. What sorts of relationships are implied? Why is it significant that she doesn't look at her children or at the camera? How do the photographs' effects change according to how much you can see of the children's faces?

3. These photographs constitute a sort of persuasive "speech." Of what, exactly, might the photographer be trying to persuade her viewers? Try to state the purpose of Lange's photographs by completing this sentence: "Lange would like the viewers of her photographs to. . . ." Write a brief essay (250 words) making the same case. Compare your written argument to Lange's visual one. Which form of persuasion do you find more effective? Why?

4. Whom do you think Lange had in mind as her original audience? What assumptions does she make about that audience? What sorts of evidence does she use to reach them?

During World War II, the U.S. government produced a series of recruitment posters bearing the legend "This is the enemy." These posters depicted racially stereotyped images of both German and Japanese soldiers, typically engaged in acts of savage violence or clandestine surveillance.

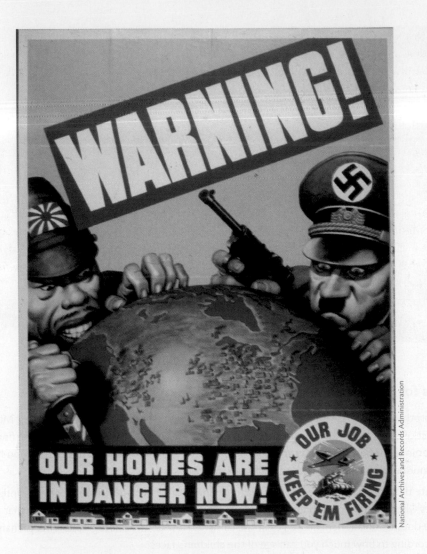

National Archives and Records Administration

Topics for Critical Thinking and Writing

1. It has been claimed that one role of propaganda is to dehumanize the enemy so that (1) soldiers will feel less remorse about killing opposing soldiers and (2) civilians will continue to support the war effort. What specific features of this poster contribute to this propaganda function?

2. Some would claim that such a racially provocative image of a Japanese soldier should never have been used because of the potential harm to all Asians, including patriotic Asian Americans. (Did you know that that the 442nd Regimental Combat Team, consisting solely of Japanese American volunteers, was by war's end the most decorated unit in U.S. military

history for its size and length of service?) Others believe that the ordinary rules do not apply in times of national crisis and that, as an old saying has it, "All's fair in love and war." In an essay of about 500 words, argue for one or the other of these propositions. Refer to this poster as one piece of your evidence.

Additional Topics for Critical Thinking and Writing

Gather some of the graphic materials used to promote and reflect your college or university — including a screen shot of its Web site, the college catalog, and the brochures and other materials sent to prospective students.

1. What is the dominant image that your college or university administration seems to be promoting? Are there different, even competing, images of your school at work? How accurate is the story that these materials tell about your campus? Write an essay (250 words) in which you explain to prospective students the ways in which the promotional materials capture, or fail to capture, the true spirit of your campus.

2. Compare the Web site of your institution to one or two from very different institutions — perhaps a community college, a large state university, or an elite private college. How do you account for the similarities and differences among the sites?

NORA EPHRON

Nora Ephron (1941–2012) attended Wellesley College and then worked as a reporter for the New York Post *and as a columnist and senior editor for* Esquire. *Ephron wrote screenplays and directed films, including* Sleepless in Seattle *(1993), and continued to write essays on a wide variety of topics. "The Boston Photographs" is from her collection* Scribble, Scribble: Notes on the Media *(1978).*

The Boston Photographs

"I made all kinds of pictures because I thought it would be a good rescue shot over the ladder . . . never dreamed it would be anything else. . . . I kept having to move around because of the light set. The sky was bright and they were in deep shadow. I was making pictures with a motor drive and he, the fire fighter, was reaching up and, I don't know, everything started falling. I followed the girl down taking pictures. . . . I made three or four frames. I realized what was going on and I completely turned around, because I didn't want to see her hit."

You probably saw the photographs. In most newspapers, there were three of them. The first showed some people on a fire escape — a fireman, a woman, and a child. The fireman had a nice strong jaw and looked very brave. The woman was holding the child. Smoke was pouring from the building behind them. A rescue ladder was approaching, just a few feet away, and the fireman had one arm around the woman and one arm reaching out toward the ladder. The second picture showed the fire escape slipping off the building. The child had fallen on the escape and seemed about to slide off the edge. The woman was grasping desperately at the legs of the fireman, who had managed to grab the ladder. The third picture showed the woman and child in midair, falling to the ground. Their arms and legs were outstretched, horribly distended. A potted plant was falling too. The caption said that the woman, Diana Bryant, nineteen, died in the fall. The child landed on the woman's body and lived.

The pictures were taken by Stanley Forman, thirty, of the *Boston Herald American.* He used a motor-driven Nikon F set at 1/250, f5.6-S. Because of the motor, the camera can click off three frames a second. More than four hundred newspapers in the United States alone carried the photographs: The tear sheets from overseas are still coming in. The *New York Times* ran them on the first page of its second section; a paper in south Georgia gave them nineteen columns; the *Chicago Tribune,* the *Washington Post*, and the *Washington Star* filled almost half their front pages, the *Star* under a somewhat redundant headline that read: SENSATIONAL PHOTOS OF RESCUE ATTEMPT THAT FAILED.

The photographs are indeed sensational. They are pictures of death in action, of that split second when luck runs out, and it is impossible to look at them without feeling their extraordinary impact and remembering, in an almost subconscious way, the morbid fantasy of falling, falling off a building, falling to one's death. Beyond that, the pictures are classics, old-fashioned but perfect examples

Stanley Forman

Stanley Forman

Stanley Forman

Stanley Forman

of photojournalism at its most spectacular. They're throwbacks, really, fire pictures, 1930s tabloid shots; at the same time they're technically superb and thoroughly modern — the sequence could not have been taken at all until the development of the motor-driven camera some sixteen years ago.

Most newspaper editors anticipate some 5 reader reaction to photographs like Forman's; even so, the response around the country was enormous, and almost all of it was negative. I have read hundreds of the letters that were printed in letters-to-the-editor sections, and they repeat the same points. "Invading the privacy of death." "Cheap sensationalism." "I thought I was reading the *National Enquirer.*" "Assigning the agony of a human being in terror of imminent death to the status of a sideshow act." "A tawdry way to sell newspapers." The *Seattle Times* received sixty letters and calls; its managing editor even got a couple of them at home. A reader wrote the *Philadelphia Inquirer:* "*Jaws* and *Towering Inferno* are playing downtown; don't take business away from people who pay good money to advertise in your own paper." Another reader wrote the *Chicago Sun-Times:* "I shall try to hide my disappointment that Miss Bryant wasn't wearing a skirt when she fell to her death. You could have had some award-winning photographs of her underpants as her skirt billowed over her head, you voyeurs." Several newspaper editors wrote columns defending the pictures: Thomas Keevil of the *Costa Mesa* (California) *Daily Pilot* printed a ballot for readers to vote on whether they would have printed the pictures; Marshall L. Stone of Maine's *Bangor Daily News,* which refused to print the famous assassination picture of the Vietcong prisoner in Saigon, claimed that the Boston pictures showed the dangers of fire escapes and raised questions about slumlords. (The

burning building was a five-story brick apartment house on Marlborough Street in the Back Bay section of Boston.)

For the last five years, the *Washington Post* has employed various journalists as ombudsmen, whose job is to monitor the paper on behalf of the public. The *Post's* current ombudsman is Charles Seib, former managing editor of the *Washington Star;* the day the Boston photographs appeared, the paper received over seventy calls in protest. As Seib later wrote in a column about the pictures, it was "the largest reaction to a published item that I have experienced in eight months as the *Post's* ombudsman. . . .

"In the *Post's* newsroom, on the other hand, I found no doubts, no second thoughts . . . the question was not whether they should be printed but how they should be displayed. When I talked to editors . . . they used words like 'interesting' and 'riveting' and 'gripping' to describe them. The pictures told of something about life in the ghetto, they said (although the neighborhood where the tragedy occurred is not a ghetto, I am told). They dramatized the need to check on the safety of fire escapes. They dramatically conveyed something that had happened, and that is the business we're in. They were news. . . .

"Was publication of that [third] picture a bow to the same taste for the morbidly sensational that makes gold mines of disaster movies? Most papers will not print the picture of a dead body except in the most unusual circumstances. Does the fact that the final picture was taken a millisecond before the young woman died make a difference? Most papers will not print a picture of a bare female breast. Is that a more inappropriate subject for display than the picture of a human being's last agonized instant of life?" Seib offered no answers to the questions he raised, but he went on to say that although as an editor he would probably have run the pictures, as a reader he was revolted by them.

In conclusion, Seib wrote: "Any editor who decided to print those pictures without giving at least a moment's thought to what purpose they served and what their effect was likely to be on the reader should ask another question: Have I become so preoccupied with manufacturing a product according to professional traditions and standards that I have forgotten about the consumer, the reader?"

It should be clear that the phone calls and letters and Seib's own reaction were occasioned by one factor alone: the death of the woman. Obviously, had she survived the fall, no one would have protested; the pictures would have had a completely different impact. Equally obviously, had the child died as well — or instead — Seib would undoubtedly have received ten times the phone calls he did. In each case, the pictures would have been exactly the same — only the captions, and thus the responses, would have been different.

But the questions Seib raises are worth discussing — though not exactly for the reasons he mentions. For it may be that the real lesson of the Boston photographs is not the danger that editors will be forgetful of reader reaction, but that they will continue to censor pictures of death precisely because of that reaction. The protests Seib fielded were really a variation on an old theme — and we saw plenty of it during the Nixon-Agnew years — the "Why doesn't the press print the good news?" argument. In this case, of course, the objections were all dressed up and cleverly disguised as righteous indignation about the privacy of death. This is a form of puritanism that is often justifiable; just as often it is merely puritanical.

Seib takes it for granted that the widespread though fairly recent newspaper policy against printing pictures of dead bodies is a sound one; I don't know that it makes any sense at all. I recognize that printing pictures of corpses raises all sorts of problems about taste and titillation and sensationalism; the fact is, however, that people die. Death happens to be one of life's main events. And it is irresponsible — and more than that, inaccurate — for newspapers to fail to show it, or to show it only when an astonishing set of photos comes in over the Associated Press wire. Most papers covering fatal automobile accidents will print pictures of mangled cars. But the significance of fatal automobile accidents is not that a great deal of steel is twisted but that people die. Why not show it? That's what accidents are about. Throughout the Vietnam War, editors were reluctant to print atrocity pictures. Why *not* print them? That's what that was about. Murder victims are almost never photographed; they are granted their privacy. But their relatives are relentlessly pictured on their way in and out of hospitals and morgues and funerals.

I'm not advocating that newspapers print these things in order to teach their readers a lesson. The *Post* editors justified their printing of the Boston pictures with several arguments in that direction; every one of them is irrelevant. The pictures don't show anything about slum life; the incident could have happened anywhere, and it did. It is extremely unlikely that anyone who saw them rushed out and had his fire escape strengthened. And the pictures were not news — at least they were not national news. It is not news in Washington, or New York, or Los Angeles that a woman was killed in a Boston fire. The only newsworthy thing about the pictures is that they were taken. They deserve to be printed because they are great pictures, breathtaking pictures of something that happened. That they disturb readers is exactly as it should be: that's why photojournalism is often more powerful than written journalism.

Topics for Critical Thinking and Writing

1. In paragraph 5, Nora Ephron refers to "the famous assassination picture of the Vietcong prisoner in Saigon" (see p. 155). The photo shows the face of a prisoner who is about to be shot in the head at close range. Jot down the reasons why you would or would not approve of printing this photo in a newspaper. Think, too, about this: If the photo on page 154 weren't about a war — if it didn't include the soldiers and the burning village in the rear but, instead, showed children fleeing from an abusive parent or an abusive sibling — would you approve of printing it in a newspaper?

2. In paragraph 9, Ephron quotes a newspaperman as saying that before printing Forman's pictures of the woman and the child falling from the fire escape, editors should have asked themselves "what purpose they served and what their effect was likely to be on the reader." If you were an editor, what would your answers be? By the way, the pictures were *not* taken in a poor neighborhood, and they did *not* expose slum conditions.

3. In 50 words or so, write a precise description of what you see in the third of the Boston photographs. Do you think readers of your description would be "revolted" by the picture (para. 8), as were many viewers, the *Washington Post*'s ombudsman among them? Why, or why not?

4. Ephron thinks it would be good for newspapers to publish more photographs of death and dying (paras. 11–13). In an essay of approximately 500 words, state her reasons and your evaluation of them.

PART TWO

Critical Writing

5

Writing an Analysis of an Argument

This is what we can all do to nourish and strengthen one another: listen to one another very hard, ask questions, too, send one another away to work again, and laugh in all the right places.

— NANCY MAIRS

I don't wait for moods. You accomplish nothing if you do that. Your mind must know it has got to get down to work.

— PEARL S. BUCK

Fear not those who argue but those who dodge.

— MARIE VON EBNER-ESCHENBACH

Analyzing an Argument

EXAMINING THE AUTHOR'S THESIS

Most of your writing in other courses will require you to write an analysis of someone else's writing. In a course in political science you may have to analyze, say, an essay first published in *Foreign Affairs,* perhaps reprinted in your textbook, that argues against raising tariff barriers to foreign trade. Or a course in sociology may require you to analyze a report on the correlation between fatal accidents and drunk drivers under the age of twenty-one. Much of your writing, in short, will set forth reasoned responses to your reading as preparation for making an argument of your own.

Obviously, you must understand an essay before you can analyze it thoughtfully. You must read it several times — not just skim it — and (the hard part) you must think critically about it. Again, you'll find that your thinking is stimulated if you take notes and if you ask yourself questions about the material. Are there any Web sites or organizations dedicated to the material you are analyzing? If there are, visit some to see what others are saying about the material you are reviewing. Notes will help you to keep track of the writer's thoughts and also of your own responses to the writer's thesis. The writer probably *does* have a thesis, a claim, a point, and if so, you must try to locate it. Perhaps the thesis is explicitly stated in the title or in a sentence or two near the beginning of the essay or in a concluding paragraph, but perhaps you will have to infer it from the essay as a whole.

Notice that we said the writer *probably* has a thesis. Much of what you read will indeed be primarily an argument; the writer explicitly or implicitly is trying to support some thesis and to convince readers to agree with it. But some of what you read will be relatively neutral, with the argument just faintly discernible — or even with no argument at all. A work may, for instance, chiefly be a report: Here are the data, or here is what *X*, *Y*, and *Z* said; make of it what you will. A report might simply state how various ethnic groups voted in an election. In a report of this sort, of course, the writer hopes to persuade readers that the facts are correct, but no thesis is advanced — at least not explicitly or perhaps even consciously; the writer is not evidently arguing a point and trying to change readers' minds. Such a document differs greatly from an essay by a political analyst who presents similar findings to persuade a candidate to sacrifice the votes of one particular ethnic bloc and thereby get more votes from other blocs.

EXAMINING THE AUTHOR'S PURPOSE

While reading an argument, try to form a clear idea of the author's **purpose**. Judging from the essay or the book, was the purpose to persuade, or was it to report? An analysis of a pure report (a work apparently without a thesis or argumentative angle) on ethnic voting will deal chiefly with the accuracy of the report. It will, for example, consider whether the sample poll was representative.

Much material that poses as a report really has a thesis built into it, consciously or unconsciously. The best evidence that the prose you are reading is argumentative is the presence of two kinds of key terms: transitions that imply the drawing of a conclusion (such as *therefore, because, for the reason that,* and *consequently*) and verbs that imply proof (such as *confirms, verifies, accounts for, implies, proves, disproves, is [in]consistent with, refutes,* and *it follows that*). Keep your eye out for such terms, and scrutinize their precise role whenever they appear. If the essay does not advance a thesis, think of one that it might support or some conventional belief that it might undermine. (See also Thinking Critically: Drawing Conclusions and Implying Proof on page 190.)

EXAMINING THE AUTHOR'S METHODS

If the essay advances a thesis, you will want to analyze the strategies or methods of argument that allegedly support the thesis.

- Does the writer quote authorities? Are these authorities competent in this field? Does the writer consider equally competent authorities who take a different view?

- Does the writer use statistics? If so, who compiled them, and are they appropriate to the point being argued? Can they be interpreted differently?

- Does the writer build the argument by using examples or analogies? Are they satisfactory?

- Are the writer's assumptions acceptable?

- Does the writer consider all relevant factors? Has he or she omitted some points that you think should be discussed? For instance, should the author recognize certain opposing positions and perhaps concede something to them?

- Does the writer seek to persuade by means of ridicule? If so, is the ridicule fair? Is it supported also by rational argument?

- Is the argument aimed at a particular audience?

In writing your analysis, you will want to tell readers something about the author's purpose and something about the author's **methods**. It is usually a good idea at the start of your analysis—if not in the first paragraph, then in the second or third—to let the reader know the purpose (and thesis, if there is one) of the work you are analyzing and then to summarize the work briefly.

Next, you will probably find it useful (readers will certainly find it helpful) to write out *your* thesis (your evaluation or judgment). You might say, for instance, that the essay is impressive but not conclusive, or is undermined by convincing contrary evidence, or relies too much on unsupported generalizations, or is wholly admirable. Remember, because your paper is itself an argument, it needs its own thesis.

And then, of course, comes the job of setting forth your analysis and the support for your thesis. There is no one way of going about this work. If, say, the author whose work you're analyzing gives four arguments (e.g., an appeal to common sense, the testimony of authorities, the evidence of comparisons, and an appeal to self-interest), you might want to do one of the following:

- Take up these four arguments in sequence.

- Discuss the simplest of the four, and then go on to the more difficult ones.

- Discuss the author's two arguments that you think are sound, and then turn to the two that you think are not sound (or perhaps the reverse).

- Apply one of these approaches, and then clinch your case by constructing a fifth argument that is absent from the work under scrutiny but is, in your view, highly important.

In short, the organization of your analysis may or may not follow the organization of the work you are analyzing.

EXAMINING THE AUTHOR'S PERSONA

You will probably also want to analyze something a bit more elusive than the author's explicit arguments: the author's self-presentation. Does the author seek to persuade readers partly by presenting himself or herself as conscientious, friendly, self-effacing, authoritative, tentative, or in some other light? Most writers do two things:

- They present evidence.

- They present themselves (or, more precisely, they present the image of themselves that they wish us to behold).

In some persuasive writing this **persona** or **voice** or presentation of the self may be no less important than the presentation of evidence. In other cases, the persona may not much matter, but our point is that you should spend a little time looking at the author's self-presentation to consider if it's significant.

In establishing a persona, writers adopt various rhetorical strategies, ranging from the use of characteristic words to the use of a particular form of organization. For instance:

- The writer who speaks of an opponent's "gimmicks" instead of "strategy" probably is trying to downgrade the opponent and also to convey the self-image of a streetwise person.

- On a larger scale, consider the way in which evidence is presented and the kind of evidence that's offered. One writer may first bombard the reader with facts and then spend relatively little time drawing conclusions. Another may rely chiefly on generalizations, waiting until the end of the essay to bring the thesis home with a few details. Another may begin with a few facts and spend most of the space reflecting on these. One writer may seem professorial or pedantic, offering examples of an academic sort; another, whose examples are drawn from ordinary life, may seem like a regular guy.

All such devices deserve comment in your analysis.

The writer's persona, then, may color the thesis and help it develop in a distinctive way. If we accept the thesis, it is partly because the writer has won our goodwill by persuading us of his or her good character (*ethos,* in Aristotle's terms). Later we talk more about the appeal to the speaker's character — the so-called *ethical appeal,* but here we may say that good writers present themselves not as wise-guys, bullies, or pompous asses but as decent people whom the reader would like to invite to dinner.

The author of an essay may, for example, seem fair-minded and open-minded, treating the opposition with great courtesy and expressing interest in hearing other views. Such a tactic is itself a persuasive device. Another author may appear to rely on hard evidence such as statistics. This reliance on seemingly objective truths is itself a way of seeking to persuade — a rational way, to be sure, but a mode of persuasion nonetheless.

Especially in analyzing a work in which the author's persona and ideas are blended, you will want to spend some time commenting on the persona. Whether you discuss it near the beginning of your analysis or near the end will depend on how you want to construct your essay, and this decision will partly depend on the work you are analyzing. For example, if the author's persona is kept in the background and is thus relatively invisible, you may want to make that point fairly early to get it out of the way and then concentrate on more interesting matters. If, however, the persona is interesting — and perhaps seductive, whether because it seems so scrupulously objective or so engagingly subjective — you may want to hint at this quality early in your essay and then develop the point while you consider the arguments.

In short, the author's self-presentation usually matters. Recognize its effect, whether positive or negative.

EXAMINING PERSONA AND INTENDED AUDIENCE

A key element in understanding an argument lies in thinking about the intended audience — how the author perceives the audience and what strategies the author uses to connect to it. We have already said something about the creation of the author's persona. An author with a loyal following is, almost by definition, someone who in earlier writings has presented an engaging persona, a persona with a trustworthy *ethos*. A trusted author can sometimes cut corners and can perhaps adopt a colloquial tone that would be unacceptable in the writing of an unknown author.

Authors who want to win the assent of their audiences need to think about how they present information and how they present *themselves*. Consider how you prefer people to talk to you. What sorts of language do you find engaging? Much of course depends on the circumstances, notably the topic, the audience, and the place. A joke may be useful in an argument about whether the government should regulate junk food, but almost surely a joke will be inappropriate — will backfire, will alienate the audience — in an argument about abortion. The *way* an author addresses the reader (through an invented persona) can have a significant impact on the reader's perception of the author, which is to say perception of the author's *views*, the author's *argument*. A slip in tone or an error of fact, however small, may be enough for the audience to dismiss the author's argument. Understanding audience means thinking about all of the possible audiences who may come into contact with your writing or your message, and thinking about the consequences of what you write and where it is published.

You may recall a tweet by Lebron James, who formerly played basketball for the Cleveland Cavaliers but left to play for the Miami Heat. After James left the Cavaliers (and his home state of Ohio), the Los Angeles Lakers beat the Cavaliers by fifty-five points, and James tweeted: "Crazy. Karma is a b****. Gets you every time. It's not good to wish bad on anybody. God sees everything!" Cleveland fans not surprisingly perceived his tweet as a slap in the face. The broader audience, too, outside of Cleveland, perceived it as inappropriate. Though he has since returned to Cleveland and been largely forgiven by fans, Lebron James clearly did not think about his audience(s). To put it in rhetorical terms, Lebron James vastly diminished his *ethos*. Doubtless he wishes he could retract the tweet, but as the ancient Roman poet Horace said, *"Nescit vox missa reverti"* ("The word once spoken can never be recalled"), or, in plain proverbial English, "Think twice before you speak."

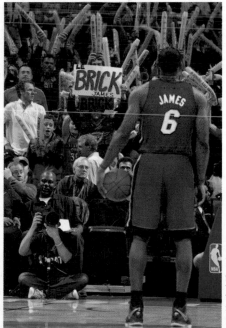

Lebron James, considering his audience while he was with the Miami Heat.

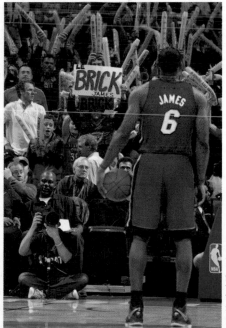Layne Murdoch/Getty Images

Consider Facebook status updates. Have you ever posted a status update and wished you could take it back only to find out it was too late? People you did not want to see it saw it before you could remove it. Have you ever tweeted or even texted something you wished you hadn't? When reading and writing more formal essays, it is equally important to think about who wrote what you are reading, and who will read what you are writing.

SUMMARY

In the last few pages we have tried to persuade you that, in writing an analysis of a reading, you must do the following:

- Read and reread thoughtfully. Composing and keeping notes will help you to think about what you are reading.

- Be aware of the purpose of the material to which you are responding.

We have also tried to point out these facts:

- Most of the nonliterary material that you will read is designed to argue, to report, or to do both.

- Most of this material also presents the writer's personality, or voice, and this voice usually merits attention in an analysis. An essay on, say, nuclear war, in a journal devoted to political science, may include a voice that moves from an objective tone to a mildly ironic tone to a hortatory tone, and this voice is worth commenting on.

Possibly all this explanation is obvious. There is yet another point, equally obvious but often neglected by students who begin by writing an analysis and end up by writing only a summary, a shortened version of the work they have read: Although your essay is an analysis of someone else's writing, and you may have to include a summary of the work you are writing about, your essay is *your* essay, your analysis, not a mere summary. The thesis, the organization, and the tone are yours.

- Your thesis, for example, may be that although the author is convinced she has presented a strong case, her case is far from proved because . . .

- Your organization may be deeply indebted to the work you are analyzing, but it need not be. The author may have begun with specific examples and then gone on to make generalizations and to draw conclusions, but you may begin with the conclusions.

- Your tone, similarly, may resemble your subject's (let's say the voice is courteous academic), but it will nevertheless have its own ring, its own tone of, say, urgency, caution, or coolness.

Most of the essays that we have included thus far are more or less in an academic style, and indeed several are by students and by professors. But argumentative writing is not limited to academicians — if it were, your college would not be requiring you to take a course in the subject. The following essay, in a breezy style, comes from a columnist who writes for the *New York Times*.

A CHECKLIST FOR ANALYZING A TEXT

Have I considered all of the following matters?

- ☐ Who is the author? What stake might he or she have in writing this piece?

- ☐ Is the piece aimed at a particular audience? A neutral audience? Persons who are already sympathetic to the author's point of view? A hostile audience? What evidence enables me to identify the target audience?

- ☐ What is the author's thesis (argument, main point, claim)?

- ☐ What assumptions does the author make? Do I share them? If not, why not?

- ☐ Does the author ever confuse facts with beliefs or opinions?

- ☐ What appeals does the author make? To reason (*logos*), for instance, with statistics, the testimony of authorities, and personal experience? To the emotions (*pathos*), for instance, by an appeal to "our better nature" or to widely shared values? To our sense that the speaker is trustworthy (*ethos*)?

- ☐ How convincing is the evidence? Why do I think so?

- ☐ Are significant objections and counterevidence adequately discussed?

(continues on next page)

An Argument, Its Elements, and a Student's Analysis of the Argument

NICHOLAS D. KRISTOF

Nicholas D. Kristof (b. 1959), a two-time Pulitzer Prize winner, grew up on a farm in Oregon. After graduating from Harvard, he was awarded a Rhodes scholarship to Oxford, where he studied law. In 1984 he joined the New York Times *as a correspondent, and since 2001 he has written as a columnist. The editorial that follows first appeared in the* New York Times *in 2005.*

For Environmental Balance, Pick Up a Rifle

Here's a quick quiz: Which large American mammal kills the most humans each year?

It's not the bear, which kills about two people a year in North America. Nor is it the wolf, which in modern times hasn't killed anyone in this country. It's not the cougar, which kills one person every year or two.

Rather, it's the deer. Unchecked by predators, deer populations are exploding in a way that is profoundly unnatural and that is destroying the ecosystem in many parts of the country. In a wilderness, there might be ten deer per square mile; in parts of New Jersey, there are up to 200 per square mile.

One result is ticks and Lyme disease, but deer also kill people more directly. A study for the insurance industry estimated that deer kill about 150 people a year in car crashes nationwide and cause $1 billion in damage. Granted, deer aren't stalking us, and they come out worse in these collisions — but it's still true that in a typical year, an American is less likely to be killed by Osama bin Laden than by Bambi.

If the symbol of the environment's being 5 out of whack in the 1960s was the Cuyahoga River in Cleveland catching fire, one such symbol today is deer congregating around what they think of as salad bars and what we think of as suburbs.

So what do we do? Let's bring back hunting.

Now, you've probably just spilled your coffee. These days, among the university-educated crowd in the cities, hunting is viewed as barbaric.

The upshot is that towns in New York and New Jersey are talking about using birth control to keep deer populations down. (Liberals presumably support free condoms, while conservatives back abstinence education.) Deer contraception hasn't been very successful, though.

Meanwhile, the same population bomb has spread to bears. A bear hunt has been scheduled for this week in New Jersey — prompting outrage from some animal rights groups (there's also talk of bear contraception: make love, not cubs).

As for deer, partly because hunting is per- 10 ceived as brutal and vaguely psychopathic, towns are taking out contracts on deer through discreet private companies. Greenwich, Connecticut, budgeted $47,000 this year to pay a company to shoot eighty deer from raised platforms over four nights — as well as $8,000 for deer birth control.

Look, this is ridiculous.

We have an environmental imbalance caused in part by the decline of hunting. Humans first wiped out certain predators — like wolves and cougars — but then expanded their own role as predators to sustain a rough ecological balance. These days, though, hunters are on the decline.

According to "Families Afield: An Initiative for the Future of Hunting," a report by an alliance of shooting organizations, for every hundred hunters who die or stop hunting, only sixty-nine hunters take their place.

I was raised on *Bambi* — but also, as an Oregon farm boy, on venison and elk meat.

But deer are not pets, and dead deer are as natural as live deer. To wring one's hands over them, perhaps after polishing off a hamburger, is soggy sentimentality.

What's the alternative to hunting? Is it 15 preferable that deer die of disease and hunger? Or, as the editor of *Adirondack Explorer* magazine suggested, do we introduce wolves into the burbs?

To their credit, many environmentalists agree that hunting can be green. The New Jersey Audubon Society this year advocated deer hunting as an ecological necessity.

There's another reason to encourage hunting: it connects people with the outdoors and creates a broader constituency for wilderness preservation. At a time when America's wilderness is being gobbled away for logging, mining, or oil drilling, that's a huge boon.

Granted, hunting isn't advisable in suburban backyards, and I don't expect many soccer moms to install gun racks in their minivans. But it's an abdication of environmental responsibility to eliminate other predators and then refuse to assume the job ourselves. In that case, the collisions with humans will simply get worse.

In October, for example, Wayne Goldsberry was sitting in a home in northwestern Arkansas when he heard glass breaking in the next room. It was a home invasion — by a buck.

Mr. Goldsberry, who is six feet one inch 20 and weighs two hundred pounds, wrestled with the intruder for forty minutes. Blood spattered the walls before he managed to break the buck's neck.

So it's time to reestablish a balance in the natural world — by accepting the idea that hunting is as natural as bird-watching.

Topics for Critical Thinking and Writing

1. What is Nicholas Kristof's chief thesis? (State it in one sentence.)

2. Does Kristof make any assumptions — tacit or explicit — with which you disagree? With which you agree? Write them down.

3. Is the slightly humorous tone of Kristof's essay inappropriate for a discussion of deliberately killing wild animals? Why, or why not?

4. If you are familiar with *Bambi*, does the story make any *argument* against killing deer, or does the story appeal only to our emotions?

5. Do you agree that "hunting is as natural as bird-watching" (para. 21)? In any case, do you think that an appeal to what is "natural" is a good argument for expanding the use of hunting?

6. To whom is Kristof talking? How do you know?

THINKING CRITICALLY *Drawing Conclusions and Implying Proof*

Look at Nicholas D. Kristof's essay on page 188. Provide two examples of sentences from Kristof's essay that use each type of conclusion or proof.

INDICATOR OF CONCLUSION OR PROOF	EXAMPLES	TWO EXAMPLES FROM KRISTOF'S ESSAY
Transitions that imply the drawing of a conclusion	*therefore, because, for the reason that, consequently*	
Verbs that imply proof	*confirms, verifies, accounts for, implies, proves, disproves, is (in)consistent with, refutes, it follows that*	

LaunchPad   To complete this activity online, go to **macmillanhighered.com/barnetbedauohara**

THE ESSAY ANALYZED

OK, time's up. Let's examine Kristof's essay with an eye to identifying those elements we mentioned earlier in this chapter (pp. 181–88) that deserve notice when examining *any* argument: the author's *thesis, purpose, methods, persona,* and *audience.* And while we're at it, let's also notice some other features of Kristof's essay that will help us appreciate its effects and evaluate it. We will thus be in a good position to write an evaluation or an argument that confirms, extends, or even rebuts Kristof's argument.

But first, a caution: Kristof's essay appeared in a newspaper where paragraphs are customarily very short, partly to allow for easy reading and partly because the columns are narrow and even short paragraphs may extend for an inch or two. If his essay were to appear in a book, doubtless the author would run many of the paragraphs together, making longer units. In analyzing a work, think about where it originally appeared. A blog, a print journal, an online magazine? Does the format in some measure influence the piece?

Title   By combining "Environmental Balance" with "Rifle"—terms that don't seem to go together—Kristof starts off with a bang. He gives a hint of his *topic* (something about the environment) and of his thesis (some sort of way of introducing ecological balance). He also conveys something of his persona by introducing a rifle into the environment. He is, the title suggests, a no-nonsense, hard-hitting guy.

Opening Paragraphs   Kristof immediately grabs hold of us ("Here's a quick quiz") and asks a simple question, but one that we probably have not thought much about: "Which large American mammal kills the most humans each year?" In paragraph 2 he tells us it is *not* the bear—the answer most readers probably come up with—nor is it the cougar. Not until paragraph 3 does Kristof give us the answer, the deer. But remember, Kristof is writing in a newspaper, where paragraphs customarily are very short. It takes us only a few seconds to get to the third paragraph and the answer.

Thesis   What is the basic thesis Kristof is arguing? Somewhat unusually, Kristof does *not* announce it in its full form until paragraph 6 ("Let's bring back hunting"), but, again, his paragraphs are very short, and if the essay were published in a book, Kristof's first two paragraphs probably would be combined, as would the third and fourth.

Purpose   Kristof's purpose is clear: He wants to *persuade* readers to adopt his view. This amounts to trying to persuade us that his thesis (stated above) is *true*. Kristof, however, does not show that his essay is argumentative or persuasive by using many of the key terms that normally mark argumentative prose. He doesn't call anything his *conclusion*, none of his statements is labeled *my premises*, and he doesn't connect clauses or sentences with *therefore* or *because*. Almost the only traces of the language of argument are "Granted" (para. 18) and "So" (i.e., *therefore*) in his final paragraph.

Despite the lack of argumentative language, the argumentative nature of his essay is clear. He has a thesis—one that will strike many readers as highly unusual—and he wants readers to accept it, so he must go on to *support* it; accordingly, after his introductory paragraphs, in which he calls attention to a problem and offers a solution (his thesis), he must offer evidence. And that is what much of the rest of the essay seeks to do.

Methods   Although Kristof will have to offer evidence, he begins by recognizing the folks on the other side, "the university-educated crowd in the cities, [for whom] hunting is viewed as barbaric" (para. 7). He goes on to spoof this "crowd" when, speaking of methods of keeping the deer population down, he says in paragraph 8, "Liberals presumably support free condoms, while conservatives back abstinence education." Ordinarily, it is a bad idea to make fun of persons who hold views other than your own — after all, they just may be on to something, they just might know something you don't know, and, in any case, impartial readers rarely want to align themselves with someone who mocks others. In the essay we are looking at, however, Kristof gets away with this smart-guy tone because he not only has loyal readers but also has written the entire essay in a highly informal or playful manner. Think again about paragraph 1, which begins "Here's a quick quiz." The informality is not only in the contraction (*Here's* versus *Here is*), but in the very idea of beginning by grabbing the readers and thrusting a quiz at them. The playfulness is evident throughout: For instance, immediately after Kristof announces his thesis, "Let's bring back hunting," he begins a new paragraph (7) with "Now, you've probably just spilled your coffee."

Kristof's methods of presenting evidence include providing *statistics* (paras. 3, 4, 10, and 13), giving *examples* (paras. 10, 19–20), and citing *authorities* (paras. 13 and 16).

Persona   Kristof presents himself as a confident, no-nonsense fellow, a persona that not many writers can get away with, but that probably is acceptable in a journalist who regularly writes a newspaper column. His readers know what to expect, and they read him with pleasure. But it would be inadvisable for an unknown writer to adopt this persona, unless perhaps he or she were writing for an audience that could be counted on to be friendly (in this instance, an audience of hunters). If this essay appeared in a hunting magazine, doubtless it would please and entertain its audience. It would not convert anybody, but conversion would not be its point if it appeared in a magazine read by hunters. In the *New York Times*, where the essay originally appeared, Kristof could count on a moderately sympathetic audience because he has a large number of faithful readers, but one can guess that many of these readers — chiefly city dwellers — read him for entertainment rather than for information about how they should actually behave.

By the way, when we speak of "faithful readers" we are in effect saying that the author has established good *ethos*, has convinced those readers that he or she is *worth* reading.

Closing Paragraphs   The first two of the last three paragraphs report an episode (the home invasion by a buck) that Kristof presumably thinks is pretty conclusive evidence. The final paragraph begins with "So," strongly implying a logical conclusion to the essay.

Let's now turn to a student's analysis of Kristof's essay and then to our own analysis of the student's analysis. (We should say that the analysis of Kristof's essay that you have just read is partly indebted to the student's essay that you are about to read.)

Betsy Swinton

Professor Knowles

English 101B

March 12, 2016

Tracking Kristof

Nicholas D. Kristof's "For Environmental Balance, Pick Up a Rifle" is an engaging piece of writing, but whether it is convincing is something I am not sure about. And I am not sure about it for two reasons: (1) I don't know much about the deer problem, and that's my fault; (2) I don't know much about the deer problem, and that's Kristof's fault. The first point needs no explanation, but let me explain the second.

Kristof is making an argument, offering a thesis: Deer are causing destruction, and the best way to reduce the destruction is to hunt deer. For all that I know, he may be correct both in his comment about what deer are doing and also in his comment about what must be done about deer. My ignorance of the situation is regrettable, but I don't think that I am the only reader from Chicago who doesn't know much about the deer problems in New Jersey, Connecticut, and Arkansas, the states that Kristof specifically mentions in connection with the deer problem. He announces his thesis early enough, in his sixth paragraph, and he is entertaining throughout his essay, but does he make a convincing case? To ask "Does he make a convincing case?" is to ask "Does he offer adequate evidence?" and "Does he show that his solution is better than other possible solutions?"

To take the first question: In a short essay Kristof can hardly give overwhelming evidence, but he does convince me that there is a problem. The most convincing evidence he gives appears in paragraph 16, where he says that the New Jersey Audubon Society "advocated deer hunting as an ecological necessity." I don't really know anything about the New Jersey Audubon Society, but I suppose that they are people with a deep interest in nature and in conservation, and if even such a group advocates deer hunting, there must be something to this solution.

I am even willing to accept his argument that, in this nation of meat-eaters, "to wring one's hands over them [dead deer], perhaps after

polishing off a hamburger, is soggy sentimentality" (para. 14). According
to Kristof, the present alternative to hunting deer is that we leave the deer
to "die of disease and hunger" (para. 15). But what I am not convinced
of is that there is no way to reduce the deer population other than by
hunting. I don't think Kristof adequately explains why some sort of birth
control is inadequate. In his eighth paragraph he makes a joke about
controlling the birth of deer ("Liberals presumably support free condoms,
while conservatives back abstinence education"), and the joke is funny, but
it isn't an argument, it's just a joke. Why can't food containing some sort of
sterilizing medicine be put out for the starving deer, food that will nourish
them and yet make them unreproductive? In short, I don't think he has
fairly informed his readers of alternatives to his own positions, and because
he fails to look at counterproposals, he weakens his own proposal.

Although Kristof occasionally uses a word or phrase that suggests
argument, such as "Granted" (para. 18), "So" (final paragraph), and "There's
another reason" (para. 17), he relies chiefly on forceful writing rather than
on reasoning. And the second of his two reasons for hunting seems utterly
unconvincing to me. His first, as we have seen, is that the deer population
(and apparently the bear population) is out of control. His second (para. 17)
is that hunting "connects people with the outdoors and creates a broader
constituency for wilderness preservation." I am not a hunter and I have
never been one. Perhaps that's my misfortune, but I don't think I am missing
anything. And when I hear Kristof say, in his final sentence—the climactic
place in his essay—that "hunting is as natural as bird-watching," I rub
my eyes in disbelief. If he had me at least half-convinced by his statistics
and his citation of the Audubon Society, he now loses me when he argues
that hunting is "natural." One might as well say that war is natural, rape is
natural, bribery is natural—all these terrible things occur, but we ought to
deplore them and we ought to make every effort to see that they disappear.

In short, I think that Kristof has written an engaging essay, and
he may well have an important idea, but I think that in his glib final
paragraph, where he tells us that "hunting is as natural as bird-watching,"
he utterly loses the reader's confidence.

AN ANALYSIS OF THE STUDENT'S ANALYSIS

Swinton's essay seems to us to be excellent, doubtless the product of a good deal of thoughtful revision. She does not cover every possible aspect of Kristof's essay—she concentrates on his reasoning and says very little about his style—but we think that given the limits of space (about 500 words), she does a good job. What makes this student's essay effective?

- The essay has a title ("Tracking Kristof") that is of at least a little interest; it picks up Kristof's point about hunting, and it gives a hint of what is to come.

- The author promptly identifies her subject (she names the writer and the title of his essay) early.

- Early in the essay she gives us a hint of where she will be going (in her first paragraph she tells us that Kristof's essay is "engaging . . . *but* . . .").

A CHECKLIST FOR WRITING AN ANALYSIS OF AN ARGUMENT

Have I asked myself the following questions?

- ❏ Early in my essay have I accurately stated the writer's thesis (claim) and summarized his or her supporting reasons? Have I explained to my reader any disagreement about definitions of important terms?

- ❏ Have I, again fairly early in my essay, indicated where I will be taking my reader (i.e., have I indicated my general response to the essay I am analyzing)?

- ❏ Have I called attention to the strengths, if any, and the weaknesses, if any, of the essay?

- ❏ Have I commented not only on the *logos* (logic, reasoning) but also on the *ethos* (character of the writer, as presented in the essay)? For instance, has the author convinced me that he or she is well informed and is a person of goodwill? Or, in contrast, does the writer seem to be chiefly concerned with ridiculing those who hold a different view?

- ❏ If there is an appeal to *pathos* (emotion, originally meaning "pity for suffering," but now interpreted more broadly to include appeals to patriotism, humor, or loyalty to family, for example), is it acceptable? If not, why not?

- ❏ Have I used occasional brief quotations to let my reader hear the author's tone and to ensure fairness and accuracy?

- ❏ Is my analysis effectively organized?

- ❏ Have I taken account of the author's audience(s)?

- ❏ Does my essay, perhaps in the concluding paragraphs, indicate my agreement or disagreement with the writer but also my view of the essay as a piece of argumentative writing?

- ❏ Is my tone appropriate?

- She recognizes Kristof's audience at the start, and she suggests that he may not have given thought to this matter of the audience.

- She uses a few brief quotations, to give us a feel for Kristof's essay and to let us hear the evidence for itself, but she does not pad her essay with long quotations.

- She takes up all of Kristof's main points.

- She gives her essay a reasonable organization, letting us hear Kristof's thesis, letting us know the degree to which she accepts it, and finally letting us know her specific reservations about the essay.

- She concludes without the formality of "in conclusion"; "in short" nicely does the trick.

- Notice, finally, that she sticks closely to Kristof's essay. She does not go off on a tangent about the virtues of vegetarianism or the dreadful politics of the *New York Times*, the newspaper that published Kristof's essay. She was asked to analyze the essay, and she has done so.

Exercise

Take one of the essays not yet discussed in class or an essay assigned now by your instructor, and in an essay of 500 words analyze and evaluate it, guided by the checklists and examples we have provided.

Arguments for Analysis

JEFF JACOBY

Jeff Jacoby (b. 1959) is a columnist for the Boston Globe, *where this essay was originally published on the op-ed page on February 20, 1997.*

Bring Back Flogging

Boston's Puritan forefathers did not indulge miscreants lightly.

For selling arms and gunpowder to Indians in 1632, Richard Hopkins was sentenced to be "whipt, & branded with a hott iron on one of his cheekes." Joseph Gatchell, convicted of blasphemy in 1684, was ordered "to stand in pillory, have his head and hand put in & have his toung drawne forth out of his mouth, & peirct through with a hott iron." When Hannah Newell pleaded guilty to adultery in 1694, the court ordered "fifteen stripes Severally to be laid on upon her naked back at the Common Whipping post." Her consort, the aptly named Lambert Despair, fared worse: He was sentenced to twenty-five lashes "and that on the next Thursday Immediately after Lecture he stand upon the Pillory for . . . a full hower with Adultery in Capitall letters written upon his brest."

Corporal punishment for criminals did not vanish with the Puritans — Delaware didn't get around to repealing it until 1972 — but for all relevant purposes, it has been out of fashion for at least 150 years. The day is long past when the stocks had an honored place on the Boston Common, or when offenders were publicly flogged. Now we practice a more enlightened, more humane way of disciplining wrongdoers: We lock them up in cages.

Imprisonment has become our penalty of choice for almost every offense in the criminal code. Commit murder; go to prison. Sell cocaine; go to prison. Kite checks; go to prison. It is an all-purpose punishment, suitable — or so it would seem — for crimes violent and nonviolent, motivated by hate or by greed, plotted coldly or committed in a fit of passion. If anything, our preference for incarceration is deepening — behold the slew of mandatory minimum sentences for drug crimes and "three-strikes-you're-out" life terms for recidivists. Some 1.6 million Americans are behind bars today. That represents a 250 percent increase since 1980, and the number is climbing.

We cage criminals at a rate unsurpassed in 5 the free world, yet few of us believe that the criminal justice system is a success. Crime is out of control, despite the deluded happy talk by some politicians about how "safe" cities have become. For most wrongdoers, the odds of being arrested, prosecuted, convicted, and incarcerated are reassuringly long. Fifty-eight percent of all murders do *not* result in a prison term. Likewise 98 percent of all burglaries.

Many states have gone on prison-building sprees, yet the penal system is choked to bursting. To ease the pressure, nearly all convicted felons are released early — or not locked up at all. "About three of every four convicted criminals," says John DiIulio, a noted Princeton criminologist, "are on the streets without meaningful probation or parole supervision." And while everyone knows that amateur thugs should be deterred before they become career criminals, it is almost unheard of for judges to send first- or second-time offenders to prison.

Meanwhile, the price of keeping criminals in cages is appalling — a common estimate is $30,000 per inmate per year. (To be sure, the cost to society of turning many inmates loose would be even higher.) For tens of thousands of convicts, prison is a graduate school of criminal studies: They emerge more ruthless and savvy than when they entered. And for many offenders, there is even a certain cachet to doing time — a stint in prison becomes a sign of manhood, a status symbol.

But there would be no cachet in chaining a criminal to an outdoor post and flogging him. If young punks were horsewhipped in public after their first conviction, fewer of them would harden into lifelong felons. A humiliating and painful paddling can be applied to the rear end of a crook for a lot less than $30,000 — and prove a lot more educational than ten years' worth of prison meals and lockdowns.

Are we quite certain the Puritans have nothing to teach us about dealing with criminals?

Of course, their crimes are not our crimes: 10 We do not arrest blasphemers or adulterers, and only gun control fanatics would criminalize the sale of weapons to Indians. (They would criminalize the sale of weapons to anybody.) Nor would the ordeal suffered by poor Joseph Gatchell — the tongue "peirct through" with a hot poker — be regarded today as anything less than torture.

But what is the objection to corporal punishment that doesn't maim or mutilate? Instead of a prison term, why not sentence at least some criminals — say, thieves and drunk drivers — to a public whipping?

"Too degrading," some will say. "Too brutal." But where is it written that being whipped is more degrading than being caged? Why is it more brutal to flog a wrongdoer than to throw him in prison — where the risk of being beaten, raped, or murdered is terrifyingly high?

The *Globe* reported in 1994 that more than two hundred thousand prison inmates are raped each year, usually to the indifference of the guards. "The horrors experienced by many young inmates, particularly those who . . . are convicted of nonviolent offenses," former Supreme Court Justice Harry Blackmun has written, "border on the unimaginable." Are those horrors preferable to the short, sharp shame of corporal punishment?

Perhaps the Puritans were more enlightened than we think, at least on the subject of punishment. Their sanctions were humiliating and painful, but quick and cheap. Maybe we should readopt a few.

Topics for Critical Thinking and Writing

1. When Jeff Jacoby says (para. 3) that today we are more "enlightened" than our Puritan forefathers because where they used flogging, "We lock them up in cages," is he being ironic? Explain.

2. Suppose you agree with Jacoby. Explain precisely (1) what you mean by *flogging* (does Jacoby explain what he means?) and (2) how much flogging is appropriate for the crimes of housebreaking, rape, robbery, and murder.

3. In an essay of 250 words, explain why you think that flogging would be more (or less) degrading and brutal than imprisonment.

4. At the end of his essay Jacoby draws to our attention the terrible risk of being raped in prison as an argument in favor of replacing imprisonment with flogging. Do you think he mentions this point at the end because he believes it is the strongest or most persuasive of all those he mentions? Why, or why not?

5. It is often said that corporal punishment does not have any effect or, if it does, that the effect is the negative one of telling the recipient that violence is an acceptable form of behavior. But suppose it were demonstrated that the infliction of physical pain reduced at least certain kinds of crimes, perhaps shoplifting or unarmed robbery. Should we adopt the practice? Why, or why not?

6. Jacoby draws the line (para. 11) at punishment that would "maim or mutilate." Why draw the line here? Some societies punish thieves by amputating a hand. Suppose we knew that this practice really did seriously reduce theft. Should we adopt it? How about adopting castration (surgical or chemical) for rapists? For child molesters? Explain your response.

GERARD JONES

Gerard Jones (b. 1957), author of several works of fiction and nonfiction, has written many comic books for Marvel Comics and other publishers. This essay was published in Mother Jones *magazine in 2000.*

Violent Media Is Good for Kids

At thirteen I was alone and afraid. Taught by my well-meaning, progressive, English-teacher parents that violence was wrong, that rage was something to be overcome and cooperation was always better than conflict, I suffocated my deepest fears and desires under a nice-boy persona. Placed in a small, experimental school that was wrong for me, afraid to join my peers in their bumptious rush into adolescent boyhood, I withdrew into passivity and loneliness. My parents, not trusting the violent world of the late 1960s, built a wall between me and the crudest elements of American pop culture.

Then the Incredible Hulk smashed through it.

One of my mother's students convinced her that Marvel Comics, despite their apparent juvenility and violence, were in fact devoted to lofty messages of pacifism and tolerance. My mother borrowed some, thinking they'd be good for me. And so they were. But not because they preached lofty messages of benevolence. They were good for me because they were juvenile. And violent.

The character who caught me, and freed me, was the Hulk: overgendered and under-socialized, half-naked and half-witted, raging against a frightened world that misunderstood and persecuted him. Suddenly I had a fantasy self to carry my stifled rage and buried desire for power. I had a fantasy self who was a self: unafraid of his desires and the world's disapproval, unhesitating and effective in action.

"Puny boy follow Hulk!" roared my fantasy self, and I followed.

I followed him to new friends—other sensitive geeks chasing their own inner brutes—and I followed him to the arrogant, self-exposing, self-assertive, superheroic decision to become a writer. Eventually, I left him behind, followed more sophisticated heroes, and finally my own lead along a twisting path to a career and an identity. In my thirties, I found myself writing action movies and comic books. I wrote some Hulk stories, and met the geek-geniuses who created him. I saw my own creations turned into action figures, cartoons, and computer games. I talked to the kids who read my stories. Across generations, genders, and ethnicities I kept seeing the same story: people pulling themselves out of emotional traps by immersing themselves in violent stories. People integrating the scariest, most fervently denied fragments of their psyches into fuller senses of selfhood through fantasies of superhuman combat and destruction.

I have watched my son living the same story—transforming himself into a blood-thirsty dinosaur to embolden himself for the plunge into preschool, a Power Ranger to muscle through a social competition in kindergarten. In the first grade, his friends started climbing a tree at school. But he was afraid: of falling, of the centipedes crawling on the trunk, of sharp branches, of his friends' derision. I took my cue from his own fantasies and read him old Tarzan comics, rich in combat

Gerard Jones

A scene from Gerard Jones and Gene Ha's comic book "Oktane"

and bright with flashing knives. For two weeks he lived in them. Then he put them aside. And he climbed the tree.

But all the while, especially in the wake of the recent burst of school shootings, I heard pop psychologists insisting that violent stories are harmful to kids, heard teachers begging parents to keep their kids away from "junk culture," heard a guilt-stricken friend with a son who loved Pokémon lament, "I've turned into the bad mom who lets her kid eat sugary cereal and watch cartoons!"

That's when I started the research.

"Fear, greed, power-hunger, rage: these are aspects of our selves that we try not to experience in our lives but often want, even need, to experience vicariously through stories of others," writes Melanie Moore, Ph.D., a psychologist who works with urban teens. "Children need violent entertainment in order to explore the inescapable feelings that they've been taught to deny, and to reintegrate those feelings into a more whole, more complex, more resilient selfhood."

Moore consults to public schools and local governments, and is also raising a daughter. For the past three years she and I have been studying the ways in which children use violent stories to meet their emotional and developmental needs — and the ways in which adults can help them use those stories healthily. With her help I developed Power Play, a program for helping young people improve their self-knowledge and sense of potency through heroic, combative storytelling.

We've found that every aspect of even the trashiest pop-culture story can have its own developmental function. Pretending to have superhuman powers helps children conquer the feelings of powerlessness that inevitably come with being so young and small. The dual-identity concept at the heart of many superhero stories helps kids negotiate the conflicts between the inner self and the public self as they work through the early stages of socialization. Identification with a rebellious, even destructive, hero helps children learn to push back against a modern culture that cultivates fear and teaches dependency.

At its most fundamental level, what we call "creative violence" — head-bonking cartoons, bloody videogames, playground karate, toy guns — gives children a tool to master their rage. Children will feel rage. Even the sweetest and most civilized of them, even those whose parents read the better class of literary magazines, will feel rage. The world is uncontrollable

10

and incomprehensible; mastering it is a terrifying, enraging task. Rage can be an energizing emotion, a shot of courage to push us to resist greater threats, take more control, than we ever thought we could. But rage is also the emotion our culture distrusts the most. Most of us are taught early on to fear our own. Through immersion in imaginary combat and identification with a violent protagonist, children engage the rage they've stifled, come to fear it less, and become more capable of utilizing it against life's challenges.

I knew one little girl who went around exploding with fantasies so violent that other moms would draw her mother aside to whisper, "I think you should know something about Emily. . . ." Her parents were separating, and she was small, an only child, a tomboy at an age when her classmates were dividing sharply along gender lines. On the playground she acted out *Sailor Moon* fights, and in the classroom she wrote stories about people being stabbed with knives. The more adults tried to control her stories, the more she acted out the roles of her angry heroes: breaking rules, testing limits, roaring threats.

Then her mother and I started helping her tell her stories. She wrote them, performed them, drew them like comics: sometimes

The title character of "Oktane" gets nasty.

bloody, sometimes tender, always blending the images of pop culture with her own most private fantasies. She came out of it just as fiery and strong, but more self-controlled and socially competent: a leader among her peers, the one student in her class who could truly pull boys and girls together.

I worked with an older girl, a middle-class 15 "nice girl," who held herself together through a chaotic family situation and a tumultuous adolescence with gangsta rap. In the mythologized street violence of Ice T, the rage and strutting of his music and lyrics, she found a theater of the mind in which she could be powerful, ruthless, invulnerable. She avoided the heavy drug use that sank many of her peers, and flowered in college as a writer and political activist.

I'm not going to argue that violent entertainment is harmless. I think it has helped inspire some people to real life violence. I am going to argue that it's helped hundreds of people for every one it's hurt, and that it can help far more if we learn to use it well. I am going to argue that our fear of "youth violence" isn't well-founded on reality, and that the fear can do more harm than the reality. We act as though our highest priority is to prevent our children from growing up into murderous thugs — but modern kids are far more likely to grow up too passive, too distrustful of themselves, too easily manipulated.

We send the message to our children in a hundred ways that their craving for imaginary gun battles and symbolic killings is wrong, or at least dangerous. Even when we don't call for censorship or forbid *Mortal Kombat*, we moan to other parents within our kids' earshot about the "awful violence" in the entertainment they love. We tell our kids that it isn't nice to play-fight, or we steer them from some monstrous action figure to a prosocial doll. Even in the most progressive households, where we make such a point of letting children feel what they feel, we rush to substitute an enlightened discussion for the raw material of rageful fantasy. In the process, we risk confusing them about their natural aggression in the same way the Victorians confused their children about their sexuality. When we try to protect our children from their own feelings and fantasies, we shelter them not against violence but against power and selfhood.

Topics for Critical Thinking and Writing

1. In his final paragraph, Gerard Jones mentions the Victorian treatment of sexuality. Why does he bring this in? Does his use of this point make for an effective ending? Explain.

2. In an essay of 300 words, explain whether you think Jones has made the case for violence in an effective and persuasive way. If so, what is it about his article that makes it effective and persuasive? If it is not, where do the problems lie?

3. What kinds of violence does Jones advocate?

4. Does violence play as large a part in the life of teenage girls as it does in the life of teenage boys? Why, or why not?

5. How would you characterize the audience Jones is addressing? What is your evidence?

JUSTIN CRONIN

Justin Cronin (b. 1962) is an award-winning novelist who teaches at Rice University in Houston, Texas. The following selection was published in the New York Times.

Confessions of a Liberal Gun Owner

I am a New England liberal, born and bred. I have lived most of my life in the Northeast — Boston, New York, and Philadelphia — and my politics are devoutly Democratic. In three decades, I have voted for a Republican exactly once, holding my nose, in a mayoral election in which the Democratic candidate seemed mentally unbalanced.

I am also a Texas resident and a gun owner. I have half a dozen pistols in my safe, all semi-automatics, the largest capable of holding twenty rounds. I go to the range at least once a week, have applied for a concealed carry license, and am planning to take a tactical training course in the spring. I'm currently shopping for a shotgun, either a Remington 870 Express Tactical or a Mossberg 500 Flex with a pistol grip and adjustable stock.

Except for shotguns (firing one feels like being punched by a prizefighter), I enjoy shooting. At the range where I practice, most of the staff knows me by sight if not by name. I'm the guy in the metrosexual eyeglasses and Ralph Lauren polo, and I ask a lot of questions: What's the best way to maintain my sight picture with both eyes open? How do I clear a stove-piped round?

There is pleasure to be had in exercising one's rights, learning something new in mid-life, and mastering the operation of a complex tool, which is one thing a gun is. But I won't deny the seductive psychological power that firearms possess. I grew up playing shooting games, pretending to be Starsky or Hutch or one of the patrolmen on *Adam-12*, the two most boring TV cops in history.

A prevailing theory holds that boys are 5 simultaneously aware of their own physical powerlessness and society's mandate that they serve as protectors of the innocent. Pretending to shoot a bad guy assuages this anxiety, which never goes away completely. This explanation makes sense to me. Another word for it is catharsis, and you could say that, as a novelist, I've made my living from it.

There are a lot of reasons that a gun feels right in my hand, but I also own firearms to protect my family. I hope I never have to use one for this purpose, and I doubt I ever will. But I am my family's last line of defense. I have chosen to meet this responsibility, in part, by being armed. It wasn't a choice I made lightly. I am aware that, statistically speaking, a gun in the home represents a far greater danger to its inhabitants than to an intruder. But not every choice we make is data-driven. A lot comes from the gut.

Apart from the ones in policemen's holsters, I don't think I saw a working firearm until the year after college, when a friend's girlfriend, after four cosmopolitans, decided to show off the .38 revolver she kept in her purse. (Half the party guests dived for cover, including me.)

It wasn't until my mid-forties that my education in guns began, in the course of writing a novel in which pistols, shotguns, and rifles, but also heavy weaponry like the AR-15 and its military analogue, the M-16, were widely used. I suspected that much of the gunplay I'd witnessed in movies and television was completely wrong (it is) and hired an instructor for a daylong private lesson "to shoot everything in the store." The gentleman who met me at the range was someone whom I would have called "a gun nut." A former New Yorker, he had relocated to Texas because of its lax gun laws and claimed to keep a pistol within arm's reach even when he showered. He was perfect, in other words, for my purpose.

My relationship to firearms might have ended there, if not for a coincidence of weather. Everybody remembers Hurricane Katrina; fewer recall Hurricane Rita, an even more intense storm that headed straight for Houston less than a month later. My wife and I arranged to stay at a friend's house in Austin, packed up the kids and dog, and headed out of town — or tried to. As many as 3.7 million people had the same idea, making Rita one of the largest evacuations in history, with predictable results.

By two in the morning, after six hours 10 on the road, we had made it all of fifty miles. The scene was like a snapshot from the Apocalypse: crowds milling restlessly, gas stations and mini-marts picked clean and heaped with trash, families sleeping by the side of the road. The situation had the hopped-up feel of barely bottled chaos. After Katrina, nobody had any illusions that help was on its way. It also occurred to me that there were probably a lot of guns out there — this was Texas, after all. Here I was with two tiny children, a couple of thousand dollars in cash, a late-model S.U.V. with half a tank of gas and not so much as a heavy book to throw. When my wife wouldn't let me get out of the car so the dog could do his business, that was it for me. We jumped the median, turned around, and were home in under an hour.

As it happened, Rita made a last-minute turn away from Houston. But what if it hadn't? I believe people are basically good, but not all of them and not all the time. Like most citizens of our modern, technological world, I am wholly reliant upon a fragile web of services to meet my most basic needs. What would happen if those services collapsed? Chaos, that's what.

It didn't happen overnight, but before too long my Northeastern liberal sensibilities, while intact on other issues, had shifted on the question of gun ownership. For my first pistol I selected a little Walther .380. I shot it enough to decide it was junk, upgraded to a full-size Springfield 9-millimeter, liked it but wanted something with a thumb safety, found a nice Smith & Wesson subcompact that fit the bill, but along the way got a little bit of a gun-crush on the Beretta M-9 — and so on.

Lots of people on both sides of the aisle own firearms, or don't, for reasons that supersede their broader political and cultural affiliations. Let me be clear: my personal armory notwithstanding. I think guns are woefully under-regulated. It's far too easy to buy a gun — I once bought one in a parking lot — and I loathe the National Rifle Association. Some of the Obama administration's proposals strike me as more symbolic than effective, with some 300 million firearms on the loose. But the White House's recommendations seem like a good starting point and nothing that would prevent me from protecting my family in a crisis. The AR-15 is a fascinating weapon, and, frankly, a gas to shoot. So is a tank, and I don't need to own a tank.

Alas, the days of à la carte politics like mine seem over, if they ever even existed. The bigger culprit is the far right and the lunatic pronouncements of those like Rush Limbaugh. But in the weeks since Newtown, I've watched my Facebook feed, which is dominated by my coastal friends, fill up with antigun dispatches that seemed divorced from reality. I agree it would be nice if the world had exactly zero guns in it. But I don't see that happening, and calling gun owners "a bunch of inbred rednecks" doesn't do much to advance rational discussion.

Thus, my secret life — though I guess it's 15 not such a secret anymore. My wife is afraid of my guns (though she also says she's glad I have them). My sixteen-year-old daughter is a different story. The week before her fall semester exams, we allowed her to skip school for a day, a tradition in our house. The rule is, she gets to do whatever she wants. This time, she asked to take a pistol lesson. She's an NPR listener like me, but she's also grown up in Texas, and the fact that one in five American women is a victim of sexual assault is not lost on her. In the windowless classroom off the range, the instructor ran her through the basics, demonstrating with a Glock 9-millimeter: how to hold it, load it, pull back the slide.

"You'll probably have trouble with that part," he said. "A lot of the women do."

"Oh really?" my daughter replied, and with a cagey smile proceeded to rack her weapon with such authority you could have heard it in the parking lot.

A proud-papa moment? I confess it was.

Topics for Critical Thinking and Writing

1. This essay could with equal accuracy be called "Confessions of a Texas Gun Owner." Why do you suppose Justin Cronin chose the title he did, rather than our imagined title? That is, why is his title better — better for his purposes — than our invented title?

2. Why does Cronin devote so many sentences to autobiographical matters, since, in fact, none of the autobiography actually involves using a gun to protect himself or his family against an intruder?

3. How would you characterize Cronin's persona as he presents it in this essay? Does he try to speak with authority, connect with his audience on a personal level, or employ another strategy to gain his reader's trust? Do you feel that his persona effectively connects with you as a reader? Why, or why not?

4. What *arguments* does Cronin offer on behalf of gun ownership? Do you think his case — his thesis, his point, his Big Idea — might have been strengthened if he had cited statistics or authorities, or do you think that such evidence probably would have been inappropriate in what is essentially a highly personal essay? Explain your response.

5. In paragraph 12, Cronin writes, "It didn't happen overnight, but before too long my North-eastern liberal sensibilities . . . had shifted on the question of gun ownership." Suppose a reader said to you, "I don't really understand exactly why his attitude shifted. What *happened* that made him shift? I don't get it." What would you say to this questioner?

6. In paragraph 13, Cronin says that he believes "guns are woefully under-regulated" and that he "loathe[s] the National Rifle Association," but he doesn't go into any detail about what sorts of regulations he favors. Do you think his essay might have been more convincing if he had given us details along these lines? Explain.

7. Each of Cronin's last three paragraphs is very short. We have discussed how, in general, a short paragraph is usually an underdeveloped paragraph. Do you think these paragraphs are underdeveloped — or do you think Cronin knows exactly what he is doing? Explain.

PETER SINGER

Peter Singer (b. 1946) is the Ira W. DeCamp Professor of Bioethics at Princeton University. A native of Australia, he is a graduate of the University of Melbourne and Oxford University and the author or editor of more than two dozen books, including Animal Liberation *(1975),* Practical Ethics *(1979),* Rethinking Life and Death *(1995), and* One World: The Ethics of Globalization *(2002). He has written on a variety of ethical issues, but he is especially known for caring about the welfare of animals.*

This essay originally appeared in the New York Review of Books *(April 5, 1973), as a review of* Animals, Men and Morals, *edited by Stanley and Roslind Godlovitch and John Harris.*

Animal Liberation

I

We are familiar with Black Liberation, Gay Liberation, and a variety of other movements. With Women's Liberation some thought we had come to the end of the road. Discrimination on the basis of sex, it has been said, is the last form of discrimination that is universally accepted and practiced without pretense, even in those liberal circles which have long prided themselves on their freedom from racial discrimination. But one should always be wary of talking of "the last remaining form of discrimination." If we have learned anything from the liberation movements, we should have learned how difficult it is to be aware of the ways in which we discriminate until they are forcefully pointed out to us. A liberation movement demands an expansion of our moral horizons, so that practices that were previously regarded as natural and inevitable are now seen as intolerable.

Animals, Men and Morals is a manifesto for an Animal Liberation movement. The contributors to the book may not all see the issue this way. They are a varied group. Philosophers, ranging from professors to graduate students, make up the largest contingent. There are five of them, including the three editors, and there is also an extract from the unjustly neglected German philosopher with an English name, Leonard Nelson, who died in 1927. There are essays by two novelist/critics, Brigid Brophy and Maureen Duffy, and another by Muriel the Lady Dowding, widow of Dowding of Battle of Britain fame and the founder of "Beauty without Cruelty," a movement that campaigns against the use of animals for furs and cosmetics. The other pieces are by a psychologist, a botanist, a sociologist, and Ruth Harrison, who is probably best described as a professional campaigner for animal welfare.

Whether or not these people, as individuals, would all agree that they are launching a liberation movement for animals, the book as a whole amounts to no less. It is a demand for a complete change in our attitudes to nonhumans. It is a demand that we cease to regard the exploitation of other species as natural and inevitable, and that, instead, we see it as a continuing moral outrage. Patrick Corbett, Professor of Philosophy at Sussex University, captures the spirit of the book in his closing words:

> We require now to extend the great principles of liberty, equality, and fraternity over the lives of animals. Let animal slavery join human slavery in the graveyard of the past.

The reader is likely to be skeptical. "Animal Liberation" sounds more like a parody of liberation movements than a serious objective. The reader may think: We support the claims of blacks and women for equality because blacks and women really are equal to whites and males — equal in intelligence and in abilities, capacity for leadership, rationality, and so on. Humans and nonhumans obviously are not equal in these respects. Since justice demands only that we treat equals equally, unequal treatment of humans and nonhumans cannot be an injustice.

This is a tempting reply, but a dangerous ⁵ one. It commits the nonracist and nonsexist to a dogmatic belief that blacks and women really are just as intelligent, able, etc., as whites and males — and no more. Quite possibly this happens to be the case. Certainly attempts to prove that racial or sexual differences in these respects have a genetic origin have not been conclusive. But do we really want to stake our demand for equality on the assumption that there are no genetic differences of this kind between the different races or sexes? Surely the appropriate response to those who claim to have found evidence for such genetic differences is not to stick to the belief that there are no differences, whatever the evidence to the contrary; rather one should be clear that the claim to equality does not depend on IQ. Moral equality is distinct from factual equality. Otherwise it would be nonsense to talk to the equality of human beings, since humans, as individuals, obviously differ in intelligence and almost any ability one cares to name. If possessing greater intelligence does not entitle one human to exploit another, why should it entitle humans to exploit nonhumans?

Jeremy Bentham expressed the essential basis of equality in his famous formula: "Each to count for one and none for more than one." In other words, the interests of every being that has interests are to be taken into account and treated equally with the like interests of any other being. Other moral philosophers, before and after Bentham, have made the same point in different ways. Our concern for others must not depend on whether they possess certain characteristics, though just what that concern involves may, of course, vary according to such characteristics.

Bentham, incidentally, was well aware that the logic of the demand for racial equality did not stop at the equality of humans. He wrote:

> The day *may* come when the rest of the animal creation may acquire those rights which never could have been withholden from them but by the hand of tyranny. The French have already discovered that the blackness of the skin is no reason why a human being should be abandoned without redress to the caprice of a tormentor. It may one day come to be recognized that the number of the legs, the villosity of the skin, or the termination of the *os sacrum*, are reasons equally insufficient for abandoning a sensitive being to the same fate. What else is it that should trace the insuperable line? Is it the faculty of reason, or perhaps the faculty of discourse? But a full-grown horse or dog is beyond comparison a more rational, as well as a more conversable animal, than an infant of a day, or a week, or even a month, old. But suppose they were

otherwise, what would it avail? The question is not, Can they *reason*? nor Can they *talk*? but, Can they *suffer*?[1]

Surely Bentham was right. If a being suffers, there can be no moral justification for refusing to take that suffering into consideration, and, indeed, to count it equally with the like suffering (if rough comparisons can be made) of any other being.

So the only question is: Do animals other than man suffer? Most people agree unhesitatingly that animals like cats and dogs can and do suffer, and this seems also to be assumed by those laws that prohibit wanton cruelty to such animals. Personally, I have no doubt at all about this and find it hard to take seriously the doubts that a few people apparently do have. The editors and contributors of *Animals, Men and Morals* seem to feel the same way, for although the question is raised more than once, doubts are quickly dismissed each time. Nevertheless, because this is such a fundamental point, it is worth asking what grounds we have for attributing suffering to other animals.

It is best to begin by asking what grounds any individual human has for supposing that other humans feel pain. Since pain is a state of consciousness, a "mental event," it can never be directly observed. No observations, whether behavioral signs such as writhing or screaming or physiological or neurological recordings, are observations of pain itself. Pain is something one feels, and one can only infer that others are feeling it from various external indications. The fact that only philosophers are ever skeptical about whether other humans feel pain shows that we regard such inference as justifiable in the case of humans.

[1] *The Principles of Morals and Legislation*, ch. XVII, sec. 1, footnote to paragraph 4. [All notes are the author's unless otherwise specified.]

Is there any reason why the same inference should be unjustifiable for other animals? Nearly all the external signs which lead us to infer pain in other humans can be seen in other species, especially "higher" animals such as mammals and birds. Behavioral signs — writhing, yelping, or other forms of calling, attempts to avoid the source of pain, and many others — are present. We know, too, that these animals are biologically similar in the relevant respects, having nervous systems like ours which can be observed to function as ours do.

So the grounds for inferring that these animals can feel pain are nearly as good as the grounds for inferring other humans do. Only nearly, for there is one behavioral sign that humans have but nonhumans, with the exception of one or two specially raised chimpanzees, do not have. This, of course, is a developed language. As the quotation from Bentham indicates, this has long been regarded as an important distinction between man and other animals. Other animals may communicate with each other, but not in the way we do. Following Chomsky,[2] many people now mark this distinction by saying that only humans communicate in a form that is governed by rules of syntax. (For the purposes of this argument, linguists allow those chimpanzees who have learned a syntactic sign language to rank as honorary humans.) Nevertheless, as Bentham pointed out, this distinction is not relevant to the question of how animals ought to be treated, unless it can be linked to the issue of whether animals suffer.

This link may be attempted in two ways. First, there is a hazy line of philosophical thought, stemming perhaps from some doctrines associated with Wittgenstein, which maintains that we cannot meaningfully attribute states of consciousness to beings without language. I have not seen this argument made explicit in print, though I have come across it in conversation. This position seems to me very implausible, and I doubt that it would be held at all if it were not thought to be a consequence of a broader view of the significance of language. It may be that the use of a public, rule-governed language is a precondition of conceptual thought. It may even be, although personally I doubt it, that we cannot meaningfully speak of a creature having an intention unless that creature can use a language. But states like pain, surely, are more primitive than either of these, and seem to have nothing to do with language.

Indeed, as Jane Goodall points out in her study of chimpanzees, when it comes to the expression of feelings and emotions, humans tend to fall back on nonlinguistic modes of communication which are often found among apes, such as a cheering pat on the back, an exuberant embrace, a clasp of hands, and so on.[3] Michael Peters makes a similar point in his contribution to *Animals, Men and Morals* when he notes that the basic signals we use to convey pain, fear, sexual arousal, and so on are not specific to our species. So there seems to be no reason at all to believe that a creature without language cannot suffer.

The second, and more easily appreciated way of linking language and the existence of pain is to say that the best evidence that we can have that another creature is in pain is when he tells us that he is. This is a distinct line of argument, for it is not being denied that a non-language-user conceivably could suffer, but

_____

[2]**Chomsky** Noam Chomsky (b. 1928), a professor of linguistics and the author of (among other books) *Language and Mind* (1972). [Editors' note.]

[3]Jane van Lawick-Goodall, *In the Shadow of Man* (Houghton Mifflin, 1971), p. 225.

only that we could know that he is suffering. Still, this line of argument seems to me to fail, and for reasons similar to those just given. "I am in pain" is not the best possible evidence that the speaker is in pain (he might be lying) and it is certainly not the only possible evidence. Behavioral signs and knowledge of the animal's biological similarity to ourselves together provide adequate evidence that animals do suffer. After all, we would not accept linguistic evidence if it contradicted the rest of the evidence. If a man was severely burned, and behaved as if he were in pain, writhing, groaning, being very careful not to let his burned skin touch anything, and so on, but later said he had not been in pain at all, we would be more likely to conclude that he was lying or suffering from amnesia than that he had not been in pain.

Even if there were stronger grounds for refusing to attribute pain to those who do not have a language, the consequences of this refusal might lead us to examine these grounds unusually critically. Human infants, as well as some adults, are unable to use language. Are we to deny that a year-old infant can suffer? If not, how can language be crucial? Of course, most parents can understand the responses of even very young infants better than they understand the responses of other animals, and sometimes infant responses can be understood in the light of later development.

This, however, is just a fact about the relative knowledge we have of our own species and other species, and most of this knowledge is simply derived from closer contact. Those who have studied the behavior of other animals soon learn to understand their responses at least as well as we understand those of an infant. (I am not referring to Jane Goodall's and other well-known studies of apes. Consider, for example, the degree of understanding achieved by

Tinbergen from watching herring gulls.[4]) Just as we can understand infant human behavior in the light of adult human behavior, so we can understand the behavior of other species in the light of our own behavior (and sometimes we can understand our own behavior better in the light of the behavior of other species).

The grounds we have for believing that other mammals and birds suffer are, then, closely analogous to the grounds we have for believing that other humans suffer. It remains to consider how far down the evolutionary scale this analogy holds. Obviously it becomes poorer when we get further away from man. To be more precise would require a detailed examination of all that we know about other forms of life. With fish, reptiles, and other vertebrates the analogy still seems strong, with molluscs like oysters it is much weaker. Insects are more difficult, and it may be that in our present state of knowledge we must be agnostic about whether they are capable of suffering.

If there is no moral justification for ignoring suffering when it occurs, and it does occur in other species, what are we to say of our attitudes toward these other species? Richard Ryder, one of the contributors to *Animals, Men and Morals*, uses the term "speciesism" to describe the belief that we are entitled to treat members of other species in a way in which it would be wrong to treat members of our own species. The term is not euphonious, but it neatly makes the analogy with racism. The nonracist would do well to bear the analogy in mind when he is inclined to defend human behavior toward nonhumans. "Shouldn't we worry about improving the lot of our own species before we concern ourselves with other species?" he may ask. If we substitute "race" for

---

[4]N. Tinbergen, *The Herring Gull's World* (Basic Books, 1961).

"species" we shall see that the question is better not asked. "Is a vegetarian diet nutritionally adequate?" resembles the slaveowner's claim that he and the whole economy of the South would be ruined without slave labor. There is even a parallel with skeptical doubts about whether animals suffer, for some defenders of slavery professed to doubt whether blacks really suffer in the way whites do.

I do not want to give the impression, however, that the case for Animal Liberation is based on the analogy with racism and no more. On the contrary, *Animals, Men and Morals* describes the various ways in which humans exploit nonhumans, and several contributors consider the defenses that have been offered, including the defense of meat-eating mentioned in the last paragraph. Sometimes the rebuttals are scornfully dismissive, rather than carefully designed to convince the detached critic. This may be a fault, but it is a fault that is inevitable, given the kind of book this is. The issue is not one on which one can remain detached. As the editors state in their Introduction:

> Once the full force of moral assessment has been made explicit there can be no rational excuse left for killing animals, be they killed for food, science, or sheer personal indulgence. We have not assembled this book to provide the reader with yet another manual on how to make brutalities less brutal. Compromise, in the traditional sense of the term, is simple unthinking weakness when one considers the actual reasons for our crude relationships with the other animals.

The point is that on this issue there are few critics who are genuinely detached. People who eat pieces of slaughtered nonhumans every day find it hard to believe that they are doing wrong; and they also find it hard to imagine what else they could eat. So for those who do not place nonhumans beyond the pale of morality, there comes a stage when further argument seems pointless, a stage at which one can only accuse one's opponent of hypocrisy and reach for the sort of sociological account of our practices and the way we defend them that is attempted by David Wood in his contribution to his book. On the other hand, to those unconvinced by the arguments, and unable to accept that they are merely rationalizing their dietary preferences and their fear of being thought peculiar, such sociological explanations can only seem insultingly arrogant.

II

The logic of speciesism is most apparent in the practice of experimenting on nonhumans in order to benefit humans. This is because the issue is rarely obscured by allegations that nonhumans are so different from humans that we cannot know anything about whether they suffer. The defender of vivisection cannot use this argument because he needs to stress the similarities between man and other animals in order to justify the usefulness to the former of experiments on the latter. The researcher who makes rats choose between starvation and electric shocks to see if they develop ulcers (they do) does so because he knows that the rat has a nervous system very similar to man's, and presumably feels an electric shock in a similar way.

Richard Ryder's restrained account of experiments on animals made me angrier with my fellow men than anything else in this book. Ryder, a clinical psychologist by profession, himself experimented on animals before he came to hold the view he puts forward in his essay. Experimenting on animals is now a large industry, both academic and commercial. In 1969, more than 5 million experiments were performed in Britain, the vast majority without anesthetic (though how many of these involved pain is not known). There are no accurate U.S. figures, since there is no federal law on the subject, and in many cases no state law either. Estimates vary from 20 million to 200 million. Ryder suggests that 80 million may be the best guess. We tend to think that this is all for vital medical research, but of course it is not. Huge numbers of animals are used in university departments from Forestry to Psychology, and even more are used for commercial purposes, to test whether cosmetics can cause skin damage, or shampoos eye damage, or to test food additives or laxatives or sleeping pills or anything else.

A standard test for foodstuffs is the "LD50." The object of this test is to find the dosage level at which 50 percent of the test animals will die. This means that nearly all of them will become very sick before finally succumbing or surviving. When the substance is a harmless one, it may be necessary to force huge doses down the animals, until in some cases sheer volume or concentration causes death.

Ryder gives a selection of experiments, taken from recent scientific journals. I will quote two, not for the sake of indulging in gory details, but in order to give an idea of what normal researchers think they may legitimately do to other species. The point is not that the individual researchers are cruel men, but that they are behaving in a way that is allowed by our speciesist attitudes. As Ryder points out, even if only 1 percent of the experiments involve severe pain, that is 50,000 experiments in Britain each year, or nearly 150 every day

(and about fifteen times as many in the United States, if Ryder's guess is right). Here then are two experiments:

O. S. Ray and R. J. Barrett of Pittsburgh gave electric shocks to the feet of 1,042 mice. They then caused convulsions by giving more intense shocks through cup-shaped electrodes applied to the animals' eyes or through pressure spring clips attached to their ears. Unfortunately some of the mice who "successfully completed Day One training were found sick or dead prior to testing on Day Two." [*Journal of Comparative and Physiological Psychology,* 1969, vol. 67, pp. 110–116]

At the National Institute for Medical Research, Mill Hill, London, W. Feldberg and S. L. Sherwood injected chemicals into the brains of cats — "with a number of widely different substances, recurrent patterns of reaction were obtained. Retching, vomiting, defecation, increased salivation and greatly accelerated respiration leading to panting were common features." . . .

The injection into the brain of a large dose of Tubocuraine caused the cat to jump "from the table to the floor and then straight into its cage, where it started calling more and more noisily whilst moving about restlessly and jerkily . . . finally the cat fell with legs and neck flexed, jerking in rapid clonic movements, the condition being that of a major [epileptic] convulsion . . . within a few seconds the cat got up, ran for a few yards at high speed, and fell in another fit. The whole process was repeated several times within the next ten minutes, during which the cat lost faeces and foamed at the mouth."

This animal finally died thirty-five minutes after the brain injection. [*Journal of Physiology,* 1954, vol. 123, pp. 148–167]

There is nothing secret about these exper- 25 iments. One has only to open any recent volume of a learned journal, such as the *Journal of Comparative and Physiological Psychology,* to find full descriptions of experiments of this sort, together with the results obtained — results that are frequently trivial and obvious. The experiments are often supported by public funds.

It is a significant indication of the level of acceptability of these practices that, although these experiments are taking place at this moment on university campuses throughout the country, there has, so far as I know, not been the slightest protest from the student movement. Students have been rightly concerned that their universities should not discriminate on grounds of race or sex, and that they should not serve the purposes of the military or big business. Speciesism continues undisturbed, and many students participate in it. There may be a few qualms at first, but since everyone regards it as normal, and it may even be a required part of a course, the student soon becomes hardened and, dismissing his earlier feelings as "mere sentiment," comes to regard animals as statistics rather than sentient beings with interests that warrant consideration.

Argument about vivisection has often missed the point because it has been put in absolutist terms: Would the abolitionist be prepared to let thousands die if they could be saved by experimenting on a single animal? The way to reply to this purely hypothetical question is to pose another: Would the experimenter be prepared to experiment on a human orphan under six months old, if it were the only way to save many lives? (I say "orphan" to avoid the complication of parental feelings, although in doing so I am being overfair to the experimenter, since the nonhuman subjects of experiments are not orphans.) A negative answer to this question indicates that the experimenter's readiness to use nonhumans is simple discrimination, for adult apes, cats, mice, and other mammals are more conscious of what is happening to them, more self-directing, and, so far as we can tell, just as sensitive to pain as a human infant. There is no characteristic that human infants possess that adult mammals do not have to the same or a higher degree.

(It might be possible to hold that what makes it wrong to experiment on a human infant is that the infant will in time develop into more than the nonhuman, but one would then, to be consistent, have to oppose abortion, and perhaps contraception, too, for the fetus and the egg and sperm have the same potential as the infant. Moreover, one would still have no reason for experimenting on a nonhuman rather than a human with brain damage severe enough to make it impossible for him to rise above infant level.)

The experimenter, then, shows a bias for his own species whenever he carries out an experiment on a nonhuman for a purpose that

Pigs at sausage-processing factory in Spain

he would not think justified him in using a human being at an equal or lower level of sentience, awareness, ability to be self-directing, etc. No one familiar with the kind of results yielded by these experiments can have the slightest doubt that if this bias were eliminated the number of experiments performed would be zero or very close to it.

III

If it is vivisection that shows the logic of speciesism most clearly, it is the use of other species for food that is at the heart of our attitudes toward them. Most of *Animals, Men and Morals* is an attack on meat eating—an attack which is based solely on concern for nonhumans, without reference to arguments derived from consideration of ecology, macrobiotics, health, or religion.

The idea that nonhumans are utilities, means to our ends, pervades our thought. Even conservationists who are concerned about the slaughter of wildfowl but not about the vastly greater slaughter of chickens for our tables are thinking in this way—they are worried about what we would lose if there were less wildlife. Stanley Godlovitch, pursuing the Marxist idea that our thinking is formed by the activities we undertake in satisfying our needs, suggests that man's first classification of his environment was into Edibles and Inedibles. Most animals came into the first category, and there they have remained.

Man may always have killed other species for food, but he has never exploited them so ruthlessly as he does today. Farming has succumbed to business methods, the objective being to get the highest possible ratio of output (meat, eggs, milk) to input (fodder, labor costs, etc.). Ruth Harrison's essay "On Factory Farming" gives an account of some aspects of modern methods, and of the unsuccessful British campaigns for effective controls, a campaign which was sparked off by her *Animal Machines* (London: Stuart, 1964).

Her article is in no way a substitute for her earlier book. This is a pity since, as she says, "Farm produce is still associated with mental pictures of animals browsing in the fields . . . of hens having a last forage before going to roost. . . ." Yet neither in her article nor elsewhere in *Animals, Men and Morals* is this false image replaced by a clear idea of the nature and extent of factory farming. We learn of this only indirectly, when we hear of the code of reform proposed by an advisory committee set up by the British government.

Among the proposals, which the government refused to implement on the grounds that they were too idealistic, were: "*Any animal should at least have room to turn around freely.*"

Factory farm animals need liberation in the most literal sense. Veal calves are kept in stalls 5 feet by 2 feet. They are usually slaughtered when about four months old, and have been too big to turn in their stalls for at least a month. Intensive beef herds, kept in stalls only proportionately larger for much longer periods, account for a growing percentage of beef production. Sows are often similarly confined when pregnant, which, because of artificial methods of increasing fertility, can be most of the time. Animals confined in this way do not waste food by exercising, nor do they develop unpalatable muscle.

"*A dry bedded area should be provided for all stock.*" Intensively kept animals usually have to stand and sleep in slatted floors without straw, because this makes cleaning easier.

"*Palatable roughage must be readily available to all calves after one week of age.*" In order to produce the pale veal housewives are said to prefer, calves are fed on an all-liquid diet until slaughter, even though they are long past the age at which they would normally eat grass. They develop a craving for roughage, evidenced by attempts to gnaw wood from their stalls. (For the same reason, their diet is deficient in iron.)

"Battery cages for poultry should be large enough for a bird to be able to stretch one wing at a time." Under current British practice, a cage for four or five laying hens has a floor area of 20 inches by 18 inches, scarcely larger than a double page of the *New York Review of Books*. In this space, on a sloping wire floor (sloping so the eggs roll down, wire so the dung drips through) the birds live for a year or eighteen months while artificial lighting and temperature conditions combine with drugs in their food to squeeze the maximum number of eggs out of them. Table birds are also sometimes kept in cages. More often they are reared in sheds, no less crowded. Under these conditions all the birds' natural activities are frustrated, and they develop "vices" such as pecking each other to death. To prevent this, beaks are often cut off, and the sheds kept dark.

How many of those who support factory farming by buying its produce know anything about the way it is produced? How many have heard something about it, but are reluctant to check up for fear that it will make them uncomfortable? To nonspeciesists, the typical consumer's mixture of ignorance, reluctance to find out the truth, and vague belief that nothing really bad could be allowed seems analogous to the attitudes of "decent Germans" to the death camps.

There are, of course, some defenders of factory farming. Their arguments are considered, though again rather sketchily, by John Harris. Among the most common: "Since they have never known anything else, they don't suffer." This argument will not be put by anyone who knows anything about animal behavior, since he will know that not all behavior has to be learned. Chickens attempt to stretch wings, walk around, scratch, and even dustbathe or build a nest, even though they have never lived under conditions that allowed these activities. Calves can suffer from maternal deprivation no matter at what age they were taken from their mothers. "We need these intensive methods to provide protein for a growing population." As ecologists and famine relief organizations know, we can produce far more protein per acre if we grow the right vegetable crop, soy beans for instance, than if we use the land to grow crops to be converted into protein by animals who use nearly 90 percent of the protein themselves, even when unable to exercise.

There will be many readers of this book who will agree that factory farming involves an unjustifiable degree of exploitation of sentient creatures, and yet will want to say that there is nothing wrong with rearing animals for food, provided it is done "humanely." These people are saying, in effect, that although we should not cause animals to suffer, there is nothing wrong with killing them.

There are two possible replies to this view. One is to attempt to show that this combination of attitudes is absurd. Roslind Godlovitch takes this course in her essay, which is an examination of some common attitudes to animals. She argues that from the combination of "animal suffering is to be avoided" and "there is nothing wrong with killing animals" it follows that all animal life ought to be exterminated (since all sentient creatures will suffer to some degree at some point in their lives). Euthanasia is a contentious issue only because we place some value on living. If we did not, the least amount of suffering would justify it. Accordingly, if we deny that we have a duty to exterminate all animal life, we must concede that we are placing some value on animal life.

This argument seems to me valid, although one could still reply that the value of animal life is to be derived from the pleasures that life can have for them, so that, provided their lives have a balance of pleasure over pain, we are justified in rearing them. But this would imply that we ought to produce animals and let them live as pleasantly as possible, without suffering.

At this point, one can make the second of the two possible replies to the view that rearing and killing animals for food is all right so long as it is done humanely. This second reply is that so long as we think that a nonhuman may be killed simply so that a human can satisfy his taste for meat, we are still thinking of nonhumans as means rather than as ends in themselves. The factory farm is nothing more than the application of technology to this concept. Even traditional methods involve castration, the separation of mothers and their young, the breaking up of herds, branding or earpunching, and of course transportation to the abattoirs and the final moments of terror when the animal smells blood and senses danger. If we were to try rearing animals so that they lived and died without suffering, we should find that to do so on anything like the scale of today's meat industry would be a sheer impossibility. Meat would become the prerogative of the rich.

I have been able to discuss only some of the contributions to this book, saying nothing about, for instance, the essays on killing for furs and for sport. Nor have I considered all the detailed questions that need to be asked once we start thinking about other species in the radically different way presented by this book. What, for instance, are we to do about genuine conflicts of interest like rats biting slum children? I am not sure of the answer, but the essential point is just that we *do* see this as a conflict of interests, that we recognize that rats have interests too. Then we may begin to think about other ways of resolving the conflict — perhaps by leaving out rat baits that sterilize the rats instead of killing them.

I have not discussed such problems because they are side issues compared with the exploitation of other species for food and for experimental purposes. On these central matters, I hope that I have said enough to show that this book, despite its flaws, is a challenge to every human to recognize his attitudes to nonhumans as a form of prejudice no less objectionable than racism or sexism. It is a challenge that demands not just a change of attitudes, but a change in our way of life, for it requires us to become vegetarians.

Can a purely moral demand of this kind succeed? The odds are certainly against it. The book holds out no inducements. It does not tell us that we will become healthier, or enjoy life more, if we cease exploiting animals. Animal Liberation will require greater altruism on the part of mankind than any other liberation movement, since animals are incapable of demanding it for themselves, or of protesting against their exploitation by votes, demonstrations, or bombs. Is man capable of such genuine altruism? Who knows? If this book does have a significant effect, however, it will be a vindication of all those who have believed that man has within himself the potential for more than cruelty and selfishness.

Topics for Critical Thinking and Writing

1. In paragraph 4, Peter Singer formulates an argument on behalf of the skeptical reader. Examine that argument closely, restate it in your own words, and evaluate it. Which of its premises is most vulnerable to criticism? Why?

2. Singer quotes with approval (para. 7) Bentham's comment, "The question is not, Can they *reason*? nor Can they *talk*? but, Can they *suffer*?" Do you find this argument persuasive? Can you think of any effective challenge to it?

3. Singer allows that although developed linguistic capacity is not necessary for a creature to have pain, perhaps such a capacity is necessary for "having an intention" (para. 12). Do you think this concession is correct? Have you ever seen animal behavior that you would be willing to describe or explain as evidence that the animal has an intention to do something, despite knowing that the animal cannot talk? Explain your response.

4. Singer thinks that the readiness to experiment on animals argues against believing that animals don't suffer pain (see para. 21). Do you agree with this reasoning? Why, or why not?

5. Singer confesses (para. 22) to being made especially angry "with my fellow men" after reading the accounts of animal experimentation. What is it that aroused his anger? Do such feelings, and the acknowledgment that one has them, have any place in a sober discussion about the merits of animal experimentation? Why, or why not?

6. What is "factory farming" (paras. 32–40)? Why is Singer opposed to it?

7. To the claim that there is nothing wrong with "rearing animals for food," provided it is done "humanely" (para. 41), Singer offers two replies (paras. 42–44). In an essay of 250 words, summarize them briefly and then indicate whether either persuades you and why or why not.

8. Suppose someone were to say to Singer: "You claim that capacity to suffer is the relevant factor in deciding whether a creature deserves to be treated as my moral equal. But you're wrong. The relevant factor is whether the creature is *alive*. Being alive is what matters, not being capable of feeling pain." In one or two paragraphs declare what you think would be Singer's reply.

9. Do you think it is worse to kill an animal for its fur than to kill, cook, and eat an animal? Is it worse to kill an animal for sport than to kill it for medical experimentation? What is Singer's view? Explain your view, making use of Singer's if you wish, in an essay of 500 words.

10. Are there any arguments, in your opinion, that show the immorality of eating human flesh (cannibalism) but that do not show a similar objection to eating animal flesh? Write a 500-word essay in which you discuss the issue.

JONATHAN SAFRAN FOER

Jonathan Safran Foer (b. 1977) is an American author best known for his novels, Everything Is Illuminated *(2002) and* Extremely Loud and Incredibly Close *(2005). In addition to writing two more recent novels, Safran Foer also wrote a nonfiction work expressing his views on vegetarianism,* Eating Animals *(2009). The following piece is from the* Wall Street Journal *around the time* Eating Animals *was published.*

Let Them Eat Dog: A Modest Proposal for Tossing Fido in the Oven

Despite the fact that it's perfectly legal in 44 states, eating "man's best friend" is as taboo as a man eating his best friend. Even the most enthusiastic carnivores won't eat dogs. TV guy and sometimes cooker Gordon Ramsay can get pretty macho with lambs and piglets when doing publicity for something he's selling, but you'll never see a puppy peeking out of one of his pots. And though he once said he'd electrocute his children if they became vegetarian, one can't help but wonder what his response would be if they poached the family pooch.

Dogs are wonderful, and in many ways unique. But they are remarkably unremarkable in their intellectual and experiential capacities. Pigs are every bit as intelligent and feeling, by any sensible definition of the words. They can't hop into the back of a Volvo, but they can fetch, run and play, be mischievous and reciprocate affection. So why don't they get to curl up by the fire? Why can't they at least be spared being tossed on the fire? Our taboo against dog eating says something about dogs and a great deal about us.

The French, who love their dogs, sometimes eat their horses.

The Spanish, who love their horses, sometimes eat their cows.

The Indians, who love their cows, some- 5 times eat their dogs.

While written in a much different context, George Orwell's words (from *Animal Farm*) apply here: "All animals are equal, but some animals are more equal than others."

So who's right? What might be the reasons to exclude canine from the menu? The selective carnivore suggests.

Don't eat companion animals. But dogs aren't kept as companions in all of the places they are eaten. And what about our petless neighbors? Would we have any right to object if they had dog for dinner?

OK, then: Don't eat animals with significant mental capacities. If by "significant mental capacities" we mean what a dog has, then good for the dog. But such a definition would also include the pig, cow and chicken. And it would exclude severely impaired humans.

Then: It's for good reason that the eternal 10 taboos — don't fiddle with your crap, kiss your sister, or eat your companions — are taboo. Evolutionarily speaking, those things are bad for us. But dog eating isn't a taboo in many places, and it isn't in any way bad for us. Properly cooked, dog meat poses no greater health risks than any other meat.

Dog meat has been described as "gamey," "complex," "buttery" and "floral." And there is a proud pedigree of eating it. Fourth-century tombs contain depictions of dogs being slaughtered along with other food animals. It was a fundamental enough habit to have informed language itself: the Sino-Korean character for "fair and proper" (yeon) literally translates into "as cooked dog meat is delicious." Hippocrates praised dog meat as a source of strength. Dakota Indians enjoyed dog liver, and not so long ago Hawaiians ate dog brains and blood. Captain Cook ate dog. Roald Amundsen famously ate his sled dogs. (Granted, he was really hungry.) And dogs are still eaten to overcome bad luck in the Philippines; as medicine in China and Korea; to enhance libido in Nigeria and in numerous places, on every continent, because they taste good. For centuries, the Chinese have raised special breeds of dogs, like the black-tongued chow, for chow, and many European countries still have laws on the books regarding postmortem examination of dogs intended for human consumption.

Of course, something having been done just about everywhere is no kind of justification for doing it now. But unlike all farmed meat, which requires the creation and maintenance of animals, dogs are practically begging to be eaten. Three to four million dogs and cats are euthanized annually. The simple disposal of these euthanized dogs is an enormous ecological and economic problem. But eating those strays, those runaways, those not-quite-cute-enough-to-take and not-quite-well-behaved-enough-to-keep dogs would be killing a flock of birds with one stone and eating it, too.

In a sense it's what we're doing already. Rendering — the conversion of animal protein unfit for human consumption into food for livestock and pets — allows processing plants to transform useless dead dogs into productive members of the food chain. In America, millions of dogs and cats euthanized in animal shelters every year become the food for our food. So let's just eliminate this inefficient and bizarre middle step.

This need not challenge our civility. We won't make them suffer any more than necessary. While it's widely believed that adrenaline makes dog meat taste better — hence the traditional methods of slaughter: hanging, boiling alive, beating to death — we can all agree that if we're going to eat them, we should kill them quickly and painlessly, right? For example, the traditional Hawaiian means of holding the dog's nose shut — in order to conserve blood — must be regarded (socially if not legally) as a no-no. Perhaps we could include dogs under the Humane Methods of Slaughter Act. That doesn't say anything about how they're treated during their lives, and isn't subject to any meaningful oversight or enforcement, but surely we can rely on the industry to "self-regulate," as we do with other eaten animals.

Few people sufficiently appreciate the 15 colossal task of feeding a world of billions of omnivores who demand meat with their potatoes. The inefficient use of dogs — conveniently already in areas of high human population (take note, local-food advocates) — should make any good ecologist blush. One could argue that various "humane" groups are the worst hypocrites, spending enormous amounts of money and energy in a futile attempt to reduce the number of unwanted dogs while at the very same time propagating the irresponsible no-dog-for-dinner taboo. If we let dogs be dogs, and breed without interference, we would create a sustainable, local meat supply with low energy inputs that would put even the most efficient grass-based farming to shame. For the ecologically-minded it's time to admit that dog is realistic food for realistic environmentalists.

For those already convinced, here's a classic Filipino recipe I recently came across. I haven't tried it myself, but sometimes you can read a recipe and just know.

STEWED DOG, WEDDING STYLE

First, kill a medium-sized dog, then burn off the fur over a hot fire. Carefully remove the skin while still warm and set aside for later (may be used in other recipes). Cut meat into 1" cubes. Marinate meat in mixture of vinegar, peppercorn, salt, and garlic for 2 hours. Fry meat in oil using a large wok over an open fire, then add onions and chopped pineapple and saute until tender. Pour in tomato sauce and boiling water, add green pepper, bay leaf, and Tabasco. Cover and simmer over warm coals until meat is tender. Blend in puree of dog's liver and cook for additional 5–7 minutes.

There is an overabundance of rational reasons to say no to factory-farmed meat: It is the No. 1 cause of global warming, it systematically forces tens of billions of animals to suffer in ways that would be illegal if they were dogs, it is a decisive factor in the development of swine and avian flus, and so on. And yet even most people who know these things still aren't inspired to order something else on the menu. Why?

Food is not rational. Food is culture, habit, craving and identity. Responding to factory farming calls for a capacity to care that dwells beyond information. We know what we see on undercover videos of factory farms and slaughterhouses is wrong. (There are those who will defend a system that allows for occasional animal cruelty, but no one defends the cruelty, itself.) And despite it being entirely reasonable, the case for eating dogs is likely repulsive to just about every reader of this paper. The instinct comes before our reason, and is more important.

Topics for Critical Thinking and Writing

1. What is the author's persona in this essay? Is his presentation effective?

2. In the headnote for this piece, you are told Jonathan Safran Foer is an outspoken vegetarian, yet the title reveals what he will be arguing. How would you characterize the author's "modest proposal" and the actual goal of his argument?

3. In paragraph 7, Safran Foer begins to address arguments against eating dog meat by "selective carnivores" who apparently do not hesitate to eat other kinds of animals. Is Safran Foer's suggestion that their arguments are not valid convincing? Why, or why not?

4. What other arguments does Safran Foer make to convince readers of the potential benefits of eating dogs? What do you think is his actual position on eating dogs? On factory farming? On using dogs as an efficient solution to factory farming? How do you know he is not serious?

5. What do you think is the purpose for providing the recipe for "Stewed Dog?"

6. Safran Foer is writing his own take on the famous satirical essay by Jonathan Swift. Swift's original "Modest Proposal" (1729) criticized cruel attitudes toward the poor by arguing that the impoverished Irish could sell their children as food to the rich ("A young healthy child well nursed, is, at one year old, a most delicious nourishing and wholesome food . . . "). Write your own "modest proposal," ironically suggesting an absurd solution to a problem. Possible topics: health care, illegal immigrants, overcrowded jails, children who have committed a serious crime, homeless people. The modern version of the problem to which the proposal should be addressed is called "population policy." How would you describe our nation's current population policy? Do we have an adequate population policy, in fact? If not, what would you propose? If we do have one, what changes could you propose?

6

Developing an Argument of Your Own

The difficult part in an argument is not to defend one's opinion but to know what it is.

— ANDRÉ MAUROIS

Imagine that you enter a parlor. You come late. When you arrive, others have long preceded you, and they are engaged in a heated discussion, a discussion too heated for them to pause and tell you exactly what it is about. In fact, the discussion had already begun long before any of them got there, so that no one present is qualified to retrace for you all the steps that had gone before. You listen for a while, until you decide that you have caught the tenor of the argument; then you put in your oar. Someone answers; you answer him; another comes to your defense; another aligns himself against you, to either the embarrassment or gratification of your opponent, depending upon the quality of your ally's assistance. However, the discussion is interminable. The hour grows late, you must depart. And you do depart, with the discussion still vigorously in progress. — KENNETH BURKE

No greater misfortune could happen to anyone than that of developing a dislike for argument.

— PLATO

Planning, Drafting, and Revising an Argument

First, hear the wisdom of Mark Twain: "When the Lord finished the world, He pronounced it good. That is what I said about my first work, too. But Time, I tell you, Time takes the confidence out of these incautious early opinions."

All of us, teachers and students, have our moments of confidence, but for the most part we know that it takes considerable effort to write clear, thoughtful, seemingly effortless prose. In a conversation we can cover ourselves with such expressions as "Well, I don't know, but I sort of think . . ." and we can always revise our position ("Oh, well, I didn't mean it that way"), but once we have handed in the final version of our writing, we are helpless. We are (putting it strongly) naked to our enemies.

GETTING IDEAS: ARGUMENT AS AN INSTRUMENT OF INQUIRY

In Chapter 1 we quoted Robert Frost, "To learn to write is to learn to have ideas," and we offered suggestions about generating ideas, a process traditionally called **invention**. A moment ago we said that we often improve our ideas when explaining them to someone else. Partly, of course, we're responding to questions or objections raised by our companion in the conversation. But partly we're responding to ourselves: Almost as soon as we hear what we have to say, we may find that it won't do, and if we're lucky, we may find a better idea surfacing. One of the best ways of getting ideas is to talk things over.

The process of talking things over usually begins with the text that you're reading: Your notes, your summary, and your annotations are a kind of dialogue between you and the author. You are also having a dialogue when you talk with friends about your topic. You are trying out and developing ideas. You're arguing, but not chiefly to persuade; rather, you're using argument in order to find the truth. Finally, after reading, taking notes, and talking, you may feel that you have some clear ideas and need only put them into writing. So you take up a sheet of blank paper, but then a paralyzing thought suddenly strikes: "I have ideas but just can't put them into words." The blank white page (or screen) stares back at you and you just can't seem to begin.

All writers, even professional ones, are familiar with this experience. Good writers know that waiting for inspiration is usually not the best strategy. You may be waiting a long time. The best thing to do is begin. Recall some of what we said in Chapter 1: *Writing is a way of thinking*. It's a way of *getting and developing ideas*. *Argument* is an instrument of inquiry as well as persuasion. It is an important part of *critical thinking*. It helps us clarify what we think. One reason we have trouble writing is our fear of putting ourselves on record, but another reason is our fear that we have no ideas worth putting down. However, by writing notes — or even free associations — and by writing a draft, no matter how weak, we can begin to think our way toward good ideas.

THREE BRAINSTORMING STRATEGIES: FREEWRITING, LISTING, AND DIAGRAMMING

If you are facing an issue, debate, or topic and don't know what to write, this is likely because you don't yet know what you think. If, after talking about the topic with yourself (via your reading notes) and others, you are still unclear on what you think, try one of these three strategies:

FREEWRITING Write for five or six minutes, nonstop, without censoring what you produce. You may use what you write to improve your thinking. You may even dim your computer screen so you won't be tempted to look up and fiddle too soon with what you've just written. Once you have spent the time writing out your ideas, you can use what you've written to look further into the subject at hand.

Freewriting should be totally free. If you have some initial ideas, a good freewrite might look like this. (As a topic, let's imagine the writer below is thinking about how children's toys are constructed for different genders. The student is reflecting on the release of the Nerf Rebelle, a type of toy gun made specifically for girls.)

FREEWRITING: This year Nerf released a new toy made for girls, the Nerf Rebelle gun, an attempt the company made to offer toys for girls traditionally made for boys. This seems good—showing an effort toward equality between the sexes. Or is Nerf just trying to broaden its market and sell more toys (after all, boys are only half the population)? Or is it both? That could be my central question. But it is not like the gun makes no distinction between boys and girls. It is pink and purple and has feminine-looking designs on it. And with its "elle" ending the gun sounds small, cute, and girly. Does this toy represent true equality between the sexes, or does it just offer more in the way of feminine stereotypes? It shoots foam arrows, unlike the boys' version of the gun, which shoots bullets. This suggests Cupid, maybe—that is, the figure whose arrows inspire love—a stereotype that girls aren't saving the world but seeking love and marriage. Maybe it's also related to Katniss Everdeen from the *Hunger Games* movie. She carries a bow and arrow, too. Like a lot of female superheroes, Katniss is presented as both strong and sexy, powerful and vulnerable, masculine and feminine at the same time. What kind of messages does this send to young girls? Is it the same message suggested by the gun? Why do powerful women have to project traditional or stereotypical femininity at the same time? How does this work in other areas of life, like business and politics?

Notice that the writer here is jumping around, generating and exploring ideas while writing. Later she can return to the freewriting and begin organizing her ideas and observations. Notice that right in the middle of the freewriting she made a connection between the toy and the *Hunger Games* movie, and by extension to the larger culture in which forms of contemporary femininity can be found. This connection seems significant, and it may help the student to broaden her argument from a critique of the company's motives early on, to a more evidence-based piece about assumptions underlying certain trends in consumer and media culture. The point is that freewriting in this case led to new paths of inquiry and may have inspired further research into different kinds of toys and media.

LISTING   Writing down keywords, just as you do when making a shopping list, is another way of generating ideas. When you make a shopping list, you write *ketchup,* and the act of writing it reminds you that you also need hamburger rolls—and *that* in turn reminds you that you also need tuna fish. Similarly, when preparing a list of ideas for a paper, just writing down one item will often generate another. Of course, when you look over the list, you'll probably drop some of these ideas—the dinner menu will change—but you'll be making progress. If you have a smartphone or tablet, use it to write down your thoughts. You can even e-mail these notes to yourself so you can access them later.

Here's an example of a student listing questions and making associations that could help him focus on a specific argument within a larger debate. The subject here is whether prostitution should be legalized.

LIST: Prostitutes—Law—How has the law traditionally policed sex?—What types of prostitutes exist?—What is prostitution?—Where is it already legal?—How does it work in places where it is legal?—Individual rights vs. public good?—Why shouldn't people be allowed to sell sex?—What are the "bad" effects of prostitution socially?—How many prostitutes are arrested every year?—Could prostitution be taxed?—Who suffers most from enforcement?—Who would suffer most if it were legal?—If it were legal, could its negative effects be better controlled?—Aren't "escort services" really prostitution rings for people with more money? — How is that dealt with? — Who goes into the "oldest business" and why?

Notice that the student doesn't really know the answers yet but is asking questions by free-associating and seeing what turns up as a productive line of analysis. The questions range from the definition of prostitution to its effects, and they might inspire the student to do some basic Internet research or even deeper research. Once you make a list, see if you can observe patterns or similarities among the items you listed, or if you invented a question worthy of its own thesis statement (e.g., "The enforcement of prostitution laws hurts *X* group unequally, and it uses a lot of public money that could better be used in other areas or toward regulating the trade rather than jailing people").

DIAGRAMMING   Sketching a visual representation of an essay is a kind of listing. Three methods of diagramming are especially common.

- *Clustering*   As we discuss on page 6, you can make an effective cluster by writing, in the middle of a sheet of paper, a word or phrase summarizing your topic (e.g., *fracking;* see diagram below), circling it, and then writing down and circling a related word (e.g., *energy independence*). Perhaps this leads you to write *lower gas prices* and *clean energy.* You then circle these phrases and continue making connections. The next thing you think of is *environmental impact,* so you draw a line to *clean energy.* Then you think of *water pollution*, write it down and circle it, and draw another line to *environmental impact*. The next thing that occurs to you is *job creation*, so you write this down and circle it. You won't connect this to *clean energy,* but you might connect it to *lower gas prices* because both are generally positive economic effects. (If you can think of negative economic impacts on other industries or workers, write them down and circle them.) Keep going, jotting down ideas and making connections where possible, indicating relationships. Notice that you appear to be detailing and weighing the economic and environmental impacts of fracking. Whether you realized it or not, an argument is taking shape.

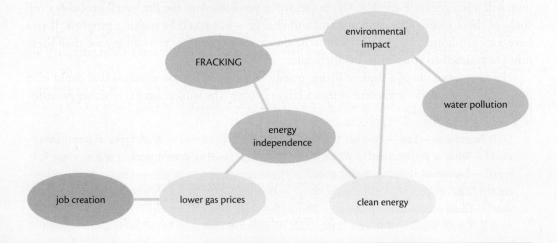

- *Branching*   Some writers find it useful to draw a tree, moving from the central topic to the main branches (chief ideas) and then to the twigs (aspects of the chief ideas).

- *Comparing in columns*   Draw a line down the middle of the page, and then set up two columns showing oppositions. For instance, if you are concerned with the environmental and economic impacts of fracking, you might head one column ENVIRONMENTAL and the other ECONOMIC. In the first column, you might write *water pollution, chemicals used,* and *other hazards?* In the second column, you might write *clean air, employment,* and *independence from unstable oil-producing countries.* You might go on to write, in the first column, *gas leaks* and *toxic waste,* and in the second, *cheaper fuel* and *cheaper electricity* — or whatever else relevant comes to mind.

All these methods can, of course, be executed with pen and paper, but you may also be able to use them on your computer depending on the capabilities of your software.

Whether you're using a computer or a pen, you put down some words and almost immediately see that they need improvement, not simply a little polishing but a substantial overhaul. You write, "Race should be counted in college admissions for two reasons," and as soon as you write those words, a third reason comes to mind. Or perhaps one of those "two reasons" no longer seems very good. As E. M. Forster said, "How can I know what I think till I see what I say?" We have to see what we say — we have to get something down on paper — before we realize that we need to make it better.

Writing, then, is really **rewriting** — that is, **revising** — and a revision is a *re-vision,* a second look. The essay that you submit — whether as hard copy or as a .doc file — should be clear and may appear to be effortlessly composed, but in all likelihood the clarity and apparent ease are the result of a struggle with yourself during which you refined your first thoughts. You begin by putting down ideas, perhaps in random order, but sooner or later comes the job of looking at them critically, developing what's useful in them and removing what isn't. If you follow this procedure you will be in the company of Picasso, who said that he "advanced by means of destruction." Any passages that you cut or destroy can be kept in another file in case you want to revisit those deletions later. Sometimes, you end up restoring them and developing what you discarded into a new essay with a new direction.

Whether you advance bit by bit (writing a sentence, revising it, writing the next, etc.) or whether you write an entire first draft and then revise it and revise it again and again is chiefly a matter of temperament. Probably most people combine both approaches, backing up occasionally but trying to get to the end fairly soon so that they can see rather quickly what they know, or think they know, and can then start the real work of thinking, of converting their initial ideas into something substantial.

FURTHER INVENTION STRATEGIES: ASKING GOOD QUESTIONS

ASKING QUESTIONS   Generating ideas, we said when talking about **topics** and **invention** strategies in Chapter 1 (p. 18) is mostly a matter of asking (and then thinking about) questions. In this book we include questions at the end of each argumentative essay, not to torment you but to help you think about the arguments — for instance, to turn your attention to especially important matters. If your instructor asks you to write an answer to one of these questions, you are lucky: Examining the question will stimulate your mind to work in a specific direction.

If your instructor doesn't assign a topic for an argumentative essay, you'll find that some ideas (possibly poor ones initially, but that doesn't matter because you'll soon revise) come to mind if you ask yourself questions. Begin determining where you stand on an issue (**stasis**) by asking the following five basic questions:

1. What is *X*?
2. What is the value of *X*?
3. What are the causes (or the consequences) of *X*?
4. What should (or ought or must) we do about *X*?
5. What is the evidence for my claims about *X*?

Let's spend a moment looking at each of these questions.

1. What is X? We can hardly argue about the number of people sentenced to death in the United States in 2000 — a glance at the appropriate government report will give the answer — but we can argue about whether capital punishment as administered in the United States is discriminatory. Does the evidence support the view that in the United States the death penalty is unfair? Similarly, we can ask whether a human fetus is a human being (in saying what something is, must we take account of its potentiality?), and even if we agree that a fetus is a human being, we can further ask whether it is a person. In *Roe v. Wade* the U.S. Supreme Court ruled that even the "viable" unborn human fetus is not a "person" as that term is used in the Fifth and Fourteenth Amendments. Here the question is this: Is the essential fact about the fetus that it is a person?

An argument of this sort makes a claim — that is, it takes a stand; but notice that it does not also have to argue for an action. Thus, it may argue that the death penalty is administered unfairly — that's a big enough issue — but it need not go on to argue that the death penalty should be abolished. After all, another possibility is that the death penalty should be administered fairly. The writer of the essay may be doing enough if he or she establishes the truth of the claim and leaves to others the possible responses.

2. What is the value of X? College courses often call for literary judgments. No one can argue if you say you prefer the plays of Tennessee Williams to those of Arthur Miller. But academic papers are not mere declarations of preferences. As soon as you say that Williams is a better playwright than Miller, you have based your preference on implicit standards, and you must support your preference by giving evidence about the relative skill, insight, and accomplishments of both Williams and Miller. Your argument is an evaluation. The question now at issue is the merits of the two authors and the standards appropriate for making such an appraisal.

In short, an essay offering an evaluation normally has two purposes:

- to set forth an assessment
- to convince the reader that the assessment is reasonable

In writing an evaluation, you have to rely on criteria, and these will vary depending on your topic. For instance, in comparing the artistic merit of plays by Williams and by Miller, you may want to talk about the quality of the characterization, the importance of the theme, and so on. But if the topic is "Which playwright is more suitable to be taught in high school?" other criteria may be appropriate, such as these:

- the difficulty of the author's language
- the sexual content of some scenes
- the presence of obscene words

Alternatively, consider a nonliterary issue: On balance, are college fraternities and sororities good or bad? If good, how good? If bad, how bad? What criteria serve best in making our evaluation? Probably some or all of the following:

- testimony of authorities (e.g., persons who can offer firsthand testimony about the good or bad effects)
- inductive evidence (examples of good or bad effects)
- appeals to logic ("it follows, therefore, that . . .")
- appeals to emotion (e.g., an appeal to our sense of fairness)

3. *What are the causes (or the consequences) of X?*   Why did the rate of auto theft increase during a specific period? If the death penalty is abolished, will that cause the rate of murder to increase? Problems such as these may be complex. The phenomena that people usually argue about — such as inflation, war, suicide, crime — have many causes, and it can be a mistake to speak of *the* cause of *X*. A writer in *Time* mentioned that the life expectancy of an average American male is about sixty-seven years, a figure that compares unfavorably with the life expectancy of males in Japan and Israel. The *Time* writer suggested that an important cause of the American male's relatively short life span is "the pressure to perform well in business." Perhaps. But the life expectancy of plumbers is no greater than that of managers and executives. Nutrition authority Jean Mayer, in an article in *Life,* attributed the relatively poor longevity of American males to a diet that is "rich in fat and poor in nutrients." Doubtless other authorities propose other causes, and in all likelihood no one cause entirely accounts for the phenomenon.

Consider a second example of discussions of causality, this one concerning the academic performance of girls in single-sex elementary schools, middle schools, and high schools. It is pretty much agreed (based on statistical evidence) that the graduates of these schools do better, as a group, than girls who graduate from coeducational schools. *Why* do girls in single-sex schools tend, as a group, to do better? What is the *cause*? The administrators of girls' schools usually attribute the success to the fact (we're putting the matter bluntly here) that young women flourish better in an atmosphere free from male intimidation: They allegedly gain confidence and become more expressive when they aren't threatened by the presence of males. This may be the answer, but skeptics have attributed the graduates' success to two other causes:

- Most single-sex schools require parents to pay tuition, and it is a documented fact that the children of well-to-do parents do better, academically, than the children of poor parents.

- Most single-sex schools are private schools, and they select students from a pool of candidates. Admissions officers select those candidates who seem to be academically promising — that is, students who have *already done well academically*.

In short, the girls who graduate from single-sex schools may owe their later academic success not to the schools' single-sex environment but to the fact that even at admission the students were academically stronger (again, we're speaking of a cohort, not of individuals) than the girls who attend coeducational schools.

The lesson? Be cautious in attributing a cause. There may be several causes.

The kinds of support that usually accompany claims of cause include the following:

- factual data, especially statistics
- analogies ("The Roman Empire declined because of *X* and *Y*"; "Our society exhibits *X* and *Y*; therefore . . .")
- inductive evidence

4. ***What should (or ought or must) we do about*** **X?**   Must we always obey the law? Should the law allow eighteen-year-olds to drink alcohol? Should eighteen-year-olds be drafted to do one year of social service? Should pornography be censored? Should steroid use by athletes be banned? Ought there to be Good Samaritan laws, making it a legal duty for a stranger to intervene to save a person from death or great bodily harm, when one might do so with little or no risk to oneself? These questions involve conduct and policy; how we answer them will reveal our values and principles.

An essay answering questions of this sort usually has the following characteristics:

- It begins by explaining what the issue (the problem) is.
- Then it states why the reader should care about the issue.
- Next, it offers the proposed solution.
- Then it considers alternative solutions.
- Finally, it reaffirms the merit of the proposed solution, especially in light of the audience's interests and needs.

You'll recall that throughout this book we have spoken about devices that help a writer to generate ideas. If in drafting an essay concerned with policy you begin by writing down your thoughts on the five bulleted items listed above, you'll almost surely uncover ideas that you didn't know you had.

Support for claims of policy usually include the following:

- statistics
- appeals to common sense and to the reader's moral sense
- testimony of authorities

5. *What is the evidence for my claims about* X? In commenting on the four previous topics, we have talked about the kinds of support that writers commonly offer. However, a few additional points are important.

Critical reading, writing, and thinking depend on identifying and evaluating the evidence for and against the claims one makes and encounters in the writings of others. It isn't enough to have an *opinion* or belief one way or the other; you need to be able to support your opinions — the bare fact of your sincere belief in what you say or write is not itself any *evidence* that what you believe is true.

What constitutes good reasons for opinions and adequate evidence for beliefs? The answer depends on the type of belief or opinion, assertion or hypothesis, claim or principle you want to assert. For example, there is good evidence that President John F. Kennedy was assassinated on November 22, 1963, because this is the date for his death reported in standard almanacs. You could further substantiate the date by checking the back issues of the *New York Times.* But a different kind of evidence is needed to support the proposition that the chemical composition of water is H_2O. And you would need still other kinds of evidence to support your beliefs about the likelihood of rain tomorrow, the probability that the Red Sox will win the pennant this year, the twelfth digit in the decimal expansion of pi, the average cumulative grades of graduating seniors over the past three years in your college, the relative merits of *Hamlet* and *Death of a Salesman*, and the moral dimensions of sexual harassment. None of these issues is merely a matter of opinion; yet about some of them, educated and informed people may disagree over the reasons, the evidence, and what they show. Sometimes, equally qualified experts examine the same evidence and draw different conclusions. Your job as a critical thinker is to be alert to the relevant reasons and evidence, as well as the basis of various conclusions, and to make the most of them as you present your views.

Again, an argument may answer two or more of our five basic questions. Someone who argues that pornography should (or should not) be censored will have to do the following:

- Mark out the territory of the discussion by defining pornography (our first question: What is *X*?).

- Examine the consequences of adopting the preferred policy (our third question).

- Perhaps argue about the value of that policy (our second question). Some people maintain that pornography produces crime, but others maintain that it provides a harmless outlet for impulses that otherwise might vent themselves in criminal behavior.

- Address the possible objection that censorship, however desirable on account of some of its consequences, may be unconstitutional and that even if censorship were constitutional, it would (or might) have undesirable side effects, such as repressing freedom of political opinion.

- Keep in mind our fifth question: What is the evidence for my claims?

Thinking about one or more of these questions may get you going. For instance, thinking about What is *X*? will require you to produce a definition; and as you do this, new ideas might arise. If a question seems relevant, it's a good idea to start writing—even just a fragmentary sentence. You'll probably find that one word leads to another and that ideas begin to appear. Even if these ideas seem weak as you write them, don't be discouraged; you will have put something on paper, and returning to these words, perhaps in five minutes or the next day, you'll probably find that some aren't at all bad and that others will stimulate you to better ones.

It may be useful to record your ideas in a special notebook or in a private digital notebook or document reserved for the purpose. Such a **journal** can be a valuable resource when it comes time to write your paper. Many students find it easier to focus their thoughts on writing if during the gestation period they've been jotting down relevant ideas on something more substantial than slips of paper or loose sheets. The very act of designating a traditional or digital notebook or document file as your journal for a course can be the first step in focusing your attention on the eventual need to write a paper.

Take advantage of the free tools at your disposal. Use the Internet and free Web tools, including RSS feeds, Google (Drive, sites, and others), Yahoo!, blogs, and wikis to organize your initial ideas and to solicit feedback. Talking with others can help, but sometimes there isn't time to chat. By using an RSS feed on a Web site that you think will provide good information on your topic (or a topic you're considering), you can receive notifications if the site has uploaded new material such as news links or op-eds. Posting a blog entry in a public space about your topic can also foster conversations about the topic and help you discover other opinions. Using the Internet to uncover and refine a topic is common practice, especially early in the research process.

If what we have just said doesn't sound convincing, and if you know from experience that you have trouble getting started with writing, don't despair. First aid is at hand in a sure-fire method that we will explain next.

THE THESIS OR MAIN POINT

Let's assume that you are writing an argumentative essay—perhaps an evaluation of an argument in this book—and you have what seems to be a pretty good draft or at least a collection of notes that are the result of hard thinking. You really do have ideas now, and you want to present them effectively. How will you organize your essay? No one formula works best for every essayist and for every essay, but it is usually advisable to formulate a basic **thesis** (a claim, a central point, a chief position) and to state it early. Every essay that is any good, even a book-length one, has a thesis (a main point), which can be stated briefly—usually, in a sentence. Remember Coolidge's remark on the preacher's sermon on sin: "He was against it." Don't confuse the **topic** (sin) with the thesis (sin is bad). The thesis is the argumentative theme, the author's primary claim or contention, the proposition that the rest of the essay will explain and defend. Of course, the thesis may sound commonplace, but the book or essay or sermon ought to develop it in an interesting and convincing way.

RAISING THE STAKES OF YOUR THESIS   Imagine walking across campus and coming upon a person ready to perform on a tightrope suspended between two buildings. He is wearing a glittering leotard and is eyeing up his challenge very seriously. Here's the thing, though: His tightrope is only *one foot off the ground*. Would you stop and watch him walk across it? Maybe, maybe not. Most people are likely to take a look and move on. If you did spend a few minutes watching, you wouldn't be very worried about the performer falling. If he lost his balance momentarily, you wouldn't gasp in horror. And if he walked across the tightrope masterfully, you might be somewhat impressed but not enraptured.

Now imagine the rope being a hundred feet off the ground. You and many others would almost certainly stop and witness the feat. The audience would likely be captivated, nervous about the performer potentially falling, "oohing" if he momentarily lost his balance, and cheering if he crossed the rope successfully.

Consider the tightrope as your thesis statement, the performer as writer, and the act of crossing as the argument. What we call "low-stakes" thesis statements are comparable to low tightropes: A low-stakes thesis statement itself may be interesting, but not much about it is vital to any particular audience. Low-stakes thesis statements lack a sense of importance or relevance. They may restate what is already widely known and accepted, or they may make a good point but not discuss any consequences. Some examples:

Good nutrition and exercise can lead to a healthy life.

Our education system focuses too much on standardized tests.

Children's beauty pageants are exploitative.

Students can write well-organized, clear, and direct papers on these topics, but if the thesis is "low stakes" like these, then the performance would be similar to that of an expert walking across a tightrope *one foot off the ground*. The argument may be well executed, but few in the audience will be inspired by it.

However, if you raise the stakes by "raising the tightrope," you can compel readers to *want* to read and keep reading. There are several ways to raise the tightrope. First, *think about what is socially, culturally, or politically important* about your thesis statement and argument. Some

Tightropes, like these, can be raised to many different levels.

writing instructors tell students to ask themselves "so what?" about the thesis, but this can be a vague directive. Here are some better questions: Why is your thesis important? What is the impact of your thesis on a particular group or demographic? What are the consequences of what you claim? What could happen if your position were *not* recognized? How can your argument benefit readers or compel them to action (by doing something or adopting a new belief)? What will readers *gain* by accepting your argument as convincing?

In formulating your thesis, keep in mind these points:

Different thesis statements may speak to different target audiences. An argument about changes in estate tax laws may not thrill all audiences, but for a defined group — accountants, lawyers, or the elderly, for instance — this may be quite controversial and highly relevant.

Not all audiences are equal — or equally interested in your thesis or argument. In this book, we generally select topics of broad importance. However, in a literature course, a film history course, or a political science course, you'll calibrate your thesis statements and arguments to an audience who is invested in those fields. In writing about the steep decline in bee populations, your argument might look quite different if you're speaking to ecologists as opposed to gardeners. (We will discuss audience in greater detail in the following section.)

Be wary of compare-and-contrast arguments. One of the most basic approaches to writing is to compare and contrast, a maneuver that produces a low-tightrope thesis. It normally looks like this: "X *and* Y *are similar in some ways and different in others.*" But if you think about it, *anything* can be compared and contrasted in this way, and doing so doesn't necessarily *tell* anything important. So, if you're writing a compare-and-contrast paper, make sure to include the reasons why it is important to compare and contrast these things. What benefit does the comparison yield? What significance does it have to some audience, some area of knowledge, some field of study?

> **A CHECKLIST FOR A THESIS STATEMENT**
>
> Consider the following questions:
>
> ☐ Does the statement make an arguable assertion rather than (1) merely assert an unarguable fact, (2) merely announce a topic, or (3) declare an unarguable opinion or belief?
>
> ☐ Is the statement broad enough to cover the entire argument that I will be presenting, and is it narrow enough for me to cover the topic in the space allotted?

IMAGINING AN AUDIENCE

Raising the tightrope of your thesis will also require you to imagine the *audience* you're addressing. The questions that you ask yourself in generating thoughts on a topic will primarily relate to the topic, but additional questions that consider the audience are always relevant:

- Who are my readers?
- What do they believe?
- What common ground do we share?

THINKING CRITICALLY *"Walking the Tightrope"*

Examine the low-stakes thesis statements provided below, and expand each one into a high-stakes thesis by including the importance of asserting it and by proposing a possible response. The first one has been done as an example.

LOW-STAKES THESIS	HIGH-STAKES THESIS
Good nutrition and exercise can lead to a healthy life.	One way to help solve the epidemic obesity problem in the United States is to remind consumers of a basic fact accepted by nearly all reputable health experts: Good nutrition and exercise can lead to a healthy life.
Every qualified American should vote.	
Spanking children is good/bad.	
Electric cars will reduce air pollution.	

LaunchPad To complete this activity online, go to **macmillanhighered.com/barnetbedauohara**

- What do I want my readers to believe?
- What do they need to know?
- Why should they care?

Let's think about these questions. The literal answer to the first probably is "my teacher," but (unless you receive instructions to the contrary) you should not write specifically for your teacher. Instead, you should write for an audience that is, generally speaking, like your classmates. In short, your imagined audience is literate, intelligent, and moderately well informed, but its members don't know everything that you know, and they don't know your response to the problem being addressed. Your audience needs more information along those lines to make an intelligent decision about the issue.

For example, in writing about how children's toys shape the minds of young boys and girls differently, it may not be enough to simply say, "Toys are part of the gender socialization process." ("Sure they are," the audience might already agree.) However, if you raise the stakes, you have an opportunity to frame the questions that result from this observation: You frame the questions, lay out the issues, identify the problems, and note the complications that arise because of your basic thesis. You could point out that toys have a significant impact on the interests, identities, skills, and capabilities that children develop and carry into adulthood.

Because toys are so significant, is it important to ask questions about whether they perpetuate gender-based stereotypes? Do toys help perpetuate social inequalities between the sexes? Most children think toys are "just fun," but they may be teaching kids to conform unthinkingly to the social expectations of their sex, to accept designated sex-based social roles, and to cultivate talents differently based on sex. Is this a good or a bad thing? Do toys facilitate growth, or do they have any limiting effects?

What audiences should be concerned with your topic? Maybe you're addressing the general public who buys toys for children at least some of the time. Maybe you're addressing parents who are raising young children. Maybe you're addressing consumer advocates, encouraging them to pressure toy manufacturers and retailers to produce more gender-neutral offerings. The point is that your essay should contain (and sustain) an assessment of the impact of your high-stakes thesis, and it should set out a clear course of action for a particular audience.

That said, if you know your audience well, you can argue for different courses of action that are most likely to be persuasive. You may not be very convincing if you argue to parents in general that they should never buy princess toys for their girls and avoid all Disney-themed toys. Perhaps you should argue simply that parents should be conscious of the gender messages that toys convey, offer their kids diverse toys, and talk to their children while playing with them about alternatives to the stereotypical messages that the toys convey. However, if you're writing for a magazine called *Radical Parenting* and your essay is titled "Buying Toys the Gender-Neutral Way," your audience and its expectations — therefore, your thesis and argument — may look far different. The bottom line is not just to know your audience but to define it.

The essays in this book are from many different sources with many different audiences. An essay from the *New York Times* addresses educated general readers; an essay from *Ms.* magazine targets readers sympathetic to feminism. An essay from *Commonweal*, a Roman Catholic publication for nonspecialists, is likely to differ in point of view or tone from one in *Time*, even though both articles may advance approximately the same position. The *Commonweal* article may, for example, effectively cite church fathers and distinguished Roman Catholic writers as authorities, whereas the *Time* article would probably cite few or none of these figures because a non-Catholic audience might be unfamiliar with them or, even if familiar, might be unimpressed by their views.

The tone as well as the gist of the argument is in some degree shaped by the audience. For instance, popular journals, such as *National Review* and *Ms.* Magazine, are more likely to use ridicule than are journals chiefly addressed to, say, an academic audience.

THE AUDIENCE AS COLLABORATOR

If you imagine a particular audience and ask yourself what it does and doesn't need to be told, you will find that material comes to mind, just as when a friend asks you what a film you saw was about, who was in it, and how you liked it.

Your readers don't have to be told that Thomas Jefferson was an American statesman in the early years of this country's history, but they do have to be told that Elizabeth Cady Stanton was a late-nineteenth-century American feminist. Why? Because it's your hunch that your classmates never heard of her, or even if they have heard the name, they can't quite identify it. But what if your class has been assigned an essay by Stanton? In that case your imagined readers know Stanton's name and at least a little about her, so you don't have to identify her as an American of the nineteenth century. But you do still have to remind readers about relevant aspects of her essay, and you have to tell them about your responses to those aspects.

After all, even if the instructor has assigned an essay by Stanton, you cannot assume that your classmates know the essay inside out. You can't say, "Stanton's third reason is also unconvincing," without reminding the reader, by means of a brief summary, of her third reason. Again:

- Think of your classmates — people like you — as your imagined readers.
- Be sure that your essay does not make unreasonable demands.

If you ask yourself,

- "What do my readers need to know?" and
- "What do I want them to believe?"

you will find some answers arising, and you will start writing.

We've said that you should imagine your audience as your classmates. But this isn't the whole truth. In a sense, your argument is addressed not simply to your classmates but to the world interested in ideas. Even if you can reasonably assume that your classmates have read only one work by Stanton, you can't begin your essay by writing, "Stanton's essay is deceptively easy." You have to name the work because it's possible that a reader is familiar with some other work by Stanton. And by precisely identifying your subject, you ease the reader into your essay.

Similarly, you won't open with a statement like this:

The majority opinion in *Walker v. City of Birmingham* held that . . .

Rather, you'll write something like this:

In *Walker v. City of Birmingham*, the U.S. Supreme Court ruled in 1966 that city authorities acted lawfully when they jailed Martin Luther King Jr. and other clergymen in 1963 for marching in Birmingham without a permit. Justice Potter Stewart delivered the majority opinion, which held that . . .

By the way, if you suffer from a writing block, the mere act of writing out such readily available facts will help you to get started. You'll find that writing a few words, perhaps merely copying the essay's title or an interesting quotation from the essay, will stimulate other thoughts that you didn't know you had.

Here, again, are the questions about audience. If you write on a computer, consider putting these questions into a file. For each assignment, copy the questions into the file you're working on, and then, as a way of generating ideas, *enter your responses, indented, under each question.*

1. Who are my readers?
2. What do they believe?
3. What common ground do we share?

4. What do I want my readers to believe?

5. What do they need to know?

6. Why should they care?

Thinking about your audience can help you get started; even more important, it can help you generate ideas. Our second and third questions about the audience ("What do they believe?" and "How much common ground do we share?") will usually help you get ideas flowing.

- Presumably, your imagined audience does not share your views, or at least does not fully share them. But why?

- How can these readers hold a position that to you seems unreasonable?

By putting yourself into your readers' shoes — and your essay will almost surely summarize the views that you're going to speak against — and by thinking about what your audience knows or thinks it knows, you will generate ideas. Spend time online reviewing Web sites dedicated to your topic. What do they have to say, and why do the authors hold these views?

Let's assume that you don't believe that people should be allowed to smoke in enclosed public places, but you know that some people hold a different view. Why do they hold it? Try to state their view *in a way that would be satisfactory to them*. Having done so, you may perceive that your conclusions and theirs differ because they're based on different premises — perhaps different ideas about human rights. Examine the opposition's premises carefully, and explain, first to yourself and ultimately to your readers, why you find some of those premises to be unacceptable.

Perhaps some facts are in dispute, such as whether exposure to tobacco is harmful to non-smokers. The thing to do, then, is to check the facts. If you find that harm to nonsmokers has not been proved but you nevertheless believe that smoking should be prohibited in enclosed public places, of course you can't premise your argument on the wrongfulness of harming the innocent (in this case, the nonsmokers). You'll have to develop arguments that take account of the facts.

Among the relevant facts there surely are some that your audience or your opponent will not dispute. The same is true of the values relevant to the discussion; both sides very likely believe in some of the same values (such as the principle mentioned above, that it is wrong to harm the innocent). These areas of shared agreement are crucial to effective persuasion in argument.

There are two good reasons for identifying and isolating the areas of agreement:

- There is no point in disputing facts or values on which you and your readers already agree.

- It usually helps to establish goodwill between yourself and your opponent when you can point to shared beliefs, assumptions, facts, and values.

> **A RULE FOR WRITERS**
> If you wish to persuade, you have to begin by finding premises that you can share with your audience.

In a few moments we will return to the need to share some of the opposition's ideas.

Recall that in composing college papers it's usually best to write for a general audience, an audience rather like your classmates but without the specific knowledge that they all share as students enrolled in one course. If the topic is smoking in public places, the audience presumably consists of smokers and nonsmokers. Thinking about our fifth question on page 236 — "What do [readers] need to know?" — may prompt you to give statistics about the harmful effects of smoking. Or if you're arguing on behalf of smokers, it may prompt you to cite studies claiming that no evidence conclusively demonstrates that cigarette smoking is harmful to nonsmokers. If indeed you are writing for a general audience and you are not advancing a highly unfamiliar view, our second question ("What does the audience believe?") is less important here; but if the audience is specialized, such as an antismoking group, a group of restaurant owners who fear that antismoking regulations will interfere with their business, or a group of civil libertarians, an effective essay will have to address their special beliefs.

In addressing their beliefs (let's assume that you don't share them — at least, not fully), you must try to establish some common ground. If you advocate requiring restaurants to provide nonsmoking areas, you should recognize the possibility that this arrangement will result in inconvenience for the proprietor. But perhaps (the good news) the restaurant will regain some lost customers or attract some new customers. This thought should prompt you to think of other kinds of evidence — perhaps testimony or statistics.

When you formulate a thesis and ask questions about it — such as who the readers are, what they believe, what they know, and what they need to know — you begin to get ideas about how to organize the material (or, at least, you realize that you'll have to work out some sort of organization). The thesis may be clear and simple, but the reasons (the argument) may take many pages. The thesis is the point; the argument sets forth the evidence that supports the thesis.

THE TITLE

It's a good idea to announce the thesis in your essay's **title**. If you scan the table of contents of this book, you'll notice that a fair number of essayists use the title to let readers know, at least in a general way, what position they will advocate. Here are a few examples of titles that take a position:

Forgive Student Loans? Worst Idea Ever

Millennials Are Selfish and Entitled, and Helicopter Parents Are to Blame

The Draft Would Compel Us to Share the Sacrifice

True, these titles are not especially engaging, but the reader welcomes them because they give some information about the writer's thesis.

Some titles don't announce the thesis, but they do announce the topic:

Are We Slaves to Our Online Selves?

On Racist Speech

Should Governments Tax Unhealthy Foods and Drinks?

Although not clever or witty, the above titles are informative.

Some titles seek to attract attention or to stimulate the imagination:

A First Amendment Junkie

Why I Don't Spare "Spare Change"

Building Baby from the Genes Up

All of these are effective, but a word of caution is appropriate here. In seeking to engage your readers' attention, be careful not to sound like a wise guy. You want to engage the readers, not turn them off.

Finally, be prepared to rethink your title *after* completing the last draft of your paper. A title somewhat different from your working title may be an improvement because the finished paper may emphasize something entirely different from what you expected when you first gave it a title.

THE OPENING PARAGRAPHS

Opening paragraphs are difficult to write, so don't worry about writing an effective opening when you're drafting. Just get some words down on paper and keep going. But when you revise your first draft, you should begin to think seriously about the effect of your opening.

A good introduction arouses readers' interest and prepares them for the rest of the paper. How? Opening paragraphs usually do at least one (and often all) of the following:

- attract readers' interest (often with a bold thesis statement or an interesting relevant statistic, quotation, or anecdote)

- prepare readers by giving some idea of the topic and often of the thesis

- give readers an idea of how the essay is organized
- define a key term

You may not wish to announce your thesis in the title, but if you don't announce it there, you should set it forth early in the argument, in the introductory paragraph or paragraphs. In an essay titled "Human Rights and Foreign Policy" (1982), U.S. ambassador to the United Nations Jeanne J. Kirkpatrick merely announces her topic (subject) as opposed to her thesis (point), but she hints at the thesis in her first paragraph, by deprecating President Jimmy Carter's policy:

> In this paper I deal with three broad subjects: first, the content and consequences of the Carter administration's human rights policy; second, the prerequisites of a more adequate theory of human rights; and third, some characteristics of a more successful human rights policy.

Alternatively, consider this opening paragraph from Peter Singer's "Animal Liberation" (p. 205):

> We are familiar with Black Liberation, Gay Liberation, and a variety of other movements. With Women's Liberation some thought we had come to the end of the road. Discrimination on the basis of sex, it has been said, is the last form of discrimination that is universally accepted and practiced without pretense, even in those liberal circles which have long prided themselves on their freedom from racial discrimination. But one should always be wary of talking of "the last remaining form of discrimination." If we have learned anything from the liberation movements, we should have learned how difficult it is to be aware of the ways in which we discriminate until they are forcefully pointed out to us. A liberation movement demands an expansion of our moral horizons, so that practices that were previously regarded as natural and inevitable are now seen as intolerable.

Although Singer's introductory paragraph nowhere mentions animal liberation, in conjunction with the essay's title it gives a good idea of what Singer is up to and where he is going. He knows that his audience will be skeptical, so he reminds them that in previous years many people were skeptical of reforms that are now taken for granted. He adopts a strategy used fairly often by writers who advance unconventional theses: Rather than beginning with a bold announcement of a thesis that may turn off some readers because it sounds offensive or absurd, Singer warms up his audience, gaining their interest by cautioning them politely that although they may at first be skeptical of animal liberation, if they stay with his essay they may come to feel that they have expanded their horizons.

Notice, too, that Singer begins by establishing common ground with his readers; he assumes, probably correctly, that they share his view that other forms of discrimination (now seen to be unjust) were once widely practiced and were assumed to be acceptable and natural. In this paragraph, then, Singer is not only showing himself to be fair-minded but is also letting readers know that he will advance a daring idea. His opening wins their attention and goodwill. A writer can hardly hope to do more. (Soon we'll talk a little more about winning the audience.)

Keep in mind the following points when writing introductory paragraphs:

- You may have to give background information that readers should keep in mind if they are to follow your essay.

- You may wish to define some terms that are unfamiliar or that you use in an unusual sense.

- If you're writing for an online publication (where your instructor or audience will encounter your argument on the Web), you might establish a context for your argument by linking to a news video that outlines the topic, or you might offer your thesis and then link to a news story that supports your claim. (Remember that using any videos, images, or links also requires a citation of some kind.) The beauty of publishing the piece in an online environment is that you can link directly to sources and use them more easily than if you were submitting a hard copy.

After announcing the topic, giving the necessary background, and stating your position (and perhaps the opposition's) in as engaging a manner as possible, you will do well to give the reader an idea of *how* you will proceed — that is, what the organization will be. In other words, use the introduction to set up the organization of your essay. Your instructors may assign four- to six-page mini-research papers or ten- to fifteen-page research papers; if they assign an online venue, ask them about the approximate word count. No matter what the length, every paper needs to have a clear organization. The introduction is where you can accomplish three key things:

- hook your reader
- reveal your thesis and topic
- explain how you will organize your discussion of the topic — what you'll do first, second, third, and so on.

Look at Kirkpatrick's opening paragraph (p. 239) for an illustration. She tells her readers that she will address three subjects, and she names them. Her approach in the paragraph is concise, obvious, and effective.

Similarly, you may want to announce fairly early that there are, say, four common objections to your thesis and that you will take them up one by one, beginning with the weakest (or most widely held) and moving to the strongest (or least familiar), after which you will advance your own view in greater detail. Not every argument begins with refuting the other side, though many arguments do. The point to remember is that you usually ought to tell readers where you will be taking them and by what route. In effect, you give them an outline.

ORGANIZING AND REVISING THE BODY OF THE ESSAY

We begin with a wise remark by a newspaper columnist, Robert Cromier: "The beautiful part of writing is that you don't have to get it right the first time — unlike, say, a brain surgeon."

In drafting an essay, you will of course begin with an organization that seems appropriate, but you may find, in rereading the draft, that some other organization is better. Here, for a start, is an organization that is common in argumentative essays:

1. Statement of the problem or issue
2. Statement of the structure of the essay (its organization)
3. Statement of alternative (but less adequate) solutions
4. Arguments in support of the proposed solution
5. Arguments answering possible objections
6. A summary, resolution, or conclusion

Let's look at each of these six steps.

   1. Statement of the problem or issue   Whether the problem is stated briefly or at length depends on the nature of the problem and the writer's audience. If you haven't already defined unfamiliar terms or terms you use in a special way, now is the time to do so. In any case, it is advisable here to state the problem objectively (thereby gaining the reader's trust) and to indicate why the reader should care about the issue.

   2. Statement of the structure of the essay   After stating the problem at the appropriate length, the writer often briefly indicates the structure of the rest of the essay. The structure used most frequently is suggested below, in points 3 and 4.

   3. Statement of alternative (but less adequate) solutions   In addition to stating the alternatives fairly (letting readers know that you've done your homework), the writer conveys a willingness to recognize not only the integrity of opposing proposals but also the (partial) merit of at least some of the alternative solutions.

   Our point in the previous sentence is important and worth amplifying. Because it is important to convey your goodwill — your sense of fairness — to the reader, it's advisable to show that you're familiar with the opposition and that you recognize the integrity of those who hold that view. You accomplish this by granting its merits as far as you can. (For more about this approach, see the essay by Carl R. Rogers on p. 375.)

   The next stage, which constitutes most of the body of the essay, usually is this:

   4. Arguments in support of the proposed solution   The evidence offered will depend on the nature of the problem. Relevant statistics, authorities, examples, or analogies may come to mind or be available. This is usually the longest part of the essay.

   5. Arguments answering possible objections   These arguments may suggest the following:

   a. The proposal won't work (perhaps it is alleged to be too expensive, to make unrealistic demands on human nature, or to fail to reach the heart of the problem).

   b. The proposed solution will create problems greater than the problem under discussion. (A good example of a proposal that produced dreadful unexpected results is the law mandating a prison term for anyone over age eighteen in possession of an illegal drug. Heroin dealers then began to use children as runners, and cocaine importers followed the practice.)

6. *A summary, resolution, or conclusion* Here the writer may seek to accommodate the opposition's views as far as possible but clearly suggest that the writer's own position makes good sense. A conclusion — the word comes from the Latin *claudere*, "to shut" — ought to provide a sense of closure, but it can be much more than a restatement of the writer's thesis. It can, for instance, make a quiet emotional appeal by suggesting that the issue is important and that the ball is now in the reader's court.

Of course, not every essay will follow this six-step pattern. But let's assume that in the introductory paragraphs you have sketched the topic (and have shown, or implied, that the reader doubtless is interested in it) and have fairly and courteously set forth the opposition's view, recognizing its merits ("I grant that," "admittedly," "it is true that") and indicating the degree to which you can share part of that view. You now want to set forth arguments explaining why you differ on some essentials.

In presenting your own position, you can begin with either your strongest or your weakest reasons. Each method of organization has advantages and disadvantages.

- If you begin with your strongest reason, the essay may seem to peter out.
- If you begin with your weakest reason, you build to a climax; but readers may not still be with you because they may have felt at the start that the essay was frivolous.

The solution to the latter possibility is to ensure that even your weakest argument demonstrates strength. You can, moreover, assure your readers that stronger points will soon follow and you offer this point first in order to show that you are aware of it and that, slight though it is, it deserves some attention. The body of the essay, then, is devoted to arguing a position, which means offering not only supporting reasons but also refutations of possible objections to these reasons.

Doubtless you'll sometimes be uncertain, while drafting an essay, whether to present a given point before or after another point. When you write, and certainly when you revise, try to put yourself into the reader's shoes: Which point do you think the reader needs to know first? Which point *leads to* which further point? Your argument should not be a mere list of points; rather, it should clearly integrate one point with another in order to develop an idea. However, in all likelihood you won't have a strong sense of the best organization until you have written a draft and have reread it.

CHECKING PARAGRAPHS   When you revise a draft, watch out for short paragraphs. Although a paragraph of only two or three sentences (like some in this chapter) may occasionally be helpful as a transition between complicated points, most short paragraphs are undeveloped paragraphs. Newspaper editors favor very short paragraphs because they can be read rapidly when printed in the narrow columns typical of newspapers. Many of the essays reprinted in this book originally were published in newspapers and, thus, consist of very short paragraphs, but they should *not* be regarded as models for your own writing.

A second note about paragraphs: Writers for online venues often "chunk" (i.e., they provide extra space for paragraph breaks) rather than write a continuous flow. These writers chunk their text for several reasons, but chiefly because breaking up paragraphs and adding space between them makes some types of writing "scannable": The screen is easier to navigate because it isn't packed with text in a 12-point font. The breaks in paragraphs also allow the reader to see a complete paragraph without having to scroll.

CHECKING TRANSITIONS   Make sure, in revising, that the reader can move easily from the beginning of a paragraph to the end and from one paragraph to the next. Transitions help to signal the connections between units of the argument. For example ("For example" is a transition, indicating that an illustration will follow), they may illustrate, establish a sequence, connect logically, amplify, compare, contrast, summarize, or concede (see Thinking Critically: Using Transitions in Argument). Transitions serve as guideposts that enable the reader to move easily through your essay.

When writers revise an early draft, they chiefly do these tasks:

- They **unify** the essay by eliminating irrelevancies.
- They **organize** the essay by keeping in mind the imagined audience.
- They **clarify** the essay by fleshing out thin paragraphs, by ensuring that the transitions are adequate, and by making certain that generalizations are adequately supported by concrete details and examples.

We are not talking here about polish or elegance; we are talking about fundamental matters. Be especially careful not to abuse the logical connectives (*thus, as a result,* and so on). If you write several sentences followed by *therefore* or a similar word or phrase, be sure that what you write after the *therefore* really *does follow* from what has gone before. Logical connectives are not mere transitional devices that link disconnected bits of prose. They are supposed to mark a real movement of thought, which is the essence of an argument.

THE ENDING

What about concluding paragraphs, in which you summarize the main points and reaffirm your position?

If you can look back over your essay and add something that both enriches it and wraps it up, fine; but don't feel compelled to say, "Thus, in conclusion, I have argued *X, Y,* and *Z,* and I have refuted Jones." After all, *conclusion* can have two meanings: (1) ending, or finish, as the ending of a joke or a novel; or (2) judgment or decision reached after deliberation. Your essay should finish effectively (the first sense), but it need not announce a judgment (the second).

If the essay is fairly short, so that a reader can keep its general gist in mind, you may not need to restate your view. Just make sure that you have covered the ground and that your last sentence is a good one. Notice that the student essay printed later in this chapter (p. 258) doesn't end with a formal conclusion, although it ends conclusively, with a note of finality.

THINKING CRITICALLY *Using Transitions in Argument*

Fill in examples of the types of transitions listed below, using topics of your choice. The first one has been done as an example.

TYPE OF TRANSITION	TYPE OF LANGUAGE USED	EXAMPLE OF TRANSITION
Illustrate	*for example, for instance, consider this case*	"Many television crime dramas contain scenes of graphic violence. For example, in the episode of *Law and Order* titled . . ."
Establish a sequence	*a more important objection, a stronger example, the best reason*	
Connect logically	*thus, as a result, therefore, so, it follows*	
Amplify	*further, in addition to, moreover*	
Compare	*similarly, in a like manner, just as, analogously*	
Contrast	*on the one hand . . . on the other hand, in contrast, however, but*	
Summarize	*in short, briefly*	
Concede	*admittedly, granted, to be sure*	

 LaunchPad To complete this activity online, go to **macmillanhighered.com/barnetbedauohara**

By "a note of finality" we do *not* mean a triumphant crowing. It's far better to end with the suggestion that you hope you have by now indicated why those who hold a different view may want to modify it and accept yours.

If you study the essays in this book or the editorials and op ed pieces in a newspaper, you will notice that writers often provide a sense of closure by using one of the following devices:

- a return to something stated in the introduction
- a glance at the wider implications of the issue (e.g., if smoking is restricted, other liberties are threatened)
- a hint toward unasked or answered questions that the audience might consider in light of the writer's argument
- a suggestion that the reader can take some specific action or do some further research (i.e., the ball is now in the reader's court)
- an anecdote that illustrates the thesis in an engaging way
- a brief summary (*Note:* This sort of ending may seem unnecessary and tedious if the paper is short and the summary merely repeats what the writer has already said.)

> **A RULE FOR WRITERS**
> Emulate John Kenneth Galbraith, a distinguished writer on economics. Galbraith said that in his fifth drafts he regularly introduced the note of spontaneity for which his writing was famous.

TWO USES OF AN OUTLINE

THE OUTLINE AS A PRELIMINARY GUIDE   Some writers sketch an **outline** as soon as they think they know what they want to say, even before writing a first draft. This procedure can be helpful in planning a tentative organization, but remember that in revising a draft you'll likely generate some new ideas and have to modify the outline accordingly. A preliminary outline is chiefly useful as a means of getting going, not as a guide to the final essay.

THE OUTLINE AS A WAY OF CHECKING A DRAFT   Whether or not you use a preliminary outline, we strongly suggest that after writing what you hope is your last draft, you make an outline of it; there is no better way of finding out whether the essay is well organized.

Go through the draft, and write down the chief points in the order in which you make them. That is, prepare a table of contents — perhaps a phrase for each paragraph. Next, examine your notes to see what kind of sequence they reveal in your paper:

- Is the sequence reasonable? Can it be improved?
- Are any passages irrelevant?
- Does something important seem to be missing?

If no coherent structure or reasonable sequence clearly appears in the outline, then the full prose version of your argument probably doesn't have any either. Therefore, produce another draft by moving things around, adding or subtracting paragraphs — cutting and pasting them into a new sequence, with transitions as needed — and then make another outline to see if the sequence now is satisfactory.

You're probably familiar with the structure known as a **formal outline**. Major points are indicated by I, II, III; points within major points are indicated by A, B, C; divisions within A, B, C are indicated by 1, 2, 3; and so on. Thus:

I. Arguments for opening all Olympic sports to professionals

   A. Fairness

      1. Some Olympic sports are already open to professionals.

      2. Some athletes who really are not professionals are classified as professionals.

   B. Quality (achievements would be higher)

You may want to outline your draft according to this principle, or you might simply write a phrase for each paragraph and indent the subdivisions. But keep these points in mind:

- It is not enough for the parts to be ordered reasonably.
- The order must be made clear to the reader, usually by means of transitions such as *for instance, on the one hand . . . on the other hand, we can now turn to an opposing view,* and so on.

Here is another way of thinking about an outline. For each paragraph, write:

- what the paragraph *says,* and
- what the paragraph *does.*

An opening paragraph might be outlined thus:

- What the paragraph *says* is that the words "under God" in the Pledge of Allegiance should be omitted.
- What the paragraph *does* is, first, inform the reader of the thesis, and second, *provide some necessary background* — for instance, that the words were not in the original wording of the Pledge.

A dual outline of this sort will help you to see whether you have a final draft or a draft that needs refinement.

A LAST WORD ABOUT OUTLINES

Outlines may seem rigid to many writers, especially to those who compose online, where we're accustomed to cutting, copying, moving, and deleting as we draft. However, as mentioned earlier, an outline — whether you write it before drafting a single word or use it to evaluate the organization of something you've already written — is meant to be a guide rather than a straitjacket. Many writers who compose electronically find that the ability to keep banging out words — typing is so much easier than pushing a pen or pencil — and to cut and paste without actually reaching for scissors makes it easy to produce an essay that readers may find difficult to follow. (There is much truth in the proverb "Easy writing makes hard reading.") If you compose electronically, and especially if you continually add, delete, and move text around without a clear organizational goal in mind, be sure to read and outline your draft, and *then* examine the outline to see if indeed there is a reasonable organization.

Outlines are especially helpful for long essays, but even short ones benefit from a bit of advanced planning, a list of a few topics (drawn from notes already taken) that keep the writer moving in an orderly way. A longer work such as an honors or a master's thesis typically requires careful planning. An outline will be a great help in ensuring that you produce something that a reader can easily follow — but, of course, you may find as you write that the outline needs to be altered.

When readers reach the end of a piece of writing, they should feel that the writer has brought them to a decisive point and is not simply stopping abruptly and unexpectedly.

TONE AND THE WRITER'S PERSONA

Although this book is chiefly about argument in the sense of rational discourse — the presentation of reasons in support of a thesis or conclusion — the appeal to reason is only one form of persuasion. Another form is the appeal to emotion — to pity, for example. Aristotle saw, in addition to appeals to reason and to emotion, a third form of persuasion — the appeal to the speaker's character. He called it the **ethical appeal** (the Greek word for this kind of appeal is **ethos,** meaning "character"). The idea is that effective speakers convey the suggestion that they are

- informed,
- intelligent,
- fair minded (persons of goodwill), and
- honest.

Because they are perceived as trustworthy, their words inspire confidence in their listeners. It is a fact that when reading an argument we're often aware of the *person* or *voice* behind the words, and our assent

---

A CHECKLIST FOR ORGANIZING AN ARGUMENT

☐ Does the introduction let the readers know where the author is taking them?

☐ Does the introduction state the problem or issue?

   ☐ Does it state the claim (the thesis)?

   ☐ Does it suggest the organization of the essay, thereby helping the reader to follow the argument?

☐ Do subsequent paragraphs support the claim?

   ☐ Do they offer evidence?

   ☐ Do they face objections to the claim and offer reasonable responses?

   ☐ Do they indicate why the author's claim is preferable?

   ☐ Do transitions (signposts such as *Furthermore, In contrast,* and *Consider as an example*) guide the reader through the argument?

☐ Does the essay end effectively, with a paragraph (at most, two paragraphs) bringing a note of closure — for instance, by indicating that the proposed solution is relatively simple? By admitting that although the proposed solution will be difficult to implement, it is certainly feasible? By reminding the reader of the urgency of the problem?

to the argument depends partly on the extent to which we can share the speaker's assumptions and see the matter from his or her point of view — in short, the extent to which we can *identify* with the speaker.

How can a writer inspire the confidence that lets readers identify with him or her? First, the writer should possess the virtues Aristotle specified: intelligence or good sense, honesty, and benevolence or goodwill. As a Roman proverb puts it, "No one gives what he does not have." Still, possession of these qualities is not a guarantee that you will convey them in your writing. Like all other writers, you'll have to revise your drafts so that these qualities become apparent; stated more moderately, you'll have to revise so that nothing in the essay causes a reader to doubt your intelligence, honesty, and goodwill. A blunder in logic, a misleading quotation, a snide remark, even an error in spelling — all such slips can cause readers to withdraw their sympathy from the writer.

Of course, all good argumentative essays do not sound exactly alike; they do not all reveal the same speaker. Each writer develops his or her own voice, or (as literary critics and instructors call it) **persona**. In fact, one writer may have several voices or personae, depending on the topic and the audience. The president of the United States delivering an address on the State of the Union has one persona; when chatting with a reporter at his summer home, he has another. This change is not a matter of hypocrisy. Different circumstances call for different language. As a French writer put it, there is a time to speak of "Paris" and a time to speak of "the capital of the nation." When Abraham Lincoln spoke at Gettysburg,

A RULE FOR WRITERS
Present yourself so that readers see you as knowledgeable, honest, open-minded, and interested in helping them to think about the significance of an issue.

he didn't say "Eighty-seven years ago"; instead, he intoned "Four score and seven years ago." We might say that just as some occasions required him to be the folksy Honest Abe, the occasion of the dedication of hallowed ground at Gettysburg, where so many Civil War soldiers lost their lives, required him to be formal and solemn — thus, as president of the United States he appropriately used biblical language. Lincoln's election campaigns called for one persona, and the dedication of a military cemetery (an entirely different rhetorical situation) called for a different persona. For examples on how to vary tone, see Thinking Critically: Varying Tone.

When we talk about a writer's persona, we mean the way in which the writer presents his or her attitudes

- toward *the self,*
- toward *the audience*, and
- toward *the subject.*

Thus, if a writer says:

I have thought long and hard about this subject, and I can say with assurance that . . .

we may feel that he is a self-satisfied egotist who probably is mouthing other people's opinions. Certainly he's mouthing clichés: "long and hard," "say with assurance."

THINKING CRITICALLY *Varying Tone*

See the example of Abraham Lincoln's tone below. In the spaces provided, rewrite Lincoln's statement in wording that reflects qualities of other tones as indicated in the middle column..

TONE	QUALITIES OF THE TONE	EXAMPLE
Abraham Lincoln	Invokes biblical rhetoric in an appeal to national unity	*Four score and seven years ago our fathers brought forth on this continent a new nation, conceived in liberty, and dedicated to the proposition that all men are created equal.*
More academic tone	Incorporates specific factual information and connects to overarching ideas	
More informal tone	Is accurate but simplified, forgoing much detail	
Too informal for most academic writing	Mischaracterizes or oversimplifies the thought process	

LaunchPad To complete this activity online, go to **macmillanhighered.com/barnetbedauohara**

Let's look at a subtler example of an utterance that reveals certain attitudes:

President Nixon was hounded out of office by journalists.

The statement above conveys a respectful attitude toward Nixon ("President Nixon") and a hostile attitude toward the press (they are beasts, curs who "hounded" our elected leader). If the writer's attitudes were reversed, she might have said something like this:

The press turned the searchlight on Tricky Dick's criminal shenanigans.

"Tricky Dick" and "criminal" are obvious enough, but notice that "shenanigans" also implies the writer's contempt for Nixon, and "turned the searchlight" suggests that the press is a source of illumination, a source of truth. The original version and the opposite version both say that the press was responsible for Nixon's resignation, but the original version ("President

Nixon was hounded") conveys indignation toward journalists, whereas the revision conveys contempt for Nixon.

These two versions suggest two speakers who differ not only in their view of Nixon but also in their manner, including the seriousness with which they take themselves. Although the passage is very short, it seems to us that the first speaker conveys righteous indignation ("hounded"), whereas the second conveys amused contempt ("shenanigans"). To our ears the tone, as well as the point, differs in the two versions.

We are talking now about **loaded words**, which convey the writer's attitude and, through their connotations, seek to win the reader to the writer's side. Compare the words in the left-hand column with those in the right:

freedom fighter	terrorist
pro-choice	pro-abortion
pro-life	antichoice
economic refugee	illegal alien
terrorist surveillance	domestic spying

The words in the left-hand column sound like good things; speakers who use them seek to establish themselves as virtuous people supporting worthy causes. The **connotations** (associations, overtones) of these pairs of words differ, even though the **denotations** (explicit meanings, dictionary definitions) are the same — just as the connotations of *mother* and *female parent* differ, although the denotations are the same. Similarly, although Lincoln's "four score and seven" and "eighty-seven" both denote "thirteen less than one hundred," they differ in connotation.

Tone is not only a matter of connotation (*hounded out of office* versus, let's say, *compelled to resign*, or *pro-choice* versus *pro-abortion*); it is also a matter of such things as the selection and type of examples. A writer who offers many examples, especially ones drawn from ordinary life, conveys a persona different from that of a writer who offers no examples or only an occasional invented instance. The first writer seems friendlier, more honest, more down-to-earth.

LAST WORDS ON TONE   On the whole, when writing an argument, it's advisable to be courteous and respectful of your topic, your audience, and people who hold views opposite to yours. It is rarely good for one's own intellectual development to regard as villains or fools persons who hold views different from one's own, especially if some of them are in the audience. Keep in mind the story of two strangers on a train who, striking up a conversation, found that both were clergymen, though of different faiths. Then one said to the other, "Well, why shouldn't we be friends? After all, we both serve God, you in your way and I in His."

Complacency is all right when telling a joke, but not when offering an argument:

- Recognize opposing views.
- Assume they are held in good faith.

- State them fairly. If you don't, you do a disservice not only to the opposition but also to your own position because the perceptive reader won't take you seriously.

- Be temperate in arguing your own position: "If I understand their view correctly . . ."; "It seems reasonable to conclude that . . ."; "Perhaps, then, we can agree that. . . ."

- Write calmly. If you become overly emotional, readers may interpret you as biased or unreasonable, and they may lose their confidence in you.

One way to practice thinking about tone and persona is to think about your professional e-mails. As a student, you probably send many e-mails to classmates and to your instructors or other offices on campus (e.g., the financial aid office, your academic advisor). As teachers, we are often surprised at how flippant and inattentive students are when e-mailing. How do you present yourself in your professional e-mails?

WE, ONE, OR I?

The use of *we* in the last sentence brings us to another point: Is it correct to use the first-person pronouns *I* and *we*? In this book, because three of us are writing, we often use *we* to mean the three authors. And we sometimes use *we* to mean the authors and the readers. This shifting use of one word can be troublesome, but we hope (clearly, the *we* here refers only to the authors) that we have avoided ambiguity. But can, or should, or must an individual use *we* instead of *I*? The short answer is no.

If you're simply speaking for yourself, use *I*. Attempts to avoid the first-person singular by saying things like "This writer thinks . . ." and "It is thought that . . ." and "One thinks that . . ." are far more irritating (and wordy) than the use of *I*. The so-called editorial *we* sounds as odd in a student's argument as the royal *we* does. (Mark Twain said that the only ones who can appropriately say *we* are kings, editors, and people with a tapeworm.) It's advisable to use *we* only when you are sure you're writing or speaking directly to an audience who holds membership in the same group, as in "We *students of* X *university* should . . ." or "We *the members of Theta Chi fraternity* need to. . . ." If the *we* you refer to has a referent, simply refer to what it means: Say "Americans are" rather than "We are," or "College students should" rather than "We should," or "Republicans need to" rather than "We need to."

Many students assume that using *one* will solve the problem of pronouns. But because one *one* leads to another, the sentence may end up sounding, as James Thurber once said, "like a trombone solo." It's best to admit that you are the author, and to use *I*. However, there is no need to preface every sentence with "I think." The reader knows that the essay is yours and that the opinions are yours; so use *I* when you must, but not needlessly. Do not write, "I think X movie is terrible"; simply say, "X movie is terrible." And do not add extra words that say more obvious things, like "*It is my idea that* the company needs a new mission statement." Just write, "*The company needs a new mission statement.*"

Often you'll see *I* in journalistic writing and autobiographical writing — and in some argumentative writing, too — but in most argumentative writing it's best to state the facts and (when drawing reasonable conclusions from them) to keep yourself in the background. Why? The more you use *I* in an essay, the more your readers will attach *you* directly to the argument and may regard your position as personal rather than as relevant to themselves.

THINKING CRITICALLY Eliminating We, One, And I

Rewrite the following sentences to eliminate unnecessary uses of *I*, *we*, *one*, and other gratuitous statements of opinion.

ORIGINAL SENTENCE	REWRITTEN SENTENCE
I think fracking is the best way to achieve energy independence and to create jobs.	Fracking is the best way to achieve energy independence and to create jobs.
In our country, we believe in equality and freedom.	
One should consider one's manners at formal dinner parties.	
In my opinion, the government should not regulate the sizes of sodas we can order.	
It is clearly the case that the new policy treats employees unfairly.	

LaunchPad   To complete this activity online, go to **macmillanhighered.com/barnetbedauohara**

A CHECKLIST FOR ATTENDING TO THE NEEDS OF THE AUDIENCE

☐ Do I have a sense of what the audience probably knows about the issue?

☐ Do I have a sense of what the audience probably thinks about the issue?

☐ Have I stated the thesis clearly and sufficiently early in the essay?

❑ How much common ground do I probably share with the audience?

❑ Have I tried to establish common ground and then moved on to advance my position?

❑ Have I supported my arguments with sufficient details?

❑ Have I used appropriate language (e.g., defined terms that are likely to be unfamiliar)?

❑ Have I indicated why readers should care about the issue and should accept my views, or at least give them serious consideration?

❑ Is the organization clear?

❑ Have I used transitions where they are needed?

❑ If visual material (charts, graphs, pictures) will enhance my arguments, have I used them?

❑ Have I presented myself as a person who is fair, informed, and worth listening to? In short, have I conveyed a strong *ethos*?

AVOIDING SEXIST LANGUAGE

Courtesy as well as common sense requires that you respect your readers' feelings. Many people today find offensive the implicit sexism in the use of male pronouns to denote not only men but also women ("As the reader follows the argument, he will find . . ."). And sometimes the use of the male pronoun to denote all people is ridiculous ("An individual, no matter what his sex, . . .").

In most contexts there is no need to use gender-specific nouns or pronouns. One way to avoid using *he* when you mean any person is to use *he or she* (or *she or he*), but the result is sometimes cumbersome — although superior to the overly conspicuous *he/she* and *s/he*.

Here are two simple ways to solve the problem:

- *Use the plural* ("As readers follow the argument, they will find . . .").
- *Recast the sentence* so that no pronoun is required ("Readers following the argument will find . . .").

Because *man* and *mankind* strike many readers as sexist when used in such expressions as "Man is a rational animal" and "Mankind has not yet solved this problem," consider using such words as *human being, person, people, humanity,* and *we.* (*Examples:* "Human beings are rational animals"; "We have not yet solved this problem.")

Peer Review

Your instructor may suggest — or require — that you submit an early draft of your essay to a fellow student or small group of students for comment. Such a procedure benefits both author and readers: You get the responses of a reader, and the student-reader gets experience in thinking about the problems of developing an argument, especially such matters as the degree of detail that a writer needs to offer to a reader and the importance of keeping the organization evident to a reader.

Oral peer reviews allow for the give and take of discussion, but probably most students and most instructors find written peer reviews more helpful because reviewers think more carefully about their responses to the draft, and they help essayists to get beyond a knee-jerk response to criticism. Online reviews on a class Web site, through e-mail, or via another file-sharing service are especially helpful precisely because they are not face to face; the peer reviewer gets practice *writing*, and the essayist is not directly challenged. Sharing documents works well for peer review.

A CHECKLIST FOR PEER REVIEW OF A DRAFT OF AN ARGUMENT

Read through the draft quickly. Then read it again, with the following questions in mind. Remember: You are reading a draft, a work in progress. You're expected to offer suggestions, and you're expected to offer them courteously.

In a sentence, indicate the degree to which the draft shows promise of fulfilling the assignment.

❏ Is the writer's tone appropriate? Who is the audience?

❏ Looking at the essay as a whole, what thesis (main idea) is advanced?

❏ Are the needs of the audience kept in mind? For instance, do some words need to be defined? Is the evidence (e.g., the examples and the testimony of authorities) clear and effective?

❏ Can I accept the assumptions? If not, why not?

❏ Is any obvious evidence (or counterevidence) overlooked?

❏ Is the writer proposing a solution? If so,

    ❏ Are other equally attractive solutions adequately examined?

    ❏ Has the writer overlooked some unattractive effects of the proposed solution?

❏ Looking at each paragraph separately,

    ❏ What is the basic point?

    ❏ How does each paragraph relate to the essay's main idea or to the previous paragraph?

❏ Should some paragraphs be deleted? Be divided into two or more paragraphs? Be combined? Be moved elsewhere? (If you outline the essay by writing down the gist of each paragraph, you'll get help in answering these questions.)

❏ Is each sentence clearly related to the sentence that precedes and to the sentence that follows? If not, in a sentence or two indicate examples of good and bad transitions.

❏ Is each paragraph adequately developed? Are there sufficient details, perhaps brief supporting quotations from the text?

❏ Are the introductory and concluding paragraphs effective?

❏ What are the paper's chief strengths?

❏ Make at least two specific suggestions that you think will assist the author to improve the paper.

A Student's Essay, from Rough Notes to Final Version

While we were revising this textbook, we asked the students in one of our classes to write a short essay (500–750 words) on some ethical problem that concerned them. Because this assignment was the first writing assignment in the course, we explained that a good way to generate ideas is to ask oneself some questions, write down responses, question those responses, and write freely for ten minutes or so, not worrying about contradictions. We invited our students to hand in their initial notes along with the finished essay, so that we could get a sense of how they proceeded as writers. Not all of them chose to hand in their notes, but we were greatly encouraged by those who did. What encouraged us was the confirmation of an old belief — we call it a fact — that students will hand in a thoughtful essay if before preparing a final version they ask themselves *why* they think this or that, write down their responses, and are not afraid to change their minds as they proceed.

Here are the first notes of a student, Emily Andrews, who elected to write about whether to give money to street beggars. She simply put down ideas, one after the other.

Help the poor? Why do I (sometimes) do it?

I feel guilty, and think I should help them: poor, cold, hungry (but also some of them are thirsty for liquor, and will spend the money on liquor, not on food).

I also feel annoyed by them — most of them.

Where does the expression "the deserving poor" come from?

And "poor but honest"? Actually, that sounds odd. Wouldn't "rich but honest" make more sense?

Why don't they work? Fellow with red beard, always by bus stop in front of florist's shop, always wants a handout. He is a regular, there all day every day, so I guess he is in a way "reliable," so why doesn't he put the same time in on a job?

Or why don't they get help? Don't they know they need it? They *must* know they need it.

Maybe that guy with the beard is just a con artist. Maybe he makes more money by panhandling than he would by working, and it's a lot easier!

Kinds of poor — how to classify??

> drunks, druggies, etc.
> mentally ill (maybe drunks belong here, too)
> decent people who have had terrible luck

Why private charity?

Doesn't it make sense to say we (fortunate individuals) should give something — an occasional handout — to people who have had terrible luck? (I suppose some people might say there's no need for any of us to give anything — the government takes care of the truly needy — but I *do* believe in giving charity. A month ago a friend of the family passed away, and the woman's children suggested that people might want to make a donation in her name to a shelter for battered women. I know my parents made a donation.)

BUT how can I tell who is who, which are which? Which of these people asking for "spare change" really need (deserve???) help, and which are phonies? Impossible to tell.

Possibilities:

> Give to no one.
> Give to no one but make an annual donation, maybe to United Way.
> Give a dollar to each person who asks. This would probably not cost me even a dollar a day.
> Occasionally do without something — maybe a CD or a meal in a restaurant — and give the money I save to people who seem worthy.

WORTHY? What am I saying? How can I, or anyone, tell? The neat-looking guy who says he just lost his job may be a phony, and the dirty bum — probably a drunk — may desperately need food. (OK, so what if he spends the money on liquor instead of food? At least he'll get a little pleasure in life. No! It's not all right if he spends it on drink.)

Other possibilities:

> Do some volunteer work?
> To tell the truth, I don't want to put in the time. I don't feel *that* guilty.

So what's the problem?

Is it, How I can help the very poor (handouts, or through an organization)? or

How I can feel less guilty about being lucky enough to be able to go to college and to have a supportive family?

I can't quite bring myself to believe I should help every beggar who approaches, but I also can't bring myself to believe that I should do nothing, on the grounds that:

a. it's probably their fault

b. if they are deserving, they can get gov't help. No, I just can't believe that. Maybe some are too proud to look for government help, or don't know that they're entitled to it.

What to do?

On balance, it seems best to:

a. give to United Way

b. maybe also give to an occasional individual, if I happen to be moved, without worrying about whether he or she is "deserving" (since it's probably impossible to know)

A day after making these notes Emily reviewed them, added a few points, and then made a very brief selection from them to serve as an outline for her first draft:

Opening para.: "poor but honest"? Deserve "spare change"?

Charity: private or through organizations?

    pros and cons

    guy at bus

    it wouldn't cost me much, but . . . better to give through organizations

Concluding para.: still feel guilty?

      maybe mention guy at bus again?

After writing and revising a draft, Emily submitted her essay to a fellow student for peer review. She then revised her work in light of the peer's suggestions and her own further thinking.

On the next page we give the final essay. If after reading the final version you reread Emily's early notes, you'll notice that some of her notes never made it into the final version. But without the notes, the essay probably wouldn't have been as interesting as it is. When Emily made the notes, she wasn't so much putting down her ideas as *finding* ideas through the process of writing.

Emily Andrews

Professor Barnet

English 102

January 15, 2016

Why I Don't Spare "Spare Change"

"Poor but honest." "The deserving poor." I don't know the origin of these quotations, but they always come to mind when I think of "the poor." But I also think of people who, perhaps through alcohol or drugs, have ruined not only their own lives but also the lives of others in order to indulge in their own pleasure. Perhaps alcoholism and drug addiction really are "diseases," as many people say, but my own feeling — based, of course, not on any serious study — is that most alcoholics and drug addicts can be classified with the "undeserving poor." And that is largely why I don't distribute spare change to panhandlers.

But surely among the street people there are also some who can rightly be called "deserving." Deserving of what? My spare change? Or simply the government's assistance? It happens that I have been brought up to believe that it is appropriate to make contributions to charity — let's say a shelter for battered women — but if I give some change to a panhandler, am I making a contribution to charity and thereby helping someone, or, on the contrary, am I perhaps simply encouraging someone not to get help? Or maybe even worse, am I supporting a con artist?

If one believes in the value of private charity, one can give either to needy individuals or to charitable organizations. In giving to a panhandler one may indeed be helping a person who badly needs help, but one cannot be certain that one is giving to a needy individual. In giving to an organization such as the United Way, in contrast, one can feel that one's money is likely to be used wisely. True, confronted by a beggar one may feel that *this* particular unfortunate individual needs help at *this* moment — a cup of coffee or a sandwich — and the need will not be met unless I put my hand in my pocket right now. But I have come to think that the beggars whom I encounter can get along without my spare change, and indeed perhaps they are actually better off for not having money to buy liquor or drugs.

It happens that in my neighborhood I encounter few panhandlers. There is one fellow who is always by the bus stop where I catch the bus to the college, and I never give him anything precisely because he is always there. He is such a regular that, I think, he ought to be able to hold a regular job. Putting him aside, I probably don't encounter more than three or four beggars in a week. (I'm not counting street musicians. These people seem quite able to work for a living. If they see their "work" as playing or singing, let persons who enjoy their performances pay them. I do not consider myself among their audience.) The truth of the matter is that since I meet so few beggars, I could give each one a dollar and hardly feel the loss. At most, I might go without seeing a movie some week. But I know nothing about these people, and it's my impression — admittedly based on almost no evidence — that they simply prefer begging to working. I am not generalizing about street people, and certainly I am not talking about street people in the big urban centers. I am talking only about the people whom I actually encounter.

That's why I usually do not give "spare change," and I don't think I will in the future. These people will get along without me. Someone else will come up with money for their coffee or their liquor, or, at worst, they will just have to do without. I will continue to contribute occasionally to a charitable organization, not simply (I hope) to salve my conscience but because I believe that these organizations actually do good work. But I will not attempt to be a mini-charitable organization, distributing (probably to the unworthy) spare change.

THE ESSAY ANALYZED

Finally, here are a few comments about the essay.

The title is informative, alerting the reader to the topic and the author's position. (By the way, the student told us that in her next-to-last draft, the title was "Is It Right to Spare 'Spare Change'?" This title, unlike the revision, introduces the topic but not the author's position.)

The opening paragraph holds a reader's interest, partly by alluding to the familiar phrase "the deserving poor" and partly by introducing the *un*familiar phrase "the *un*deserving poor." Notice, too, that this opening paragraph ends by clearly asserting the author's thesis. Writers need not always announce their thesis early, but it is usually advisable to do so.

Paragraph 2 begins by voicing what probably is the reader's somewhat uneasy — perhaps even negative — response to the first paragraph. That is, *the writer has a sense of her audience;* she knows how her reader feels, and she takes account of the feeling.

Paragraph 3 clearly sets forth the alternatives. A reader may disagree with the writer's attitude, but the alternatives seem to be stated fairly.

Paragraphs 4 and 5 are more personal than the earlier paragraphs. The writer, more or less having stated what she takes to be the facts, now is entitled to offer a highly personal response to them.

The final paragraph nicely wraps things up by means of the words "spare change," which go back to the title and to the end of the first paragraph. The reader thus experiences a sensation of completeness. The essayist, of course, hasn't solved the problem for all of us for all time, but she presents a thoughtful argument and ends the essay effectively.

Exercise

In a brief essay, state a claim and support it with evidence. Choose an issue in which you are genuinely interested and about which you already know something. You may want to interview a few experts and do some reading, but don't try to write a highly researched paper. Sample topics:

1. Students in laboratory courses should not be required to participate in the dissection of animals.

2. Washington, D.C., should be granted statehood.

3. In wartime, women should be subject to the military draft.

4. The annual Miss America contest is an insult to women.

5. The government should not offer financial support to the arts.

6. The chief fault of the curriculum in high school was . . .

7. No specific courses should be required in colleges or universities.

7

Using Sources

Research is formalized curiosity. It is poking and prying with a purpose.

— ZORA NEALE HURSTON

There is no way of exchanging information that does not involve an act of judgment.

— JACOB BRONOWSKI

For God's sake, stop researching for a while and begin to think.   — WALTER HAMILTON MOBERLY

A problem adequately stated is a problem on its way to being solved.

— R. BUCKMINSTER FULLER

I have yet to see any problem, however complicated, which, when you looked at it in the right way, did not become still more complicated.   — POUL ANDERSON

Why Use Sources?

We have pointed out that one gets ideas by writing. In the exercise of writing a draft, ideas begin to form, and these ideas stimulate further ideas, especially when one questions — when one *thinks about* — what one has written. But of course in writing about complex, serious questions, nobody is expected to invent all the answers. On the contrary, a writer is expected to be familiar with the chief answers already produced by others and to make use of them through selective incorporation and criticism. In short, writers are not expected to reinvent the wheel; rather, they are expected to make good use of it and perhaps round it off a bit or replace a defective spoke. In order to think out your own views in writing, you are expected to do some preliminary research into the views of others.

When you are trying to understand an issue, high-quality sources will inform you of the various approaches others have taken and will help you establish what the facts are. Once you are informed enough to take a position, the sources you present to your readers will inform and persuade them, just as expert witnesses are sometimes brought in to inform and persuade a jury.

Research isn't limited to the world of professors and scientists. In one way or another, everyone does research at some point. If you want to persuade your city council to increase the number of bicycle lanes on city streets, you could bolster your argument with statistics on how much money the city could save if more people rode their bikes to work. If you decide to open your own business, you would do plenty of market research to persuade the bank that you could repay a loan. Sources (whether published information or data you gather yourself through interviews, surveys, or observation) are not only useful for background information; well-chosen and carefully analyzed sources are evidence for your readers that you know what you're talking about and that your interpretation is sound.

In Chapters 5 and 6 we discussed *ethos* as an appeal that establishes credibility with readers. When you do competent research and thereby let your audience see that you have done your homework, it increases your *ethos*; your audience will trust you because they see that you are well informed, offering them not just your opinions but also an awareness of other opinions and of the relevant facts. Conducting thorough research not only helps you to develop your argument, but it also shows respect for your audience.

Research is often misconstrued as the practice of transcribing information. In fact, it's a process of asking questions and gathering information that helps you come to conclusions about an issue. By using the information you find as evidence, you can develop an effective argument. But don't spend too much time searching and then waiting until the last minute to start writing. As you begin your search, write down observations and questions. When you find a useful source, take notes on what you think it means in your own words. This way, you won't find yourself with a pile of printouts and books and no idea what to say about them. What you have to say will flow naturally out of the prewriting you've already done — and that prewriting will help guide your search.

The process of research isn't always straightforward and neat. It involves scanning what other people have said about a topic and seeing what kinds of questions have been raised. As you poke and pry, you will learn more about the issue, and that, in turn, will help you develop a question to focus your efforts. Once you have a central idea — a thesis — you can sharpen your search to seek out the evidence that will make your readers sit up and take notice.

Consider arguments about whether athletes should be permitted to take anabolic steroids, drugs that supposedly build up muscle, restore energy, and enhance aggressiveness. A thoughtful argument on this subject will have to take account of information that the writer can gather only by doing some research.

- Do steroids really have the effects commonly attributed to them?
- Are they dangerous?
- If they are dangerous, how dangerous are they?

After all, competitive sports are inherently dangerous, some of them highly so. Many boxers, mixed martial arts fighters, jockeys, and football players have suffered severe injury, even death, from competing. Does anyone believe that anabolic steroids are more dangerous than the contests themselves? Obviously, again, a respectable argument about steroids will have to show awareness of what is known about them.

Or consider this question:

Why did President Truman order that atomic bombs be dropped on Hiroshima and Nagasaki?

The most obvious answer is to end the war, but some historians believe he had a very different purpose. In their view, Japan's defeat was ensured before the bombs were dropped, and the Japanese were ready to surrender; the bombs were dropped not to save American (or Japanese) lives but to show Russia that the United States would not be pushed around. Scholars who hold this view, such as Gar Alperovitz in *Atomic Diplomacy* (1965), argue that Japanese civilians in Hiroshima and Nagasaki were incinerated not to save the lives of American soldiers who otherwise would have died in an invasion of Japan but to teach Stalin a lesson. Dropping the bombs, it is argued, marked not the end of the Pacific War but the beginning of the cold war.

One must ask: What evidence supports this argument or claim or thesis, which assumes that Truman could not have thought the bomb was needed to defeat the Japanese because the Japanese knew they were defeated and would soon surrender without a hard-fought defense that would cost hundreds of thousands of lives? What about the momentum that had built up to use the bomb? After all, years of effort and $2 billion had been expended to produce a weapon with the intention of using it to end the war against Germany. But Germany had been defeated without the use of the bomb. Meanwhile, the war in the Pacific continued unabated. If the argument we are considering is correct, all this background counted for little or nothing in Truman's decision, a decision purely diplomatic and coolly indifferent to human life. The task for the writer is to evaluate the evidence available and then to argue for or against the view that Truman's purpose in dropping the bomb was to impress the Soviet government.

A student writing on the topic will certainly want to consult the chief books on the subject (Alperovitz's, cited above, Martin Sherwin's *A World Destroyed* [1975], and John Toland's *The Rising Sun* [1970]) and perhaps reviews of them, especially the reviews in journals devoted to political science. (Reading a searching review of a serious scholarly book is a good way to identify quickly some of the book's main contributions and controversial claims.) Truman's letters and statements, and books and articles about Truman, are also clearly relevant, and doubtless important articles are to be found in recent issues of scholarly journals and electronic sources. In fact, even an essay on such a topic as whether Truman was morally justified in using the atomic bomb for *any* purpose will be a stronger essay if it is well informed about such matters as the estimated loss of life that an invasion would have cost, the international rules governing weapons, and Truman's own statements about the issue.

How does one go about finding the material needed to write a well-informed argument? We will provide help, but first we want to offer a few words about choosing a topic.

Choosing A Topic

We will be brief. If a topic is not assigned, choose one that

- interests you, and
- can be researched with reasonable thoroughness in the allotted time.

Topics such as censorship, the environment, and sexual harassment obviously impinge on our lives, and it may well be that one such topic is of especial interest to you. But the scope of these topics makes researching them potentially overwhelming. Type the word *censorship* into an **Internet** search engine, and you will be referred to millions of information sources.

This brings us to our second point — a manageable topic. Any of the previous topics would need to be narrowed substantially before you could begin searching in earnest. Similarly, a topic such as the causes of World War II can hardly be mastered in a few weeks or argued in a ten-page paper. It is simply too big.

You can, however, write a solid paper analyzing, evaluating, and arguing for or against General Eisenhower's views on atomic warfare. What were they, and when did he hold them? (In his books written in 1948 and 1963 Eisenhower says that he opposed the use of the bomb before Hiroshima and that he argued with Secretary of War Henry Stimson against dropping it, but what evidence supports these claims? Was Eisenhower attempting to rewrite history in his books?) Eisenhower's own writings and books and other information sources on Eisenhower will, of course, be the major sources for a paper on this topic, but you will also want to look at books and articles about Stimson and at publications that contain information about the views of other generals, so that, for instance, you can compare Eisenhower's view with Marshall's or MacArthur's.

Spend a little time exploring a topic to see if it will be interesting and manageable by taking one or more of these approaches:

- **Do a Web search on the topic.** Though you may not use any of the sites that turn up, you can quickly put your finger on the pulse of popular approaches to the issue by scanning the first page or two of results to see what issues are getting the most attention.
- **Plug the topic into one of the library's article databases.** Again, just by scanning titles you can get a sense of what questions are being raised.
- **Browse the library shelves where books on the topic are kept.** A quick check of the tables of contents of recently published books may give you ideas of how to narrow the topic.
- **Ask a librarian to show you where specialized reference books on your topic are found.** Instead of general encyclopedias, try sources like these:

CQ Researcher

Encyclopedia of Applied Ethics

Encyclopedia of Bioethics

Encyclopedia of Crime and Justice

Encyclopedia of Science, Technology, and Ethics

- **Talk to an expert.** Members of the faculty who specialize in the area of your topic might be able to spell out some of the most significant controversies around a topic and may point you toward key sources.

Finding Material

What strategy you use for finding good sources will depend on your topic. Researching a current issue in politics or popular culture may involve reading recent newspaper articles, scanning information on government Web sites, and locating current statistics. Other topics may be best tackled by seeking out books and scholarly journal articles that are less timely but more in-depth and analytical. You may want to supplement library and Web sources with your own fieldwork by conducting surveys or interviews.

Critical thinking is crucial to every step of the research process. Whatever strategy you use, remember that you will want to find material that is authoritative, represents a balanced approach to the issues, and is persuasive. As you choose your sources, bear in mind they will be serving as your "expert witnesses" as you make a case to your audience. Their quality and credibility are crucial to your argument.

If you find what seems to be an excellent source, look at some of the sources that this author repeatedly cites.

FINDING QUALITY INFORMATION ONLINE

The Web is a valuable source of information for many topics and less helpful for others. In general, if you're looking for information on public policy, popular culture, current events, legal affairs, or any subject of interest to agencies of the federal or state government, the Web is likely to have useful material. If you're looking for literary criticism or scholarly analysis of historical or social issues, you will be better off using library databases, described later in this chapter.

To make good use of the Web, try these strategies:

- Use the most specific terms possible when using a general search engine; put phrases in quotes.
- Use the advanced search option to limit a search to a domain (e.g., *.gov* for government sites) or by date (such as Web sites updated in the past week or month).
- If you're not sure which sites might be good ones for research, try starting with one of the selective directories listed below instead of a general search engine.

- Consider which government agencies and organizations might be interested in your topic, and go directly to their Web sites.

- Follow "about" links to see who is behind a Web site and why they put the information on the Web. If there is no "about" link, delete everything after the first slash in the URL to go to the parent site to see if it provides information.

- Use clues in URLs to see where sites originate. For example, URLs containing *.k12* are hosted at elementary and secondary schools, so they may be intended for a young audience; those ending in *.gov* are government agencies, so they tend to provide official information.

- Always bear in mind that the sources you choose must be persuasive to your audience. Avoid sites that may be dismissed as unreliable or biased.

Some useful Web sites include the following:

Selective Web Site Directories
 ipl2 www.ipl.org
 Open Directory Project www.dmoz.org

Current News Sources
 Google News news.google.com
 Reuters www.reuters.com
 WikiNews en.wikinews.org/wiki/Main_Page
 World Newspapers www.world-newspapers.com
 World Press www.worldpress.org

Digital Primary Sources
 American Memory memory.loc.gov
 American Rhetoric www.americanrhetoric.com
 Avalon Project avalon.law.yale.edu/default.asp
 National Archives www.archives.gov
 Smithsonian Source www.smithsoniansource.org

Government Information
 GPO Access www.gpoaccess.gov
 Thomas (federal legislation) thomas.loc.gov
 U.S. Department of Labor www.dol.gov

Scholarly or Scientific Information
 CiteSeer citeseerx.ist.psu.edu/index
 Google Scholar scholar.google.com
 Microsoft Academic academic.microsoft.com/
 Taylor and Francis Open Access Journals www.tandfonline.com/page/openaccess

Statistical Information
 American FactFinder factfinder2.census.gov
 Fedstats www.fedstats.gov

Pew Global Attitudes Project pewglobal.org
U.S. Census Bureau www.census.gov
U.S. Data and Statistics www.usa.gov/statistics
United Nations Statistics Division unstats.un.org
U.S. Bureau of Labor Statistics Guide to U.S. and World Statistical Information
    http://www.bls.gov/bls/other.htm

A WORD ABOUT WIKIPEDIA   Links to Wikipedia (http://www.wikipedia.org) often rise to the top of Web search results. This vast and decentralized site provides over a million articles on a wide variety of topics. However, anyone can contribute to the online encyclopedia, so the accuracy of articles varies, and in some cases, the coverage of a controversial issue is one-sided or disputed. Even when the articles are accurate, they provide only basic information. Wikipedia's founder, Jimmy Wales, cautions students against using it as a source, except for obtaining general background knowledge: "You're in college; don't cite the encyclopedia."[1] Still, Wikipedia often provides valuable bibliographies that will help you to get going.

FINDING ARTICLES USING LIBRARY DATABASES

Your library has a wide range of general and specialized databases available through its Web site. Some databases provide references to articles (and perhaps abstracts or summaries) or may provide direct links to the entire text of articles. General and interdisciplinary databases include Academic Search Premier (produced by the EBSCOhost company) and Expanded Academic Index (from InfoTrac).

More specialized databases include PsycINFO (for psychology research) and ERIC (focused on topics in education). Others, such as JSTOR, are full-text digital archives of scholarly journals. You will likely have access to newspaper articles through LexisNexis or Proquest Newsstand, particularly useful for articles that are not available for free on the Web. Look at your library's Web site to see what your options are, or stop by the reference desk for a quick personalized tutorial.

When using databases, first think through your topic using the listing and diagramming techniques described on pages 223–25. List synonyms for your key search terms. As you search, look at words used in titles and descriptors for alternative ideas and make use of the "advanced search" option so that you can easily combine multiple terms. Rarely will you find exactly what you're looking for right away. Try different search terms and different ways to narrow your topic.

Most databases have an advanced search option that offers forms for combining multiple terms. In Figure 7.1, a search on "anabolic steroids" retrieved far too many articles. In this advanced search, three concepts are being combined in a search: anabolic steroids, legal aspects

---

[1]"Wikipedia Founder Discourages Academic Use of His Creation." *Chronicle of Higher Education: The Wired Campus,* 12 June 2006. chronicle.com/wiredcampus/article/1328/wikipedia-founder-discourages-academic-use-of-his-creation

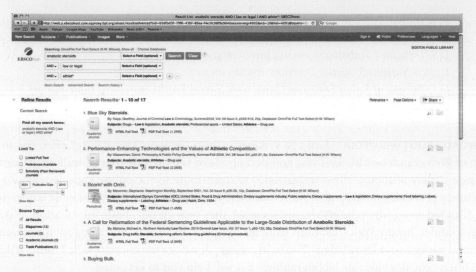

Figure 7.1 An Advanced Web Search

of their use, and use of them by athletes. Related terms are combined with the word "or": *law* or *legal*. The last letters of a word have been replaced with an asterisk so that any ending will be included in the search. *Athlet** will search for *athlete, athletes,* or *athletics*. Options on both sides of the list of articles retrieved offer opportunities to refine a search by date of publication or to restrict the results to only academic journals, magazines, or newspapers.

As with a Web search, you'll need to make critical choices about which articles are worth pursuing. In this example, the first article may not be useful because it concerns German law. The second and third look fairly current and potentially useful. Only the third has a full text link, but the others may be available in another database. Many libraries have a program that will check other databases for you at the push of a button; in this case it's indicated by the "Find full text" button.

As you choose sources, keep track of them by selecting them. Then you can print off, save, or e-mail yourself the references you have selected. You may also have an option to export references to a citation management program such as RefWorks or EndNote. These programs allow you to create your own personal database of sources in which you can store your references and take notes. Later, when you're ready to create a bibliography, these programs will automatically format your references in MLA, APA, or another style. Ask a librarian if one of these programs is available to students on your campus.

LOCATING BOOKS

The books that your library owns can be found through its online catalog. Typically, you can search by author or title or, if you don't have a specific book in mind, by keyword or subject. As with databases, think about different search terms to use, keeping an eye out for subject headings used for books that appear relevant. Take advantage of an "advanced search" option. You may, for example, be able to limit a search to books on a particular topic in English published within recent years. In addition to books, the catalog will also list DVDs, audio and video recordings, and other formats.

Unlike articles, books tend to cover broad topics, so be prepared to broaden your search terms. It may be that a book has a chapter or ten pages that are precisely what you need, but the catalog typically doesn't index the contents of books in detail. Think instead of what kind of book might contain the information you need.

Once you've found some promising books in the catalog, note down the call numbers, find them on the shelves, and then browse. Since books on the same topic are shelved together, you can quickly see what additional books are available by scanning the shelves. As you browse, be sure to look for books that have been published recently enough for your purposes. You do not have to read a book cover-to-cover to use it in your research. Instead, skim the introduction to see if it will be useful, then use its table of contents and index to pinpoint the sections of the book that are the most relevant.

If you are searching for a very specific name or phrase, you might try typing it into Google Book Search (books.google.com), which searches the contents of over seven million scanned books. Though it tends to retrieve too many results for most topics, and you may only be able to see a snippet of content, it can help you locate a particular quote or identify which books might include an unusual name or phrase. There is a "find in a library" link that will help you determine whether the books are available in your library.

Interviewing Peers and Local Authorities

You ought to try to consult experts—for instance, members of the faculty or other local authorities on art, business, law, and so forth. You can also consult interested laypersons. Remember, however, that experts have their biases and that "ordinary" people may have knowledge that experts lack. When interviewing experts, keep in mind Picasso's comment: "You mustn't always believe what I say. Questions tempt you to tell lies, particularly when there is no answer."

If you are interviewing your peers, you will probably want to make an effort to get a representative sample. Of course, even within a group not all members share a single view—many African Americans favor affirmative action, but not all do; some lawmakers support capital punishment, but again, many do not. Make an effort to talk to a range of people who might offer varied opinions. You may learn some unexpected things.

Here we will concentrate, however, on interviews with experts.

1. Finding subjects for interviews   If you are looking for expert opinions, you may want to start with a faculty member on your campus. You may already know the instructor, or you may have to scan the catalog to see who teaches courses relevant to your topic. Department secretaries and college Web sites are good sources of information about the special interests of the faculty and also about lecturers who will be visiting the campus.

2. *Doing preliminary homework* (a) In requesting the interview, make evident your interest in the topic and in the person. (If you know something about the person, you'll be able to indicate why you are asking.) (b) Request the interview, preferably in writing, a week in advance, and ask for ample time — probably half an hour to an hour. Indicate whether the material will be confidential, and (if you want to use a recorder) ask if you may record the interview. (c) If the person accepts the invitation, ask if he or she recommends any preliminary reading, and establish a time and a suitable place, preferably not the cafeteria during lunchtime.

3. *Preparing thoroughly* (a) If your interviewee recommended any reading or has written on the topic, read the material. (b) Tentatively formulate some questions, keeping in mind that (unless you are simply gathering material for a survey of opinions) you want more than yes or no answers. Questions beginning with *Why* and *How* will usually require the interviewee to go beyond yes and no.

Even if your subject has consented to let you bring a recorder, be prepared to take notes on points that strike you as especially significant; without written notes, you will have nothing if the recorder has malfunctioned. Further, by taking occasional notes you will give the interviewee some time to think and perhaps to rephrase or to amplify a remark.

4. *Conducting the interview* (a) Begin by engaging in brief conversation, without taking notes. If the interviewee has agreed to let you use a recorder, settle on the place where you will put it. (b) Come prepared with an opening question or two, but as the interview proceeds, don't hesitate to ask questions that you hadn't anticipated asking. (c) Near the end (you and your subject have probably agreed on the length of the interview) ask the subject if he or she wishes to add anything, perhaps by way of clarifying some earlier comment. (d) Conclude by thanking the interviewee and by offering to provide a copy of the final version of your paper.

5. *Writing up the interview* (a) As soon as possible — certainly, within twenty-four hours after the interview — review your notes and clarify them. At this stage, you can still remember the meaning of your abbreviated notes and shorthand devices (maybe you've been using *n* to stand for *nurses* in clinics where abortions are performed), but if you wait even a whole day you may be puzzled by your own notes. If you have recorded the interview, you may want to transcribe all of it — the laboriousness of this task is one good reason why many interviewers don't use recorders — and you may then want to scan the whole and mark the parts that now strike you as especially significant. If you have taken notes by hand, type them up, along with your own observations (e.g., "Jones was very tentative on this matter, but she said she was inclined to believe that . . ."). (b) Be especially careful to indicate which words are direct quotations. If in doubt, check with the interviewee.

Evaluating Your Sources

Each step of the way, you will be making choices about your sources. As your research proceeds, from selecting promising items in a database search to browsing the book collection, you will want to use the techniques for previewing and skimming detailed on pages 35–37 in order to make your first selection. Ask yourself some basic questions:

- Is this source relevant?
- Is it current enough?
- Does the title and/or abstract suggest it will address an important aspect of my topic?
- Am I choosing sources that represent a range of ideas, not simply ones that support my opinion?
- Do I have a reason to believe that these sources are trustworthy?

Once you have collected a number of likely sources, you will want to do further filtering. Examine each one with these questions in mind:

- *Is this source credible? Does it include information about the author and his or her credentials that can help me decide whether to rely on it?* In the case of books, you might check a database for book reviews for a second opinion. In the case of Web sites, find out where the site came from and why it has been posted online. Don't use a Web source if you can't determine its authorship or purpose.

- *Will my audience find this source credible and persuasive?* Some publishers are more selective about which books they publish than others. University presses, for instance, have several experts read and comment on manuscripts before they decide which to publish. A story about U.S. politics from the *Washington Post*, whose writers conduct firsthand reporting in the nation's capital, carries more clout than a story from a small-circulation newspaper that is drawing its information from a wire service. A scholarly source may be more impressive than a magazine article.

- *Am I using the best evidence available?* Quoting directly from a government report may be more effective than quoting a news story that summarizes the report. Finding evidence that supports your claims in a president's speeches or letters is more persuasive than drawing your conclusions from a page or two of a history textbook.

- *Am I being fair to all sides?* Make sure you are prepared to address alternate perspectives, even if you ultimately take a position. Avoid sources that clearly promote an agenda in favor of ones that your audience will consider balanced and reliable.

- *Can I corroborate my key claims in more than one source?* Compare your sources to ensure that you aren't relying on facts that can't be confirmed. If you're having trouble confirming a source, check with a librarian.

- *Do I really need this source?* It's tempting to use all the books and articles you have found, but if two sources say essentially the same thing, choose the one that is likely to carry the most weight with your audience.

The information you will look for as you evaluate a Web source is often the same as what you need to record in a citation. You can streamline the process of creating a list of works cited by identifying these elements as you evaluate a source.

In Figure 7.2, the URL includes the ending *.gov* — meaning it is a government Web site, an official document that has been vetted. There is an "about" link that will explain the government agency's mission. The date is found above the title of the page: "Revised March 2016." This appears to be a high-quality source of basic information on the issue.

The information you need to cite this report is also on the page; make sure you keep track of where you found the source and when, since Web sites can change. One way to do this is by creating an account at a social bookmarking site such as Delicious (delicious.com) or Diigo (diigo.com) where you can store and annotate Web sites.

Figure 7.2   A Page from a Government Web Site

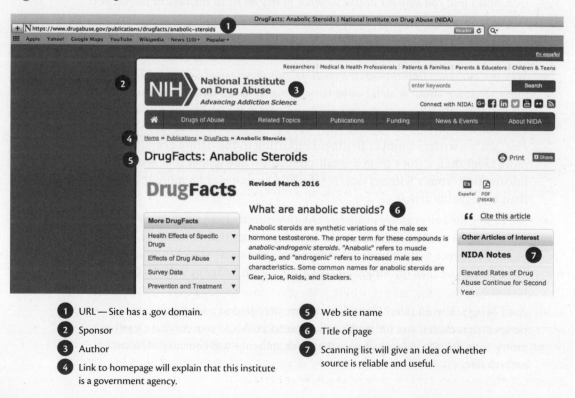

1 URL — Site has a .gov domain.

2 Sponsor

3 Author

4 Link to homepage will explain that this institute is a government agency.

5 Web site name

6 Title of page

7 Scanning list will give an idea of whether source is reliable and useful.

Figure 7.3 A Page from a Commercial Web Site

1. This is a .com (commercial) site.
2. The additional links provided in the user menu are suspect.
3. The information on the site promotes performance enhancement, not health.
4. Ads promote steroid use for cash prizes.
5. Steroids are for sale through the site.

Figure 7.3 shows how the information on a Web page might lead you to reject it as a source. Clearly, though this site purports to provide educational information, its primary purpose is to sell products. The graphics and text on the page emphasize the supposed benefits of these performance-enhancing drugs, promoting their use. The focus on performance enhancement and marketing rather than health sends up a red flag.

Taking Notes

When it comes to taking notes, all researchers have their own habits that they swear by, and they can't imagine any other way of working. We still prefer to take notes on four-by-six-inch index cards, while others use a notebook or a computer for note taking. If you use a citation management program, such as RefWorks or EndNote, you can store your personal notes and commentary with the citations you have saved. Using the program's search function, you can easily pull together related notes and citations, or you can create project folders for your references so that you can easily review what you've collected.

Whatever method you use, the following techniques should help you maintain consistency and keep organized during the research process:

A CHECKLIST FOR EVALUATING PRINT SOURCES

For Books:

- ☐ Is the book recent? If not, is the information I will be using from it likely or unlikely to change over time?

- ☐ What are the author's credentials?

- ☐ Is the book titled toward entertainment, or is it in-depth and even-handed?

- ☐ Is the book broad enough in its focus and written in a style I can understand?

- ☐ Does the book relate directly to my tentative thesis, or is it of only tangential interest?

- ☐ Do the arguments in the book seem sound, based on what I have learned about skillful critical reading and writing?

For Articles from Periodicals:

- ☐ Is the periodical recent?

- ☐ Is the author's name given? Does he or she seem a credible source?

- ☐ Does the article treat the topic superficially or in-depth? Does it take sides, or does it offer enough context so that I can make up my own mind?

- ☐ How directly does the article speak to my topic and tentative thesis?

- ☐ If the article is from a scholarly journal, am I sure I understand it?

1. If you use a notebook or cards, write in ink (pencil gets smudgy), and write on only one side of the card or paper. (Notes on the backs of cards tend to get lost, and writing on the back of paper will prevent you from later cutting up and rearranging your notes.) Consider using an online tool to keep up with your notes and ideas, for instance, a Google Doc, private blog, or wiki.

2. Summarize, for the most part, rather than quote at length.

3. Quote only passages in which the writing is especially effective or passages that are in some way crucial. These will be easy to access and use if kept in an online venue.

4. Make sure that all quotations are exact. Enclose quoted words within quotation marks, indicate omissions by ellipses (three spaced periods: . . .), and enclose within square brackets ([]) any insertions or other additions you make.

5. *Never* copy a passage, changing an occasional word. *Either* copy it word for word, with punctuation intact, and enclose it within quotation marks, *or* summarize it drastically. If you copy a passage but change a word here and there, you may later make the mistake of using your note verbatim in your essay, and you will be guilty of plagiarism.

6. Give the page number of your source, whether you summarize or quote. If a quotation you have copied runs in the original from the bottom of page 210 to the top of page 211, in your notes put a diagonal line (/) after the last word on page 210, so that later, if in your paper you quote only the material from page 210, you will know that you must cite 210 and not 210–11.

7. Indicate the source. The author's last name is enough if you have consulted only one work by the author; but if you consult more than one work by an author, you need further identification, such as both the author's name and a short title.

8. Add your own comments about the substance of what you are recording. Such comments as "but contrast with Sherwin" or "seems illogical" or "evidence?" will ensure that you are thinking as well as writing and will be of value when you come to transform your notes into a draft. Be sure, however, to enclose such notes within double diagonals (//), or to mark them in some other way, so that later you will know they are yours and not your source's. If you use a computer for note taking, you may wish to write your comments in italics or in a different font.

9. In a separate computer file or notebook page or on separate index cards, write a bibliographic entry for each source. The information in each entry will vary, depending on whether the source is a book, a periodical, an electronic document, and so forth. The kind of information (e.g., author and title) needed for each type of source can be found in the sections on MLA Format: The List of Works Cited (p. 293) or APA Format: The List of References (p. 304).

A Note on Plagiarizing, Paraphrasing, and Using Common Knowledge

Plagiarism is the unacknowledged use of someone else's work. The word comes from a Latin word for "kidnapping," and plagiarism is indeed the stealing of something engendered by someone else. We won't deliver a sermon on the dishonesty (and folly) of

A CHECKLIST FOR EVALUATING ELECTRONIC SOURCES

An enormous amount of valuable material is available online — but so is an enormous amount of junk. True, there is also plenty of junk in books and journals, but most printed material has been subjected to a review process: Book publishers and editors of journals send manuscripts to specialized readers who evaluate them and recommend whether the material should or should not be published. Publishing online is quite different. Anyone can publish online with no review process: All that is needed is sufficient access to the Internet. Ask yourself:

❏ What person or organization produced the site (a commercial entity, a nonprofit entity, a student, an expert)? Check the electronic address to get a clue about the authorship. If there is a link to the author's homepage, check it out to learn about the author. Does the author have an affiliation with a respectable institution?

❏ What is the site's purpose? Is the site in effect an infomercial, or is it an attempt to contribute to a thoughtful discussion?

❏ Are the sources of information indicated and verifiable? If possible, check the sources.

❏ Is the site authoritative enough to use? (If it seems to contain review materials or class handouts, you probably don't want to take it too seriously.)

❏ When was the page made available? Is it out of date?

plagiarism; we intend only to help you understand exactly what plagiarism is. The first thing to say is that plagiarism is not limited to the unacknowledged quotation of words.

A *paraphrase* is a sort of word-by-word or phrase-by-phrase translation of the author's language into your own language. Unlike a summary, then, a paraphrase is approximately as long as the original. Why would anyone paraphrase something? There are two good reasons:

- You may, as a reader, want to paraphrase a passage in order to make certain that you are thinking carefully about each word in the original.
- You may, as a writer, want to paraphrase a difficult passage in order to help your reader.

Paraphrase thus has its uses, but writers often use it unnecessarily, and students who overuse it may find themselves crossing the border into plagiarism. True, if you paraphrase you are using your own words, but

- you are also using someone else's ideas, and, equally important,
- you are using this other person's sequence of thoughts.

Even if you change every third word in your source, you are plagiarizing.

Here is an example of this sort of plagiarism, based on the previous sentence:

Even if you alter every second or third word that your source gives, you still are plagiarizing.

Further, even if the writer of this paraphrase had cited a source after the paraphrase, he or she would still have been guilty of plagiarism. How, you may ask, can a writer who cites a source be guilty of plagiarism? Easy. Readers assume that only the gist of the idea is the source's and that the development of the idea — the way it is set forth — is the present writer's work. A paraphrase that runs to several sentences is in no significant way the writer's work: The writer is borrowing not only the idea but the shape of the presentation, the sentence structure. What the writer needs to do is to write something like this:

Changing an occasional word does not free the writer from the obligation to cite a source.

And the source would still need to be cited, if the central idea were not a commonplace one.

We cannot overemphasize the point that even if you cite a source for your paraphrase you are nevertheless plagiarizing — unless you clearly indicate that the entire passage is a paraphrase of the source.

You are plagiarizing if, without giving credit, you use someone else's ideas — even if you put these ideas entirely into your own words. When you use another's ideas, you must indicate your indebtedness by saying something like "Alperovitz points out that . . ." or "Secretary of War Stimson, as Martin Sherwin notes, never expressed himself on this point." Alperovitz and Sherwin pointed out something that you had not thought of, and so you must give them credit if you want to use their findings.

Again, even if after a paraphrase you cite your source, you are plagiarizing. A reader assumes that the citation refers to information or an opinion, *not* to the presentation or development of the idea; and of course, in a paraphrase you are not presenting or developing the material in your own way.

Now consider this question: *Why* paraphrase? Often there is no good answer. Since a paraphrase is as long as the original, you may as well quote the original, if you think that a passage of that length is worth quoting. Probably it is *not* worth quoting in full; probably you should *not* paraphrase but rather should drastically *summarize* most of it, and perhaps quote a particularly effective phrase or two. As we explained on pages 47–52, the chief reason to paraphrase a passage is to clarify it — that is, to ensure that you and your readers understand a passage that — perhaps because it is badly written — is obscure.

Generally, what you should do is

- Take the idea and put it entirely into your own words, perhaps reducing a paragraph of a hundred words to a sentence of ten words, but you must still give credit for the idea.

- If you believe that the original hundred words are so perfectly put that they cannot be transformed without great loss, you'll have to quote them in full and cite your source. You may in this case want to tell the reader *why* you are quoting at such great length.

In short, chiefly you will quote or you will summarize, and only rarely will you paraphrase, but in all cases you will cite your source. There is no point in paraphrasing an author's hundred words into a hundred of your own. Either quote or summarize, but cite the source.

Keep in mind, too, that almost all generalizations about human nature, no matter how common and familiar (e.g., "males are innately more aggressive than females") are not indisputable facts; they are at best hypotheses on which people differ and therefore should either not

A CHECKLIST FOR AVOIDING PLAGIARISM

- ☐ In my notes did I *always* put quoted material within quotation marks?

- ☐ In my notes did I summarize *in my own words* and give credit to the source for the idea?

- ☐ In my notes did I avoid paraphrasing, that is, did I avoid copying, keeping the structure of the source's sentences but using some of my own words? (Paraphrases of this sort, even with a footnote citing the source, are *not* acceptable, since the reader incorrectly assumes that the writing is essentially yours.)

- ☐ If in my paper I set forth a borrowed idea, do I give credit, even though the words and the structure of the sentences are entirely my own?

- ☐ If in my paper I quote directly, do I put the words within quotation marks and cite the source?

- ☐ Do I *not* cite material that can be considered common knowledge (material that can be found in numerous reference works, such as the date of a public figure's birth or the population of San Francisco or the fact that *Hamlet* is regarded as a great tragedy)?

- ☐ If I have the slightest doubt about whether I should or should not cite a source, have I taken the safe course and cited the source?

be asserted at all or should be supported by some cited source or authority. Similarly, because nearly all statistics (whether on the intelligence of criminals or the accuracy of lie detectors) are the result of some particular research and may well have been superseded or challenged by other investigators, it is advisable to cite a source for any statistics you use unless you are convinced they are indisputable, such as the number of registered voters in Memphis in 1988.

In contrast, there is something called **common knowledge,** and the sources for such information need not be cited. The term does not, however, mean exactly what it seems to. It is common knowledge, of course, that Ronald Reagan was an American president (so you don't cite a source when you make that statement), and under the conventional interpretation of this doctrine, it is also common knowledge that he was born in 1911. In fact, of course, few people other than Reagan's relatives know this date. Still, information that can be found in many places and that is indisputable belongs to all of us; therefore, a writer need not cite her source when she says that Reagan was born in 1911. Probably she checked a dictionary or an encyclopedia for the date, but the source doesn't matter. Dozens of sources will give exactly the same information, and in fact, no reader wants to be bothered with a citation on such a point.

Some students have a little trouble developing a sense of what is and what is not common knowledge. Although, as we have just said, readers don't want to hear about the sources for information that is indisputable and can be documented in many places, if you are in doubt about whether to cite a source, cite it. Better risk boring the reader a bit than risk being accused of plagiarism.

Your college or your class instructor probably has issued a statement concerning plagiarism. If there is such a statement, be sure to read it carefully.

Compiling an Annotated Bibliography

When several sources have been identified and gathered, many researchers prepare an annotated bibliography. This is a list providing all relevant bibliographic information (just as it will appear in your Works Cited list or References list) as well as a brief descriptive and evaluative summary of each source — perhaps one to three sentences. Your instructor may ask you to provide an annotated bibliography for your research project.

An annotated bibliography serves four main purposes:

- First, constructing such a document helps you to master the material contained in any given source. To find the heart of the argument presented in an article or book, to phrase it briefly, and to comment on it, you must understand it fully.

- Second, creating an annotated bibliography helps you to think about how each portion of your research fits into the whole of your project, how you will use it, and how it relates to your topic and thesis.

- Third, an annotated bibliography helps your readers: They can quickly see which items may be especially helpful in their own research.

- Fourth, in constructing an annotated bibliography at this early stage, you will get some hands-on practice at bibliographic format, thereby easing the job of creating your final bibliography (the Works Cited list or References list for your paper).

Following are two examples of entries for an annotated bibliography in MLA (Modern Language Association) format for a project on the effect of violence in the media. The first is for a book, the second for an article from a periodical. Notice that each entry does two things:

- It begins with a bibliographic entry — author (last name first), title, and so forth.

- Then it provides information about the content of the work under consideration, suggesting how each may be of use to the final research paper.

Clover, Carol J. *Men, Women, and Chain Saws: Gender in the Modern Horror Film*. Princeton UP, 1992. The author focuses on Hollywood horror movies of the 1970s and 1980s. She studies representations of women and girls in these movies and the responses of male viewers to female characters, suggesting that this relationship is more complex and less exploitative than the common wisdom claims.

Winerip, Michael. "Looking for an Eleven O'Clock Fix." *New York Times Magazine,* 11 Jan. 1998, pp. 30–40. The article focuses on the rising levels of violence on local television news and highlights a station in Orlando, Florida, that tried to reduce its depictions of violence and lost viewers as a result. Winerip suggests that people only claim to be against media violence, while their actions prove otherwise.

As you construct your annotated bibliography, consider posting your Word document in Google Drive for easy access and sharing.

CITATION GENERATORS There are many citation generators available online. These generators allow you to enter the information about your source, and, with a click, they will create Works Cited entries in APA or MLA format. But just as you cannot trust spell- and grammar-checkers in Microsoft Word, you cannot trust these generators. You can use them to cite works, but if you do, be sure to double-check what they produce before submitting your essay. Always remember that responsible writers take care to cite their sources properly and that failure to do so puts you at risk for accusations of plagiarism.

Writing the Paper

ORGANIZING YOUR NOTES

If you have read thoughtfully, taken careful (and, again, thoughtful) notes on your reading, and then (yet again) thought about these notes, you are well on the way to writing a good paper. You have, in fact, already written some of it in your notes. By now you should clearly have in mind the thesis you intend to argue. But you still have to organize the material, and, doubtless, even as you set about organizing it, you will find points that will require you to do some additional research and much additional thinking.

Divide your notes into clusters, each devoted to one theme or point (e.g., one cluster on the extent of use of steroids, another on evidence that steroids are harmful, yet another on arguments that even if harmful they should be permitted). If your notes are in a computer file, rearrange them into appropriate clusters. If you use index cards, simply sort them into packets. If you take notes in a notebook, either mark each note with a number or name indicating the cluster to which it belongs, or cut the notes apart and arrange them as you would cards. Put aside all notes that — however interesting — you now see are irrelevant to your paper.

Next, arrange the clusters or packets into a tentative sequence. In effect, you are preparing a **working outline.** At its simplest, say, you will give three arguments on behalf of *X* and then three counterarguments. (Or you might decide that it's better to alternate material from the two sets of three clusters each, following each argument with an objection. At this stage, you can't be sure of the organization you will finally use, but you can make a tentative decision.)

THE FIRST DRAFT

Draft the essay, without worrying much about an elegant opening paragraph. Just write some sort of adequate opening that states the topic and your thesis. When you revise the whole later, you can put some effort into developing an effective opening. (Most experienced writers find that the opening paragraph in the final version is almost the last thing they write.)

If your notes are on cards or notebook paper, carefully copy into the draft all quotations that you plan to use. If your notes are in a computer, you may simply cut and paste them from one file to another. Do keep in mind, however, that rewriting or retyping quotations will make you think carefully about them and may result in a more focused and thoughtful paper. (In the next section of this chapter we will talk briefly about leading into quotations and about the form of quotations.) Be sure to include citations in your drafts so that if you must check a reference later it will be easy to do so.

LATER DRAFTS

Give the draft, and yourself, a rest — perhaps for a day or two — and then go back to it. Read it over, make necessary revisions, and then **outline** it. That is, on a sheet of paper chart the organization and development, perhaps by jotting down a sentence summarizing each paragraph or each group of closely related paragraphs. Your outline or map may now show you that the paper obviously suffers from poor organization. For instance, it may reveal that you neglected to respond to one argument or that you needlessly treated one point in two places. It may also help you to see that if you gave three arguments and then three counterarguments, you probably should instead have followed each argument with its rebuttal. However, if you alternated arguments and objections, it may now seem better to use two main groups — all the arguments and then all the criticisms.

No one formula is always right. Much will depend on the complexity of the material. If the arguments are highly complex, it is better to respond to them one by one than to expect a reader to hold three complex arguments in mind before you get around to responding. If, however, the arguments can be stated briefly and clearly, it is effective to state all three and then to go on to the responses. If you write on a computer, you will find it easy, even fun, to move passages of text around. Even so, you will probably want to print out a hard copy from time to time to review the structure of your paper. Allow enough time to produce several drafts.

A FEW MORE WORDS ABOUT ORGANIZATION

There is a difference between

- a paper that *has* an organization, and
- a paper that helpfully lets the reader know what the organization is.

You should write papers of the second sort, but (there is always a "but") take care not to belabor the obvious. Inexperienced writers sometimes either hide the organization so thoroughly that a reader cannot find it or they so ploddingly lay out the structure ("Eighth, I will show . . .") that the reader becomes impatient. Yet it is better to be overly explicit than to be obscure.

The ideal, of course, is the middle route. Make the overall strategy of your organization evident by occasional explicit signs at the beginning of a paragraph ("We have seen . . . ," "It is time to consider the objections . . . ," "By far the most important . . ."); elsewhere make certain that the implicit structure is evident to the reader. When rereading your draft, if you try to imagine that you are one of your classmates, you will probably be able to sense exactly where explicit signs are needed and where they are not needed. Better still, exchange drafts with a classmate in order to exchange (tactful) advice.

Another strategy for organizing an essay is to determine early on whether your approach uses **classification** or **division**. These two terms refer to the development of essays and to the function of individual paragraphs, so they may be used profitably together. **Classification** normally suggests surveying many items or aspects of an issue. You might be examining the various roles played by celebrities in international relations, or looking at many types of GMOs, or analyzing a range of characters in a novel. Classification suggests a collection of numerous things within the purview of your thesis. **Division**, in contrast, suggests looking at one thing very closely, and dividing it into parts — perhaps as a key example of your broader thesis. If you are using division, you might be examining the role of one celebrity in international relations (e.g., Bono), or looking at one particular GMO, or analyzing the role of one character within a novel. We can illustrate the difference in a hypothetical essay about the dangers of steroid use. If you're using classification, you might be looking at many different types of drugs and their uses in various sports by various athletes. You might be further pointing out the many effects of these substances and the controversies that surround each to support an overall thesis about the issue. If you're using division, you might be emphasizing a key drug, a key athlete, or a key case study to understand thoroughly its specific effects as representative of the whole.

Classification may be thought of as utilizing many *parts* to understand a *whole*. Division may be thought of as using a *whole* to understand many *parts*.

CHOOSING A TENTATIVE TITLE

By now a couple of tentative titles for your essay should have crossed your mind. If possible, choose a title that is both interesting and informative. Consider these three titles:

> Are Steroids Harmful?
>
> The Fuss over Steroids
>
> Steroids: A Dangerous Game

"Are Steroids Harmful?" is faintly interesting and lets the reader know the gist of the subject, but it gives no clue about the writer's thesis, the writer's contention or argument. "The Fuss over Steroids" is somewhat better, for it gives information about the writer's position. "Steroids: A Dangerous Game" is still better; it announces the subject ("steroids") and the thesis ("dangerous"), and it also displays a touch of wit because "game" glances at the world of athletics.

Don't try too hard, however; better a simple, direct, informative title than a strained, puzzling, or overly cute one. And remember to make sure that everything in your essay is relevant to your title. In fact, your title should help you to organize the essay and to delete irrelevant material.

THE FINAL DRAFT

When at last you have a draft that is for the most part satisfactory, check to make sure that **transitions** from sentence to sentence and from paragraph to paragraph are clear ("Further evidence," "In contrast," "A weakness, however, is apparent"), and then worry about your opening and closing paragraphs. Your **opening paragraph** should be clear, interesting, and focused; if neither the title nor the first paragraph announces your thesis, the second paragraph probably should do so.

The **final paragraph** need not say, "In conclusion, I have shown that. . . ." It should effectively end the essay, but it need not summarize your conclusions. We have already offered a few words about final paragraphs (p. 243–45), but the best way to learn how to write such paragraphs is to study the endings of some of the essays in this book and to adopt the strategies that appeal to you.

Be sure that all indebtedness is properly acknowledged. We have talked about plagiarism; now we will turn to the business of introducing quotations effectively.

Quoting from Sources

INCORPORATING YOUR READING INTO YOUR THINKING:
THE ART AND SCIENCE OF SYNTHESIS

At the beginning of Chapter 6 we quoted a passage by Kenneth Burke (1887–1993), a college dropout who became one of America's most important twentieth-century students of rhetoric. It is worth repeating:

> Imagine that you enter a parlor. You come late. When you arrive, others have long preceded you, and they are engaged in a heated discussion, a discussion too heated for them to pause and tell you exactly what it is about. In fact, the discussion had already begun long before any of them got there, so that no one present is qualified to retrace for you all the steps that had gone before. You listen for a while, until you decide that you have caught the tenor of the argument; then you put in your oar. Someone answers; you answer him; another comes to your defense; another aligns himself against you, to either the embarrassment or gratification of your opponent, depending upon the quality of your ally's assistance. However, the discussion is interminable. The hour grows late, you must depart. And you do depart, with the discussion still vigorously in progress.
>
> — *The Philosophy of Literary Form* (Baton Rouge: Louisiana State University Press, 1941), 110–11.

Why do we quote this passage? Because it is your turn to join the unending conversation.

During the process of reading, and afterward, you will want to listen, think, say to yourself something like this:

- "No, no, I see things very differently; it seems to me that . . ." or
- "Yes, of course, but on one large issue I think I differ," or
- "Yes, sure, I agree, but I would go further and add . . ." or
- "Yes, I agree with your conclusion, but I hold this conclusion for reasons very different from the ones that you offer."

During your composition courses at least (and we think during your entire life), you will be reading or listening and will sometimes want to put in your oar — you will sometimes want to respond in writing, for example in the form of a Letter to the Editor or in a memo at your place of employment. In the course of your response you almost surely will have to summarize the idea or ideas you are responding to, so that your readers will understand the context of your remarks. These ideas may not come from a single source; you may be responding to several sources. For instance, you may be responding to a report and also to some comments that the report evoked. In any case, you will state these ideas briefly and fairly and will then set forth your thoughtful responses, thereby giving the reader a statement that you hope represents an advance in the argument, even if only a tiny one. That is, you will **synthesize** sources, combining existing material into something new, drawing nourishment from what has already been said (giving credit, of course), and converting it into something new — a view that you think is worth considering.

Let's pause for a moment and consider this word *synthesis*. You probably are familiar with *photosynthesis*, the chemical process in green plants that produces carbohydrates from carbon dioxide and hydrogen. Synthesis, again, combines pre-existing elements and produces something new. In our use of the word *synthesis*, even a view that you utterly reject becomes a part of your new creation *because it helped to stimulate you to formulate your view*; without the idea that you reject, you might not have developed the view that you now hold. Consider the words of Francis Bacon, Shakespeare's contemporary:

> Some books are to be tasted, others to be swallowed, and some few to be chewed and digested.

Your instructor will expect you to digest your sources — this doesn't mean you need to accept them but only that you need to read them thoughtfully — and that, so to speak, you make them your own thoughts by refining them. Your readers will expect you to tell them *what you make out of your sources*, which means that you will go beyond writing a summary and will synthesize the material into your own contribution. *Your* view is what is wanted, and readers expect this view to be thoughtful — not mere summary and not mere tweeting.

THE USE AND ABUSE OF QUOTATIONS

When is it necessary, or appropriate, to quote? Sometimes, the reader must see the exact words of your source; the gist won't do. If you are arguing that Z's definition of *rights* is too inclusive, your readers have to know exactly how Z defined *rights*. Your brief summary of the definition may be unfair to Z; in fact, you want to convince your readers that you're being fair, and so you quote Z's definition, word for word. Moreover, if the passage is only a sentence or two long, or even if it runs to a paragraph, it may be so compactly stated that it defies summary. And to attempt to paraphrase it — substituting *natural* for *inalienable*, and so forth — saves no space and only introduces imprecision. There is nothing to do but to quote it, word for word.

Second, you may want to quote a passage that could be summarized but that is so effectively stated that you want the readers to have the pleasure of reading the original. Of course, readers won't give you credit for writing these words, but they will appreciate your taste and your effort to make especially pleasant the business of reading your paper.

In short, use (but don't overuse) quotations. Speaking roughly, quotations

- should occupy no more than 10 to 15 percent of your paper, and
- they may occupy much less.

Most of your paper should set forth your ideas, not other people's ideas.

HOW TO QUOTE

Long and Short Quotations   **Long quotations** (more than four lines of typed prose or three or more lines of poetry) are set off from the text. To set off material, start on a new line, indent one-half inch from the left margin, and type the quotation double-spaced. Do not enclose quotations within quotation marks if you are setting them off.

Short quotations are treated differently. They are embedded within the text; they are enclosed within quotation marks, but otherwise they do not stand out.

All quotations, whether set off or embedded, must be exact. If you omit any words, you must indicate the ellipsis by substituting three spaced periods for the omission; if you insert any words or punctuation, you must indicate the addition by enclosing it within square brackets, not to be confused with parentheses.

Original	The Montgomery bus boycott not only brought national attention to the discriminatory practices of the South, but elevated a twenty-six-year-old preacher to exalted status in the civil rights movement.
Quotation in student paper	"The Montgomery bus boycott . . . elevated [King] to exalted status in the civil rights movement."

Leading into a Quotation   Now for a less mechanical matter: the way in which a quotation is introduced. To say that it is "introduced" implies that one leads into it, though on rare occasions a quotation appears without an introduction, perhaps immediately after the title. Normally one leads into a quotation by giving any one or more of the following (*warning*: using them all at once can get unwieldy and produce awkward sentences):

- the *name of the author* and (no less important) the author's expertise or authority
- an indication of *the source of the quotation, by title and/or year*
- *clues signaling the content of the quotation and the purpose* it serves in the present essay

For example:

William James provides a clear answer to Huxley when he says that ". . ."

Psychologist William James provides a clear answer to Huxley when he says that ". . ."

In *The Will to Believe* (1897), psychologist William James *provides a clear answer* to Huxley when he says that ". . ."

Any of these work, especially because William James is quite well known. When you're quoting from a lesser-known author, it becomes more important to identify his or her expertise and perhaps the source, as in "Biographer Theodora Bosanquet, author of *Henry James at Work* (1982), subtly criticized Huxley's vague ideas on religion by writing '. . .'"

Note that in all of the above samples, the writer uses the lead-in to signal to readers the general tone of the quotation to follow. The writer uses "a clear answer" to signal that what's coming is, in fact, clear. The writer uses "subtly criticized" and "vague" to indicate that the following words by Bosanquet will be critical and will point out a shortcoming in Huxley's ideas. In this way, the writer anticipates and controls the meaning of the quotation for the reader. If the writer believed otherwise, the lead-ins might have run thus:

William James attempts to answer Huxley, but his response does not really meet the difficulty Huxley calls attention to. James writes, "..."

or thus:

Biographer Theodora Bosanquet, author of *Henry James at Work* (1982), unjustly criticized Huxley's complex notion of religion by writing "..."

In this last example, clearly the words "unjustly criticized" imply that the essayist wants the reader to interpret the quotation as an unjust criticism. Similarly, Huxley's idea is presented as "complex," not vague.

Signal Phrases Think of your writing as a conversation between you and your sources. As in conversation, you want to be able to move smoothly between different, sometimes contrary, points of view. You also want to be able to set your thoughts apart from those of your sources. Signal phrases make it easy for readers to know where your information came from and why it's trustworthy by pointing to key facts about the source:

According to psychologist Stephen Ceci . . .

A report published by the U.S. Bureau of Justice Statistics *concludes* . . .

Feminist philosopher Sandra Harding *argues* . . .

To avoid repetitiveness, vary your sentence structure:

. . . *claims* Stephen Ceci.

. . . *according to* a report published by the U.S. Bureau of Statistics.

Some useful verbs to introduce sources include the following:

acknowledges	disputes
argues	observes
believes	points out
claims	recommends
contends	reports
denies	suggests

Note that papers written using MLA style refer to sources in the present tense (*acknowledge, argue, believe*). Papers written in APA style use the past tense (*acknowledged, argued, believed*).

THINKING CRITICALLY *Using Signal Phrases*

In the space provided, rewrite each signal phrase using a different structure. The first has been done as an example. Use different verbs to introduce each source.

ORIGINAL SIGNAL PHRASE	REVISED SIGNAL PHRASE
According to political economist Robert Reich . . .	. . . claims Robert Reich.
The National Health Council reports . . .	
The *Harvard Law Review* claims . . .	
As science essayist Jennifer Ackerman suggests . . .	

LaunchPad   To complete this activity online, go to **macmillanhighered.com/barnetbedauohara**

Leading Out of a Quotation   You might think of providing quotations as a three-stage process that includes the **lead-in**, the **quotation** itself, and the **lead-out**. The lead-out gives you a chance to interpret the quoted material, further controlling the intended meaning, telling the reader what is most important. In the lead-out, you have a chance to reflect upon the quotation and to shift back toward your own ideas and analysis. Consider this three-stage process applied in the following two ways:

> In his first book, *A World Restored* (1954), future Secretary of Defense Henry Kissinger wrote the famous axiom "History is the memory of states." It is the collective story of an entire people, displayed in public museums and libraries, taught in schools, and passed on from generation to generation.

> In his first book, *A World Restored* (1954), Nixon's former Secretary of Defense Henry Kissinger wrote glibly, "History is the memory of states." By asserting that history is largely the product of self-interested propaganda, Kissinger's words suggest that the past is maintained and controlled by whatever groups happen to hold power.

Note the three-step process, and note especially how the two examples convey different meanings of Kissinger's famous phrase. In the lead-in to the first sample, Kissinger's "future" role suggests hope. It signals a figure whose influence is growing. By using *famous* and *axiom*, the author presents the quotation as "true" or even timeless. In the lead-out, the role of the state in preserving history is optimistic and idealistic.

In the second sample, "former" is used in the lead-in, suggesting Kissinger's later association with the ousted president. Readers are told that Kissinger "wrote glibly" even before they are told what he wrote, so readers may tend to read the quoted words that way. In the lead-out, the state becomes a more nefarious source of history-keeping, one not interested in accommodating marginal voices or alternative perspectives, or remembering events inconvenient to its authority or righteousness.

Again, we hope you can see in these examples how the three-step process facilitates a writer's control over the meanings of quotations. Returning to our earlier example, if after reading something by Huxley the writer had merely stated that "William James says . . . ," readers wouldn't know whether they were getting confirmation, refutation, or something else. The essayist would have put a needless burden on the readers. Generally speaking, the more difficult the quotation, the more important is the introductory or explanatory lead-in, but even the simplest quotation profits from some sort of brief lead-in, such as "James reaffirms this point when he says. . . ."

> **A RULE FOR WRITERS**
> In introducing a quotation, it is usually advisable to signal the reader *why* you are using the quotation by means of a lead-in consisting of a verb or a verb and adverb, such as *claims*, or *convincingly shows*, or *admits*.

Documentation

In the course of your essay, you will probably quote or summarize material derived from a source. You must give credit, and although there is no one form of documentation to which all scholarly fields subscribe, you will probably be asked to use one of two. One, established by the Modern Language Association (MLA), is used chiefly in the humanities; the other, established by the American Psychological Association (APA), is used chiefly in the social sciences.

We include two papers that use sources. "An Argument for Corporate Responsibility" (p. 309) uses the MLA format. "The Role of Spirituality and Religion in Mental Health" (p. 316) follows the APA format. (You may notice that various styles are illustrated in other selections we have included.)

In some online venues you can link directly to your sources. If your assignment is to write a blog or some other online text, linking helps the reader to look at a note or citation or the direct source quickly and easily. For example, in describing or referencing a scene in a movie, you can link to reviews of the movie, or to a YouTube of the trailer, or to the exact scene that you're discussing. These kinds of links can help your audience get a clearer sense of your point. When formatting such a link in your text, make sure the link opens in a new window so that readers won't lose their place in your original text. In a blog, linking to sources usually is easy and helpful.

A NOTE ON FOOTNOTES (AND ENDNOTES)

Before we discuss these two formats, a few words about footnotes are in order. Before the MLA and the APA developed their rules of style, citations commonly appeared in footnotes. Although today footnotes are not so frequently used to give citations, they still may be useful for another purpose. (The MLA suggests endnotes rather than footnotes, but most readers seem to think that, in fact, footnotes are preferable to endnotes. After all, who wants to keep shifting from a page of text to a page of notes at the rear?) If you want to include some material that may seem intrusive in the body of the paper, you may relegate it to a footnote: for example, you might translate a quotation given in a foreign language, or you might demote from text to footnote a paragraph explaining why you aren't taking account of such-and-such a point. By putting the matter in a footnote you signal to the reader that it is dispensable; it's relevant but not essential, something extra that you are, so to speak, tossing in. Don't make a habit of writing this sort of note, but there are times when it is appropriate to do so.

MLA FORMAT: CITATIONS WITHIN THE TEXT

Brief citations within the body of the essay give credit, in a highly abbreviated way, to the sources for material you quote, summarize, or make use of in any other way. These *in-text citations* are made clear by a list of sources, titled Works Cited, appended to the essay. Thus, in your essay you may say something like this:

> Commenting on the relative costs of capital punishment and life imprisonment, Ernest van den Haag says that he doubts "that capital punishment really is more expensive" (33).

The **citation,** the number 33 in parentheses, means that the quoted words come from page 33 of a source (listed in the Works Cited) written by van den Haag. Without a Works Cited, a reader would have no way of knowing that you are quoting from page 33 of an article that appeared in the February 8, 1985, issue of the *National Review*.

Usually, the parenthetic citation appears at the end of a sentence, as in the example just given, but it can appear elsewhere; its position will depend chiefly on your ear, your eye, and the context. You might, for example, write the sentence thus:

> Ernest van den Haag doubts that "capital punishment really is more expensive" than life imprisonment (33), but other writers have presented figures that contradict him.

Five points must be made about these examples:

1. *Quotation marks* The closing quotation mark appears after the last word of the quotation, *not* after the parenthetic citation. Since the citation is not part of the quotation, the citation is not included within the quotation marks.

2. *Omission of words (ellipsis)* If you are quoting a complete sentence or only a phrase, as in the examples given, you do not need to indicate (by three spaced periods) that you are omitting material before or after the quotation. But if for some reason you want to omit an interior part of the quotation, you must indicate the omission by inserting an *ellipsis,* the three spaced dots. To take a simple example, if you omit the word "really" from van den Haag's phrase, you must alert the reader to the omission:

> Ernest van den Haag doubts that "capital punishment . . . is more expensive" than life imprisonment (33).

Suppose you're quoting a sentence but wish to omit material from the end of the sentence. Suppose, also, that the quotation forms the end of your sentence. Write a lead-in phrase, quote what you need from the source, then type the ellipses for the omission, close the quotation, give the parenthetic citation, and finally type a fourth period to indicate the end of your sentence.

Here's an example. Suppose you want to quote the first part of a sentence that runs, "We could insist that the cost of capital punishment be reduced so as to diminish the differences." Your sentence would incorporate the desired extract as follows:

> Van den Haag says, "We could insist that the cost of capital punishment be reduced . . ." (33).

3. *Punctuation with parenthetic citations* In the preceding examples, the punctuation (a period or a comma in the examples) *follows* the citation. If, however, the quotation ends with a question mark, include the question mark *within* the quotation, since it is part of the quotation, and put a period *after* the citation:

> Van den Haag asks, "Isn't it better — more just and more useful — that criminals, if they do not have the certainty of punishment, at least run the risk of suffering it?" (33).

But if the question mark is your own and not in the source, put it after the citation, thus:

> What answer can be given to van den Haag's doubt that "capital punishment really is more expensive" (33)?

4. *Two or more works by an author* If your list of Works Cited includes two or more works by an author, you cannot, in your essay, simply cite a page number because the reader will not know which of the works you are referring to. You must give additional information. You can give it in your lead-in, thus:

> In "New Arguments against Capital Punishment," van den Haag expresses doubt that "capital punishment really is more expensive" than life imprisonment (33).

Or you can give the title, in a shortened form, within the citation:

> Van den Haag expresses doubt that "capital punishment really is more expensive" than life imprisonment ("New Arguments" 33).

5. *Citing even when you do not quote* Even if you don't quote a source directly, but use its point in a paraphrase or a summary, you will give a citation:

> Van den Haag thinks that life imprisonment costs more than capital punishment (33).

Note that in all of the previous examples, the author's name is given in the text (rather than within the parenthetic citation). But there are several other ways of giving the citation, and we shall look at them now. (We've already seen, in the example given under paragraph 4, that the title and the page number can appear within the citation.)

AUTHOR AND PAGE NUMBER IN PARENTHESES

> It has been argued that life imprisonment is more costly than capital punishment (van den Haag 33).

AUTHOR, TITLE, AND PAGE NUMBER IN PARENTHESES

We have seen that if the Works Cited list includes two or more works by an author, you will have to give the title of the work on which you are drawing, either in your lead-in phrase or within the parenthetic citation. Similarly, if you're citing someone who is listed more than once in the Works Cited, and for some reason you don't mention the name of the author or the work in your lead-in, you must add the information in the citation:

> Doubt has been expressed that capital punishment is as costly as life imprisonment (van den Haag, "New Arguments" 33).

A GOVERNMENT DOCUMENT OR A WORK OF CORPORATE AUTHORSHIP

Treat the issuing body as the author. Thus, you will write something like this:

> The Commission on Food Control, in *Food Resources Today*, concludes that there is no danger (37-38).

A WORK BY TWO AUTHORS

If a work is by *two authors,* give the names of both authors, either in the parenthetic citation (the first example below) or in a lead-in (the second example below):

> There is not a single example of the phenomenon (Christakis and Fowler 293).

> Christakis and Fowler insist there is not a single example of the phenomenon (293).

A WORK BY MORE THAN TWO AUTHORS

If there are *more than two authors,* give the last name of the first author, followed by *et al.* (an abbreviation for *et alii,* Latin for "and others"), thus:

> Gittleman et al. argue (43) that . . .

or

> On average, the cost is even higher (Gittleman et al. 43).

PARENTHETIC CITATION OF AN INDIRECT SOURCE (CITATION OF MATERIAL THAT ITSELF WAS QUOTED OR SUMMARIZED IN YOUR SOURCE)

Suppose you're reading a book by Jones in which she quotes Smith and you wish to use Smith's material. Your citation must refer the reader to Jones — the source you're using — but of course, you cannot attribute the words to Jones. You will have to make it clear that you are quoting Smith, and so after a lead-in phrase like "Smith says," followed by the quotation, you will give a parenthetic citation along these lines:

> (qtd. in Jones 324-25).

PARENTHETIC CITATION OF TWO OR MORE WORKS

> The costs are simply too high (Smith 301; Jones 28).

Notice that a semicolon, followed by a space, separates the two sources.

A WORK IN MORE THAN ONE VOLUME

This is a bit tricky. If you have used only one volume, in the Works Cited you will specify the volume, and so in the parenthetic in-text citation you won't need to specify the volume. All you need to include in the citation is a page number, as illustrated by most of the examples that we have given.

If you have used more than one volume, the parenthetic citation will have to specify the volume as well as the page, thus:

Jackson points out that fewer than 150 people fit this description (2: 351).

The reference is to page 351 in volume 2 of a work by Jackson.

If, however, you are citing not a page but an entire volume — let's say volume 2 — your parenthetic citation will look like this:

Jackson exhaustively studies this problem (vol. 2).

or

Jackson (vol. 2) exhaustively studies this problem.

Notice the following points:

- In citing a volume and page, the volume number, like the page number, is given in arabic (not roman) numerals, even if the original used roman numerals to indicate the volume number.
- The volume number is followed by a colon, then a space, then the page number.
- If you cite a volume number without a page number, as in the last example quoted, the abbreviation is *vol.* Otherwise, do *not* use such abbreviations as *vol.* and *p.* and *pg.*

AN ANONYMOUS WORK

For an anonymous work, give the title in your lead-in, or give it in a shortened form in your parenthetic citation:

A Prisoner's View of Killing includes a poll taken of the inmates on death row (32).

or

A poll is available (*Prisoner's View* 32).

AN INTERVIEW

Probably you won't need a parenthetic citation because you'll say something like

Vivian Berger, in an interview, said . . .

or

According to Vivian Berger, in an interview . . .

and when your reader turns to the Works Cited, he or she will see that Berger is listed, along with the date of the interview. But if you don't mention the source's name in the lead-in, you'll have to give it in the parentheses, thus:

> Contrary to popular belief, the death penalty is not reserved for serial killers and depraved murderers (Berger).

AN ELECTRONIC SOURCE

Electronic sources, such as Web sites, are generally not divided into pages. Therefore, the in-text citation for such sources cites only the author's name (or, if a work is anonymous, the title):

> According to the Web site for the American Civil Liberties Union . . .

If the source does use pages or breaks down further into paragraphs or screens, insert the appropriate identifier or abbreviation (*p.* or *pp.* for page or pages; *par.* or *pars.* for paragraph or paragraphs; *screen* or *screens*) before the relevant number:

> The growth of day care has been called "a crime against posterity" by a spokesman for the Institute for the American Family (Terwilliger, screens 1-2).

MLA FORMAT: THE LIST OF WORKS CITED

As the previous pages explain, parenthetic documentation consists of references that become clear when the reader consults the list titled Works Cited at the end of an essay.

The list of Works Cited begins on its own page and continues the pagination of the essay: If the last page of text is 10, then the Works Cited begins on page 11. Type the page number in the upper right corner, a half inch from the top of the sheet and flush with the right margin. Next, type the heading Works Cited (*not* enclosed within quotation marks and not italic), centered, one inch from the top, and then double-space and type the first entry.

Here are some general guidelines.

FORM ON THE PAGE

- Begin each entry flush with the left margin, but if an entry runs to more than one line, indent a half inch for each succeeding line of the entry. This is known as a hanging indent, and most word processing programs can achieve this effect easily.

- Double-space each entry, and double-space between entries.

- Italicize titles of works published independently (which the MLA also calls *containers*; see page 294), such as books, pamphlets, and journals. Enclose within quotation marks a work not published independently — for instance, an article in a journal or a short story.

- If you are citing a book that includes the title of another book, italicize the main title, but do *not* italicize the title mentioned. Example:

    A Study of Mill's On Liberty

- In the sample entries below, pay attention to the use of commas, colons, and the space after punctuation.

ALPHABETICAL ORDER

- Arrange the list alphabetically by author, with the author's last name first.
- For information about anonymous works, works with more than one author, and two or more works by one author, see below.

Here is more detailed advice.

THE AUTHOR'S NAME

Notice that the last name is given first, but otherwise the name is given as on the title page. Do not substitute initials for names written out on the title page.

If your list includes two or more works by an author, do not repeat the author's name for the second title; instead represent it by three hyphens followed by a period. The sequence of the works is determined by the alphabetical order of the titles. Thus, Smith's book titled *Poverty* would be listed ahead of her book *Welfare*. See the example on page 295, listing two works by Roger Brown.

Anonymous works are listed under the first word of the title or the second word if the first is *A, An,* or *The* or a foreign equivalent. We discuss books by more than one author, government documents, and works of corporate authorship on pages 295–96.

CONTAINERS AND PUBLICATION INFORMATION

When a source being documented comes from a larger source, the larger source is considered a *container*, because it contains the smaller source you are citing. For example, a container might be an anthology, a periodical, a Web site, a television program, a database, or an online archive. The context of a source will help you determine what counts as a container.

In Works Cited lists, the title of a container is listed after the period following the author's name. The container title is generally italicized and followed by a comma, since the information that follows describes the container. (More on this below.) Disregard any unusual typography, such as the use of all capital letters or the use of an ampersand (&) for *and*. Italicize the container title (and subtitle, if applicable; separate them by a colon), but do not italicize the period that concludes this part of the entry.

- Capitalize the first word and the last word of the title.
- Capitalize all nouns, pronouns, verbs, adjectives, adverbs, and subordinating conjunctions (e.g., *although, if, because*).
- Do not capitalize (unless it's the first or last word of the title or the first word of the subtitle) articles (e.g., *a, an, the*), prepositions (e.g., *in, on, toward, under*), coordinating conjunctions (e.g., *and, but, or, for*), or the *to* in infinitives.

When citing a source within a container, the title of the source should be the first element following the author's name. The source title should be set within quotation marks with a period inside the closing quotation mark. The title of the container is then listed, followed by a comma, with additional information—including publication information, dates, and page ranges—about the container set off by commas.

Boyle, T. C. "Achates McNeil." *After the Plague: Stories*, Viking Penguin, 2001, pp. 82-101.

This example cites a story, "Achates McNeil," from an anthology—or container—called *After the Plague: Stories*. The anthology was published by Viking Penguin in 2001, and the story appears on pages 82 through 101.

Note that the full name of the publisher is listed. Always include the full names of publishers, except for terms such as "Inc." and "Company." Retain terms such as "Books" and "Publisher." The only exception is university presses, which are abbreviated thus: *Yale UP, U of Chicago P, State U of New York P.*

Sample Entries   Here are some examples illustrating the points we have covered thus far:

Brown, Roger. *Social Psychology*. Free Press, 1965.

- - - . *Words and Things*. Free Press, 1958.

Haidt, Jonathan. "The Uses of Adversity." *The Happiness Hypothesis: Finding Modern Truth in Ancient Wisdom*, Basic Books, 2006, pp. 135-154.

Hartman, Chester. *The Transformation of San Francisco*. Rowman and Littlefield Publishers, 1984.

Kellerman, Barbara. *The Political Presidency: Practice of Leadership from Kennedy through Reagan*. Oxford UP, 1984.

These examples provide general guidelines for the kind of information you need to include in your Works Cited list. On the following pages, you will find more specific information for listing different kinds of sources.

A BOOK BY MORE THAN ONE AUTHOR

The book is alphabetized under the last name of the first author named on the title page. If there are *two authors*, the name of the second author is given in the normal order, *first name first, after the first author's name.*

Gilbert, Sandra M., and Susan Gubar. *The Madwoman in the Attic: The Woman Writer and the Nineteenth-Century Literary Imagination*. Yale UP, 1979.

Notice, again, that although the first author's name is given *last name first*, the second author's name is given in the normal order, first name first. Notice, too, that a comma is added after the first name of the first author, separating the authors.

If there are *more than two authors*, give the name only of the first, followed by a comma, and then add *et al.* (Latin for "and others").

Zumeta, William, et al. *Financing American Higher Education in the Era of Globalization*. Harvard Education Press, 2012.

GOVERNMENT DOCUMENTS

If the writer is not known, treat the government and the agency as the author. Most federal documents are issued by the Government Printing Office (abbreviated to *GPO*) in Washington, D.C.

United States, Office of Technology Assessment. *Computerized Manufacturing Automation: Employment, Education, and the Workplace*. GPO, 1984.

WORKS OF CORPORATE AUTHORSHIP

Begin the citation with the corporate author, even if the same body is also the publisher, as in the first example:

American Psychiatric Association. *Psychiatric Glossary*. American Psychiatric Association, 1984.

Human Rights Watch. *World Report of 2015: Events of 2014*. Seven Stories Press, 2015.

A REPRINT (E.G., A PAPERBACK VERSION OF AN OLDER CLOTHBOUND BOOK)

After the title, give the date of original publication (it can usually be found on the reverse of the title page of the reprint you are using), then a period, and then the publisher and date of the edition you are using. The example indicates that de Mille's book was originally published in 1951 and that the student is using the 2015 reprint with an introduction by Joan Acocella.

de Mille, Agnes. *Dance to the Piper*. 1951. Introduction by Joan Acocella, New York Review Books, 2015.

A BOOK IN SEVERAL VOLUMES

If you have used more than one volume, in a citation within your essay you will (as explained on p. 292) indicate a reference to, say, page 250 of volume 3 thus: (3: 250).

If, however, you have used only one volume of the set — let's say volume 3 — in your entry in the Works Cited, specify which volume you used, as in the next example:

Friedel, Frank. *Franklin D. Roosevelt*. Vol. 3, Little Brown, 1973. 4 vols.

With such an entry in the Works Cited, the parenthetic citation within your essay would be to the page only, not to the volume and page, because a reader who consults the Works Cited will understand that you used only volume 3. In the Works Cited, you may specify volume 3 and not give the total number of volumes, or you may add the total number of volumes, as in the preceding example.

BOOK WITH MORE THAN ONE PUBLISHER

If a book is listed as having been published by two or more publishers, separate the publishers with a slash, and include a space before and after the slash.

Hornby, Nick. *About a Boy*. Riverhead / Penguin Putnam, 1998.

A BOOK WITH AN AUTHOR AND AN EDITOR

Kant, Immanuel. *The Philosophy of Kant: Immanuel Kant's Moral and Political Writings*. Edited by Carl J. Friedrich, Modern Library, 1949.

If you are making use of the editor's introduction or other editorial material rather than the author's work, list the book under the name of the editor rather than of the author, as shown below under An Introduction, Foreword, or Afterword.

A REVISED EDITION OF A BOOK

Arendt, Hannah. *Eichmann in Jerusalem*. Revised and enlarged ed., Viking, 1965.

Honour, Hugh, and John Fleming. *The Visual Arts: A History*. 7th ed., Laurence King Publishing, 2013.

A TRANSLATED BOOK

Ullmann, Regina. *The Country Road: Stories*. Translated by Kurt Beals, New Directions Publishing, 2015.

AN INTRODUCTION, FOREWORD, OR AFTERWORD

Dunham, Lena. Foreword. *The Liars' Club*, by Mary Karr, Penguin Classics, 2015, pp. xi-xiii.

Usually, an introduction or comparable material is listed under the name of the author of the book (here Karr) rather than under the name of the writer of the foreword (here Dunham), but if you are referring to the apparatus rather than to the book itself, use the form just given. The words *Introduction, Preface, Foreword,* and *Afterword* are neither enclosed within quotation marks nor italicized.

A BOOK WITH AN EDITOR BUT NO AUTHOR

Let's assume that you have used a book of essays written by various people but collected by an editor (or editors), whose name(s) appears on the collection.

Horner, Avril, and Anne Rowe, editors. *Living on Paper: Letters from Iris Murdoch*. Princeton UP, 2016.

A WORK WITHIN A VOLUME OF WORKS BY ONE AUTHOR

The following entry indicates that a short work by Susan Sontag, an essay called "The Aesthetics of Silence," appears in a book by Sontag titled *Styles of Radical Will*. Notice that the inclusive page numbers of the short work are cited, not merely page numbers that you may happen to refer to but the page numbers of the entire piece.

Sontag, Susan. "The Aesthetics of Silence." *Styles of Radical Will*, Farrar, Straus, and Giroux, 1969, pp. 3-34.

A BOOK REVIEW

Here is an example, citing Walton's review of Mitchell's book. Walton's review was published in a journal: *The New York Review of Books*.

Walton, James. "Noble, Embattled Souls." Review of *The Bone Clocks and Slade House*, by David Mitchell. *The New York Review of Books*, 3 Dec. 2015, pp. 55-58.

In this case, Walton's review has a title ("Noble, Embattled Souls") that appears between the period following the reviewer's name and *Review*.

If a review is anonymous, list it under the first word of the title, or under the second word if the first is *A*, *An*, or *The*. If an anonymous review has no title, begin the entry with *Review of*, and then give the title of the work reviewed; alphabetize the entry under the title of the work reviewed.

AN ARTICLE OR ESSAY IN A COLLECTION

A book may consist of a collection (edited by one or more persons) of new essays by several authors. Here is a reference to one essay in such a book. (The essay by Sayrafiezadeh occupies pages 3 to 29 in a collection edited by Marcus.)

Sayrafiezadeh, Saïd. "Paranoia." *New American Stories*, edited by Ben Marcus, Vintage Books, 2015, pp. 3-29.

MULTIPLE WORKS FROM THE SAME COLLECTION

You may find that you need to cite multiple sources from within a single container, such as several essays from the same edited anthology. In these cases, provide an entry for the entire anthology (the entry for Marcus below) and a shortened entry for each selection. Alphabetize the entries by authors' or editors' last names.

Eisenberg, Deborah. "Some Other, Better Otto." Marcus, pp. 94-136.

Marcus, Ben, editor. *New American Stories*. Vintage Books, 2015.

Sayrafiezadeh, Saïd. "Paranoia." Marcus, pp. 3-29.

BOOK WITH A TITLE IN ITS TITLE

If the book title contains a title that is normally italicized, do not italicize the title within the book title. If the book title contains a title normally placed in quotation marks, retain the quotation marks and italicize the entire title.

Masur, Louis P. *Runaway Dream:* Born to Run *and Bruce Springsteen's American Vision*. Bloomsbury, 2009.

Lethem, Jonathan. *"Lucky Alan" and Other Stories*. Doubleday, 2015.

BOOK IN A SERIES

After the publication information, list the series name as it appears on the title page.

Denham, A. E., editor. *Plato on Art and Beauty*. Palgrave Macmillan, 2012. Philosophers in Depth.

AN ARTICLE IN A REFERENCE WORK (INCLUDING A WIKI)

For a *signed* article, begin with the author's last name. (If the article is signed with initials, check elsewhere in the volume for a list of abbreviations, which will inform you who the initials stand for, and use the following form.) Provide the name of the article, the publication title, edition number (if applicable), the publisher, and the copyright year.

Robinson, Lisa Clayton. "Harlem Writers Guild." *Africana: The Encyclopedia of the African and African American Experience*. 2nd ed., Oxford UP, 2005.

For an unsigned article, begin with the title of the article:

"Ball's in Your Court, The." *The American Heritage Dictionary of Idioms*. 2nd ed., Houghton Mifflin Harcourt, 2013.

For an online reference work, such as a wiki, include the author name and article name followed by the name of the Web site, the date of publication or the most recent update, and the URL (without *http*:// before it).

Durante, Amy M. "Finn Mac Cumhail." *Encyclopedia Mythica*, 17 Apr. 2011, www.pantheon .org/articles/f/finn_mac_cumhail.html.

"House Music." *Wikipedia*, 16 Nov. 2015, en.wikipedia.org/wiki/House_music.

A TELEVISION OR RADIO PROGRAM

Be sure to include the title of the episode or segment (in quotation marks), the title of the show (italicized), the producer or director of the show, the network, and the date of the airing. Other information, such as performers, narrator, and so forth, may be included if pertinent.

"Fast Times at West Philly High." *Frontline*, produced by Debbie Morton, PBS, 17 July 2012.

"Federal Role in Support of Autism." *Washington Journal*, narrated by Robb Harleston, C-SPAN, 1 Dec. 2012.

AN ARTICLE IN A SCHOLARLY JOURNAL

The title of the article is enclosed within quotation marks, and the title of the journal is italicized.

Some journals are paginated consecutively; the pagination of the second issue begins where the first issue leaves off. Other journals begin each issue with page 1.

Matchie, Thomas. "Law versus Love in The Round House." *Midwest Quarterly*, vol. 56, no. 4, Summer 2015, pp. 353-64.

Matchie's article occupies pages 353 to 364 in volume 56, which was published in 2015. When available, give the issue number as well. (If the journal is, for instance, a quarterly, there will be four page 1's each year, so the issue number must be given.)

AN ARTICLE IN A WEEKLY, BIWEEKLY, MONTHLY, OR BIMONTHLY PUBLICATION

Do not include volume or issue numbers, even if given.

> Thompson, Mark. "Sending Women to War: The Pentagon Nears a Historic Decision on Equality at the Front Lines." *Time*, 14 Dec. 2015, pp. 53-55.

AN ARTICLE IN A NEWSPAPER

Because a newspaper usually consists of several sections, a section number or a capital letter may precede the page number. The example indicates that an article appears on page 1 of section C.

> Bray, Hiawatha. "As Toys Get Smarter, Privacy Issues Emerge." *The Boston Globe*, 10 Dec. 2015, p. C1.

AN UNSIGNED EDITORIAL

> "The Religious Tyranny Amendment." *New York Times,* 15 Mar. 1998, p. 16. Editorial.

A LETTER TO THE EDITOR

> Lasken, Douglas. *New York Times.* 15 Mar. 1998, p. 16. Letter.

A PUBLISHED OR BROADCAST INTERVIEW

Give the name of the interview subject and the interviewer, followed by the relevant publication or broadcast information, in the following format:

> Weddington, Sarah. "Sarah Weddington: Still Arguing for *Roe*." Interview by Michele Kort, *Ms.*, Winter 2013, pp. 32-35.

> Tempkin, Ann, and Anne Umland. Interview by Charlie Rose. *Charlie Rose: The Week*, PBS, 9 Oct. 2015.

AN INTERVIEW YOU CONDUCT

> Akufo, Dautey. Personal interview, 11 Apr. 2016.

A PERSONAL OR PROFESSIONAL WEB SITE

Include the following elements, separated by periods: the name of the person who created the site (omit if not given, as in Figure 7.4), site title (italicized), name of any sponsoring institution or organization; date of electronic publication or of the latest update (if given; if not, provide the date you accessed the site at the end of the citation); and the URL (without *http://*).

> *Legal Guide for Bloggers*. Electronic Frontier Foundation, www.eff.org/issues/bloggers/legal. Accessed 5 Apr. 2016.

Figure 7.4   Citing a Blog

1 URL

2 Sponsor of Web site

3 No author given; start citation with the title.

4 No date of publication given; include date of access in citation.

AN ARTICLE IN AN ONLINE PERIODICAL

Give the same information as you would for a print article, plus the URL. (See Figure 7.5.)

> Acocella, Joan. "In the Blood: Why Do Vampires Still Thrill?" *New Yorker,* 16 March 2009.
> www.newyorker.com/magazine/2009/03/16/in-the-blood.

A POSTING TO AN ONLINE DISCUSSION LIST

The citation includes the author's name, the subject line of the posting, the name of the forum, the host of the forum, the date the material was posted, and the URL.

> Robin, Griffith. "Write for the Reading Teacher." *Developing Digital Literacies,* NCTE,
> 23 Oct. 2015, ncte.connectedcommunity.org/communities/community-home/digestviewer
> /viewthread?GroupId=1693&MID=24520&tab=digestviewer&CommunityKey=628d2ad6
> -8277-4042-a376-2b370ddceabf.

Figure 7.5   Citing an Online Magazine

1 URL
2 Title of periodical
3 Title of article
4 Subtitle of article
5 Author
6 Publication date. If the article doesn't have a publication date, include the date you accessed it.

A FACEBOOK POST OR COMMENT

Include the name of the Facebook page on which the post appeared, the name of the post (or the post on which the comment appears), the name of the site, the date, and the URL of the post or comment.

> Bedford English. "Stacey Cochran Explores Reflective Writing in the Classroom and as a Writer: http://ow.ly/YkjVB." *Facebook*, 15 Feb. 2016, www.facebook.com/BedfordEnglish /posts/10153415001259607.

AN E-MAIL MESSAGE

Include the name of the sender, the title of the message, the name of the recipient, and the date of the message.

> Thornbrugh, Caitlin. "Coates Lecture." Received by Rita Anderson, 20 Oct. 2015.

A TEXT MESSAGE

Include the name of the sender, the title of the message, the name of the recipient, and the date of the message.

> Naqvi, Sahin. Message to the author, 18 Nov. 2015.

TWITTER POST (TWEET)

Include the handle of the poster, the content of the Tweet (enclosed in quotation marks), the name of the site, the date and time of the post, and the URL.

> Curiosity Rover. "Can you see me waving? How to spot #Mars in the night sky: https://youtu
> .be/hv8hVvJlcJQ." *Twitter*, 5 Nov. 2015, 11:00 a.m., twitter.com/marscuriosity/status
> /672859022911889408.

A DATABASE SOURCE

Treat material obtained from a database like other printed material, but at the end of the entry add (if available) the title of the database (italicized), and a permalink or DOI (digital object identifier) if the source has one. If a source does not, then include a URL (without the protocol, such as *http://*).

> Coles, Kimberly Anne. "The Matter of Belief in John Donne's Holy Sonnets." *Renaissance Quarterly*,
> vol. 68, no. 3, Fall 2015, pp. 899-931. JSTOR, doi:10.1086/683855.

> Macari, Anne Marie. "Lyric Impulse in a Time of Extinction." *American Poetry Review*, vol. 44,
> no. 4, July/Aug. 2015, pp. 11-14. *General OneFile*, go.galegroup.com/.

Caution: Although we have covered many kinds of sources, it's entirely possible that you will come across a source that doesn't fit any of the categories that we have discussed. For greater explanations of these matters, covering the proper way to cite all sorts of troublesome and unbelievable (but real) sources, see the *MLA Handbook*, Eighth Edition (Modern Language Association of America, 2016).

APA FORMAT: CITATIONS WITHIN THE TEXT

Your paper will conclude with a separate page headed References, on which you list all of your sources. If the last page of your essay is numbered 10, number the first page of the References 11.

The APA style emphasizes the date of publication; the date appears not only in the list of references at the end of the paper but also in the paper itself, when you give a brief parenthetic citation of a source that you have quoted or summarized or in any other way used. Here is an example:

> Statistics are readily available (Smith, 1989, p. 20).

The title of Smith's book or article will be given at the end of your paper in the list titled References. We discuss the form of the material listed in the References after we look at some typical citations within the text of a student's essay.

A SUMMARY OF AN ENTIRE WORK

Smith (1988) holds the same view.

or

Similar views are held widely (Smith, 1988; Jones & Metz, 1990).

A REFERENCE TO A PAGE OR TO PAGES

Smith (1988) argues that "the death penalty is a lottery, and blacks usually are the losers" (p. 17).

A REFERENCE TO AN AUTHOR WHO HAS MORE THAN ONE WORK IN THE LIST OF REFERENCES

If in the References you list two or more works that an author published in the same year, the works are listed in alphabetical order, by the first letter of the title. The first work is labeled *a*, the second *b*, and so on. Here is a reference to the second work that Smith published in 1989:

Florida presents "a fair example" of how the death penalty is administered (Smith, 1989b, p. 18).

APA FORMAT: THE LIST OF REFERENCES

Your brief parenthetic citations are made clear when the reader consults the list you give in the References. Type this list on a separate page, continuing the pagination of your essay.

An Overview   Here are some general guidelines.

FORM ON THE PAGE

- Begin each entry flush with the left margin, but if an entry runs to more than one line, indent five spaces for each succeeding line of the entry.
- Double-space each entry, and double-space between entries.

ALPHABETICAL ORDER

- Arrange the list alphabetically by author.
- Give the author's last name first and then the initial of the first name and of the middle name (if any).
- If there is more than one author, name all of the authors up to seven, again inverting the name (last name first) and giving only initials for first and middle names. (But do not invert the editor's name when the entry begins with the name of an author who has written an article in an edited book.) When there are two or more authors, use an ampersand (&) before the name of the last author. Example (here, of an article in the tenth volume of a journal called *Developmental Psychology*):

Drabman, R. S., & Thomas, M. H. (1974). Does media violence increase children's tolerance of real-life aggression? *Developmental Psychology, 10,* 418-421.

- For eight or more authors, list the first six followed by three ellipsis dots and then the last author. If you list more than one work by an author, do so in the order of publication, the earliest first. If two works by an author were published in the same year, give them in alphabetical order by the first letter of the title, disregarding *A, An,* or *The,* and their foreign equivalent. Designate the first work as *a,* the second as *b.* Repeat the author's name at the start of each entry.

Donnerstein, E. (1980a). Aggressive erotica and violence against women. *Journal of Personality and Social Psychology, 39,* 269-277.

Donnerstein, E. (1980b). Pornography and violence against women. *Annals of the New York Academy of Sciences, 347,* 227-288.

Donnerstein, E. (1983). Erotica and human aggression. In R. Green & E. Donnerstein (Eds.), *Aggression: Theoretical and empirical reviews* (pp. 87-103). New York, NY: Academic Press.

FORM OF TITLE

- In references to books, capitalize only the first letter of the first word of the title (and of the subtitle, if any) and capitalize proper nouns. Italicize the complete title (but not the period at the end).

- In references to articles in periodicals or in edited books, capitalize only the first letter of the first word of the article's title (and subtitle, if any) and all proper nouns. Do not put the title within quotation marks or italicize it. Type a period after the title of the article. For the title of the journal and the volume and page numbers, see the next instruction.

- In references to periodicals, give the volume number in arabic numerals, and italicize it. Do *not* use *vol.* before the number, and do not use *p.* or *pg.* before the page numbers.

Sample References   Here are some samples to follow.

A BOOK BY ONE AUTHOR

Pavlov, I. P. (1927). *Conditioned reflexes* (G. V. Anrep, Trans.). London, England: Oxford University Press.

A BOOK BY MORE THAN ONE AUTHOR

Belenky, M. F., Clinchy, B. M., Goldberger, N. R., & Torule, J. M. (1986). *Women's ways of knowing: The development of self, voice, and mind.* New York, NY: Basic Books.

A COLLECTION OF ESSAYS

Christ, C. P., & Plaskow, J. (Eds.). (1979). *Woman-spirit rising: A feminist reader in religion.* New York, NY: Harper & Row.

A WORK IN A COLLECTION OF ESSAYS

Fiorenza, E. (1979). Women in the early Christian movement. In C. P. Christ & J. Plaskow (Eds.), *Woman-spirit rising: A feminist reader in religion* (pp. 84-92). New York, NY: Harper & Row.

GOVERNMENT DOCUMENTS

If the writer is not known, treat the government and the agency as the author. Most federal documents are issued by the U.S. Government Printing Office in Washington, D.C. If a document number has been assigned, insert that number in parentheses between the title and the following period.

United States Congress. Office of Technology Assessment. (1984). *Computerized manufacturing automation: Employment, education, and the workplace*. Washington, DC: U.S. Government Printing Office.

AN ARTICLE IN A JOURNAL WITH CONTINUOUS PAGINATION

Tversky, A., & Kahneman, D. (1981). The framing of decisions and the psychology of choice. *Science, 211,* 453-458.

AN ARTICLE IN A JOURNAL THAT PAGINATES EACH ISSUE SEPARATELY

Foot, R. J. (1988-89). Nuclear coercion and the ending of the Korean conflict. *International Security, 13*(4), 92-112.

The reference informs us that the article appeared in issue number 4 of volume 13.

AN ARTICLE FROM A MONTHLY OR WEEKLY MAGAZINE

Greenwald, J. (1989, February 27). Gimme shelter. *Time, 133,* 50-51.

Maran, S. P. (1988, April). In our backyard, a star explodes. *Smithsonian, 19,* 46-57.

AN ARTICLE IN A NEWSPAPER

Connell, R. (1989, February 6). Career concerns at heart of 1980s campus protests. *Los Angeles Times*, pp. 1, 3.

(*Note:* If no author is given, simply begin with the title followed by the date in parentheses.)

A CHECKLIST FOR CRITICAL PAPERS USING SOURCES

Ask yourself the following questions:

❑ Are all borrowed words and ideas credited, including those from Internet sources?

❑ Are all summaries and paraphrases acknowledged as such?

❑ Are quotations and summaries not too long?

❑ Are quotations accurate? Are omissions of words indicated by three spaced periods? Are additions of words enclosed within square brackets?

❑ Are quotations provided with helpful lead-ins?

❑ Is documentation in proper form?

And, of course, you will also ask yourself the questions that you would ask of a paper that did not use sources, such as:

❑ Is the topic sufficiently narrowed?

❑ Is the thesis (to be advanced or refuted) stated early and clearly, perhaps even in the title?

❑ Is the audience kept in mind? Are opposing views stated fairly and as sympathetically as possible? Are controversial terms defined?

❑ Are assumptions likely to be shared by readers? If not, are they argued rather than merely asserted?

❑ Is the focus clear (evaluation, recommendation of policy)?

❑ Is evidence (examples, testimony, statistics) adequate and sound?

❑ Are inferences valid?

❑ Is the organization clear (effective opening, coherent sequence of arguments, unpretentious ending)?

❑ Is all worthy opposition faced?

❑ Is the tone appropriate?

❑ Has the paper been carefully proofread?

❑ Is the title effective?

❑ Is the introduction effective?

❑ Is the structure reader-friendly?

❑ Is the ending effective?

A BOOK REVIEW

Daniels, N. (1984). Understanding physician power [Review of the book *The social transformation of American medicine*]. *Philosophy and Public Affairs, 13,* 347-356.

Daniels is the reviewer, not the author of the book. The book under review is called *The Social Transformation of American Medicine,* but the review, published in volume 13 of *Philosophy and Public Affairs,* had its own title, "Understanding Physician Power."

If the review does not have a title, retain the square brackets, and use the material within as the title. Proceed as in the example just given.

A WEB SITE

American Psychological Association. (1995). Lesbian and gay parenting. Retrieved June 12, 2000, from http://www.apa.org/pi/parent.html

AN ARTICLE IN AN ONLINE PERIODICAL

Carpenter, S. (2000, October). Biology and social environments jointly influence gender development. *Monitor on Psychology 31*(9). Retrieved from http://www.apa.org/monitor/

For a full account of the APA method of dealing with all sorts of unusual citations, see the sixth edition (2010) of the APA manual, *Publication Manual of the American Psychological Association.*

An Annotated Student Research Paper in MLA Format

The following argument makes good use of sources. Early in the semester the students were asked to choose one topic from a list of ten and to write a documented argument of 750 to 1,250 words (three to five pages of double-spaced typing). The completed paper was due two weeks after the topics were distributed. The assignment, a prelude to working on a research paper of 2,500 to 3,000 words, was in part designed to give students practice in finding and in using sources. Citations are given in the MLA form.

Lesley Timmerman

Professor Jennifer Wilson

English 102

15 August 2016

An Argument for Corporate Responsibility

Opponents of corporate social responsibility (CSR) argue that a company's sole duty is to generate profits. According to them, by acting for the public good, corporations are neglecting their primary obligation to make money. However, as people are becoming more and more conscious of corporate impacts on society and the environment, separating profits from company practices and ethics does not make sense. Employees want to work for institutions that share their values, and consumers want to buy products from companies that are making an impact and improving people's lives. Furthermore, businesses exist in an interdependent world where the health of the environment and the well-being of society really do matter. For these reasons, corporations have to take responsibility for their actions, beyond making money for shareholders. For their own benefit as well as the public's, companies must strive to be socially responsible.

In his article "The Case against Corporate Social Responsibility," *Wall Street Journal* writer Aneel Karnani argues that CSR will never be able to solve the world's problems. Thinking it can, Karnani says, is a dangerous illusion. He recommends that instead of expecting corporate managers to act in the public interest, we should rely on philanthropy and government regulation. Karnani maintains that "Managers who sacrifice profit for the common good [. . .] are in effect imposing a tax on their shareholders and arbitrarily deciding how that money should be spent." In other words, according to Karnani, corporations should not be determining what constitutes socially responsible behavior; individual donors and the government should. Certainly, individuals should continue to make charitable gifts, and governments should maintain laws and regulations to protect the public interest. However, Karnani's reasoning for why corporations should be exempt from social responsibility is flawed. With very few exceptions, corporations' socially responsible actions are not arbitrary and do not sacrifice long-term profits.

Annotations (right margin):

- Title is focused and announces the thesis.
- Double-space between the title and first paragraph—and throughout the essay.
- Brief statement of one side of the issue.
- Summary of the opposing view.
- Lead-in to quotation.
- 1" margin on each side and at bottom.
- Essayist's response to the quotation.

Author concisely
states her
position.

Transitions ("For
example," "also")
alert readers to
where the writer
is taking them.

In fact, corporations have already proven that they can contribute profitably and meaningfully to solving significant global problems by integrating CSR into their standard practices and long-term visions. Rather than focusing on shareholders' short-term profits, many companies have begun measuring their success by "profit, planet and people" — what is known as the "triple bottom line." Businesses operating under this principle consider their environmental and social impacts, as well as their financial impacts, and make responsible and compassionate decisions. For example, such businesses use resources efficiently, create healthy products, choose suppliers who share their ethics, and improve economic opportunities for people in the communities they serve. By doing so, companies often save money. They also contribute to the sustainability of life on earth and ensure the sustainability of their own businesses. In their book *The Triple Bottom Line: How Today's Best-Run Companies Are Achieving Economic, Social, and Environmental Success*, coauthors Savitz and Weber demonstrate that corporations need to become sustainable, in all ways. They argue that "the only way to succeed in today's interdependent world is to embrace sustainability" (xi). The authors go on to show that, for the vast majority of companies, a broad commitment to sustainability enhances profitability (Savitz and Weber 39).

For example, PepsiCo has been able to meet the financial expectations of its shareholders while demonstrating its commitment to the triple bottom line. In addition to donating over $16 million to help victims of natural disasters, Pepsi has woven concerns for people and for the planet into its company practices and culture (Bejou 4). For instance, because of a recent water shortage in an area of India where Pepsi runs a plant, the company began a project to build community wells (Savitz and Weber 160). Though Pepsi did not cause the water shortage nor was its manufacturing threatened by it, "Pepsi realizes that the well-being of the community is part of the company's responsibility" (Savitz and Weber 161). Ultimately, Pepsi chose to look beyond the goal of maximizing short-term profits. By doing so, the company improved its relationship with this Indian community, improved people's daily lives and opportunities, and improved its own reputation. In other words, Pepsi embraced CSR and ensured a more sustainable future for everyone involved.

Another example of a wide-reaching company that is working toward greater sustainability on all fronts is Walmart. The corporation has issued a CSR policy that includes three ambitious goals: "to be fully supplied by renewable energy, to create zero waste and to sell products that sustain people and the environment" ("From Fringe to Mainstream"). As Dr. Doug Guthrie, dean of George Washington University's School of Business, noted in a recent lecture, if a company as powerful as Walmart were to succeed in these goals, the impact would be huge. To illustrate Walmart's potential influence, Dr. Guthrie pointed out that the corporation's exports from China to the United States are equal to Mexico's total exports to the United States. In committing to CSR, the company's leaders are acknowledging how much their power depends on the earth's natural resources, as well as the communities who produce, distribute, sell, and purchase Walmart's products. The company is also well aware that achieving its goals will "ultimately save the company a great deal of money" ("From Fringe to Mainstream"). For good reason, Walmart, like other companies around the world, is choosing to act in everyone's best interest.

Recent research on employees' and consumers' social consciousness offers companies further reason to take corporate responsibility seriously. For example, studies show that workers care about making a difference (Meister). In many cases, workers would even take a pay cut to work for a more responsible, sustainable company. In fact, 45% of workers said they would take a 15% reduction in pay "for a job that makes a social or environmental impact" (Meister). Even more said they would take a 15% cut in pay to work for a company with values that match their own (Meister). The numbers are most significant among Millennials (those born between, approximately, 1980 and the early 2000s). Fully 80% of Millennials said they "wanted to work for a company that cares about how it impacts and contributes to society," and over half said they would not work for an "irresponsible company" (Meister). Given this more socially conscious generation, companies are going to find it harder and harder to ignore CSR.

Author now introduces statistical evidence that, if introduced earlier, might have turned the reader off.

To recruit and retain employees, employers will need to earn the admiration, respect, and loyalty of their workers by becoming "good corporate citizen[s]" (qtd. in "From Fringe to Mainstream").

Similarly, studies clearly show that CSR matters to today's consumers. According to an independent report, 80% of Americans say they would switch brands to support a social cause (Cone Communications 6). Fully 88% say they approve of companies' using social or environmental issues in their marketing (Cone Communications 5). And 83% say they "wish more of the products, services and retailers would support causes" (Cone Communications 5). Other independent surveys corroborate these results, confirming that today's customers, especially Millennials, care about more than just price ("From Fringe to Mainstream"). Furthermore, plenty of companies have seen what happens when they assume that consumers do not care about CSR. For example, in 1997, when Nike customers discovered that their shoes were manufactured by child laborers in Indonesia, the company took a huge financial hit (Guthrie). Today, Information Age customers are even more likely to educate themselves about companies' labor practices and environmental records. Smart corporations will listen to consumer preferences, provide transparency, and commit to integrating CSR into their long-term business plans.

In this increasingly interdependent world, the case against CSR is becoming more and more difficult to defend. Exempting corporations and relying on government to be the world's conscience does not make good social, environmental, or economic sense. Contributors to a recent article in the online journal *Knowledge@Wharton,* published by the Wharton School of Business, agree. Professor Eric Orts maintains that "it is an outmoded view to say that one must rely only on the government and regulation to police business responsibilities. What we need is re-conception of what the purpose of business is" (qtd. in "From Fringe to Mainstream"). The question is, what should the purpose of a business be in today's world? Professor of Business Administration David Bejou of Elizabeth City State University has a thoughtful and sensible answer to that question. He writes,

> Author argues that it is in the *companies'* interest to be socially responsible.

> Author's lead-in to the quotation guides the reader's response to the quotation.

> . . . it is clear that the sole purpose of a business is not merely that of generating profits for its owners. Instead, because compassion provides the necessary equilibrium between a company's purpose and the needs of its communities, it should be the new philosophy of business. (Bejou 1)

As Bejou implies, the days of allowing corporations to act in their own financial self-interest with little or no regard for their effects on others are over. None of us can afford such a narrow view of business. The world is far too interconnected. A seemingly small corporate decision — to buy coffee beans directly from local growers or to install solar panels — can affect the lives and livelihoods of many people and determine the environmental health of whole regions. A business, just like a government or an individual, therefore has an ethical responsibility to act with compassion for the public good.

Fortunately, corporations have many incentives to act responsibly. Customer loyalty, employee satisfaction, overall cost-saving, and long-term viability are just some of the advantages businesses can expect to gain by embracing comprehensive CSR policies. Meanwhile, companies have very little to lose by embracing a socially conscious view. These days, compassion is profitable. Corporations would be wise to recognize the enormous power, opportunity, and responsibility they have to effect positive change.

Upbeat ending.

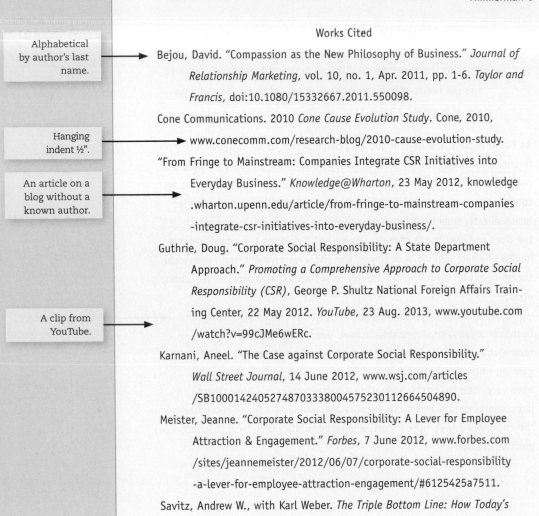

Works Cited

Bejou, David. "Compassion as the New Philosophy of Business." *Journal of Relationship Marketing*, vol. 10, no. 1, Apr. 2011, pp. 1-6. *Taylor and Francis*, doi:10.1080/15332667.2011.550098.

Cone Communications. 2010 *Cone Cause Evolution Study*. Cone, 2010, www.conecomm.com/research-blog/2010-cause-evolution-study.

"From Fringe to Mainstream: Companies Integrate CSR Initiatives into Everyday Business." *Knowledge@Wharton*, 23 May 2012, knowledge .wharton.upenn.edu/article/from-fringe-to-mainstream-companies -integrate-csr-initiatives-into-everyday-business/.

Guthrie, Doug. "Corporate Social Responsibility: A State Department Approach." *Promoting a Comprehensive Approach to Corporate Social Responsibility (CSR)*, George P. Shultz National Foreign Affairs Train- ing Center, 22 May 2012. *YouTube*, 23 Aug. 2013, www.youtube.com /watch?v=99cJMe6wERc.

Karnani, Aneel. "The Case against Corporate Social Responsibility." *Wall Street Journal*, 14 June 2012, www.wsj.com/articles /SB10001424052748703338004575230112664504890.

Meister, Jeanne. "Corporate Social Responsibility: A Lever for Employee Attraction & Engagement." *Forbes*, 7 June 2012, www.forbes.com /sites/jeannemeister/2012/06/07/corporate-social-responsibility -a-lever-for-employee-attraction-engagement/#6125425a7511.

Savitz, Andrew W., with Karl Weber. *The Triple Bottom Line: How Today's Best-Run Companies Are Achieving Economic, Social, and Environmental Success*, Jossey-Bass, 2006.

Alphabetical by author's last name.

Hanging indent ½".

An article on a blog without a known author.

A clip from YouTube.

An Annotated Student Research Paper in APA Format

The following paper is an example of a student paper that uses APA format.

The APA-style cover page gives title, author, and course information.

The Role of Spirituality and Religion
in Mental Health
Laura DeVeau
English 102
Professor Gardner
April 12, 2016

The Role of Spirituality and Religion
in Mental Health

It has been called "a vestige of the childhood of mankind," "the feeling of something true, total and absolute," "an otherworldly answer as regards the meaning of life" (Jones, 1991, p. 1; Amaro, 1998; Kristeva, 1987, p. 27). It has been compared to medicine, described as a psychological cure for mental illness, and also referred to as the cause of a dangerous fanaticism. With so many differing opinions on the impact of religion in people's lives, where would one begin a search for the truth? Who has the answer: Christians, humanists, objectivists, atheists, psychoanalysts, Buddhists, philosophers, cults? This was my dilemma at the advent of my research into how religion and spirituality affect the mental health of society as a whole.

In this paper, I explore the claims, widely accepted by professionals in the field of psychology, that religious and spiritual practices have a negative impact on mental health. In addition, though, I cannot help but reflect on how this exploration has changed my beliefs as well. Religion is such a personal experience that one cannot be dispassionate in reporting it. One can, however, subject the evidence provided by those who have studied the issue to critical scrutiny. Having done so, I find myself in disagreement with those who claim religious feelings are incompatible with sound mental health. There is a nearly limitless number of beliefs regarding spirituality. Some are organized and involve rituals like mass or worship. Many are centered around the existence of a higher being, while others focus on the self. I have attempted to uncover the perfect set of values that lead to a better lifestyle, but my research has pointed me in an entirely different direction, where no single belief seems to be adequate but where spiritual belief in general should be valued more highly than it is currently in mental health circles.

I grew up in a moderately devout Catholic family. Like many young people raised in a household where one religion is practiced by both parents, it never occurred to me to question those beliefs. I went through a spiritual cycle, which I believe much of Western society also

Short form of title and page number as running head.

Citation of multiple works from references.

Acknowledgment of opposing viewpoints.

Thesis explicitly introduced.

experiences. I attended religious services because I had to. I possessed a blind, unquestioning acceptance of what I was being taught because the adults I trusted said it was so. Like many adolescents and young adults, though, I stopped going to church when I was old enough to decide because I thought I had better things to do. At this stage, we reach a point when we begin searching for a meaning to our existence. For some, this search is brought on by a major crisis or a feeling of emptiness in their daily lives, while for others it is simply a part of growing up. This is where we begin to make personal choices, but with the barrage of options, where do we turn?

> **Author and date cited for summary or paraphrase.**

Beginning with the holistic health movement in the eighties, there has been a mass shift from traditional religions to less structured spiritual practices such as meditation, yoga, the Cabala, and mysticism (Beyerman, 1989). They venture beyond the realm of conventional dogmatism and into the new wave of spirituality. Many of these practices are based on the notion that health of the mind and spirit equals health of the body. Associated with this movement is a proliferation of retreats offering a chance to get in touch with the beauty and silence of nature and seminars where we can take "a break from our everyday environment where our brains are bustling and our bodies are exhausting themselves" ("Psychological benefits," 1999).

> **Anonymous source cited by title and date.**

A major concept of the spiritual new wave is that it focuses inward toward the individual psyche, rather than outward toward another being like a god. Practitioners do not deny the existence of this being, but they believe that to fully love another, we must first understand ourselves. Many find this a preferable alternative to religions where the individual is seen as a walking dispenser of sin who is very fortunate to have a forgiving creator. It is also a relief from the scare tactics like damnation used by traditional religions to make people behave. Many, therefore, praise the potential psychological benefits of such spirituality.

> **Clear transition refers to previous paragraph.**

While I believe strongly in the benefits of the new wave, I am not willing to do away with structured religion, for I find that it also has its benefits. Without the existence of churches and temples, it would be harder to expose the public to values beneficial to mental stability. It is much more difficult to hand a child a copy of the Cabala and say "Read this, and then get back to me on it" than it is to bring a child to a service where the ideas are represented with concrete examples. My religious upbringing presented me with a set of useful morals and values, and it does the same for millions of others who are brought up in this manner. Many people, including some followers of the new wave, are bitter toward Christianity because of events in history like the Crusades, the Inquisition, the Salem witch trials, and countless other horrific acts supposedly committed in the name of God. But these events were based not on biblical teachings but on pure human greed and lust for power. We should not reject the benevolent possibilities of organized religion on the basis of historical atrocities any more than we should abandon public education because a few teachers are known to mistreat children.

Another factor contributing to the reluctance concerning religion is the existence of cults that seduce people into following their extreme teachings. The victims are often at vulnerable times in their lives, and the leaders are usually very charming, charismatic, and sometimes also psychotic or otherwise mentally unstable. Many argue that if we acknowledge these groups as dangerous cults, then we must do the same for traditional religions such as Christianity and Islam, which are likewise founded on the teachings of charismatic leaders. Again, though, critics are too quick to conflate all religious and spiritual practice; we must distinguish between those who pray and attend services and those who commit group suicide because they think that aliens are coming to take over the world. Cults have provided many psychologists, who are eager to discount religion as a factor in improving mental health, with an easy target. Ellis (1993), the founder of rational-emotive therapy, cites many extreme examples of religious commitment, such as cults and antiabortion killings, to show that commitment is hazardous to one's sanity. Anomalies like these should not be used to speak of religion as a whole, though. Religion is clearly the least of these people's mental problems.

When the author's name appears in text, only the date is cited in parentheses.

Besides Ellis, there are many others in the field of psychology who do not recognize religion as a potential aid for improving the condition of the psyche. Actually, fewer than 45% of the members of the American Psychiatric Association even believe in God. The general American public has more than twice that percentage of religious devotees (Larson, 1998). Going back to the days of Freud, many psychologists have held atheist views. The father of psychoanalysis himself called religion a "universal obsessional neurosis." Psychologists have long rejected research that demonstrates the benefits of spirituality by saying that this research is biased. They claim that such studies are out to prove that religion helps because the researchers are religious people who need to justify their beliefs.

While this may be true in some instances, there is also some quite empirical research available to support the claims of those who promote religion and spirituality. The *Journal for the Scientific Study of Religion* has conducted many studies examining the effects of religion on individuals and groups. In one example, the relationship between religious coping methods and positive recovery after major stressful events was observed. The results indicated not only that spirituality was not harmful to the mind but that "the positive religious coping pattern was tied to benevolent outcomes, including fewer symptoms of psychological distress, [and] reports of psychological and spiritual growth as a result of the stressor" (Pargament, Smith, Koening, and Perez, 1998, p. 721). Clearly, the benefits of piety can, in fact, be examined empirically, and in some cases the results point to a positive correlation between religion and mental health.

But let us get away from statistics and studies. If religion is both useless and dangerous, as so many psychologists claim, we must ask why has it remained so vital a part of humanity for so long. Even if it can be reduced to a mere coping method that humans use to justify their existence and explain incomprehensible events, is it futile? I would suggest that this alone represents a clear benefit to society. Should religion, if it cannot be proven as "true," be eliminated and life be based on scientific fact alone?

Bracketed word in quotation not in original source.

Author, date, and page number are cited for a direct quotation.

Surely many would find this a pointless existence. With all the conflicting knowledge I have gained about spirituality during my personal journey and my research, one idea is clear. It is not the depth of devotion, the time of life when one turns to religion, or even the particular combination of beliefs one chooses to adopt that will improve the quality of life. There is no right or wrong answer when it comes to self-fulfillment. It is whatever works for the individual, even if that means holding no religious or spiritual beliefs at all. But clearly there *are* benefits to be gained, at least for some individuals, and mental health professionals need to begin acknowledging this fact in their daily practice.

Conclusion restates and strengthens thesis.

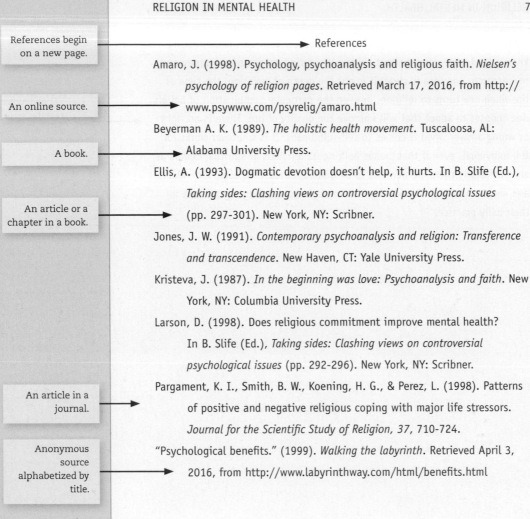

References

Amaro, J. (1998). Psychology, psychoanalysis and religious faith. *Nielsen's psychology of religion pages*. Retrieved March 17, 2016, from http://www.psywww.com/psyrelig/amaro.html

Beyerman A. K. (1989). *The holistic health movement*. Tuscaloosa, AL: Alabama University Press.

Ellis, A. (1993). Dogmatic devotion doesn't help, it hurts. In B. Slife (Ed.), *Taking sides: Clashing views on controversial psychological issues* (pp. 297-301). New York, NY: Scribner.

Jones, J. W. (1991). *Contemporary psychoanalysis and religion: Transference and transcendence*. New Haven, CT: Yale University Press.

Kristeva, J. (1987). *In the beginning was love: Psychoanalysis and faith*. New York, NY: Columbia University Press.

Larson, D. (1998). Does religious commitment improve mental health? In B. Slife (Ed.), *Taking sides: Clashing views on controversial psychological issues* (pp. 292-296). New York, NY: Scribner.

Pargament, K. I., Smith, B. W., Koening, H. G., & Perez, L. (1998). Patterns of positive and negative religious coping with major life stressors. *Journal for the Scientific Study of Religion, 37*, 710-724.

"Psychological benefits." (1999). *Walking the labyrinth*. Retrieved April 3, 2016, from http://www.labyrinthway.com/html/benefits.html

Labels (left margin):

References begin on a new page.

An online source.

A book.

An article or a chapter in a book.

An article in a journal.

Anonymous source alphabetized by title.

PART THREE

Further Views on Argument

A Philosopher's View: The Toulmin Model

All my ideas hold together, but I cannot elaborate them all at once. —JEAN-JACQUES ROUSSEAU

Clarity has been said to be not enough. But perhaps it will be time to go into that when we are within measurable distance of achieving clarity on some matter. —J. L. AUSTIN

[Philosophy is] a peculiarly stubborn effort to think clearly. —WILLIAM JAMES

Philosophy is like trying to open a safe with a combination lock: Each little adjustment of the dials seems to achieve nothing, only when everything is in place does the door open. —LUDWIG WITTGENSTEIN

In Chapter 3, we explained the contrast between making *deductive* and *inductive* arguments, the two main methods people use to reason. Either:

- we make explicit something concealed in what we already accept (**deduction**), or
- we use what we have observed as a basis for asserting or proposing something new (**induction**).

These two types of reasoning share some structural features, as we also noticed. Both deductive and inductive reasoning seek to establish a **thesis** (or conclusion) by offering **reasons** for accepting the conclusion. Thus, every argument contains both a thesis and one or more supportive reasons.

After a little scrutiny, we can in fact point to several features shared by all arguments, whether deductive or inductive, good or bad. We use the vocabulary popularized by Stephen Toulmin, Richard Rieke, and Allan Janik in their book *An Introduction to Reasoning* (1979; second edition 1984) to explore the various elements of argument. Once these elements are understood, it is possible to analyze an argument using their approach and their vocabulary in what has come to be known as "The Toulmin Method."

The Claim

Every argument has a purpose, goal, or aim — namely, to establish a **claim** (*conclusion* or *thesis*). Suppose you are arguing in favor of equal rights for women. You might state your thesis or claim as follows:

> Men and women ought to have equal rights.

A more precise formulation of the claim might be this:

> Men and women ought to have equal legal rights.

A still more precise formulation might be this:

> Equal legal rights for men and women ought to be protected by our Constitution.

The third version of this claim states what the controversy in the 1970s over the Equal Rights Amendment was all about. (Both houses of Congress passed it in 1972, but the number of state legislatures that needed to ratify it before the Amendment could be added to the Constitution failed to do so before Congress's mandated deadline of June 30, 1982.)

In other words, the *claim* being made in an argument is the whole point of making the argument in the first place. Consequently, when you read or analyze someone else's argument, the first questions you should ask are these:

- What is the argument intended to prove or establish?
- *What claim is it making?*
- Has this claim been clearly and precisely formulated, so that it unambiguously asserts what its advocate wants it to assert?

Grounds

Once we have the argument's purpose or point clearly in mind and thus know what the arguer is aiming to establish, then we can look for the evidence, reasons, support — in short, for the **grounds** — on which that claim is based. In a *deductive* argument, these grounds are the premises from which the claim is deduced; in an *inductive* argument, the grounds are the evidence — which could be based on a sample, an observation, or an experiment — that makes the claim plausible or probable.

Not every kind of claim can be supported by every kind of ground, and, conversely, not every kind of ground gives equally good support for every kind of claim. Suppose, for instance, that I claim half the students in the classroom are women. I can establish the *grounds* for this claim in any of several ways. For example:

1. I can count all the women and all the men. Suppose the total equals fifty. If the number of women is twenty-five and the number of men is twenty-five, I have vindicated my claim.

2. I can count a sample of ten students — perhaps the first ten to walk into the classroom — and find that in the sample five of the students are women. I thus have inductive — plausible but not conclusive — grounds for my claim.

3. I can point out that the students in the college divide equally into men and women and then claim that this class is a representative sample of the whole college.

Clearly, ground 1 is stronger than ground 2, and 2 is much stronger than 3.

Up to this point, we have merely restated points about premises and conclusions that were covered in Chapter 3. We want now to consider four additional features of arguments.

Warrants

Once we have the claim or the point of an argument fixed in mind and have isolated the evidence or reasons offered in its support, the next question to ask is this:

Exactly how do the reasons offered in support of the conclusion work? In other words, what kind of guarantee — **warrant** — is provided to demonstrate that the reasons proffered actually do support the claim or lead to the conclusion? (A *warrant* in this context is like the *warranty* you get when you buy something.)

In ordinary and straightforward *deductive* arguments, warrants take different forms. In the simplest cases, we can point to the way in which the *meanings* of the key terms are really equivalent. Thus, if John is taller than Bill, then Bill must be shorter than John. We know this because we know what "is shorter than" and "is taller than" mean. If A is taller than B, it must be the case that B is shorter than A; those are the meanings of the phrases being used here. Of course, everyone involved does have to know the language well enough to understand the relationship between "is taller than" and "is shorter than." The *warrant* in this case is the common understanding of what those two phrases mean.

In other cases, we may need to be more resourceful. A reliable tactic is to think up a simple *parallel argument*, an argument exactly parallel in form and structure to the argument we are trying to defend. If the two arguments really do have the same form and structure, and we are ready to accept the simpler one, then we can point out that the more complex argument must be accepted — because the two arguments have exactly the same structure. For example, if we want to argue that it is reasonable for FedEx to charge more for its delivery services than the U.S. Postal Service (USPS) does, we could point out that since it seems entirely reasonable to pay higher costs for special services from the USPS such as overnight delivery promised by a certain time (depending on factors such as location), then it is reasonable to pay even higher fees for similar overnight delivery by FedEx because that service includes sending someone to pick up what you want delivered.

In simple *inductive* arguments, we are likely to point to the way in which observations or sets of data constitute a *representative sample* of a whole population, even if not every member of the sample is strictly in evidence. For instance, when scattered information is plotted on a graph, the trend line does not have to touch each (or even any) of the data points as long as they are scattered above and below the line in roughly equal numbers in pairs that are roughly equidistant from the trend line. We can defend this projection on the grounds that it takes all of the points into account in the least complicated way. In such a case, the warrant is this combination of *inclusiveness* and *simplicity*.

Establishing the warrants for our reasoning—that is, explaining why our grounds really do support our claims—can quickly become a highly technical and exacting procedure that goes far beyond the aims of this book. Even so, developing a "feel" for why reasons or grounds are or are not relevant to what they are alleged to support is important. "That's just my view" is *not* a convincing warrant for any argument. Even without formal training, however, one can sense that something is wrong with many bad arguments. Here is one example: British professor C. E. M. Joad found himself standing on a station platform, annoyed because he had just missed his train. Then another train, making an unscheduled stop, pulled up to the platform in front of him. Joad decided to jump aboard, only to hear the conductor say, "I'm afraid you'll have to get off, Sir. This train doesn't stop here." "In that case," replied the professor, "don't worry. I'm not on it."

Backing

A really solid argument may need even further support, especially if what we're arguing is complicated. *Warrants*, remember, explain the way our *grounds* support our *claims*. The next task, however, is to be able to show that we can back up what we have claimed by showing that the reasons we have given for a claim are good reasons. To establish that kind of further support for an argument is to provide **backing**.

What is appropriate backing for one kind of argument might be quite inappropriate for another kind of argument. For example, the kinds of reasons relevant to support an amendment to the Constitution are completely different from the kinds appropriate to settle the question of what caused the defeat of Napoleon's invasion of Russia in 1812. Arguments for the amendment might be rooted in an appeal to fairness, whereas arguments about the military defeat might be rooted in letters and other documents in French and Russian archives. The *canons* (established conventions) of good argument in two such dramatically different cases have to do with the means that scholarly communities in law and history, respectively, have developed over the years to support, defend, challenge, and undermine a given kind of argument.

Another way of stating this point is to recognize that once you have given reasons for a claim, you are then likely to be challenged to explain why your reasons are good reasons — why, that is, anyone should believe your reasons rather than regard them skeptically. They have to be the right kinds of reasons, given the field you are arguing about. Why (to give a simple example) should we accept the testimony of Dr. *X* when Dr. *Y*, equally renowned, supports the opposite side? What more do we need to know before "expert testimony" is appropriately invoked? For a different kind of case: When and why is it safe to rest a prediction on a small though admittedly carefully selected sample? And still another: Why is it legitimate to argue that (1) if I dream I am the king of France, then I must exist, whereas it is illegitimate to argue that (2) if I dream I am the king of France, then the king of France must exist?

To answer challenges of these sorts is to back up one's reasons, to give them legitimate *backing*. No argument is any better than its backing.

Modal Qualifiers

As we have seen, all arguments are made up of assertions or propositions that can be sorted into four categories:

- the *claim* (conclusion, thesis to be established)
- the *grounds* (explicit reasons advanced)
- the *warrant* (guarantee, evidence, or principle that legitimates the ground by connecting it to the claim)
- the *backing* (relevant support, implicit assumptions)

All of the kinds of propositions that emerge when we assert something in an argument have what philosophers call a **modality**. This means that propositions generally indicate — explicitly or tacitly — the *character* and *scope* of what is believed to be their likely truth.

Character has to do with the nature of the claim being made, the extent of an argument's presumed reach. Both making and evaluating arguments require being clear about whether they are *necessary, probable, plausible,* or *possible.* Consider, for example, a claim that it is to the advantage of a college to have a racially diverse student body. Is that *necessarily* or only *probably* true? What about an argument that a runner who easily wins a 100-meter race should also be able to win at 200 meters? Is this *plausible* — or only *possible*? Indicating the *character* with which an assertion is advanced is crucial to any argument for or against it. Furthermore, if there is more than one reason for making a claim, and all of those reasons are *good*, it is still possible that one of those good reasons may be *better* than the others. If so, the better reason should be stressed.

Indicating the *scope* of an assertion is equally crucial to how an argument plays out. *Scope* entails such considerations as whether the proposition is thought to be true *always* or just *sometimes.* Further, is the claim being made supposed to apply in *all* instances or just in *some*? Assertions are usually clearer, as well as more likely to be true, if they are explicitly *quantified* and *qualified.* Suppose, for example, that you are arguing against smoking, and the ground for your claim is this:

Heavy smokers cut short their life span.

In this case, there are three obvious alternative quantifications to choose among: *All* smokers cut short their life span, *most* do, or only *some* do. Until the assertion is quantified in one of these ways, we really don't know what is being asserted — and so we don't know what degree and kind of evidence or counterevidence is relevant. Other quantifiers include *few, rarely, often, sometimes, perhaps, usually, more or less, regularly, occasionally.*

Scope also has to do with the fact that empirical generalizations are typically *contingent* on various factors. Indicating such contingencies clearly is an important way to protect a generalization against obvious counterexamples. Thus, consider this empirical generalization:

Students do best on final examinations if they study hard for them.

Are we really to believe that students who cram ("study hard" in that concentrated sense) for an exam will do better than those who do the work diligently throughout the whole course ("study hard" in that broader sense) and therefore do not need to cram for the final? Probably not; what is really meant is that *all other things being equal* (in Latin, *ceteris paribus*), concentrated study just before an exam will yield good results. Alluding in this way to the contingencies — the things that might derail the argument — shows that the writer is aware of possible exceptions and is conceding them from the start.

In sum, sensitivity to both character and (especially) scope — paying attention to the role played by quantifiers, qualifiers, and contingencies and making sure you use appropriate ones for each of your assertions — will strengthen your arguments enormously. Not least of the benefits is that you will reduce the peculiar vulnerabilities of an argument that is undermined by exaggeration and other misguided generalizations.

Rebuttals

Very few arguments of any interest are beyond dispute, conclusively knockdown affairs. Only very rarely is the claim of an argument so rigidly tied to its grounds, warrants, and backing — and with its quantifiers and qualifiers argued in so precise a manner — that it proves its conclusion beyond any possibility of doubt. On the contrary, most arguments have many counterarguments, and sometimes one of these counterarguments is more convincing than the original argument.

Suppose someone has taken a sample that appears to be random: An interviewer on your campus accosts the first ten students she encounters, and seven of them are fraternity or sorority members. She is now ready to argue that seven-tenths of enrolled students belong to Greek organizations.

You believe, however, that the Greeks are in the minority; you point out that she happens to have conducted her interview around the corner from the Panhellenic Society's office just off Sorority Row. Her random sample is anything but random. The ball is now back in her court as you await her response to your rebuttal.

As this example illustrates, it is safe to say that we do not understand our own arguments very well until we have tried to get a grip on the places in which they are vulnerable to criticism, counterattack, or refutation. We have already, in Chapter 3, quoted Edmund Burke — but the passage is worth repeating: "He that wrestles with us strengthens our nerves, and sharpens our skill. Our antagonist is our helper."

To be sure, in everyday conversation we may not enjoy being in the company of people who interrupt to ask what are our grounds, warrants, backing, and so forth. The poet T. S. Eliot amusingly characterized himself as such a person:

How Unpleasant to Meet Mr. Eliot!

How unpleasant to meet Mr. Eliot!
With his features of clerical cut.
And his brow so grim

And his mouth so prim
And his conversation, so nicely
Restricted to What Precisely
And If and Perhaps and But . . .
How unpleasant to meet Mr. Eliot!
(Whether his mouth be open or shut.)

Still, if we wish to make serious progress in thinking and arguing about significant issues, cultivating alertness to possible weak spots in arguments — our own arguments as well as those of others — and incorporating thoughtful responses to anticipated criticisms will always be helpful.

Corbis

Would you want to argue with Mr. Eliot?

THINKING CRITICALLY *Constructing a Toulmin Argument*

Choose a topic or issue that interests you. In the spaces provided, supply a sentence or two for each step of a Toulmin argument about your topic.

STEP OF TOULMIN ARGUMENT	QUESTION THIS STEP ADDRESSES	YOUR SENTENCE(S)
Claim	*What is your argument?*	
Grounds	*What is your evidence?*	
Warrant	*What reasoning connects your evidence to your argument?*	
Backing	*Why should the reader agree with your grounds?*	
Rebuttal	*What are the objections to this argument?*	
Qualifier	*What are the limits of your argument?*	

🔲 **LaunchPad**   To complete this activity online, go to **macmillanhighered.com/barnetbedauohara**

PUTTING THE TOULMIN METHOD TO WORK:

Responding to an Argument

Let's take a look at another argument — it happens to be on why buying directly from farmers near you won't save the planet — and see how the Toulmin method can be applied. The checklist on page 333 can help you focus your thoughts as you read.

JAMES E. McWILLIAMS

> *James E. McWilliams (b. 1968), the author of* Just Food, *is an associate professor of history at Texas State University. This piece first appeared in* Forbes Magazine *on August 3, 2009.*

The Locavore Myth: Why Buying from Nearby Farmers Won't Save the Planet

Buy local, shrink the distance food travels, save the planet. The locavore movement has captured a lot of fans. To their credit, they are highlighting the problems with industrialized food. But a lot of them are making a big mistake. By focusing on transportation, they overlook other energy-hogging factors in food production.

Take lamb. A 2006 academic study (funded by the New Zealand government) discovered that it made more environmental sense for a Londoner to buy lamb shipped from New Zealand than to buy lamb raised in the U.K. This finding is counterintuitive — if you're only counting food miles. But New Zealand lamb is raised on pastures with a small carbon footprint, whereas most English lamb is produced under intensive factory-like conditions with a big carbon footprint. This disparity overwhelms domestic lamb's advantage in transportation energy.

New Zealand lamb is not exceptional. Take a close look at water usage, fertilizer types, processing methods, and packaging techniques and you discover that factors other than shipping far outweigh the energy it takes to transport food. One analysis, by Rich Pirog of the Leopold Center for Sustainable Agriculture, showed that transportation accounts for only 11 percent of food's carbon footprint. A fourth of the energy required to produce food is expended in the consumer's kitchen. Still more energy is consumed per meal in a restaurant, since restaurants throw away most of their leftovers.

Locavores argue that buying local food supports an area's farmers and, in turn, strengthens the community. Fair enough. Left unacknowledged, however, is the fact that it also hurts farmers in other parts of the world. The U.K. buys most of its green beans from Kenya. While it's true that the beans almost always arrive in airplanes — the form of transportation that consumes the most energy — it's also true that a campaign to shame English consumers with small airplane stickers affixed to flown-in produce threatens the livelihood of 1.5 million sub-Saharan farmers.

Another chink in the locavores' armor 5 involves the way food miles are calculated. To choose a locally grown apple over an apple trucked in from across the country might seem easy. But this decision ignores economies of scale. To take an extreme example, a shipper sending a truck with 2,000 apples over 2,000 miles would consume the same amount of fuel per apple as a local farmer who takes a pickup 50 miles to sell 50 apples at his stall at the green market. The critical measure here is not food miles but apples per gallon.

The one big problem with thinking beyond food miles is that it's hard to get the information you need. Ethically concerned consumers know very little about processing practices, water availability, packaging waste, and fertilizer application. This is an opportunity for watchdog groups. They should make life-cycle carbon counts available to shoppers.

Until our food system becomes more transparent, there is one thing you can do to shrink the carbon footprint of your dinner: Take the meat off your plate. No matter how you slice it, it takes more energy to bring meat, as opposed to plants, to the table. It takes 6 pounds of grain to make a pound of chicken and 10 to 16 pounds to make a pound of beef. That difference translates into big differences in inputs. It requires 2,400 liters of water to make a burger and only 13 liters to grow a tomato. A majority of the water in the American West goes toward the production of pigs, chickens, and cattle.

The average American eats 273 pounds of meat a year. Give up red meat once a week and you'll save as much energy as if the only food miles in your diet were the distance to the nearest truck farmer.

If you want to make a statement, ride your bike to the farmer's market. If you want to reduce greenhouse gases, become a vegetarian.

A CHECKLIST FOR USING THE TOULMIN METHOD

Have I asked the following questions?

- ☐ What claim does the argument make?
- ☐ What grounds are offered for the claim?
- ☐ What warrants the inferences from the grounds to the claim?
- ☐ What backing supports the claim?
- ☐ With what modalities are the claim and grounds asserted?
- ☐ To what rebuttals are the claim, grounds, and backing vulnerable?

Thinking with Toulmin's Method

Remember to make use of the checklist above as you work to find the claim(s), grounds, and warrant(s) that McWilliams puts forward in this short essay.

- First and foremost, what **claim** is the author making? Is it in his title? The opening sentence? Or is it buried in the first paragraph?

McWilliams really gives away his game in his title, even though he opens the essay itself in a way that might make the reader think he is about to launch into a defense of the locavore movement. He even goes out of his way to praise its members ("To their credit . . ."). The signal that his claim really appears already in the title and that he is *not* going to defend the locavore movement is the way he begins the fourth sentence. Notice that although you may have been told that starting a sentence with *But* isn't the best way to write, McWilliams here does so to good effect. Not only does he dramatically counter what he said just prior to that; he also sets up the final sentence of the paragraph, which turns out to be crucial. In this way, he draws sharp attention to his *claim*. How would you state his claim?

- Second, what are the **grounds,** the evidence or reasons, that the author advances in support of his claim?

As it turns out, McWilliams spells out only one example as evidence for his claim. What is it? Is it convincing? Should he have provided more evidence or reasons at this point? It turns out that he does have other grounds to offer—but he mentions them only later. What are those other pieces of evidence?

- Third, what **warrants** does McWilliams offer to show why we should accept his grounds? What authority does he cite? How effective and convincing is this way of trying to get us to accept the grounds he offered in support of his claim?

The essence of the Toulmin method lies in these three elements: the claim(s), the grounds, and the warrant(s). If you have extracted these from McWilliams's essay, you are well on the way to being able to identify the argument he is putting forward. So far, so good. Further probing, however—looking for the other three elements of the Toulmin method (the backing, the modal qualifiers and quantifiers, and the rebuttal)—is essential before you are in a position to actually evaluate the argument. So let's go on.

- Fourth, what **backing** does McWilliams provide? What reasons does he give that might persuade us to accept his argument? Look for what he claimed came out of the analysis that was his basic warrant. He certainly seems to be using factual information—but what if you challenged him? Has he provided adequate reasons for us to believe him? What could he (or would he have to) be able to tell us if we challenged him with questions like "How do you know . . . ?" or "Why do you believe . . . ?" In other words, has he provided adequate backing? Or does he want us to just accept his statement of the facts?

- Fifth, does McWilliams use **modal qualifiers**? Can you find phrases like "in most cases" or "generally it is true that . . . "? Or does he write so boldly—with little in the way of qualifiers or quantifiers—that readers are left uncertain about whether to accept his position? Where might he have effectively used qualifiers?

- Finally, does McWilliams use **rebuttals,** the reasons given in anticipation of some- one rejecting the author's claim, or conceding the claim but rejecting the grounds? Does McWilliams anticipate rejections and prepare rebuttals? Does he offer anything to forestall criticisms? If so, what is it that he does? If not, what could or should he have done?

Just how good an argument has McWilliams made? Is he convincing? If you identified weak points in his argument, what are they? Can you help strengthen the argument? If so, how?

9

A Logician's View: Deduction, Induction, Fallacies

Logic is the anatomy of thought.
— JOHN LOCKE

Logic takes care of itself; all we have to do is to look and see how it does it. — LUDWIG WITTGENSTEIN

I n Chapter 3 we introduced the terms *deduction*, *induction*, and *fallacy*. Here we discuss them in greater detail.

Deduction

The basic aim of deductive reasoning is to start with some assumption or premise and extract from it a conclusion—a logical consequence—that is concealed but implicit in it. Thus, taking the simplest case, if I assert as a premise

1a.   Nuclear power poses more risks of harm to the environment than fossil fuels.

then it is a matter of simple deduction to infer the conclusion that

1b.   Fossil fuels pose fewer risks of harm to the environment than nuclear power.

Anyone who understands English would grant that 1b follows 1a—or equivalently, that 1b can be validly deduced from 1a—because whatever two objects, *A* and *B*, you choose, if *A* does *more things than B*, then *B* must do *fewer things than A*.

Thus, in this and all other cases of valid deductive reasoning, we can say not only that we are entitled to *infer* the conclusion from the premise—in this case, infer 1b from 1a—but that the premise *implies* the conclusion. Remember, too, the conclusion (1b) that fossil fuels pose fewer risks than nuclear power—inferred or deduced from the statement (1a) that nuclear power poses more risks—does not depend on the truth of the statement that nuclear power poses more risks. If the speaker (falsely) asserts that nuclear power poses more risks, then the hearer validly (i.e., logically) concludes that fossil fuels pose fewer risks. Thus, 1b follows from 1a whether or not 1a is true; consequently, if 1a is true, then so is 1b; but if 1a is false, then 1b must be false also.

Let's take another example — more interesting but comparably simple:

2a.   President Truman was underrated by his critics.

Given 2a, a claim amply verified by events of the 1950s, one is entitled to infer that

2b.   His critics underrated President Truman.

On what basis can we argue that 2a implies 2b? The two propositions are equivalent because a rule of English grammar assures us that we can convert the position of subject and predicate phrases in a sentence by shifting from the passive to the active voice (or vice versa) without any change in the conditions that make the proposition true (or false).

Both pairs of examples illustrate that in deductive reasoning, our aim is to transform, reformulate, or restate in our conclusion some (or, as in the two examples above, all) of the information contained in our premises.

Remember, even though a proposition or statement follows from a previous proposition or statement, the statements need not be true. We can see why if we consider another example. Suppose someone asserts or claims that

3a.   The Gettysburg Address is longer than the Declaration of Independence.

As every student of American history knows, 3a is false. But false or not, we can validly deduce from it that

3b.   The Declaration of Independence is shorter than the Gettysburg Address.

This inference is valid (even though the conclusion is untrue) because the conclusion follows logically (more precisely, deductively) from 3a: In English, as we know, the meaning of "*A* is shorter than *B*," which appears in 3b, is simply the converse of "*B* is longer than *A*," which appears in 3a.

The deductive relation between 3a and 3b reminds us again that the idea of validity, which is so crucial to deduction, is not the same as the idea of truth. False propositions have implications — logical consequences — too, just as true propositions do.

In the three pairs of examples so far, what can we point to as the warrant for our claims? Well, look at the reasoning in each case; the arguments rely on rules of ordinary English, on the accepted meanings of words like *on*, *under*, and *underrated*.

In many cases, of course, the deductive inference or pattern of reasoning is much more complex than that which we have seen in the examples so far. When we introduced the idea of deduction in Chapter 3, we gave as our primary example the *syllogism*. Here is another example:

4.   Texas is larger than California; California is larger than Arizona; therefore, Texas is larger than Arizona.

The conclusion in this syllogism can be derived from the two premises; that is, anyone who asserts the two premises is committed to accepting the conclusion as well, whether or not one thinks of it.

Notice again that the *truth* of the conclusion is not established merely by validity of the inference. The conclusion in this syllogism happens to be true. And the premises of this syllogism imply the conclusion. But the argument establishes the conclusion only because both of the premises on which the conclusion depends are true. Even a Californian admits that Texas is larger than California, which in turn is larger than Arizona. In other words, argument 4 is a *sound* argument because (as we explained in Chapter 3) it is valid and all its premises are true. All — and only — arguments that *prove* their conclusions have these two traits.

How might we present the warrant for the argument in 4? Short of a crash course in formal logic, either of two strategies might suffice. One is to argue from the fact that the validity of the inference depends on the meaning of a key concept, *being larger than*. This concept has the property of *transitivity,* a property that many concepts share (e.g., *is equal to, is to the right of, is smarter than* — all are transitive concepts). Consequently, whatever A, B, and C are, if A is larger than B, and B is larger than C, then A will be larger than C. The final step is to substitute "Texas," "California," and "Arizona" for A, B, and C, respectively.

A second strategy, less abstract and more graphic, is to think of representing Texas, California, and Arizona by nested circles. Thus, the first premise in argument 4 would look like this:

The second premise would look like this:

The conclusion would look like this:

We can see that this conclusion follows from the premises because it amounts to nothing more than what one gets by superimposing the two premises on each other. Thus, the whole argument can be represented like this:

$$\left(\text{TX}\ \widehat{\text{CA}}\right) + \left(\text{CA}\ \widehat{\text{AZ}}\right) = \left(\text{TX}\ \widehat{\text{AZ}}\right)$$

The so-called middle term in the argument — California — disappears from the conclusion; its role is confined to be the link between the other two terms, Texas and Arizona, in the premises. (This is an adaptation of the technique used in elementary formal logic known as Venn diagrams.) In this manner one can give graphic display to the important fact that the conclusion follows from the premises because one can literally *see* the conclusion represented by nothing more than a representation of the premises.

Both of these strategies bring out the fact that validity of deductive inference is a purely *formal* property of argument. Each strategy abstracts the form from the content of the propositions involved to show how the concepts in the premises are related to the concepts in the conclusion.

For the sake of illustration, here is another syllogistic argument with the same logical features as argument 4. (A nice exercise is to restate argument 5 using diagrams in the manner of argument 4.)

5. African American slaves were treated worse than white indentured servants. Indentured white servants were treated worse than free white labor. Therefore, African American slaves were treated worse than free white labor.

Not all deductive reasoning occurs in syllogisms, however, or at least not in syllogisms like the ones in 4 and 5. (The term *syllogism* is sometimes used to refer to any deductive argument of any form, provided only that it has two premises.) In fact, syllogisms such as 4 are not the commonest form of our deductive reasoning at all. Nor are they the simplest (and, of course, not the most complex). For an argument that is even simpler, consider this:

6. If a youth is an African American slave, he is probably treated worse than a youth in indentured service. This youth is an African American slave. Therefore, he is probably treated worse than if he had been an indentured servant.

Here the pattern of reasoning has the form: If *A*, then *B*; *A*; therefore, *B*. Notice that the content of the assertions represented by *A* and *B* don't matter; any set of expressions having the same form or structure will do equally well, including assertions built out of meaningless terms, as in this example:

7. If the slithy toves, then the gyres gimble. The slithy toves. Therefore, the gyres gimble.

Argument 7 has the form: If *A*, then *B*; *A*; therefore *B*. As a piece of deductive inference it is every bit as good as argument 6. Unlike 6, however, 7 is of no interest to us because none of its assertions make any sense (unless you're a reader of Lewis Carroll's "Jabberwocky," and even then the sense of 7 is doubtful). You cannot, in short, use a valid deductive argument to prove anything unless the premises and the conclusion are *true,* but they can't be true unless they *mean* something in the first place.

This parallel between arguments 6 and 7 shows once again that deductive validity in an argument rests on the *form* or structure of the argument, and not on its content or meaning. If all one can say about an argument is that it is valid — that is, its conclusion follows from the premises — one has not given a sufficient reason for accepting the argument's conclusion. It has been said that the devil can quote scripture; similarly, an argument can be deductively valid and of no further interest or value whatever because valid (but false) conclusions can be drawn from false or even meaningless assumptions. For example:

8. New York's Metropolitan Museum of Art has the finest collection of abstract impressionist paintings in the world. The finest collection of abstract impressionist paintings includes dozens of canvases by Winslow Homer. Therefore, the Metropolitan Museum of Art has dozens of paintings by Winslow Homer.

Here the conclusion follows validly from the premises, even though all three propositions are false. Nevertheless, although validity by itself is not enough, it is a necessary condition of any deductive argument that purports to establish its conclusion.

Now let's consider another argument with the same form as 8, only more interesting:

9. If President Truman knew the Japanese were about to surrender, then it was immoral of him to order that atom bombs be dropped on Hiroshima and Nagasaki. Truman knew the Japanese were about to surrender. Therefore, it was immoral of him to order dropping those bombs.

As in the two previous examples, anyone who assents to the premises in argument 9 must assent to the conclusion; the form of arguments 8 and 9 is identical. But do the premises of argument 9 *prove* the conclusion? That depends on whether both premises are true. Well, are they? This turns on a number of considerations, and it is worthwhile pausing to examine this argument closely to illustrate the kinds of things that are involved in answering this question.

Let's begin by examining the second (minor) premise. Its truth is controversial even to this day. Autobiography, memoranda, other documentary evidence — all are needed to assemble the evidence to back up the grounds for the thesis or claim made in the conclusion of this valid argument. Evaluating this material effectively will probably involve not only further deductions but inductive reasoning as well.

Now consider the first (major) premise in argument 9. Its truth doesn't depend on what history shows but on the moral principles one accepts. The major premise has the form of a hypothetical proposition ("if . . . then . . .") and asserts a connection between two very different kinds of things. The antecedent of the hypothetical (the clause following "if") mentions facts about Truman's *knowledge,* and the consequent of the hypothetical (the clause following "then") mentions facts about the *morality* of his conduct in light of such knowledge. The major premise as a whole can thus be seen as expressing *a principle of moral responsibility.*

Such principles can, of course, be controversial. In this case, for instance, is the principle peculiarly relevant to the knowledge and conduct of a president of the United States? Probably not; it is far more likely that this principle is merely a special case of a more general proposition about anyone's moral responsibility. (After all, we know a great deal more about the conditions of our own moral responsibility than we do about those of high government officials.) We might express this more general principle in this way: If we have knowledge that would make our violent conduct unnecessary, then we are immoral if we deliberately act violently anyway. Thus, accepting this general principle can serve as a basis for defending the major premise of argument 9.

We have examined this argument in some detail because it illustrates the kinds of considerations needed to test not only whether a given argument is valid but also whether its premises are true — that is, whether its premises really prove the conclusion.

The great value of the form of argument known as hypothetical syllogism, exemplified by arguments 6 and 7, is that the structure of the argument is so simple and so universally applicable in reasoning that it is often both easy and worthwhile to formulate one's claims so that they can be grounded by an argument of this sort.

Before leaving the subject of deductive inference, let's consider three other forms of argument, each of which can be found in actual use elsewhere in the readings in this volume. The simplest of these is **disjunctive syllogism,** so called because its major premise is a **disjunction.** For example:

10. Either censorship of television shows is overdue, or our society is indifferent to the education of its youth. Our society is not indifferent to the education of its youth. Therefore, censorship of television is overdue.

Notice, by the way, that the validity of an argument, as in this case, does not turn on pedantic repetition of every word or phrase as the argument moves along; nonessential elements can be dropped, or equivalent expressions substituted for variety without adverse effect on the reasoning. Thus, in conversation or in writing, the argument in 10 might actually be presented like this:

11. Either censorship of television is overdue, or our society is indifferent to the education of its youth. But, of course, we aren't indifferent; it's censorship that's overdue.

The key feature of disjunctive syllogism, as example 11 suggests, is that the conclusion is whichever of the disjuncts is left over after the others have been negated in the minor premise. Thus, we could easily have a very complex disjunctive syllogism, with a dozen disjuncts in the major premise, and seven of them denied in the minor premise, leaving a conclusion of the remaining five. Usually, however, a disjunctive argument is formulated in this manner: Assert a disjunction with two or more disjuncts in the major premise; then *deny all but one* in the minor premise; and infer validly the remaining disjunct as the conclusion. That was the form of argument 11.

Another type of argument, especially favored by orators and rhetoricians, is the **dilemma.** Ordinarily, we use the term *dilemma* in the sense of an awkward predicament, as when we say, "His dilemma was that he didn't have enough money to pay the waiter." But when logicians refer to a dilemma, they mean a forced choice between two or more equally unattractive alternatives. For example, the predicament faced by the U.S. government in 2014 in deciding how to deal with the growth of the Islamic State in Syria can be posed as a dilemma. Two major choices emerged. The United States could ally itself with the Syrian government, or it could support rebel groups inside Syria who fight against ISIS. The dilemma is that the Syrian government, a dictatorship under Bashar al-Assad, has attempted to crush political reform movements in Syria, and it actively supports groups the United

States deems terrorist organizations, such as Hamas and Hezbollah. Also, some important U.S. allies such as Saudi Arabia oppose the al-Assad regime. On the other hand, if the United States were to support resistance groups within Syria, it would open itself up to charges that it was funding and arming groups hostile to the al-Assad regime, making them vulnerable to attack from the Syrian government and angering Syrian allies such as Russia, which may well be called upon to support strikes against the United States. The dilemma might be phrased as such:

12. If the United States supports the Syrian government, it would also be supporting a dictatorship that has been linked to terrorism and crimes against humanity, and that furthermore is an enemy of some of our closest Middle Eastern allies. If the United States supports rebel groups within Syria, it may be subject to attack by the al-Assad regime, extending the Syrian civil war and inviting potentially dangerous conflict with Russia. Either the United States supports a dictatorship, or it supports internal resistance groups. In either case, unattractive consequences follow.

Notice first the structure of the argument: two conditional propositions asserted as premises, followed by another premise that states a **necessary truth**. (The premise, "Either we support the Libyan dictatorship, or we support the Libyan rebels," is a disjunction; since its two alternatives are exhaustive, one of the two alternatives must be true. Such a statement is often called analytically true, or a *tautology*.) No doubt the conclusion of this dilemma follows from its premises.

But does the argument prove, as it purports to do, that whatever the U.S. government does, it will suffer "unattractive consequences"? It is customary to speak of "the horns of the dilemma," as though the challenge posed by the dilemma were like a bull ready to gore us no matter which direction we turn. But if the two conditional premises failed to exhaust the possibilities, then we can escape from the dilemma by going "between the horns," that is, by finding a third alternative. If (as in this case) that isn't possible, we can still ask whether both of the main premises are true. (In this argument, it should be clear that neither of the main premises spells out all or even most of the consequences that could be foreseen.) Even so, in cases where both of these conditional premises are true, it may be that the consequences of one alternative are nowhere nearly so bad as those of the other. If that is true, but our reasoning stops before evaluating that fact, we may be guilty of failing to distinguish between the greater and the lesser of two admitted evils. The logic of the dilemma itself cannot decide this choice for us. Instead, we must bring to bear empirical inquiry and imagination to the evaluation of the grounds of the dilemma itself.

Writers commonly use the term *dilemma* without explicitly formulating the dilemma to which they refer, leaving it for the readers to do. And sometimes, what is called a dilemma really isn't one. (Remember the dog's tail? Calling it a leg doesn't make it a leg.) As an example, consider the plight of Sophie in William Styron's novel, *Sophie's Choice*. The scene is Birkenau, the main Nazi extermination camp during World War II. Among the thousands arriving at the prison gates are Sophie and her two children, Jan and Eva. On the train platform a Nazi SS medical officer confronts them. He will decide which are the lucky ones; they will live to work in the camp. The rest will go to their death in the gas chambers. When Sophie insists she is Polish but not Jewish, the officer says she may choose one of her children to be saved. Which of the two should she save? On what basis ought Sophie resolve her dilemma? It looks as if she has only two alternatives, each of which presents an agonizing outcome. Or is there a third way out?

Finally, one of the most powerful and dramatic forms of argument is **reductio ad absurdum** (from the Latin, meaning "reduction to absurdity"). The idea of a reductio argument is to disprove a proposition by showing the absurdity of its inevitable conclusion. It is used, of course, to refute your opponent's position and prove your own. For example, in Plato's *Republic,* Socrates asks an old gentleman, Cephalus, to define right conduct. Cephalus says that it consists of paying your debts and keeping your word. Socrates rejects this answer by showing that it leads to a contradiction. He argues that Cephalus cannot have given the correct answer because if we believe that he did, we will quickly encounter contradictions; in some cases, when you keep your word you will nonetheless be doing the wrong thing. For suppose, says Socrates, that you borrowed a weapon from a man, promising to return it when he asks for it. One day he comes to your door, demanding his weapon and swearing angrily that he intends to murder a neighbor. Keeping your word under those circumstances would be absurd, Socrates implies, and the reader of the dialogue is left to infer that Cephalus's definition, which led to this result, has been refuted.

Let's take a closer look at another example. Suppose you are opposed to any form of gun control, whereas I am in favor of gun control. I might try to refute your position by attacking it with a reductio argument. To do that, I start out by assuming the very opposite of what I believe or favor; instead, I try to establish a contradiction that results from following out the consequences of this initial assumption. My argument might look like this:

13. Let's assume your position — namely, that there ought to be no legal restrictions of any kind on the sale and ownership of guns. That means that you'd permit having every neighborhood hardware store sell pistols and rifles to whoever walks in the door. But that's not all. You apparently also would permit selling machine guns to children, antitank weapons to lunatics, small-bore cannons to the nearsighted, as well as guns and ammunition to anyone with a criminal record. But this is utterly preposterous. No one could favor such a dangerous policy. So the only question worth debating is what kind of gun control is necessary.

Now in this example, my reductio of your position on gun control is not based on claiming to show that you have strictly contradicted yourself, for there is no purely logical contradiction in opposing all forms of gun control. Instead, what I have tried to do is to show that there is a contradiction between what you profess — no gun controls at all — and what you probably really believe, if only you'll stop to think about it — which is that no lunatic should be allowed to buy a loaded machine gun.

My refutation of your position rests on whether I succeed in establishing an inconsistency among your own beliefs. If it turns out that you really believe lunatics should be free to purchase guns and ammunition, then my attempted refutation fails.

In explaining reductio ad absurdum, we have had to rely on another idea fundamental to logic, that of **contradiction,** or inconsistency. (We used this idea, remember, to define validity in Chapter 3. A deductive argument is valid if and only if the process of affirming the premises and denying the conclusion results in a contradiction.) The opposite of contradiction is **consistency,** a notion of hardly less importance to good reasoning than validity. These concepts deserve a few words of further explanation and illustration. Consider this pair of assertions:

14. Abortion is homicide.
15. Racism is unfair.

No one would plausibly claim that we can infer or deduce 15 from 14, or, for that matter, 14 from 15. This almost goes without saying because there is no evident connection between these two assertions. They are unrelated assertions; logically speaking, they are *independent* of each other. In such cases the two assertions are mutually *consistent;* that is, both could be true—or both could be false. But now consider another proposition:

16. Euthanasia is not murder.

Could a person assert 14 (*Abortion is homicide*) and also assert 16 (*Euthanasia is not murder*) and be consistent? This question is equivalent to asking whether one could assert the **conjunction** of these two propositions—namely:

17. Abortion is homicide, and euthanasia is not murder.

It's not so easy to say whether 17 is consistent or inconsistent. The kinds of moral scruples that might lead a person to assert one of these conjuncts (i.e., one of the two initial propositions, *Abortion is homicide* and *Euthanasia is not murder*) might lead to the belief that the other one must be false and thus to the conclusion that 17 is inconsistent. (Notice that if 14 were the assertion that *Abortion is murder,* instead of *Abortion is homicide,* the problem of asserting consistently both 14 and 16 would be more acute.) Yet if we think again, we might imagine someone being convinced that there is no inconsistency in asserting that *Abortion is homicide,* say, and that *Euthanasia is not murder,* or even the reverse. (For instance, suppose you believed that the unborn deserve a chance to live and that putting terminally ill persons to death in a painless manner and with their consent confers a benefit on them.)

Let us generalize: We can say of any set of propositions that they are *consistent* if and only if *all could be true together.* (Notice that it follows from this definition that propositions mutually imply each other, as do *Seabiscuit was America's fastest racehorse* and *America's fastest racehorse was Seabiscuit.*) Remember that, once again, the truth of the assertions in question doesn't matter. Two propositions can be consistent or not, quite apart from whether they are true. Not so with falsehood: It follows from our definition of consistency that an *inconsistent* proposition must be *false.* (We have relied on this idea in explaining how a reductio ad absurdum argument works.)

Assertions or claims that are not consistent can take either of two forms. Suppose you assert proposition 14, that abortion is homicide, early in an essay you are writing, but later you assert that

18. Abortion is harmless.

You have now asserted a position on abortion that is strictly contrary to the one with which you began — contrary in the sense that both assertions 14 and 18 cannot be true. It is simply not true that if an abortion involves killing a human being (which is what *homicide* strictly means), then it causes no one any harm (killing a person always causes harm — even if it is excusable, justifiable, not wrong, the best thing to do in the circumstances, and so on). Notice that although 14 and 18 cannot both be true, they *can* both be false. In fact, many people who are perplexed about the morality of abortion believe precisely this. They concede that abortion does harm the fetus, so 18 must be false; but they also believe that abortion doesn't kill a person, so 14 must also be false.

Let's consider another, simpler case. If you describe the glass as half empty and I describe it as half full, both of us can be right; the two assertions are consistent, even though they sound vaguely incompatible. (This is the reason that disputing over whether the glass is half full or half empty has become the popular paradigm of a futile, purely *verbal disagreement*.) But if I describe the glass as half empty whereas you insist that it is two-thirds empty, then we have a real disagreement; your description and mine are strictly contrary, in that both cannot be true — although both *can* be false. (Both are false if the glass is only one-quarter full.)

This, by the way, enables us to define the difference between a pair of **contradictory** propositions and a pair of **contrary** propositions. Two propositions are contrary if and only if both cannot be true (though both can be false); two propositions are contradictory if and only if they are such that if one is true the other must be false, and vice versa. Thus, if Jack says that Alice Walker's *The Color Purple* is a better novel than Mark Twain's *Huckleberry Finn*, and Jill says, "No, *Huckleberry Finn* is better than *The Color Purple*," she is contradicting Jack. If what either one of them says is true, then what the other says must be false.

A more subtle case of contradiction arises when two or more of one's own beliefs implicitly contradict each other. We may find ourselves saying "Travel is broadening," and saying an hour later "People don't really change." Just beneath the surface of these two beliefs lies a self-contradiction: How can travel broaden us unless it influences — and changes — our beliefs, values, and outlook? But if we can't really change ourselves, then traveling to new places won't change us, either. (Indeed, there is a Roman saying to the effect that travelers change the skies above them, not their hearts.) "Travel is broadening" and "People don't change" collide with each other; something has to give.

Our point, of course, is not that you must never say today something that contradicts something you said yesterday. Far from it; if you think you were mistaken yesterday, of course you will take a different position today. But what you want to avoid is what George Orwell called *doublethink* in his novel *1984*: "*Doublethink* means the power of holding two contradictory beliefs in one's mind simultaneously, and accepting them both."

Genuine contradiction, and not merely contrary assertion, is the situation we should expect to find in some disputes. Someone advances a thesis — such as the assertion in 14, *Abortion is homicide* — and someone else flatly contradicts it by the simple expedient of negating it, thus:

19. Abortion is not homicide.

If we can trust public opinion polls, many of us are not sure whether to agree with 14 or with 19. But we should agree that whichever is true, *both* cannot be true, and *both* cannot be false. The two assertions, between them, exclude all other possibilities; they pose a forced choice for our belief. (Again, we have met this idea, too, in a reductio ad absurdum.)

Now it is one thing for Jack and Jill in a dispute or argument to contradict each other. It is quite another matter for Jack to contradict himself. One wants (or should want) to avoid self-contradiction because of the embarrassing position that results: Once I have contradicted myself, what are others to believe I really believe? What, indeed, *do* I believe, for that matter?

It may be, as Emerson observed, that a "foolish consistency is the hobgoblin of little minds" — that is, it may be shortsighted to purchase a consistency in one's beliefs at the expense of flying in the face of common sense. But making an effort to avoid a foolish inconsistency is the hallmark of serious thinking.

While we're speaking of inconsistency, let's spend a moment on **paradox.** The word refers to two different things:

- an assertion that is essentially self-contradictory and therefore cannot be true
- a seemingly contradictory assertion that nevertheless may be true

An example of the first might be "Evaluations concerning quality in literature are all a matter of personal judgment, but Shakespeare is the world's greatest writer." It is hard to make any sense out of this assertion. Contrast it with a paradox of the second sort, a *seeming* contradiction that may make sense, such as "The longest way around is the shortest way home," or "Work is more fun than fun," or "The best way to find happiness is not to look for it." Here we have assertions that are striking because as soon as we hear them we realize that although they seem inconsistent and self-defeating, they contain (or may contain) profound truths. Paradoxes of this second sort are especially common in religious texts, where they may imply a mysterious reality concealed by a world of contradictory appearances. Examples are "Some who are last shall be first, and some who are first shall be last" (Jesus, quoted in Luke 13:30), and "Death, thou shalt die" (the poet John Donne, alluding to the idea that the person who has faith in Jesus dies to this world but lives eternally). If you use the word *paradox* in your own writing — for instance, to characterize an argument that you're reading — be sure that the reader will understand in which sense you're using the word. (And, of course, you won't want to write paradoxes of the first, self-contradictory sort.)

Induction

Deduction involves logical thinking that applies to absolutely any assertion or claim — because every possible statement, true or false, has deductive logical consequences. Induction is relevant to one kind of assertion only; namely, to **empirical** or *factual* claims. Other kinds of assertions (such as definitions, mathematical equations, and moral or legal norms) simply are not the product of inductive reasoning and cannot serve as a basis for further inductive thinking.

And so, in studying the methods of induction, we are exploring tactics and strategies useful in gathering and then using **evidence** — empirical, observational, experimental — in support of a belief as its ground. Modern scientific knowledge is the product of these methods, and they differ somewhat from one science to another because they depend on the theories and technology appropriate to each of the sciences. Here all we can do is discuss generally the more abstract features common to inductive inquiry generally. For fuller details, you must eventually consult a physicist, chemist, geologist, or their colleagues and counterparts in other scientific fields.

OBSERVATION AND INFERENCE

Let's begin with a simple example. Suppose we have evidence (actually we don't, but that won't matter for our purposes) in support of the claim that

1. In a sample of 500 smokers, 230 persons observed have cardiovascular disease.

The basis for asserting 1 — the evidence or ground — would be, presumably, straightforward physical examination of the 500 persons in the sample, one by one.

With this claim in hand, we can think of the purpose and methods of induction as pointing in two opposite directions: toward establishing the basis or ground of the very empirical proposition with which we start (in this example, the observation stated in 1) or toward understanding what that observation indicates or suggests as a more general, inclusive, or fundamental fact of nature.

In each case, we start from something we *do* know (or take for granted and treat as a sound starting point) — some fact of nature, perhaps a striking or commonplace event that we have observed and recorded — and then go on to something we do *not* fully know and perhaps cannot directly observe. In example 1, only the second of these two orientations is of any interest, so let's concentrate exclusively on it. Let's also generously treat as a *method* of induction any regular pattern or style of nondeductive reasoning that we could use to support a claim such as that in 1.

Anyone truly interested in the observed fact that *230 of 500 smokers have cardiovascular disease* is likely to start speculating about, and thus be interested in finding out, whether any or all of several other propositions are also true. For example, one might wonder whether

2. *All* smokers have cardiovascular disease or will develop it during their lifetimes.

This claim is a straightforward generalization of the original observation as reported in claim 1. When we think inductively about the linkage between 1 and 2, we are reasoning from an observed sample (some smokers — i.e., 230 of the 500 *observed*) to the entire membership of a more inclusive class (*all* smokers, whether observed or not). The fundamental question raised by reasoning from the narrower claim 1 to the broader claim 2 is whether we have any ground for believing that what is true of *some* members of a class is true of them *all*. So the difference between 1 and 2 is that of *quantity* or scope.

We can also think inductively about the *relation* between the factors mentioned in 1. Having observed data as reported in 1, we may be tempted to assert a different and more profound kind of claim:

3. Smoking *causes* cardiovascular disease.

Here our interest is not merely in generalizing from a sample to a whole class; it is the far more important one of *explaining* the observation with which we began in claim 1. Certainly, the preferred, even if not the only, mode of explanation for a natural phenomenon is a *causal* explanation. In proposition 3, we propose to explain the presence of one phenomenon (cardiovascular disease) by the prior occurrence of an independent phenomenon (smoking). The observation reported in 1 is now serving as evidence or support for this new conjecture stated in 3.

Our original claim in 1 asserted no causal relation between anything and anything else; whatever the cause of cardiovascular disease may be, that cause is not observed, mentioned, or assumed in assertion 1. Similarly, the observation asserted in claim 1 is consistent with many explanations. For example, the explanation of 1 might not be 3, but some other, undetected, carcinogenic factor unrelated to smoking — for instance, exposure to high levels of radon. The question one now faces is what can be added to 1, or teased out of it, to produce an adequate ground for claiming 3. (We shall return to this example for closer scrutiny.)

But there is a third way to go beyond 1. Instead of a straightforward generalization, as we had in 2, or a pronouncement on the cause of a phenomenon, as in 3, we might have a more complex and cautious further claim in mind, such as this:

4. Smoking is a factor in the causation of cardiovascular disease in some persons.

This proposition, like 3, advances a claim about causation. But 4 is obviously a weaker claim than 3. That is, other observations, theories, or evidence that would require us to reject 3 might be consistent with 4; evidence that would support 4 could easily fail to be enough to support 3. Consequently, it is even possible that 4 is true although 3 is false, because 4 allows for other (unmentioned) factors in the causation of cardiovascular disease (e.g., genetic or dietary factors) that may not be found in all smokers.

Propositions 2, 3, and 4 differ from proposition 1 in an important respect. We began by assuming that 1 states an empirical fact based on direct observation, whereas these others do not. Instead, they state empirical *hypotheses* or conjectures — tentative generalizations not fully confirmed — each of which goes beyond the observed facts asserted in 1. Each of 2, 3, and 4 can be regarded as an *inductive inference* from 1. We can also say that 2, 3, and 4 are hypotheses relative to 1, even if they are not relative to some other starting point (such as all the information that scientists today really have about smoking and cardiovascular disease).

PROBABILITY

Another way of formulating the last point is to say that whereas proposition 1, a statement of observed fact (*230 out of 500 smokers have cardiovascular disease*), has a **probability** of 1.0 — that is, it is absolutely certain — the probability of each of the hypotheses stated in 2, 3, and 4, *relative* to 1, is smaller than 1.0. (We need not worry here about how much smaller than 1.0 the probabilities are, nor about how to calculate these probabilities precisely.) Relative to some starting point other than 1, however, the probability of the same three hypotheses might be quite different. Of course, it still wouldn't be 1.0, absolute certainty. But it takes only a moment's reflection to realize that no matter what the probability of 2 or 3 or 4 may be relative to 1, those probabilities in each case will be quite different relative to different information, such as this:

5. Ten persons observed in a sample of 500 smokers have cardiovascular disease.

The idea that a *given proposition can have different probabilities* relative to different bases is fundamental to all inductive reasoning. The following example makes a convincing illustration. Suppose we want to consider the probability of this proposition being true:

6. Susanne Smith will live to be eighty.

Taken as an abstract question of fact, we cannot even guess what the probability is with any assurance. But we can do better than guess; we can in fact even calculate the answer, if we get some further information. Thus, suppose we are told that

7. Susanne Smith is seventy-nine.

Our original question then becomes one of determining the probability that 6 is true given 7; that is, relative to the evidence contained in proposition 7. No doubt, if Susanne Smith really is seventy-nine, then the probability that she will live to be eighty is greater than if we know only that

8. Susanne Smith is more than nine years old.

Obviously, a lot can happen to Susanne in the seventy years between nine and seventy-nine that isn't very likely to happen in the one year between seventy-nine and eighty. And so, proposition 6 is more probable relative to proposition 7 than it is relative to proposition 8.

Let's suppose for the sake of the argument that the following is true:

9. Ninety percent of women alive at age seventy-nine live to be eighty.

Given this additional information, and the information that Susanne is seventy-nine, we now have a basis for answering our original question about proposition 6 with some precision. But suppose, in addition to 8, we are also told that

10. Susanne Smith is suffering from inoperable cancer.

and also that

11. The survival rate for women suffering from inoperable cancer is 0.6 years (i.e., the average life span for women after a diagnosis of inoperable cancer is about seven months).

With this new information, the probability that 6 will be true drops significantly, all because we can now estimate the probability in relation to a new body of evidence.

The probability of an event, thus, is not a fixed number but one that varies because it is always relative to some evidence — and given different evidence, one and the same event can have different probabilities. In other words, the probability of any event is always relative to how much is known (assumed, believed), and because different persons may know different things about a given event, or the same person may know different things at different times, one and the same event can have two or more probabilities. This conclusion is not a paradox but a logical consequence of the concept of what it is for an event to have (i.e., to be assigned) a probability.

If we shift to the *calculation* of probabilities, we find that generally there are two ways to calculate them. One way to proceed is by the method of **a priori** or **equal probabilities** — that is, by reference to the relevant possibilities taken abstractly and apart from any other information. Thus, in an election contest with only two candidates, Smith and Jones, each of the candidates has a fifty-fifty chance of winning (whereas in a three-candidate race, each candidate would have one chance in three of winning). Therefore, the probability that Smith will win is 0.5, and the probability that Jones will win is also 0.5. (The sum of the probabilities of all possible independent outcomes must always equal 1.0, which is obvious enough if you think about it.)

But in politics the probabilities are not reasonably calculated so abstractly. We know that many empirical factors affect the outcome of an election and that a calculation of probabilities in ignorance of those factors is likely to be drastically misleading. In our example of the two-candidate election, suppose Smith has strong party support and is the incumbent, whereas Jones represents a party long out of power and is further handicapped by being relatively unknown. No one who knows anything about electoral politics would give Jones the same chance of winning as Smith. The two events are not equiprobable in relation to all the information available.

Moreover, a given event can have more than one probability. This happens whenever we calculate a probability by relying on different bodies of data that report how often the event in question has been observed to happen. Probabilities calculated in this way are **relative frequencies.** Our earlier hypothetical example of Susanne Smith provides an illustration. If she is a smoker and we have observed that 100 out of a random set of 500 smokers have cardiovascular disease, we have a basis for claiming that she has a probability of 100 in 500, or 0.2 (one fifth), of having this disease. However, if other data have shown that 250 out of 500 women smokers ages eighty or older have cardiovascular disease, we have a basis for believing that there is a probability of 250 in 500, or 0.5 (one-half), that she has this disease. Notice that in both calculations we assume that Susanne Smith is not among the persons we have examined. In both cases we infer the probability of her having this disease from observing its frequency in populations that exclude her.

Both methods of calculating probabilities are legitimate; in each case the calculation is relative to observed circumstances. But as the examples show, it is most reasonable to have recourse to the method of equiprobabilities only when few or no other factors affecting possible outcomes are known.

S. Harris/Cartoonstock

MILL'S METHODS

Now let's return to our earlier discussion of smoking and cardiovascular disease and consider in greater detail the question of a causal connection between the two phenomena. We began thus:

1. In a sample of 500 smokers, 230 persons observed have cardiovascular disease.

We regarded 1 as an observed fact, though in truth, of course, it is mere supposition. Our question now is how we might augment this information so as to strengthen our confidence that

3. Smoking *causes* cardiovascular disease.

or at least that

4. Smoking is a factor in the causation of cardiovascular disease in some persons.

Suppose further examination showed that

12. In the sample of 230 smokers with cardiovascular disease, no other suspected factor (such as genetic predisposition, lack of physical exercise, age over fifty) was also observed.

Such an observation would encourage us to believe that 3 or 4 is true. Why? Because we're inclined to believe also that no matter what the cause of a phenomenon is, it must *always* be present when its effect is present. Thus, the inference from 1 to 3 or 4 is supported by 12, using **Mill's Method of Agreement,** named after the British philosopher, John Stuart Mill (1806–1873), who first formulated it. It's called a method of agreement because of the way in which the inference relies on *agreement* among the observed phenomena where a presumed cause is thought to be *present*.

Let's now suppose that in our search for evidence to support 3 or 4 we conduct additional research and discover that

13. In a sample of 500 nonsmokers, selected to be representative of both sexes, different ages, dietary habits, exercise patterns, and so on, none is observed to have cardiovascular disease.

This observation would further encourage us to believe that we had obtained significant additional confirmation of 3 or 4. Why? Because we now know that factors present (such as male sex, lack of exercise, family history of cardiovascular disease) in cases where the effect is absent (no cardiovascular disease observed) cannot be the cause. This is an example of **Mill's Method of Difference,** so called because the cause or causal factor of an effect must be *different* from whatever factors are present when the effect is *absent.*

Suppose now that, increasingly confident we've found the cause of cardiovascular disease, we study our first sample of 230 smokers ill with the disease, and we discover this:

14. Those who smoke two or more packs of cigarettes daily for ten or more years have cardiovascular disease either much younger or much more severely than those who smoke less.

This is an application of **Mill's Method of Concomitant Variation,** perhaps the most convincing of the three methods. Here we deal not merely with the presence of the conjectured cause (smoking) or the absence of the effect we are studying (cardiovascular disease), as we were previously, but with the more interesting and subtler matter of the *degree and regularity of the correlation* of the supposed cause and effect. According to the observations reported in 14, it strongly appears that the more we have of the "cause" (smoking), the sooner or the more intense the onset of the "effect" (cardiovascular disease).

Notice, however, what happens to our confirmation of 3 and 4 if, instead of the observation reported in 14, we had discovered that

15. In a representative sample of 500 nonsmokers, cardiovascular disease was observed in 34 cases.

(We won't pause here to explain what makes a sample more or less representative of a population, although the representativeness of samples is vital to all statistical reasoning.) Such an observation would lead us almost immediately to suspect some other or additional causal factor: Smoking might indeed be *a* factor in causing cardiovascular disease, but it can hardly be *the* cause because (using Mill's Method of Difference) we cannot have the effect, as we do in the observed sample reported in 15, unless we also have the cause.

An observation such as the one in 15, however, is likely to lead us to think our hypothesis that *smoking causes cardiovascular disease* has been disconfirmed. But we have a fallback position ready — we can still defend a weaker hypothesis; namely, 4: *Smoking is a factor in the causation of cardiovascular disease in some persons.* Even if 3 stumbles over the evidence in 15, 4 does not. It is still quite possible that smoking is a factor in causing this disease, even if it isn't the *only* factor — and if it is, then 4 is true.

Notice that in the discussion so far, we have spoken of the *confirmation* of a hypothesis, such as our causal claim in 4, but not of its *verification*. (Similarly, we have imagined very different evidence, such as that stated in 15, leading us to speak of the *disconfirmation* of 3, though not of its *falsification*.) Confirmation (getting some evidence for) is weaker than verification (getting sufficient evidence to regard as true), and our (imaginary) evidence so far in favor of 4 falls well short of conclusive support. Further research—the study of more representative or much larger samples, for example—might yield very different observations. It might lead us to conclude that although initial research had confirmed our hypothesis about smoking as the cause of cardiovascular disease, the additional information obtained subsequently disconfirmed the hypothesis. For most interesting hypotheses, both in detective stories and in modern science, there is both confirming and disconfirming evidence simultaneously. The challenge is to evaluate the hypothesis by considering such conflicting evidence.

As long as we confine our observations to *correlations* of the sort reported in our several (imaginary) observations, such as proposition 1, *230 smokers in a group of 500 have cardiovascular disease,* or 12, *230 smokers with the disease share no other suspected factors,* such as lack of exercise, any defense of a *causal* hypothesis such as claim 3, *Smoking causes cardiovascular disease,* or claim 4, *Smoking is a factor in causing the disease,* is not likely to convince the skeptic or lead those with beliefs alternative to 3 and 4 to abandon them and agree with us. Why is that? It is because a causal hypothesis without any account of the *underlying mechanism* by means of which the (alleged) cause produces the effect will seem superficial. Only when we can specify in detail *how* the (alleged) cause produces the effect will the causal hypothesis be convincing.

In other cases, in which no mechanism can be found, we seek instead to embed the causal hypothesis in a larger *theory,* one that rules out as incompatible any causal hypothesis except the favored one. (That is, we appeal to the test of consistency and thereby bring deductive reasoning to bear on our problem.) Thus, perhaps we cannot specify any mechanism—any underlying structure that generates a regular sequence of events, one of which is the effect we are studying—to explain why, for example, the gravitational mass of a body causes it to attract other bodies. But we can embed this claim in a larger context of physical theory that rules out as inconsistent any alternative causal explanation. To do that convincingly in regard to any given causal hypothesis, as this example suggests, requires detailed knowledge of the current state of the relevant body of scientific theory—something far beyond our need to consider in further detail here.

Fallacies

The straight road on which sound reasoning proceeds gives little latitude for cruising about. Irrationality, carelessness, passionate attachment to one's unexamined beliefs, and the sheer complexity of some issues occasionally spoil the reasoning of even the best of us. Although in this book we reprint many varied voices and arguments, we hope we've reprinted no readings that exhibit the most flagrant errors or commit the graver abuses against the canons of good reasoning. Nevertheless, an inventory of those abuses and their close examination can be an instructive (as well as an amusing) exercise — instructive because the diagnosis and repair of error help to fix more clearly the principles of sound reasoning on which such remedial labors depend; amusing because we are so constituted that our perception of the nonsense of others can stimulate our minds, warm our hearts, and give us comforting feelings of superiority.

The discussion that follows, then, is a quick tour through the twisting lanes, mudflats, forests, and quicksands of the faults that one sometimes encounters in reading arguments that stray from the highway of clear thinking.

FALLACIES OF AMBIGUITY

Ambiguity   Near the center of the town of Concord, Massachusetts, is an empty field with a sign reading "Old Calf Pasture." Hmm. A pasture in former times in which calves grazed? A pasture now in use for old calves? An erstwhile pasture for old calves? These alternative readings arise because of **ambiguity;** brevity in the sign has produced a group of words that give rise to more than one possible interpretation, confusing the reader and (presumably) frustrating the sign writer's intentions.

Consider a more complex example. Suppose someone asserts *People have equal rights* and also *Everyone has a right to property.* Many people believe both these claims, but their combination involves an ambiguity. According to one interpretation, the two claims entail that everyone has an *equal right* to property. (That is, you and I each have an equal right to whatever property we have.) But the two claims can also be interpreted to mean that everyone has a *right to equal property.* (That is, whatever property you have a right to, I have a right to the same, or at least equivalent, property.) The latter interpretation is revolutionary, whereas the former is not. Arguments over equal rights often involve this ambiguity.

Division   In the Bible, we read that the apostles of Jesus were twelve and that Matthew was an apostle. Does it follow that Matthew was twelve years old? No. To argue in this way from a property of a group to a property of a member of that group is to commit the **fallacy of division.** The example of the apostles may not be a very tempting instance of this error; here is a classic version that is a bit more interesting: If it is true that the average American family has 1.8 children, does it follow that your brother and sister-in-law are likely to have 1.8 children? If you think it does, you have committed the fallacy of division.

Composition   Could an all-star team of professional basketball players beat the Boston Celtics in their heyday — say, the team of 1985–1986? Perhaps in one game or two, but probably not in seven out of a dozen games in a row. As students of the game know, teamwork is an indispensable part of outstanding performance, and the 1985–1986 Celtics were famous for their self-sacrificing style of play.

The **fallacy of composition** can be convincingly illustrated, therefore, in this argument: *A team of five NBA all-stars is the best team in basketball if each of the five players is the best* *at his position.* The fallacy is called composition because the reasoning commits the error of arguing from the true premise that each member of a group has a certain property to the not necessarily true conclusion that the group (the composition) itself has the property. (That is, because *A* is the best player at forward, *B* is the best center, and so on, therefore, the team of *A, B, . . .* is the best team.)

Equivocation In a delightful passage in Lewis Carroll's *Through the Looking-Glass*, the king asks his messenger, "Who did you pass on the road?" and the messenger replies, "Nobody." This prompts the king to observe, "Of course, Nobody walks slower than you," provoking the messenger's sullen response: "I do my best. I'm sure nobody walks much faster than I do." At this the king remarks with surprise, "He can't do that or else he'd have been here first!" (This, by the way, is the classic predecessor of the famous comic dialogue "Who's on First?" between the comedians Bud Abbott and Lou Costello.) The king and the messenger are equivocating on the term *nobody*. The messenger uses it in the normal way as an indefinite pronoun equivalent to "not anyone." But the king uses the word as though it were a proper noun, *Nobody*, the rather odd name of some person. No wonder the king and the messenger talk right past each other.

Equivocation (from the Latin for "equal voice" — i.e., giving utterance to two meanings at the same time in one word or phrase) can ruin otherwise good reasoning, as in this example: *Euthanasia is a good death; one dies a good death when one dies peacefully in old age; therefore, euthanasia is dying peacefully in old age.* The etymology of *euthanasia* is literally "a good death," so the first premise is true. And the second premise is certainly plausible. But the conclusion of this syllogism is false. Euthanasia cannot be defined as a peaceful death in one's old age, for two reasons. First, euthanasia requires the intervention of another person who kills someone (or lets the person die); second, even a very young person can be euthanized. The problem arises because "a good death" works in the second premise in a manner that does not apply to euthanasia. Both meanings of "a good death" are legitimate, but when used together, they constitute an equivocation that spoils the argument.

The fallacy of equivocation takes us from the discussion of confusions in individual claims or grounds to the more troublesome fallacies that infect the linkages between the claims we make and the grounds (or reasons) for them. These are the fallacies that occur in statements that, following the vocabulary of the Toulmin method, are called the *warrant* of reasoning. Each fallacy is an example of reasoning that involves a **non sequitur** (Latin for "It does not follow"). That is, the *claim* (the conclusion) does not follow from the *grounds* (the premises).

For a start, here is an obvious non sequitur: "He went to the movies on three consecutive nights, so he must love movies." Why doesn't the claim ("He must love movies") follow from the grounds ("He went to the movies on three consecutive nights")? Perhaps the person was just fulfilling an assignment in a film course (maybe he even hated movies so much that he had postponed three assignments to see films and now had to see them all in quick succession), or maybe he went with a girlfriend who was a movie buff, or maybe . . . — well, there are any number of other possible reasons.

FALLACIES OF PRESUMPTION

Distorting the Facts   Facts can be distorted either intentionally (to deceive or mislead) or unintentionally, and in either case usually (but not invariably) to the benefit of whoever is doing the distortion. Consider this not entirely hypothetical case. A pharmaceutical company spends millions of dollars to develop a new drug that will help pregnant women avoid spontaneous abortion. The company reports its findings, but it doesn't also report that its researchers have learned of a serious downside for this drug in many cases, resulting in deformed limbs in the neonate. Had the company informed the public of this fact, the drug would not have been certified for use.

Here is another case. Half a century ago the surgeon general reported that smoking cigarettes increased the likelihood that smokers would eventually suffer from lung cancer. The cigarette manufacturers vigorously protested that the surgeon general relied on inconclusive research and was badly misleading the public about the health risks of smoking. It later turned out that the tobacco companies knew that smoking increased the risk of lung cancer — a fact established by the company's own laboratories but concealed from the public. Today, thanks to public access to all the facts, it is commonplace knowledge that inhaled smoke — including secondhand smoke — is a risk factor for many illnesses.

Post Hoc, Ergo Propter Hoc   One of the most tempting errors in reasoning is to ground a claim about causation on an observed temporal sequence; that is, to argue "after this, therefore because of this" (which is what the phrase ***post hoc, ergo propter hoc*** means in Latin). Nearly forty years ago, when the medical community first announced that smoking tobacco caused lung cancer, advocates for the tobacco industry replied that doctors were guilty of this fallacy.

These industry advocates argued that medical researchers had merely noticed that in some people, lung cancer developed *after* considerable smoking, indeed, years after; but (they insisted) this correlation was not at all the same as a causal relation between smoking and lung cancer. True enough. The claim that *A causes B* is not the same as the claim that *B comes after A*. After all, it was possible that smokers as a group had some other common trait and that this factor was the true cause of their cancer.

As the long controversy over the truth about the causation of lung cancer shows, to avoid the appearance of fallacious *post hoc* reasoning one needs to find some way to link the observed phenomena (the correlation between smoking and the onset of lung cancer). This step requires some further theory and preferably some experimental evidence for the exact sequence or physical mechanism, in full detail, of how ingestion of tobacco smoke is a crucial factor — and is not merely an accidental or happenstance prior event — in the subsequent development of the cancer.

Many Questions   The old saw, "When did you stop beating your wife?" illustrates the **fallacy of many questions.** This question, as one can readily see, is unanswerable unless all three of its implicit presuppositions are true. The questioner presupposes that (1) the addressee has or had a wife, (2) he has beaten her, and (3) he has stopped beating her. If any of these presuppositions is false, then the question is pointless; it cannot be answered strictly and simply with a date or time.

Hasty Generalization　　From a logical point of view, **hasty generalization** is the precipitous move from true assertions about *one* or a *few* instances to dubious or even false assertions about *all*. For example, while it may be true that the only native Hungarians you personally know do not speak English very well, that is no basis for asserting that all Hungarians do not speak English very well. Or if the clothes you recently ordered online turn out not to fit very well, it doesn't follow that *all* online clothes turn out to be too large or too small. A hasty generalization usually lies behind a **stereotype** — that is, a person or event treated as typical of a whole class. Thus, in 1914, after the German invasion of Belgium, during which the invaders committed numerous atrocities, the German troops were quickly stereotyped by the Allies as brutal savages who skewered helpless babies on their bayonets.

The Slippery Slope　　One of the most familiar arguments against any type of government regulation is that if it is allowed, then it will be just the first step down the path that leads to ruinous interference, overregulation, and totalitarian control. Fairly often we encounter this mode of argument in the public debates over handgun control, the censorship of pornography, and physician-assisted suicide. The argument is called the **slippery slope argument** (or the **wedge argument,** from the way people use the thin end of a wedge to split solid things apart; it is also called, rather colorfully, "letting the camel's nose under the tent"). The fallacy here is in implying that the first step necessarily leads to the second, and so on down the slope to disaster, when in fact there is no necessary slide from the first step to the second. (Would handgun registration lead to a police state? Well, it hasn't in Switzerland.) Sometimes, the argument takes the form of claiming that a seemingly innocent or even attractive principle that is being applied in a given case (censorship of pornography, to avoid promoting sexual violence) requires one for the sake of consistency to apply the same principle in other cases, only with absurd and catastrophic results (censorship of everything in print, to avoid hurting anyone's feelings).

Here's an extreme example of this fallacy in action:

> Automobiles cause more deaths than handguns do. If you oppose handguns on the ground that doing so would save lives of the innocent, you'll soon find yourself wanting to outlaw the automobile.

Does opposition to handguns have this consequence? Not necessarily. Most people accept without dispute the right of society to regulate the operation of motor vehicles by requiring drivers to have a license, a greater restriction than many states impose on gun ownership. Besides, a gun is a lethal weapon designed to kill, whereas an automobile or truck is a vehicle designed for transportation. Private ownership and use in both cases entail risks of death to the innocent. But there is no inconsistency in a society's refusal to tolerate this risk in the case of guns and its willingness to do so in the case of automobiles.

Closely related to the slippery slope is what lawyers call a **parade of horrors,** an array of examples of terrible consequences that will or might follow if we travel down a certain path. A good example appears in Justice William Brennan's opinion for the Supreme Court in *Texas v. Johnson* (1989), regarding a Texas law against burning the American flag in political protest. If this law is allowed to stand, Brennan suggests, we may next find laws against burning the presidential seal, state flags, and the Constitution.

False Analogy   Argument by analogy, as we point out in Chapter 3 and as many of the selections in this book show, is a familiar and even indispensable mode of argument. But it can be treacherous because it runs the risk of the **fallacy of false analogy.** Unfortunately, we have no simple or foolproof way of distinguishing between the useful, legitimate analogies and the others. The key question to ask yourself is this: Do the two things put into analogy differ in any essential and relevant respect, or are they different only in unimportant and irrelevant aspects?

In a famous example from his discussion in support of suicide, philosopher David Hume rhetorically asked: "It would be no crime in me to divert the Nile or Danube from its course, were I able to effect such purposes. Where then is the crime of turning a few ounces of blood from their natural channel?" This is a striking analogy, except that it rests on a false assumption. No one has the right to divert the Nile or the Danube or any other major international watercourse; it would be a catastrophic crime to do so without the full consent of people living in the region, their government, and so forth. Therefore, arguing by analogy, one might well say that no one has the right to take his or her own life, either. Thus, Hume's own analogy can be used to argue against his thesis that suicide is no crime. But let's ignore the way in which his example can be turned against him. The analogy is a terrible one in any case. Isn't it obvious that the Nile, regardless of its exact course, would continue to nourish Egypt and the Sudan, whereas the blood flowing out of someone's veins will soon leave that person dead? The fact that the blood is the same blood, whether in a person's body or in a pool on the floor (just as the water of the Nile is the same body of water no matter what path it follows to the sea) is, of course, irrelevant to the question of whether one has the right to commit suicide.

Let's look at a more complex example. During the 1960s, when the United States was convulsed over the purpose and scope of its military involvement in Southeast Asia, advocates of more vigorous U.S. military participation appealed to the so-called domino effect, supposedly inspired by a passing remark from President Eisenhower in the 1950s. The analogy refers to the way in which a row of standing dominoes will collapse, one after the other, if the first one is pushed. If Vietnam turns Communist, according to this analogy, so too will its neighbors, Laos and Cambodia, followed by Thailand and then Burma, until the whole region is as communist as China to the north. The domino analogy (or metaphor) provided, no doubt, a vivid illustration and effectively portrayed the worry of many anti-Communists. But did it really shed any light on the likely pattern of political and military developments in the region? The history of events there during the 1970s and 1980s did not bear out the domino analogy.

Straw Man   It is often tempting to reframe or report your opponent's thesis to make it easier to attack and perhaps refute it. If you do this in the course of an argument, you are creating a straw man, a thing of no substance that's easily blown away. The straw man you've constructed is usually a radically conservative or extremely liberal thesis, which few if any would want to defend. That's why it is easier to refute than the view your opponent actually holds. "So you defend the death penalty — and all the horrible things done in its name. No one in his right mind would hold such a view." It's highly unlikely that your opponent supports *everything* that has been done in the name of capital punishment — crucifixion and beheading, for example, or execution of the children of the guilty offender.

Special Pleading   We all have our favorites — relatives, friends, and neighbors — and we're all too likely to show that favoritism in unacceptable ways. How about this: "Yes, I know Billy hit Sally first, but he's my son. He's a good boy, and I know he must have had a good reason." Or this: "True, she's late for work again — the third time this week! — but her uncle's my friend, and it will be embarrassing to me if she's fired, so we'll just ignore it." Special pleading inevitably leads to unmerited advantages.

Begging the Question   The argument over whether the death penalty is a deterrent illustrates another fallacy. From the fact that you live in a death-penalty state and were not murdered yesterday, we cannot infer that the death penalty was a deterrent. Yet it is tempting to make this inference, perhaps because — all unaware — we are relying on the **fallacy of begging the question.** If someone tacitly assumes from the start that the death penalty is an effective deterrent, then the fact that you weren't murdered yesterday certainly looks like evidence for the truth of that assumption. But it isn't, so long as there are competing but unexamined alternative explanations, as in this case. (The fallacy is called "begging the question," *petitio principii* in Latin, because the conclusion of the argument is hidden among its assumptions — and so the conclusion, not surprisingly, follows from the premises.)

Of course, the fact that you weren't murdered is *consistent* with the claim that the death penalty is an effective deterrent, just as someone else's being murdered is also consistent with that claim (because an effective deterrent need not be a *perfect* deterrent). In general, from the fact that two propositions are consistent with each other, we cannot infer that either is evidence for the other.

Note: The term "begging the question" is often wrongly used to mean "raises the question," as in "His action of burning the flag begs the question, What drove him to do such a thing?"

False Dichotomy   Sometimes, oversimplification takes a more complex form, in which contrary possibilities are wrongly presented as though they were exhaustive and exclusive. "Either we get tough with drug users, or we must surrender and legalize all drugs." Really? What about doing neither and instead offering education and counseling, detoxification programs, and incentives to "Say no"? A favorite of debaters, **either/or reasoning** always runs the risk of ignoring a third (or fourth) possibility. Some disjunctions are indeed exhaustive: "Either we get tough with drug users, or we do not." This proposition, though vague (what does "get tough" really mean?), is a tautology; it cannot be false, and there is no third alternative. But most disjunctions do not express a pair of *contradictory* alternatives: They offer only a pair of *contrary* alternatives, and mere contraries do not exhaust the possibilities (recall our discussion of contraries versus contradictories on pp. 342–45).

An example of **false dichotomy** appears in the essay by Jeff Jacoby on flogging (pp. 196–98). His entire discussion is built on the relative superiority of whipping over imprisonment, as though there was no alternative punishment worth considering. But of course, there is — notably, community service (especially for white-collar offenders, juveniles, and many first offenders).

Oversimplification   "Poverty causes crime," "Taxation is unfair," "Truth is stranger than fiction" — these are examples of generalizations that exaggerate and therefore oversimplify the truth. Poverty as such can't be the sole cause of crime because many poor people do not break the law. Some taxes may be unfairly high, others unfairly low — but there is no reason to believe that *every* tax is unfair to all those who have to pay it. Some true stories do amaze us as much or more than some fictional stories, but the reverse is true, too. (In the language of the Toulmin method, **oversimplification** is the result of a failure to use suitable modal qualifiers in formulating one's claims or grounds or backing.)

Red Herring   The fallacy of **red herring,** less colorfully named irrelevant thesis, occurs when one tries to distract one's audience by invoking a consideration that is irrelevant to the topic under discussion. (This fallacy probably gets its name from the fact that a rotten herring, or a cured herring, which is reddish, will throw pursuing hounds off the right track.) Consider this case: Some critics, seeking to defend our government's refusal to sign the Kyoto accords to reduce global warming, argue that signing is supported mainly by left-leaning scientists. This argument supposedly shows that global warming — if there is such a thing — is not a serious, urgent issue. But claiming that the supporters of these accords are left-inclined is a red herring, an irrelevant thesis. By raising doubts about the political views of the advocates of signing, critics distract attention from the scientific question (Is there global warming?) and also from the separate political question (Ought the U.S. government sign the accords?). The refusal of a government to sign the accords doesn't show there is no such thing as global warming. And even if all the advocates of signing were left-leaning (they aren't), this fact (if it were a fact, but it isn't) would not show that worries about global warming are exaggerated.

FALLACIES OF RELEVANCE

Tu Quoque   The Romans had a word for it: *Tu quoque* means "you, too." Consider this: "You're a fine one, trying to persuade me to give up smoking when you indulge yourself with a pipe and a cigar from time to time. Maybe I should quit, but then so should you. As things stand now, however, it's hypocritical of you to complain about my smoking when you persist in the same habit." The fallacy is this: The merit of a person's argument has nothing to do with the person's character or behavior. Here the assertion that smoking is bad for one's health is *not* weakened by the fact that a smoker offers the argument.

The Genetic Fallacy   A member of the family of fallacies that includes poisoning the well and ad hominem (see below) is the **genetic fallacy.** Here the error takes the form of arguing against a claim by pointing out that its origin (genesis) is tainted or that it was invented by someone deserving our contempt. Thus, one might attack the ideas of the Declaration of Independence by pointing out that its principal author, Thomas Jefferson, was a slaveholder. Assuming that it is not anachronistic and inappropriate to criticize a public figure of two centuries ago for practicing slavery, and conceding that slavery is morally outrageous, it is nonetheless fallacious to attack the ideas or even the sincerity of the Declaration by attempting to impeach the credentials of its author. Jefferson's moral faults do not by themselves falsify, make improbable, or constitute counterevidence to the truth or other merits of the claims made in his writings. At most, one's faults cast doubt on one's integrity or sincerity if one makes claims at odds with one's practice.

The genetic fallacy can take other forms less closely allied to ad hominem argument. For example, an opponent of the death penalty might argue this:

> Capital punishment arose in barbarous times; but we claim to be civilized; therefore, we should discard this relic of the past.

Such reasoning shouldn't be persuasive because the question of the death penalty for our society must be decided by the degree to which it serves our purposes—justice and defense against crime, presumably—to which its historic origins are irrelevant. The practices of beer- and wine-making are as old as human civilization, but their origin in antiquity is no reason to outlaw them in our time. The curious circumstances in which something originates usually play no role in its validity. Anyone who would argue that nothing good could possibly come from molds and fungi is refuted by Sir Alexander Fleming's discovery of penicillin in 1928.

Poisoning the Well   During the 1970s some critics of the Equal Rights Amendment (ERA) argued against it by pointing out that Marx and Engels, in their *Communist Manifesto*, favored equality of women and men—and therefore the ERA was immoral, undesirable, and perhaps even a Communist plot. This kind of reasoning is an attempt to **poison the well**; that is, an attempt to shift attention from the merits of the argument—the validity of the reasoning, the truth of the claims—to the source or origin of the argument. Such criticism deflects attention from the real issue; namely, whether the view in question is true and what the quality of evidence is in its support. The mere fact that Marx (or Hitler, for that matter) believed something does not show that the belief is false or immoral; just because some scoundrel believes the world is round, that is no reason for you to believe it is flat.

Appeal to Ignorance   In the controversy over the death penalty, the issues of deterrence and executing the innocent are bound to be raised. Because no one knows how many innocent persons have been convicted for murder and wrongfully executed, it is tempting for abolitionists to argue that the death penalty is too risky. It is equally tempting for proponents of the death penalty to argue that since no one knows how many people have been deterred from murder by the threat of execution, we abolish it at society's peril.

Each of these arguments suffers from the same flaw: the **fallacy of appeal to ignorance.** Each argument invites the audience to draw an inference from a premise that is unquestionably true—but what is that premise? It asserts that there is something "we don't know." But what we *don't* know cannot be *evidence* for (or against) anything. Our ignorance is no reason for believing anything, except perhaps that we ought to undertake an appropriate investigation in order to replace our ignorance with reliable information.

Ad Hominem   Closely allied to poisoning the well is another fallacy, **ad hominem** argument (from the Latin for "against the person"). A critic can easily yield to the temptation to attack an argument or theory by trying to impeach or undercut the credentials of its advocates.

Example: Jones is arguing that prayer should not be permitted in public schools, and Smith responds by pointing out that Jones has twice been convicted of assaulting members of the clergy. Jones's behavior doubtless is reprehensible, but the issue is not Jones, it is prayer in school, and what must be scrutinized is Jones's argument, not his police record or his character.

Appeal to Authority   The example of Jefferson that we gave to illustrate the genetic fallacy can be turned around to illustrate another fallacy. One might easily imagine someone from the South in 1860 defending the slave-owning society of that day by appealing to the fact that no less a person than Jefferson — a brilliant public figure, thinker, and leader by any measure — owned slaves. Or today one might defend capital punishment on the ground that Abraham Lincoln, surely one of the nation's greatest presidents, signed many death warrants during the Civil War, authorizing the execution of Union soldiers. No doubt the esteem in which such figures as Jefferson and Lincoln are deservedly held amounts to impressive endorsement for whatever acts and practices, policies, and institutions, they supported. But the **authority** of these figures in itself is not evidence for the truth of their views, so their authority cannot be a reason for anyone to agree with them. Obviously, Jefferson and Lincoln themselves could not support their beliefs by pointing to the fact that they held them. Because their own authority is no reason for them to believe what they believe, it is no reason for anyone else, either.

Sometimes, the appeal to authority is fallacious because the authoritative person is not an expert on the issue in dispute. The fact that a high-energy physicist has won the Nobel Prize is no reason for attaching any special weight to her views on the causes of cancer, the reduction of traffic accidents, or the legalization of marijuana. However, one would be well advised to attend to her views on the advisability of ballistic missile-defense systems, for there may be a connection between the kind of research for which she received the prize and the defense research projects.

All of us depend heavily on the knowledge of various experts and authorities, so we tend to respect their views. Conversely, we should resist the temptation to accord their views on diverse subjects the same respect that we grant them in the area of their expertise.

Appeal to Fear   The Romans called this fallacy *ad baculum*, "resorting to violence" (*baculum* means "stick" or "club"). Trying to persuade people to agree with you by threatening them with painful consequences is obviously an appeal that no rational person would contemplate. The violence need not be physical; if you threaten someone with the loss of a job, for instance, you are still using a stick. Violence or the threat of harmful consequences in the course of an argument is beyond reason and always shows the haste or impatience of those who appeal to it. It is also an indication that the argument on its merits would be unpersuasive, inconclusive, or worse. President Teddy Roosevelt's epigrammatic doctrine for the kind of foreign policy he favored — "Speak softly but carry a big stick" — illustrates an attempt to have it both ways; an appeal to reason for starters but a recourse to coercion, or the threat of coercion, as a backup if needed.

Finally, we add two fallacies, not easily embraced by Engels's three categories that have served us well thus far (ambiguity, erroneous presumption, and irrelevance): death by a thousand qualifications and protecting the hypothesis

Death by a Thousand Qualifications   In a letter of recommendation sent in support of an applicant for a job on your newspaper, you find this sentence: "Young Smith was the best student I've ever taught in an English course." Pretty strong endorsement, you think, except that you don't know, because you haven't been told, that the letter writer is a very junior faculty member, has been teaching for only two years, is an instructor in the history department, taught a section of freshman English as a courtesy for a sick colleague, and had only eight students enrolled in the course. Thanks to these implicit qualifications, the letter writer did not lie or exaggerate in his praise; but the effect of his sentence on you, the unwitting reader, is quite misleading. The explicit claim in the letter, and its impact on you, is quite different from the tacitly qualified claim in the mind of the writer.

Death by a thousand qualifications gets its name from the ancient torture of death by a thousand small cuts. Thus, a bold assertion can be virtually killed, its true content reduced to nothing, bit by bit, as all the appropriate or necessary qualifications are added to it. Consider another example. Suppose you hear a politician describing another country (let's call it Ruritania so as not to offend anyone) as a "democracy" — except it turns out that Ruritania doesn't have regular elections, lacks a written constitution, has no independent judiciary, prohibits religious worship except of the state-designated deity, and so forth. So what remains of the original claim that Ruritania is a democracy is little or nothing. The qualifications have taken all the content out of the original description.

Protecting the Hypothesis   In Chapter 3, we contrasted *reasoning* and *rationalization* (or the finding of bad reasons for what one intends to believe anyway). Rationalization can take subtle forms, as the following example indicates. Suppose you're standing with a friend on the shore or on a pier, and you watch as a ship heads out to sea. As it reaches the horizon, it slowly disappears — first the hull, then the upper decks, and finally the tip of the mast. Because the ship (you both assume) isn't sinking, it occurs to you that this sequence of observations provides evidence that the earth's surface is curved. Nonsense, says your companion. Light waves sag, or bend down, over distances of a few miles, and so a flat surface (such as the ocean) can intercept them. Hence, the ship, which appears to be going "over" the horizon, really isn't: It's just moving steadily farther and farther away in a straight line. Your friend, you discover to your amazement, is a card-carrying member of the Flat Earth Society (yes, there really is such an organization). Now most of us would regard the idea that light rays bend down in the manner required by the Flat Earther's argument as a rationalization whose sole purpose is to protect the flat-earth doctrine against counterevidence. We would be convinced it was a rationalization, and not a very good one at that, if the Flat Earther held to it despite a patient and thorough explanation from a physicist that showed modern optical theory to be quite incompatible with the view that light waves sag.

This example illustrates two important points about the *backing* of arguments. First, it is always possible to protect a hypothesis by abandoning adjacent or connected hypotheses;

this is the tactic our Flat Earth friend has used. This maneuver is possible, however, only because — and this is the second point — whenever we test a hypothesis, we do so by taking for granted (usually, quite unconsciously) many other hypotheses as well. So the evidence for the hypothesis we think we are confirming is impossible to separate entirely from the adequacy of the connected hypotheses. As long as we have no reason to doubt that light rays travel in straight lines (at least over distances of a few miles), our Flat Earth friend's argument is unconvincing. But once that hypothesis is itself put in doubt, the idea that seemed at first to be a pathetic rationalization takes on an even more troublesome character.

There are, then, not one but two fallacies exposed by this example. The first and perhaps graver one is in rigging your hypothesis so that *no matter what* observations are brought against it, you will count nothing as falsifying it. The second and subtler one is in thinking that as you test one hypothesis, all of your other background beliefs are left safely to one side, immaculate and uninvolved. On the contrary, our beliefs form a corporate structure, intertwined and connected to one another with great complexity, and no one of them can ever be singled out for unique and isolated application, confirmation, or disconfirmation to the world around us.

A CHECKLIST FOR EVALUATING AN ARGUMENT FROM A LOGICAL POINT OF VIEW

- ❑ Is the argument purely deductive, purely inductive, or a mixture of the two?
- ❑ If it is deductive, is it valid?
- ❑ If it is valid, are all its premises and assumptions true?
- ❑ If it is not valid, what fallacy does it commit?
- ❑ If it is not valid, are the claims at least consistent with each other?
- ❑ If it is not valid, can you think of additional plausible assumptions that would make it valid?
- ❑ If the argument is inductive, on what observations is it based?
- ❑ If the argument is deductive, how probable are its premises and its conclusion?
- ❑ In any case, can you think of evidence that would further confirm the conclusion? Disconfirm the conclusion?

Exercise: Fallacies — or Not?

Here, for diversion and practice, are some fallacies in action. Some of these statements, however, are not fallacies. Can you tell which is which? Can you detect *what* has gone wrong in the cases where something has gone wrong? Please explain your reasoning.

1. Abortion is murder — and it doesn't matter whether we're talking about killing a human embryo or a human fetus.

2. Euthanasia is not a good thing, it's murder — and it doesn't matter how painful one's dying may be.

3. Never loan a tool to a friend. I did once and never got it back.

4. If the neighbors don't like our loud music, that's just too bad. After all, we have a right to listen to the music we like when and where we want to play it.

5. The Good Samaritan in the Bible was pretty foolish; he was taking grave risks with no benefits for him in sight.

6. "Shoot first and ask questions afterward" is a good epigram for the kind of foreign policy we need.

7. "You can fool some of the people all of the time, and you can fool all the people some of the time, but you can't fool all the people all of the time." That's what Abraham Lincoln said, and he was right.

8. It doesn't matter whether Shakespeare wrote the plays attributed to him. What matters is whether the plays are any good.

9. The Golden Gate Bridge in San Francisco ought to be closed down. After all, just look at all the suicides that have occurred there.

10. Reparations for African Americans are way overdue; it's just another version of the reparations eventually paid to the Japanese Americans who were wrongly interned in 1942 during World War II.

11. Animals don't have rights any more than do trees or stones. They don't have desires, either. What they have are feelings and needs.

12. The average American family is said to have 2.1 children. This is absurd — did you ever meet 2.1 children?

13. My marriage was a failure, which just proves my point: Don't ever get married in the first place.

14. The Red Queen in *Alice in Wonderland* was right: Verdict first, evidence later.

15. Not until astronauts sailed through space around the moon and could see its back side for themselves did we have adequate reason to believe that the moon even had a back side.

16. If you start out with a bottle of beer a day and then go on to a glass or two of wine on the weekends, you're well on your way to becoming a hopeless drunk.

17. Two Indians are sitting on a fence. The small Indian is the son of the big Indian, but the big Indian is not the small Indian's father. How is that possible?

18. If you toss a coin five times and each time it comes up heads, is it more likely than not that on the sixth throw you'll come up heads again — or is it more likely that you'll come up tails? Or is neither more likely?

19. Going to church on a regular basis is bad for your health. Instead of sitting in a pew for an hour each Sunday, you'd be better off taking an hour's brisk walk.

20. You can't trust anything he says. When he was young, he was an avid Communist.

21. Since 9/11 we've tried and convicted few terrorists, so our defense systems must be working.

22. We can trust the White House in its press releases because it's a reliable source of information.

23. Intelligent design must be true because the theory of evolution can't explain how life began.

24. Andreas Serrano's notorious photograph called *Piss Christ* (1989), showing a small plastic crucifix submerged in a glass of urine, never should have been put on public display, let alone financed by public funds.

25. Doubting Thomas was right — you need more than somebody's say-so to support a claim of resurrection.

26. You are a professional baseball player and you have a good-luck charm. When you wear it, the team wins. When you don't wear it, the team loses. What do you infer?

27. Resolve the following dilemma: When it rains, you can't fix the hole in the roof. When it's not raining, there is no need to mend the roof. Conclusion: Leave the roof as it is.

28. You are at the beach, and you watch a ship steaming toward the horizon. Bit by bit it disappears from view — first the masts, then the upper deck, then the main deck, then the stern, and then it's gone. Why would it be wrong to infer that the ship is sinking?

29. How can it be true that "it's the exception that proves the rule"? If anything, isn't it the exception that *dis*proves the rule?

30. How come herbivores don't eat herbs?

31. In the 1930s it was commonplace to see ads announcing "More Doctors Smoke Camels." What do you make of such an ad?

32. Suppose the only way you could save five innocent people was by killing one of them. Would you do it? Suppose the only way you could save one innocent person was by killing five others. Would you do it?

MAX SHULMAN

Having read about proper and improper arguments, you are now well equipped to read a short story on the topic.

Max Shulman (1919–1988) began his career as a writer when he was a journalism student at the University of Minnesota. Later he wrote humorous novels, stories, and plays. One of his novels, Barefoot Boy with Check *(1943), was made into a musical, and another,* Rally Round the Flag, Boys! *(1957), was made into a film starring Paul Newman and Joanne Woodward. The Tender Trap (1954), a play he wrote with Robert Paul Smith, still retains its popularity with theater groups.*

"Love Is a Fallacy" was first published in 1951, when demeaning stereotypes about women and minorities were widely accepted in the marketplace as well as the home. Thus, jokes about domineering mothers-in-law or about dumb blondes routinely met with no objection.

Love Is a Fallacy

Cool was I and logical. Keen, calculating, perspicacious, acute, and astute — I was all of these. My brain was as powerful as a dynamo, as precise as a chemist's scales, as penetrating as a scalpel. And — think of it! — I was only eighteen.

It is not often that one so young has such a giant intellect. Take, for example, Petey Bellows, my roommate at the university. Same age, same background, but dumb as an ox. A nice enough fellow, you understand, but nothing upstairs. Emotional type. Unstable.

Impressionable. Worst of all, a faddist. Fads, I submit, are the very negation of reason. To be swept up in every new craze that comes along, to surrender yourself to idiocy just because everybody else is doing it — this, to me, is the acme of mindlessness. Not, however, to Petey.

One afternoon I found Petey lying on his bed with an expression of such distress on his face that I immediately diagnosed appendicitis. "Don't move," I said. "Don't take a laxative. I'll call a doctor."

"Raccoon," he mumbled thickly.

"Raccoon?" I said, pausing in my flight. 5

"I want a raccoon coat," he wailed.

I perceived that his trouble was not physical, but mental. "Why do you want a raccoon coat?"

"I should have known it," he cried, pounding his temples. "I should have known they'd come back when the Charleston came back. Like a fool I spent all my money for textbooks, and now I can't get a raccoon coat."

"Can you mean," I said incredulously, "that people are actually wearing raccoon coats again?"

"All the Big Men on Campus are wearing 10 them. Where've you been?"

"In the library," I said, naming a place not frequented by Big Men on Campus.

He leaped from the bed and paced the room. "I've got to have a raccoon coat," he said passionately. "I've got to!"

"Petey, why? Look at it rationally. Raccoon coats are unsanitary. They shed. They smell bad. They weigh too much. They're unsightly. They——"

"You don't understand," he interrupted impatiently. "It's the thing to do. Don't you want to be in the swim?"

"No," I said truthfully. 15

"Well, I do," he declared. "I'd give anything for a raccoon coat. Anything!"

My brain, that precision instrument, slipped into high gear. "Anything?" I asked, looking at him narrowly.

"Anything," he affirmed in ringing tones.

I stroked my chin thoughtfully. It so happened that I knew where to get my hands on a raccoon coat. My father had had one in his undergraduate days; it lay now in a trunk in the attic back home. It also happened that Petey had something I wanted. He didn't *have* it exactly, but at least he had first rights on it. I refer to his girl, Polly Espy.

I had long coveted Polly Espy. Let me 20 emphasize that my desire for this young woman was not emotional in nature. She was, to be sure, a girl who excited the emotions, but I was not one to let my heart rule my head. I wanted Polly for a shrewdly calculated, entirely cerebral reason.

I was a freshman in law school. In a few years I would be out in practice. I was well aware of the importance of the right kind of wife in furthering a lawyer's career. The successful lawyers I had observed were, almost without exception, married to beautiful, gracious, intelligent women. With one omission, Polly fitted these specifications perfectly.

Beautiful she was. She was not yet of pin-up proportions, but I felt sure that time would supply the lack. She already had the makings.

Gracious she was. By gracious I mean full of graces. She had an erectness of carriage, an ease of bearing, a poise that clearly indicated the best of breeding. At table her manners were exquisite. I had seen her at the Kozy Kampus Korner eating the specialty of the house — a sandwich that contained scraps of pot roast, gravy, chopped nuts, and a dipper of sauerkraut — without even getting her fingers moist.

Intelligent she was not. In fact, she veered in the opposite direction. But I believed that under my guidance she would smarten up. At any rate, it was worth a try. It is, after all, easier to make a beautiful dumb girl smart than to make an ugly smart girl beautiful.

"Petey," I said, "are you in love with Polly Espy?" [25]

"I think she's a keen kid," he replied, "but I don't know if you'd call it love. Why?"

"Do you," I asked, "have any kind of formal arrangement with her? I mean are you going steady or anything like that?"

"No. We see each other quite a bit, but we both have other dates. Why?"

"Is there," I asked, "any other man for whom she has a particular fondness?"

"Not that I know of. Why?" [30]

I nodded with satisfaction. "In other words, if you were out of the picture, the field would be open. Is that right?"

"I guess so. What are you getting at?"

"Nothing, nothing," I said innocently, and took my suitcase out of the closet.

"Where you going?" asked Petey.

"Home for the weekend." I threw a few [35] things into the bag.

"Listen," he said, clutching my arm eagerly, "while you're home, you couldn't get some money from your old man, could you, and lend it to me so I can buy a raccoon coat?"

"I may do better than that," I said with a mysterious wink and closed my bag and left.

"Look," I said to Petey when I got back Monday morning. I threw open the suitcase and revealed the huge, hairy, gamy object that my father had worn in his Stutz Bearcat in 1925.

"Holy Toledo!" said Petey reverently. He plunged his hands into the raccoon coat and then his face. "Holy Toledo!" he repeated fifteen or twenty times.

"Would you like it?" I asked. [40]

"Oh yes!" he cried, clutching the greasy pelt to him. Then a canny look came into his eyes. "What do you want for it?"

"Your girl," I said, mincing no words.

"Polly?" he said in a horrified whisper. "You want Polly?"

"That's right."

He flung the coat from him. "Never," he [45] said stoutly.

I shrugged. "Okay. If you don't want to be in the swim, I guess it's your business."

I sat down in a chair and pretended to read a book, but out of the corner of my eye I kept watching Petey. He was a torn man. First he looked at the coat with the expression of a waif at a bakery window. Then he turned away and set his jaw resolutely. Then he looked back at the coat, with even more longing in his face. Then he turned away, but with not so much resolution this time. Back and forth his head swiveled, desire waxing, resolution waning. Finally he didn't turn away at all; he just stood and stared with mad lust at the coat.

"It isn't as though I was in love with Polly," he said thickly. "Or going steady or anything like that."

"That's right," I murmured.

"What's Polly to me, or me to Polly?" [50]

"Not a thing," said I.

"It's just been a casual kick—just a few laughs, that's all."

"Try on the coat," said I.

He complied. The coat bunched high over his ears and dropped all the way down to his shoe tops. He looked like a mound of dead raccoons. "Fits fine," he said happily.

I rose from my chair. "Is it a deal?" I asked, [55] extending my hand.

He swallowed. "It's a deal," he said and shook my hand.

I had my first date with Polly the following evening. This was in the nature of a survey; I wanted to find out just how much work I had to do to get her mind up to the standard I required. I took her first to dinner. "Gee, that was a delish dinner," she said as we left the restaurant. Then I took her to a movie. "Gee, that was a marvy movie," she said as we left the theater. And then I took her home. "Gee, I had a sensaysh time," she said as she bade me good night.

I went back to my room with a heavy heart. I had gravely underestimated the size of my task. This girl's lack of information was terrifying. Nor would it be enough merely to supply her with information. First she had to be taught to *think*. This loomed as a project of no small dimensions, and at first I was tempted to give her back to Petey. But then I got to thinking about her abundant physical charms and about the way she entered a room and the way she handled a knife and fork, and I decided to make an effort.

I went about it, as in all things, systematically. I gave her a course in logic. It happened that I, as a law student, was taking a course in logic myself, so I had all the facts at my fingertips. "Polly," I said to her when I picked her up on our next date, "tonight we are going over to the Knoll and talk."

"Oo, terrif," she replied. One thing I will say 60 for this girl: You would go far to find another so agreeable.

We went to the Knoll, the campus trysting place, and we sat down under an old oak, and she looked at me expectantly: "What are we going to talk about?" she asked.

"Logic."

She thought this over for a minute and decided she liked it. "Magnif," she said.

"Logic," I said, clearing my throat, "is the science of thinking. Before we can think correctly, we must first learn to recognize the common fallacies of logic. These we will take up tonight."

"Wow-dow!" she cried, clapping her hands 65 delightedly.

I winced, but went bravely on. "First let us examine the fallacy called Dicto Simpliciter."

"By all means," she urged, batting her lashes eagerly.

"Dicto Simpliciter means an argument based on an unqualified generalization. For example: Exercise is good. Therefore everybody should exercise."

"I agree," said Polly earnestly. "I mean exercise is wonderful. I mean it builds the body and everything."

"Polly," I said gently, "the argument is a fal- 70 lacy. *Exercise is good* is an unqualified generalization. For instance, if you have heart disease, exercise is bad, not good. Many people are ordered by their doctors *not* to exercise. You must *qualify* the generalization. You must say exercise is *usually* good, or exercise is good *for most people.* Otherwise you have committed a Dicto Simpliciter. Do you see?"

"No," she confessed. "But this is marvy. Do more! Do more!"

"It will be better if you stop tugging at my sleeve," I told her, and when she desisted, I continued. "Next we take up a fallacy called Hasty Generalization. Listen carefully: You can't speak French. I can't speak French. Petey Bellows can't speak French. I must therefore conclude that nobody at the University of Minnesota can speak French."

"Really?" said Polly, amazed. "*Nobody?*"

I hid my exasperation. "Polly, it's a fallacy. The generalization is reached too hastily. There are too few instances to support such a conclusion."

"Know any more fallacies?" she asked 75 breathlessly. "This is more fun than dancing even."

I fought off a wave of despair. I was getting nowhere with this girl, absolutely nowhere. Still, I am nothing if not persistent. I continued. "Next comes Post Hoc. Listen to this: Let's not take Bill on our picnic. Every time we take him out with us, it rains."

"I know somebody just like that," she exclaimed. "A girl back home—Eula Becker, her name is. It never fails. Every single time we take her on a picnic ——"

"Polly," I said sharply, "it's a fallacy. Eula Becker doesn't *cause* the rain. She has no connection with the rain. You are guilty of Post Hoc if you blame Eula Becker."

"I'll never do it again," she promised contritely. "Are you mad at me?"

I sighed. "No, Polly, I'm not mad." 80

"Then tell me some more fallacies."

"All right. Let's try Contradictory Premises."

"Yes, let's," she chirped, blinking her eyes happily.

I frowned, but plunged ahead. "Here's an example of Contradictory Premises: If God can do anything, can He make a stone so heavy that He won't be able to lift it?"

"Of course," she replied promptly. 85

"But if He can do anything, He can lift the stone," I pointed out.

"Yeah," she said thoughtfully. "Well, then I guess He can't make the stone."

"But He can do anything," I reminded her.

She scratched her pretty, empty head. "I'm all confused," she admitted.

"Of course you are. Because when the 90 premises of an argument contradict each other, there can be no argument. If there is an irresistible force, there can be no immovable object. If there is an immovable object, there can be no irresistible force. Get it?"

"Tell me some more of this keen stuff," she said eagerly.

I consulted my watch. "I think we'd better call it a night. I'll take you home now, and you go over all the things you've learned. We'll have another session tomorrow night."

I deposited her at the girls' dormitory, where she assured me that she had had a perfectly terrif evening, and I went glumly home to my room. Petey lay snoring in his bed, the raccoon coat huddled like a great hairy beast at his feet. For a moment I considered waking him and telling him that he could have his girl back. It seemed clear that my project was doomed to failure. The girl simply had a logic-proof head.

But then I reconsidered. I had wasted one evening; I might as well waste another. Who knew? Maybe somewhere in the extinct crater of her mind a few embers still smoldered. Maybe somehow I could fan them into flame. Admittedly it was not a prospect fraught with hope, but I decided to give it one more try.

Seated under the oak the next evening 95 I said, "Our first fallacy tonight is called Ad Misericordiam."

She quivered with delight.

"Listen closely," I said. "A man applies for a job. When the boss asks him what his qualifications are, he replies that he has a wife and six children at home, the wife is a helpless cripple, the children have nothing to eat, no clothes to wear, no shoes on their feet, there are no beds in the house, no coal in the cellar, and winter is coming."

A tear rolled down each of Polly's pink cheeks. "Oh, this is awful, awful," she sobbed.

"Yes, it's awful," I agreed, "but it's no argument. The man never answered the boss's question about his qualifications. Instead he appealed to the boss's sympathy. He committed the fallacy of Ad Misericordiam. Do you understand?"

"Have you got a handkerchief?" she 100 blubbered.

I handed her a handkerchief and tried to keep from screaming while she wiped her eyes. "Next," I said in a carefully controlled tone, "we will discuss False Analogy. Here is an example: Students should be allowed to look at their textbooks during examinations. After all, surgeons have X rays to guide them during an operation, lawyers have briefs to guide them during a trial, carpenters have blueprints to guide them when they are building a house. Why, then, shouldn't students be allowed to look at their textbooks during an examination?"

"There now," she said enthusiastically, "is the most marvy idea I've heard in years."

"Polly," I said testily, "the argument is all wrong. Doctors, lawyers, and carpenters aren't taking a test to see how much they have learned, but students are. The situations are altogether different, and you can't make an analogy between them."

"I still think it's a good idea," said Polly.

"Nuts," I muttered. Doggedly I pressed on. 105 "Next we'll try Hypothesis Contrary to Fact."

"Sounds yummy," was Polly's reaction.

"Listen: If Madame Curie had not happened to leave a photographic plate in a drawer with a chunk of pitchblende, the world today would not know about radium."

"True, true," said Polly, nodding her head. "Did you see the movie? Oh, it just knocked me out. That Walter Pidgeon is so dreamy. I mean he fractures me."

"If you can forget Mr. Pidgeon for a moment," I said coldly, "I would like to point out that the statement is a fallacy. Maybe Madame Curie would have discovered radium at some later date. Maybe somebody else would have discovered it. Maybe any number of things would have happened. You can't start with a hypothesis that is not true and then draw any supportable conclusions from it."

"They ought to put Walter Pidgeon in 110 more pictures," said Polly. "I hardly ever see him any more."

One more chance, I decided. But just one more. There is a limit to what flesh and blood can bear. "The next fallacy is called Poisoning the Well."

"How cute!" she gurgled.

"Two men are having a debate. The first one gets up and says, 'My opponent is a notorious liar. You can't believe a word that he is going to say.' . . . Now, Polly, think. Think hard. What's wrong?"

I watched her closely as she knit her creamy brow in concentration. Suddenly a glimmer of intelligence — the first I had seen — came into her eyes. "It's not fair," she said with indignation. "It's not a bit fair. What chance has the second man got if the first man calls him a liar before he even begins talking?"

"Right!" I cried exultantly. "One hundred 115 percent right. It's not fair. The first man has *poisoned the well* before anybody could drink from it. He has hamstrung his opponent before he could even start. . . . Polly, I'm proud of you."

"Pshaw," she murmured, blushing with pleasure.

"You see, my dear, these things aren't so hard. All you have to do is concentrate. Think — examine — evaluate. Come now, let's review everything we have learned."

"Fire away," she said with an airy wave of her hand.

Heartened by the knowledge that Polly was not altogether a cretin, I began a long, patient review of all I had told her. Over and over and over again I cited instances, pointed out flaws, kept hammering away without letup. It was like digging a tunnel. At first everything was work, sweat, and darkness. I had no idea when I would reach the light, or even *if* I would. But I persisted. I pounded and clawed and scraped, and finally I was rewarded. I saw a chink of light. And then the chink got bigger and the sun came pouring in and all was bright.

Five grueling nights this took, but it was 120 worth it. I had made a logician out of Polly; I had taught her to think. My job was done. She was worthy of me at last. She was a fit wife for me, a proper hostess for my many mansions, a suitable mother for my well-heeled children.

It must not be thought that I was without love for this girl. Quite the contrary. Just as Pygmalion loved the perfect woman he had fashioned, so I loved mine. I decided to acquaint her with my feelings at our very next meeting. The time had come to change our relationship from academic to romantic.

"Polly," I said when next we sat beneath our oak, "tonight we will not discuss fallacies."

"Aw, gee," she said, disappointed.

"My dear," I said, favoring her with a smile, "we have now spent five evenings together. We have gotten along splendidly. It is clear that we are well matched."

"Hasty Generalization," said Polly brightly. 125

"I beg your pardon," said I.

"Hasty Generalization," she repeated. "How can you say that we are well matched on the basis of only five dates?"

I chuckled with amusement. The dear child had learned her lessons well. "My dear," I said, patting her hand in a tolerant manner, "five dates is plenty. After all, you don't have to eat a whole cake to know that it's good."

"False Analogy," said Polly promptly. "I'm not a cake. I'm a girl."

I chuckled with somewhat less amuse- 130 ment. The dear child had learned her lesson perhaps too well. I decided to change tactics. Obviously the best approach was a simple, strong, direct declaration of love. I paused for a moment while my massive brain chose the proper words. Then I began:

"Polly, I love you. You are the whole world to me, and the moon and the stars and the constellations of outer space. Please, my darling, say that you will go steady with me, for if you will not, life will be meaningless. I will languish. I will refuse my meals. I will wander the face of the earth, a shambling, hollow-eyed hulk."

There, I thought, folding my arms, that ought to do it.

"Ad Misericordiam," said Polly.

I ground my teeth. I was not Pygmalion; I was Frankenstein, and my monster had me by the throat. Frantically I fought back the tide of panic surging through me. At all costs I had to keep cool.

"Well, Polly," I said, forcing a smile, "you 135 certainly have learned your fallacies."

"You're darn right," she said with a vigorous nod.

"And who taught them to you, Polly?"

"You did."

"That's right. So you do owe me something, don't you, my dear? If I hadn't come along you never would have learned about fallacies."

"Hypothesis Contrary to Fact," she said 140 instantly.

I dashed perspiration from my brow. "Polly," I croaked, "you mustn't take all these things so literally. I mean this is just classroom stuff. You know that the things you learn in school don't have anything to do with life."

"Dicto Simpliciter," she said, wagging her finger at me playfully.

That did it. I leaped to my feet, bellowing like a bull. "Will you or will you not go steady with me?"

"I will not," she replied.

"Why not?" I demanded. 145

"Because this afternoon I promised Petey Bellows that I would go steady with him."

I reeled back, overcome with the infamy of it. After he promised, after he made a deal, after he shook my hand! "That rat!" I shrieked, kicking up great chunks of turf. "You can't go with him, Polly. He's a liar. He's a cheat. He's a rat."

"Poisoning the Well," said Polly, "and stop shouting. I think shouting must be a fallacy too."

With an immense effort of will, I modulated my voice. "All right," I said. "You're a logician. Let's look at this thing logically. How could you choose Petey Bellows over me? Look at me — a brilliant student, a tremendous intellectual, a man with an assured future. Look at Petey — a knothead, a jitterbug, a guy who'll never know where his next meal is coming from. Can you give me one logical reason why you should go steady with Petey Bellows?"

"I certainly can," declared Polly. "He's got a raccoon coat." 150

Topic for Critical Thinking and Writing

After you have finished reading "Love Is a Fallacy," you may want to write an argumentative essay of 500 to 750 words on one of the following topics: (1) the story, rightly understood, is not antiwoman; (2) if the story is antiwoman, it is equally antiman; (3) the story is antiwoman but nevertheless belongs in this book; or (4) the story is antiwoman and does not belong in the book.

10

A Psychologist's View: Rogerian Argument

Real communication occurs . . . when we listen with understanding. —CARL ROGERS

The first duty of a wise advocate is to convince his opponents that he understands their arguments, and sympathizes with their just feelings. —SAMUEL TAYLOR COLERIDGE

Rogerian Argument: An Introduction

Carl R. Rogers (1902–1987), perhaps best known for his book entitled *On Becoming a Person* (1961), was a psychotherapist, not a teacher of writing. This short essay by Rogers (on pp. 375–80) has, however, exerted much influence on instructors who teach argument. Written in the 1950s, this essay reflects the political climate of the cold war between the United States and the Soviet Union, which dominated headlines for more than forty years (1947–1989). Several of Rogers's examples of bias and frustrated communication allude to the tensions of that era.

On the surface, many arguments seem to show *A* arguing with *B*, presumably seeking to change *B*'s mind; but *A*'s argument is really directed not to *B* but to *C*. This attempt to persuade a nonparticipant is evident in the courtroom, where neither the prosecutor (*A*) nor the defense lawyer (*B*) is really trying to convince the opponent. Rather, both are trying to convince a third party, the jury (*C*). Prosecutors don't care whether they convince defense lawyers; they don't even mind infuriating defense lawyers because

Carl R. Rogers leading a panel discussion in 1966.

their only real goal is to convince the jury. Similarly, the writer of a letter to a newspaper, taking issue with an editorial, doesn't expect to change the paper's policy. Rather, the writer hopes to convince a third party, the reader of the newspaper.

But suppose *A* really does want to bring *B* around to *A*'s point of view. Suppose Mary really wants to persuade the teacher to allow her little lamb to stay in the classroom. Rogers points out that when we engage in an argument, if we feel our integrity or our identity is threatened, we will stiffen our position. (The teacher may feel that his or her dignity is compromised by the presence of the lamb and will scarcely attend to Mary's argument.) The sense of threat may be so great that we are unable to consider the alternative views being offered, and we therefore remain unpersuaded. Threatened, we may defend ourselves rather than our argument, and little communication will take place. Of course, a third party might say that we or our opponent presented the more convincing case, but we, and perhaps the opponent, have scarcely listened to each other, and so the two of us remain apart.

Rogers suggests, therefore, that a writer who wishes to communicate with someone (as opposed to convincing a third party) needs to reduce the threat. In a sense, the participants in the argument need to become partners rather than adversaries. Rogers writes, "Mutual communication tends to be pointed toward solving a problem rather than toward attacking a person or group." Thus, in an essay on whether schools should test students for use of drugs, the writer need not—and probably should not—see the issue as black or white, as *either/or*. Such an essay might indicate that testing is undesirable because it may have bad effects, *but in some circumstances* it may be acceptable. This qualification does not mean that one must compromise. Thus, the essayist might argue that the potential danger to liberty is so great that no circumstances justify testing students for drugs. But even such an essayist should recognize the merit (however limited) of the opposition and should grant that the position being advanced itself entails great difficulties and dangers.

A writer who wishes to reduce the psychological threat to the opposition and thus facilitate partnership in the study of some issue can do several things:

- show sympathetic understanding of the opposing argument
- recognize what is valid in it
- recognize and demonstrate that those who take the other side are nonetheless persons of goodwill

Advocates of Rogerian argument are likely to contrast it with Aristotelian argument, saying that the style of argument associated with Aristotle (384–322 B.C., Greek philosopher and rhetorician) has these two characteristics:

- It is adversarial, seeking to refute other views.
- It sees the listener as wrong, as someone who now must be overwhelmed by evidence.

In contrast to the confrontational Aristotelian style, which allegedly seeks to present an airtight case that compels belief, Rogerian argument (it is said) has the following characteristics:

- It is nonconfrontational, collegial, and friendly.

- It respects other views and allows for multiple truths.
- It seeks to achieve some degree of assent rather than convince utterly.

Thus, in the first part of an argumentative essay, a writer who takes Rogers seriously will usually

1. state the problem,
2. give the opponent's position, and
3. grant whatever validity the writer finds in that position — for instance, will recognize the circumstances in which the position would indeed be acceptable.

Next, the writer will, if possible,

4. attempt to show how the opposing position will be improved if the writer's own position is accepted.

Sometimes, of course, the differing positions may be so far apart that no reconciliation can be proposed, in which case the writer will probably seek to show how the problem can best be solved by adopting the writer's own position. We have discussed these matters in Chapter 6, but not from the point of view of a psychotherapist, and so we reprint Rogers's essay here. (This essay was orginally presented on October 11, 1951, at Northwestern University's Centennial Conference on Communication.)

CARL R. ROGERS

Communication: Its Blocking and Its Facilitation

It may seem curious that a person whose whole professional effort is devoted to psychotherapy should be interested in problems of communication. What relationship is there between providing therapeutic help to individuals with emotional maladjustments and the concern of this conference with obstacles to communication? Actually the relationship is very close indeed. The whole task of psychotherapy is the task of dealing with a failure in communication. The emotionally maladjusted person, the "neurotic," is in difficulty first because communication within himself has broken down, and second because as a result of this his communication with others has been damaged. If this sounds somewhat strange, then let me put it in other terms. In the "neurotic" individual, parts of himself which have been termed unconscious, or repressed, or denied to awareness, become blocked off so that they no longer communicate themselves to the conscious or managing part of himself. As long as this is true, there are distortions in the way he communicates himself to others, and so he suffers both within himself, and in his interpersonal relations. The task of psychotherapy is to help the person achieve, through a special relationship with a therapist, good communication within himself. Once this is achieved he can communicate more freely and more effectively with others. We may say then that psychotherapy is good communication, within and between men. We may also turn that statement around and it will still be true. Good communication, free communication, within or between men, is always therapeutic.

It is, then, from a background of experience with communication in counseling and psychotherapy that I want to present here two ideas. I wish to state what I believe is one of the major factors in blocking or impeding communication, and then I wish to present what in our experience has proven to be a very important way to improving or facilitating communication.

I would like to propose, as an hypothesis for consideration, that the major barrier to mutual interpersonal communication is our very natural tendency to judge, to evaluate, to approve or disapprove, the statement of the person, or the other group. Let me illustrate my meaning with some very simple examples. As you leave the meeting tonight, one of the statements you are likely to hear is, "I didn't like that man's talk." Now what do you respond? Almost invariably your reply will be either approval or disapproval of the attitude expressed. Either you respond, "I didn't either. I thought it was terrible," or else you tend to reply, "Oh, I thought it was really good." In other words, your primary reaction is to evaluate what has just been said to you, to evaluate it from *your* point of view, your own frame of reference.

Or take another example. Suppose I say with some feeling, "I think the Republicans are behaving in ways that show a lot of good sound sense these days," what is the response that arises in your mind as you listen? The overwhelming likelihood is that it will be evaluative.

You will find yourself agreeing, or disagreeing, or making some judgment about me such as "He must be a conservative," or "He seems solid in his thinking." Or let us take an illustration from the international scene. Russia says vehemently, "The treaty with Japan is a war plot on the part of the United States." We rise as one person to say "That's a lie!"

This last illustration brings in another 5 element connected with my hypothesis. Although the tendency to make evaluations is common in almost all interchange of language, it is very much heightened in those situations where feelings and emotions are deeply involved. So the stronger our feelings, the more likely it is that there will be no mutual element in the communication. There will be just two ideas, two feelings, two judgments, missing each other in psychological space. I'm sure you recognize this from your own experience. When you have not been emotionally involved yourself, and have listened to a heated discussion, you often go away thinking, "Well, they actually weren't talking about the same thing." And they were not. Each was making a judgment, an evaluation, from his own frame of reference. There was really nothing which could be called communication in any genuine sense. This tendency to react to any emotionally meaningful statement by forming an evaluation of it from our own point of view, is, I repeat, the major barrier to interpersonal communication.

But is there any way of solving this problem, of avoiding this barrier? I feel that we are making exciting progress toward this goal and I would like to present it as simply as I can. Real communication occurs, and this evaluative tendency is avoided, when we listen with understanding. What does that mean? It means *to see the expressed idea and attitude from the other person's point of view, to sense how it feels to him, to achieve his frame of reference in regard to the thing he is talking about.*

Stated so briefly, this may sound absurdly simple, but it is not. It is an approach which we have found extremely potent in the field of psychotherapy. It is the most effective agent we know for altering the basic personality structure of an individual, and improving his relationships and his communications with others. If I can listen to what he can tell me, if I can understand how it seems to him, if I can see its personal meaning for him, if I can sense the emotional flavor which it has for him, then I will be releasing potent forces of change in him. If I can really understand how he hates his father, or hates the university, or hates communists — if I can catch the flavor of his fear of insanity, or his fear of atom bombs, or of Russia — it will be of the greatest help to him in altering those very hatreds and fears, and in establishing realistic and harmonious relationships with the very people and situations toward which he has felt hatred and fear. We know from our research that such empathic understanding — understanding *with* a person, not *about* him — is such an effective approach that it can bring about major changes in personality.

Some of you may be feeling that you listen well to people, and that you have never seen such results. The chances are very great indeed that your listening has not been of the type I have described. Fortunately I can suggest a little laboratory experiment which you can try to test the quality of your understanding. The next time you get into an argument with your wife, or your friend, or with a small group of friends, just stop the discussion for a moment and for an experiment, institute this rule. "Each person can speak up for himself only *after* he has first restated the ideas and feelings of the previous speaker accurately, and to that speaker's satisfaction." You see what this would

mean. It would simply mean that before presenting your own point of view, it would be necessary for you to really achieve the other speaker's frame of reference — to understand his thoughts and feelings so well that you could summarize them for him. Sounds simple, doesn't it? But if you try it you will discover it one of the most difficult things you have ever tried to do. However, once you have been able to see the other's point of view, your own comments will have to be drastically revised. You will also find the emotion going out of the discussion, the differences being reduced, and those differences which remain being of a rational and understandable sort.

Can you imagine what this kind of an approach would mean if it were projected into larger areas? What would happen to a labor-management dispute if it was conducted in such a way that labor, without necessarily agreeing, could accurately state management's point of view in a way that management could accept; and management, without approving labor's stand, could state labor's case in a way that labor agreed was accurate? It would mean that real communication was established, and one could practically guarantee that some reasonable solution would be reached.

If then this way of approach is an effective [10] avenue to good communication and good relationships, as I am quite sure you will agree if you try the experiment I have mentioned, why is it not more widely tried and used? I will try to list the difficulties which keep it from being utilized.

In the first place it takes courage, a quality which is not too widespread. I am indebted to Dr. S. I. Hayakawa, the semanticist, for pointing out that to carry on psychotherapy in this fashion is to take a very real risk, and that courage is required. If you really understand another person in this way, if you are willing to enter his private world and see the way life appears to him, without any attempt to make evaluative judgments, you run the risk of being changed yourself. You might see it his way, you might find yourself influenced in your attitudes or your personality. This risk of being changed is one of the most frightening prospects most of us can face. If I enter, as fully as I am able, into the private world of a neurotic or psychotic individual, isn't there a risk that I might become lost in that world? Most of us are afraid to take that risk. Or if we had a Russian communist speaker here tonight, or Senator Joe McCarthy, how many of us would dare to try to see the world from each of these points of view? The great majority of us could not *listen;* we would find ourselves compelled to *evaluate,* because listening would seem too dangerous. So the first requirement is courage, and we do not always have it.

But there is a second obstacle. It is just when emotions are strongest that it is most difficult to achieve the frame of reference of the other person or group. Yet it is the time the attitude is most needed, if communication is to be established. We have not found this to be an insuperable obstacle in our experience in psychotherapy. A third party, who is able to lay aside his own feelings and evaluations, can assist greatly by listening with understanding to each person or group and clarifying the views and attitudes each holds. We have found this very effective in small groups in which contradictory or antagonistic attitudes exist. When the parties to a dispute realize that they are being understood, that someone sees how the situation seems to them, the statements grow less exaggerated and less defensive, and it is no longer necessary to maintain the attitude, "I am 100 percent right and you are 100 percent wrong." The influence of such an understanding catalyst in the group permits the members

to come closer and closer to the objective truth involved in the relationship. In this way mutual communication is established and some type of agreement becomes much more possible. So we may say that though heightened emotions make it much more difficult to understand *with* an opponent, our experience makes it clear that a neutral, understanding, catalyst type of leader or therapist can overcome this obstacle in a small group.

This last phrase, however, suggests another obstacle to utilizing the approach I have described. Thus far all our experience has been with small face-to-face groups — groups exhibiting industrial tensions, religious tensions, racial tensions, and therapy groups in which many personal tensions are present. In these small groups our experience, confirmed by a limited amount of research, shows that this basic approach leads to improved communication, to greater acceptance of others and by others, and to attitudes which are more positive and more problem-solving in nature. There is a decrease in defensiveness, in exaggerated statements, in evaluative and critical behavior. But these findings are from small groups. What about trying to achieve understanding between larger groups that are geographically remote? Or between face-to-face groups who are not speaking for themselves, but simply as representatives of others, like the delegates at Kaesong?[1] Frankly we do not know the answers to these questions. I believe the situation might be put this way. As social scientists we have a tentative test-tube solution of the problem of breakdown in communication. But to confirm the validity of this test-tube solution, and to adapt it to the enormous problems of communication

---

[1] **the delegates at Kaesong** Representatives of North and South Korea met at the border town of Kaesong to arrange terms for an armistice to hostilities during the Korean War (1950–1953). [All notes are the editors'.]

breakdown between classes, groups, and nations, would involve additional funds, much more research, and creative thinking of a high order.

Even with our present limited knowledge we can see some steps which might be taken, even in large groups, to increase the amount of listening *with,* and to decrease the amount of evaluation *about.* To be imaginative for a moment, let us suppose that a therapeutically oriented international group went to the Russian leaders and said, "We want to achieve a genuine understanding of your views and even more important, of your attitudes and feelings, toward the United States. We will summarize and resummarize the views and feelings if necessary, until you agree that our description represents the situation as it seems to you." Then suppose they did the same thing with the leaders in our own country. If they then gave the widest possible distribution to these two views, with the feelings clearly described but not expressed in name-calling, might not the effect be very great? It would not guarantee the type of understanding I have been describing, but it would make it much more possible. We can understand the feelings of a person who hates us much more readily when his attitudes are accurately described to us by a neutral third party, than we can when he is shaking his fist at us.

But even to describe such a first step is to suggest another obstacle to this approach of understanding. Our civilization does not yet have enough faith in the social sciences to utilize their findings. The opposite is true of the physical sciences. During the war[2] when a test-tube solution was found to the problem of synthetic rubber, millions of dollars and an army of talent was turned loose on the problem of using that finding. If synthetic rubber could be made in milligrams, it could and would be made in the thousands of tons. And it was. But in the social science realm, if a way is found of facilitating communication and mutual understanding in small groups, there is no guarantee that the finding will be utilized. It may be a generation or more before the money and the brains will be turned loose to exploit that finding.

In closing, I would like to summarize this small-scale solution to the problem of barriers in communication, and to point out certain of its characteristics.

I have said that our research and experience to date would make it appear that breakdowns in communication, and the evaluative tendency which is the major barrier to communication, can be avoided. The solution is provided by creating a situation in which each of the different parties come to understand the other from the *other's* point of view. This has been achieved, in practice, even when feelings run high, by the influence of a person who is willing to understand each point of view empathically, and who thus acts as a catalyst to precipitate further understanding.

This procedure has important characteristics. It can be initiated by one party, without waiting for the other to be ready. It can even be initiated by a neutral third person, providing he can gain a minimum of cooperation from one of the parties.

This procedure can deal with the insincerities, the defensive exaggerations, the lies, the "false fronts" which characterize almost every failure in communication. These defensive distortions drop away with astonishing speed as people find that the only intent is to understand, not judge.

This approach leads steadily and rapidly toward the discovery of the truth, toward a realistic appraisal of the objective barriers

---

[2]**the war** World War II.

to communication. The dropping of some defensiveness by one party leads to further dropping of defensiveness by the other party, and truth is thus approached.

This procedure gradually achieves mutual communication. Mutual communication tends to be pointed toward solving a problem rather than toward attacking a person or group. It leads to a situation in which I see how the problem appears to you, as well as to me, and you see how it appears to me, as well as to you. Thus accurately and realistically defined, the problem is almost certain to yield to intelligent attack, or if it is in part insoluble, it will be comfortably accepted as such.

This then appears to be a test-tube solution to the breakdown of communication as it occurs in small groups. Can we take this small-scale answer, investigate it further, refine it; develop it and apply it to the tragic and well-nigh fatal failures of communication which threaten the very existence of our modern world? It seems to me that this is a possibility and a challenge which we should explore.

> ## A CHECKLIST FOR ANALYZING ROGERIAN ARGUMENT
>
> ❏ Have I stated the problem and indicated that a dialogue is possible?
>
> ❏ Have I stated at least one other point of view in a way that would satisfy its proponents?
>
> ❏ Have I been courteous to those who hold views other than mine?
>
> ❏ Have I enlarged my own understanding to the extent that I can grant validity, at least in some circumstances, to at least some aspects of other positions?
>
> ❏ Have I stated my position and indicated the contexts in which I believe it is valid?
>
> ❏ Have I pointed out the ground that we share?
>
> ❏ Have I shown how other positions will be strengthened by accepting some aspects of my position?

EDWARD O. WILSON

Edward O. Wilson, born in Birmingham, Alabama, in 1929, is an emeritus professor of evolutionary biology at Harvard University. A distinguished writer as well as a researcher and teacher, Wilson has twice won the Pulitzer Prize for General Non-Fiction. We reprint a piece first published in 2006 in Wilson's book The Creation: An Appeal to Save Life on Earth.

Letter to a Southern Baptist Minister

Dear Pastor:

We have not met, yet I feel I know you well enough to call you friend. First of all, we grew up in the same faith. As a boy I too answered the altar call; I went under the water. Although I no longer belong to that faith, I am confident that if we met and spoke privately of our deepest beliefs, it would be in a spirit of mutual respect and good will. I know we share many precepts of moral behavior. Perhaps it also matters that we are both Americans and, insofar as it might still affect civility and good manners, we are both Southerners.

I write to you now for your counsel and help. Of course, in doing so, I see no way to avoid the fundamental differences in our respective worldviews. You are a literalist interpreter of Christian Holy Scripture. You reject the conclusion of science that mankind evolved from lower forms. You believe that each person's soul is immortal, making this planet a way station to a second, eternal life. Salvation is assured those who are redeemed in Christ.

I am a secular humanist. I think existence is what we make of it as individuals. There is no guarantee of life after death, and heaven and hell are what we create for ourselves, on this planet. There is no other home. Humanity originated here by evolution from lower forms over millions of years. And yes, I will speak plain, our ancestors were apelike animals. The human species has adapted physically and mentally to life on Earth and no place else. Ethics is the code of behavior we share on the basis of reason, law, honor, and an inborn sense of decency, even as some ascribe it to God's will.

For you, the glory of an unseen divinity; for me, the glory of the universe revealed at last. For you, the belief in God made flesh to save mankind; for me, the belief in Promethean[1] fire seized to set men free. You have found your final truth; I am still searching. I may be wrong, you may be wrong. We may both be partly right.

Does this difference in worldview separate us in all things? It does not. You and I and every other human being strive for the same

imperatives of security, freedom of choice, personal dignity, and a cause to believe in that is larger than ourselves.

Let us see, then, if we can, and you are willing, to meet on the near side of metaphysics in order to deal with the real world we share. I put it this way because you have the power to help solve a great problem about which I care deeply. I hope you have the same concern. I suggest that we set aside our differences in order to save the Creation. The defense of living Nature is a universal value. It doesn't rise from, nor does it promote, any religious or ideological dogma. Rather, it serves without discrimination the interests of all humanity.

Pastor, we need your help. The Creation—living Nature—is in deep trouble. Scientists estimate that if habitat conversion and other destructive human activities continue at their present rates, half the species of plants and animals on Earth could be either gone or at least fated for early extinction by the end of the century. A full quarter will drop to this level during the next half century as a result of climate change alone. The ongoing extinction rate is calculated in the most conservative estimates to be about a hundred times above that prevailing before humans appeared on Earth, and it is expected to rise to at least a thousand times greater or more in the next few decades. If this rise continues unabated, the cost to humanity, in wealth, environmental security, and quality of life, will be catastrophic.

Surely we can agree that each species, however inconspicuous and humble it may seem to us at this moment, is a masterpiece of biology, and well worth saving. Each species possesses a unique combination of genetic traits that fits it more or less precisely to a particular part of the environment. Prudence alone dictates that we act quickly to prevent the extinction of

---

[1]**Promethean** In Greek mythology, Prometheus was a Titan who looked after mankind, going so far as to steal fire from Mount Olympus to give it to humans. [Editors' note.]

species and, with it, the pauperization of Earth's ecosystems — hence of the Creation.

You may well ask at this point, Why me? Because religion and science are the two most powerful forces in the world today, including especially the United States. If religion and science could be united on the common ground of biological conservation, the problem would soon be solved. If there is any moral precept shared by people of all beliefs, it is that we owe ourselves and future generations a beautiful, rich, and healthful environment.

I am puzzled that so many religious lead- [10] ers, who spiritually represent a large majority of people around the world, have hesitated to make protection of the Creation an important part of their magisterium.[2] Do they believe that human-centered ethics and preparation for the afterlife are the only things that matter? Even more perplexing is the widespread conviction among Christians that the Second Coming is imminent, and that therefore the condition of the planet is of little consequence. Sixty percent of Americans, according to a 2004 poll, believe that the prophecies of the book of Revelation are accurate. Many of these, numbering in the millions, think the End of Time will occur within the life span of those now living. Jesus will return to Earth, and those redeemed by Christian faith will be transported bodily to heaven, while those left behind will struggle through severe hard times and, when they die, suffer eternal damnation. The condemned will remain in hell, like those already consigned in the generations before them, for a trillion trillion years, enough for the universe to expand to its own, entropic death, time enough for countless universes like it afterward to be born, expand, and likewise die away. And that is just

the beginning of how long condemned souls will suffer in hell — all for a mistake they made in choice of religion during the infinitesimally small time they inhabited Earth.

For those who believe this form of Christianity, the fate of 10 million other life forms indeed does not matter. This and other similar doctrines are not gospels of hope and compassion. They are gospels of cruelty and despair. They were not born of the heart of Christianity. Pastor, tell me I am wrong!

However you will respond, let me here venture an alternative ethic. The great challenge of the twenty-first century is to raise people everywhere to a decent standard of living while preserving as much of the rest of life as possible. Science has provided this part of the argument for the ethic: the more we learn about the biosphere, the more complex and beautiful it turns out to be. Knowledge of it is a magic well: the more you draw from it, the more there is to draw. Earth, and especially the razor-thin film of life enveloping it, is our home, our wellspring, our physical and much of our spiritual sustenance.

I know that science and environmentalism are linked in the minds of many with evolution, Darwin, and secularism. Let me postpone disentangling all this (I will come back to it later) and stress again: to protect the beauty of Earth and of its prodigious variety of life forms should be a common goal, regardless of differences in our metaphysical beliefs.

To make the point in good Gospel manner, let me tell the story of a young man, newly trained for the ministry, and so fixed in his Christian faith that he referred all questions of morality to readings from the Bible. When he visited the cathedral-like Atlantic rainforest of Brazil, he saw the manifest hand of God and in his notebook wrote, "It is not possible to give an adequate idea of the higher feelings of

---

[2]**magisterium** The official teaching of the Roman Catholic Church. [Editors' note.]

wonder, admiration, and devotion which fill and elevate the mind."

That was Charles Darwin in 1832, early into the voyage of HMS *Beagle*, before he had given any thought to evolution.

And here is Darwin, concluding *On the Origin of Species* in 1859, having first abandoned Christian dogma and then, with his newfound intellectual freedom, formulated the theory of evolution by natural selection: "There is grandeur in this view of life, with its several powers, having been originally breathed into a few forms or into one; and that, whilst this planet has gone cycling on according to the fixed law of gravity, from so simple a beginning endless forms most beautiful and most wonderful have been, and are being, evolved."

Darwin's reverence for life remained the same as he crossed the seismic divide that divided his spiritual life. And so it can be for the divide that today separates scientific humanism from mainstream religion. And separates you and me.

You are well prepared to present the theological and moral arguments for saving the Creation. I am heartened by the movement growing within Christian denominations to support global conservation. The stream of thought has arisen from many sources, from evangelical to unitarian. Today it is but a rivulet. Tomorrow it will be a flood.

I already know much of the religious argument on behalf of the Creation, and would like to learn more. I will now lay before you and others who may wish to hear it the scientific argument. You will not agree with all that I say about the origins of life — science and religion do not easily mix in such matters — but I like to think that in this one life-and-death issue we have a common purpose

Topics for Critical Thinking and Writing

1. Wilson claims to be a "secular humanist" (para. 3). How would you define that term? Are you a secular humanist? Why, or why not?

2. What does Wilson mean by "metaphysics" (para. 6)? Which if any of his views qualify as metaphysical?

3. Wilson obviously seeks to present his views in a fashion that makes them as palatable as possible. Do you think he succeeds in this endeavor? Write an essay of 500 words arguing for or against his achievement in this regard.

11

A Literary Critic's View:
Arguing about Literature

Literary criticism [is] a reasoned account of the feeling produced upon the critic by the book he is reading.

— D. H. LAWRENCE

A writer is someone for whom writing is more difficult than it is for other people.

— THOMAS MANN

You can never draw the line between aesthetic criticism and social criticism. . . . You start with literary criticism, and however rigorous an aesthete you may be, you are over the frontier into something else sooner or later. The best you can do is to accept these conditions and know what you are doing when you are doing it.

— T. S. ELIOT

Nothing is as easy as it looks.

— MURPHY'S LAW #23

Everything is what it is and not another thing.

— BISHOP JOSEPH BUTLER

You might think that literature — fiction, poetry (including songs), drama — is meant only to be enjoyed, not to be argued about. Yet literature is constantly the subject of argumentative writing — not all of it by teachers of English. For instance, if you glance at the current issue of *Time* or *The New Yorker*, you probably will find a review of a play suggesting that the play is worth seeing or is not worth seeing. Or in the same magazine you may find an article reporting that a senator or member of Congress argued that the National Endowment for the Humanities wasted its grant money by funding research on such-and-such an author or that the National Endowment for the Arts insulted taxpayers by making an award to a writer who defamed the American family.

Probably most writing about literature, whether done by college students, their professors, journalists, members of Congress, or whomever, is devoted to interpreting, judging (evaluating), and theorizing. Let's look at each of these, drawing our examples chiefly from comments about Shakespeare's *Macbeth*.

Interpreting

Interpreting is a matter of setting forth the *meaning* or the meanings of a work. For some readers, a work has *a* meaning, the one intended by the writer, which we may or may not perceive. For most critics today, however, a work has *many* meanings — for instance, the meaning it had for the writer, the meanings it has accumulated over time, and the meanings it has for each of today's readers. Take *Macbeth*, a play about a Scottish king, written soon after a Scot — James VI of Scotland — had been installed as James I, King of England. The play must have meant something special to the king — we know that it was presented at court — and something a little different to the ordinary English citizen. And surely it means something different to us. For instance, few if any people today believe in the divine right of kings, although James I certainly did; and few if any people today believe in malevolent witches, although witches play an important role in the tragedy. What *we* see in the play must be rather different from what Shakespeare's audience saw in it.

Many interpretations of *Macbeth* have been offered. Let's take two fairly simple and clearly opposed views:

1. Macbeth is a villain who, by murdering his lawful king, offends God's rule, so he is overthrown by God's earthly instruments, Malcolm and Macduff. Macbeth is justly punished; the reader or spectator rejoices in his defeat.

One can offer a good deal of evidence — and if one is taking this position in an essay, of course one must *argue* it — by giving supporting reasons rather than merely asserting the position.

2. Macbeth is a hero-villain, a man who commits terrible crimes but who never completely loses the reader's sympathy; although he is justly punished, the reader believes that with the death of Macbeth the world has become a smaller place.

Again, one *must* offer evidence in an essay that presents this thesis or indeed presents any interpretation. For instance, one might offer as evidence the fact that the survivors, especially Macduff and Malcolm, have not interested us nearly as much as Macbeth has. One might argue, too, that although Macbeth's villainy is undeniable, his conscience never deserts him — here one would point to specific passages and would offer some brief quotations. Macbeth's pained awareness of what he has done, one can argue, enables the reader to sympathize with him continually.

Or consider an interpretation of Lady Macbeth. Is she simply evil through and through, or are there mitigating reasons for her actions? Might one argue, perhaps in a feminist interpretation, that despite her intelligence and courage she had no outlet for expression except through her husband? To make this argument, the writer might want to go beyond the text of the play, offering as evidence Elizabethan comments about the proper role of women.

Judging (or Evaluating)

Literary criticism is also concerned with such questions as these: Is *Macbeth* a great tragedy? Is *Macbeth* a greater tragedy than *Romeo and Juliet*? The writer offers an opinion about the worth of the literary work, but the opinion must be supported by an argument, expressed in sentences that offer supporting evidence.

Let's pause for a moment to think about evaluation in general. When we say "This is a great play," are we in effect saying only "I like this play"? That is, are we merely *expressing* our taste rather than *asserting* something independent of our tastes and feelings? (The next few paragraphs won't answer this question, but they may start you thinking about your own answer.) Consider these three sentences:

1. It's raining outside.
2. I like vanilla.
3. This is a really good book.

If you are indoors and you say that it is raining outside, a hearer may ask for verification. Why do you say what you say? "Because," you reply, "I'm looking out the window." Or "Because Jane just came in, and she is drenched." Or "Because I just heard a weather report." If, however, you say that you like vanilla, it's almost unthinkable that anyone would ask you why. No one expects you to justify — to support, to give a reason for — an expression of taste.

Now consider the third statement, "This is a really good book." It is entirely reasonable, we think, for someone to ask you *why* you say that. And you reply, "Well, the characters are realistic, and the plot held my interest," or "It really gave me an insight into what life among the rich [or the poor] must be like," or some such thing.

That is, statement 3 at least seems to be stating a fact, and it seems to be something we can discuss, even argue about, in a way that we cannot argue about a personal preference for vanilla. Almost everyone would agree that when offering an aesthetic judgment we ought to be able to give reasons for it. At the very least, we might say, we hope to show *why* we evaluate the work as we do and to suggest that if readers try to see it from our point of view they may then accept our evaluation.

Evaluations are always based on assumptions, although these assumptions may be unstated, and in fact the writer may even be unaware of them. Some of these assumptions play the role of criteria; they control the sort of evidence the writer believes is relevant to the evaluation. What sorts of assumptions may underlie value judgments? We will mention a few, merely as examples. Other assumptions are possible, and all of these assumptions can themselves become topics of dispute:

1. A good work of art, although fictional, says something about real life.
2. A good work of art is complex yet unified.
3. A good work of art sets forth a wholesome view of life.
4. A good work of art is original.
5. A good work of art deals with an important subject.

Let's look briefly at these views, one by one.

1. A good work of art, although fictional, says something about real life. If you hold the view that literature is connected to life and believe that human beings behave in fairly consistent ways—that is, that each of us has an enduring "character"—you probably will judge as inferior a work in which the figures behave inconsistently or seem to be inadequately motivated. (We must point out, however, that different literary forms or genres are governed by different rules. For instance, consistency of character is usually expected in tragedy but not in melodrama or in comedy, where last-minute reformations may be welcome and greeted with applause. The novelist Henry James said, "You will not write a good novel unless you possess the sense of reality." He's probably right—but does his view hold for the writer of farces?) In the case of *Macbeth* you might well find that the characters are consistent: Although the play begins by showing Macbeth as a loyal defender of King Duncan, Macbeth's later treachery is understandable, given the temptation and the pressure. Similarly, Lady Macbeth's descent into madness, although it may come as a surprise, may strike you as entirely plausible: At the beginning of the play she is confident that she can become an accomplice to a murder, but she has overestimated herself (or, we might say, she has underestimated her own humanity, the power of her guilty conscience, which drives her to insanity).

2. A good work of art is complex yet unified. If Macbeth is only a "tyrant" (Macduff's word) or a "butcher" (Malcolm's word), he is a unified character, but he may be too simple and too uninteresting a character to be the subject of a great play. But, one argument holds, Macbeth in fact is a complex character, not simply a villain but a hero-villain, and the play as a whole is complex. *Macbeth* is a good work of art, one might argue, partly because it shows us so many aspects of life (courage, fear, loyalty, treachery, for a start) through richly varied language (the diction ranges from a grand passage in which Macbeth says that his bloody hands will "incarnadine," or make red, "the multitudinous seas" to colloquial passages such as the drunken porter's "Knock, knock"). The play shows the heroic Macbeth tragically destroying his own life, and it shows the comic porter making coarse jokes about deceit and damnation, jokes that (although the porter doesn't know it) connect with Macbeth's crimes.

3. A good work of art sets forth a wholesome view of life. The general public widely believes that a work should be judged partly or largely on the moral view that it sets forth. (Esteemed philosophers, notably Plato, have felt the same way.) Thus, a story that demeans women—perhaps one that takes a casual view of rape—would receive a low rating, as would a play that treats a mass murderer as a hero.

A seventeenth-century artist's interpretation of Macbeth's murder of King Duncan.

Implicit in this approach is what is called an *instrumentalist* view — the idea that a work of art is an instrument, a means, to some higher value. Thus, many people hold that reading great works of literature makes us better — or at least does not make us worse. In this view, a work that is pornographic or in some other way considered immoral will receive a low value. At the time we are writing this chapter, a law requires the National Endowment for the Arts to take into account standards of decency when making awards.

Moral judgments, it should be noted, do not come only from the conservative right; the liberal left has been quick to detect political incorrectness. In fact, except for those people who subscribe to the now unfashionable view that a work of art is an independent aesthetic object with little or no connection to the real world — something like a pretty floral arrangement or a wordless melody — most people judge works of literature largely by their content, by what the works seem to say about life.

- Marxist critics, for instance, have customarily held that literature should make the reader aware of the political realities of life.

- Feminist critics are likely to hold that literature should make us aware of gender relationships — for example, aware of patriarchal power and of women's accomplishments.

4. A good work of art is original. This assumption puts special value on new techniques and new subject matter. Thus, the *first* playwright who introduces a new subject (say, AIDS) gets extra credit, so to speak. Or to return to Shakespeare, one sign of his genius, it is held, is that he was so highly varied; none of his tragedies seems merely to duplicate another, each is a world of its own, a new kind of achievement. Compare, for instance, *Romeo and Juliet*, with its two youthful and innocent heroes, with *Macbeth*, with its deeply guilty hero. Both plays are tragedies, but we can hardly imagine two more different plays — even if a reader perversely argues that the young lovers are guilty of impetuosity and of disobeying appropriate authorities.

5. A good work of art deals with an important subject. Here we are concerned with theme: Great works, in this view, must deal with great themes. Love, death, patriotism, and God, say, are great themes; a work that deals with these may achieve a height, an excellence, that, say, a work describing a dog scratching for fleas may not achieve. (Of course, if the reader feels that the dog is a symbol of humanity plagued by invisible enemies, then the poem about the dog may reach the heights; but then, too, it is *not* a poem about a dog and fleas: It is really a poem about humanity and the invisible.)

The point: In writing an evaluation you must let the reader know *why* you value the work as you do. Obviously, it is not enough just to keep saying that *this* work is great whereas *that* work is not so great; the reader wants to know *why* you offer the judgments that you do, which means that you

- must set forth your criteria, and then
- offer evidence that is in accord with them.

Theorizing

Some literary criticism is concerned with such theoretical questions as these:

> What is tragedy? Can the hero be a villain? How does tragedy differ from melodrama?
>
> Why do tragedies — works showing good or at least interesting people destroyed — give us pleasure?
>
> Does a work of art — a play or a novel, say, a made-up world with imagined characters — offer anything that can be called "truth"? Does our experience of a work of art affect our character?
>
> Does a work of art have meaning in itself, or is the meaning simply whatever anyone wishes to say it is? Does *Macbeth* tell us anything about life, or is it just an invented story?

And, yet again, one hopes that anyone asserting a thesis concerned with any of these topics will offer evidence — will, indeed, *argue* rather than merely assert.

A CHECKLIST FOR AN ARGUMENT ABOUT LITERATURE

❏ Is my imagined reader like a typical classmate of mine, someone who is not a specialist in literature but who is open-minded and interested in hearing my point of view about a work?

❏ Is the essay supported with evidence, usually from the text itself but conceivably from other sources (such as a statement by the author, a statement by a person regarded as an authority, or perhaps the evidence of comparable works)?

❏ Is the essay inclusive? Does it take into account all relevant details (which is not to say that it includes everything the writer knows about the work — for instance, that it was made into a film or that the author died poor)?

❏ Is the essay focused? Does the thesis stay steadily before the reader?

❏ Does the essay use quotations, but as evidence, not as padding? Whenever possible, does it abridge or summarize long quotations?

❏ Are all sources fully acknowledged? (For the form of documentation, see Chapter 7.)

Examples:
Two Students Interpret Robert Frost's "Mending Wall"

Let's consider two competing interpretations of a poem, Robert Frost's "Mending Wall." We say "competing" because these interpretations clash head-on. Differing interpretations need not be incompatible, of course. For instance, a historical interpretation of *Macbeth*, arguing that an understanding of the context of English–Scottish politics around 1605 helps us to appreciate the play, need not be incompatible with a psychoanalytic interpretation that tells us that Macbeth's murder of King Duncan is rooted in an Oedipus complex, the king being a father figure. Different approaches thus can illuminate different aspects of the work, just as they can emphasize or subordinate different elements in the plot or characters portrayed. But, again, in the next few pages we will deal with mutually incompatible interpretations of the meaning of Frost's poem.

After reading the poem and the two interpretations written by students, spend a few minutes thinking about the questions that we raise after the second interpretation.

ROBERT FROST

Robert Frost (1874–1963) studied for part of one term at Dartmouth College in New Hampshire, then did odd jobs (including teaching), and from 1897 to 1899 was enrolled as a special student at Harvard. He then farmed in New Hampshire, published a few poems in newspapers, did some more teaching, and in 1912 left for England, where he hoped to achieve success as a writer. By 1915 he was known in England, and he returned to the United States. By the time of his death he was the nation's unofficial poet laureate. "Mending Wall" was first published in 1914.

Mending Wall

Something there is that doesn't love a wall,
That sends the frozen-ground-swell under it,
And spills the upper boulders in the sun;
And makes gaps even two can pass abreast.
The work of hunters is another thing: 5
I have come after them and made repair
Where they have left not one stone on a stone,
But they would have the rabbit out of hiding,
To please the yelping dogs. The gaps I mean,
No one has seen them made or heard them
      made,
But at spring mending-time we find them there.   10
I let my neighbor know beyond the hill;
And on a day we meet to walk the line
And set the wall between us once again.
We keep the wall between us as we go.   15
To each the boulders that have fallen to each.
And some are loaves and some so nearly balls
We have to use a spell to make them balance:
"Stay where you are until our backs are turned!"
We wear our fingers rough with handling them.   20
Oh, just another kind of outdoor game,
One on a side. It comes to little more:
There where it is we do not need the wall:

He is all pine and I am apple orchard.
My apple trees will never get across   25
And eat the cones under his pines, I tell him.
He only says, "Good fences make good
      neighbors."
Spring is the mischief in me, and I wonder
If I could put a notion in his head:
"*Why* do they make good neighbors? Isn't it   30
Where there are cows? But here there are no cows.
Before I built a wall I'd ask to know
What I was walling in or walling out,
And to whom I was like to give offense.
Something there is that doesn't love a wall,   35
That wants it down." I could say "Elves" to him,
But it's not elves exactly, and I'd rather
He said it for himself. I see him there
Bringing a stone grasped firmly by the top
In each hand, like an old-stone savage armed.   40
He moves in darkness as it seems to me,
Not of woods only and the shade of trees.
He will not go behind his father's saying,
And he likes having thought of it so well
He says again, "Good fences make good
      neighbors."   45

Jonathan Deutsch
Professor Walton
English 102
5 March 2016

The Deluded Speaker in Frost's "Mending Wall"

Our discussions of "Mending Wall" in high school showed that most people think Frost is saying that walls between people are a bad thing and that we should not try to separate ourselves from each other unnecessarily. Perhaps the wall, in this view, is a symbol for race prejudice or religious differences, and Frost is suggesting that these differences are minor and that they should not keep us apart. In this common view, the neighbor's words, "Good fences make good neighbors" (lines 27 and 45), show that the neighbor is shortsighted. I disagree with this view, but first I want to present the evidence that might be offered for it, so that we can then see whether it really is substantial.

First of all, someone might claim that in lines 23 to 26 Frost offers a good argument against walls:

There where it is we do not need the wall:
He is all pine and I am apple orchard.
My apple trees will never get across
And eat the cones under his pines, I tell him.

The neighbor does not offer a valid reply to this argument; in fact, he doesn't offer any argument at all but simply says, "Good fences make good neighbors."

Another piece of evidence supposedly showing that the neighbor is wrong, it is said, is found in Frost's description of him as "an old-stone savage" and someone who "moves in darkness" (40, 41). And a third piece of evidence is said to be that the neighbor "will not go behind his father's saying" (43), but he merely repeats the saying.

There is, however, another way of looking at the poem. As I see it, the speaker is a very snide and condescending person. He is confident that he knows it all and that his neighbor is an ignorant savage; he is even willing to tease his supposedly ignorant neighbor. For instance, the speaker admits to "the mischief in me" (28), and he is confident that he could tell the truth to the neighbor but arrogantly thinks that it would be a more effective form of teaching if the neighbor "said it for himself" (38).

The speaker is not only unpleasantly mischievous and condescending toward his neighbor, but he is also shallow, for he does not see the great wisdom that there is in proverbs. The *American Heritage Dictionary of the English Language*, Third Edition, defines a proverb as "A short, pithy saying in frequent and widespread use that expresses a basic truth." Frost, or at least the man who speaks this poem, does not seem to realize that proverbs express truths. He just dismisses them, and he thinks the neighbor is wrong not to "go behind his father's saying" (43). But there is a great deal of wisdom in the sayings of our fathers. For instance, in the Bible (in the Old Testament) there is a whole book of proverbs, filled with wise sayings such as "Reprove not a scorner, lest he hate thee: rebuke a wise man, and he will love thee" (9:8); "He that trusteth in his riches shall fall" (11:28); "The way of a fool is right in his own eyes" (12:15; this might be said of the speaker of "Mending Wall"); "A soft answer turneth away wrath" (15:1); and (to cut short what could be a list many pages long), "Whoso diggeth a pit shall fall therein" (26:27).

The speaker is confident that walls are unnecessary and probably bad, but he doesn't realize that even where there are no cattle, walls serve the valuable purpose of clearly marking out our territory. They help us to preserve our independence and our individuality. Walls — man-made structures — are a sign of civilization. A wall more or less says, "*This* is mine, but I respect *that* as yours." Frost's speaker is so confident of his shallow view that he makes fun of his neighbor for repeating that "Good fences make good neighbors" (27, 45). But he himself repeats his own saying, "Something there is that doesn't love a wall" (1, 35). And at least the neighbor has age-old tradition on his side, since the proverb is the saying of his father. In contrast, the speaker has only his own opinion, and he can't even say what the "something" is.

It may be that Frost meant for us to laugh at the neighbor and to take the side of the speaker, but I think it is much more likely that he meant for us to see that the speaker is mean-spirited (or at least given to unpleasant teasing), too self-confident, foolishly dismissing the wisdom of the old times, and entirely unaware that he has these unpleasant characteristics.

Felicia Alonso

Professor Walton

English 102

5 March 2016

The Debate in Robert Frost's "Mending Wall"

I think the first thing to say about Frost's "Mending Wall" is this: The poem is not about a debate over whether good fences do or do not make good neighbors. It is about two debaters: one of the debaters is on the side of vitality, and the other is on the side of an unchanging, fixed — dead, we might say — tradition.

How can we characterize the speaker? For one thing, he is neighborly. Interestingly, it is *he*, and not the neighbor, who initiates the repairing of the wall: "I let my neighbor know beyond the hill" (line 12). This seems strange, since the speaker doesn't see any point in this wall, whereas the neighbor is all in favor of walls. Can we explain this apparent contradiction? Yes; the speaker is a good neighbor, willing to do his share of the work and willing (perhaps in order not to upset his neighbor) to maintain an old tradition even though he doesn't see its importance. It may not be important, he thinks, but it is really rather pleasant, "another kind of outdoor game" (21). In fact, sometimes he even repairs fences on his own, after hunters have destroyed them.

Second, we can say that the speaker is on the side of nature. "Something there is that doesn't love a wall," he says (1, 35), and of course, the "something" is nature itself. Nature "sends the frozen-ground-swell" under the wall and "spills the upper boulders in the sun; / And makes gaps even two can pass abreast" (2–4). Notice that nature itself makes the gaps and that "two can pass abreast" — that is, people can walk together in a companionable way. It is hard to imagine the neighbor walking side by side with anyone.

Third, we can say that the speaker has a sense of humor. When he thinks of trying to get his neighbor interested in the issue, he admits that "the mischief" is in him (28), and he amusingly attributes his playfulness to a natural force, the spring. He playfully toys with the obviously preposterous idea of suggesting to his neighbor that elves caused the stones to fall, but he stops short of making this amusing suggestion to his very serious neighbor. Still, the mere thought assures us that he has a playful, genial nature, and the idea also again implies that not only the speaker but also some sort of mysterious natural force dislikes walls.

Finally, though, of course, he thinks he is right and that his neighbor is mistaken, he at least is cautious in his view. He does not call his neighbor "an old-stone savage" (40); rather, he uses a simile ("like") and then adds that this is only his opinion, so the opinion is softened quite a bit. Here is the description of the neighbor, with italics added to clarify my point. The neighbor is . . .

> *like* an old-stone savage armed.
> He moves in darkness *as it seems to me* . . . (40–41)

Of course, the only things we know about the neighbor are those things that the speaker chooses to tell us, so it is not surprising that the speaker comes out ahead. He comes out ahead not because he is right about walls (real or symbolic) and his neighbor is wrong — that's an issue that is not settled in the poem. He comes out ahead because he is a more interesting figure, someone who is neighborly, thoughtful, playful. Yes, maybe he seems to us to feel superior to his neighbor, but we can be certain that he doesn't cause his neighbor any embarrassment. Take the very end of the poem. The speaker tells us that the neighbor

> . . . will not go behind his father's saying,
> And he likes having thought of it so well
> He says again, "Good fences make good neighbors."

The speaker is telling *us* that the neighbor is utterly unoriginal and that the neighbor confuses *remembering* something with *thinking*. But the speaker doesn't get into an argument; he doesn't rudely challenge his neighbor and demand reasons, which might force the neighbor to see that he can't think for himself. And in fact we probably like the neighbor just as he is, and we don't want him to change his mind. The words that ring in our ears are not the speaker's but the neighbor's: "Good fences make good neighbors." The speaker of the poem is a good neighbor. After all, one can hardly be more neighborly than to let the neighbor have the last word.

Topics for Critical Thinking and Writing

1. State the thesis of each essay. Do you believe the theses are sufficiently clear and appear sufficiently early in the essays? Why, or why not?

2. Consider the evidence that each essay offers by way of supporting its thesis. Do you find some of the evidence unconvincing? Explain.

3. Putting aside the question of which interpretation you prefer, comment on the organization of each essay. Is the organization clear? Do you want to propose some other pattern that you think might be more effective? Explain your responses.

4. Consult the Checklist for Peer Review on pages 254–55, and offer comments on one of the two essays. Or: If you were the instructor in the course in which these two essays were submitted, what might be your final comments on each of them? Or: Write an analysis (250–500 words) of the strengths and weaknesses of either essay.

EXERCISES: READING A POEM AND A STORY

ANDREW MARVELL

Andrew Marvell (1621–1678), born in Hull, England, and educated at Trinity College, Cambridge, was traveling in Europe when the civil war between the Royalists and the Puritans broke out in England in 1642. The Puritans were victorious and established the Commonwealth (the monarchy was restored later, in 1660), and Marvell became a tutor to the daughter of the victorious Lord-General. In 1657 he became an assistant to the blind poet John Milton, who held the title of Latin Secretary (Latin was the language of international diplomacy). In 1659 Marvell was elected to represent Hull in Parliament. As a man of letters, during his lifetime he was known chiefly for some satiric prose and poetry; most of the writings for which he is now esteemed were published posthumously. The following poem was first published in 1681.

To His Coy Mistress°

Had we but world enough, and time,
This coyness,° Lady, were no crime.
We would sit down, and think which way
To walk, and pass our long love's day.
Thou by the Indian Ganges' side   5
Shouldst rubies find; I by the tide
Of Humber° would complain. I would
Love you ten years before the Flood,
And you should, if you please, refuse

Till the Conversion of the Jews.°   10
My vegetable° love should grow
Vaster than empires and more slow;
An hundred years should go to praise
Thine eyes, and on thy forehead gaze;
Two hundred to adore each breast,   15
But thirty thousand to the rest;
An age at least to every part,
And the last age should show your heart.

Mistress Beloved woman.
2 coyness Reluctance.
7 Humber An estuary at Hull, Marvell's birthplace.

10 Conversion of the Jews Something that would take place in the remote future, at the end of history.
11 vegetable Vegetative or growing.

For, Lady, you deserve this state,°
Nor would I love at lower rate.   20

    But at my back I always hear
Time's wingèd chariot hurrying near;
And yonder all before us lie
Deserts of vast eternity.
Thy beauty shall no more be found,   25
Nor, in thy marble vault, shall sound
My echoing song; then worms shall try°
That long-preserved virginity,
And your quaint° honour turn to dust,
And into ashes all my lust: 30
The grave's a fine and private place,
But none, I think, do there embrace.

    Now therefore, while the youthful hue

Sits on thy skin like morning dew,
And while thy willing soul transpires   35
At every pore with instant fires,
Now let us sport us while we may,
And now, like amorous birds of prey,
Rather at once our time devour
Than languish in his slow-chapt° power.   40
Let us roll all our strength and all
Our sweetness up into one ball,
And tear our pleasures with rough strife
Thorough° the iron gates of life:
Thus, though we cannot make our sun   45
Stand still,° yet we will make him run.

---

19 state Ceremonious treatment.
27 try Test.
29 quaint Fastidious or finicky, with a pun on a coarse word defined in an Elizabethan dictionary as "a woman's privities."

40 slow-chapt Slow-jawed.
44 Thorough Through.
46 make our sun stand still An allusion to Joshua, the ancient Hebrew who, according to the Book of Joshua (10.12–13), made the sun stand still.

Topics for Critical Thinking and Writing

1. The motif that life is short and that we should seize the day (Latin: *Vita brevis carpe diem*) is old. Marvell's poem, in fact, probably has its ultimate source in a classical text called *The Greek Anthology*, a collection of about six thousand short Greek poems composed between the first century B.C. and the tenth century A.D. One poem goes thus, in a fairly literal translation:

   > You spare your maidenhead, and to what profit? For when you come to Hades
   > you will not find your lover, girl. Among the living are the delights of Venus, but,
   > maiden, we shall lie in the underworld mere bones and dust.

   If you find Marvell's poem more impressive, offer reasons for your belief.

2. A student, working from the translation just given, produced this rhyming version:

   > You keep your virginity, but to what end?
   > Below, in Hades, you won't find your friend.
   > On earth we enjoy Venus' sighs and moans;
   > Buried below, we are senseless bones.

   What do you think of this version? Why? Prepare your own version — your instructor may divide the class into groups of four, and each group can come up with a collaborative version — and then compare it with other versions, giving reasons for your preferences.

3. Marvell's poem takes the form of a syllogism (see pp. 90–95). It can be divided into three parts:

   a. "Had we" (i.e., "If we had") (line 1), a supposition, or suppositional premise;
   b. "But at my back" (line 21), a refutation;
   c. "Now therefore" (line 33), a deduction.

Look closely at the poem and develop the argument using these three parts, devoting a few sentences to each part.

4. A student wrote of this poem:

> As a Christian I can't accept the lover's statement that "yonder all before us lie / Deserts of vast eternity" (lines 23–24). The poem may contain beautiful lines, and it may offer clever reasoning, but the reasoning is based on what my religion tells me is wrong. I not only cannot accept the idea of the poem, but I also cannot enjoy the poem, since it presents a false view of reality.

What assumptions is this student making about a reader's response to a work of literature? Do you agree or disagree? Why?

5. Here are three additional comments by students. For each, list the writer's assumptions, and then evaluate each comment. You may agree or disagree, in whole or in part, with any comment, but give your reasons.

> a. The poem is definitely clever, and that is part of what is wrong with it. It is a blatant attempt at seduction. The man seems to think he is smarter than the woman he is speaking to, and he "proves" that she should go to bed with him. Since we don't hear her side of the argument, Marvell implies that she has nothing to say and that his argument is sound. What the poet doesn't seem to understand is that there is such a thing as virtue, and a woman need not sacrifice virtue just because death is inevitable.
>
> b. On the surface, "To His Coy Mistress" is an attempt to persuade a woman to go to bed with the speaker, but the poem is really less about sex than it is about the terrifying shortness of life.
>
> c. This is not a love poem. The speaker admits that his impulse is "lust" (line 30), and he makes fun of the girl's conception of honor and virginity. If we enjoy this poem at all, our enjoyment must be in the hope that this would-be date-rapist is unsuccessful.

6. Read the poem several times slowly, perhaps even aloud. Do certain lines seem especially moving, especially memorable? If so, which ones? Give reasons for your belief.

7. In *On Deconstruction* (1982), a study of contemporary literary theory, Jonathan Culler remarks that feminist criticism has often stressed "reading as a woman." This concept, Culler says, affirms the "continuity between women's experience of social and familial structures and their experiences as readers." Do you agree with his suggestion that men and women often interpret literary works differently? Consider Marvell's poem in particular: Identify and discuss phrases and images in it to which men and women readers might (or might not) respond very differently.

8. A small point, but perhaps one of some interest. In the original text, line 34 ends with *glew*, not with *dew*. Most editors assume that the printer made an error, and — looking for a word to rhyme with *hue* — they replace *glew* with *dew*. Another possible emendation is *lew*, an archaic word meaning "warmth." But the original reading has been defended, as a variant of the word *glow*. Your preference? Your reasons?

KATE CHOPIN

Kate Chopin (1851–1904) was born in St. Louis and named Katherine O'Flaherty. At the age of nineteen she married a cotton broker in New Orleans, Oscar Chopin (the name is pronounced something like "show pan"), who was descended from the early French settlers in Louisiana. After her husband's death in 1883, Kate Chopin turned to writing fiction. The following story was first published in 1894.

The Story of an Hour

Knowing that Mrs. Mallard was afflicted with a heart trouble, great care was taken to break to her as gently as possible the news of her husband's death.

It was her sister Josephine who told her, in broken sentences, veiled hints that revealed in half concealing. Her husband's friend Richards was there, too, near her. It was he who had been in the newspaper office when intelligence of the railroad disaster was received, with Brently Mallard's name leading the list of "killed." He had only taken the time to assure himself of its truth by a second telegram, and had hastened to forestall any less careful, less tender friend in bearing the sad message.

She did not hear the story as many women have heard the same, with a paralyzed inability to accept its significance. She wept at once, with sudden, wild abandonment, in her sister's arms. When the storm of grief had spent itself she went away to her room alone. She would have no one follow her.

There stood, facing the open window, a comfortable, roomy armchair. Into this she sank, pressed down by a physical exhaustion that haunted her body and seemed to reach into her soul.

She could see in the open square before 5 her house the tops of trees that were all aquiver with the new spring life. The delicious breath of rain was in the air. In the street below a peddler was crying his wares. The notes of a distant song which some one was singing reached her faintly, and countless sparrows were twittering in the eaves.

There were patches of blue sky showing here and there through the clouds that had met and piled one above the other in the west facing her window.

She sat with her head thrown back upon the cushion of the chair, quite motionless, except when a sob came up into her throat and shook her, as a child who has cried itself to sleep continues to sob in its dreams.

She was young, with a fair, calm face, whose lines bespoke repression and even a certain strength. But now there was a dull stare in her eyes, whose gaze was fixed away off yonder on one of those patches of blue sky. It was not a glance of reflection, but rather indicated a suspension of intelligent thought.

There was something coming to her and she was waiting for it, fearfully. What was it? She did not know; it was too subtle and elusive to name. But she felt it, creeping out of the sky, reaching toward her through the sounds, the scents, the color that filled the air.

Now her bosom rose and fell tumultuously. 10 She was beginning to recognize this thing that was approaching to possess her, and she was striving to beat it back with her will — as powerless as her two white slender hands would have been.

When she abandoned herself a little whispered word escaped her slightly parted lips. She said it over and over under her breath: "Free, free, free!" The vacant stare and the look of terror that had followed it went from her eyes. They stayed keen and bright. Her pulses beat fast, and the coursing blood warmed and relaxed every inch of her body.

She did not stop to ask if it were not a monstrous joy that held her. A clear and exalted perception enabled her to dismiss the suggestion as trivial.

She knew that she would weep again when she saw the kind, tender hands folded in death; the face that had never looked save with love upon her, fixed and gray and dead. But she saw beyond that bitter moment a long procession of years to come that would belong to her absolutely. And she opened and spread her arms out to them in welcome.

There would be no one to live for her during those coming years; she would live for herself. There would be no powerful will bending her in that blind persistence with which men and women believe they have a right to impose a private will upon a fellow creature. A kind intention or a cruel intention made the act seem no less a crime as she looked upon it in that brief moment of illumination.

And yet she had loved him — sometimes. 15 Often she had not. What did it matter! What could love, the unsolved mystery, count for in face of this possession of self-assertion which she suddenly recognized as the strongest impulse of her being.

"Free! Body and soul free!" she kept whispering.

Josephine was kneeling before the closed door with her lips to the keyhole, imploring for admission. "Louise, open the door! I beg; open the door — you will make yourself ill. What are you doing, Louise? For heaven's sake open the door."

"Go away. I am not making myself ill." No; she was drinking in a very elixir of life through that open window.

Her fancy was running riot along those days ahead of her. Spring days, and summer days, and all sorts of days that would be her own. She breathed a quick prayer that life might be long. It was only yesterday she had thought with a shudder that life might be long.

She arose at length and opened the door 20 to her sister's importunities. There was a feverish triumph in her eyes, and she carried herself unwittingly like a goddess of Victory. She clasped her sister's waist, and together they descended the stairs. Richards stood waiting for them at the bottom.

Some one was opening the front door with a latchkey. It was Brently Mallard who entered, a little travel-stained, composedly carrying his gripsack and umbrella. He had been far from the scene of accident, and did not even know there had been one. He stood amazed at Josephine's piercing cry; at Richards' quick motion to screen him from the view of his wife.

But Richards was too late.

When the doctors came they said she had died of heart disease — of joy that kills.

Topics for Critical Thinking and Writing

Read the following assertions, and consider whether you agree or disagree, and why. For each assertion, draft a paragraph with your arguments.

1. The railroad accident is a symbol of the destructiveness of the industrial revolution.

2. The story claims that women rejoice in the deaths of their husbands.

3. Mrs. Mallard's death at the end is a just punishment for the joy she takes in her husband's death.

4. The story is rich in irony. Some examples: (1) The other characters think she is grieving, but she is rejoicing; (2) she prays for a long life, but she dies almost immediately, (3) the doctors say she died of "the joy that kills," but they think her joy was seeing her husband alive.

5. The story is excellent because it has a surprise ending.

Thinking about the Effects of Literature

Works of art are artifacts — things constructed, made up, fashioned, just like chairs and houses and automobiles. In analyzing works of literature it is therefore customary to keep one's eye on the complex, constructed object and not simply tell the reader how one feels about it. Instead of reporting their feelings, critics usually analyze the relationships between the parts and the relationship of the parts to the whole.

For instance, in talking about literature we can examine the relationship of plot to character, of one character to another, or of one stanza in a poem to the next. Still, although we may try to engage in this sort of analysis as dispassionately as possible, we all know that inevitably

- we are not only examining something out there,
- but also examining our own responses.

Why? Because literature has an effect on us. Indeed, it probably has several kinds of effects, ranging from short-range emotional responses ("I really enjoyed this," "I burst out laughing," "It revolted me") to long-range effects ("I have always tried to live up to a line in *Hamlet*, 'This above all, to thine own self be true'"). Let's first look, very briefly, at immediate emotional responses.

Analysis usually begins with a response: "This is marvelous," or "What a bore," and we then go on to try to account for our response. A friend mentions a book or a film to us, and we say, "I couldn't stay with it for five minutes." The friend expresses surprise, and we then go on to explain, giving reasons (to the friend and also to ourselves) why we couldn't stay with it. Perhaps the book seemed too remote from life or perhaps it seemed to be nothing more than a transcript of the boring talk that we can overhear on a bus or in an elevator.

In such discussions, when we draw on our responses, as we must, the work may disappear; we find ourselves talking about ourselves. Let's take two extreme examples: "I can't abide *Huckleberry Finn*. How am I expected to enjoy a so-called masterpiece that has a character in it called 'Nigger Jim?'" Or: "T. S. Eliot's anti-Semitism is too much for me to take. Don't talk to me about Eliot's skill with meter, when he has such lines as 'Rachel, *née* Rabinovitch / Tears at the grapes with murderous paws.'"

Although everyone agrees that literature can evoke this sort of strong emotional response, not everyone agrees on how much value we should put on our personal experience. Several of the Topics for Critical Thinking and Writing below invite you to reflect on this issue.

What about the *consequences of the effects* of literature? Does literature shape our character and therefore influence our behavior? It is generally believed that it does have an effect. One hears, for example, that literature (like travel) is broadening, that it makes us aware of, and tolerant of, kinds of behavior that differ from our own and from what we see around us. One of the chief arguments against pornography, for instance, is that it desensitizes us, makes us too tolerant of abusive relationships, relationships in which people (usually men) use other people (usually women) as mere things or instruments for pleasure. (A contrary view: Some people argue that pornography provides a relatively harmless outlet for fantasies that otherwise might be given release in the real world. In this view, pornography acts as a sort of safety valve.)

Discussions of the effects of literature that get into the popular press almost always involve pornography, but other topics are also the subjects of controversy. For instance, in recent decades parents and educators have been much concerned with fairy tales. Does the violence in some fairy tales ("Little Red Riding Hood," "The Three Little Pigs") have a bad effect on children? Do some of the stories teach the wrong lessons, implying that women should be passive, men active ("Sleeping Beauty," for instance, in which the sleeping woman is brought to life by the action of the handsome prince)? The Greek philosopher Plato (427–347 B.C.) strongly believed that the literature we hear or read shapes our later behavior, and since most of the ancient Greek traditional stories (notably Homer's *Odyssey* and *Iliad*) celebrate acts of love and war rather than of justice, he prohibited the reading of such material in his ideal society. (We reprint a relevant passage from Plato on page 404.)

Topics for Critical Thinking and Writing

1. If you have responded strongly (favorably or unfavorably) to some aspect of the social content of a literary work — for instance, its depiction of women or of a particular minority group — in an essay of 250 to 500 words analyze the response, and try to determine whether you are talking chiefly about yourself or the work. (Two works widely regarded as literary masterpieces but nonetheless often banned from classrooms are Shakespeare's *The Merchant of Venice* and Mark Twain's *Huckleberry Finn*. If you have read either of these, you may want to write about it and your response.) Can we really see literary value — *really* see it — in a work that deeply offends us?

2. Most people believe that literature influences life — that in some mysterious way it helps to shape character. Certainly, anyone who believes that some works should be censored, or at least should be made unavailable to minors, assumes that they can have a bad influence, so why not assume that other works can have a good influence?

   Read the following brief claims about literature; then choose one and write a 250-word essay offering support or taking issue with it.

   The pen is mightier than the sword.   — EDWARD BULWER LYTTON

   The writer isn't made in a vacuum. Writers are witnesses. The reason we need writers is because we need witnesses to this terrifying century.   — E. L. DOCTOROW

When we read of human beings behaving in certain ways, with the approval of the author, who gives his benedictions to this behavior by his attitude towards the result of the behavior arranged by himself, we can be influenced towards behaving in the same way.   — T. S. ELIOT

Poetry makes nothing happen.   — W. H. AUDEN

Literature is *without proofs*. By which it must be understood that it cannot prove, not only *what* it says, but even that it is worth the trouble of saying it.   — ROLAND BARTHES

Of course the illusion of art is to make one believe that great literature is very close to life, but exactly the opposite is true. Life is amorphous, literature is formal.   — FRANÇOISE SAGAN

3. At least since the time of Plato (see the piece directly following), some thoughtful people have wanted to ban certain works of literature because they allegedly stimulate the wrong sorts of pleasure or cause us to take pleasure in the wrong sorts of things. Consider, by way of comparison, bullfighting and cockfighting. Of course, they cause pain to the animals, but branding animals also causes pain and is not banned. Bullfighting and cockfighting probably are banned in the United States largely because most of us believe that people should not take pleasure in these activities. Now to return to literature: Should some kinds of writing be prohibited because they offer the wrong sorts of pleasure?

PLATO

Plato (427–347 B.C.), an Athenian aristocrat by birth, was the student of one great philosopher (Socrates) and the teacher of another (Aristotle). His legacy of more than two dozen dialogues — imaginary discussions between Socrates and one or more other speakers, usually young Athenians — has been of such influence that the whole of Western philosophy can be characterized, A. N. Whitehead wrote, as "a series of footnotes to Plato." Plato's interests encompassed the full range of topics in philosophy: ethics, politics, logic, metaphysics, epistemology, aesthetics, psychology, and education.

This selection from Plato's Republic, *one of his best-known and longest dialogues, is about the education suitable for the rulers of an ideal society. The Republic begins, typically, with an investigation into the nature of justice. Socrates (who speaks for Plato) convincingly explains to Glaucon that we cannot reasonably expect to achieve a just society unless we devote careful attention to the moral education of the young men who are scheduled in later life to become the rulers. (Here as elsewhere, Plato's elitism and aristocratic bias shows itself; as readers of* The Republic *soon learn, Plato is no admirer of democracy or of a classless society.) Plato cares as much about what the educational curriculum should exclude as what it should include. His special target was the common practice in his day of using for pedagogy the Homeric tales and other stories about the gods. He readily embraces the principle of censorship, as the excerpt explains, because he thinks it is a necessary means to achieve the ideal society.*

"The Greater Part of the Stories Current Today We Shall Have to Reject"

"What kind of education shall we give them then? We shall find it difficult to improve on the time-honored distinction between the physical training we give to the body and the education we give to the mind and character."

"True."

"And we shall begin by educating mind and character, shall we not?"

"Of course."

"In this education you would include stories, would you not?"

"Yes."

"These are of two kinds, true stories and fiction.[1] Our education must use both, and start with fiction."

"I don't know what you mean."

"But you know that we begin by telling children stories. These are, in general, fiction, though they contain some truth. And we tell children stories before we start them on physical training."

"That is so."

"That is what I meant by saying that we must start to educate the mind before training the body."

"You are right," he said.

"And the first step, as you know, is always what matters most, particularly when we are dealing with those who are young and tender. That is the time when they are easily molded and when any impression we choose to make leaves a permanent mark."

"That is certainly true."

"Shall we therefore readily allow our children to listen to any stories made up by anyone, and to form opinions that are for the most part the opposite of those we think they should have when they grow up?"

"We certainly shall not."

"Then it seems that our first business is to supervise the production of stories, and choose only those we think suitable, and reject the rest. We shall persuade mothers and nurses to tell our chosen stories to their children, and by means of them to mold their minds and characters which are more important than their bodies. The greater part of the stories current today we shall have to reject."

"Which are you thinking of?"

"We can take some of the major legends as typical. For all, whether major or minor, should be cast in the same mold and have the same effect. Do you agree?"

"Yes: but I'm not sure which you refer to as major."

"The stories in Homer and Hesiod and the poets. For it is the poets who have always made up fictions and stories to tell to men."

"What sort of stories do you mean and what fault do you find in them?"

"The worst fault possible," I replied, "especially if the fiction is an ugly one."

"And what is that?"

"Misrepresenting the nature of gods and heroes, like a portrait painter whose portraits bear no resemblance to their originals."

"That is a fault which certainly deserves censure. But give me more details."

"Well, on the most important of subjects, there is first and foremost the foul story about Ouranos[2] and the things Hesiod says he did,

---

[1] The Greek word *pseudos* and its corresponding verb meant not only "fiction" — stories, tales — but also "what is not true" and so, in suitable contexts, "lies": and this ambiguity should be borne in mind. [Editors' note: All footnotes are by the translator, but some have been omitted.]

[2] **Ouranos** The sky, the original supreme god. Ouranos was castrated by his son Cronos to separate him from Gaia (mother earth). Cronos was in turn deposed by Zeus in a struggle in which Zeus was helped by the Titans.

and the revenge Cronos took on him. While the story of what Cronos did, and what he suffered at the hands of his son, is not fit as it is to be lightly repeated to the young and foolish, even if it were true; it would be best to say nothing about it, or if it must be told, tell it to a select few under oath of secrecy, at a rite which required, to restrict it still further, the sacrifice not of a mere pig but of something large and difficult to get."

"These certainly are awkward stories."

"And they shall not be repeated in our state, Adeimantus," I said. "Nor shall any young audience be told that anyone who commits horrible crimes, or punishes his father unmercifully, is doing nothing out of the ordinary but merely what the first and greatest of the gods have done before."

"I entirely agree," said Adeimantus, "that 30 these stories are unsuitable."

"Nor can we permit stories of wars and plots and battles among the gods; they are quite untrue, and if we want our prospective guardians to believe that quarrelsomeness is one of the worst of evils, we must certainly not let them be told the story of the Battle of the Giants or embroider it on robes, or tell them other tales about many and various quarrels between gods and heroes and their friends and relations. On the contrary, if we are to persuade them that no citizen has ever quarreled with any other, because it is sinful, our old men and women must tell children stories with this end in view from the first, and we must compel our poets to tell them similar stories when they grow up. But we can admit to our state no stories about Hera being tied up by her son, or Hephaestus being flung out of Heaven by his father for trying to help his mother when she was getting a beating, nor any of Homer's Battles of the Gods, whether their intention is allegorical or not. Children cannot distinguish between what is allegory and what isn't, and opinions formed

at that age are usually difficult to eradicate or change; we should therefore surely regard it as of the utmost importance that the first stories they hear shall aim at encouraging the highest excellence of character."

"Your case is a good one," he agreed, "but if someone wanted details, and asked what stories we were thinking of, what should we say?"

To which I replied, "My dear Adeimantus, you and I are not engaged on writing stories but on founding a state. And the founders of a state, though they must know the type of story the poet must produce, and reject any that do not conform to that type, need not write them themselves."

"True: but what are the lines on which our poets must work when they deal with the gods?"

"Roughly as follows," I said. "God must 35 surely always be represented as he really is, whether the poet is writing epic, lyric, or tragedy."

"He must."

"And in reality of course god is good, and he must be so described."

"Certainly."

"But nothing good is harmful, is it?"[3]

"I think not."
40

"Then can anything that is not harmful do harm?"

"No."

"And can what does no harm do evil?"

"No again."

"And can what does no evil be the cause of 45 any evil?"

"How could it?"

"Well then; is the good beneficial?"

---

[3]The reader of the following passage should bear the following ambiguities in mind: (1) the Greek word for good (*agathos*) can mean (a) morally good, (b) beneficial or advantageous; (2) the Greek word for evil (*kakos*) can also mean harm or injury; (3) the adverb of *agathos* (*eu* — the well) can imply either morally right or prosperous. The word translated "cause of" could equally well be rendered "responsible for."

"Yes."

"So it must be the cause of well-being."

"Yes." 50

"So the good is not the cause of everything, but only of states of well-being and not of evil."

"Most certainly," he agreed.

"Then god, being good, cannot be responsible for everything, as is commonly said, but only for a small part of human life, for the greater part of which he has no responsibility. For we have a far smaller share of good than of evil, and while god must be held to be the sole cause of good, we must look for some factors other than god as cause of the evil."

"I think that's very true," he said.

"So we cannot allow Homer or any other 55 poet to make such a stupid mistake about the gods, as when he says that

> Zeus has two jars standing on the floor of his palace, full of fates, good in one and evil in the other

and that the man to whom Zeus allots a mixture of both has 'varying fortunes sometimes good and sometimes bad,' while the man to whom he allots unmixed evil is 'chased by ravening despair over the face of the earth.'[4] Nor can we allow references to Zeus as 'dispenser of good and evil.' And we cannot approve if it is said that Athene and Zeus prompted the breach of solemn treaty and oath by Pandarus,

_____
[4] Quotations from Homer are generally taken from the translations by Dr. Rieu in the Penguin series. At times (as here) the version quoted by Plato differs slightly from the accepted text.

or that the strife and contentions of the gods were due to Themis and Zeus. Nor again can we let our children hear from Aeschylus that

> God implants a fault in man, when he wishes to destroy a house utterly.

No: We must forbid anyone who writes a play about the sufferings of Niobe (the subject of the play from which these last lines are quoted), or the house of Pelops, or the Trojan war, or any similar topic, to say they are acts of god; or if he does he must produce the sort of interpretation we are now demanding, and say that god's acts were good and just, and that the sufferers were benefited by being punished. What the poet must not be allowed to say is that those who were punished were made wretched through god's action. He may refer to the wicked as wretched because they needed punishment, provided he makes it clear that in punishing them god did them good. But if a state is to be run on the right lines, every possible step must be taken to prevent anyone, young or old, either saying or being told, whether in poetry or prose, that god, being good, can cause harm or evil to any man. To say so would be sinful, inexpedient, and inconsistent."

"I should approve of a law for this purpose and you have my vote for it," he said.

"Then of our laws laying down the principles which those who write or speak about the gods must follow, one would be this: *God is the cause, not of all things, but only of good.*"

"I am quite content with that," he said.

Topics for Critical Thinking and Writing

1. In the beginning of the dialogue Plato says that adults recite fictions to very young children and that these fictions help to mold character. Think of some stories that you heard or read when young, such as "Snow White and the Seven Dwarfs" or "Ali Baba and the Forty Thieves." Try to think of a story that, in the final analysis, is not in accord with what you consider to be proper morality, such as a story in which a person triumphs through trickery

or a story in which evil actions — perhaps murders — are set forth without unfavorable comment. (Was it naughty of Jack to kill the giant?) On reflection, do you think children should not be told such stories? Why, or why not? Or think of the early film westerns, in which, on the whole, the Indians (except for an occasional Uncle Tonto) are depicted as bad guys and the whites (except for an occasional coward or rustler) are depicted as good guys. Many people who now have gray hair enjoyed such films in their childhood. Are you prepared to say that such films are not damaging? Or, in contrast, are you prepared to say they are damaging and should be prohibited?

2. It is often objected that censorship of reading matter and of television programs available to children underrates their ability to think for themselves and to discount the dangerous, obscene, and tawdry. Do you agree with this objection? Does Plato? Explain your response.

3. Plato says that allowing poets to say what they please about the gods in his ideal state would be "inconsistent." Explain what he means by this criticism, and then explain why you agree or disagree with it.

4. Do you believe that parents should censor the "fiction" their children encounter (literature, films, pictures, music) but that the community should not censor the "fiction" of adults? Write an essay of 500 words on one of these topics: "Censorship and Rock Lyrics"; "X-Rated Films"; "Ethnic Jokes." (These topics are broadly worded; you can narrow one and offer any thesis you wish.)

5. Were you taught that any of the founding fathers ever acted disreputably or that any American hero had any serious moral flaw? Or that America ever acted immorally in its dealings with other nations? Do you think it appropriate for children to hear such things? Explain your responses.

Thinking about Government Funding for the Arts

Our government supports the arts, including writers, by giving grants to numerous institutions. However, the amount that the government contributes is extremely small when compared to the amounts given to the arts by most European governments. Consider the following questions.

1. Should taxpayers' dollars be used to support the arts? Why, or why not?

2. What possible public benefit can come from supporting the arts? Can one argue that we should support the arts for the same reasons that we support public schools, that is, to have a civilized society? Explain your response.

3. If dollars are given to the arts, should the political content of the works be taken into account, or only the aesthetic merit? Can we separate content from aesthetic merit? (The best way to approach this issue probably is to begin by thinking of a strongly political work.)

4. Is it censorship not to award public funds to writers whose work is not approved of, or is it simply a matter of refusing to reward them with taxpayers' dollars?

5. Should decisions about grants to writers be made chiefly by government officials or chiefly by experts in the field? Why?

12

A Debater's View: Individual Oral Presentations and Debate

He who knows only his own side of the case knows little of that.
— JOHN STUART MILL

A philosopher who is not taking part in discussions is like a boxer who never goes into the ring.
— LUDWIG WITTGENSTEIN

Freedom is hammered out on the anvil of dissension, dissent, and debate.
— HUBERT HUMPHREY

Individual Oral Presentations

Forensic comes from the Latin word *foris,* meaning "out of doors," which also produced the word *forum,* an open space in front of a public building. In the language of rhetoricians, the place where one delivers a speech to an audience is the forum — whether it is a classroom, a court of law, or the steps of the Lincoln Memorial.

Your instructor may ask you to make an oral presentation (in this case, the forum is the classroom), and if he or she doesn't make such a demand, later life almost certainly will: You'll find that at a job interview you will be expected to talk persuasively about what good qualities or experience you can bring to the place of employment. When you have a job, you'll sometimes have to summarize a report orally or orally argue a case — for instance, that your colleagues should do something they may be hesitant to do.

The goal of your classroom talk is to persuade the audience to share your view, or, if you can't get them to agree completely, to get them to see that at least there is something to be said for this view — that it is a position a reasonable person can hold.

Elsewhere in this book we have said that the subjects of persuasive writing are usually

- matters of fact (e.g., statistics show that the death penalty does — or does not — deter crime), or
- matters of value (abortion is — or is not — immoral), or

- matters of policy (government should — or should not — give money to faith-based institutions).

No matter what your subject is, when you draft and revise your talk, make certain that a thesis statement underlies the whole (e.g., "Proposition 2 is a bad idea because . . .").

The text of an oral presentation ought not to be identical with the text of a written presentation. Both must have a clear **organization,** but oral presentations usually require making the organization a bit more obvious, with abundant **signposts** such as "Before I talk about X," "When I discussed Y, I didn't mention such-and-such because I wanted to concentrate on a single instance, but now is the time to consider Y," and so on. You will also have to repeat a bit more than you would in a written presentation. After all, a reader can turn back to check a sentence or a statistic, but a listener cannot; so rather than saying (as one might in a printed text), "When we think further about Smith's comment, we realize. . .," you'll repeat what Smith said before you go on to analyze the statement.

You will want to think carefully about the organization of your talk. We've already stressed the need to develop essays with clear thesis statements and logical supporting points. Oral presentations are no different, but remember that when you are speaking in public, a clear organization will always help alleviate anxiety and reassure you. Thus, you can deliver a powerful message without getting tripped up yourself. We suggest you try the following:

- Outline your draft in advance in order to make sure that it has clear organization.

- Inform the audience at the start what the organization of your presentation will be. Early in the talk you probably should say something along these lines, though not in so abbreviated a form:

  > "In talking about A, I'll have to define a few terms, B and C, and I will also have to talk about two positions that differ from mine, D and E. I'll then try to show why A is the best policy to pursue, clearly better than D and E."

- So that the listeners can easily follow you, be sure to use transitions such as "Furthermore," "Therefore," "Although it is often said," and "It may be objected that," so that the listeners can easily follow your train of thought. Sometimes, you may even remind the listeners what the previous stages were, with such a comment as "We have now seen three approaches to the problem of. . ."

METHODS OF DELIVERY

After thinking about helping the audience to follow your speech, consider how much help you'll need delivering it. Depending on your comfort level with the topic and your argument, you might decide to

- deliver a memorized talk without notes,
- read the talk from a text, or
- speak from an outline, perhaps with quotations and statistics written down.

Each of these methods has strengths and weaknesses. A memorized talk allows for plenty of eye contact with the audience but unless you are a superb actor it is almost surely going to seem a bit mechanical. A talk that you read from a text will indeed let you say to an audience exactly what you intend (with the best possible wording), but reading a text inevitably establishes some distance between you and the audience, even if you occasionally glance up from your pages. If you talk from a mere outline, almost surely some of your sentences will turn out to be a bit awkward — though a little awkwardness may help to convey sincerity and therefore be a plus.

No matter what form of delivery you choose, try to convey the impression that you're conversing with the audience, not talking down to them — even though if you're standing on a platform you will be literally talking down.

You may want to use **audiovisual aids** in your presentation. These can range from such low-tech materials as handouts, blackboards, and whiteboards to high-tech PowerPoint presentations. Each has advantages and disadvantages. For instance, if you distribute handouts when the talk begins, the audience may start thumbing through them during your opening comments. And although PowerPoint can be a highly useful aid, some speakers make too much use of it simply because it's available. It happens that the day before writing this discussion the author witnessed a PowerPoint presentation that began with the speaker projecting on the screen the date, the speaker's name, and the name of the university at which the talk was being delivered. Well, most of us knew the date, and we all knew the speaker's name and the name of the university. It seemed like overkill. The truth is, the talk simply didn't need any images at all, and we ended up wondering why the speaker bothered with PowerPoint.

For a delightful parody of this sort of talk, consider "The Gettysburg Powerpoint Presentation" (http://norvig.com/Gettysburg/). It begins thus:

And now please welcome President Abraham Lincoln.
Good morning. Just a second while I get this connection to work. Do I press this button here? Function-F7? No, that's not right. Hmmm. Maybe I'll have to reboot. Hold on a minute. Um, my name is Abe Lincoln and I'm your president. While we're waiting, I want to thank Judge David Wills, chairman of the committee supervising the dedication of the Gettysburg cemetery. It's great to be here, Dave, and you and the committee are doing a great job. Gee, sometimes this new **technology** does have glitches, but **we couldn't live without it, could we?** Oh — is it ready? OK, here we go.

The lesson? Yes, use audiovisual material if it will help you to present your material, but don't use it if it adds nothing or if you haven't mastered the technology.

One final point: If you do use visual material, *make certain that any words on the images are large enough to be legible to the audience:* A graph with tiny words won't impress your audience, even if you read the words aloud.

The Audience

It is not merely because topics are complicated that we cannot agree that one side is reasonable and right and the other side irrational and wrong. The truth is, we are swayed not only by reason (*logos*) but also by appeals to the emotions (*pathos*) and by the speaker's character (*ethos*). We can combine these last two factors, and put it this way: Sometimes we are inclined to agree with X rather than with Y because X strikes us as a more appealing person (perhaps more open-minded, more intelligent, better informed, more humane, and less cold). X is the sort of person we want to have as a friend. We disagree with Y — or at least we're unwilling to associate ourselves with Y — because Y is, well, Y just isn't the sort of person we want to agree with. Y's statistics don't sound right, or Y seems like a bully; for some reason, we just don't have confidence in Y. Confidence is easily lost: Alas, even a mispronunciation will diminish the audience's confidence in Y. As Peter de Vries said, "You can't be happy with someone who pronounces both *d*'s in Wednesday."

Earlier in the book we talked about the importance of **tone** and of the writer's **persona**. And we have made the point that the writer's tone will depend partly on the audience. A person writing for a conservative journal whose readership is almost entirely conservatives can adopt a highly satiric manner in talking about liberals and will win much approval. But if this conservative writer is writing in a liberal journal and hopes to get a sympathetic hearing, he or she will have to avoid satire and wisecracks and, instead, present himself or herself as a person of goodwill who is open-minded and eager to address the issue seriously.

The **language** that you use — the degree to which it is formal as opposed to colloquial, and the degree to which it is technical as opposed to general — will also depend on the audience. Speaking broadly, in oral argument you should speak politely but not formally. You do *not* want to be one of those people who "talk like a book." But you also don't want to be overly colloquial. Choose a middle course, probably a notch below the style you would use in a written paper. For instance, in an oral presentation you might say, "We'll consider this point in a minute or two," whereas in a written paper you probably would write, "We will consider this point shortly."

Technical language is entirely appropriate *if* your audience is familiar with it. If you are arguing before members of Amnesty International about the use of torture, you can assume certain kinds of specialized knowledge. You can, for ins tance, breezily speak of the DRC and of KPCS, and your listeners will know what you're talking about because Amnesty International has been active with issues concerning the Democratic Republic of Congo and the Kimberley Process Certification Scheme. In contrast, if you are arguing the same case before a general public, you'll have to explain these abbreviations, and you may even have to explain what Amnesty International is.

If you are arguing before an audience of classmates, you probably have a good idea of what they know and don't know.

Delivery

Your audience will in some measure determine not only your tone but also the way you appear when giving the speech. Part of the delivery is the speaker's **appearance.** The medium is part of the message. The president can appear in jeans when he chats about his reelection plans, but he wears a suit and a tie when he delivers the State of the Union address. Just as we wear one kind of **clothing** when playing tennis, another when attending classes, and yet another when going for a job interview, an effective speaker dresses appropriately. A lawyer arguing before the Supreme Court wears a dark suit or dress, and if the lawyer is male he wears a necktie. The same lawyer, arguing at a local meeting, speaking as a community resident who objects to a proposal to allow a porno store to open near a school, may well dress informally—maybe in jeans—to show that he is not at all stuffy but still feels that a porno store goes too far.

Your appearance when you speak is not merely a matter of clothing; it includes your **facial expressions,** your **posture,** your **gestures,** your general demeanor. All that we can say here is that you should avoid those bodily motions—swaying, thumping the table, putting on and taking off eyeglasses, craning your neck, smirking—that are so distracting that they cause the audience to concentrate on the distraction rather than on the argument. ("That's the third time he straightened his necktie. I wonder how many more times he will—oops, that's the fourth!") Most of us are unaware of our annoying habits; if you're lucky, a friend, when urged, will tell you about them. You may lose a friend, but you will gain some good advice.

You probably can't do much about your **voice**—it may be high-pitched, or it may be gravelly—but you can make sure you speak loudly enough for the audience members to hear you, slowly enough for them to understand you, and clearly enough for them to understand you.

We have some advice about **quotations.** First, if possible, use an effective quotation or two, partly because—we'll be frank here—the quotations probably are more impressively worded than anything you come up with on your own. A quotation may be the chief thing that your audience comes away with: "Hey, yes, I liked that: 'War is too important to be left to the generals'" or "When it comes down to it, I agree with that Frenchman who said 'If we are to abolish the death penalty, I should like to see the first step taken by the murderers'" or "You know, I think it was all summed up in that line by Margaret Mead, something like, 'No one would remember the Good Samaritan if he'd had only good intentions. He had money as well.' Yes, that's pretty convincing. Morality isn't enough. You need money." You didn't invent the words that you quote, but you did bring them to your listeners' attention, and they will be grateful to you.

A second bit of advice about quotations: When quoting, do *not* begin by saying "quote," and do not end by saying "end quote" (or as we once heard a speaker endlessly say, quotation after quotation, "unquote"), and do not hook the air with your fingers. How do you make it clear that you are quoting and that you have finished quoting? Begin with a clear lead-in ("In *Major Barbara* George Bernard Shaw touches on this issue, when Barbara says, . . ."), slightly pause, and then slightly change (e.g., elevate) your voice. When you have finished quoting — again, a slight pause and a return to your normal voice — be sure to use words that clearly indicate the quotation is finished, such as "Shaw here says what everyone thinks," or "Shaw's comment is witty but short-sighted," or "Barbara's point, then, is. . . ."

Our third and last piece of advice concerning quotations is this: If the quotation is only a phrase or a brief sentence, you can memorize it and be confident that you'll remember it, but if it's longer than a sentence, write it on a sheet in your notes or on a four-by-six-inch card in print large enough for you to read easily. You have chosen these words because they are effectively put, so you don't want to misquote them or hesitate in delivering them.

The Talk

As for the talk itself, well, we have been touching on it in our discussion of such matters as the speaker's relation to the audience, the need to provide signposts, and the use of quotations. All of our comments in earlier chapters about developing a written argument are relevant also to oral arguments, but here we should merely emphasize that because the talk is oral and the audience cannot look back to an earlier page to remind itself of some point, the speaker may have to repeat and summarize a bit more than is usual in a written essay.

Remember, too, that a reader can *see* when the essay ends — there is blank space at the end of the page — but a listener depends on aural cues. Nothing is more embarrassing — and less effective as argument — than a speaker who seems (to the audience) to suddenly stop and sit down. In short, give your hearers ample clues that you are ending (post such signs as "Finally" or "Last" or "Let me end by saying"), and be sure to end with a strong sentence. It probably won't be as good as the end of the Gettysburg address ("government of the people, by the people, for the people, shall not perish from the earth"), nor will it be as good as the end of Martin Luther King Jr.'s "I Have a Dream" speech ("Free at last! Free at last! Thank God Almighty, we are free at last!"), but those are the models to emulate.

Formal Debates

It would be nice if all arguments ended with everyone, participants and spectators, agreeing that the facts are clear, that one presentation is more reasonable than the other, and therefore that one side is right and the other side is wrong. But in life, most issues are complicated. High school students may earnestly debate — this is a real topic in a national debate —

Resolved: That education has failed its mission in the United States,

but it takes only a moment of reflection to see that neither the affirmative nor the negative can be true. Yes, education has failed its mission in many ways, but, No, it has succeeded in many ways. Its job now is (in the words of Samuel Beckett) to try again: "Fail. Fail again. Fail better."

Debates of this sort, conducted before a judge and guided by strict rules concerning "Constructive Speeches," "Rebuttal Speeches," and "Cross-Examinations" are not attempts to get at the truth; like lawsuits, they are attempts to win a case. Each speaker seeks not to persuade the opponent but only to convince the judge. Although most of this section is devoted not to forensics in the strictest sense but more generally to the presentation of oral arguments, we begin with the standard format.

STANDARD DEBATE FORMAT

Formal debates occur within a structure that governs the number of speeches, their order, and the maximum time for each one. The format may vary from place to place, but there is always a structure. In most debates, a formal resolution states the reason for the debate ("Resolved: That capital punishment be abolished in juvenile cases"). The affirmative team supports the resolution; the negative team denies its legitimacy. The basic structure has three parts:

- *The constructive phase,* in which the debaters construct their cases and develop their arguments (usually for ten minutes).

- *The rebuttal,* in which debaters present their responses and also present their final summary (usually for five minutes).

- *The preparation,* in which the debater prepares for presenting the next speech. (During the preparation — a sort of time-out — the debater is not addressing the opponent or audience. The total time allotted to a team is usually six or eight minutes, which the individual debaters divide as they wish.)

We give, very briefly, the usual structure of each part, though we should mention that another common format calls for a cross-examination of the First Affirmative Construction

U.S. Democratic presidential candidates Hillary Clinton and Bernie Sanders during a debate at the University of New Hampshire in Durham on February 4, 2016. A successful debate can help change the tide of a candidate's campaign.

by the Second Negative, a cross-examination of the First Negative Construction by the First Affirmative, a cross-examination of the Second Affirmative by the First Negative, and a cross-examination of the Second Negative by the Second Affirmative:

First Affirmative Constructive Speech: Serves as introduction, giving summary overview, definitions, criteria for resolution, major claims and evidence, statement, and intention to support the resolution.

First Negative Constructive Speech: Responds by introducing the basic position, challenges the definitions and criteria, suggests the line of attack, emphasizes that the burden of proof lies with the affirmative, rejects the resolution as unnecessary or dangerous, and supports the status quo.

Second Affirmative Constructive: Rebuilds the affirmative case; refutes chief attacks, especially concerning definitions, criteria, and rationale (philosophic framework); and further develops the affirmative case.

Second Negative Constructive: Completes the negative case, if possible advances it by rebuilding portions of the first negative construction, and contrasts the entire negative case with the entire affirmative case.

First Negative Rebuttal: Attacks the opponents' arguments and defends the negative constructive arguments (but a rebuttal may *not* introduce new constructive arguments).

First Affirmative Rebuttal: Usually responds first to the second negative construction and then to the first negative rebuttal.

Second Negative Rebuttal: Constitutes final speech for the negative, summarizing the case and explaining to the judge why the negative should be declared the winner.

Second Affirmative Rebuttal: Summarizes the debate, responds to issues pressed by the second negative rebuttal, and suggests to the judge that the affirmative team should win.

A CHECKLIST FOR PREPARING FOR A DEBATE

❏ Have I done adequate preparation in my research?

❏ Are my notes legible, with accurate quotations and credible sources?

❏ Am I prepared to take good notes during the debate?

❏ Is my proposition clearly stated?

❏ Do I have adequate evidence to support the thesis (main point)?

❏ Do I have backup points in mind?

❏ Have I given thought to issues my opponents might raise?

❏ Does the opening properly address the instructor, the audience, the opponents? (Remember, you are addressing an audience, not merely the opponents.)

❏ Are my visual aids focused on major points?

❏ Is my demeanor professional, and is my dress appropriate?

PART FOUR

A Casebook on the State and the Individual

13

How Free Is the Will of the Individual within Society?

Thoughts about Free Will

All theory is against the freedom of the will; all experience for it.

— SAMUEL JOHNSON

Free will is doing gladly and freely that which one must do.

— CARL G. JUNG

The will is never free — it is always attached to an object, a purpose. It is simply the engine in the car — it can't steer.

— JOYCE CARY

A man may be a pessimistic determinist before lunch and an optimistic believer in the will's freedom after it.

— ALDOUS HUXLEY

Fatalism, whose solving word in all crises of behavior is all striving is vain, will never reign supreme, for the impulse to take life strivingly is indestructible in the race. Moral creeds which speak to that impulse will be widely successful in spite of inconsistency, vagueness, and shadowy determination of expectancy. Man needs a rule for his will, and will invent one if one be not given him.

— WILLIAM JAMES

Man is a masterpiece of creation if for no other reason than that, all the weight of evidence for determinism notwithstanding, he believes he has free will.

— GEORG C. LICHTENBERG

We human beings do have some genuine freedom of choice and therefore some effective control over our own destinies. I am not a determinist. But I also believe that the decisive choice is seldom the latest choice in the series. More often than not, it will turn out to be some choice made relatively far back in the past.

— ARNOLD TOYNBEE

We are responsible human beings, not blind automatons; persons, not puppets. By endowing us with freedom, God relinquished a measure of his own sovereignty and imposed certain limitations upon himself. If his children are free, they must do his will by a voluntary choice.

— MARTIN LUTHER KING JR.

Life is a card game. You play the hand that is dealt to you.

— PROVERBIAL

We must believe in free will. We have no choice.

— ISAAC BASHEVIS SINGER

Topics for Critical Thinking and Writing

1. If any one of these passages especially appeals to you, make it the thesis of an essay of about 500 words.

2. Take two of these passages — perhaps one that you especially like and one that you think is wrong-headed — and write a dialogue of about 500 words in which the two authors converse. They may each try to convince the other, or they may find that to some degree they share views and they may then work out a statement that both can accept. If you do take the position that one writer is on the correct track but the other is utterly mistaken, try to be fair to the view that you think is mistaken. (As an experiment in critical thinking, imagine that you accept it, and make the best case for it that you possibly can.)

PLATO

Plato (427–347 B.C.), an Athenian aristocrat by birth, was the student of one great philosopher (Socrates) and the teacher of another (Aristotle). His legacy of more than two dozen dialogues — imaginary discussions between Socrates and one or more other speakers, usually young Athenians — has been of such influence that the whole of Western philosophy can be characterized, A. N. Whitehead wrote, as "a series of footnotes to Plato." Plato's interests encompassed the full range of topics in philosophy: ethics, politics, logic, metaphysics, epistemology, aesthetics, psychology, and education.

The selection reprinted here, Crito, is the third of four dialogues telling the story of the final days of Socrates (469–399 B.C.). The first in the sequence, Euthyphro, portrays Socrates in his typical role, questioning someone about his beliefs (in this case, the young aristocrat Euthyphro). The discussion is focused on the nature of piety, but the conversation breaks off before a final answer is reached — perhaps none is possible — because Socrates is on his way to stand trial before the Athenian assembly. He has been charged with "preaching false gods" (heresy) and "corrupting the youth" by causing them to doubt or disregard the wisdom of their elders. (How faithful to any actual event or discussion Euthyphro and Plato's other Socratic dialogues really are, scholars cannot say with assurance.)

In Apology, the second dialogue in the sequence, Plato (who remains entirely in the background, as he does in all the dialogues) recounts Socrates's public reply to the charges against him. During the speech, Socrates explains his life, reminding his fellow citizens that if he is (as the oracle had pronounced) "the wisest of men," then it is only because he knows that he doesn't know what others believe or pretend they do know. The dialogue ends with Socrates being found guilty and duly sentenced to death.

The third in the series is Crito, but we will postpone comment on it for a moment and glance at the fourth dialogue, Phaedo, in which Plato portrays Socrates's final philosophical discussion. The topic, appropriately, is whether the soul is immortal. It ends with Socrates, in the company of his closest friends, bidding them a last farewell and drinking the fatal cup of hemlock.

Crito, the whole text of which is reprinted here, is the debate provoked by Crito, an old friend and admirer of Socrates. He visits Socrates in prison and urges him to escape while he still has the chance. After all, Crito argues, the guilty verdict was wrong and unfair, few Athenians really want to have Socrates put to death, his family and friends will be distraught, and so forth. Socrates will not have it. He patiently but firmly examines each of Crito's arguments and explains why it would be wrong to follow his advice.

Plato's Crito thus ranks with Sophocles's tragedy Antigone as one of the first explorations in Western literature of the perennial theme of our responsibility for obeying laws that challenge our conscientious moral convictions. Antigone concludes that she must disobey the law of Creon, tyrant of Thebes; Socrates concludes that he must obey the law of democratic Athens. In Crito, we have not only a superb illustration of Socratic dialogue and argument but also a portrait of a virtuous thinker at the end of a long life, reflecting on its course and on the moral principles that have guided him. We see Socrates living an "examined life," the only life he thought was worth living.

This translation is by Hugh Tredennick.

Crito

(SCENE: *A room in the State prison at Athens in the year 399 B.C. The time is half an hour before dawn, and the room would be almost dark but for the light of a little oil lamp. There is a pallet bed against the back wall. At the head of it a small table supports the lamp; near the foot of it Crito is sitting patiently on a stool. He is an old man, kindly, practical, simple-minded; at present he is suffering from acute emotional strain. On the bed lies Socrates asleep. He stirs, yawns, opens his eyes, and sees Crito.)*

SOCRATES: Here already, Crito? Surely it is still early?

CRITO: Indeed it is.

SOCRATES: About what time?

CRITO: Just before dawn.

SOCRATES: I wonder that the warder paid any attention to you.

CRITO: He is used to me now, Socrates, because I come here so often; besides, he is under some small obligation to me.

SOCRATES: Have you only just come, or have you been here for long?

CRITO: Fairly long.

SOCRATES: Then why didn't you wake me at once, instead of sitting by my bed so quietly?

CRITO: I wouldn't dream of such a thing, Socrates. I only wish I were not so sleepless and depressed myself. I have been wondering at you, because I saw how comfortably you were sleeping; and I deliberately didn't wake you because

I wanted you to go on being as comfortable as you could. I have often felt before in the course of my life how fortunate you are in your disposition, but I feel it more than ever now in your present misfortune when I see how easily and placidly you put up with it.

SOCRATES: Well, really, Crito, it would be hardly suitable for a man of my age to resent having to die.

CRITO: Other people just as old as you are get involved in these misfortunes, Socrates, but their age doesn't keep them from resenting it when they find themselves in your position.

SOCRATES: Quite true. But tell me, why have you come so early?

CRITO: Because I bring bad news, Socrates; not so bad from your point of view, I suppose, but it will be very hard to bear for me and your other friends, and I think that I shall find it hardest of all.

SOCRATES: Why, what is this news? Has the boat come in from Delos — the boat which ends my reprieve when it arrives?[1]

CRITO: It hasn't actually come in yet, but I expect that it will be here today, judging from the report of some people who have just arrived from Sunium and left it there. It's quite clear from their account that it will be here today; and so by tomorrow, Socrates, you will have to — to end your life.

SOCRATES: Well, Crito, I hope that it may be for the best; if the gods will it so, so be it. All the same, I don't think it will arrive today.

CRITO: What makes you think that?

SOCRATES: I will try to explain. I think I am right in saying that I have to die on the day after the boat arrives?

CRITO: That's what the authorities say, at any rate.

SOCRATES: Then I don't think it will arrive on this day that is just beginning, but on the day after. I am going by a dream that I had in the night, only a little while ago. It looks as though you were right not to wake me up.

CRITO: Why, what was the dream about?

SOCRATES: I thought I saw a gloriously beautiful woman dressed in white robes, who came up to me and addressed me in these words: "Socrates, to the pleasant land of Phthia on the third day thou shalt come."

CRITO: Your dream makes no sense, Socrates.

SOCRATES: To my mind, Crito, it is perfectly clear.

CRITO: Too clear, apparently. But look here, Socrates, it is still not too late to take my advice and escape. Your death means a double calamity for me. I shall not only lose a friend whom I can never possibly replace, but besides a great many people who don't know you and me very well will be sure to think that I let you down, because I could have saved you if I had been willing to spend the money; and what could be more contemptible than to get a name for thinking more of money than of your friends? Most people will never believe that it was you who refused to leave this place although we tried our hardest to persuade you.

SOCRATES: But my dear Crito, why should we pay so much attention to what "most people" think? The really reasonable people, who have more claim to be considered, will believe that the facts are exactly as they are.

---

[1]**Delos . . . arrives** Ordinarily execution was carried out immediately after sentencing, but the day before Socrates's trial was the first day of an annual ceremony that involved sending a ship to Delos. When the ship was absent — in this case for about a month — executions could not be performed. As Crito goes on to say, Socrates could easily escape, and indeed he could have left the country before being tried. [All notes are the editors'.]

CRITO: You can see for yourself, Socrates, that one has to think of popular opinion as well. Your present position is quite enough to show that the capacity of ordinary people for causing trouble is not confined to petty annoyances, but has hardly any limits if you once get a bad name with them.

SOCRATES: I only wish that ordinary people *had* unlimited capacity for doing harm; then they might have an unlimited power for doing good; which would be a splendid thing, if it were so. Actually they have neither. They cannot make a man wise or stupid; they simply act at random.

CRITO: Have it that way if you like; but tell me this, Socrates. I hope that you aren't worrying about the possible effects on me and the rest of your friends, and thinking that if you escape we shall have trouble with informers for having helped you to get away, and have to forfeit all our property or pay an enormous fine, or even incur some further punishment? If any idea like that is troubling you, you can dismiss it altogether. We are quite entitled to run that risk in saving you, and even worse, if necessary. Take my advice, and be reasonable.

SOCRATES: All that you say is very much in my mind, Crito, and a great deal more besides.

CRITO: Very well, then, don't let it distress you. I know some people who are willing to rescue you from here and get you out of the country for quite a moderate sum. And then surely you realize how cheap these informers are to buy off; we shan't need much money to settle them; and I think you've got enough of my money for yourself already. And then even supposing that in your anxiety for my safety you feel that you oughtn't to spend my money, there are these foreign gentlemen staying in Athens who are quite willing to spend theirs. One

30

of them, Simmias of Thebes, has actually brought the money with him for this very purpose; and Cebes and a number of others are quite ready to do the same. So as I say, you mustn't let any fears on these grounds make you slacken your efforts to escape; and you mustn't feel any misgivings about what you said at your trial, that you wouldn't know what to do with yourself if you left this country. Wherever you go, there are plenty of places where you will find a welcome; and if you choose to go to Thessaly, I have friends there who will make much of you and give you complete protection, so that no one in Thessaly can interfere with you.

Besides, Socrates, I don't even feel that it is right for you to try to do what you are doing, throwing away your life when you might save it. You are doing your best to treat yourself in exactly the same way as your enemies would, or rather did, when they wanted to ruin you. What is more, it seems to me that you are letting your sons down too. You have it in your power to finish their bringing up and education, and instead of that you are proposing to go off and desert them, and so far as you are concerned they will have to take their chance. And what sort of chance are they likely to get? The sort of thing that usually happens to orphans when they lose their parents. Either one ought not to have children at all, or one ought to see their upbringing and education through to the end. It strikes me that you are taking the line of least resistance, whereas you ought to make the choice of a good man and a brave one, considering that you profess to have made goodness your object all through life. Really, I am ashamed, both on your account and on ours your friends'; it will look as though we had played something like a coward's part all through this affair of yours. First, there was the way you came into court when it was quite unnecessary — that was the first act; then there was the conduct of the defense — that was the second; and finally, to complete the farce, we get this situation, which makes it appear that we have let you slip out of our hands through some lack of courage and enterprise on our part, because we didn't save you, and you didn't save yourself, when it would have been quite possible and practicable, if we had been any use at all.

There, Socrates; if you aren't careful, besides the suffering there will be all this disgrace for you and us to bear. Come, make up your mind. Really it's too late for that now; you ought to have it made up already. There is no alternative; the whole thing must be carried through during this coming night. If we lose any more time, it can't be done, it will be too late. I appeal to you, Socrates, on every ground; take my advice and please don't be unreasonable!

SOCRATES: My dear Crito, I appreciate your warm feelings very much — that is, assuming that they have some justification; if not, the stronger they are, the harder they will be to deal with. Very well, then; we must consider whether we ought to follow your advice or not. You know that this is not a new idea of mine; it has always been my nature never to accept advice from any of my friends unless reflection shows that it is the best course that reason offers. I cannot abandon the principles which I used to hold in the past simply because this accident has happened to me; they seem to me to be much as they were, and I respect and regard the same principles now as before.

So unless we can find better principles on this occasion, you can be quite sure that I shall not agree with you; not even if the power of the people conjures up fresh hordes of bogies to terrify our childish minds, by subjecting us to chains and executions and confiscations of our property.

Well, then, how can we consider the question most reasonably? Suppose that we begin by reverting to this view which you hold about people's opinions. Was it always right to argue that some opinions should be taken seriously but not others? Or was it always wrong? Perhaps it was right before the question of my death arose, but now we can see clearly that it was a mistaken persistence in a point of view which was really irresponsible nonsense. I should like very much to inquire into this problem, Crito, with your help, and to see whether the argument will appear in any different light to me now that I am in this position, or whether it will remain the same; and whether we shall dismiss it or accept it.

Serious thinkers, I believe, have always held some such view as the one which I mentioned just now: that some of the opinions which people entertain should be respected, and others should not. Now I ask you, Crito, don't you think that this is a sound principle? — You are safe from the prospect of dying tomorrow, in all human probability; and you are not likely to have your judgment upset by this impending calamity. Consider, then; don't you think that this is a sound enough principle, that one should not regard all the opinions that people hold, but only some and not others? What do you say? Isn't that a fair statement?

CRITO: Yes, it is.

SOCRATES: In other words, one should regard the good ones and not the bad?

CRITO: Yes.

SOCRATES: The opinions of the wise being good, and the opinions of the foolish bad?

CRITO: Naturally.

SOCRATES: To pass on, then: What do you think of the sort of illustration that I used to employ? When a man is in training, and taking it seriously, does he pay attention to all praise and criticism and opinion indiscriminately, or only when it comes from the one qualified person, the actual doctor or trainer?

CRITO: Only when it comes from the one qualified person.

SOCRATES: Then he should be afraid of the criticism and welcome the praise of the one qualified person, but not those of the general public.

CRITO: Obviously.

SOCRATES: So he ought to regulate his actions and exercises and eating and drinking by the judgment of his instructor, who has expert knowledge, rather than by the opinions of the rest of the public.

CRITO: Yes, that is so.

SOCRATES: Very well. Now if he disobeys the one man and disregards his opinion and commendations, and pays attention to the advice of the many who have no expert knowledge, surely he will suffer some bad effect?

CRITO: Certainly.

SOCRATES: And what is this bad effect? Where is it produced? — I mean, in what part of the disobedient person?

CRITO: His body, obviously; that is what suffers.

SOCRATES: Very good. Well now, tell me, Crito — we don't want to go through all the examples one by one — does this apply as a general rule, and above all to the sort of actions which we are trying to decide about: just and unjust, honorable and dishonorable, good and bad? Ought we to be guided and intimidated by the opinion of the many or by that of the one — assuming that there is someone with expert knowledge? Is it true that we ought to respect and fear this person more than all the rest put together; and that if we do not follow his guidance we shall spoil and mutilate that part of us which, as we used to say, is improved by right conduct and destroyed by wrong? Or is this all nonsense?

CRITO: No, I think it is true, Socrates.

SOCRATES: Then consider the next step. There is a part of us which is improved by healthy actions and ruined by unhealthy ones. If we spoil it by taking the advice of nonexperts, will life be worth living when this part is once ruined? The part I mean is the body; do you accept this?

CRITO: Yes.

SOCRATES: Well, is life worth living with a body which is worn out and ruined by health?

CRITO: Certainly not.

SOCRATES: What about the part of us which is mutilated by wrong actions and benefited by right ones? Is life worth living with this part ruined? Or do we believe that this part of us, whatever it may be, in which right and wrong operate, is of less importance than the body?

CRITO: Certainly not.

SOCRATES: It is really more precious?

CRITO: Much more.

SOCRATES: In that case, my dear fellow, what we ought to consider is not so much what people in general will say about us but how we stand with the expert in right and wrong, the one authority, who represents the actual truth. So in the first place your proposition is not correct when you say that we should consider popular opinion in questions of what is right and honorable and good, or the opposite. Of course one might object "All the same, the people have the power to put us to death."

CRITO: No doubt about that! Quite true, Socrates; it is a possible objection.

SOCRATES: But so far as I can see, my dear 65 fellow, the argument which we have just been through is quite unaffected by it. At the same time I should like you to consider whether we are still satisfied on this point: that the really important thing is not to live, but to live well.

CRITO: Why, yes.

SOCRATES: And that to live well means the same thing as to live honorably or rightly?

CRITO: Yes.

SOCRATES: Then in the light of this agreement we must consider whether or not it is right for me to try to get away without an official discharge. If it turns out to be right, we must make the attempt; if not, we must let it drop. As for the considerations you raise about expense and reputation and bringing up children, I am afraid, Crito, that they represent the reflections of the ordinary public, who put people to death, and would bring them back to life if they could, with equal indifference to reason. Our real duty, I fancy, since the argument leads that way, is to consider one question only, the one which we raised just now: Shall we be acting rightly in paying money and showing gratitude to these people who are going to rescue me, and in escaping or arranging the escape ourselves, or shall we really be acting wrongly in doing all this? If it becomes clear that such conduct is wrong, I cannot help thinking that the question whether we are sure to die, or to suffer any other ill effect for that matter, if we stand our ground and take no action, ought not to weigh with us at all in comparison with the risk of doing what is wrong.

CRITO: I agree with what you say, Socrates; but 70 I wish you would consider what we ought to *do.*

SOCRATES: Let us look at it together, my dear fellow; and if you can challenge any of my arguments, do so and I will listen to you; but if you can't, be a good fellow and stop telling me over and over again that I ought to leave this place without official permission. I am very anxious to obtain your approval before I adopt the course which I have in mind; I don't want to act against your convictions. Now give your attention to the starting point of this inquiry — I hope that you will be satisfied with my way of stating it — and try to answer my questions to the best of your judgment.

CRITO: Well, I will try.

SOCRATES: Do we say that one must never willingly do wrong, or does it depend upon circumstance? Is it true, as we have often agreed before, that there is no sense in which wrongdoing is good or honorable? Or have we jettisoned all our former convictions in these last few days? Can you and I at our age, Crito, have spent all these years in serious discussions without realizing that we were no better than a pair of children? Surely the truth is just what we have always said. Whatever the popular view is, and whether the alternative is pleasanter than the present one or even harder to bear, the fact remains that to do wrong is in every sense bad and dishonorable for the person who does it. Is that our view, or not?

CRITO: Yes, it is.

SOCRATES: Then in no circumstances must one 75 do wrong.

CRITO: No.

SOCRATES: In that case one must not even do wrong when one is wronged, which most people regard as the natural course.

CRITO: Apparently not.

SOCRATES: Tell me another thing, Crito: Ought one to do injuries or not?

CRITO: Surely not, Socrates.

SOCRATES: And tell me: Is it right to do an injury in retaliation, as most people believe, or not?

CRITO: No, never.

SOCRATES: Because, I suppose, there is no difference between injuring people and wronging them.

CRITO: Exactly.

SOCRATES: So one ought not to return a wrong or an injury to any person, whatever the provocation is. Now be careful, Crito, that in making these single admissions you do not end by admitting something contrary to your real beliefs. I know that there are and always will be few people who think like this; and consequently between those who do think so and those who do not there can be no agreement on principle; they must always feel contempt when they observe one another's decisions. I want even you to consider very carefully whether you share my views and agree with me, and whether we can proceed with our discussion from the established hypothesis that it is never right to do a wrong or return a wrong or defend one's self against injury by retaliation; or whether you dissociate yourself from any share in this view as a basis for discussion. I have held it for a long time, and still hold it; but if you have formed any other opinion, say so and tell me what it is. If, on the other hand, you stand by what we have said, listen to my next point.

CRITO: Yes, I stand by it and agree with you. Go on.

SOCRATES: Well, here is my next point, or rather question. Ought one to fulfill all one's agreements, provided that they are right, or break them?

CRITO: One ought to fulfill them.

SOCRATES: Then consider the logical consequence. If we leave this place without first persuading the State to let us go, are we or are we not doing an injury, and doing it in a quarter where it is least justifiable? Are we or are we not abiding by our just agreements?

CRITO: I can't answer your question, Socrates; I am not clear in my mind.

SOCRATES: Look at it in this way. Suppose that while we were preparing to run away from here (or however one should describe it) the Laws and Constitution of Athens were to come and confront us and ask this question: "Now, Socrates, what are you proposing to do? Can you deny that by this act which you are contemplating you intend, so far as you have the power, to destroy us, the Laws, and the whole State as well? Do you imagine that a city can continue to exist and not be turned upside down, if the legal judgments which are pronounced in it have no force but are nullified and destroyed by private persons?" — how shall we answer this question, Crito, and others of the same kind? There is much that could be said, especially by a professional advocate, to protest against the invalidation of this law which enacts that judgments once pronounced shall be binding. Shall we say "Yes, I do intend to destroy the laws, because the State wronged me by passing a faulty judgment at my trial"? Is this to be our answer, or what?

CRITO: What you have just said, by all means, Socrates.

SOCRATES: Then what supposing the Laws say, "Was there provision for this in the agreement between you and us, Socrates? Or did you undertake to abide by whatever judgments the State pronounced?" If we expressed surprise at such language, they would probably say: "Never mind our language, Socrates, but answer our questions; after all, you are accustomed to the method of question and answer. Come now, what charge do you bring against us and the State, that you are trying to destroy us? Did we not give you life in the first place? Was it not through us that your father married your mother and begot you? Tell us, have you any complaint against those of us Laws that deal with marriage?" "No, none," I should say. "Well, have you any against the laws which deal with children's upbringing and education, such as you had yourself? Are you not grateful to those of us Laws which were instituted for this end, for requiring your father to give you a cultural and physical education?" "Yes," I should say. "Very good. Then since you have been born and brought up and educated, can you deny, in the first place, that you were our child and servant, both you and your ancestors? And if this is so, do you imagine that what is right for us is equally right for you, and that whatever we try to do to you, you are justified in retaliating? You did not have equality of rights with your father, or your employer (supposing that you had had one), to enable you to retaliate; you were not allowed to answer back when you were scolded or to hit back when you were beaten, or to do a great

many other things of the same kind. Do you expect to have such license against your country and its laws that if we try to put you to death in the belief that it is right to do so, you on your part will try your hardest to destroy your country and us its Laws in return? And will you, the true devotee of goodness, claim that you are justified in doing so? Are you so wise as to have forgotten that compared with your mother and father and all the rest of your ancestors your country is something far more precious, more venerable, more sacred, and held in greater honor both among gods and among all reasonable men? Do you not realize that you are even more bound to respect and placate the anger of your country than your father's anger? That if you cannot persuade your country you must do whatever it orders, and patiently submit to any punishment that it imposes, whether it be flogging or imprisonment? And if it leads you out to war, to be wounded or killed, you must comply, and it is right that you should do so; you must not give way or retreat or abandon your position. Both in war and in the law courts and everywhere else you must do whatever your city and your country commands, or else persuade it in accordance with universal justice; but violence is a sin even against your parents, and it is a far greater sin against your country" — What shall we say to this, Crito? — that what the Laws say is true, or not?

CRITO: Yes, I think so.

SOCRATES: "Consider, then, Socrates," the Laws would probably continue, "whether it is also true for us to say that what you are now trying to do to us is not right. Although we have brought you into the world and reared you and educated you, and given you and all your fellow citizens a share in all the good things at our disposal, nevertheless by the very fact of granting our permission we openly proclaim this principle: that any Athenian, on attaining to manhood and seeing for himself the political organization of the State and us its Laws, is permitted, if he is not satisfied with us, to take his property and go away wherever he likes. If any of you chooses to go to one of our colonies, supposing that he should not be satisfied with us and the State, or to emigrate to any other country, not one of us Laws hinders or prevents him from going away wherever he likes, without any loss of property. On the other hand, if any one of you stands his ground when he can see how we administer justice and the rest of our public organization, we hold that by so doing he has in fact undertaken to do anything that we tell him; and we maintain that anyone who disobeys is guilty of doing wrong on three separate counts: first because we are his parents, and secondly because we are his guardians; and thirdly because, after promising obedience, he is neither obeying us nor persuading us to change our decision if we are at fault in any way; and although all our orders are in the form of proposals, not of savage commands, and we give him the choice of either persuading us or doing what we say, he is actually doing neither. These are the charges, Socrates, to which we say that you will be liable if you do what you are contemplating; and you will not be the least culpable of your fellow countrymen, but one of the most guilty." If I said "Why do you say that?" they would no doubt pounce upon

me with perfect justice and point out that there are very few people in Athens who have entered into this agreement with them as explicitly as I have. They would say "Socrates, we have substantial evidence that you are satisfied with us and with the State. You would not have been so exceptionally reluctant to cross the borders of your country if you had not been exceptionally attached to it. You have never left the city to attend a festival or for any other purpose, except on some military expedition; you have never traveled abroad as other people do, and you have never felt the impulse to acquaint yourself with another country or constitution; you have been content with us and with our city. You have definitely chosen us, and undertaken to observe us in all your activities as a citizen; and as the crowning proof that you are satisfied with our city, you have begotten children in it. Furthermore, even at the time of your trial you could have proposed the penalty of banishment, if you had chosen to do so; that is, you could have done then with the sanction of the State what you are now trying to do without it. But whereas at that time you made a noble show of indifference if you had to die, and in fact preferred death, as you said, to banishment, now you show no respect for your earlier professions, and no regard for us, the Laws, whom you are trying to destroy; you are behaving like the lowest type of menial, trying to run away in spite of the contracts and undertakings by which you agreed to live as a member of our State. Now first answer this question: Are we or are we not speaking the truth when we say that you have undertaken, in deed if not in word, to live your life as a citizen in obedience to us?" What are we to say to that, Crito? Are we not bound to admit it?

CRITO: We cannot help it, Socrates.

SOCRATES: "It is a fact, then," they would say, "that you are breaking covenants and undertakings made with us, although you made them under no compulsion or misunderstanding, and were not compelled to decide in a limited time; you had seventy years in which you could have left the country, if you were not satisfied with us or felt that the agreements were unfair. You did not choose Sparta or Crete — your favorite models of good government — or any other Greek or foreign state; you could not have absented yourself from the city less if you had been lame or blind or decrepit in some other way. It is quite obvious that you stand by yourself above all other Athenians in your affection for this city and for us its Laws; — who would care for a city without laws? And now, after all this, are you not going to stand by your agreement? Yes, you are, Socrates, if you will take our advice; and then you will at least escape being laughed at for leaving the city.

"We invite you to consider what good you will do to yourself or your friends if you commit this breach of faith and stain your conscience. It is fairly obvious that the risk of being banished and either losing their citizenship or having their property confiscated will extend to your friends as well. As for yourself, if you go to one of the neighboring states, such as Thebes or Megara, which are both well governed, you will enter them as an enemy to their constitution[2] and all good patriots will eye you with suspicion as a destroyer of law and order. Incidentally you will confirm the opinion of the jurors who tried you that they gave a correct verdict; a destroyer of laws might very well be supposed to have a destructive influence upon young and foolish human beings. Do you intend, then, to avoid well governed states and the higher forms of human society? And if you do, will life be worth living? Or will you approach these people and have the impudence to converse with them? What arguments will you use, Socrates? The same which you used here, that goodness and integrity, institutions and laws, are the most precious possessions of mankind? Do you not think that Socrates and everything about him will appear in a disreputable light? You certainly ought to think so. But perhaps you will retire from this part of the world and go to Crito's friends in Thessaly? That is the home of indiscipline and laxity, and no doubt they would enjoy hearing the amusing story of how you managed to run away from prison by arraying yourself in some costume or putting on a shepherd's smock or some other conventional runaway's disguise, and altering your personal appearance. And will no one comment on the fact that an old man of your age, probably with only a short time left to live, should dare to cling so greedily to life, at the price of violating the most stringent laws? Perhaps not, if you avoid irritating anyone. Otherwise, Socrates, you will hear a good many humiliating comments. So you will live as the toady and slave of all the populace, literally 'roistering in Thessaly,' as though you had left this country for Thessaly to attend a banquet there; and where will your discussions about goodness and uprightness be then, we should like to

---

[2] **as an enemy to their constitution** As a lawbreaker.

know? But of course you want to live for your children's sake, so that you may be able to bring them up and educate them. Indeed! by first taking them off to Thessaly and making foreigners of them, so that they may have that additional enjoyment? Or if that is not your intention, supposing that they are brought up here with you still alive, will they be better cared for and educated without you, because of course your friends will look after them? Will they look after your children if you go away to Thessaly, and not if you go away to the next world? Surely if those who profess to be your friends are worth anything, you must believe that they would care for them.

"No, Socrates; be advised by us your guardians, and do not think more of your children or of your life or of anything else than you think of what is right; so that when you enter the next world you may have all this to plead in your defense before the authorities there. It seems clear that if you do this thing, neither you nor any of your friends will be the better for it or be more upright or have a cleaner conscience here in this world, nor will it be better for you when you reach the next. As it is, you will leave this place, when you do, as the victim of a wrong done not by us, the Laws, but by your fellow men. But if you leave in that dishonorable way, returning wrong for wrong and evil for evil, breaking your agreements and covenants with us, and injuring those whom you least ought to injure — yourself, your friends, your country, and us — then you will have to face our anger in your lifetime, and in that place beyond when the laws of the other world know that you have tried, so far as you could, to destroy even us their brothers, they will not receive you with a kindly welcome. Do not take Crito's advice, but follow ours."

That, my dear friend Crito, I do assure you, is what I seem to hear them saying, just as a mystic seems to hear the strains of music; and the sound of their arguments rings so loudly in my head that I cannot hear the other side. I warn you that, as my opinion stands at present, it will be useless to urge a different view. However, if you think that you will do any good by it, say what you like.

CRITO: No, Socrates, I have nothing to say.

SOCRATES: Then give it up, Crito, and let us follow this course, since God points out the way.

Topics for Critical Thinking and Writing

1. State as precisely as you can all the arguments Crito uses to try to convince Socrates that he ought to escape. Which of these arguments seems to you to be the best? The worst? Why?

2. Socrates says to Crito, "I cannot abandon the principles which I used to hold in the past simply because this accident [the misfortune of being convicted by the Athenian assembly and then sentenced to death] has happened to me" (para. 35). Does this remark strike you as self-righteous? Stubborn? Smug? Stupid? Explain.

3. Socrates declares that "serious thinkers" have always held the view that "some of the opinions which people entertain should be respected, and others should not" (para. 37). There are two main alternatives to this principle: (a) One should respect *all* the opinions that others hold, and (b) one should respect *none* of the opinions of others. Socrates attacks

(a), but he ignores (b). What are his objections to (a)? Do you find them convincing? Why, or why not? Can you think of any convincing arguments against (b)?

4. As Socrates shows in his reply to Crito, he seems ready to believe (para. 63) that there are "expert[s] in right and wrong" — that is, persons with expert opinion or even authoritative knowledge on matters of right and wrong conduct — and that their advice should be sought and followed. Do you agree? Consider the thesis that there are no such experts, and write a 500-word essay defending or attacking it.

5. Socrates, as he comments to Crito, believes that "it is never right to do a wrong or return a wrong or defend one's self against injury by retaliation" (para. 85). He does not offer any argument for this thesis in the dialogue (although he does elsewhere). It was a very strange doctrine in his day, and even now it is not generally accepted. Write a 1,000-word essay defending or attacking this thesis.

6. Socrates seems to argue that (a) no one ought to do wrong, (b) it would injure the state for someone in Socrates's position to escape, and (c) this act would break a "just agreement" between the citizen and his state; therefore, (d) no one in Socrates's position should escape. Do you think this argument is valid? If not, what further assumptions would be needed to make it valid? Do you think the argument is sound (i.e., both valid and true in all its premises)? If not, explain. If you had to attack premise (b) or (c), which do you think is the more vulnerable, and why?

7. In the imaginary speech by the Laws of Athens to Socrates, especially in paragraph 93, the Laws convey a picture of the supremacy of the state over the individual — and Socrates seems to assent to this picture. Do you? Why, or why not?

8. The Laws (para. 95) claim that if Socrates were to escape, he would be "guilty of doing wrong on three separate counts." What are they? Do you agree with all or any? Why, or why not? Read the essay by Martin Luther King Jr., "Letter from Birmingham Jail" (p. 447), and decide how King would have responded to the judgment of the Laws of Athens.

9. At the end of their peroration (para. 99), the Laws of Athens say to Socrates: Take your punishment as prescribed, and at your death "you will leave this place . . . as the victim of a wrong done not by us, the Laws, but by your fellow men." To what wrong do the Laws allude? Do you agree that it is men and not laws who perpetrated this wrong? If you were in Socrates's position, would it matter to you if you were being wronged not by laws but only by men? Explain your response.

10. Compose a letter from Socrates to Martin Luther King Jr. in which Socrates responds to King's "Letter from Birmingham Jail" (p. 447).

GEORGE ORWELL

George Orwell was the pen name adopted by Eric Blair (1903–1950), an Englishman born in India. Orwell was educated at Eton, in England, but in 1921 he went back to the East and served for five years as a police officer in Burma (now Myanmar). Disillusioned with colonial imperialism, he returned to Europe, doing odd jobs while writing novels and stories. In 1936 he fought in the Spanish Civil War on the side of the Republicans, an experience he reported in Homage to Catalonia *(1938). His last years were spent writing in England. His best-known work probably is the satiric allegory* 1984 *(1949), showing a totalitarian state in which the citizens are perpetually under the eye of Big Brother. The following essay is from* Shooting an Elephant and Other Essays *(1950).*

Shooting an Elephant

In Moulmein, in Lower Burma, I was hated by large numbers of people—the only time in my life that I have been important enough for this to happen to me. I was subdivisional police officer of the town, and in an aimless, petty kind of way anti-European feeling was very bitter. No one had the guts to raise a riot, but if a European woman went through the bazaars alone somebody would probably spit betel juice over her dress. As a police officer I was an obvious target and was baited whenever it seemed safe to do so. When a nimble Burman tripped me up on the football field and the referee (another Burman) looked the other way, the crowd yelled with hideous laughter. This happened more than once. In the end the sneering yellow faces of young men that met me everywhere, the insults hooted after me when I was at a safe distance, got badly on my nerves. The young Buddhist priests were the worst of all. There were several thousands of them in the town and none of them seemed to have anything to do except stand on street corners and jeer at Europeans.

All this was perplexing and upsetting. For at that time I had already made up my mind that imperialism was an evil thing and the sooner I chucked up my job and got out of it the better. Theoretically—and secretly, of course—I was all for the Burmese and all against their oppressors, the British. As for the job I was doing, I hated it more bitterly than I

can perhaps make clear. In a job like that you see the dirty work of Empire at close quarters. The wretched prisoners huddling in the stinking cages of the lock-ups, the grey, cowed faces of the long-term convicts, the scarred buttocks of the men who had been flogged with bamboos—all these oppressed me with an intolerable sense of guilt. But I could get nothing into perspective. I was young and ill-educated and I had had to think out my problems in the utter silence that is imposed on every Englishman in the East. I did not even know that the British Empire is dying, still less did I know that it is a great deal better than the younger empires that are going to supplant it. All I knew was that I was stuck between my hatred of the empire I served and my rage against the evil-spirited little beasts who tried to make my job impossible. With one part of my mind I thought of the British Raj[1] as an unbreakable tyranny, as something clamped down, *in saecula saeculorum*,[2] upon the will of prostrate peoples; with another part I thought that the greatest joy in the world would be to drive a bayonet into a Buddhist priest's guts. Feelings like these are the normal

---

[1] **British Raj** British imperial government in India and Burma. [All notes are the editors'.]

[2] *in saecula saeculorum* Forever (Latin). A term used in Christian liturgy.

by-products of imperialism; ask any Anglo-Indian official, if you can catch him off duty.

One day something happened which in a roundabout way was enlightening. It was a tiny incident in itself, but it gave me a better glimpse than I had had before of the real nature of imperialism — the real motives for which despotic governments act. Early one morning the sub-inspector at a police station the other end of the town rang me up on the 'phone and said that an elephant was ravaging the bazaar. Would I please come and do something about it? I did not know what I could do, but I wanted to see what was happening and I got on to a pony and started out. I took my rifle, an old .44 Winchester and much too small to kill an elephant, but I thought the noise might be useful *in terrorem*.[3] Various Burmans stopped me on the way and told me about the elephant's doings. It was not, of course, a wild elephant, but a tame one which had gone "must."[4] It had been chained up, as tame elephants always are when their attack of "must" is due, but on the previous night it had broken its chain and escaped. Its mahout, the only person who could manage it when it was in that state, had set out in pursuit, but had taken the wrong direction and was now twelve hours' journey away, and in the morning the elephant had suddenly reappeared in the town. The Burmese population had no weapons and were quite helpless against it. It had already destroyed somebody's bamboo hut, killed a cow and raided some fruit-stalls and devoured the stock; also it had met the municipal rubbish van and, when the driver jumped out and took to his heels, had turned the van over and inflicted violences upon it.

The Burmese sub-inspector and some Indian constables were waiting for me in the quarter where the elephant had been seen. It was a very poor quarter, a labyrinth of squalid bamboo huts, thatched with palm-leaf, winding all over a steep hillside. I remember that it was a cloudy, stuffy morning at the beginning of the rains. We began questioning the people as to where the elephant had gone and, as usual, failed to get any definite information. That is invariably the case in the East; a story always sounds clear enough at a distance, but the nearer you get to the scene of events the vaguer it becomes. Some of the people said that the elephant had gone in one direction, some said that he had gone in another, some professed not even to have heard of any elephant. I had almost made up my mind that the whole story was a pack of lies, when we heard yells a little distance away. There was a loud, scandalized cry of "Go away, child! Go away this instant!" and an old woman with a switch in her hand came round the corner of a hut, violently shooing away a crowd of naked children. Some more women followed, clicking their tongues and exclaiming; evidently there was something that the children ought not to have seen. I rounded the hut and saw a man's dead body sprawling in the mud. He was an Indian, a black Dravidian coolie, almost naked, and he could not have been dead many minutes. The people said that the elephant had come suddenly upon him round the corner of the hut, caught him with its trunk, put its foot on his back and ground him into the earth. This was the rainy season and the ground was soft, and his face had scored a trench a foot deep and a couple of yards long. He was lying on his belly with arms crucified and head sharply twisted to one side. His face was coated with mud, the eyes wide open, the teeth bared and grinning

---

[3]*in terrorem* As a warning.
[4]**"must"** Into sexual heat.

with an expression of unendurable agony. (Never tell me, by the way, that the dead look peaceful. Most of the corpses I have seen looked devilish.) The friction of the great beast's foot had stripped the skin from his back as neatly as one skins a rabbit. As soon as I saw the dead man I sent an orderly to a friend's house nearby to borrow an elephant rifle. I had already sent back the pony, not wanting it to go mad with fright and throw me if it smelt the elephant.

The orderly came back in a few minutes 5 with a rifle and five cartridges, and meanwhile some Burmans had arrived and told us that the elephant was in the paddy fields below, only a few hundred yards away. As I started forward practically the whole population of the quarter flocked out of the houses and followed me. They had seen the rifle and were all shouting excitedly that I was going to shoot the elephant. They had not shown much interest in the elephant when he was merely ravaging their homes, but it was different now that he was going to be shot. It was a bit of fun to them, as it would be to an English crowd; besides they wanted the meat. It made me vaguely uneasy. I had no intention of shooting the elephant — I had merely sent for the rifle to defend myself if necessary — and it is always unnerving to have a crowd following you. I marched down the hill, looking and feeling a fool, with the rifle over my shoulder and an ever-growing army of people jostling at my heels. At the bottom, when you got away from the huts, there was a metalled road and beyond that a miry waste of paddy fields a thousand yards across, not yet ploughed but soggy from the first rains and dotted with coarse grass. The elephant was standing eight yards from the road, his left side towards us. He took not the slightest notice of the crowd's approach. He was tearing up bunches of grass, beating them against his knees to clean them and stuffing them into his mouth.

I had halted on the road. As soon as I saw the elephant I knew with perfect certainty that I ought not to shoot him. It is a serious matter to shoot a working elephant — it is comparable to destroying a huge and costly piece of machinery — and obviously one ought not to do it if it can possibly be avoided. And at that distance, peacefully eating, the elephant looked no more dangerous than a cow. I thought then and I think now that his attack of "must" was already passing off; in which case he would merely wander harmlessly about until the mahout came back and caught him. Moreover, I did not in the least want to shoot him. I decided that I would watch him for a little while to make sure that he did not turn savage again, and then go home.

But at that moment I glanced round at the crowd that had followed me. It was an immense crowd, two thousand at the least and growing every minute. It blocked the road for a long distance on either side. I looked at the sea of yellow faces above the garish clothes — faces all happy and excited over this bit of fun, all certain that the elephant was going to be shot. They were watching me as they would watch a conjurer about to perform a trick. They did not like me, but with the magical rifle in my hands I was momentarily worth watching. And suddenly I realized that I should have to shoot the elephant after all. The people expected it of me and I had got to do it; I could feel their two thousand wills pressing me forward, irresistibly. And it was at this moment, as I stood there with the rifle in my hands, that I first grasped the hollowness, the futility of the white man's dominion in the East. Here was I, the white man with his gun, standing in front of the unarmed native crowd — seemingly the leading actor of the piece; but in reality I was only an absurd puppet pushed to and fro by the will of those yellow faces behind. I perceived in this moment that when the white man turns tyrant it is his own freedom that he destroys. He becomes a sort of hollow, posing dummy, the conventionalized figure of a sahib. For it is the condition of his rule that he shall spend his life in trying to impress the "natives," and so in every crisis he has got to do what the "natives" expect of him. He wears a mask, and his face grows to fit it. I had got to shoot the elephant. I had committed myself to doing it when I sent for the rifle. A sahib has got to act like a sahib; he has got to appear resolute, to know his own mind and do definite things. To come all that way, rifle in hand, with two thousand people marching at my heels, and then to trail feebly away, having done nothing — no, that was impossible. The crowd would laugh at me. And my whole life, every white man's life in the East, was one long struggle not to be laughed at.

But I did not want to shoot the elephant. I watched him beating his bunch of grass against his knees, with that preoccupied grandmotherly air that elephants have. It seemed to me that it would be murder to shoot him. At that age I was not squeamish about killing animals, but I had never shot an elephant and never wanted to. (Somehow it always seems worse to kill a *large* animal.) Besides, there was the beast's owner to be considered. Alive, the elephant was worth at least a hundred pounds; dead, he would only be worth the value of his tusks, five pounds, possibly. But I had got to act quickly. I turned to some experienced-looking Burmans who had been there when we arrived, and asked them how the elephant had been behaving. They all said the same thing; he took no notice of you if you left him alone, but he might charge if you went too close to him.

It was perfectly clear to me what I ought to do. I ought to walk up to within, say, twenty-five yards of the elephant and test his behavior. If he charged, I could shoot; if he took no notice of me, it would be safe to leave him until the mahout came back. But also I knew that I was going to do no such thing. I was a poor shot with a rifle and the ground was soft mud into which one would sink at every step. If the elephant charged and I missed him, I should have about as much chance as a toad under a steamroller. But even then I was not thinking particularly of my own skin, only of the watchful yellow faces behind. For at that moment, with the crowd watching me, I was not afraid in the ordinary sense, as I would have been if I had been alone. A white man mustn't be frightened in front of "natives"; and so, in general, he isn't frightened. The sole thought in my mind was that if anything went wrong those two thousand Burmans would see me pursued, caught, trampled on and reduced to a grinning corpse like that Indian up the hill. And if that happened it was quite probable that some of them would laugh. That would never do. There was only one alternative. I shoved the cartridges into the magazine and lay down on the road to get a better aim.

The crowd grew very still, and a deep, low, 10 happy sigh, as of people who see the theatre curtain go up at last, breathed from innumerable throats. They were going to have their bit of fun after all. The rifle was a beautiful German thing with cross-hair sights. I did not then know that in shooting an elephant one would shoot to cut an imaginary bar running from ear-hole to ear-hole. I ought, therefore, as the elephant was sideways on, to have aimed straight at his ear-hole; actually I aimed several inches in front of this, thinking the brain would be further forward.

When I pulled the trigger I did not hear the bang or feel the kick — one never does when a shot goes home — but I heard the devilish roar of glee that went up from the crowd. In that instant, in too short a time, one would have thought, even for the bullet to get there, a mysterious, terrible change had come over the elephant. He neither stirred nor fell, but every line of his body had altered. He looked suddenly stricken, shrunken, immensely old, as though the frightful impact of the bullet had paralyzed him without knocking him down. At last, after what seemed a long time — it might have been five seconds, I dare say — he sagged flabbily to his knees. His mouth slobbered. An enormous senility seemed to have settled upon him. One could have imagined him thousands of years old. I fired again into the same spot. At the second shot he did not collapse but climbed with desperate slowness to his feet and stood weakly upright, with legs sagging and head dropping. I fired a third time. That was the shot that did for him. You could see the agony of it jolt his whole body and knock the last remnant of strength from his legs. But in falling he seemed for a moment to rise, for as his hind legs collapsed beneath him he seemed to tower upward like a huge rock toppling, his trunk reaching skywards like a tree. He trumpeted, for the first and only time. And then down he came, his belly towards me, with a crash that seemed to shake the ground even where I lay.

I got up. The Burmans were already racing past me across the mud. It was obvious that the elephant would never rise again, but he was not dead. He was breathing very rhythmically with long rattling gasps, his great mound of a side painfully rising and falling. His mouth was wide open — I could see far down into caverns of pale pink throat. I waited a long time for him to die, but his breathing did not weaken. Finally I fired my two remaining shots into the spot where I thought his heart must be. The thick blood welled out of him like red velvet, but still he did not die. His body did not even jerk when the shots hit him, the tortured breathing continued without a pause. He was dying, very slowly and in great agony, but in some world remote from me where not even a bullet could damage him further. I felt that I had got to put an end to that dreadful noise. It seemed dreadful to see the great beast lying there, powerless to move and yet powerless to die, and not even to be able to finish him. I sent back for my small rifle and poured shot after shot into his heart and down his throat. They seemed to make no impression. The tortured gasps continued as steadily as the ticking of a clock.

In the end I could not stand it any longer and went away. I heard later that it took him half an hour to die. Burmans were bringing dahs[5] and baskets even before I left, and I was told they had stripped his body almost to the bones by the afternoon.

Afterwards, of course, there were endless discussions about the shooting of the elephant. The owner was furious, but he was only an Indian and could do nothing. Besides, legally I had done the right thing, for a mad elephant has to be killed, like a mad dog, if its owner fails to control it. Among the Europeans opinion was divided. The older men said I was right, the younger men said it was a damn shame to shoot an elephant for killing a coolie, because an elephant was worth more than any damn Coringhee coolie. And afterwards I was very glad that the coolie had been killed; it put me legally in the right and it gave me a sufficient pretext for shooting the elephant. I often wondered whether any of the others grasped that I had done it solely to avoid looking a fool.

---

[5]**dahs** Large knives.

Topics for Critical Thinking and Writing

1. Did George Orwell shoot the elephant of his own free will? Or did he shoot the elephant because he *had* to shoot it? What does he say about this? Do you find his judgment convincing or not? Write a 500-word essay explaining your answer.

2. Was Orwell justified in shooting the elephant? Did he do the right thing in killing it? In the aftermath, did he think he did the right thing? Do you? Write a 500-word essay explaining your answers.

3. Orwell says, "As soon as I saw the elephant I knew with perfect certainty that I ought not to shoot him" (para. 6). How could he claim to "know" this, when moments later he did shoot the elephant?

4. Orwell says in passing, "Somehow it always seems worse to kill a *large* animal" (para. 8). Explain why you think Orwell says this and whether you agree.

5. A biographer who did research on Orwell in Burma reported that he could find no supporting documentation, either in the local newspapers or in the files of the police, that this episode ever occurred. Suppose that Orwell made it up. If so, is your response different? Explain.

6. If, pressured by circumstances, you have ever acted against what you might think is your reason or your nature, report the experience, and give your present evaluation of your behavior.

WALTER T. STACE

Walter T. Stace (1886–1967), a professor of philosophy at Princeton University for many years, was the author of several books, including Religion and the Modern Mind *(1952), from which this selection is taken. The title is the editors'.*

Is Determinism Inconsistent with Free Will?

The second great problem which the rise of scientific naturalism has created for the modern mind concerns the foundations of morality. The old religious foundations have largely crumbled away, and it may well be thought that the edifice built upon them by generations of men is in danger of collapse. A total collapse of moral behavior is, as I pointed out before, very unlikely. For a society in which this occurred could not survive. Nevertheless the danger to

moral standards inherent in the virtual disappearance of their old religious foundations is not illusory.

I shall first discuss the problem of free will, for it is certain that if there is no free will there can be no morality. Morality is concerned with what men ought and ought not to do. But if a man has no freedom to choose what he will do, if whatever he does is done under compulsion, then it does not make sense to tell him that he ought not to have done what he did and that he ought to do something different. All moral precepts would in such case be meaningless. Also if he acts always under compulsion, how can he be held morally responsible for his actions? How can he, for example, be punished for what he could not help doing?

It is to be observed that those learned professors of philosophy or psychology who deny the existence of free will do so only in their professional moments and in their studies and lecture rooms. For when it comes to doing anything practical, even of the most trivial kind, they invariably behave as if they and others were free. They inquire from you at dinner whether you will choose this dish or that dish. They will ask a child why he told a lie, and will punish him for not having chosen the way of truthfulness. All of which is inconsistent with a disbelief in free will. This should cause us to suspect that the problem is not a real one; and this, I believe, is the case. The dispute is merely verbal, and is due to nothing but a confusion about the meanings of words. It is what is now fashionably called a semantic problem.

How does a verbal dispute arise? Let us consider a case which, although it is absurd in the sense that no one would ever make the mistake which is involved in it, yet illustrates the principle which we shall have to use in the solution of the problem. Suppose that someone believed that the word "man" means a certain sort of five-legged animal; in short that "five-legged animal" is the correct *definition* of man. He might then look around the world, and rightly observing that there are no five-legged animals in it, he might proceed to deny the existence of men. This preposterous conclusion would have been reached because he was using an incorrect definition of "man." All you would have to do to show him his mistake would be to give him the correct definition; or at least to

show him that his definition was wrong. Both the problem and its solution would, of course, be entirely verbal. The problem of free will, and its solution, I shall maintain, is verbal in exactly the same way. The problem has been created by the fact that learned men, especially philosophers, have assumed an incorrect definition of *free will*, and then finding that there is nothing in the world which answers to their definition, have denied its existence. As far as logic is concerned, their conclusion is just as absurd as that of the man who denies the existence of men. The only difference is that the mistake in the latter case is obvious and crude, while the mistake which the deniers of free will have made is rather subtle and difficult to detect.

Throughout the modern period, until quite recently, it was assumed, both by the philosophers who denied free will and by those who defended it, that *determinism is inconsistent with free will*. If a man's actions were wholly determined by chains of causes stretching back into the remote past, so that they could be predicted beforehand by a mind which knew all the causes, it was assumed that they could not in that case be free. This implies that a certain definition of actions done from free will was assumed, namely that they are actions *not* wholly determined by causes or predictable beforehand. Let us shorten this by saying that free will was defined as meaning indeterminism. This is the incorrect definition which has led to the denial of free will. As soon as we see what the true definition is we shall find that the question whether the world is deterministic, as Newtonian science implied, or in a measure indeterministic, as current physics teaches, is wholly irrelevant to the problem.

Of course there is a sense in which one can define a word arbitrarily in any way one pleases. But a definition may nevertheless be called correct or incorrect. It is correct if it accords with a *common usage* of the word defined. It is incorrect if it does not. And if you give an incorrect definition, absurd and untrue results are likely to follow. For instance, there is nothing to prevent you from arbitrarily defining a man as a five-legged animal, but this is incorrect in the sense that it does not accord with the ordinary meaning of the word. Also it has the absurd result of leading to a denial of the existence of men. This shows that *common usage is the criterion for deciding whether a definition is correct or not*. And this is the principle which I shall apply to free will. I shall show that indeterminism is not what is meant by the phrase "free will" *as it is commonly used*. And I shall attempt to discover the correct definition by inquiring how the phrase is used in ordinary conversation.

Here are a few samples of how the phrase might be used in ordinary conversation. It will be noticed that they include cases in which the question whether a man acted with free will is asked in order to determine whether he was morally and legally responsible for his acts.

JONES: I once went without food for a week.
SMITH: Did you do that of your own free will?
JONES: No. I did it because I was lost in a desert and could find no food.

But suppose that the man who had fasted was Mahatma Gandhi. The conversation might then have gone:

GANDHI: I once fasted for a week.
SMITH: Did you do that of your own free will?
GANDHI: Yes. I did it because I wanted to compel the British Government to give India its independence.

Take another case. Suppose that I had stolen some bread, but that I was as truthful as George Washington. Then, if I were charged with the crime in court, some exchange of the following sort might take place:

JUDGE: Did you steal the bread of your own free will?
STACE: Yes. I stole it because I was hungry.

Or in different circumstances the conversation might run: [10]

JUDGE: Did you steal of your own free will?
STACE: No. I stole because my employer threatened to beat me if I did not.

At a recent murder trial in Trenton some of the accused had signed confessions, but afterwards asserted that they had done so under police duress. The following exchange might have occurred:

JUDGE: Did you sign this confession of your own free will?
PRISONER: No. I signed it because the police beat me up.

Now suppose that a philosopher had been a member of the jury. We could imagine this conversation taking place in the jury room.

FOREMAN OF THE JURY: The prisoner says he signed the confession because he was beaten, and not of his own free will.
PHILOSOPHER: This is quite irrelevant to the case. There is no such thing as free will.
FOREMAN: Do you mean to say that it makes no difference whether he signed because his conscience made him want to tell the truth or because he was beaten?
PHILOSOPHER: None at all. Whether he was caused to sign by a beating or by some

desire of his own — the desire to tell the truth, for example — in either case his signing was causally determined, and therefore in neither case did he act of his own free will. Since there is no such thing as free will, the question whether he signed of his own free will ought not to be discussed by us.

The foreman and the rest of the jury would rightly conclude that the philosopher must be making some mistake. What sort of a mistake could it be? There is only one possible answer. The philosopher must be using the phrase "free will" in some peculiar way of his own which is not the way in which men usually use it when they wish to determine a question of moral responsibility. That is, he must be using an incorrect definition of it as implying action not determined by causes.

Suppose a man left his office at noon, and were questioned about it. Then we might hear this:

JONES: Did you go out of your own free will?
SMITH: Yes. I went out to get my lunch.

But we might hear:

JONES: Did you leave your office of your own free will?
SMITH: No. I was forcibly removed by the police.

We have now collected a number of cases of actions which, in the ordinary usage of the English language, would be called cases in which people have acted of their own free will. We should also say in all these cases that they *chose* to act as they did. We should also say that they could have acted otherwise, if they had chosen. For instance, Mahatma Gandhi was not compelled to fast; he chose to do so. He could have eaten if he had wanted

to. When Smith went out to get his lunch, he chose to do so. He could have stayed and done some more work, if he had wanted to. We have also collected a number of cases of the opposite kind. They are cases in which men were not able to exercise their free will. They had no choice. They were compelled to do as they did. The man in the desert did not fast of his own free will. He had no choice in the matter. He was compelled to fast because there was nothing for him to eat. And so with the other cases. It ought to be quite easy, by an inspection of these cases, to tell what we ordinarily mean when we say that a man did or did not exercise free will. We ought therefore to be able to extract from them the proper definition of the term. Let us put the cases in a table:

Free Acts	Unfree Acts
Gandhi fasting because he wanted to free India.	The man fasting in the desert because there was no food.
Stealing bread because one is hungry.	Stealing because one's employer threatened to beat one.
Signing a confession because one wanted to tell the truth.	Signing because the police beat one.
Leaving the office because one wanted one's lunch.	Leaving because forcibly removed.

It is obvious that to find the correct definition of free acts we must discover what characteristic is common to all the acts in the left-hand column, and is, at the same time, absent from all the acts in the right-hand

15

column. This characteristic which all free acts have, and which no unfree acts have, will be the defining characteristic of free will.

Is being uncaused, or not being determined by causes, the characteristic of which we are in search? It cannot be, because although it is true that all the acts in the right-hand column have causes, such as the beating by the police or the absence of food in the desert, so also do the acts in the left-hand column. Mr. Gandhi's fasting was caused by his desire to free India, the man leaving his office by his hunger, and so on. Moreover there is no reason to doubt that these causes of the free acts were in turn caused by prior conditions, and that these were again the results of causes, and so on back indefinitely into the past. Any physiologist can tell us the causes of hunger. What caused Mr. Gandhi's tremendously powerful desire to free India is no doubt more difficult to discover. But it must have had causes. Some of them may have lain in peculiarities of his glands or brain, others in his past experiences, others in his heredity, others in his education. Defenders of free will have usually tended to deny such facts. But to do so is plainly a case of special pleading, which is unsupported by any scrap of evidence. The only reasonable view is that all human actions, both those which are freely done and those which are not, are either wholly determined by causes, or at least as much determined as other events in nature. It may be true, as the physicists tell us, that nature is not as deterministic as was once thought. But whatever degree of determinism prevails in the world, human actions appear to be as much determined as anything else. And if this is so, it cannot be the case that what distinguishes actions freely chosen from those which are not free is that the latter are determined by causes while the former

are not. Therefore, being uncaused or being undetermined by causes must be an incorrect definition of free will.

What, then, is the difference between acts which are freely done and those which are not? What is the characteristic which is present to all the acts in the left-hand column and absent from all those in the right-hand column? Is it not obvious that, although both sets of actions have causes, the causes of those in the left-hand column are *of a different kind* from the causes of those in the right-hand column? The free acts are all caused by desires, or motives, or by some sort of internal psychological states of the agent's mind. The unfree acts, on the other hand, are all caused by physical forces or physical conditions, outside the agent. Police arrest means physical force exerted from the outside; the absence of food in the desert is a physical condition of the outside world. We may therefore frame the following rough definitions. *Acts freely done are those whose immediate causes are psychological states in the agent. Acts not freely done are those whose immediate causes are states of affairs external to the agent.*

It is plain that if we define free will in this 20 way, then free will certainly exists, and the philosopher's denial of its existence is seen to be what it is — nonsense. For it is obvious that all those actions of men which we should ordinarily attribute to the exercise of their free will, or of which we should say that they freely chose to do them, are in fact actions which have been caused by their own desires, wishes, thoughts, emotions, impulses, or other psychological states.

In applying our definition we shall find that it usually works well, but that there are some puzzling cases which it does not seem exactly to fit. These puzzles can always be solved by paying careful attention to the ways in which words are used, and remembering that they are not always used consistently. I have space for only one example. Suppose that a thug threatens to shoot you unless you give him your wallet, and suppose that you do so. Do you, in giving him your wallet, do so of your own free will or not? If we apply our definition, we find that you acted freely, since the immediate cause of the action was not an actual outside force but the fear of death, which is a psychological cause. Most people, however, would say that you did not act of your own free will but under compulsion. Does this show that our definition is wrong? I do not think so. Aristotle, who gave a solution of the problem of free will substantially the same as ours (though he did not use the term "free will"), admitted that there are what he called "mixed" or borderline cases in which it is difficult to know whether we ought to call the acts free or compelled. In the case under discussion, though no actual force was used, the gun at your forehead so nearly approximated to actual force that we tend to say the case was one of compulsion. It is a borderline case.

Here is what may seem like another kind of puzzle. According to our view an action may be free though it could have been predicted beforehand with certainty. But suppose you told a lie, and it was certain beforehand that you would tell it. How could one then say, "You could have told the truth"? The answer is that it is perfectly true that you could have told the truth *if* you had wanted to. In fact you would have done so, for in that case the causes producing your action, namely your desires, would have been different, and would therefore have produced different effects. It is a delusion that predictability and free will are incompatible. This

agrees with common sense. For if, knowing your character, I predict that you will act honorably, no one would say when you do act honorably, that this shows you did not do so of your own free will.

Since free will is a condition of moral responsibility, we must be sure that our theory of free will gives a sufficient basis for it. To be held morally responsible for one's actions means that one may be justly punished or rewarded, blamed or praised, for them. But it is not just to punish a man for what he cannot help doing. How can it be just to punish him for an action which it was certain beforehand that he would do? We have not attempted to decide whether, as a matter of fact, all events, including human actions, are completely determined. For that question is irrelevant to the problem of free will. But if we assume for the purposes of argument that complete determinism is true, but that we are nevertheless free, it may then be asked whether such a deterministic free will is compatible with moral responsibility. For it may seem unjust to punish a man for an action which it could have been predicted with certainty beforehand that he would do.

But that determinism is incompatible with moral responsibility is as much a delusion as that it is incompatible with free will. You do not excuse a man for doing a wrong act because, knowing his character, you felt certain beforehand that he would do it. Nor do you deprive a man of a reward or prize because, knowing his goodness or his capabilities, you felt certain beforehand that he would win it.

Volumes have been written on the justification of punishment. But so far as it affects the question of free will, the essential principles involved are quite simple. The punishment of a man for doing a wrong act is justified, either on the ground that it will correct his own character, or that it will deter other people from doing similar acts. The instrument of punishment has been in the past, and no doubt still is, often unwisely used; so that it may often have done more harm than good. But that is not relevant to our present problem. Punishment, if and when it is justified, is justified only on one or both of the grounds just mentioned. The question then is how, if we assume determinism, punishment can correct character or deter people from evil actions.

Suppose that your child develops a habit of telling lies. You give him a mild beating. Why? Because you believe that his personality is such that the usual motives for telling the truth do not cause him to do so. You therefore supply the missing cause, or motive, in the shape of pain and the fear of future pain if he repeats his untruthful behavior. And you hope that a few treatments of this kind will condition him to the habit of truth-telling, so that he will come to tell the truth without the infliction of pain. You assume that his actions are determined by causes, but that the usual causes of truth-telling do not in him produce their usual effects. You therefore supply him with an artificially injected motive, pain and fear, which you think will in the future cause him to speak truthfully.

The principle is exactly the same where you hope, by punishing one man, to deter others from wrong actions. You believe that the fear of punishment will cause those who might otherwise do evil to do well.

We act on the same principle with nonhuman, and even with inanimate, things, if they do not behave in the way we think they ought to behave. The rose bushes in the garden produce only small and poor blooms, whereas we want large and rich ones. We supply a cause which will produce large blooms, namely fertilizer. Our automobile does not go properly. We supply a cause which will make it go better, namely oil in the works. The punishment for the man, the fertilizer for the plant, and the oil for the car are all justified by the same principle and in the same way. The only difference is that different kinds of things require different kinds of causes to make them do what they should. Pain may be the appropriate remedy to apply, in certain cases, to human beings, and oil to the machine. It is, of course, of no use to inject motor oil into the boy or to beat the machine.

Thus we see that moral responsibility is not only consistent with determinism, but requires it. The assumption on which punishment is based is that human behavior is causally determined. If pain could not be a cause of truth-telling there would be no justification at all for punishing lies. If human actions and volitions were uncaused, it would be useless either to punish or reward, or indeed to do anything else to correct people's bad behavior. For nothing that you could do would in any way influence them. Thus moral responsibility would entirely disappear. If there were no determinism of human beings at all, their actions would be completely unpredictable and capricious, and therefore irresponsible. And this is in itself a strong argument against the common view of philosophers that free will means being undetermined by causes.

Topics for Critical Thinking and Writing

1. Walter Stace asserts that "if there is no free will there can be no morality" (para. 2). What is his reasoning (see para. 23)? Do you agree? Why, or why not?

2. "The dispute is merely verbal," Stace proclaims in paragraph 3. What "dispute"? Why "merely verbal"? What would Stace say to someone who insists that the existence or nonexistence of free will is a question of *fact*?

3. What is *determinism* (para. 5)? Why does Stace seem to think that philosophers are strongly inclined to believe in it?

4. Stace claims that he will show that "indeterminism is not what is meant by . . . 'free will' *as it is commonly used*" (para. 6). What is his argument? What does he think *free will* means as the term is "commonly used"? Are you convinced? Why, or why not? Write a 500-word essay answering these questions.

5. Stace insists that "all human actions . . . are . . . at least as much determined as other events in nature" (para. 18). How might one argue against this?

6. Complete the following definition so that it captures Stace's view: "When Smith did *X*, he acted freely if and only if . . ."

7. Stace mentions some "puzzling cases" (para. 21) that do not quite fit, he admits, his analysis of free will. Give an example of such a case, and explain why it is puzzling.

8. Why does Stace conclude in paragraph 22 that "it is a delusion that predictability and free will are incompatible"? Do you agree? Why, or why not?

9. It seems paradoxical to assert, as Stace does in his last paragraph, that "moral responsibility is not only consistent with determinism, but requires it." Explain Stace's view here in no more than 250 words.

MARTIN LUTHER KING JR.

Martin Luther King Jr. (1929–1968) was born in Atlanta and educated at Morehouse College, Crozer Theological Seminary, and Boston University. In 1954 he was called to serve as a Baptist minister in Montgomery, Alabama. During the next two years he achieved national fame when, using a policy of nonviolent resistance, he successfully led the boycott against segregated bus lines in Montgomery. He then organized the Southern Christian Leadership Conference, which furthered civil rights, first in the South and then nationwide. In 1964 he was awarded the Nobel Peace Prize. Four years later he was assassinated in Memphis, Tennessee, while supporting striking garbage workers.

In 1963 King was arrested in Birmingham, Alabama, for participating in a march for which no parade permit had been issued by city officials. In jail he wrote a response to a letter that eight local clergymen had published in a newspaper.

Note: Their letter, titled "A Call for Unity," is printed here, followed by King's response.

A CALL FOR UNITY

April 12, 1963

We the undersigned clergymen are among those who, in January, issued "An Appeal for Law and Order and Common Sense," in dealing with racial problems in Alabama. We expressed understanding that honest convictions in racial matters could properly be pursued in the courts, but urged that decisions of those courts should in the meantime be peacefully obeyed.

Since that time there had been some evidence of increased forebearance and a willingness to face facts. Responsible citizens have undertaken to work on various problems which cause racial friction and unrest. In Birmingham, recent public events have given indication that we all have opportunity for a new constructive and realistic approach to racial problems.

However, we are now confronted by a series of demonstrations by some of our Negro citizens, directed and led in part by outsiders. We recognize the natural impatience of people who feel that their hopes are slow in being realized. But we are convinced that these demonstrations are unwise and untimely.

We agree rather with certain local Negro leadership which has called for honest and open negotiation of racial issues in our area. And we believe this kind of facing of issues can best be accomplished by citizens of our own metropolitan area, white and Negro, meeting with their knowledge and experience of the local situation. All of us need to face that responsibility and find proper channels for its accomplishment.

Just as we formerly pointed out that "hatred and violence have no sanction in our religious and political traditions," we also point out that such actions as incite to hatred and violence, however technically peaceful those actions may be, have not contributed to the resolution of our local problems. We do not believe that these days of new hope are days when extreme measures are justified in Birmingham.

We commend the community as a whole, and the local news media and law enforcement officials in particular, on the calm manner in which these demonstrations have been handled. We urge the public to continue to show restraint should the demonstrations continue, and the law enforcement officials to remain calm and continue to protect our city from violence.

We further strongly urge our own Negro community to withdraw support from these demonstrations, and to unite locally in working peacefully for a better Birmingham. When rights are consistently denied, a cause should be pressed in the courts and in negotiations among local leaders, and not in the streets. We appeal to both our white and Negro citizenry to observe the principles of law and order and common sense.

—C.C.J. CARPENTER, D.D., L.L.D., BISHOP OF ALABAMA; JOSEPH A. DURICK, D.D., AUXILIARY BISHOP, DIOCESE OF MOBILE-BIRMINGHAM; RABBI MILTON L. GRAFMAN, TEMPLE EMANU-EL, BIRMINGHAM, ALABAMA; BISHOP PAUL HARDIN, BISHOP OF THE ALABAMA-WEST FLORIDA CONFERENCE OF THE METHODIST CHURCH; BISHOP NOLAN B. HARMON, BISHOP OF THE NORTH ALABAMA CONFERENCE OF THE METHODIST CHURCH; GEORGE M. MURRAY, D.D., L.L.D., BISHOP COADJUTOR, EPISCOPAL DIOCESE OF ALABAMA; EDWARD V. RAMAGE, MODERATOR, SYNOD OF THE ALABAMA PRESBYTERIAN CHURCH IN THE UNITED STATES; EARL STALLINGS, PASTOR, FIRST BAPTIST CHURCH, BIRMINGHAM, ALABAMA.

Letter from Birmingham Jail

April 16, 1963

My Dear Fellow Clergymen:

While confined here in the Birmingham city jail, I came across your recent statement calling my present activities "unwise and untimely."[1] Seldom do I pause to answer criticism of my work and ideas. If I sought to answer all the criticisms that cross my desk, my secretaries would have little time for anything other than such correspondence in the course of the day, and I would have no time for constructive work. But since I feel that you are men of genuine good will and that your criticisms are sincerely set forth, I want to try to answer your statement in what I hope will be patient and reasonable terms.

I think I should indicate why I am here in Birmingham, since you have been influenced by the view which argues against "outsiders coming in." I have the honor of serving as president of the Southern Christian Leadership Conference, an organization operating in every southern state, with headquarters in Atlanta, Georgia. We have some eighty-five affiliated organizations across the South, and one of them is the Alabama Christian Movement for Human Rights. Frequently we share staff, educational, and financial resources with our affiliates. Several months ago the affiliate here in Birmingham asked us to be on call to engage in a nonviolent direct-action program if such were deemed necessary. We readily consented, and when the hour came we lived up to our promise. So I, along with several members of my staff, am here because I was invited here. I am here because I have organizational ties here.

But more basically, I am in Birmingham because injustice is here. Just as the prophets of the eighth century B.C. left their villages and carried their "thus saith the Lord" far beyond the boundaries of their home towns, and just as the Apostle Paul left his village of Tarsus and carried the gospel of Jesus Christ to the far corners of the Greco-Roman world, so am I compelled to carry the gospel of freedom beyond my own home town. Like Paul, I must constantly respond to the Macedonian call for aid.

Moreover, I am cognizant of the interrelatedness of all communities and states. I cannot sit idly by in Atlanta and not be concerned about what happens in Birmingham. Injustice anywhere is a threat to justice everywhere. We are caught in an inescapable network of mutuality; tied in a single garment of destiny. Whatever affects one directly, affects all indirectly. Never again can we afford to live with the narrow, provincial "outside agitator" idea. Anyone who lives inside the United States can never be considered an outsider anywhere within its bounds.

You deplore the demonstrations taking [5] place in Birmingham. But your statement, I am sorry to say, fails to express a similar concern for the conditions that brought about the demonstrations. I am sure that none of you would want to rest content with the superficial kind of social analysis that deals merely with

---

[1] This response to a published statement by eight fellow clergymen from Alabama (Bishop C.C.J. Carpenter, Bishop Joseph A. Durick, Rabbi Milton L. Grafman, Bishop Paul Hardin, Bishop Nolan B. Harmon, the Reverend George M. Murray, the Reverend Edward V. Ramage, and the Reverend Earl Stallings) was composed under somewhat constricting circumstances. Begun on the margins of the newspaper in which the statement appeared while I was in jail, the letter was continued on scraps of writing paper supplied by a friendly Negro trusty, and concluded on a pad my attorneys were eventually permitted to leave me. Although the text remains in substance unaltered, I have indulged in the author's prerogative of polishing it for publication. [King's note.]

effects and does not grapple with underlying causes. It is unfortunate that demonstrations are taking place in Birmingham, but it is even more unfortunate that the city's white power structure left the Negro community with no alternative.

In any nonviolent campaign there are four basic steps: collection of the facts to determine whether injustices exist; negotiation; self-purification; and direct action. We have gone through all these steps in Birmingham. There can be no gainsaying the fact that racial injustice engulfs this community. Birmingham is probably the most thoroughly segregated city in the United States. Its ugly record of brutality is widely known. Negroes have experienced grossly unjust treatment in the courts. There have been more unsolved bombings of Negro homes and churches in Birmingham than in any other city in the nation. These are the hard, brutal facts of the case. On the basis of these conditions, Negro leaders sought to negotiate with the city fathers. But the latter consistently refused to engage in good-faith negotiation.

Then, last September, came the opportunity to talk with leaders of Birmingham's economic community. In the course of the negotiations, certain promises were made by the merchants — for example, to remove the stores' humiliating racial signs. On the basis of these promises, the Reverend Fred Shuttlesworth and the leaders of the Alabama Christian Movement for Human Rights agreed to a moratorium on all demonstrations. As the weeks and months went by, we realized that we were the victims of a broken promise. A few signs, briefly removed, returned; the others remained.

As in so many past experiences, our hopes had been blasted, and the shadow of deep disappointment settled upon us. We had no alternative except to prepare for direct action, whereby we would present our very bodies as a means of laying our case before the conscience of the local and the national community. Mindful of the difficulties involved, we decided to undertake a process of self-purification. We began a series of workshops on nonviolence, and we repeatedly asked ourselves: "Are you able to accept blows without retaliating?" "Are you able to endure the ordeal of jail?" We decided to schedule our direct-action program for the Easter season, realizing that except for Christmas, this is the main shopping period of the year. Knowing that a strong economic-withdrawal program would be the by-product of direct action, we felt that this would be the best time to bring pressure to bear on the merchants for the needed change.

Then it occurred to us that Birmingham's mayoralty election was coming up in March, and we speedily decided to postpone action until after election day. When we discovered that the Commissioner of Public Safety, Eugene "Bull" Connor, had piled up enough votes to be in the run-off, we decided again to postpone action until the day after the run-off so that the demonstrations could not be used to cloud the issues. Like many others, we waited to see Mr. Connor defeated, and to this end we endured postponement after postponement. Having aided in this community need, we felt that our direct-action program could be delayed no longer.

You may well ask: "Why direct action? [10] Why sit-ins, marches, and so forth? Isn't negotiation a better path?" You are quite right in calling for negotiation. Indeed, this is the very purpose of direct action. Nonviolent direct action seeks to create such a crisis and foster such a tension that a community which has constantly refused to negotiate is forced to confront the issue. It seeks so to dramatize the issue that it can no longer be ignored. My citing the creation of tension as part of the work of the nonviolent-resister may sound rather shocking. But I must confess that I am not afraid of the word "tension." I have earnestly opposed violent tension, but there is a type of constructive, nonviolent tension which is necessary for growth. Just as Socrates felt that it was necessary to create a tension in the mind so that individuals could rise from the bondage of myths and half-truths to the unfettered realm of creative analysis and objective appraisal, so must we see the need for nonviolent gadflies to create the kind of tension in society that will help men rise from the dark depths of prejudice and racism to the majestic heights of understanding and brotherhood.

The purpose of our direct-action program is to create a situation so crisis-packed that it will inevitably open the door to negotiation. I therefore concur with you in your call for negotiation. Too long has our beloved Southland been bogged down in a tragic effort to live in monologue rather than dialogue.

One of the basic points in your statement is that the action that I and my associates have taken in Birmingham is untimely. Some have asked: "Why didn't you give the new city administration time to act?" The only answer that I can give to this query is that the new Birmingham administration must be prodded about as much as the outgoing one, before it will act. We are sadly mistaken if we feel that the election of Albert Boutwell as mayor will bring the millennium to Birmingham. While Mr. Boutwell is a much more gentle person than Mr. Connor, they are both segregationists, dedicated to maintenance of the status quo. I have hope that Mr. Boutwell will be reasonable enough to see the futility of massive resistance to desegregation. But he will not see this without pressure from devotees of civil rights. My friends, I must say to you that we have not made a single gain in civil rights without determined legal and nonviolent pressure. Lamentably, it is an historical fact that privileged groups seldom give up their privileges voluntarily. Individuals may see the moral light and voluntarily give up their unjust posture; but as Reinhold Niebuhr[2] has reminded us, groups tend to be more immoral than individuals.

We know through painful experience that freedom is never voluntarily given by the oppressor; it must be demanded by the oppressed. Frankly, I have yet to engage in a direct-action campaign that was "well timed" in the view of those who have not suffered unduly from the disease of segregation. For years now I have heard the word "Wait!" It rings in the ear of every Negro with piercing familiarity. This "Wait" has almost always meant "Never." We must come to see, with one of our distinguished jurists, that "justice too long delayed is justice denied."[3]

We have waited for more than 340 years for our constitutional and God-given rights. The nations of Asia and Africa are moving with jetlike speed toward gaining political independence, but we still creep at horse-and-buggy pace toward gaining a cup of coffee at a lunch counter. Perhaps it is easy for those who have never felt the stinging darts of segregation to say, "Wait." But when you have seen vicious mobs lynch your mothers and fathers at will and drown your sisters and brothers at whim; when you have seen hate-filled policemen curse, kick, and even kill your black brothers and sisters; when you see the vast majority of your twenty million Negro brothers smothering in an airtight cage of poverty in the midst of an

[2]**Reinhold Niebuhr** Niebuhr (1892–1971) was a minister, political activist, author, and professor of applied Christianity at Union Theological Seminary. [All notes are the editors' unless otherwise specified.]
[3]**Justice . . . denied** A quotation attributed to William E. Gladstone (1809–1898), British statesman and prime minister.

affluent society; when you suddenly find your tongue twisted and your speech stammering as you seek to explain to your six-year-old daughter why she can't go to the public amusement park that has just been advertised on television, and see tears welling up in her eyes when she is told that Funtown is closed to colored children, and see ominous clouds of inferiority beginning to form in her little mental sky, and see her beginning to distort her personality by developing an unconscious bitterness toward white people; when you have to concoct an answer for a five-year-old son who is asking: "Daddy, why do white people treat colored people so mean?"; when you take a cross-country drive and find it necessary to sleep night after night in the uncomfortable corners of your automobile because no motel will accept you; when you are humiliated day in and day out by nagging signs reading "white" and "colored"; when your first name becomes "nigger," your middle name becomes "boy" (however old you are) and your last name becomes "John," and your wife and mother are never given the respected title "Mrs."; when you are harried by day and haunted by night by the fact that you are a Negro, living constantly at tiptoe stance, never quite knowing what to expect next, and are plagued with inner fears and outer resentments; when you are forever fighting a degenerating sense of "nobodiness"—then you will understand why we find it difficult to wait. There comes a time when the cup of endurance runs over, and men are no longer willing to be plunged into the abyss of despair. I hope, sirs, you can understand our legitimate and unavoidable impatience.

You express a great deal of anxiety over our 15 willingness to break laws. This is certainly a legitimate concern. Since we so diligently urge people to obey the Supreme Court's decision of 1954 outlawing segregation in the public schools, at first glance it may seem rather paradoxical for us consciously to break laws. One may well ask: "How can you advocate breaking some laws and obeying others?" The answer lies in the fact that there are two types of laws: just and unjust. I would be the first to advocate obeying just laws. One has not only a legal but a moral responsibility to obey just laws. Conversely, one has a moral responsibility to disobey unjust laws. I would agree with St. Augustine[4] that "an unjust law is no law at all."

Now, what is the difference between the two? How does one determine whether a law is just or unjust? A just law is a man-made code that squares with the moral law or the law of God. An unjust law is a code that is out of harmony with the moral law. To put it in the terms of St. Thomas Aquinas:[5] An unjust law is a human law that is not rooted in eternal law and natural law. Any law that uplifts human personality is just. Any law that degrades human personality is unjust. All segregation statutes are unjust because segregation distorts the soul and damages the personality. It gives the segregator a false sense of superiority and the segregated a false sense of inferiority. Segregation, to use the terminology of the Jewish philosopher Martin Buber, substitutes an "I-it" relationship for an "I-thou" relationship and ends up relegating persons to the status of things. Hence segregation is not only politically, economically, and sociologically unsound, it is morally wrong and sinful. Paul Tillich[6] has said that sin is separation. Is not segregation an

---

[4]**St. Augustine** Augustine of Hippo (354–430), an early Christian philosopher.

[5]**St. Thomas Aquinas** Aquinas (1225–1274) was a Catholic priest and an important medieval philosopher and theologian.

[6]**Paul Tillich** Tillich (1886–1965), born in Germany, taught theology at several German universities, but in 1933 he was dismissed from his post at the University of Frankfurt because of his opposition to the Nazi regime. At the invitation of Reinhold Niebuhr, he came to the United States and taught at Union Theological Seminary.

existential expression of man's tragic separation, his awful estrangement, his terrible sinfulness? Thus it is that I can urge men to obey the 1954 decision of the Supreme Court, for it is morally right; and I can urge them to disobey segregation ordinances, for they are morally wrong.

Let us consider a more concrete example of just and unjust laws. An unjust law is a code that a numerical or power majority group compels a minority group to obey but does not make binding on itself. This is *difference* made legal. By the same token, a just law is a code that a majority compels a minority to follow and that it is willing to follow itself. This is *sameness* made legal.

Let me give another explanation. A law is unjust if it is inflicted on a minority that, as a result of being denied the right to vote, had no part in enacting or devising the law. Who can say that the legislature of Alabama which set up that state's segregation laws was democratically elected? Throughout Alabama all sorts of devious methods are used to prevent Negroes from becoming registered voters, and there are some counties in which, even though Negroes constitute a majority of the population, not a single Negro is registered. Can any law enacted under such circumstances be considered democratically structured?

Sometimes a law is just on its face and unjust in its application. For instance, I have been arrested on a charge of parading without a permit. Now, there is nothing wrong in having an ordinance which requires a permit for a parade. But such an ordinance becomes unjust when it is used to maintain segregation and to deny citizens the First Amendment privilege of peaceful assembly and protest.

I hope you are able to see the distinction 20 I am trying to point out. In no sense do I advocate evading or defying the law, as would the rabid segregationist. That would lead to anarchy. One who breaks an unjust law must do so openly, lovingly, and with a willingness to accept the penalty. I submit that an individual who breaks a law that conscience tells him is unjust, and who willingly accepts the penalty of imprisonment in order to arouse the conscience of the community over its injustice, is in reality expressing the highest respect for law.

Of course, there is nothing new about this kind of civil disobedience. It was evidenced sublimely in the refusal of Shadrach, Meshach, and Abednego to obey the laws of Nebuchadnezzar, on the ground that a higher moral law was at stake. It was practiced superbly by the early Christians, who were willing to face hungry lions and the excruciating pain of chopping blocks rather than submit to certain unjust laws of the Roman Empire. To a degree, academic freedom is a reality today because Socrates practiced civil disobedience. In our own nation, the Boston Tea Party represented a massive act of civil disobedience.

We should never forget that everything Adolf Hitler did in Germany was "legal" and everything the Hungarian freedom fighters did in Hungary was "illegal." It was "illegal" to aid and comfort a Jew in Hitler's Germany. Even so, I am sure that, had I lived in Germany at the time, I would have aided and comforted my Jewish brothers. If today I lived in a Communist country where certain principles dear to the Christian faith are suppressed, I would openly advocate disobeying that country's antireligious laws.

I must make two honest confessions to you, my Christian and Jewish brothers. First, I must confess that over the past few years I have been gravely disappointed with the white moderate. I have almost reached the regrettable conclusion that the Negro's great stumbling block in his stride toward freedom is not the White Citizen's Counciler or the Ku Klux

Klanner, but the white moderate, who is more devoted to "order" than to justice; who prefers a negative peace which is the absence of tension to a positive peace which is the presence of justice; who constantly says: "I agree with you in the goal you seek, but I cannot agree with your methods or direct action"; who paternalistically believes he can set the timetable for another man's freedom; who lives by a mythical concept of time and who constantly advises the Negro to wait for a "more convenient season." Shallow understanding from people of good will is more frustrating than absolute misunderstanding from people of ill will. Lukewarm acceptance is much more bewildering than outright rejection.

I had hoped that the white moderate would understand that law and order exist for the purpose of establishing justice and that when they fail in this purpose they become the dangerously structured dams that block the flow of social progress. I had hoped that the white moderate would understand that the present tension in the South is a necessary phase of the transition from an obnoxious negative peace, in which the Negro passively accepted his unjust plight, to a substantive and positive peace, in which all men will respect the dignity and worth of human personality. Actually, we who engage in nonviolent direct action are not the creators of tension. We merely bring to the surface the hidden tension that is already alive. We bring it out in the open, where it can be seen and dealt with. Like a boil that can never be cured so long as it is covered up but must be opened with all its ugliness to the natural medicines of air and light, injustice must be exposed, with all the tension its exposure creates, to the light of human conscience and the air of national opinion before it can be cured.

In your statement you assert that our actions, even though peaceful, must be condemned because they precipitate violence. But is this a logical assertion? Isn't this like condemning a robbed man because his possession of money precipitated the evil act of robbery? Isn't this like condemning Socrates because his unswerving commitment to truth and his philosophical inquiries precipitated the act by the misguided populace in which they made him drink hemlock? Isn't this like condemning Jesus because his unique God-consciousness and never-ceasing devotion to God's will precipitated the evil act of crucifixion? We must come to see that, as the federal courts have consistently affirmed, it is wrong to urge an individual to cease his efforts to gain his basic constitutional rights because the quest may precipitate violence. Society must protect the robbed and punish the robber.

I had also hoped that the white moderate would reject the myth concerning time in relation to the struggle for freedom. I have just received a letter from a white brother in Texas. He writes: "All Christians know that the colored people will receive equal rights eventually, but it is possible that you are in too great a religious hurry. It has taken Christianity almost two thousand years to accomplish what it has. The teachings of Christ take time to come to earth." Such an attitude stems from a tragic misconception of time, from the strangely irrational notion that there is something in the very flow of time that will inevitably cure all ills. Actually, time itself is neutral; it can be used either destructively or constructively. More and more I feel that the people of ill will have used time much more effectively than have the people of good will. We will have to repent in this generation not merely for the hateful words and actions of the bad people but for the appalling silence of the good people. Human progress never rolls in on wheels of inevitability; it comes through the tireless efforts of men willing to be co-workers with God, and without this hard work, time itself becomes an ally of the forces of social stagnation. We must use time creatively, in the knowledge that the time is always ripe to do right. Now is the time to make real the promise of democracy and transform our pending national elegy into a creative psalm of brotherhood. Now is the time to lift our national policy from the quicksand of racial injustice to the solid rock of human dignity.

You speak of our activity in Birmingham as extreme. At first I was rather disappointed that fellow clergymen would see my nonviolent efforts as those of an extremist. I began thinking about the fact that I stand in the middle of two opposing forces in the Negro community. One is a force of complacency, made up in part of Negroes who, as a result of long years of oppression, are so drained of self-respect and a sense of "somebodiness" that they have adjusted to segregation; and in part of a few middle class Negroes who, because of a degree of academic and economic security and because in some ways they profit by segregation, have become insensitive to the problems of the masses. The other force is one of bitterness and hatred, and it comes perilously close to advocating violence. It is expressed in the various black nationalist groups that are springing up across the nation, the largest and best-known being Elijah Muhammad's Muslim movement. Nourished by the Negro's frustration over the continued existence of racial discrimination, this movement is made up of people who have lost faith in America, who have absolutely repudiated Christianity, and who have concluded that the white man is an incorrigible "devil."

I have tried to stand between these two forces, saying that we need emulate neither the "do-nothingism" of the complacent nor the hatred and despair of the black nationalist. For there is the more excellent way of love and nonviolent protest. I am grateful to God that, through the influence of the Negro church, the way of nonviolence became an integral part of our struggle.

If this philosophy had not emerged, by now many streets of the South should, I am convinced, be flowing with blood. And I am further convinced that if our white brothers dismiss as "rabble-rousers" and "outside agitators" those of us who employ nonviolent direct action, and if they refuse to support our nonviolent efforts, millions of Negroes will, out of frustration and despair, seek solace and security in black-nationalist ideologies — a development that would inevitably lead to a frightening racial nightmare.

Oppressed people cannot remain oppressed forever. The yearning for freedom eventually manifests itself, and that is what has happened to the American Negro. Something within has reminded him of his birthright of freedom, and something without has reminded him that it can be gained. Consciously or unconsciously, he has been caught up by the *Zeitgeist,*[7] and with his black brothers of Africa and his brown and yellow brothers of Asia, South America, and the Caribbean, the United States Negro is moving with a sense of great urgency toward the promised land of racial justice. If one recognizes this vital urge that has engulfed the Negro community, one should readily understand why public demonstrations are taking place. The Negro has many pent-up resentments and latent frustrations, and he must release them. So let him march; let him make prayer pilgrimages to the city hall; let him go on freedom rides — and try to understand why he must do so. If his repressed emotions are not released in nonviolent ways, they will seek expression through violence; this is not a threat but a fact

30

---

[7]*Zeitgeist* Spirit of the age (German).

of history. So I have not said to my people: "Get rid of your discontent." Rather, I have tried to say that this normal and healthy discontent can be channeled into the creative outlet of nonviolent direct action. And now this approach is being termed extremist.

But though I was initially disappointed at being categorized as an extremist, as I continued to think about the matter I gradually gained a measure of satisfaction from the label. Was not Jesus an extremist for love: "Love your enemies, bless them that curse you, do good to them that hate you, and pray for them which despitefully use you, and persecute you." Was not Amos an extremist for justice: "Let justice roll down like waters and righteousness like an ever-flowing stream." Was not Paul an extremist for the Christian gospel: "I bear in my body the marks of the Lord Jesus." Was not Martin Luther an extremist: "Here I stand; I cannot do otherwise, so help me God." And John Bunyan: "I will stay in jail to the end of my days before I make a butchery of my conscience." And Abraham Lincoln: "This nation cannot survive half slave and half free." And Thomas Jefferson: "We hold these truths to be self-evident, that all men are created equal...." So the question is not whether we will be extremists, but what kind of extremists we will be. Will we be extremists for hate or for love? Will we be extremists for the preservation of injustice or for the extension of justice? In that dramatic scene on Calvary's hill three men were crucified. We must never forget that all three were crucified for the same crime — the crime of extremism. Two were extremists for immorality, and thus fell below their environment. The other, Jesus Christ, was an extremist for love, truth, and goodness, and thereby rose above his environment. Perhaps the South, the nation, and the world are in dire need of creative extremists.

I had hoped that the white moderate would see this need. Perhaps I was too optimistic; perhaps I expected too much. I suppose I should have realized that few members of the oppressor race can understand the deep groans and passionate yearnings of the oppressed race, and still fewer have the vision to see that injustice must be rooted out by strong, persistent, and determined action. I am thankful, however, that some of our white brothers in the South have grasped the meaning of this social revolution and committed themselves to it. They are still all too few in quantity, but they are big in quality. Some — such as Ralph McGill, Lillian Smith, Harry Golden, James McBride Dabbs, Ann Braden, and Sarah Patton Boyle — have written about our struggle in eloquent and prophetic terms. Others have marched with us down nameless streets of the South. They have languished in filthy, roach-infested jails, suffering the abuse and brutality of policemen who view them as "dirty nigger-lovers." Unlike so many of their moderate brothers and sisters, they have recognized the urgency of the moment and sensed the need for powerful "action" antidotes to combat the disease of segregation.

Let me take note of my other major disappointment. I have been so greatly disappointed with the white church and its leadership. Of course, there are some notable exceptions. I am not unmindful of the fact that each of you has taken some significant stands on this issue. I commend you, Reverend Stallings, for your Christian stand on this past Sunday, in welcoming Negroes to your worship service on a nonsegregated basis. I commend the Catholic leaders of this state for integrating Spring Hill College several years ago.

But despite these notable exceptions, I must honestly reiterate that I have been disappointed with the church. I do not say this as one of those negative critics who can always find something wrong with the church. I say this as a minister of the gospel, who loves the church; who was nurtured in its bosom; who has been sustained by its spiritual blessings and who will remain true to it as long as the cord of life shall lengthen.

When I was suddenly catapulted into the 35 leadership of the bus protest in Montgomery, Alabama, a few years ago, I felt we would be supported by the white church. I felt that the white ministers, priests, and rabbis of the South would be among our strongest allies. Instead, some have been outright opponents, refusing to understand the freedom movement and misrepresenting its leaders; all too many others have been more cautious than courageous and have remained silent behind the anesthetizing security of stained-glass windows.

In spite of my shattered dreams, I came to Birmingham with the hope that the white religious leadership of this community would see the justice of our cause and, with deep moral concern, would serve as the channel through which our just grievances could reach the power structure. I had hoped that each of you would understand. But again I have been disappointed.

I have heard numerous southern religious leaders admonish their worshipers to comply with a desegregation decision because it is the law, but I have longed to hear white ministers declare: "Follow this decree because integration is morally right and because the Negro is your brother." In the midst of blatant injustices inflicted upon the Negro, I have watched white churchmen stand on the sideline and mouth pious irrelevancies and sanctimonious trivialities. In the midst of a mighty struggle to rid our nation of racial and economic injustice, I have heard many ministers say: "Those are social issues, with which the gospel has no real concern." And I have watched many churches commit themselves to a completely otherworldly religion which makes a strange, unbiblical distinction between body and soul, between the sacred and the secular.

I have traveled the length and breadth of Alabama, Mississippi, and all the other southern states. On sweltering summer days and crisp autumn mornings I have looked at the South's beautiful churches with their lofty spires pointing heavenward. I have beheld the impressive outlines of her massive religious-education buildings. Over and over I have found myself saying: "What kind of people worship here? Who is their God? Where were their voices when the lips of Governor Barnett dripped with words of interposition and nullification? Where were they when Governor Wallace gave a clarion call for defiance and hatred? Where were their voices of support when bruised and weary Negro men and women decided to rise from the dark dungeons of complacency to the bright hills of creative protest?"

Yes, these questions are still in my mind. In deep disappointment I have wept over the laxity of the church. But be assured that my tears have been tears of love. There can be no deep disappointment where there is not deep love. Yes, I love the church. How could I do otherwise? I am in the rather unique position of being the son, the grandson, and the great-grandson of preachers. Yes, I see the church as the body of Christ. But, Oh! How we have blemished and scarred that body through social neglect and through fear of being nonconformists.

There was a time when the church was 40 very powerful—in the time when the early Christians rejoiced at being deemed worthy to suffer for what they believed. In those days the church was not merely a thermometer that recorded the ideas and principles of popular opinion; it was a thermostat that transformed the mores of society. Whenever the early Christians entered a town, the people in power became disturbed and immediately sought to convict the Christians for being "disturbers of the peace" and "outside agitators." But the Christians pressed on, in the conviction that they were "a colony of heaven," called to obey God rather than man. Small in number, they were big in commitment. They were too God-intoxicated to be "astronomically intimidated." By their effort and example they brought an end to such ancient evils as infanticide and gladiatorial contests.

Things are different now. So often the contemporary church is a weak, ineffectual voice with an uncertain sound. So often it is an arch-defender of the status quo. Far from being disturbed by the presence of the church, the power structure of the average community is consoled by the church's silent—and often even vocal—sanction of things as they are.

But the judgment of God is upon the church as never before. If today's church does not recapture the sacrificial spirit of the early church, it will lose its authenticity, forfeit the loyalty of millions, and be dismissed as an irrelevant social club with no meaning for the twentieth century. Every day I meet young people whose disappointment with the church has turned into outright disgust.

Perhaps I have once again been too optimistic. Is organized religion too inextricably bound to the status quo to save our nation and the world? Perhaps I must turn my faith to the inner spiritual church, the church within the church, as the true *ekklesia*[8] and the hope of the world. But again I am thankful to God that some noble souls from the ranks of organized religion have broken loose from the paralyzing chains of conformity and joined us as active partners in the struggle for freedom. They have left their secure congregations and walked the streets of Albany, Georgia, with us. They have gone down the highways of the South on tortuous rides for freedom. Yes, they have gone to jail with us. Some have been dismissed from their churches, have lost the support of their bishops and fellow ministers. But they have acted in the faith that right defeated is stronger than evil triumphant. Their witness has been the spiritual salt that has preserved the true meaning of the gospel in these troubled times. They have carved a tunnel of hope through the dark mountain of disappointment.

I hope the church as a whole will meet the challenge of this decisive hour. But even if the church does not come to the aid of justice, I have no despair about the future. I have no fear about the outcome of our struggle in Birmingham, even if our motives are at present misunderstood. We will reach the goal of freedom in Birmingham and all over the nation, because the goal of America is freedom. Abused and scorned though we may be, our destiny is tied up with America's destiny. Before the pilgrims landed at Plymouth, we were here. Before the pen of Jefferson etched the majestic words of the Declaration of Independence across the pages of history, we were here. For more than two centuries our forebears labored in this country without wages; they made cotton king; they built the homes of their masters while suffering gross injustice and shameful humiliation — and yet out of a bottomless vitality they continue to thrive and develop. If the inexpressible cruelties of slavery could not stop us, the opposition we now face will surely fail. We will win our freedom because the sacred heritage of our nation and the eternal will of God are embodied in our echoing demands.

---

[8]*ekklesia* A gathering or assembly of citizens (Greek).

Before closing I feel impelled to mention one other point in your statement that has troubled me profoundly. You warmly commended the Birmingham police force for keeping "order" and "preventing violence." I doubt that you would have so warmly commended the police force if you had seen its dogs sinking their teeth into unarmed, non-violent Negroes. I doubt that you would so quickly commend the policemen if you were to observe their ugly and inhumane treatment of Negroes here in the city jail; if you were to watch them push and curse old Negro women and young Negro girls; if you were to see them slap and kick old Negro men and young boys; if you were to observe them, as they did on two occasions, refuse to give us food because we wanted to sing our grace together. I cannot join you in your praise of the Birmingham police department.

It is true that the police have exercised a degree of discipline in handling the demonstrators. In this sense they have conducted themselves rather "nonviolently" in public. But for what purpose? To preserve the evil system of segregation. Over the past few years I have consistently preached that nonviolence demands that the means we use must be as pure as the ends we seek. I have tried to make clear that it is wrong to use immoral means to attain moral ends. But now I must affirm that it is just as wrong, or perhaps even more so, to use moral means to preserve immoral ends. Perhaps Mr. Connor and his policemen have been rather nonviolent in public, as was Chief Pritchett in Albany, Georgia, but they used the moral means of nonviolence to maintain the immoral end of racial injustice. As T. S. Eliot has said: "The last temptation is the greatest treason: To do the right deed for the wrong reason."

I wish you had commended the Negro sit-inners and demonstrators of Birmingham for their sublime courage, their willingness to suffer, and their amazing discipline in the midst of great provocation. One day the South will recognize its real heroes. They will be the James Merediths, with the noble sense of purpose that enables them to face jeering and hostile mobs, and with the agonizing loneliness that characterizes the life of the pioneer. They will be old, oppressed, battered Negro women, symbolized in a seventy-two-year-old woman in Montgomery, Alabama, who rose up with a sense of dignity and with her people decided not to ride segregated buses, and who responded with ungrammatical profundity to one who inquired about her weariness: "My feets is tired, but my soul is at rest." They will be the young high school and college students, the young ministers of the gospel and a host of their elders, courageously and nonviolently sitting in at lunch counters and willingly going to jail for conscience's sake. One day the South will know that when these disinherited children of God sat down at lunch counters, they were in reality standing up for what is best in the American dream and for the most sacred values in our Judaeo-Christian heritage, thereby bringing our nation back to those great wells of democracy which were dug deep by the founding fathers in their formulation of the Constitution and the Declaration of Independence.

Never before have I written so long a letter. I'm afraid it is much too long to take your precious time. I can assure you that it would have been much shorter if I had been writing from a comfortable desk, but what else can one do when he is alone in a narrow jail cell, other than write long letters, think long thoughts, and pray long prayers?

If I have said anything in this letter that overstates the truth and indicates an unreasonable impatience, I beg you to forgive me. If I have said anything that understates the truth and indicates my having a patience that allows me to settle for anything less than brotherhood, I beg God to forgive me.

I hope this letter finds you strong in the faith. I also hope that circumstances will soon make it possible for me to meet each of you, not as an integrationist or a civil-rights leader but as a fellow clergyman and a Christian brother. Let us all hope that the dark clouds of racial prejudice will soon pass away and the deep fog of misunderstanding will be lifted from our fear-drenched communities, and in some not too distant tomorrow the radiant stars of love and brotherhood will shine over our great nation with all their scintillating beauty.

Yours for the cause of Peace and Brotherhood,
Martin Luther King Jr.

Topics for Critical Thinking and Writing

1. In his first five paragraphs of the "Letter," how does Martin Luther King assure his audience that he is not a meddlesome intruder but a man of goodwill?

2. In paragraph 3, King refers to Hebrew prophets and to the Apostle Paul, and later (para. 10) he refers to Socrates. What is the point of these references?

3. In paragraph 11, what does King mean when he says that "our beloved Southland" has long tried to "live in monologue rather than dialogue"?

4. King begins paragraph 23 with "I must make two honest confessions to you, my Christian and Jewish brothers." What would have been gained or lost if he had used this paragraph as his opening?

5. King's last three paragraphs do not advance his argument. What do they do?

6. Why does King advocate breaking unjust laws "openly, lovingly" (para. 20)? What does he mean by these words? What other motives or attitudes do these words rule out?

7. Construct two definitions of *civil disobedience,* and explain whether and to what extent it is easier (or harder) to justify civil disobedience, depending on how you have defined the expression.

8. If you feel that you wish to respond to King's letter on some point, write a letter nominally addressed to King. You may, if you like, adopt the persona of one of the eight clergymen whom King initially addressed.

9. King writes (para. 46) that "nonviolence demands that the means we use must be as pure as the ends we seek." How do you think King would evaluate the following acts: (a) occupying a college administration building to protest the administration's unsatisfactory response to a racial incident on campus or its failure to hire minority persons as staff and faculty; (b) occupying an abortion clinic to protest abortion? Set down your answer in an essay of 500 words.

10. Compose a letter from King in which he responds to Plato's "Crito" (p. 420).

PETER CAVE

Peter Cave (b. 1952) teaches philosophy at the Open University and City University of London. He is the author of Can a Robot Be Human? 33 Perplexing Philosophy Puzzles *(2007) and* What's Wrong with Eating People? 33 More Perplexing Philosophy Puzzles *(2008). We reprint an essay from the second book.*

Man or Sheep?

Thomas Hobbes, a key political philosopher of the seventeenth century, wrote that man's life was "solitary, poor, nasty, brutish, and short." The obvious reply is, "It could have been worse, Thomas; it could have been solitary, poor, nasty, brutish — and long."

Hobbes was describing life before the existence of a state, government, and law. Humans are competitive. They lack reason to trust each other, unless there is a powerful authority that sets laws and punishes law-breakers. In a state of nature, individuals would be in constant conflict or, at least, always on their guard, insecure, and ready for battle. The state of nature, of life pre-government, is a state of war. With the state of nature so horrible, human beings would obviously want to get out, into something better. According to Hobbes, they would come together and agree on a sovereign, an absolute authority, to represent and rule over them, giving them security and opportunity to lead reasonable lives.

There are many puzzles, not least why individuals in the state of nature would risk trusting each other to keep to any agreement. Let us, though, not worry about how government arises. Here we are, living within a state. Let us assume we have a government democratically elected. However, whatever the degree of democracy, laws are imposed that restrict what we may do. We may disapprove of some laws because of some moral or religious principles;

we may disapprove of other laws simply because they prevent us from getting what we want. The general concern becomes: By what authority does any government rightfully rule over us?

WHY SHOULD WE OBEY THE STATE AND ITS LAWS?

We may answer in practical terms. We obey the law because we are scared of the consequences of disobedience, not wanting to risk fines and imprisonment. The rational thing to do, given the aim of getting on with our lives as best we can, is to obey. When asked whether man or mouse, some of us tend to squeak and take the cheese. Even more so may most of us squeak, when the tentacles of the law and the long arm of the police take hold. We mice may, indeed, be more akin to sheep, sheepishly following each other in our general obedience. Our puzzle though is what, if anything, makes obeying the law the *right* thing to do — even if we could get away with disobeying.

Many of us benefit because of the state's 5 existence: We are defended from others, receive state education, health services, in return for paying taxes. We are better off with law than without. So, we are obligated, in return, to obey the laws that confer those benefits. One immediate objection is that this justification for lawful obedience fails to work for those who overall do not benefit. A significant number do very badly, sleeping rough, being denied state benefits, and being avoided by those better off. Why should they obey? Also, some at society's top may argue that they contribute more than they receive — probably forgetting that they secured the more because of society's stability and protection of gross inequalities often inherited.

Even when overall we do benefit from the state's existence, it does not follow that we are under any obligation to the benefactor. Did we ever sign up, agreeing that we would accept benefits in return for obeying the law? If someone buys us a drink, without our asking, are we under an obligation to buy one in return?

Reference to "signing up" casts us along another line, a line orientated toward the "social contract." What justifies the state and our obedience is that we consented to the set-up. Some philosophers, John Locke and arguably Hobbes, believed that historically some individuals made contracts to be governed by an authority acting in their interests, leading to our societies. Of course, there is no reason to believe in such historical events; but, even if they occurred, whatever relevance do they have for us today? We were not around hundreds of years ago, engaged in any contractual deals.

The response to that last thought is to spot features of our current lives that may indicate consent. We make use of the state's services; we travel freely on the King's highway, notes Locke — well, today the Queen's highway. This shows that we tacitly consent to the state — or does it? Just because we remain in this country, using its facilities, it does not follow that we consent: After all, what other options are available? Can most people afford to go elsewhere? Would other countries, with acceptable laws, permit entry? It is as if we find ourselves on a ship in the middle of the ocean, with the captain making the point that we are free to leave.

Rationality is often wheeled out, to come to the rescue. True, we were not involved in any original social contract; true, our remaining within our society fails to establish consent. But suppose we were rational, not yet in a society, and needing to create society's laws. Suppose, too, we were ignorant of our sex, race, abilities, and the position we probably would reach in society, be it through chance or talent. In such an original position, behind a veil of ignorance, where everything is fair between us, our thinking, even though we remain as individuals, would not be distorted by a distinctive self-interest differing from the self-interest of others. Rather, our common rationality and interests should lead us to see and accept what would be fair laws, benefits, and rights for all. Behind the veil of ignorance, it would seem rational to consent to a society that permitted basic freedoms, did not discriminate between individuals on irrelevant grounds, and provided welfare benefits for when things go badly. After all, behind the veil of ignorance, we have no idea whether we may end up belonging to minority groups or hitting on hard times. If our current society possesses the features it would be rational to consent to behind the veil, then our obedience today is justified by this hypothetical consent, by what is seen as a hypothetical contract.

The response, by way of jibe, is that hypothetical contracts are not worth the paper they are not written upon. Hypothetical consent is not consent. The jibe, though, misses the point. Justifications can rightly involve hypotheticals. Why did you battle with the man, yanking him from the cliff's path, despite his protests? "Because, had he been sober, he would have consented to the yanking, to save him from risking a fatal fall." 10

The resort to the veil of ignorance, to rationality, and the hypothetical, though, raises its own puzzles. Quite what does rationality involve behind such a veil? Is it rational, for example, to place liberty higher than greater welfare benefits requiring higher levels of taxation?

Whatever justifications are offered for general obedience to the state, sometimes we morally ought to disobey. Had only many, many consulted their conscience instead of the law, various atrocities, instituted by governments, could have been avoided. Had only many, many been aware of their humanity rather than going along with the mice and the sheep . . .

Mind you, that is so easy for me to say and you to read as, in all likelihood, we sit reasonably well off, looking at this book, not having to stand up and be counted — and also not scraping a living in desperate circumstances. We are cocooned, indeed, from millions of dispossessed in the world for whom life is certainly nasty, brutish, and short.

Topics for Critical Thinking and Writing

1. Name five things or services (e.g., paved sidewalks, the police) that you did not create or establish but from which you benefit (para. 6).

2. Why is the "social contract" so called (paras. 6–8)?

3. Did the voyagers on the *Mayflower* (1620) create a social contract among themselves? How can you tell?

4. Is the following proposition — "We are not morally obligated by the deeds of our predecessors" — true? Why, or why not? Explain your answer.

5. What counts as a free, voluntary compact to obey some laws? What would you have to do to show that you (no longer) consent to be governed by the government under which you live?

THOMAS HARDY

Thomas Hardy (1840–1928) was born in Dorset, England, the son of a stonemason. Despite great obstacles, he studied the classics and architecture, and in 1862 he moved to London to study and practice as an architect. Ill health forced him to return to Dorset, where he continued to work as an architect and to write. Best known for his novels, Hardy ceased writing fiction after the hostile reception of Jude the Obscure *in 1896 and turned to writing lyric poetry. We print a poem of 1902.*

The Man He Killed

"Had he and I but met
By some old ancient inn,
We should have sat us down to wet
Right many a nipperkin°!

"But ranged an infantry,   5
And staring face to face,
I shot at him as he at me,
And killed him in his place.

---
4 **nipperkin** Cup.

"I shot him dead because —
Because he was my foe,
Just so: my foe of course he was;
That's clear enough; although

"He thought he'd 'list, perhaps,
Off-hand like — just as I —

Was out of work — had sold his traps° — 15
No other reason why.

"Yes; quaint and curious war is!
You shoot a fellow down
You'd treat if met where any bar is,
Or help to half-a-crown." 20

---

15 traps Personal belongings. [Both notes are the editors'.]

Topics for Critical Thinking and Writing

1. Thomas Hardy published this poem in 1902, at the conclusion of the Boer War (1899–1902, also called the South African War), a war between the Boers (Dutch) and the British for possession of part of Africa. The speaker of the poem is an English veteran of the war. Do you think such a poem might just as well have been written by an English (or American) soldier in World War II? Explain your response.

2. Characterize the speaker. What sort of man does he seem to be? Pay special attention to the punctuation in the third and fourth stanzas — what do the pauses indicated by the dashes, the colons, and the semicolons tell us about him? — and pay special attention to the final stanza, in which he speaks of war as "quaint and curious" (line 17). Do you think that Hardy too would speak of war this way? Why, or why not? Can you imagine an American soldier in the Vietnam War speaking of the war as "quaint and curious"? Explain.

3. Do you think we can reasonably say that the speaker of Hardy's poem possesses free will? Explain your position.

T. S. ELIOT

Thomas Stearns Eliot (1888–1965) was born into a New England family that had moved to St. Louis. He attended a preparatory school in Massachusetts, graduated from Harvard University, and then continued his studies in literature in France, Germany, and England. In 1914 he began working for Lloyds Bank in London, and three years later he published his first book of poems, which included "Prufrock." In 1925 he joined a publishing firm, and in 1927 he became a British citizen and a member of the Church of England. In 1948 he received the Nobel Prize for Literature.

The Love Song of J. Alfred Prufrock

S'io credesse che mia risposta fosse
A persona che mai tornasse al mondo,
Questa fiamma staria senza più scosse.
Ma perciocchè giammai di questo fondo
Non torno vivo alcun, s' i' odo il vero,
Senza tema d'infamia ti rispondo.°

Let us go then, you and I,
When the evening is spread out against the
    sky
Like a patient etherised upon a table;
Let us go, through certain half-deserted
    streets,
The muttering retreats   5
Of restless nights in one-night cheap hotels
And sawdust restaurants with oyster-shells:
Streets that follow like a tedious argument
Of insidious intent
To lead you to an overwhelming question . . .   10
Oh, do not ask, "What is it?"
Let us go and make our visit.

In the room the women come and go
Talking of Michelangelo.

The yellow fog that rubs its back upon the   15
    window-panes,
The yellow smoke that rubs its muzzle on the
    window-panes
Licked its tongue into the corners of the
    evening,
Lingered upon the pools that stand in drains,

Let fall upon its back the soot that falls from
    chimneys,
Slipped by the terrace, made a sudden leap,   20
And seeing that it was a soft October night,
Curled once about the house, and fell asleep.

And indeed there will be time
For the yellow smoke that slides along the
    street,
Rubbing its back upon the window-panes;   25
There will be time, there will be time
To prepare a face to meet the faces that you
    meet;
There will be time to murder and create,
And time for all the works and days° of hands
That lift and drop a question on your plate;   30
Time for you and time for me,
And time yet for a hundred indecisions,
And for a hundred visions and revisions,
Before the taking of a toast and tea.

In the room the women come and go   35
Talking of Michelangelo
And indeed there will be time
To wonder, "Do I dare?" and, "Do I dare?"
Time to turn back and descend the stair,
With a bald spot in the middle of my hair —   40
[They will say: "How his hair is growing
    thin!"]
My morning coat, my collar mounting firmly
    to the chin,
My necktie rich and modest, but asserted by a
    simple pin —
[They will say: "But how his arms and legs are
    thin!"]
Do I dare   45
Disturb the universe?

S'io . . . rispondo The Italian epigraph that begins the poem is a quotation from Dante's *Divine Comedy* (1321). In this passage, a damned soul in hell who had sought absolution before committing a crime addresses Dante, thinking that his words will never reach the earth. He says: "If I thought that my answer were to someone who could ever return to the world, this flame would be still, without further motion. But because no one has ever returned alive from this depth, if what I hear is true, without fear of shame I answer you." [All notes are the editors'.]

---

29 works and days The title of a poem on farm life by Hesiod (Greek, eighth century B.C.).

In a minute there is time
For decisions and revisions which a minute
    will reverse.

For I have known them all already, known
    them all: —
Have known the evenings, mornings,   50
    afternoons,
I have measured out my life with coffee spoons;
I know the voices dying with a dying fall°
Beneath the music from a farther room.
        So how should I presume?

And I have known the eyes already, known   55
    them all —
The eyes that fix you in a formulated phrase,
And when I am formulated, sprawling on a pin,
When I am pinned and wriggling on the wall,
Then how should I begin
To spit out all the butt-ends of my days and   60
    ways? And how should I presume?

And I have known the arms already, known
    them all —
Arms that are braceleted and white and bare
[But in the lamplight, downed with light
    brown hair!]
Is it perfume from a dress   65
That makes me so digress?
Arms that lie along a table, or wrap about a
    shawl.
        And should I then presume?
        And how should I begin?
            . . . . .

Shall I say, I have gone at dusk through   70
    narrow streets
And watched the smoke that rises from the
    pipes
Of lonely men in shirt-sleeves, leaning out of
    windows? . . .

I should have been a pair of ragged claws
Scuttling across the floors of silent seas.

            . . . . .

And the afternoon, the evening, sleeps so   75
    peacefully!
Smoothed by long fingers,
Asleep . . . tired . . . or it malingers,
Stretched on the floor, here beside you
    and me.
Should I, after tea and cakes and ices,
Have the strength to force the moment to its   80
    crisis?
But though I have wept and fasted, wept and
    prayed,
Though I have seen my head [grown slightly
    bald] brought in upon a platter,°
I am no prophet — and here's no great
    matter;
I have seen the moment of my greatness
    flicker,
And I have seen the eternal Footman hold my
    coat, and snicker,   85
And in short, I was afraid.

And would it have been worth it, after all,
After the cups, the marmalade, the tea,
Among the porcelain, among some talk of you
    and me,
Would it have been worth while,   90
To have bitten off the matter with a smile,
To have squeezed the universe into a ball
To roll° it toward some overwhelming
    question,
To say: "I am Lazarus,° come from the dead,
Come back to tell you all, I shall tell you   95
    all" —

---

82 head . . . platter Alludes to John the Baptist, whose head
was delivered on a platter to Salome.
92–93 ball / To roll Echoes Andrew Marvell's "To His Coy
Mistress," lines 41–42 (see p. 398).
94 Lazarus Mentioned in the New Testament: John 11; Lazarus
rises from the dead at the command of Jesus.

---

52 dying fall Echoes Shakespeare's *Twelfth Night* 1.1.4.

If one, settling a pillow by her head,
      Should say: "That is not what I meant
at all.
      That is not it, at all."

And would it have been worth it, after all,
Would it have been worth while,   100
After the sunsets and the dooryards and the
      sprinkled streets,
After the novels, after the teacups, after the
      skirts that trail along the floor—
And this, and so much more?—
It is impossible to say just what I mean!
But as if a magic lantern threw the nerves in   105
      patterns on a screen:
Would it have been worth while
If one, settling a pillow or throwing off a
      shawl,
And turning toward the window, should say:
      "That is not it at all,
      That is not what I meant, at all."   110
                  . . . . .

No! I am not Prince Hamlet,° nor was meant
      to be;
Am an attendant lord, one that will do
To swell a progress, start a scene or two,
Advise the prince; no doubt, an easy tool.
Deferential, glad to be of use,   115

Politic, cautious, and meticulous;
Full of high sentence,° but a bit obtuse;
At times, indeed, almost ridiculous—
Almost, at times, the Fool.

I grow old . . . I grow old . . .   120
I shall wear the bottoms of my trousers
      rolled.

Shall I part my hair behind? Do I dare to eat
      a peach?
I shall wear white flannel trousers, and walk
      upon the beach.
I have heard the mermaids singing, each to
      each.
I do not think that they will sing to me.   125

I have seen them riding seaward on the
      waves
Combing the white hair of the waves blown
      back
When the wind blows the water white and
      black.

We have lingered in the chambers of the sea
By sea-girls wreathed with seaweed red and   130
      brown
Till human voices wake us, and we drown.

---

111 Prince Hamlet The next few lines allude to lesser figures in Shakespeare's tragedy, specifically to Polonius, a self-satisfied fatuous courtier.

117 Full of high sentence Full of thoughtful sayings; comes from Chaucer's description of the Oxford student in *The Canterbury Tales*.

Topics for Critical Thinking and Writing

1. One of the most famous images of the poem compares the evening to "a patient ether-ised upon a table" (line 3). Does the image also suggest that individuals—for instance, Prufrock—may not be fully conscious and therefore are not responsible for their actions or their inactions? Explain your response.

2. Are lines 57 to 60 meant to evoke the reader's pity for the speaker? If not, what (if any) response are these lines intended to evoke?

3. The speaker admits he is "At times, indeed, . . . / Almost . . . the Fool" (lines 118–19). Where, if at all, in the poem do we see him not at all as a fool?

4. Do you take the poem to be a criticism of an individual, a society, neither, or both? Why?

5. Evaluate this critical judgment, offering evidence to support your view: "The poem is obscure: It begins in Italian, and it includes references that most readers can't know. It is not at all uplifting. In fact, in so far as it is comprehensible, it is depressing. These are not the characteristics of a great poem."

6. The poem is chiefly concerned with the thoughts of a man, J. Alfred Prufrock. Do you think it therefore is of more interest to men than to women? Explain your response.

7. The speaker describes the streets he walks as "follow[ing] like a tedious argument" (line 8). Is the simile apt? When do you think an argument becomes tedious?

SUSAN GLASPELL

Susan Glaspell (1882–1948) was born in Davenport, Iowa, and educated at Drake University in Des Moines. In 1903 she married George Cram Cook and, with Cook and other writers, actors, and artists, in 1915 founded the Provincetown Players, a group that remained vital until 1929. Glaspell wrote Trifles *(1916) for the Provincetown Players, but she also wrote stories, novels, and a biography of her husband. In 1931 she won the Pulitzer Prize for* Alison's House, *a play about the family of a deceased poet who in some ways resembles Emily Dickinson.*

Trifles

(SCENE: *The kitchen in the now abandoned farmhouse of John Wright, a gloomy kitchen, and left without having been put in order — unwashed pans under the sink, a loaf of bread outside the breadbox, a dish towel on the table — other signs of incompleted work. At the rear the outer door opens, and the Sheriff comes in, followed by the County Attorney and Hale. The Sheriff and Hale are men in middle life, the County Attorney is a young man; all are much bundled up and go at once to the stove. They are followed by the two women — the Sheriff's Wife first; she is a slight wiry woman, a thin nervous face. Mrs. Hale is larger and would ordinarily be called more comfortable looking, but she is disturbed now and looks fearfully about as she enters. The women have come in slowly and stand close together near the door.)*

COUNTY ATTORNEY (*rubbing his hands*). This feels good. Come up to the fire, ladies.

MRS. PETERS (*after taking a step forward*). I'm not — cold.

SHERIFF (*unbuttoning his overcoat and stepping away from the stove as if to the beginning of official business*). Now, Mr. Hale, before we move things about, you explain to Mr. Henderson just what you saw when you came here yesterday morning.

COUNTY ATTORNEY. By the way, has anything been moved? Are things just as you left them yesterday?

SHERIFF (*looking about*). It's just the same. When it dropped below zero last night,

5

I thought I'd better send Frank out this morning to make a fire for us — no use getting pneumonia with a big case on; but I told him not to touch anything except the stove — and you know Frank.

COUNTY ATTORNEY. Somebody should have been left here yesterday.

SHERIFF. Oh — yesterday. When I had to send Frank to Morris Center for that man who went crazy — I want you to know I had my hands full yesterday. I knew you could get back from Omaha by today, and as long as I went over everything here myself —

COUNTY ATTORNEY. Well, Mr. Hale, tell just what happened when you came here yesterday morning.

HALE. Harry and I had started to town with a load of potatoes. We came along the road from my place; and as I got here, I said, "I'm going to see if I can't get John Wright to go in with me on a party telephone." I spoke to Wright about it once before, and he put me off, saying folks talked too much anyway, and all he asked was peace and quiet — I guess you know about how much he talked himself; but I thought maybe if I went to the house and talked about it before his wife, though I said to Harry that I didn't know as what his wife wanted made much difference to John —

COUNTY ATTORNEY. Let's talk about that later, Mr. Hale. I do want to talk about that, but tell now just what happened when you got to the house.

HALE. I didn't hear or see anything; I knocked at the door, and still it was all quiet inside. I knew they must be up, it was past eight o'clock. So I knocked again, and I thought I heard somebody say, "Come in." I wasn't sure, I'm not sure yet, but I opened the door — this door (*indicating the door by which the two women are still standing*),

and there in that rocker — (*pointing to it*) sat Mrs. Wright. (*They all look at the rocker.*)

COUNTY ATTORNEY. What — was she doing?

HALE. She was rockin' back and forth. She had her apron in her hand and was kind of — pleating it.

COUNTY ATTORNEY. And how did she — look?

HALE. Well, she looked queer.

COUNTY ATTORNEY. How do you mean — queer?

HALE. Well, as if she didn't know what she was going to do next. And kind of done up.

COUNTY ATTORNEY. How did she seem to feel about your coming?

HALE. Why, I don't think she minded — one way or other. She didn't pay much attention. I said, "How do, Mrs. Wright, it's cold, ain't it?" And she said, "Is it?" — and went on kind of pleating at her apron. Well, I was surprised; she didn't ask me to come up to the stove, or to set down, but just sat there, not even looking at me, so I said, "I want to see John." And then she — laughed. I guess you would call it a laugh. I thought of Harry and the team outside, so I said a little sharp: "Can't I see John?" "No," she says, kind o' dull like. "Ain't he home?" says I. "Yes," says she, "he's home." "Then why can't I see him?" I asked her, out of patience. "'Cause he's dead," says she. *"Dead?"* says I. She just nodded her head, not getting a bit excited, but rockin' back and forth. "Why — where is he?" says I, not knowing what to say. She just pointed upstairs — like that (*himself pointing to the room above*). I got up, with the idea of going up there. I walked from there to here — then I says, "Why, what did he die of?" "He died of a rope around his neck," says she, and just went on pleatin' at her apron. Well, I went out and called Harry. I thought I might — need help. We went upstairs, and there he was lyin' —

COUNTY ATTORNEY. I think I'd rather have you go into that upstairs, where you can point it all out. Just go on now with the rest of the story.

HALE. Well, my first thought was to get that rope off. I looked . . . (Stops, his face twitches.) . . . but Harry, he went up to him, and he said, "No, he's dead all right, and we'd better not touch anything." So we went back downstairs. She was still sitting that same way. "Has anybody been notified?" I asked. "No," says she, unconcerned. "Who did this, Mrs. Wright?" said Harry. He said it businesslike — and she stopped pleatin' of her apron. "I don't know," she says. "You don't *know*?" says Harry. "No," says she. "Weren't you sleepin' in the bed with him?" says Harry. "Yes," says she, "but I was on the inside." "Somebody slipped a rope round his neck and strangled him, and you didn't wake up?" says Harry. "I didn't wake up," she said after him. We must 'a looked as if we didn't see how that could be, for after a minute she said, "I sleep sound." Harry was going to ask her more questions, but I said maybe we ought to let her tell her story first to the coroner, or the sheriff, so Harry went fast as he could to Rivers' place, where there's a telephone.

COUNTY ATTORNEY. And what did Mrs. Wright do when she knew that you had gone for the coroner?

HALE. She moved from that chair to this over here . . . (Pointing to a small chair in the corner.) . . . and just sat there with her hands held together and looking down. I got a feeling that I ought to make some conversation, so I said I had come in to see if John wanted to put in a telephone, and at that she started to laugh, and then she stopped and looked at me — scared. (The County Attorney, who has had his notebook out, makes a note.) I dunno, maybe it wasn't scared. I wouldn't like to say it was. Soon Harry got back, and then Dr. Lloyd came, and you, Mr. Peters, and so I guess that's all I know that you don't.

COUNTY ATTORNEY (looking around). I guess we'll go upstairs first — and then out to the barn and around there. (To the Sheriff.) You're convinced that there was nothing important here — nothing that would point to any motive?

SHERIFF. Nothing here but kitchen things. (The County Attorney, after again looking around the kitchen, opens the door of a cupboard closet. He gets up on a chair and looks on a shelf. Pulls his hand away, sticky.)

COUNTY ATTORNEY. Here's a nice mess. (The women draw nearer.)

MRS. PETERS (to the other woman). Oh, her fruit; it did freeze. (To the Lawyer.) She worried about that when it turned so cold. She said the fire'd go out and her jars would break.

SHERIFF. Well, can you beat the woman! Held for murder and worryin' about her preserves.

COUNTY ATTORNEY. I guess before we're through she may have something more serious than preserves to worry about.

HALE. Well, women are used to worrying over trifles. (The two women move a little closer together.)

COUNTY ATTORNEY. (with the gallantry of a young politician). And yet, for all their worries, what would we do without the ladies? (The women do not unbend. He goes to the sink, takes a dipperful of water from the pail and, pouring it into a basin, washes his hands. Starts to wipe them on the roller towel, turns it for a cleaner place.) Dirty towels!

(*Kicks his foot against the pans under the sink.*) Not much of a housekeeper, would you say, ladies?

MRS. HALE (*stiffly*). There's a great deal of work to be done on a farm.

COUNTY ATTORNEY. To be sure. And yet . . . (*With a little bow to her.*) . . . I know there are some Dickson county farmhouses which do not have such roller towels. (*He gives it a pull to expose its full length again.*)

MRS. HALE. Those towels get dirty awful quick. Men's hands aren't always as clean as they might be.

COUNTY ATTORNEY. Ah, loyal to your sex. I see. 35 But you and Mrs. Wright were neighbors. I suppose you were friends, too.

MRS. HALE (*shaking her head*). I've not seen much of her of late years. I've not been in this house — it's more than a year.

COUNTY ATTORNEY. And why was that? You didn't like her?

MRS. HALE. I liked her all well enough. Farmers' wives have their hands full, Mr. Henderson. And then —

COUNTY ATTORNEY. Yes — ?

MRS. HALE (*looking about*). It never seemed a 40 very cheerful place.

COUNTY ATTORNEY. No — it's not cheerful. I shouldn't say she had the homemaking instinct.

MRS. HALE. Well, I don't know as Wright had, either.

COUNTY ATTORNEY. You mean they didn't get on very well?

MRS. HALE. No, I don't mean anything. But I don't think a place'd be any cheerfuller for John Wright's being in it.

COUNTY ATTORNEY. I'd like to talk more of that 45 a little later. I want to get the lay of things upstairs now. (*He goes to the left, where three steps lead to a stair door.*)

SHERIFF. I suppose anything Mrs. Peters does'll be all right. She was to take in some clothes for her, you know, and a few little things. We left in such a hurry yesterday.

COUNTY ATTORNEY. Yes, but I would like to see what you take, Mrs. Peters, and keep an eye out for anything that might be of use to us.

MRS. PETERS. Yes, Mr. Henderson. (*The women listen to the men's steps on the stairs, then look about the kitchen.*)

MRS. HALE. I'd hate to have men coming into my kitchen, snooping around and criticizing. (*She arranges the pans under the sink which the Lawyer had shoved out of place.*)

MRS. PETERS. Of course it's no more than their 50 duty.

MRS. HALE. Duty's all right, but I guess that deputy sheriff that came out to make the fire might have got a little of this on. (*Gives the roller towel a pull.*) Wish I'd thought of that sooner. Seems mean to talk about her for not having things slicked up when she had to come away in such a hurry.

MRS. PETERS (*who has gone to a small table in the left rear corner of the room, and lifted one end of a towel that covers a pan*). She had bread set. (*Stands still.*)

MRS. HALE (*eyes fixed on a loaf of bread beside the breadbox, which is on a low shelf at the other side of the room. Moves slowly toward it*). She was going to put this in there. (*Picks up loaf, then abruptly drops it. In a manner of returning to familiar things.*) It's a shame about her fruit. I wonder if it's all gone. (*Gets up on the chair and looks.*) I think there's some here that's all right, Mrs. Peters. Yes — here; (*Holding it toward the window.*) this is cherries, too. (*Looking again.*) I declare I believe that's the only one. (*Gets down, bottle in her hand. Goes*

to the sink and wipes it off on the outside.)
She'll feel awful bad after all her hard work
in the hot weather. I remember the afternoon I put up my cherries last summer.
(She puts the bottle on the big kitchen table,
center of the room. With a sigh, is about to
sit down in the rocking chair. Before she is
seated realizes what chair it is; with a slow
look at it, steps back. The chair, which she
has touched, rocks back and forth.)

MRS. PETERS. Well, I must get those things from
the front room closet. (She goes to the door
at the right, but after looking into the other
room steps back.) You coming with me,
Mrs. Hale? You could help me carry them.
(They go into the other room; reappear, Mrs.
Peters carrying a dress and skirt, Mrs. Hale
following with a pair of shoes.)

MRS. PETERS. My, it's cold in there. (She puts the
cloth on the big table, and hurries to the
stove.)

MRS. HALE (examining the skirt). Wright was
close. I think maybe that's why she kept
so much to herself. She didn't even belong
to the Ladies' Aid. I suppose she felt she
couldn't do her part, and then you don't
enjoy things when you feel shabby. She
used to wear pretty clothes and be lively,
when she was Minnie Foster, one of
the town girls singing in the choir. But
that — oh, that was thirty years ago. This all
you was to take in?

MRS. PETERS. She said she wanted an apron.
Funny thing to want, for there isn't much
to get you dirty in jail, goodness knows.
But I suppose just to make her feel more
natural. She said they was in the top
drawer in this cupboard. Yes, here. And
then her little shawl that always hung
behind the door. (Opens stair door and
looks.) Yes, here it is. (Quickly shuts door
leading upstairs.)

MRS. HALE (abruptly moving toward her).
Mrs. Peters?

MRS. PETERS. Yes, Mrs. Hale?

MRS. HALE. Do you think she did it? 60

MRS. PETERS (in a frightened voice). Oh, I don't
know.

MRS. HALE. Well, I don't think she did. Asking
for an apron and her little shawl. Worrying
about her fruit.

MRS. PETERS (starts to speak, glances up, where
footsteps are heard in the room above. In a
low voice). Mr. Peters says it looks bad for
her. Mr. Henderson is awful sarcastic in
speech, and he'll make fun of her sayin' she
didn't wake up.

MRS. HALE. Well, I guess John Wright didn't
wake when they was slipping that rope
under his neck.

MRS. PETERS. No, it's strange. It must have been 65
done awful crafty and still. They say it was
such a — funny way to kill a man, rigging it
all up like that.

MRS. HALE. That's just what Mr. Hale said. There
was a gun in the house. He says that's what
he can't understand.

MRS. PETERS. Mr. Henderson said coming
out that what was needed for the case
was a motive; something to show anger
or — sudden feeling.

MRS. HALE (who is standing by the table). Well,
I don't see any signs of anger around here.
(She puts her hand on the dish towel which
lies on the table, stands looking down at the
table, one half of which is clean, the other
half messy.) It's wiped here. (Makes a move
as if to finish work, then turns and looks at
loaf of bread outside the breadbox. Drops
towel. In that voice of coming back to familiar things.) Wonder how they are finding
things upstairs? I hope she had it a little
more red-up there. You know, it seems
kind of sneaking. Locking her up in town

and then coming out here and trying to get her own house to turn against her!

MRS. PETERS. But, Mrs. Hale, the law is the law.

MRS. HALE. I s'pose 'tis. (*Unbuttoning her coat.*) Better loosen up your things, Mrs. Peters. You won't feel them when you go out. (*Mrs. Peters takes off her fur tippet, goes to hang it on hook at the back of room, stands looking at the under part of the small corner table.*)

MRS. PETERS. She was piecing a quilt. (*She brings the large sewing basket, and they look at the bright pieces.*)

MRS. HALE. It's log cabin pattern. Pretty, isn't it? I wonder if she was goin' to quilt or just knot it? (*Footsteps have been heard coming down the stairs. The Sheriff enters, followed by Hale and the County Attorney.*)

SHERIFF. They wonder if she was going to quilt it or just knot it. (*The men laugh, the women look abashed.*)

COUNTY ATTORNEY (*rubbing his hands over the stove*). Frank's fire didn't do much up there, did it? Well, let's go out to the barn and get that cleared up. (*The men go outside.*)

MRS. HALE (*resentfully*). I don't know as there's anything so strange, our takin' up our time with little things while we're waiting for them to get the evidence. (*She sits down at the big table, smoothing out a block with decision.*) I don't see as it's anything to laugh about.

MRS. PETERS (*apologetically*). Of course they've got awful important things on their minds. (*Pulls up a chair and joins Mrs. Hale at the table.*)

MRS. HALE (*examining another block*). Mrs. Peters, look at this one. Here, this is the one she was working on, and look at the sewing! All the rest of it has been so nice and even. And look at this! It's all over the place! Why, it looks as if she didn't know what she was about! (*After she has said

this, they look at each other, then start to glance back at the door. After an instant Mrs. Hale has pulled at a knot and ripped the sewing.*)

MRS. PETERS. Oh, what are you doing, Mrs. Hale?

MRS. HALE (*mildly*). Just pulling out a stitch or two that's not sewed very good. (*Threading a needle.*) Bad sewing always made me fidgety.

MRS. PETERS (*nervously*). I don't think we ought to touch things.

MRS. HALE. I'll just finish up this end. (*Suddenly stopping and leaning forward.*) Mrs. Peters?

MRS. PETERS. Yes, Mrs. Hale?

MRS. HALE. What do you suppose she was so nervous about?

MRS. PETERS. Oh — I don't know. I don't know as she was nervous. I sometimes sew awful queer when I'm just tired. (*Mrs. Hale starts to say something, looks at Mrs. Peters, then goes on sewing.*) Well, I must get these things wrapped up. They may be through sooner than we think. (*Putting apron and other things together.*) I wonder where I can find a piece of paper, and string.

MRS. HALE. In that cupboard, maybe.

MRS. PETERS (*looking in cupboard*). Why, here's a birdcage. (*Holds it up.*) Did she have a bird, Mrs. Hale?

MRS. HALE. Why, I don't know whether she did or not — I've not been here for so long. There was a man around last year selling canaries cheap, but I don't know as she took one; maybe she did. She used to sing real pretty herself.

MRS. PETERS (*glancing around*). Seems funny to think of a bird here. But she must have had one, or why should she have a cage? I wonder what happened to it?

MRS. HALE. I s'pose maybe the cat got it.

MRS. PETERS. No, she didn't have a cat. She's got that feeling some people have about cats — being afraid of them. My cat got in her room, and she was real upset and asked me to take it out.

MRS. HALE. My sister Bessie was like that. Queer, ain't it?

MRS. PETERS *(examining the cage)*. Why, look at this door. It's broke. One hinge is pulled apart.

MRS. HALE *(looking, too)*. Looks as if someone must have been rough with it.

MRS. PETERS. Why, yes. *(She brings the cage forward and puts it on the table.)*

MRS. HALE. I wish if they're going to find any evidence they'd be about it. I don't like this place.

MRS. PETERS. But I'm awful glad you came with me, Mrs. Hale. It would be lonesome for me sitting here alone.

MRS. HALE. It would, wouldn't it? *(Dropping her sewing.)* But I tell you what I do wish, Mrs. Peters. I wish I had come over sometimes when *she* was here. I — *(Looking around the room.)* — wish I had.

MRS. PETERS. But of course you were awful busy, Mrs. Hale — your house and your children.

MRS. HALE. I could've come. I stayed away because it weren't cheerful — and that's why I ought to have come. I — I've never liked this place. Maybe because it's down in a hollow, and you don't see the road. I dunno what it is, but it's a lonesome place and always was. I wish I had come over to see Minnie Foster sometimes. I can see now — *(Shakes her head.)*

MRS. PETERS. Well, you mustn't reproach yourself, Mrs. Hale. Somehow we just don't see how it is with other folks until — something comes up.

MRS. HALE. Not having children makes less work — but it makes a quiet house, and Wright out to work all day, and no company when he did come in. Did you know John Wright, Mrs. Peters?

MRS. PETERS. Not to know him; I've seen him in town. They say he was a good man.

MRS. HALE. Yes — good; he didn't drink, and kept his word as well as most, I guess, and paid his debts. But he was a hard man, Mrs. Peters. Just to pass the time of day with him. *(Shivers.)* Like a raw wind that gets to the bone. *(Pauses, her eye falling on the cage.)* I should think she would 'a' wanted a bird. But what do you suppose went with it?

MRS. PETERS. I don't know, unless it got sick and died. *(She reaches over and swings the broken door, swings it again; both women watch it.)*

MRS. HALE. You weren't raised around here, were you? *(Mrs. Peters shakes her head.)* You didn't know — her?

MRS. PETERS. Not till they brought her yesterday.

MRS. HALE. She — come to think of it, she was kind of like a bird herself — real sweet and pretty, but kind of timid and — fluttery. How — she — did — change. *(Silence; then as if struck by a happy thought and relieved to get back to everyday things.)* Tell you what, Mrs. Peters, why don't you take the quilt in with you? It might take up her mind.

MRS. PETERS. Why, I think that's a real nice idea, Mrs. Hale. There couldn't possible be any objection to it, could there? Now, just what would I take? I wonder if her patches are in here — and her things. *(They look in the sewing basket.)*

MRS. HALE. Here's some red. I expect this has got sewing things in it. *(Brings out a fancy box.)* What a pretty box. Looks like something somebody would give you. Maybe her scissors are in here. *(Opens box. Suddenly puts her hand to her nose.)* Why — *(Mrs. Peters bends nearer, then turns her face away.)* There's something wrapped up in this piece of silk.

MRS. PETERS. Why, this isn't her scissors. 110

MRS. HALE (lifting the silk). Oh, Mrs. Peters — it's — (Mrs. Peters bends closer.)

MRS. PETERS. It's the bird.

MRS. HALE (jumping up). But, Mrs. Peters — look at it. Its neck! Look at its neck! It's all — other side to.

MRS. PETERS. Somebody — wrung — its neck. (Their eyes meet. A look of growing comprehension of horror. Steps are heard outside. Mrs. Hale slips box under quilt pieces, and sinks into her chair. Enter Sheriff and County Attorney, Mrs. Peters rises.)

COUNTY ATTORNEY (as one turning from serious 115 things to little pleasantries). Well, ladies, have you decided whether she was going to quilt it or knot it?

MRS. PETERS. We think she was going to — knot it.

COUNTY ATTORNEY. Well, that's interesting, I'm sure. (Seeing the birdcage.) Has the bird flown?

MRS. HALE. (putting more quilt pieces over the box). We think the — cat got it.

COUNTY ATTORNEY (preoccupied). Is there a cat? (Mrs. Hale glances in a quick covert way at Mrs. Peters.)

MRS. PETERS. Well, not now. They're super- 120 stitious, you know. They leave.

COUNTY ATTORNEY (to Sheriff Peters, continu- ing an interrupted conversation). No sign at all of anyone having come from the outside. Their own rope. Now let's go up again and go over it piece by piece. (They start upstairs.) It would have to have been someone who knew just the — (Mrs. Peters sits down. The two women sit there not looking at one another, but as if peering into something and at the same time holding back. When they talk now, it is the manner of feeling their way over strange ground, as if afraid of what they are saying, but as if they cannot help saying it.)

MRS. HALE. She liked the bird. She was going to bury it in that pretty box.

MRS. PETERS (in a whisper). When I was a girl — my kitten — there was a boy took a hatchet, and before my eyes — and before I could get there — (Covers her face an instant.) If they hadn't held me back, I would have — (Catches herself, looks upstairs where steps are heard, falters weakly.) — hurt him.

MRS. HALE (with a slow look around her). I won- der how it would seem never to have had any children around. (Pause.) No, Wright wouldn't like the bird — a thing that sang. She used to sing. He killed that, too.

MRS. PETERS (moving uneasily). We don't know 125 who killed the bird.

MRS. HALE. I knew John Wright.

MRS. PETERS. It was an awful thing was done in this house that night, Mrs. Hale. Killing a man while he slept, slipping a rope around his neck that choked the life out of him.

MRS. HALE. His neck. Choked the life out of him. (Her hand goes out and rests on the birdcage.)

MRS. PETERS (with a rising voice). We don't know who killed him. We don't know.

MRS. HALE (her own feeling not interrupted). If 130 there'd been years and years of nothing, then a bird to sing to you, it would be awful — still, after the bird was still.

MRS. PETERS (something within her speaking). I know what stillness is. When we home- steaded in Dakota, and my first baby died — after he was two years old, and me with no other then —

MRS. HALE (moving). How soon do you suppose they'll be through, looking for evidence?

MRS. PETERS. I know what stillness is. (*Pulling herself back.*) The law has got to punish crime, Mrs. Hale.

MRS. HALE (*not as if answering that*). I wish you'd seen Minnie Foster when she wore a white dress with blue ribbons and stood up there in the choir and sang. (*A look around the room.*) Oh, I *wish* I'd come over here once in a while! That was a crime! That was a crime! Who's going to punish that?

MRS. PETERS (*looking upstairs*). We mustn't — take on.   135

MRS. HALE. I might have known she needed help! I know how things can be — for women. I tell you, it's queer, Mrs. Peters. We live close together and we live far apart. We all go through the same things — it's all just a different kind of the same thing. (*Brushes her eyes, noticing the bottle of fruit, reaches out for it.*) If I was you, I wouldn't tell her her fruit was gone. Tell her it *ain't*. Tell her it's all right. Take this in to prove it to her. She — she may never know whether it was broke or not.

MRS. PETERS (*takes the bottle, looks about for something to wrap it in; takes petticoat from the clothes brought from the other room, very nervously begins winding this around the bottle. In a false voice*). My, it's a good thing the men couldn't hear us. Wouldn't they just laugh! Getting all stirred up over a little thing like a — dead canary. As if that could have anything to do with — with — wouldn't they *laugh*! (*The men are heard coming downstairs.*)

MRS. HALE (*under her breath*). Maybe they would — maybe they wouldn't.

COUNTY ATTORNEY. No, Peters, it's all perfectly clear except a reason for doing it. But you know juries when it comes to women. If there was some definite thing. Something

to show — something to make a story about — a thing that would connect up with this strange way of doing it. (*The women's eyes meet for an instant. Enter Hale from outer door.*)

HALE. Well, I've got the team around. Pretty   140
cold out there.

COUNTY ATTORNEY. I'm going to stay here a while by myself. (*To the Sheriff.*) You can send Frank out for me, can't you? I want to go over everything. I'm not satisfied that we can't do better.

SHERIFF. Do you want to see what Mrs. Peters is going to take in? (*The Lawyer goes to the table, picks up the apron, laughs.*)

COUNTY ATTORNEY. Oh, I guess they're not very dangerous things the ladies have picked up. (*Moves a few things about, disturbing the quilt pieces which cover the box. Steps back.*) No, Mrs. Peters doesn't need supervising. For that matter, a sheriff's wife is married to the law. Ever think of it that way, Mrs. Peters?

MRS. PETERS. Not — just that way.

SHERIFF (*chuckling*). Married to the law. (*Moves   145
toward the other room.*) I just want you to come in here a minute, George. We ought to take a look at these windows.

COUNTY ATTORNEY (*scoffingly*). Oh, windows!

SHERIFF. We'll be right out, Mr. Hale. (*Hale goes outside. The Sheriff follows the County Attorney into the other room. Then Mrs. Hale rises, hands tight together, looking intensely at Mrs. Peters, whose eyes take a slow turn, finally meeting Mrs. Hale's. A moment Mrs. Hale holds her, then her own eyes point the way to where the box is concealed. Suddenly Mrs. Peters throws back quilt pieces and tries to put the box in the bag she is carrying. It is too big. She opens box, starts to take the bird out, cannot touch it, goes to pieces, stands there helpless.*)

Sound of a knob turning in the other room. Mrs. Hale snatches the box and puts it in the pocket of her big coat. Enter County Attorney and Sheriff.)

COUNTY ATTORNEY *(facetiously).* Well, Henry, at least we found out that she was not going to quilt it. She was going to — what is it you call it, ladies?

MRS. HALE *(her hand against her pocket).* We call it — knot it, Mr. Henderson.

Topics for Critical Thinking and Writing

1. The dead canary in the box isn't evidence that Mrs. Wright has killed her husband. So what is the point of the dead canary in the play?

2. Do you think the play is immoral? Explain your response.

3. Assume that Minnie is indicted for murder and that you are asked to serve as her defense lawyer. If you somehow know that the evidence of the canary has been suppressed, would you accept the case? Why, or why not? (It is unlawful for *prosecutors* to suppress evidence, but it is not unlawful for defense lawyers to withhold incriminating evidence.)

4. Assume that you have accepted Minnie's case. In 500 words, set forth the defense you will offer for her. (Take any position that you wish. You may, for example, argue that she committed justifiable homicide or that — on the basis of her behavior as reported by Mr. Hale — she is innocent by reason of insanity.)

5. Assume that Minnie has been found guilty. Compose the speech she might give before being sentenced.

6. "*Trifles* is badly dated. It cannot speak to today's audience." In an essay of 500 words, evaluate this view: Offer an argument supporting or rejecting it, or take a middle position.

MITSUYE YAMADA

Mitsuye Yamada, the daughter of Japanese immigrants to the United States, was born in Japan in 1923, during her mother's return visit to her native land. Yamada was raised in Seattle, but in 1942 she and her family were incarcerated and then relocated to a camp in Idaho, when Executive Order 9066 (signed by President Franklin D. Roosevelt that year) gave military authorities the right to remove any and all persons from "military areas." In 1954 she became an American citizen. A professor of English at Cypress Junior College in San Luis Obispo, California, until she retired in 1989, Yamada is the author of poems and stories.

Yamada's poem concerns the compliant response to Executive Order 9066, which brought about the incarceration and relocation of the entire Japanese and Japanese American population on the Pacific coast — about 120,000 people. More than two-thirds of the people moved were native-born citizens of the United States. (The 158,000 Japanese residents of the Territory of Hawaii were not affected.) There was virtually no protest at the time, but in recent years the order has been widely regarded as an outrageous infringement on liberty, and some younger Japanese Americans cannot fathom why their parents and grandparents complied with it. This poem first appeared in Camp Notes and Other Poems *in 1976.*

To the Lady

The one in San Francisco who asked:
Why did the Japanese Americans let
the government put them in
those camps without protest?

Come to think of it I   5
    should've run off to Canada
    should've hijacked a plane to
        Algeria
    should've pulled myself up from my
    bra straps
    and kicked'm in the groin   10
    should've bombed a bank
    should've tried self-immolation
    should've holed myself up in a
    woodframe house
    and let you watch me   15
    burn up on the six o'clock news
    should've run howling down the street
    naked and assaulted you at breakfast
    by AP wirephoto

should've screamed bloody murder   20
like Kitty Genovese°

Then
YOU would've
come to my aid in shining armor
laid yourself across the railroad track   25
marched on Washington
tattooed a Star of David on your arm
written six million enraged
letters to Congress
But we didn't draw the line   30
anywhere
law and order Executive Order 9066
social order moral order internal order
YOU let'm
I let'm   35
All are punished.

---

21 Kitty Genovese In 1964 Kitty Genovese of Kew Gardens, New York, was stabbed to death when she left her car and walked toward her home. Thirty-eight persons heard her screams, but no one came to her assistance. [Editors' note.]

Topics for Critical Thinking and Writing

1. Has the lady's question (lines 2–4) ever crossed your mind? If so, what answers did you think of?

2. What, in effect, is the speaker really saying in lines 5–21? And in lines 22–29?

3. What possible arguments can you offer for and against the removal of Japanese Americans in 1942?

4. Do you think the survivors of the relocation are entitled to some sort of redress? Why, or why not? If you think they merit compensation, what should the compensation be?

TEXT CREDITS

Derek Bok, "Protecting Freedom of Expression on the Campus," originally published as "Protecting Freedom of Expression at Harvard." From *The Boston Globe,* May 21, 1991. Copyright © 1991 by Derek Bok. Reprinted by permission of the author.

Susan Brownmiller, "Let's Put Pornography Back in the Closet," originally published in *Newsday,* 1979. Copyright © 1979 by Susan Brownmiller. Reprinted by permission of the author.

Peter Cave, "Man or Sheep?" from *What's Wrong with Eating People?* is reprinted by permission of Oneworld Publications.

Justin Cronin, "Confessions of a Liberal Gun Owner," from *The New York Times,* Jan. 28, 2013. Copyright © 2013 by *The New York Times.* All rights reserved. Used by permission and protected by the copyright laws of the United States. The printing, copying, redistribution, or retransmission of this content without express written permission is prohibited.

Alfred Edmond, Jr., "Why Asking for a Job Applicant's Facebook Password Is Fair Game," from *Black Enterprise,* April 2, 2012. Copyright © 2012 Black Enterprise. 98107:313PF. Used with permission.

T. S. Eliot, "The Love Song of J. Alfred Prufrock," from *Collected Poems 1909–1962.* Reprinted with the permission of Faber & Faber Ltd.

Nora Ephron, "The Boston Photographs," copyright © 1975 by Nora Ephron. All rights reserved. Used by permission.

Nina Fedoroff, "The Genetically Engineered Salmon Is a Boon for Consumers and Sustainability," from *The New York Times,* December 2, 2015 issue. Copyright © 2015 by *The New York Times.* All rights reserved. Used by permission and protected by the copyright laws of the United States. The printing, copying, redistribution, or retransmission of this content without express written permission is prohibited.

Stanley Fish, "When Identity Politics Is Rational," from *The New York Times,* Feb. 17, 2008. Copyright © 2008 by *The New York Times.* All rights reserved. Used by permission and protected by the copyright laws of the United States. The printing, copying, redistribution, or retransmission of this content without express written permission is prohibited.

Jonathan Safran Foer, "Let Them Eat Dog: A Modest Proposal for Tossing Fido in the Oven," *Wall Street Journal,* 10/31/2009. Copyright © 2009 by Dow Jones. Republished with permission of Dow Jones, permission conveyed through Copyright Clearance Center, Inc.

Robert Frost, "Mending Wall," from the book *The Poetry of Robert Frost,* ed. by Edward Connery Lathem. Copyright © 1930, 1939, 1969 by Henry Holt and Company, copyright © 1958, copyright © 1967 by Lesley Frost Ballantine. Used by arrangement with Henry Holt and Company, LLC. Users are warned that this Selection is protected under copyright laws and downloading is strictly prohibited. The right to reproduce or transfer the Selection via any medium must be secured from Henry Holt and Company, LLC.

Sanjay Gupta, "Why I Changed My Mind on Weed," from CNN, August 2013. All rights reserved. Used by permission and protected by the copyright laws of the United States. The printing, copying, redistribution, or retransmission of the material without express written permission is prohibited.

Jeff Jacoby, "Bring Back Flogging," from *The Boston Globe,* Feb. 20, 1997, copyright © 1997 by *The Boston Globe.* All rights reserved. Used by permission and protected by the copyright laws of the United States. The printing, copying, redistribution, or retransmission of this content without express written permission is prohibited.

Susan Jacoby, "A First Amendment Junkie," by Susan Jacoby. Copyright © 1978 by Susan Jacoby. Originally appeared in *The New York Times* (January 26, 1978). Reprinted by permission of Georges Borchardt, Inc. on behalf of the author.

Gerard Jones, "Violent Media Is Good for Kids," from *Mother Jones,* Op-Ed, June 20, 2000. Reprinted by permission of the author.

Index of Authors and Titles

Index of Terms